Carnivals and Dreams

Pieter Bruegel and the History of the Imagination

by

Louise S. Milne

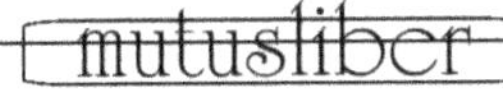

London

Revised Edition
Monochrome

First published in 2007
Revised edition published in 2011
by Mutus Liber
BM Mutus Liber
London WC1N 3XX

A CIP catalogue record for this book is available from the British Library

ISBN 978-0-9555230-8-3

www.mutusliber.com

Acknowledgements

Many acknowledgements could be made in a work of this kind. The debts I owe my teachers, past and present, will be evident to the reader. The errors, naturally, are my own. Much of the present book has at its core my doctoral work on Bruegel at Boston University. At that time I thanked my supervisors, Fred Licht and Helmut Wohl, my mentors Wendy Steadman Sheard and Lionel Rothkrug, and my friends Jay Dunn and Jan Nicholson for their Herculean gifts of time, support and assistance. I thank them again most sincerely. Over the years, the ideas in this book have benefitted especially from conversations with Walter Gibson, Donald Preziosi and Susan Hiller. Some of the materials have also been presented as conference papers: of these, in particular I thank Whitney Davis, who gave me the first opportunity to present the germ of what was to become Chapter 5, at the CAA conference in Boston in 1996; Jane Carroll and Alison Stewart, who invited me to present at the Dulle Griet Workshop, Museum Mayer van den Bergh, Historians of Netherlandish Art Conference, Antwerp, 2002, and the International Association for the Study of Dreams, where I presented material from Chapter One in 2006. Here in Edinburgh, as I started the task of interrogating that research from an entirely new perspective, I have received sterling encouragement and support from Sean Martin at Mutus Liber, best of publishers; Jenny Triggs, who designed the cover and edited the revised edition; Jay Hetrick and Zeynep Arman, who designed the pages; my most excellent research assistant Jules Hodges, who also drew the diagram; and Lina Löfström, for invaluable help in the final stages of preparing the MS. I thank Lorna Gilbertson for help with the image preparation, and Ariadne Xenou, who checked the bibliography. I would like to thank my family, Robert O. Milne, and Norma and Ian Dorward, for their support and faith in me. I am grateful also for financial help from the School of Creative Industries at Edinburgh Napier University, and from Edinburgh College of Art, which made the illustrations possible. To my students at both these institutions, I owe a special debt: their enthusiasm for the subject of this book over the years has been inspirational.

This second revised edition was made possible by a grant from the Carnegie Foundation.

Louise S. Milne
Edinburgh, 2011

To the dear memory of my father

Robert O. Milne

1932-1968

Quem di diligunt, adolescens moritur

Table of Contents

List of Illustrations

Intro

Chapter 1

21d Pieter Bruegel, egg-laying goose-angel, detail, *Fall of the Rebel Angels*

22 Frans Floris, *The Fall of the Rebellious Angels*, 1564. Oil on panel, 308 x 220 cm. Koninklijk Museum voor Schone Kunsten, Antwerp. © Reproductiefonds - Lukas Art in Flanders

23 Rogier van der Weyden, *Fall of the Damned*, far right wing of *Last Judgement* polyptych, 1446-52. Oil on panel, 215 x 560 cm. Musée de l'Hôtel Dieu, Beaune

24 Hieronymus Bosch, *Fall of the Rebel Angels and The Creation*, left inner wing of *Last Judgement* triptych, c 1506. Oil on panel, 167.7 x 60 cm. Gemäldegalerie der Akademie der Bildenden Künste, Vienna

24a Hieronymus Bosch, *Fall of the Rebel Angels*, detail, left inner wing of *Last Judgement* triptych

25 Anon, Pliny's human monsters, woodcut, from Sebastian Münster, *Cosmographia* (Basel, 1558) Staatsbibliothek Bamberg. Geogr. f 21

26 Anon, Barbarians, Savages and Monsters (The World's People), woodcut, from Sebastian Münster, *Cosmographia* (Basel, 1552), Biblioteca Lazzerini, Prato © Istituto Internazionale di Storia Economica e Sociale "F. Datini"

27a Anon, *Seven nymphs turn into trees*, woodcut, from Francesco Colonna, *Hypnerotomachia Poliphili* (Venice, 1499), Chapter 14: 174. Photo: Delft University of Technology and MIT Press, 1997

27b Anon, *Polia witnesses the massacre of two maidens by Eros*, woodcut, from Francesco Colonna, *Hypnerotomachia Poliphili* (Venice, 1499), Chapter 27: 401. Photo: Delft University of Technology and MIT Press, 1997

28 Marcantonio Raimondi, *The "Dream of Raphael"*, c. 1505. Engraving, 23.7 x 33.4 cm. Graphische Sammlung Albertina, Vienna

29 Guilio Campagnola, *The Astrologer*, 1509. Engraving, 99 x 152 mm. British Museum, London. 1845-8.25.771

30 Battista Dossi, *"Night" (The Dream)*, 1544. Oil on canvas, 82 x 149.5cm. Gemäldegalerie Alte Meister, Staatliche Kunstsammlungen Dresden

31 Pieter van der Heyden, after Pieter Bruegel, *The Pedlar Pillaged by Apes*, 1562. Engraving, 22.5 x 29 cm. Bibliothèque Royale Belgique, Brussels. S V 70758

32 Pieter van der Heyden, after Pieter Bruegel, *The Temptation of St.Anthony*, 1556. Engraving, 24.5 x 32 cm. Bibliothèque Royale Belgique, Brussels. S I 7602

33a Francois Desprez, XLIV soup-spoon creature; XLVI wheel-feet man, from *Les songes drolatiques de Pantagruel* (Paris, 1565). Photo: after Jules Morel (1869)

33b Francois Desprez, XCIII fish man; XCVI guitar man, from *Les songes drolatiques de Pantagruel* (Paris, 1565). Photo: after Jules Morel (1869)

Chapter 2

Chapter 3

Chapter 4

Chapter 5

90 Pieter Bruegel, *Caritas*, 1559. Pen and brown ink on paper, 22.4 x 29.9 cm. Museum Boijmans van Beuningen, Rotterdam

91 Pieter van der Heyden, after Pieter Bruegel, *Christ's Descent into Limbo*, 1561. Engraving, 23.2 x 29.1 cm. Bibliothèque Royale Belgique, Brussels. S 11 31214

92 Pieter Bruegel, *Death of the Virgin*, c 1564. Oil on panel, 36 x 55 cm. ©NTPL/Angelo Hornak Upton House, The Bearsted Collection (The National Trust)

93 Michael Osendorfer, *Pilgrimages to the Church of the Schonen Maria*, 1521. Engraving. Kunstsammlung der Veste, Coburg / Germany

94 Master of Alkmaar, *Seven Works of Mercy*, polyptych, after restoration. Oil on panel, 101 x 54 cm. Rijksmuseum, Amsterdam. Sk-A-2815.

94a Master of Alkmaar, Burial of the Dead, from *Seven Works of Mercy*, central panel, before restoration after iconoclast attack c. 1566

94b Master of Alkmaar, Burial of the Dead, *Seven Works of Mercy*, after restoration

95 Pieter Bruegel, *The Sermon of St John the Baptist*, 1566, Oil on panel, 95 x 160.5 cm. Museum of Fine Arts, Budapest

96 Anon, *Armenseelen attacking from a graveyard*, German, c 1520. Wall painting (destroyed), Marienkirche, Frankfort an de Oder. After Bucheit (1934), courtesy of Widener Library, Harvard College Library. 25212.164

97 Ligier Richier, Tomb of René de Châlons, after 1544, Marble. St Étienne, Bar-le-Duc

98 Michael Wohlgemut, *Dance of Death*, coloured woodcut from the *Nuremberg Chronicle*, f. CCLXIIIIv, by Hartmann Schedel,(1440-1514). University of Iowa Libraries, Iowa City, Iowa

99 Philip Galle (?), after Pieter Bruegel, *The Triumph of Time*, published 1574. Engraving, Bibliothèque Royale Belgique, Brussels. S IV 2183

100 Pieter van der Heyden, after Pieter Bruegel, *The Last Judgement*, 1558. Engraving, 22.5 x 29.5 cm. Bibliothèque Royale Belgique, Brussels. S1 7609

101a Hans Holbein the Younger, *The Cardinal*, from *The Dance of Death*, c. 1526. Cleveland Museum of Art. Inv 1922.149

101b Hans Holbein the Younger, *The King*, from *The Dance of Death*, c. 1526. Cleveland Museum of Art

102 Pieter Bruegel, *The Misanthrope*, 1568. Oil on panel, 86 x 85 cm. Museo di Capodimonte, Naples. Photo © 2003. SCALA, Florence - courtesy of the Ministero Beni e Att. Culturali

103 Philip Galle, after Pieter Bruegel, *Justitia*, 1559. Engraving, 23.3 x 28.7 cm. Bibliothèque Royale Belgique, Brussels. S II 135128

Introduction

> Multa pinxit, hic Bruegelius, quae pingi non possunt, quod Plinius de Apelle. In omnibus eius operibus intelligitur plus semper quam pingitur.
>
> [As Pliny said of Apelles, our Bruegel has painted well the things which cannot be painted. In all his works there is always more thought than painting.]
>
> Abraham Ortelius, *Album Amicorum* (after 1550)

This is a book about Renaissance surrealism: a study of Pieter Bruegel the Elder's mysterious paintings and prints of carnivals and dreams. It is also a book about how and why dreams and carnivals underwent a revolution in representation in the later Renaissance, and how this re-shaped the ways we experience public and private fantasy. I will argue that Bruegel's art brought about a convergence between traditions of dream representation and carnivalesque imagery. Successive chapters explore the visual cultures of masquerade, dream and nightmare in the sixteenth-century, to explain how Bruegel and his contemporaries saw these phenomena, and how this imagery was used to reshape the landscape of the Western imaginary.

Born at the end of a century of astonishing artistic achievement and innovation, Pieter Bruegel is now best known for landscape and peasant paintings (figs. 1, 2, 82), such as his famous *Hunters in the Snow*, *Peasant Dances* and *Peasant Weddings*. In art historical terms, what this means is that Bruegel devised not one but two new, interlinked genres: the stand-alone landscape and the scene of peasant life. He thus engineered a decisive shift in the subject matter of Western art, away from the representation of gods and saints, towards the material and the secular. Bruegel is unique among the great artists of the Renaissance in his attention to folk culture and fantasy as subjects for fine art. Contemporaries hailed him as *a new Bosch who brings his master's ingenious dreams to life once more* — famous for his work in the idiom of Hieronymus Bosch (c. 1450-1516), master of the surreal and the otherworldly. Bruegel's "Boschian" designs include his *Seven Deadly Sins* (figs. 9-15), the *Fall of the Rebel Angels* (fig. 21), *Dulle Griet* (fig. 35) and the *Triumph of Death* (fig. 89). My object in this volume is to explore the sources and meaning of these surreal works, in order to discover not just what they mean, but how they mean. Hence the present title: carnivals and dreams. This rubric suggests the common psychological territory of Bruegel's work as an ethnographer of the imaginary. For Bruegel fused many novel materials into his reinvention of Bosch. He took much from the world of the popular imagination, from traditional lore and festivals, masks and stories, rituals, rhymes and metaphors, games, processions, plays and costumes. He was interested in monsters and nightmares, in sin, in the "irrational" aspects of Carnival practices and carnivalesque imagery, and in the traditions and rituals of popular religion.

The way that Bruegel approached these materials opens deep questions about how the discourses of carnivals and dreams were structured in the social and mental world in which he lived. Broadly speaking, dreams were inside and carnivals outside his *milieu*. Bruegel was not, of course, himself a peasant. He worked for the educated cosmopolitan elites of the Spanish Netherlands; his friends and customers were merchants and bankers, government officials, fellow craftsmen, printers and scholars. He shared their Humanist, mercantile view of the world. Therefore when he depicted subjects drawn from folk-culture, such as feast-days and proverbial wisdom, he did so from a self-consciously external viewpoint. In this sense, his art mediated with, as much as it meditated on, the popular imagination.

The major event that framed this artist's life (and the lives of everyone around him) was the Reformation. This complex struggle between Catholics and Reformers redrew the map of Europe, put an end to the ideal of a unified Christendom, and redefined the mental world of Europeans. In the long run, it marked the rise of modern secular capitalism, heralded the demise of the Papacy as a world power, and the beginning of the end of the divine rights of kings. For the Netherlands, then under Spanish control, the geo-political dimensions of these theological debates and struggles were very clear. Relations with the Hapsburg Imperial government worsened year by year under the pressure of competing financial and confessional demands. Shortly after Bruegel's death, following a bloody civil war and revolution, the Netherlands were partitioned into Northern and Southern provinces, the origins of the present division between the Netherlands and what is now Belgium.

The efforts of reformers on both sides of the Catholic-Protestant divide to "clean up" popular culture (particularly popular Christianity) had equally far-reaching consequences. The Reformation constituted a war on Carnival and carnivalesque performances, as well as a war against Catholic ritual. Peter Burke speaks of this as the "Triumph of Lent"[1] — at first most visible in the culture of Puritanism, ultimately spreading its norms through the whole of the West. Lenten values triumphed both in the streets and in the minds of individuals. City authorities took to themselves increasingly greater powers to police the behaviour of their citizens; at the same time, new codes of civility and self-control induced individuals to police their own behaviour. Writing about the later eighteenth-century, Foucault called this change a shift to the *microphysics of power*: an internalisation of Lenten codes, the *sine qua non* of modern urban capitalist society.[2]

These seismic events shaped Bruegel's thinking about matters of belief and provided him with the subjects for many satires (his attitude to the issues of the Reformation is discussed in Chapters 4 and 5). Most of the works where he deals with religion are fantastical, and they seem at first sight to have little to do with the war of ideas being conducted on every street. But, as we will see, these fantasies draw on contemporary ideas about the imagination. They can be thought of as studies on the upheavals taking place in people's minds, as the lines separating supernatural from natural were redrawn and reorganized.

It seems best to start by setting out a range of key contexts which intersect in the figure of Pieter Bruegel. The first of these deals with chronologies: the basic facts about Bruegel's life and the main ways in which his art has been assessed and interpreted over the last century. The next context is the intellectual background to Renaissance surrealism: theories of the creative faculty, and of the unconscious mind. Early modern psychology started from the problem of the inspired mind: novel concepts of the mechanism of inspiration, as envisaged by the Neo-Platonic Humanists, widened and deepened concepts of psychology and creativity in the century before Bruegel. How sixteenth-century people understood the unconscious mind is then illustrated with a short case-history: Bruegel's designs for the Seven Deadly Sins. Finally, the sociological context: a brief account of the issues involved in "translating" folk and popular culture for literate audiences. All these themes overlap and inform each other; from different angles and tangents they converge on and construct our subject: Bruegel and the history of the imagination.

Life and Times

First, let us meet the man himself. The outline of Bruegel's life is well-known, though facts are sparse.[3] Born around 1528, probably in the province of Brabant, to fairly well-off parents, Bruegel seems to have received his early training at Malines, a centre specializing in paintings on linen. The main source for his career is Karel van Mander (c. 1548-1606), writing his *Lives of the Netherlandish Artists*, in imitation of Giorgio Vasari (c. 1511-1574), a generation after Bruegel's death.[4] Bruegel was apprenticed to the workshop of Pieter Coecke van Aelst (c. 1502-1550), and Mayeken Verhulst Bessemers, whose daughter he married in 1563. Bessemers is one

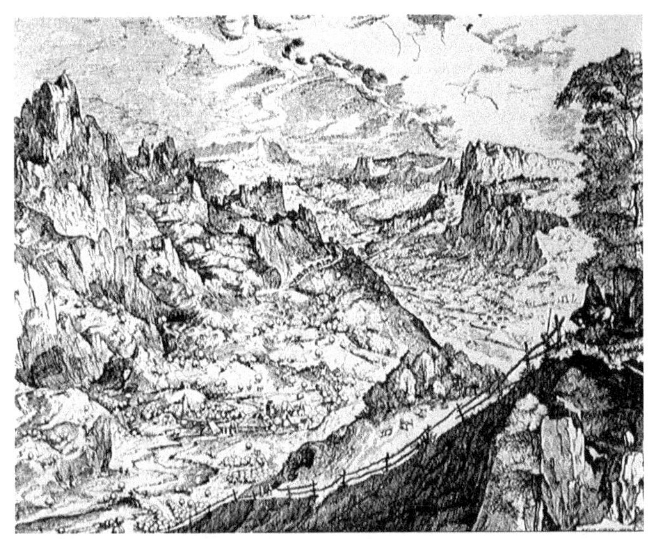

1 Joannes and Lucas van Doetecum, after Pieter Bruegel the Elder, Large Alpine Landscape, 1555-6. Etching with engraving, 36.8 x 46.8 cm. Museum Boijmans Van Beuningen, Rotterdam BdH 23963. Photo: ArtServe/ANU

of the possible candidates for the identity of the enigmatic early sixteenth-century painter known as the Brunswick Monogrammist, often cited as a close predecessor for Bruegel's style.

Bruegel's training thus took place in an unusually cosmopolitan workshop. Bessemers was a famous miniaturist, mentioned by Lodovico Guicciardini (c. 1521-1589), and Vasari. Coecke is known, among other things, for his ethnographical drawings of Turkish costumes and customs. He died in Brussels in 1550 (where members of the Bruegel family were already living) and the next year, we find Bruegel enrolled as a Master in the Guild of St. Luke at Antwerp. Both guild and city were then at the zenith of their powers.

In 1552, Bruegel travelled to Italy by way of Lyons and the Alps. He visited the Gulf of Naples, and may have withessed the sea-battle there against the Turks. At Rome in 1553, possibly using his training from Bessemers, he collaborated on several miniatures with the Serb artist Giulio

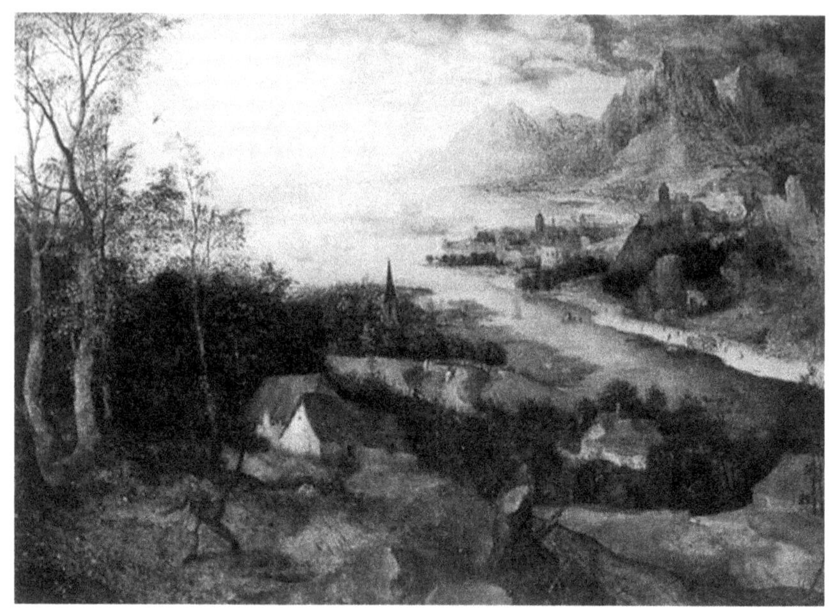

2 Pieter Bruegel the Elder, *Landscape with Parable of the Sower*, 1557. Oil on wood, 29 x 40.5" Putnam Foundation, Timken Museum of Art, San Diego

Clovio (c. 1498-1578), then moving in the aristocratic circles of the Farnese family. At his death, the inventory of Clovio's possessions listed nine compositions by Bruegel. Bruegel may already have been sponsored by the entrepreneur print-seller, Hieronymus Cock (d. 1570) to make drawings which could be engraved and sold as prints during this trip. By 1555, he was back in Antwerp designing prints for Cock; the first of which were two series of landscape prints, presumably based on drawings he made while travelling through the Alps (fig. 1). His earliest extant figurative works are also print designs: the series of the Seven Vices and Seven Virtues. He continued working for Cock throughout the 1560s.

Bruegel's first ascribed and dated painting also follows his return from Italy, and uses a similar composition to the landscape print designs: a large vista with one or two small figures in a corner of the foreground (1557; fig. 2). In 1559 he embarked on a series of ambitious large-scale paintings known as the *theatrum mundi* works: *Netherlandish Proverbs* (1559;

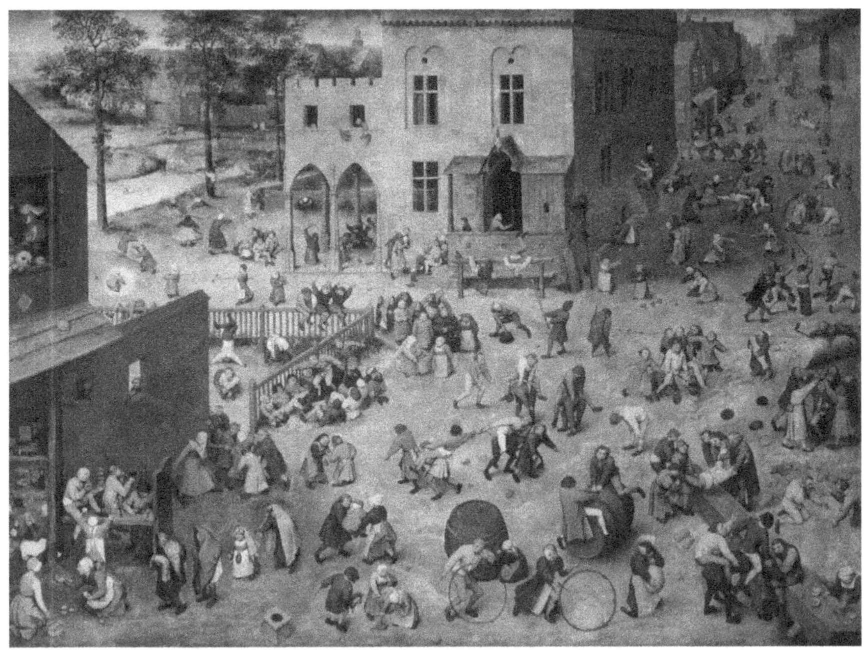

3 Pieter Bruegel the Elder, Children's Games, 1560. Oil on wood, 118 x 161 cm. Kunsthistorisches Museum Wien oder KHM, Vienna. Inv. GG 1017

fig. 63), *The Battle Between Carnival and Lent* (1559; fig. 71), *Children's Games* (1560; fig. 3). Around 1562, he turned fully from prints to painting; in 1563, following his marriage, he moved to Brussels, the seat of the Imperial administration. He died there on the 5th of September 1569.

During his lifetime, known owners of his paintings include: Clovio, Nicholas Jonghelinck (fl.1550-66), a merchant; Cardinal Granvelle (c. 1517-86), governor of the Spanish Netherlands; and Abraham Ortelius (c. 1527-98), the map-illuminator and geographer. This chronology and this *milieu* generated the content of Bruegel's art: novel depictions of fantasies and folk culture; magical subjects and lampoons on proverbial thinking. How, then, would an artist of the mid-sixteenth-century approach the various philosophical and popular discourses involved in the culture of carnivals and dreams? What were the available starting points, and possible perspectives on these matters?

The first important perspective is that of his profession. Bruegel was a trained artist, a guild master, who could hardly help but be aware that the prestige of his craft as a painter was a relatively new phenomenon.[5] This rise in status had happened in the recent past: Jan van Eyck and Leonardo were the first world-famous artists; Titian and Michaelangelo were living legends when Bruegel was a young man. These people transcended the previous social status of artists as craftsmen (manual labourers); now ranked as closer to philosophers (mental labourers), they were seen as inspired and praised for their originality. This issue of originality in art was bound up with the subjects of temperament and theories of the imagination.

The recent elevation of Bruegel's profession thus leads into the discourse of the imagination on several levels. Renaissance theories about personal creativity and the mechanisms of inspiration provided the first framework for thinking about individual psychology in general. The same, Renaissance theories of inspiration and genius still shape current efforts to comprehend how far outside his or her culture an artist can operate, and to define what is meant by "original" thought. All this has a bearing on how the workings of the mind, and the zone of dreams were understood in sixteenth-century terms, and how we understand these concerns now.

Originality remains a key guiding concept in the history of art. Since the Renaissance, to credit an artist with an innovation is to automatically increase his or her importance within the general scheme of things. The whole subject of originality remains vexed because ideas about it emanate from this Renaissance matrix. The more "unprecedented" an artwork appears to be, the harder it is to understand. Clearly, all imagery has precedents: new work does not emerge from a vacuum. The paradox is that, while claims of "originality" remain central to the rhetoric of assigning value, actually this value is more often ascribed only to work that has a visible following.

This has a particular bearing on efforts to place Bruegel's oeuvre in the canon of Western art. In Bruegel's case, the works which we regard as his most original are not at all the same as those works for which he was most acclaimed in his time as the *second Bosch*. The meaning of his surreal imagery really is, of course, obscure, often turning on puns and allusions whose key referents are now lost or buried. But barriers to interpretation exist also on the methodological level: in terms of the way art historians (and art history as a whole) "set up" Bruegel's art as worthy of attention in the first place on account of its originality.

Bruegel and the Art Historians

Bruegel's originality was first supposed to lie in his landscapes and peasant (or genre) pictures. The founders of art history as a discipline were concerned both with identifying and praising originality, and with constructing clear genealogies of artists, and classification schemes of periods, styles and genres. Bruegel's landscapes and genre scenes (figs. 1, 2) had an obvious lineage in the works of successive generations of painters. Indeed, by the nineteenth-century, genre painting was the predominant mode. Landscape and "scenes of everyday life" were effectively all that were left in Western painting, of the much greater range of subjects available to Renaissance artists. This coloured the views of the first scholarly art historians to turn their attention to Bruegel.

Bruegel's surreal works, like the works of Bosch himself, did not fit this picture of development; with a few exceptions such as Goya, the later paths of Western art did not appear to have followed this direction. By the 1930s, this view had changed again: André Breton and the Surrealists hailed Bosch as an ancestor. They understood their new word, *surrealism,* also to refer to a type of fantasy, usually (though not always) expressed in the visual arts (perhaps particularly in painting), which had existed for centuries. From this tradition, they derived their chief formal tools:

hybridisation, especially of human and animal; change of scale; concern with the passions. Among writers of the period whose eyes were opened by this contemporary art, the art historian Charles de Tolnay became convinced that some of Bruegel's pictures, like those of Bosch, must have some connection with dreams and systems of dream representation.

Still, the first students of Bruegel's folkloric pictures took a different line. Following the Warburg style of iconographical research in the 1940s and 50s,[6] Stridbeck, Zupnick et al decided Bruegel must be aligned with his contemporaries. Humanism in the North was seen as having a strongly didactic and sententious bent: preoccupied with the (Lenten) Reformation goals of educating and "raising" public taste and behaviour. Bruegel's folkloric and fantastic works could then be assimilated to the Humanist-emblematist circles of Christopher Plantin (c. 1514-89) and Maarten van Heemskerck's (c. 1498–1574) Antwerp.[7] Plantin was a famous printer, translator, classicist and closet Reformer; van Heemskerck adapted the Italian visual language of allegorical nudes and personifications to make didactic images of a social reforming character (fig. 54). So it was reasoned that the vogue for printed emblem books and designs with moralising messages (in fact reaching its zenith in the seventeenth century) would provide the key to unlock the meaning of Bruegel's obscure fantasy. Since all the other contemporary artists and writers who dealt with folk culture took this moralising line, it was safe to assume that Bruegel did too. Where revelry or feastdays were depicted, the point must be, as in the emblem tradition, to rail against drunkenness and waste. Thus was born what is still a prevailing orthodoxy about Bruegel's folkloric works: that they are diatribes against *folly*. Though much useful research came of this conception, I argue that it is a misconception — perhaps it would be better to call it a mistranslation — of Bruegel's relationship to the preoccupations of his contemporaries. They may have been concerned with folly: he was concerned with madness (see Chapter 2).

The issue of determining the artist's social class operated here in several respects. Bruegel's most famous subject matter made his familiarity with the peasant world obvious to nineteenth-century collectors. However, when this art was reassessed in the early twentieth century, it was necessary to get rid of the soubriquet, *Peasant Bruegel.* The desire to place Bruegel among the Humanists meant that his work was divided into *genre* scenes and *didactic* (or "moralising") designs. The former had a clear lineage in seventeenth-century Netherlandish art, and established Bruegel's situation in the main line of descent of later art. The latter could be understood, like the works of the emblematists, in terms of civic Humanist moralism. Bruegel's works in the Boschian idiom did not easily fit either category. Since they were clearly not *scenes of everyday life* (genre), they had to be classed as didactic. They tended also to be viewed as backward-looking (the art of Bosch himself was regarded at that time as late medieval rather than Renaissance), and glossed over as a youthful passing phase. The insights of De Tolnay and the Surrealists (about both Bosch and Bruegel) were lost at this point. Where the surrealism could not be recuperated as moralism, it was ignored.

As ideas about the interaction of class and ideas changed towards the middle of the twentieth century, efforts were made to interpret Bruegel's folklorish pictures anew, as expressions of sympathy for the life of the common people. The artist's political and religious beliefs were re-scrutinised: could he have been an incipient democrat? Or at least a nationalist? Attempts to see him as an illustrator of current events faced another set of difficulties.[8] Bruegel seems to have resolutely refused to take sides in the quarrels of the Reformation. The nationalist cause was barely articulated in the 1560s, and we know that his work was highly thought of by the Spanish appointee Governor, Cardinal Granvelle. The artist died too soon (September 1569)[9] to see the "Spanish Fury," when Imperial soldiers ran riot in the streets of Antwerp, killing seven thousand residents. This was the event which sparked the Prince of Orange's revolt, and the subsequent establishment of the Dutch Republic.

In the 1980s and 90s, art historical work on Bruegel concentrated on setting in order his achievement as a draughtsman,[10] and considering more complex possible attitudes embodied in his depictions of peasant festivities.[11] Scholars engaged in both endeavours continued to try to fit the pictures into the Humanist *milieu*.[12] The activities of Bruegel's main publisher, Hieronymus Cock, at the print shop of the Four Winds, for example, have been well studied.[13] The issue of surreality attracted less scholarly attention, but two ground-breaking essays are particularly relevant here. The folklorists Dundes and Stibbe tabulated anew all the proverbs in the *Netherlandish Proverbs* (fig. 63). They realised for the first time that Bruegel's "illustrations" of these sayings in fact subverted the meaning of their proverbial sources. At the same time, the hegemony of the *folly* interpretation received its first serious blow when Edward Snow conducted a visual analysis of *Children's Games* (fig. 3) and demonstrated the gulf between Bruegel's approach to this popular subject matter and the Lenten concerns of the emblematists (this subject is explored in Chapters 3 and 4).[14]

These were important steps in reframing Bruegel's attitudes to popular culture. What of his relationship to the wider intellectual culture of the day? The first great writers on Bruegel, Max Dvorak, Max Friedlander and De Tolnay placed his art firmly in the context of European intellectual history. Their observations on the broader meanings of his work tended to be laid aside by later scholars as too obvious or too speculative. This was as much a rejection of the sweeping essay-like nature of the prose (too Romantic), as it was a rejection of assumptions implicit in the methodology (too Hegelian).

The relation of intellectual history and philosophy to art remains problematic: in what sense can philosophical systems lie behind paintings, and changes in the thought of an era parallel changes in its art? For De Tolnay the connection between Bruegel's vision and the Neo-Platonic philosophers of the previous century simply required to be stated in order to be understood:

> In Bruegel, it is the whole image of the world which becomes an animated organism. The origin of this world image finds itself in the philosophy of Humanists of the 15th century. For the first time, Nicholas Cusanus said of the earth, that it is, so to speak, a great animal, the rocks of which are bones, the rivers of which are veins, the trees, hair. To this thought, which Leonardo da Vinci, Marsilio Ficino, and others took up, Bruegel first gave a plastic form....
>
> Bruegel, founding his landscapes on both Netherlandish and Italian points of view, becomes at one and the same time the Northern artist and the European artist *par excellence*. The sympathetic regard which he throws on the life of the little Brabant villages, on the people unconscious of their true misery, is not that of the soul of the peasant but of the soul of the Humanist who has the whole world for his country.[15]

Broadly speaking there is nothing wrong with this. But the link between the art and the concepts invoked is asserted, or pointed to, rather than demonstrated. For example, the same Neo-Platonic principles which gave rise to the concept of the animate landscape could also be seen as re-stating an archaic or folk world-view, wherein the earth naturally swarmed with unseen spirits and demons. Even radical Protestant groups, otherwise very far from sharing from Neo-Platonic ideas, believed that spirits (conceived of as wholly negative) could animate matter. In other words, we could find intellectual evidence for some form of the animate landscape emanating from any number of otherwise opposed sixteenth-century platforms. On its own, De Tolnay's insight does not establish a specifically Neo-Platonic connection.

Efforts to build more definite bridges between Bruegel and the Neo-Platonic *zeitgeist* tended to founder on this kind of issue. There is a general lack of biographical bricks in the case of Bruegel.[16] We know Bruegel was in Italy, but we know very little about who he met and what he did there. Similar obstacles apply to efforts to fit him into Northern moralist contexts in Antwerp or Brussels.

There are other problems with the assumption that the intellectual content of an era is contained in the philosophies of its elite, and that this content is accessed mainly through reading. In very few cases can it be shown that a certain painter read a certain philosopher. Where this can be done, this fact gives no assurance that this same philosophy is somehow "contained" in a painter's works, as if painting stood to philosophy as a jug to water. Similarly, in cases where philosophical ideas demonstrably do inform particular artworks, and where one can show that the creator of the work had specific texts in mind, this still does not mean that the meaning of the artwork is "the same as" that of the parent text. Reading, in any case, is not the only means of transmitting ideas: some ideas are *in the air,* in conversation, in turns of phrase or style. To speak of *Humanist art* glides over this difficulty. The connotations of *Humanist,* as the term came to be used in connection with Bruegel, are too narrow and too text-oriented to describe the range of ideas signified by the art.

Looking at the whole range of images and visual conceptions within Bruegel's culture, a different approach is needed to establish the artist's relationship to Italian and Northern Humanist ideals, motivations and ways of thinking. Let me try then to re-graft De Tolnay's insight back on to the stem of art-historical thinking about Bruegel. A change of vocabulary helps. The point of all quintessentially Renaissance activity was to redraw the universe, expecting to find its science divine and its divinity scientific. The visual arts were at the centre of this project — arguably more central than conventional philosophy. These mapping and re-mapping exercises were bound, here and there, to come across the limits of what was known. An artist might then apply the tools of *spatialising philosophy* — including the collection and comparison of data — as a means of expressing and investigating the paradoxes thrown up by the clash of competing, or incommensurable systems of representation. As Snow suggested:

> The act of painting was for Bruegel a rethinking and often a refusal of his culture's attitudes, not an automatic mirroring of them... those

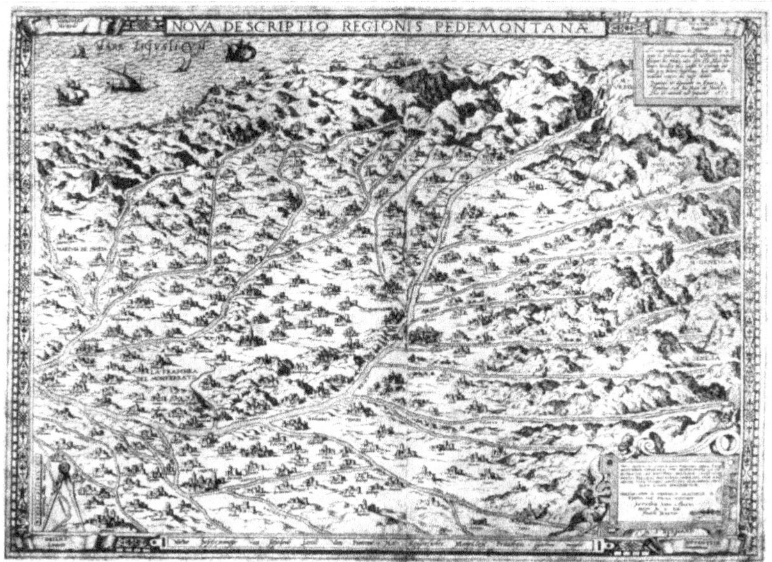

4 *Map of Piedmont*, published by Hieronymus Cock, Antwerp, 1552. Engraving, 53.3 x 74.3 cm. Bibliothèque National, Paris

> attitudes were at any rate such conglomerates of warring differences that they cannot serve as "given" points of reference with which to stabilise his meanings.
>
> [It is] more fruitful to regard Bruegel's work as a perspective from which to make sense of the ambiguities of its historical context. The paintings... suggest that this is how he himself regarded his enterprise.[17]

What we all agree is *original* in Bruegel's art is its capacity to invert and alter (*détourner*) the previous arrangements (or signifying fields) of inherited visual traditions. Bruegel's particular *spatialising philosophy* (Renaissance perspective) was cartographic in the widest sense: this was the experimental platform from which he could choreograph anew a variety of visual codes; folkloric, classical, Christian, even pagan. Cartography was a key ingredient in this project; bear in mind that Cock himself published maps (fig. 4), as well as fine art prints, and that Ortelius, the author of the first atlas, was also part of this circle. Looked at in this way, Bruegel's surreal designs share the same principles as his landscapes. We can see his general approach — the way his mind set about constructing innovative images — in the techniques he perfected for creating the illusion of a co-extensive landscape. Before Bruegel, the traditional "marks for landscape" were transmitted through pattern books; literally part of the cultural capital of the painters' guilds. They existed as separable sets of schemata — for mountains, trees, rivers etc. Starting with his designs for the Alpine landscapes, Bruegel devised a new graphic schema that would create a different kind of jigsaw — interlocking irregular parallelograms set along a horizontal axis (see figs. 1, 2, 82). The resulting pattern generates illusory space. The same technique was used to orchestrate his figurative panoramas, notably the *theatrum mundi* works (figs. 3, 63, 71), the *Dulle Griet*, and the *Triumph of Death* (figs. 35, 89).

This typically Bruegelian procedure can also be seen as a variation on the ruling "mannerist" aesthetic described by Vasari: "selecting" ideal parts to create an ideal whole. If we inflect the meaning of *ideal* to signify *existing only in the mind*, then we can see that even the hybrids in Bruegel's works as a *second Bosch* were created by this same technical process (*châine operatoire*).[18] This aesthetic project of selection and recombination had far-reaching results in the field of visual fantasy. To understand its resonance, we can borrow some explanatory concepts from outside art history, in particular from the kind of analysis which Jacques Le Goff called *archaeopsychology*.[19] Visual artists are specialists in representation. Their power resides, as it were, on the cusp of cultural change, where shifts in collective visualisation can first be perceived and made visible; manifested in art. The situation addressed by the new imagery may suddenly leap into view, as if the creation of the imagery itself speeds up the arrival of the situation into full consciousness. At the same time, folk visual culture is conservative; its repertoire remains stable over long periods. This conservatism evokes the *longue durée* of the *Annales* school; the longest cycle of duration within cultural history. Such continuities experienced a crisis with the coming of printing, when the rate and range of distribution of pictorial models increased astronomically. Folk traditions underwent profound alteration as they were translated from oral to "fixed" media. As Bruegel drew folk materials through the double prism of literacy and perspective, his finished imagery expressed and compressed the weight of these larger, collective changes in meaning.

Many monographs use the concept of considering an artist's work as a kind of concentrated window into time, through which the concerns of the age are funnelled to become visible in the art. This book is designed rather to suggest the shape of an hourglass or prism, wherein the "raw" materials of culture enter into the condensed semiotic space of the artwork, and emerge in a different legible order, with some elements suppressed, some distorted, some stressed. Making use of the *longue durée* perspective, we can regard Bruegel's artwork as a kind of terminus for older traditions. One can go further than this, and say that the moment at which a subject matter which the culture as a whole had conserved as images emerges into a fine art medium, marks a decisive change in the significance of that subject matter.

The attention of Bruegel's synthetic mind to carnivals and dreams at this time is itself revealing. The distinctions we need to make here cannot be entirely resolved in terms of printed or written matter versus an oral tradition, though the surreal art of the Renaissance to a great extent marks the experience of transition between the two forms. Cultural transformations brought about by printing were manifested as much in broadsheets and printed pictures as in printed books. The illiterate majority participated in the upheavals of their time, as well as those who could read. There is no simple dichotomy between the categories *high* culture and *low* culture when the *milieu* in question is an early modern independent city, ruled by an oligarchy rather than an aristocracy, and inhabited by multilingual craftsmen. When considering the production of novel images in early modern Europe (or indeed at any other time), we are always dealing with people who partake of both *high* and *low cultures*.

Better than *high* versus *low*, or *literate* versus *illiterate,* is the anthropological formulation *cognitive* versus *non-cognitive*: to distinguish between the aspects of their culture that a people openly know, understand, and have explanations for, and those aspects that are not explained or discussed because they *go without saying*, because they are taboo in some sense, or because they contradict or compensate for elements in the cognitive version. The presence of folkloric traditions in the minds of literate sixteenth-century people can be described as non-cognitive. Their appearance in conscious art can then be thought of as marking a change of status in this subject matter, from non-cognitive to cognitive, within the whole society: the collective culture.

That collective states of mind — comprised of superstitions, beliefs, ritualized behaviour — operate powerfully in everyday life has been demonstrated beyond doubt for the early modern period, notably by Jacques Le Goff, Keith Thomas, Pierre Francastel, Carlo Ginzburg and Lionel Rothkrug.[20] Rothkrug, for, studied changes in the cultural use and construction of sacred places over two millennia, and refered to these group patterns of behaviour "collectivities," as we will se in Chapter 5. [21] In this sense, the imagery of rural and urban festivals manifests collective attitudes to seasonal time. Some of the non-cognitive aspects of his society that interested Bruegel — such as proverbial images — express collective psychology: they configure common mental states and express common attitudes about mental states. Thus proverbs to do with *uppity* women encode the misogynist assumptions of the day; these meanings are explored in the *Dulle Griet* (fig. 35; Chapter 2). In Bruegel's surreal art, non-cognitive subject-matter coincides closely with what is now regarded as the sphere of the unconscious: the irrational and fantastic side of human thought.

The Unconscious in the Sixteenth Century

Let us be clear about what is meant by this word, the *unconscious*. Sigmund Freud, in establishing the concept, *was careful to say that it was not a place, but still it has achieved that status*.[22] Klein warned that there is a danger of,

> [humanity] being endowed with two minds, namely a conscious mind and an unconscious mind. [There is] a not uncommon tendency to personify or reify the unconscious into some sort of spectral homunculus or psychic entity controlling the content of dreams, initiating blunders of speech and action, and even solving problems while the conscious mind is asleep.[23]

He proposed instead that,

> the concept of non-sensory ideation as a synonym for reflection, thinking, judging, and other cognitive processes [better] suggests the unity of mental life.[24]

States commented,

> The notion that the unconscious is a *spectral homunculus* or even a discrete region of the brain is not held by many brain specialists. But one encounters the metaphor of the homunculus, or something like it, often enough in both clinical and literary commentary to suggest that it has some force, if only as an unexamined assumption. In typical usage, it is something less than an anatomical fact and more than a verbal convenience.[25]

This last is the *commonsensical* usage I adopt here and in subsequent discussions. By Bruegel's time, this *spectral* aspect of the mind had been formulated anew in Neo-Platonic terms. To understand how this was done involves returning to the subject of originality and the mind of the artist from a somewhat different perspective.

Any investigation of how the unconscious mind was conceived of in the sixteenth century must begin with the theory of humours: the central paradigm of ancient and medieval medicine. Aristotle and Galen thought that there were four kinds of fluids present in the human body in various combinations. An imbalance of humours, a deficiency or a preponderance of one or another caused disease; different proportions determined the temperament of the individual. Aristotle devoted a good deal of time and study to the problem of why artistic inspiration was found in people dominated by black bile, the humour that causes melancholy.[26]

The question of the connection between creativity and melancholy was picked up intermittently throughout the Middle Ages by various authors, but it was not until a professor at Padua, Antonio Guainerio (d. 1440), took up the subject that the study of melancholy began to evolve out of the field of medieval medicine into the new field of Renaissance psychology. Guainerio suggested that the stars influence the melancholic. He believed that, in the state of ecstasy to which melancholics are liable, hampering bodily senses are dampened. The soul of the melancholic can therefore perceive first, the divine innate ideas that every soul had before birth, and second, the influence of the presiding star of that individual.

The doctor thus solved Aristotle's problem. The black humour clears the mind of its corporeal muddling. The soul can then receive creative inspiration either by remembering divine ideas put there before birth by God (Plato's theory of knowledge), or by directly intuiting signals from its ruling star. This, says Guainerio, explains why any melancholic, even the most uneducated peasant, can produce works of inspiration while in the grip of his controlling humour.

The philosopher, doctor and translator of Plato, Marsilio Ficino (1433-99) gathered up this material in the 1480s in his famous *De Vita Triplici*, "On the Triple Life."[27] Here as elsewhere, Ficino tried to reconcile Aristotelian and Platonic doctrine. In the melancholic's state of ecstasy, Ficino recognised Plato's divine frenzy, creativity. Plato describes how the poet sings in a state of intoxication, in elation, in a trance, not conscious of what he does. For Ficino, this divine *furor* is equivalent to being wholly caught up in a love of beauty, which is indistinguishable from the love of God.

Ficino identified several species of *furor*. At the top of the list is the frenzy which leads one directly to God, the soul travelling upwards in its Phaedran chariot. Secondly, the human can travel towards God through loving another person and recognizing the spark of the divine in that individual, since all forms of love are subsets of the soul's basic passion for God. He ranked third and last the form of divine frenzy which produces creative art. Deep implications followed from Ficino's work. One might note in passing his audacity in including carnal love, however implicitly, in the realm of the transcendent. From the point of view of defining the artistic mind, the consequences were large enough. From Ficino's philosophy derived the threefold classification of melancholy. The first and highest kind produces theologians; the second, philosophers; the third, artists.[28]

Ficino himself was a saturnine melancholic. One of the most interesting aspects of the way in which he developed this idea of melancholy was derived from his own experience of having a very unpromising star-chart. The *De Vita Triplici*, published in 1489, took a decisive step towards redefining the experiential bridge between soul and temperament in the person of a melancholic in such a way as to bring it much closer to what we now understand by individual psychology. As a consequence, creativity itself became further interiorized. Unlike any of its predecessors, the *De Vita Triplici* was a handbook designed to help the melancholic control his fearsome humour. Moreover, in the course of encouraging the melancholic to achieve this control, which would enable him to lead a normal life, the book gave the sufferer a powerful motivation for cultivating and even harnessing melancholy in the pursuit of illumination. This was an important change. Previously, the process of inspiration had been thought of as a non-volitional phenomenon. Now an element of individual volition was felt to be desirable for inspiration to take place to full effect.

The psychoanalyst Ernst Kris analysed Plato's description of inspiration in "primitive", or radically oral, societies, in terms of modern psychological mechanisms:

> We are perhaps thus justified in saying that the inspired leadership of primitive society consists of individuals who are distinguished, among other qualities... by a certain disposition to communicate with the repressed wishes and fantasies in themselves by the use of special mechanisms. These mechanisms are in the nature of projection and introjection. What comes from inside is believed to come from without. The "voice of the unconscious" is externalized and becomes the voice of God, who speaks through the mouth of the chosen... The knowledge which the voice communicates is not only derived from God, but literally given by him. The awareness itself is the result of inspiration as well as a part of it, and thus the driving of the unconscious towards consciousness, the process of becoming conscious, is attributed to the influence of the Divine. In other words, an alteration of cathexis inside the person, the bursting of the frontiers between the unconscious and the conscious, is experienced as an intrusion from without.[29]

Kris is of course describing a state of affairs which has not existed in its "pure" form for millennia (and may never have had a "pure" form). Even by Roman times, he adds, the word *ingenium* no longer had its full mythological meaning (i.e., *possessed by a genius or spirit*). But as a theory of the artistic process, the ancient metaphor was individualised (and effectively psychologised) much further by Ficino.

Instead of the poet or seer abdicating the burden of responsibility associated with constructing and composing his revelation, the melancholic was now urged to take a conscious role in handling and activating the catalyst of revelation, which he bears within him. The states of mind to which a melancholic could fall prey were carefully differentiated. Dürer's famous print, *Melancholia I* (fig. 5) is a bitter and powerful description of the by then well-known melancholic state, where the creative powers lie fallow in a kind of latent torpor.

Recall now the astrological signals, which Guainerio felt that the ecstatic melancholic could receive. In the *De Vita Triplici* Ficino advocated that the melancholic try to attract such heavenly influences as a form of therapy, to balance out and ameliorate the exigencies of melancholy.[30] Minerals, plants and foods, associated with Saturn's opposite numbers, Jupiter and Venus, were the keys to this astrological medicine. Ficino recommended the cultivation of Platonic love and the singing of Orphic hymns, felt to be akin to the music of the spheres. It is significant that the stars were now being credited with the kind of powers of inspiration previously ascribed solely to God. Of course, the ultimate source of this inspiration was still God, but He was now considered to have delegated divine wisdom to the heavenly bodies. In this form, it could be materially manipulated in a way not possible before.

To summarise, whereas previously inspiration was attributable wholly to God, with the human as a passive recipient, from Ficino's time there were, notionally at least, two other factors: an additional divine source, the stars, and the self-consciousness of the melancholic seeking inspiration. The

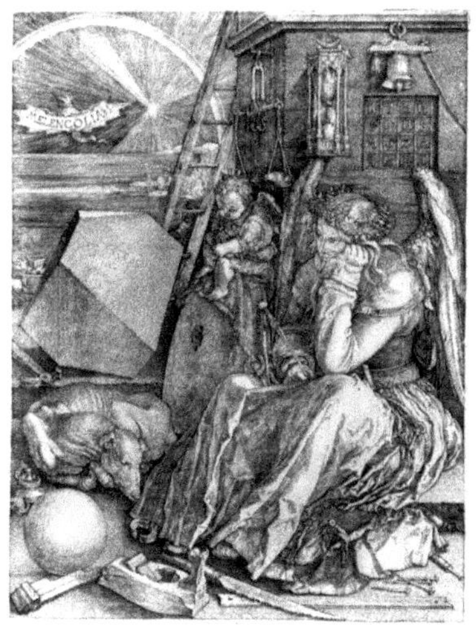

5 Albrecht Dürer, *Melancholia I*, 1514.
Engraving, 31 H 26 cm.
National Galleries of Scotland, Edinburgh

relevance of this for the artist is clear. Kris has this to say about the inspired individual and responsibility:

> Through the idea of inspiration, the communication gains in authority, and the person who communicates it is relieved of the burden of responsibility... [Such] revealed truth... is beyond criticism as well as beyond doubt... The problem of responsibility is more complicated... In speaking of archaic social conditions, we may say that the tale the poet tells derives from or touches upon, the forbidden sphere of wishes, desires, and impulses. Under the assumption of inspiration, not he but the Divine is acting; he is not responsible, his feelings of guilt are relieved, and no anxiety need arise.[31]

This is what Ficino's theories changed; he strengthened the role for will and desire in accounting for creativity. Ficino's importance thus has less to do with his enthusiastic espousal of astrological magic, as with his attempts to shed light, however gropingly, on what Kris calls the *special mechanisms* which allow the conscious mind to communicate with the unconscious. His astrological magic was simply a tool recommended for this purpose. But to posit the existence of such tools called attention for the first time to the *mechanisms* themselves.

At the same time, new responsibility was conferred upon the artist for the content of his work. Leonardo's belief that portraiture should show *the movements of the mind* heralded what was to become a preoccupation of artists in the sixteenth century. Of course, what we now refer to as the unconscious in Ficino's day was regarded as, at best, a gateway to the divine (as we have seen), but at worst, a descent into bestiality, equated with the full assertion of man's animal nature. It lay, in other words, at the top and bottom of everyday existence. On the one hand, sacred intrusions from above, on the other, the overthrow of higher thought by lower impulses conceived of as rooted in the animal human body.

As twenty-first century people who no longer believe in God or humours, we can legitimately ask, what did this sixteenth-century unconscious actually consist of? Anthropology and psychoanalysis suggest some answers. Any individual *en route* to maturity assembles his or her own mind out of the available elements of his or her culture. At a microcosmic level — the level of the individual — the raw materials and the ways in which they can be assembled are, naturally, infinitely varied. However, at the macrocosmic level — the level of collective culture — the general end results of this internalisation — for example, distinctions between conscious and unconscious, responses to sacred structures and taboos — are startlingly uniform.

Geza Ròheim and Jackson Lincoln — followed by Erica Bourgignon, Francis Hsu, and more recently, Suzette Heald, Ariane Deluz and Barbara Tedlock — have studied ideas and images of the sexual, the sacred and the taboo in dreams in tribal or radically oral cultures.[32] "Primitive" dreams and visions take shape within an organisational framework provided by the culture's religious and mythological beliefs.[33] Through these given visual patterns and models, the individual can understand, and to some extent control, those encounters of the waking mind with the unconscious which correspond to experiences of the kind described by Kris. The most common of these, of course, is dreaming.

There may be a real sense in which patterns of the sacred actually organize the structure of the brain itself; a hypothesis which neurology can so far neither confirm nor disprove. It can be said with certainty, however, that, in pre-literate or radically oral cultures, ideas about the sacred are intimately connected with the control of sexuality, with one's relation to one's parents, and with ideas about death. Ethnographical evidence broadly confirms psychoanalytic conclusions about the contents and structure of the unconscious.

None of this is incompatible with the sixteenth century's own ideas about what we now call the unconscious. If the materials which shape the mind during infancy – visual gestural, linguistic – come from culture, they are amenable to study in the same way as any other part of the historical record. And, in fact, a massive literature now exists on official and unofficial sixteenth-century attitudes to the subjects central to the cultural interfaces of the unconscious: sexuality, death, and the sacred. This is the sense in which a common cultural inheritance of and about the unconscious mind informs the content of Renaissance surreal art.

Bruegel's *Vices*

Let us consider how these concerns operate in some of Bruegel's earliest figurative works: the prints of the *Seven Deadly Sins*.[34] The artist commenced this study of human vice around the age of 30, immediately after publishing his *Large* and *Small Landscapes* series. Significantly, perhaps (as discussed in Chapter 2), he began with *Avaritia* (fig. 10), the drawing for which bears the date 1556. The rest of the drawings were made in 1557. The series as a whole was published in 1558 at the Four Winds in Antwerp; a companion series of *Virtues* followed. There is nothing new about the subject itself, personifications of the Seven Deadly sins were centuries-old.[35] However, Bruegel's representations were highly innovative, as we can see by comparing them with two notable versions by famous predecessors: Andrea Mantegna's *Pallas Expelling the Vices from the Garden of Virtue* (c. 1499-1502, fig. 6), and the *Tabletop of the Seven Deadly Sins and Four Last Things* (c 1500-25; fig. 7), by Bosch or his workshop.

Around 1500, Mantegna made his allegory, now in the Louvre.[36] In the picture, idiosyncratically personified Vices are driven by Pallas Athena from a vision of classically-ordered nature, into a dark pool. The conceit involves one of these fusions between classical and Christian forms for which Mantegna was renowned. There are three occult portals in the picture: in the sky, into the garden, and through the surface of the pond. This *Garden of Virtue* is a kind of classicised, allegorised Eden. Pallas Athena is Wisdom; wisdom or knowledge, derived from eating the apple, was what first drove

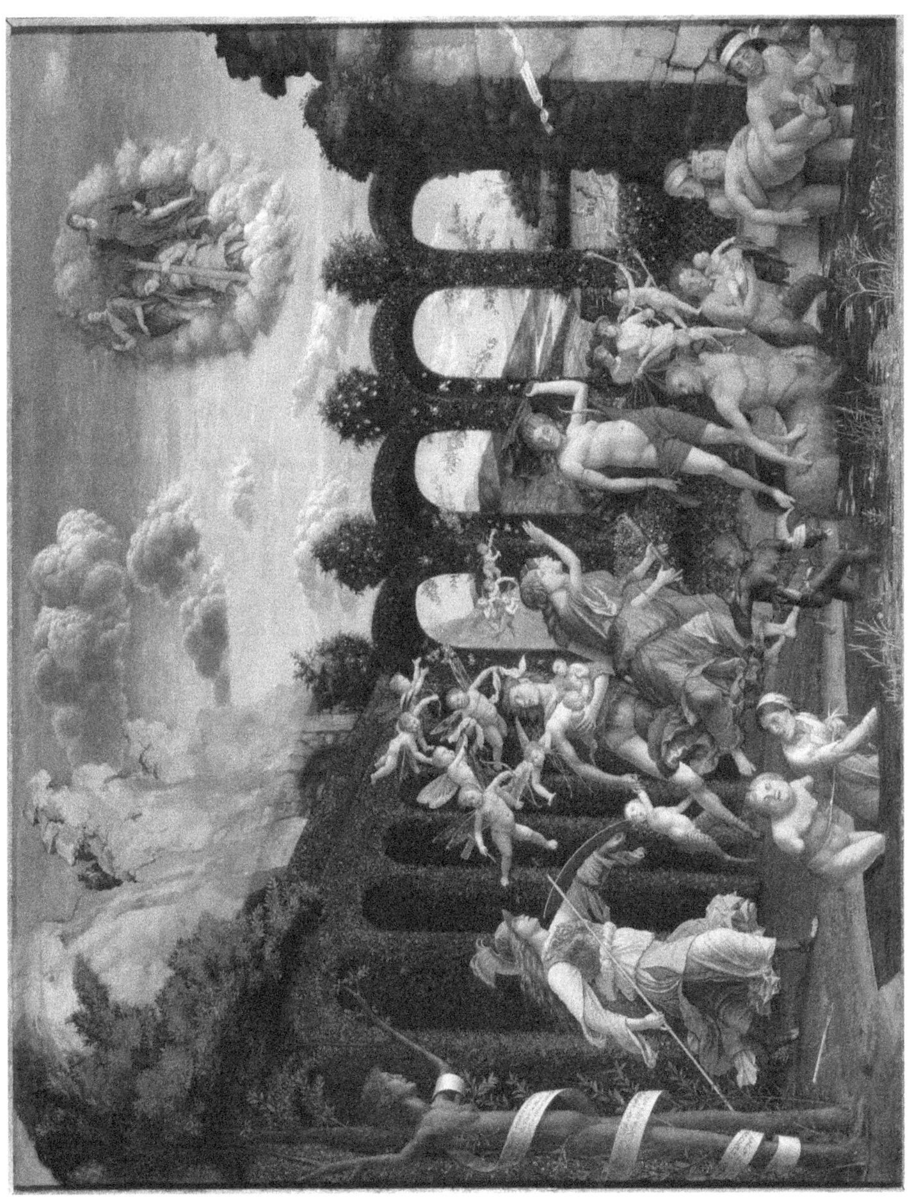

6 Andrea Mantegna, *Pallas Expelling the Vices from the Garden of Virtue*, c 1499-1502. Tempera on canvas, 160 x 192 cm. Musée du Louvre, Paris. Photo: RMN/© Christian Jean

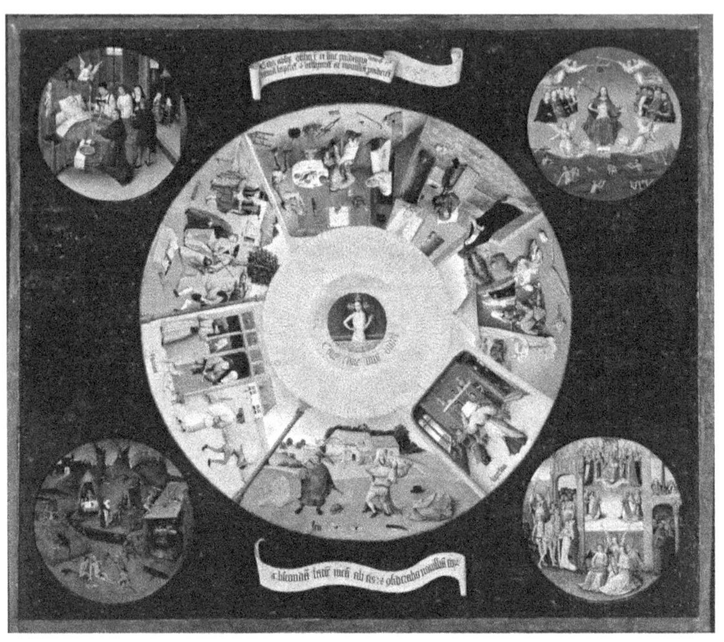

7 Hieronymus Bosch or his workshop, *Tabletop of the Seven Deadly Sins and Four Last Things*, c 1500-25. Oil on wood, 120 x 150 cm. © Museo Nacional del Prado, Madrid

humanity from Eden. Mantegna turns the meaning of the garden around, in line with prevailing Neo-Platonic optimism about human destiny, which held that the ability to choose between good and evil is a mark of human kinship with the divine. This expulsion is a victory over evil. The Garden of Virtue is a sacred space defended by Pallas; it can only be glimpsed from the outside. The Vices are expelled from the double-order of antiquity/nature into black water, wherein they disappear, below the surface of the visible. They are envisaged as deformed, hybrid figures. Possibly Mantegna was aware of Bosch, and shaped the forms of his Vices in response to this imagery, though of course he also drew on straight classical models — centaurs and satyrs — for his monstrous composite sins.

The imagery Bruegel used for his illustrations of each sin derives much more directly from Bosch. Much of the symbolism of *Ira* (fig. 11) is

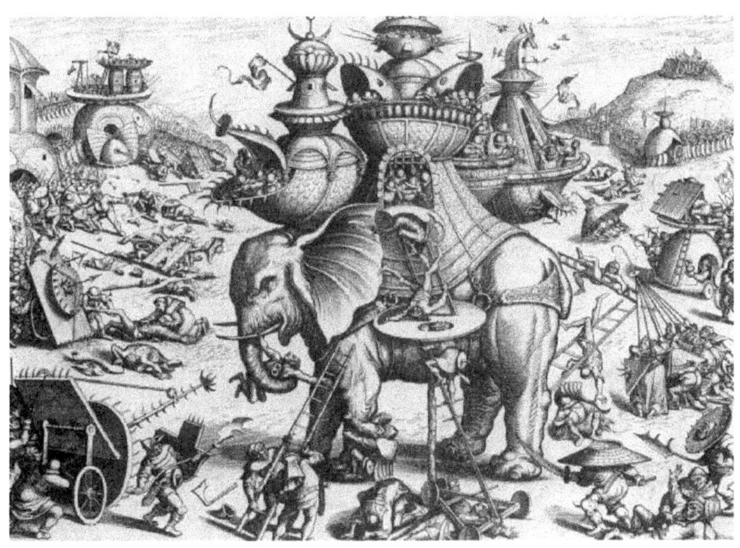

8 Master of St George's Kermis, after Alart Duhameel (School of Hieronymus Bosch), *The Besieging of an Elephant*, mid-sixteenth-century. Engraving, 39.4 x 53.8 cm. Graphische Sammlung Albertina Vienna. Photo: Sotheby's, London, 1990

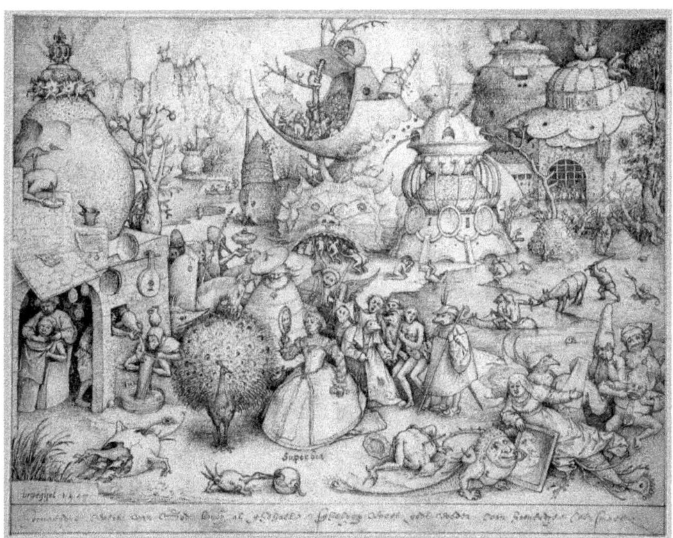

9 Pieter Bruegel, Superbia, 1557. Drawing, pen on paper, 22.9 x 30 cm. Collection Frits Lugt, Institut néerlandais, Paris

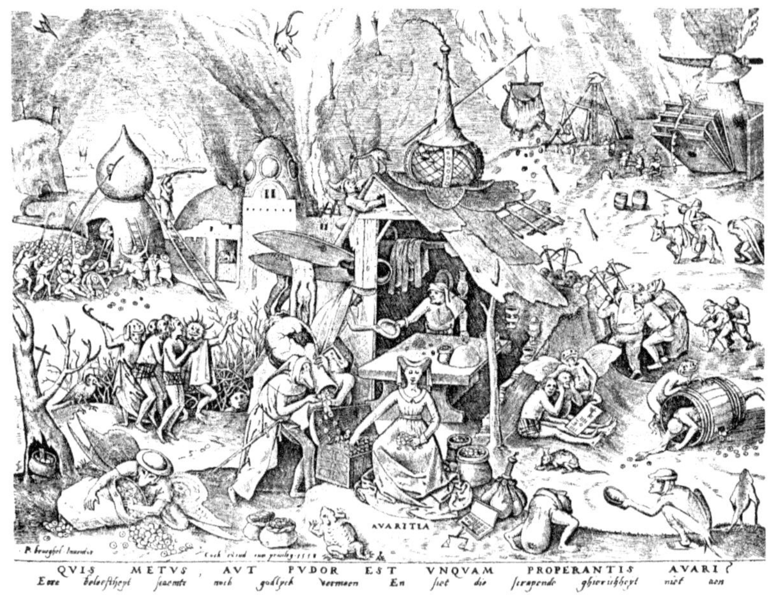

10 Pieter van der Heyden, after Pieter Bruegel, *Avaritia*, 1556. Engraving, 22.4 x 29.3 cm. Bibliothèque Royale Belgique, Brussels. S I 7606

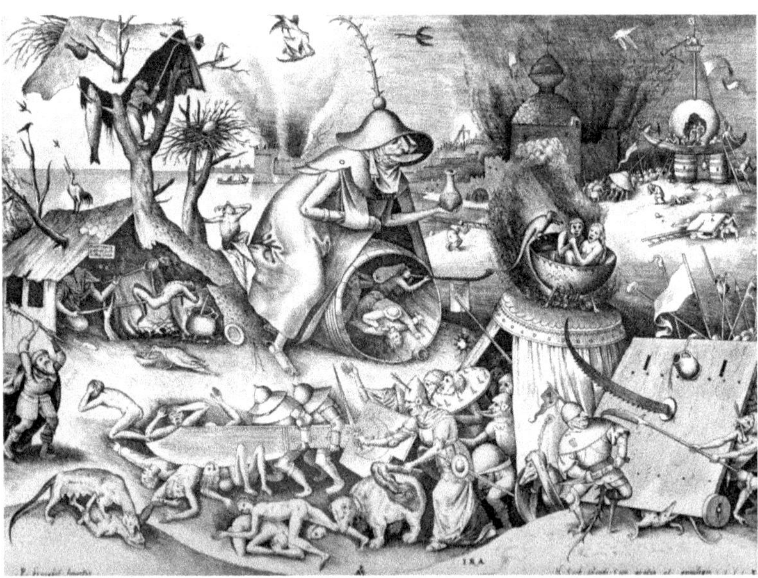

11 Pieter van der Heyden, after Pieter Bruegel, *Ira*, 1558. Engraving, 22.5 x 29.2 cm. Bibliothèque Royale Belgique, Brussels. S IV 22001

taken from the Boschian print, *The Besieging of an Elephant* (mid-16C; fig. 8) — one of the earliest such works published by Cock.

Bruegel's *Superbia* (fig. 9) quite literally unpacks and expands the details of the *Elephant*: the bizarre architecture that fills the top right quadrant of the Vice design is a displaced and scaled-up version of the elements from the "fantastic castle" on the elephant's back.[37] The relationship between Bosch and Bruegel will be examined in Chapter 1; here, I want simply to focus on one notable point of difference between Bosch and Bruegel in their visualisation of Vices. Bosch typically used his hybrid fauna to illustrate and elaborate on material drawn from Jewish legend, Christian apocrypha, the alchemical cycle, and even popular culture. But Bosch's one treatment of actual Vices, the *Tabletop* of the Sins (fig. 7) contains a minimum of the imagery for which he is famous.[38] In the *Tabletop*, each Vice appears in a recognizable, everyday setting; three of them contemporary interiors.[39]

A single vice in a fantastic landscape as the sole subject for a picture was not a Boschian idea. Bruegel, on the other hand, visualised each of his vices set firmly in the middle of a grotesque dreamscape, associated with all that is lowest in human nature. As we will see in Chapter 1, the affinity between dream-representation and Boschian hybrids derives from the context of Neo-Platonic explorations of desire and sexuality. For the moment, I want to consider them as links between sixteenth-century and modern theories of the unconscious. On their own terms, Bruegel's *Vice* designs constitute strong evidence for interpreting Renaissance surreal fantasy as representing the world of dreams and nightmares.

Though also comic, Bruegel's *Vices* describe the underbelly of human society in unreal, imaginary terms. Each personified Vice is surrounded by a myriad of little figures, part-human, part-beast. These figures represent breaches of the law of nature. The suggestion is that, when humans sin, the whole world goes wrong. In *Avaritia* and *Ira* (figs. 10, 11), fish sprout wings and fly in the sky. In *Superbia* (fig. 9), trees grow through the fantastic

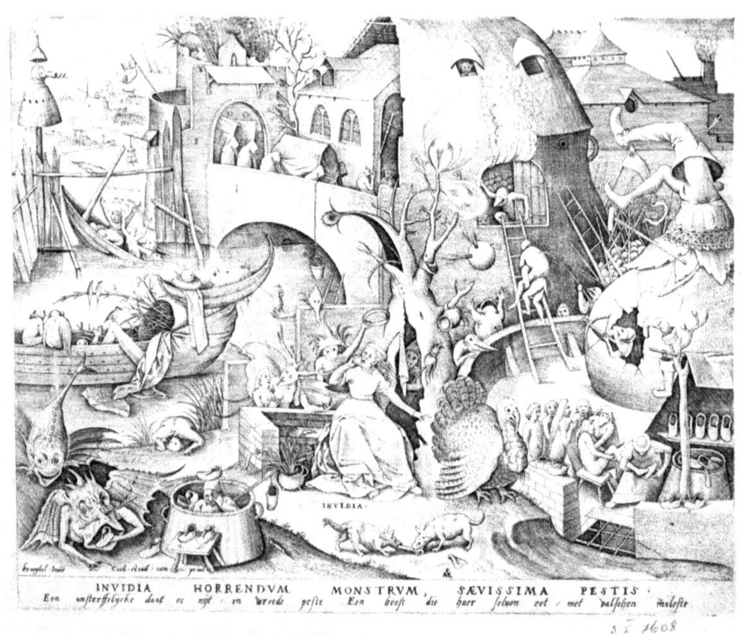

12 Pieter van der Heyden, after Pieter Bruegel, *Invidia*, 1558. Engraving, 22.5 x 29.5 cm. Bibliothèque Royal Belgique, Brussels. S I 7608

pavilions which arise shakily from the ground. In *Invidia* and *Desidia* (figs. 12, 13), dwellings have eyes, mouths or arms. In *Avaritia* and *Gula* (fig. 10, 14), bird-like fish are confined in cages. This imagery disturbs because it erases the categories, manmade and natural, which keep things in their place and make the world comprehensible. Many of the structures in the *Vices* appear to be grown rather than built, like the entirely foliate pavilion in the background of *Luxuria* (fig. 15), the animated house-giants of *Gula*, or the ramshackle structures in *Desidia*. None provide safety or shelter.

Since Sigmund Freud, desire has been seen as impelling both lust and dreams. Modern and sixteenth-century paradigms of the unconscious might be expected, then, to coincide most clearly in *Luxuria* (fig. 15). In Bruegel's design, the landscape of Lust centres on a living bark tent, where Lady Lust is debauched by an animal-headed man. Three branches grow from this structure: a tree encased in a wicket fence; a branch that metamorphoses into the head of stag with an apple in its mouth; a central branch impaling a huge oyster shell containing a glass bubble, inside which a couple make love.

In the foreground, a head, its mouth extended in an "O" has no body. Two limbs sprout suggestively on either side of the mouth orifice. The head douses itself with liquid from a cracked egg with a knife through it. This effective image (which recurs in Bruegel's fantasies) makes a derogatory equation of the head with the genitals (see below). In a corner, left of the title Luxuria, there is probably the first depiction ever of a castration fantasy. A cloaked figure, with indentations for eyes and no mouth, holds in his right hand a severed penis. In his left hand, he holds a knife; he is about

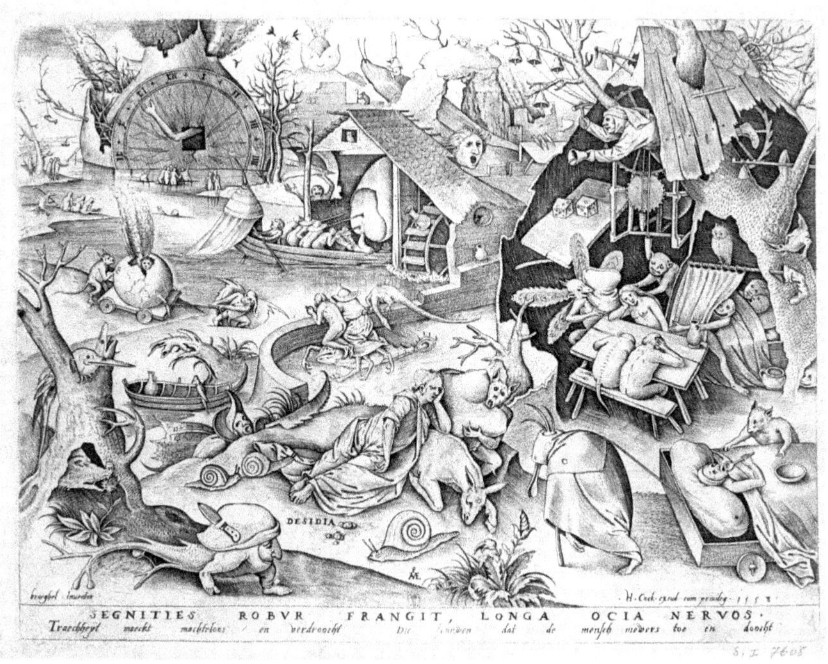

13 Pieter van der Heyden, after Pieter Bruegel, *Desidia*, 1558, Engraving, 22.5 x 29.2 cm. Bibliothèque Royale Belgique, Brussels. S I 7605

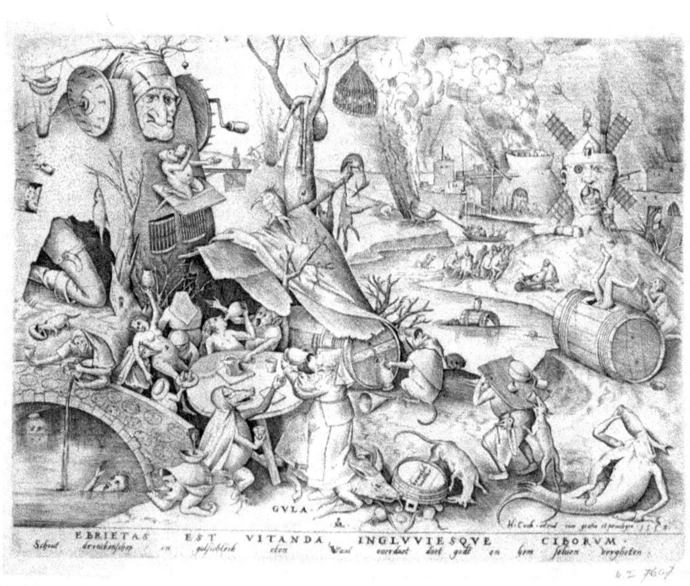

14 Pieter van der Heyden, after Pieter Bruegel, *Gula*, 1558. Engraving, 22.3 x 29.3 cm. Bibliothèque Royale Belgique, Brussels. S I 7607

15 Pieter van der Heyden, after Pieter Bruegel, *Luxuria*, 1558. Engraving, 22.5 x 29.6 cm. Bibliothèque Royale Belgique, Brussels. S II 22656

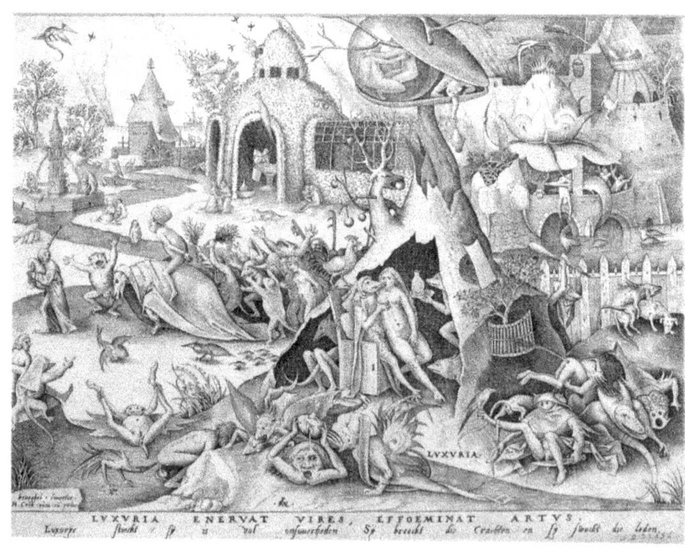

to castrate himself. He sits partly under an entangled group of copulating monsters; one prehensile foot clutches a bird.

Mottoes in Flemish and Latin appear at the foot of each print. The captions for *Luxuria* invoke sixteenth-century theories about the mind and body. The Flemish verse runs, loosely translated, *Unchastity stinks, it is drenched with dirt, it weakens men's bodies and does them hurt.* More precisely, the last line reads, *It weakens a man's fibers, and undermines his powers,* literally "unmans" a man. The resonance of the Latin motto deserves to be given in the original: *Luxuria enervat vires effoeminat artus.*

There is a good deal of sexual symbolism in the other *Vices* too. At the central table in *Gula,* naked drunken figures embrace anthropomorphic monsters. In *Avaritia,* a man's body dangles limply from the grip of a giant pair of scissors, which grows out of the central structure in the middle of the picture. There are cracked eggs at the bottom left of *Superbia*; in *Invidia,* an egg has an orifice, which appears to have half swallowed a giant humanoid. In *Superbia,* liquid excrement falls into a pan from a human anus, on which a bird perches. Anal imagery features prominently in *Luxuria,* filled with copulating beasts, and in *Desidia,* where a hunched band of hatted figures prod at a giant house-man to make him excrete.

An interest in contemporary formulations of the unconscious links this imagery with the captions. The mottoes for each print spell out the role played by vice in sixteenth-century moralising and medical terms. The Flemish tag for *Avarice*: *Grasping Avarice does not understand honour, decency, shame, or divine command.* The Latin motto for *Superbia*: *Those who are proud do not love the gods, nor do the gods love those who are proud.* The verses for *Invidia*: *Envy, endless death and sickness cruel unpent, is a self-devouring beast and merciless torment* and in Latin, *Envy, a hideous monster, a most savage disease.* The reference to humours clouding the mind is explicit in *Ira,* where the Flemish runs, *Anger congests the mouth, poisons the mood, disrupts the spirit, blackens the blood.* And the very close Latin, *Anger swells the mouth and blackens the veins with blood.*

Cock, rather than Bruegel, probably composed the captions for the prints. But the difference between the captions and the designs has an significance beyond this issue of authorship. The visual "illustration" of each vice spectacularly exceeds in metaphoric scope the commonplace observations in the mottoes. This clear disparity evokes some fundamental observations by Freud on the interpretation of dreams:

> The first thing that becomes clear to anyone who compares the dream-content with the dream-thoughts is that a work of *condensation* on a large scale has been done here. Dream are brief, meagre and laconic, in comparison to the range and wealth of the dream-thoughts.[40]

Freud analysed the relationship between dream-content (the overt, remembered imagery of the dream), and dream-thoughts (the great mass of psychic associations and materials encoded in the dream-content). At the heart of the difference is a pattern of distortion:

> As a corollary [what] is clearly the essence of the dream-thoughts need not be represented in the dream at all. The dream is, as it were, *differently centred* from the dream-thoughts - its content has different elements as its central point... a transference and displacement of psychical intensities occurs [in] dream formation [causing] difference between the text of the dream-content and that of the dream-thoughts.[41]

He identified two "governing factors" at work in this distortion or transformation: *displacement* and *condensation*.

The relationship of *meagre* dream-content to the *wealth* of dream-thoughts fits the disparity of style and content between the mottoes and the imagery in the *Vices*. The sense of the mental world of the mottoes as *differently centred* from the swarming surreality overhead is equally clear. However, the most startling level on which Freud's analysis fits Bruegel's art resides in the technique used to create the imagery itself. The processes of condensation and displacement exactly describe the visual transformations which Bruegel used to create his hybrid creatures and environments. Of course, Bruegel's art is the ancestor of Freud's theories, and not the other way round. Also, Bruegel's surreal expositions in these designs do not precisely stand to the *dream-thoughts* of his culture as the commonplace mottos stand to the *dream-content*: both are conscious manipulations of collective culture, language, and traditions. But the terminology of condensation and displacement effectively describes techniques of image production characteristic of both dream and surreal imagery.

The most important connection between Bruegel's imagery and Freudian dream theory is therefore located not only through an interest in the issue of vice, unconscious or otherwise, or in relation to the Humanist psychology of the humours, but precisely in visual practice: in processes of visualisation which render the representation of things dream-like.

Bruegel and Folk Culture

Individual details of the *Seven Deadly Sins* have sources in the proverbs and folkloric associations of Bruegel's time.[42] *Luxuria*, for instance, includes a *charivari* procession; a traditional village way of mocking a mis-matched bride and groom (see Chapter 4). However, as the fusion of this detail into a *Vice* design suggests, Bruegel's use of folk-culture is never a matter of simple illustration. His interest in surreal extrapolation places him at some distance from, and at an angle to, the Lenten view of popular culture occupied by contemporary moralists.

To discover Bruegel's relationship to folk culture, the art itself is the first port of call. Without wanting to push the comparison too far, there are points of similarity between the position of the artist/spectator in Bruegel's pictures, and Ficino's concept of the artist-melancholic, who perceives a gulf between self and society. The elements of detachment in Bruegel's art are of several kinds. There is his panoramic perspective, the farseeing, elevated vantage that he developed for landscapes and used for the *theatrum mundi* paintings (*Proverbs*; *Games*; *Carnival and Lent*; figs. 63, 3, 71), and *The Triumph of Death* (fig. 89). This built on the work of the cosmic landscapists, notably Patinir and Altdorfer at the start of the century.[43] Formally, the high viewpoint also evokes cartography. Cock published maps as well as fine-art prints (e.g. fig. 4); Bruegel knew Ortelius, the atlas-maker.[44] The panoramic viewpoint conveys a pleasurable effect of all-encompassing information, of omniscience.

Another form of detachment is intrinsic in attitudes the pictures express about the subjects of proverbial lore and carnivalesque traditions. These are more difficult to pin down. Let us take the subject of proverbs and proverbial language first. Consider, for instance, the parallels between Bruegel's interest in proverbs and that of his countryman, the Humanist scholar Erasmus (c.1466-1536). Erasmus produced a famous collection of proverbial sayings, *Adagia* (1500), and a hugely popular allegorical satire, *Praise of Folly* (1511), both in Latin. Bruegel's massive *Proverbs* is also both a compendium and a satire, undermining the "wisdom" of many of its proverbial sayings. Like Erasmus, Bruegel's work on proverbs reveals a sophisticated separation from popular mental attitudes. Unlike Erasmus, Bruegel took his raw materials from the vernacular culture of his own times and region: children's games, proverbial language and carnival customs.

Encyclopedism — the impulse to classify — itself presupposes detachment from the object of study. On the subject of proverbs — leaving aside for the moment Bruegel's equally impressive tabulation of games and customs — the extent of the artist's encyclopaedism was unusual: to the forty proverbs in the Frans Hoghenberg print (fig. 70) on which the *Netherlandish Proverbs* is based, he managed to add more than seventy. In fact, the activity of collecting was part of a wider cultural movement — what we might term the ethnographic attitude — manifested in many areas of late Renaissance life and thought, under many different guises and motivations. At the date of Bruegel's painting (1559), popular customs were beginning to be observed and catalogued by the literate. This was rarely seen as a morally neutral activity. The contemporaries of Bruegel who wrote about these subjects generally did so in the context of a pro-reform, anti-carnivalesque discourse. But their work also tended to assume encyclopaedic shape, betraying a fascination with the material, which belays somewhat their professed intent. Burke describes Philip Stubbes' *Anatomie of Abuses* (1583) as,

> [a] comprehensive indictment of Lords of Misrule, May games, Christmas feasting, church ales, wakes, bear baiting, cock fighting, and dancing; [it] is an irony he would scarcely have appreciated that his [book] (like *his Popish Kingdom*) is read today mainly by people who are interested in the popular recreations he condemned.[45]

What Bruegel's pictures share with the works of Stubbes and others is a novel sense of the gap between traditional popular forms and contemporary cultural goals. This sense both fired and was fuelled by the impetus for religious reform. Cultural relativism is visible in a whole range of broadly "Reformation" projects, from Plantin's efforts to produce a polyglot bible, to the increasing sophistication of Catholic overseas missions. Missionaries were at work in Europe also, in *the dark corners of the land*, and it was now possible for them to compare their problems with those of their colleagues in the Indies. Jesuits working in the south of Spain in the late sixteenth century found that the inhabitants *resembled Indians rather than Spaniards*.[46] A Spanish officer rescued from shipwreck during the retreat of the Armada by a young Irish girl from Donegal later testified that she was *a Christian in like manner as Mahomet*.[47]

The will to reform or purify popular festivities shows the ethnographic attitude at its most sweeping. Jean Delumeau spoke of a fundamental division between popular piety in a late medieval Christendom, whose pagan survivals and animist mentality were seen most clearly in its festivals, and in the state of religion after the Reformation: *After a millennium of assimilating animism came a total rejection of it, and the religion of a few was to be imposed on millions*.[48]

Historical consciousness was also an intrinsic aspect of Humanism.

Classically educated early modern people learned, among other things, to see through the eyes of another culture. Historians developed new theories of causation and change, based on comparative attitudes. The study of Roman law, for instance, led scholars, *to appreciate that customs in jurisprudence were bound up with the society of which they formed part and not to be isolated and appropriated for a different context.*[49] In art, the revival of classical form enabled Vasari and his readers to distinguish between historical styles: the antique, the modern (meaning Gothic), and the contemporary. In Bruegel's own milieu, Peter Coeck van Aelst studied Turkish civilization at first hand, producing a beautifully illustrated book, *Manners and Fashions of the Turks*, published posthumously in 1553.

Ethnographic awareness informed aspects of Bruegel's art which have otherwise little to do with dreams or popular culture, such as the studies of oriental costume incorporated into *John the Baptist Preaching In the Wilderness* (fig. 95) and the London *Adoration of the Magi*. But most of all, it is manifest in Bruegel's fascination with the folklore of his own region.

On this issue of detachment, fundamentally, class difference was, of course, the most significant shaper of elite attitudes to peasant culture (see Chapters 3 and 4). But the issue of what interested the artist can be distinguished from what interested the moralist, the scholar, or the reformer. There is an aesthetic aspect of attention to the folkloric, complexly bound up with its formation as an object of study. This has both a late medieval and a precociously modern dimension. Le Goff spoke of *folkloric resurgences* in art and literature from the twelfth and thirteenth century onward.[50] Each of these can be envisaged as an increase of (literate) self-consciousness about the "ground pattern" of folk culture. Periodically, as it were, the cultural envelope widened, so that town-dwellers, though still participants in folk *mentalité*, achieved some perceptual distance within it, and thus recognised *différance* where none was previously visible. This recognition itself could take the form of interest in, or desire for, aspects of the folk culture which would now appear mysterious, funny, or frightening.

At the same time, the systematic study of folklore, even at this early modern date, became bound up with what James Clifford called the *salvage paradigm*.[51] The sense of a disappearing subject was intrinsic to the phenomenon of one part of a culture studying itself, and thus simultaneously discovering and producing a split within itself. The part scrutinised was constructed, in the act of looking, as *other*. Aesthetically, the scrutiniser experienced the phenomenon from the other side, so to speak: the folkloric became attractive *because* it appeared strange (*unheimlich*); the site of a lost authenticity. Combining these two views, we can surmise that what attracted Bruegel to the folkloric was the potential for surrealism inherent in mixed metaphors and nonsense, as viewed/constructed *from a distance*, coupled with a nostalgic awareness of the fragility of popular traditions: the sense of their passing.

Bruegel's art in the years following his return from Italy concerned itself with this kind of doubly ethnographic and aesthetic research: exploring how the familiar could be rendered strange, and what was strange about the familiar. The experience of travel, his years abroad, the conflicting world-views of his contemporaries, catalysed the comparativist attitudes of the time for him on many levels. He became the artist as anthropologist, looking with new eyes, as if from a distance, on the customary life of his countrymen, and their imaginary, inner life.

The Reformation and the Counter-Reformation are only the largest, most visible symptoms of the upheavals in cosmology and psychology depicted in Bruegel's pictures. His characteristic technique was to combine highly abstract form with very earthy subject matter: working out symbolic actions appropriate to the pictorial representation of children's games, wedding feasts, or the transition from Carnival to Lent. Detachment was central to the selection of subject as well as to the visual effect of the work. Pollution in the real world is *matter in the wrong place*, the dangerous mingling of categories which human culture keeps strictly regulated. In the virtual realm of art, Bruegel's imagery regularly juxtaposes raw and cooked, dead and living, beast and human. *The Triumph of Death* represents the artist's darkest entry into this zone, but even here, as in earlier works, the detail is comic. Predicated on the structural similarity between pollution and jokes, some of his most hideously hybridised mannikins wear engaging smiles, perform tightrope tricks, or amuse us in other fashions.

It is Bruegel's choice of subjects, presented roughly in chronological order, that determines the order of chapters in this book Chapter 1 starts with the cultural roots of hybrid monsters in dreams and metamorphosis, showing how Renaissance surrealism was informed by philosophical and theological traditions of visualising the dreaming soul and the imagination, and how Bruegel developed this brand of imagery away from the definitions given it by Bosch. Novel hybrid inventions are seen as responses to conscious and unconscious ideas about the semi-divine, semi-material nature of people, their divided opinions about God and images, their changing beliefs about dreams and nightmares.

After Ficino, a century-long meditation on melancholia informed shifts in concepts of the supernatural, re-shaping the status of witchcraft in the popular imagination. Chapter 2 explores how Bruegel tackled these subjects in his great painting of money madness and crazy women: the comic and nightmarish *Dulle Griet*. The surrealism of this painting draws on the psychology of money and infernal themes in the sixteenth-century imagination.

Chapter 3 analyses Bruegel's folkloric pictures in terms of the *Land of Cockaigne* and examines changing attitudes to popular speech and nonsense. Chapter 4 deals with the subject of Carnival proper, together with other carnivalesque institutions, traditions and imagery over this period. Successive sections explain the debates and struggles which inform the *Battle between Carnival and Lent* and its related print designs. Bruegel derived both ethnographic and surreal materials from Carnival and the carnivalesque in the course of this most visual aspect of the cultural reformation, operating on private conduct and dreams as well as in public culture.

Finally, Chapter 5 considers images which deal directly with the divisive issues of religion and of the fate of the dead. Carnivals and folk dreams were interwoven in the great panorama of the *Triumph of Death* which shows the artist's interest in the *high* and *low* strands of the visual culture of death. Here, imagery from folk practice and legend is used to respond in concept and in detail to the ongoing crisis in penitential and funerary beliefs.

Working in a time when the mind was not yet wholly mental, when the body was not yet wholly physical, and when the natural world was not yet wholly material, Bruegel, his friends, his patrons and his contemporaries were fascinated by the chaotic half-world of dreams, superstitions and signs of the occult. Five centuries ago, as today, all minds can be regarded as shaped — waking and sleeping — by the cultural repertoire of carnivals and dreams. Basic to Bruegel's art, as I shall try to show, are changes in psychology and behaviour. As old kinds of performances took on the character of dreams, dreams themselves took over the old imagery of performance. The alteration of culture and collective psychology this entailed is the theme of this book.

Notes to Introduction

---

[1] P. Burke, *Popular Culture in Early Modern Europe* (New York, 1978), 207-243. K. Thomas describes this effort: *By obsessive attention to trivia... the Puritans signified their desire to eliminate all ceremonies, superstitions and observances which had non-Christian or magical overtones; Religion and the Decline of Magic* (New York, 1971), 67; cf 58-89.
[2] M. Foucault, *Discipline and Punish: The Birth of the Prison*, trans. A. Sheridan (New York, 1979), 26.
[3] Chronologies and the supporting documents for Bruegel's life can be found in P. Bianconi, *The Complete Paintings of Bruegel* (New York, 1967), 83-6, and in R. Marijnissen and M. Seidel, *Bruegel* (New York, 1984), 338-343; see Chapter Three, n. 5. On Mayeken Bessemers and the Brunswick Monogrammist, see S. Bergmans, "Le Problème de Jan van Hemessen, Monogrammiste de Brunswick," *Revue Belge d'archéologie et de l'Histoire d'Art*, 24 (1955), 133-57; on Pieter Coecke, see G. Marlier, *Pierre Coeck d'Alost. La Renaissance Flamande* (Brussels, 1966). Information on the Bruegel family at Brussels is given in P. De Ridder, "Het Testament van Everard Bruegel (d. 1530) Klein Kanunnik van Sint-Goedele te Brussel," *Jaarboek van het Koninklijk Museum voor Schone Kunsten-Antwerpen* (1981), 7-16. Everard Bruegel was a Humanist and canon of St. Gudule, with connections to Erasmus' circle; also mentioned are a Pieter Bruegel who taught at Louvain and worked as an Imperial civil servant at Brussels, and the lawyer William Bruegel, a member of the Council of Brabant. Of course there is no way of conclusively connecting any of these people with the artist, but their presence in Brussels may partly explain Bruegel's move there in 1563. A useful summary of recent scholarship is P. Zagorin, "Looking for Pieter Bruegel," *Journal of the History of Ideas* 64,1 (2003), 73-96.
[4] Karel van Mander, *The Lives of the Illustrious Netherlandish and German Painters, from the First Edition of the "schilderboek" (1603–4)*, trans. and ed. Hessel Miedema (Doornspij, the Netherlands: Davaco, 1994–99).
[5] A. Martindale, *The Rise of the Artist In the Middle Ages and Early Renaissance* (New York, 1972).
[6] Cases for Bruegel as an intellectual painter were first made by R. Van Bastelaer and G. H. De Loo, *Pieter Bruegel l'Ancien, Son Oeuvres et Son Temps* (Brussels, 1905-7); M. Dvorak (1921), reprinted as ch. 5 of his *The History of Art as the History of Ideas*, trans. J. Hardy (Boston, 1984); M. Friedlander, *Pieter Bruegel* (Leyden, 1976). Important iconographical studies are: C. G. Stridbeck, *Bruegelstudien. Untersuchungen zu den ikonologischen Problemen bei Pieter Bruegel d. Ä sowie dessen Biziehungen zum nïederlandischen Romanismus* (Stockholm, 1956); and two articles by I. L. Zupnick: "Bruegel's *Virtues* as the Epitome of Folly," in E. Castelli, ed., *L'Umanesimo e La Follia* (Rome, n.d.), 89-106; and "Appearance and Reality in Bruegel's *Virtues*," *Actes du XXIIe Congrès International d'Histoire de l'Art* I (1972), 745-753. The literature on

Bruegel is too vast to be listed here; see bibliographies in Marijnissen and Seidel up to 1960; Friedlander, 48-9 up to 1976; F. Grossman, "Bruegel, Pieter, the Elder," in *Encyclopedia of World Art*, vol. II (New York-Toronto-London, 1960). For a useful short critical history by F. Grossman, see *Bruegel, une dynastie de peintres*, Palais des Beaux-Arts, Brussels (1980), 34-48; for recent bibliography, see W. Seipel, ed., *Pieter Bruegel d. Ä im Kunsthistorisches Museum, Wien* (Milan-Vienna, 1998), E. M. Kavaler, *Pieter Bruegel: parables of order and enterprise* (Cambridge,1999), and W. S. Gibson, *Pieter Bruegel and the art of laughter* (Berkeley, 2006).

[7] On Plantin and his circle, see L. Vöet, *The Golden Compasses: A History and Evaluation of the Printing and Publishing Activities of the "Officina Plantiniana" at Antwerp*, 2 v. (Amsterdam, 1969), and C. Clair, *Christopher Plantin* (London, 1960) on van Heemskerck, see I.M. Veldman, *Maerten van Heemskerck and Dutch Humanism in the Sixteenth Century* (Maarsen, 1977).

[8] E.g., I. L. Zupnick, "Bruegel and the Revolt of the Netherlands," *Art Journal* XXIII (4) (Summer 1964), 283-9, on references to current events in Bruegel and, for the opposite viewpoint, A. Deblaere, "Bruegel and the Religious Problems of His Time," *Apollo* CV (181) (March 1977), 176-180.

[9] Cf. S. Ferber, "Pieter Bruegel and the Duke of Alba," *Renaissance News* XIX (1966), 205-19, and Deblaere, 178.

[10] Most notably the massive reattribution of the drawings by H. Mielke, Pieter Bruegel: die Zeichnungen (Brepols, 1996); see also the exhibition catalogues: the Berlin Staatliche Museen Preussischer Kulturbesitz, Kupferstichkabinett, *Pieter Bruegel d. Ä. als. Zeichner: Herkunft und Nachfolge* (1975); Washington National Gallery, *The Age of Bruegel: Netherlandish Drawings in the Sixteenth Century* (Cambridge, 1986); Museum Boijmans Van Beuningen, Rotterdam and the Metropolitan Museum of Art, *Pieter Bruegel the Elder: Drawings and Prints*, ed. Nadine M. Orenstein, et al. (New York, 2001), with bibliographies.

[11] Important contributions to this controversy are M. D. Carroll, "Peasant Festivity and Political Identity in the Sixteenth Century," *Art History* 10(3) (September, 1987), 289-314, and K. Moxey, *Peasants, Warriors and Wives: Popular Imagery in the Reformation* (Chicago, 1989); see Chapter 4, nn. 150-3, below.

[12] See studies by W. S. Gibson, *Bruegel* (Oxford, 1977); "Some Flemish Popular Prints from Hieronymous Cock and His Contemporaries," *Art Bulletin* LX (1978), 673-81; "Pieter Bruegel, Dulle Griet, and Sexist Politics in the Sixteenth Century," in O. Von Simson and M. Winner, ed., *Pieter Bruegel und seine Welt* (Berlin, 1979), 9-16; and "Artists and *Rederijkers* in the Age of Bruegel," *Art Bulletin* LXIII/3 (September, 1981), 426-46; and the works in von Simson and Winner.

[13] T. A. Riggs, *Hieronymous Cock (1510-70): Printmaker and Publisher in Antwerp at the Sign of the Four Winds* (1971; New York, 1977); "Bruegel and his Publisher," in von Simson and Winner, 165-73; and L. De Pauw-De Veen, *Jérôme Cock, Editeur d"Estampes et Graveur, 1507?-1570*, exhibition Catalogue, Bibliothèque Royale Albert Ier (Brussels, 1970).

[14] A. Dundes and C.A. Stibbe, "The Art of Mixing Metaphors. A Folkloristic Interpretation of the *Netherlandish Proverbs*, by Pieter Bruegel the Elder," *Folklore Fellows Communications*, No. 230. Helsinki, 1981; E. Snow, *Inside Bruegel: the Play of Images in Children's Games* (New York: North Point Press, 1997; his original study was: "'Meaning' in *Children's Games*: On the Limitations of the Iconographic Approach to Bruegel," *Representations* 2 (Spring, 1983), 27-60.
[15] Trans. from C. De Tolnay, *Pierre Bruegel l''ancien* (Brussels, 1935), 7-8.
[16] J. Wegg comments that there are no biographical facts for any citizen in the first half of the sixteenth century; *Antwerp, 1477-1559* (London, 1916), 252.
[17] Snow (1983), 53.
[18] On the concept of *châine operatoire*, see A. Leroi-Gourhan, *Gesture and Speech* (1964), trans. A. Bostock Berger (MIT Press; Cambridge, MA, 1993); and analyses in F. Auduze, "Leroi-Gourhan, a philosopher of technique and evolution," *Journal of Archaeological Research* 10(4) (2002), 277-306.
[19] On the concept of *châine operatoire*, see A. Leroi-Gourhan, *Gesture and Speech* (1964), trans. A. Bostock Berger (MIT Press; Cambridge, MA, 1993); and analyses in F. Auduze, "Leroi-Gourhan, a philosopher of technique and evolution," *Journal of Archaeological Research* 10(4) (2002), 277-306.
[20] E.g., K. Thomas (1971); P. Francastel, *La Figure et le Lieu: L''Ordre Visuel du Quattrocento* (Paris, 1967); C. Ginzburg, *The Night Battles. Witchcraft and Agrarian Cults in the Sixteenth and Seventeenth Centuries*, trans. J. and A. Tedeschi (Harmondsworth, 1985).
[21] See L. Rothkrug, *Death, Trust, & Society: Mapping Religion & Culture* (Berkeley, CA: c2006); his key Reformation studies appeared in special issues of *Historical Reflections/Réflexions historiques*: "Religious Practices and Collective Perceptions: Hidden Homologies in the Renaissance and Reformation," 7 (1980); "Peasant and Jew: Fears of Pollution and German Collective Perceptions," 10 (1983), 59-77; "Holy Shrines, Religious Dissonance and Satan in the Origins of the German Reformation," 14 (1987), 143–286; "German Holiness and Western Sanctity in Medieval and Modern History," 15 (1988), 161-249.
[22] B. O. States, *The Rhetoric of Dreams* (Ithaca, 1988), 22.
[23] D. B. Klein, *The Unconscious: Invention or Discovery? A Historical-Critical Inquiry* (Santa Monica, 1977), 215.
[24] Ibid.
[25] States, 22.
[26] This and subsequent material on the history of melancholy is taken from R. Klibansky, E. Panofsky and F. Saxl, *Saturn and Melancholy* (London, 1964), 96ff; cf. R. and N. Wittkower, *Born Under Saturn. The Character and Conduct of Artists: A Documented History from Antiquity to the French Revolution* (New York, 1969).
[27] M. Ficino, *Marsilio Ficino: The Book of Life. A Translation by Charles Boer of Liber de Vita (or De Vita Triplici* (Irving, 1980), Book 3, ch. 1-4. Ficino's thought and its dissemination in the sixteenth century is discussed in more detail in Chapter One.

[28] Cf. R. and M. Wittkower, especially ch. 3 and 5.
[29] E. Kris, *Psychoanalytic Explorations in Art* (New York, 1952), ch. 13, "On Inspiration," 293-4.
[30] Ficino, Book 3, especially ch. 4, 6, 11, 21. The heading for ch. 21, for example, is "On the power of words and songs in obtaining heavenly gifts."
[31] Kris, 294.
[32] G. Ròheim, *The Gates of the Dream* (New York, 1973); J. S. Lincoln, *The Dream in Primitive Cultures* (New York-London, 1970). F. Hsu, ed., *Psychological anthropology; approaches to culture and personality* (Homewood, IL, 1961); *Ethos* 9(4) (Winter, 1981), ed. and intro. J. G. Kennedy and L. L. Langness, summarises the ethnographical literature on dreams to that date. C.f. R. K. Dentan, "Ethnographic Considerations of the Cross Cultural Study of Dreams" in J. Gackenbach, ed., *Sleep and Dreams. A Sourcebook*. (New York-London, 1986), 317-358; see intros. and bibliography in: B. Tedlock, ed., *Dreaming: anthropological and psychological interpretations* (Cambridge-New York, 1987); S. Heald and A. Deluz, eds., *Anthropology and psychoanalysis: an encounter through culture* (London-New York, 1994); D. Shulman and G. G. Stroumsa, eds., *Dream cultures: explorations in the comparative history of dreaming* (New York, 1999).
[33] C. Levi-Strauss, *The Savage Mind* (Chicago, 1966). Cf. also the bibliography given in Le Goff, 177, nn. 9-10; 178-9. For a short critique of these concepts, see E. Leach, *Claude Levi-Strauss*, rev. ed. (Harmondsworth, 1976), 35-56; 137-142.
[34] See N. Serebrennikov, *Pieter Bruegel the Elder's series of "Virtues" and "Vices,"* PhD diss., University of North Carolina, Chapel Hill, 1986; and the articles by Zupnick cited in n. 7.
[35] On their long history and distribution, see A. Katzenellenbogen, *Allegories of the Virtues and the Vices in Medieval Art*, trans. A. J. P. Crick (New York, 1964).
[36] On this painting, see J.Martineau, ed., *Andrea Mantegna*, Royal Academy of Arts, London — Metropolitan Museum of Art, NYC (1992), cat. 136; 427-430.
[37] For the *Elephant*, see Hollstein 43; Riggs (1977), 11; the relation between the two designs is summarised by N. Serebrennikov, "Pieter Bruegel the Elder: The Draftsman Revealed," *Art Bulletin* (September 2002), LXXXIV (3), 501-9; and first noted by N. Corwin, "The Fire Landscape: Its Sources and Its Development from Bosch through Jan Brueghel I, with Special Emphasis on the Mid-Sixteenth Century Bosch Revival," Ph.D. diss., Univ. of Washington, 1976, 375.
[38] I am excluding here the so-called *"Allegory of Gluttony and Lust,"* the left inside bottom panel of a fragmented Bosch triptych (c 1490-1500; Yale University Art Gallery, New Haven, CT); this is the bottom piece of *The Ship of Fools* (Louvre; for its drawing, see fig. 54); the other extant parts are *Death and the Usurer* (Nat. Gall. Art, Washington, DC) and the Rotterdam *Pedlar* (Museum Boijmans Van Beuningen); see J. Koldeweij et al., *Hieronymus Bosch: The Complete Paintings and Drawings* (Rotterdam, 2001), 29, 88. Little can be said about the original principal subject; as a fragment, the imagery in the *"Allegory"* indeed references the sins of

Gluttony and Lust. But nowhere else does Bosch make representations of the Sins the sole theme of a triptych.

[39] W. Gibson, "Hieronymus Bosch and the Mirror of Man. The authorship and iconography of the tabletop of the Seven Deadly Sins," *Oud Holland*, 87 (1973), 205-226.

[40] S. Freud, *The Interpretation of Dreams* (1900), trans J. Strachey (1958; Pelican Freud Library, v. 4, London, 1976), 383; compare J. A. Underwood's alternative translation of *Verdichtung* as "compression" in the Penguin Classics edition, *Interpreting Dreams* (1900), trans. J. A. Underwood (London, 2006), 295.

[41] Freud (1976), 414-7.

[42] On proverbs in the *Vices*, see A. Barnouw, *The Fantasy of Pieter Bruegel* (New York, 1947), 16ff.

[43] On this development see Walter S. Gibson, *Mirror of the earth: the world landscape in sixteenth-century Flemish painting* (Princeton, 1989).

[44] See Chapter Three, section 4, for a discussion of these analogues to Bruegel's art.

[45] Burke, 1978.

[46] Ibid., 208.

[47] E. Monter, *Ritual, Myth and Magic in Early Modern Europe* (Athens, 1983), 79.

[48] This formulation is from Jean Delumeau's inaugural lecture at the Collège de France in 1975, quoted in Monter, *Ritual, Myth and Magic in Early Modern Europe* (Athens, 1983), 90. See also J. Delumeau, *Catholicism between Luther and Voltaire* (London, 1977), 129-202.

[49] Thomas, 428.

[50] See his remarks on "the marvellous" in J. Le Goff, *The Medieval Imagination*, trans. A. Goldhammer (Chicago, 1988), 27-44.

[51] James Clifford, "Beyond the 'Salvage' Paradigm," in Hal Foster, ed., *Discussions in Contemporary Culture 1* (Seattle: Bay Press, 1987), 122.

1 The Image of the Metamorphic Body

> From this Ignorance of how to distinguish Dreams and other strong fancies from Vision and Sense did arise the greater part of the religion of the Gentiles in times past that worshipped Satyres, Faunes, Nymphs and the like; and nowadays the opinion that rude people have of Fayries, Ghosts, and Goblins, and of the power of Witches.
>
> Thomas Hobbes, *Leviathan*, XII

Introduction

An astonishing variety of "metamorphic" figures appear in Bruegel's works from the late 1550s to the mid-60s.[1] There are crosses between species. Some are half man, half beast; others almost wholly bestial. Mouths, tails, fins and limbs sprout in the wrong places. Rocks and shelters grow heads, eyes, mouths; bodies grow into cracked eggshells or trees. Monstrous humans defecate gold. This imagery as a kind of coherent genre in Northern painting originates with Hieronymus Bosch, but the extraordinary interest in Boschian forms in later sixteenth-century art goes well beyond the desire simply to copy that very successful artist. Of Bosch's many "followers" only a tiny proportion made a living by copying his actual compositions for Biblical and other scenes. The vast majority of these imitators remain shadowy figures. Among the best-known are Jan Wellens de Cock (c 1480-1527), Jan Mandyn (c 1500-60), and Pieter Huys (c 1520-84); he and his brother worked as engravers for Cock and Plantin). Like their anonymous brethren, they produced paintings based on Bosch's hybrid imagery (such as Huys, fig. 16), using a handful of Boschian subjects: the Temptation of St. Anthony, St Christopher in the river, Hell and Limbo.[2] Some School of Bosch artists recycled specific motifs from Bosch; the best developed distinctive brands of metamorphic imagery.

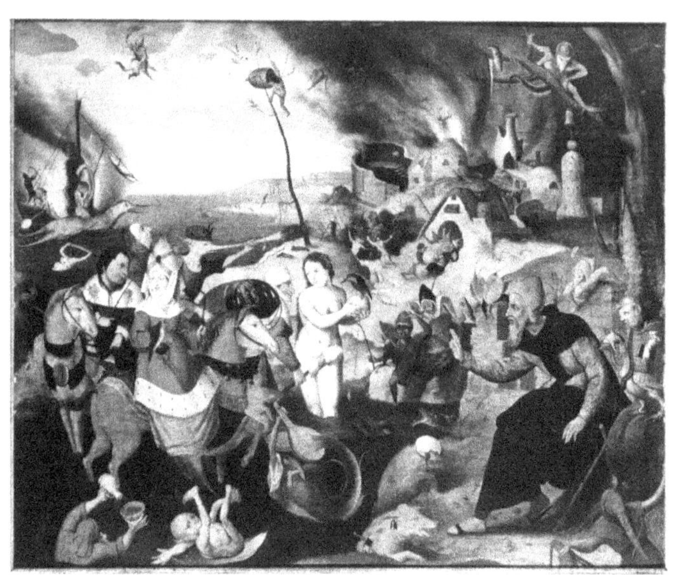

16 Pieter Huys, *Temptation of St. Anthony*, c 1555. Oil on canvas, 94.5 x 116.5 cm. Musées Royaux des Beaux-Arts, Brussels. Inv. 6001

The most original in this respect among these later artists was, of course, Pieter Bruegel. Bruegel did produce versions of the most popular Boshian vehicles: a *Temptation of St. Anthony* (1556; fig. 32), a *Descent into Limbo* (1561; fig. 91). But his main contributions in this vein turned the surreal imagery to new ends. Even when the subject was indeed First and Last Things, as in his *The Fall of the Rebel Angels* (c 1562; fig. 21), or diabolic, as in the two prints of *St James and the Magician* (1565; fig. 41 & 74), Bruegel's inventions were satirical, and quite distinct from those of Bosch or the rest of the School of Bosch. To understand how Bruegel developed the Boschian vocabulary in new directions, we must first establish the original significance of the imagery.

Most interpretations of Bosch concentrate on his human protagonists as a way of mapping a story onto the pictures. The prevalence of *Temptations* and *Hells* among Boschian imitators (at least until Bruegel) has encouraged the view that the crowds of hybrid figures — proliferating around St.

Anthony, in the landscapes of the Creations, or in the nether worlds — illustrate demonic elements in these stories. Sixteenth-century metamorphs, in other words, are seen as demonic extras; hence the generic term, *diablerie*. Apart from focusing on the "protagonist" figure in particular pictures, the issue of what the metamorphic figures might signify has also been approached by studying specific motifs in Boschian scenes. Scholars have looked for, and sometimes found, late medieval ancestors (e.g. fig. 50b) from which Bosch could have developed particular types of monster. Here and there, a hybrid can be decoded by reference to Netherlandish folklore: one is discovered to be a visual rendering of a verbal pun; another, an alchemical reference; another, a reversed Christian type.[3] Attention to the props, or attributes, of the metamorphs, the objects around which and in which they play, has proved particularly illuminating. All such researches are useful starting-points for my project here: to explain the *general* (as opposed to *generic*) significance of metamorphic imagery in works by Bosch and Bruegel.

Take, for instance, the question of the props: non-animate accoutrements in the hybrid crowds. In Bosch's triptych, *The Garden of Earthly Delights* (c 1510; fig. 17), the musical instruments in the Purgatory panel (fig. 17c) can be interpreted as representing the baser human passions which music was thought to stir.[4] The glass vessels in the central panel reveal a concern with alchemical symbolism, itself running like a musical theme through the triptych.[5] In the Eden scene (left panel; fig. 17a), male and female elements decay following this congress (fig. 18), and are reborn as a more powerful hermaphroditic spirit in the next stage (fig. 19). This sequence, as Jung realised, was understood to symbolize a psychological process.[6] The stage of reduction to *prima materia* referred to the confrontation of the self with its inner, base components, out of which would spring the gold of enlightenment.[7] So, the choice of these particular props and alchemical implements, accompanying metamorphic hybrids in the *Garden* panels, reveals concerns with human psychology. This is a considerable

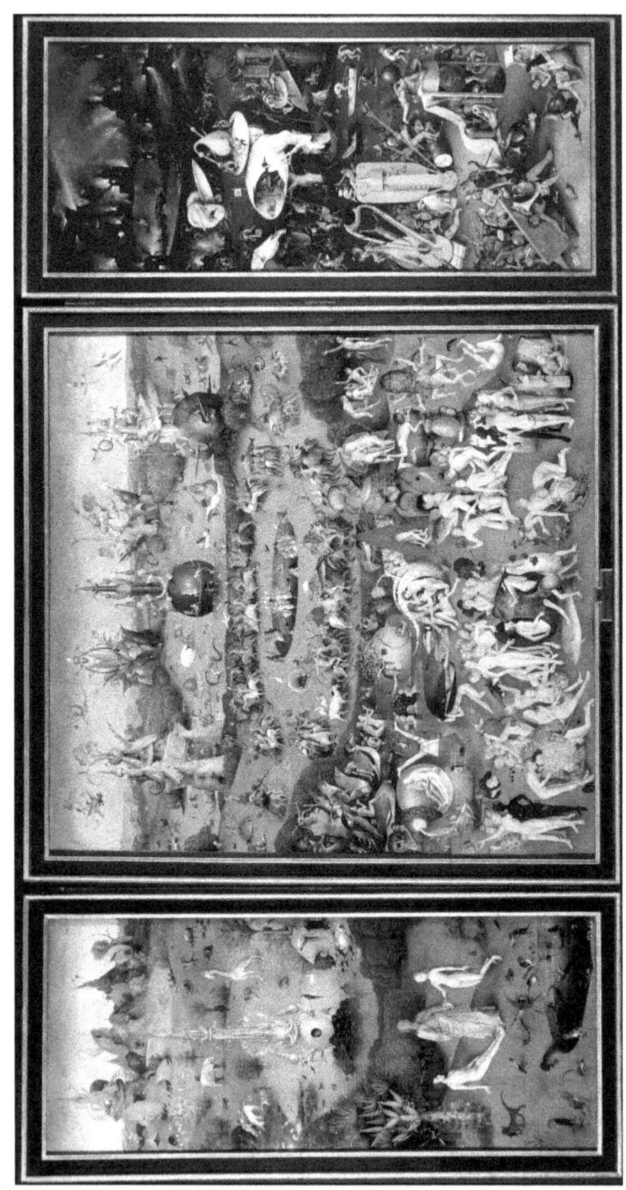

17 Hieronymus Bosch, triptych of *The Garden of Earthly Delights*, c.1510. Oil on wood: centre panel, 220 x 195 cm; wings, 220 x 97 cm. © Museo Nacional del Prado, Madrid

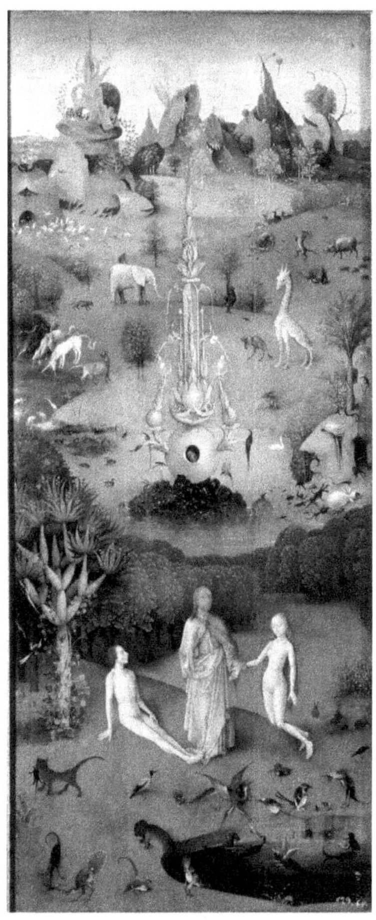

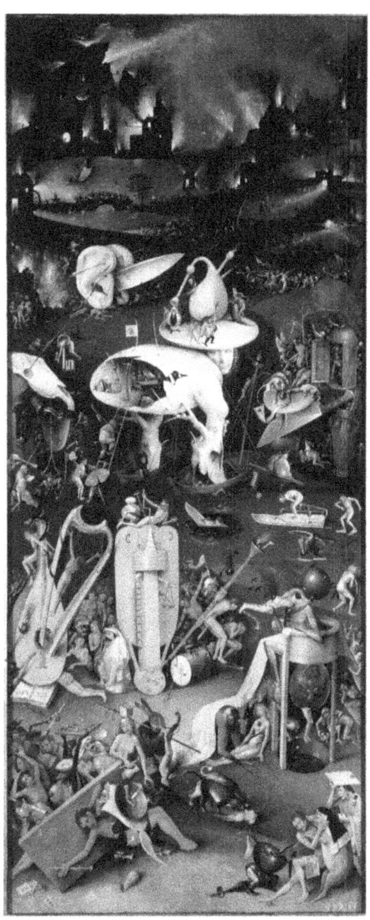

17a Hieronymus Bosch, *Creation*, left inner wing, *The Garden of Earthly Delights*
17c Hieronymus Bosch, *Purgatory*, right inner wing, *The Garden of Earthly Delights*

stage forward in unraveling Boschian surreal thought. The next step is to examine the form of the *diablerie* itself. This is the main focus of the present chapter.

Part of the trouble with interpreting the metamorphic imagery through cataloguing its prototypes in the visual arts is that the medieval sources themselves are not well understood. Following Panofsky's suggestions, *diablerie* prototypes have been located in the marginalia of medieval books, in cathedral grotesques, and in medieval synesthetic poetry.[8] Still, the general meaning of this imagery, and the reasons for its proliferation in the mid-sixteenth century, remain mysterious. What was Bosch doing when he introduced surreal creatures into large-scale oil painting? Why did this imagery become so popular in the decades after his death? What did people think it meant? How do Boschian and Bruegelian *diablerie* differ, and why?

Explanations for the *diablerie* as illustrations of folkloric or legendary texts are not much help with these questions. In Bruegel's art, proliferating metamorphs fill the picture space, and greatly outnumber the ostensible protagonists, St. Anthony, St. James, Dulle Griet, etc. Written sources of such legends contain no visual descriptions of metamorphic *diablerie*. The life of St. Anthony does not mention hybrid creatures in any of the encounters the saint has with diabolic forces.[9] It seems that the story of Anthony's Temptation became, in sixteenth-century art, an open framework into which aspects of the contemporary imagination were projected. Other contemporary subjects were also treated in this way. The return of the Prodigal Son, for example, became a useful scaffolding for exploring brothel, tavern and feasting scenes.[10] Bruegel proved adept at identifying themes no one else had thought of opening out in this fashion.

If these surreal elaborations are not called for by narrative necessity, then what do they mean? How were they supposed to be read? Suppose, for example, that we agree that some of the imagery has folkloric roots. This does not shed much light on the stylistic issue. Where an element can be identified as, say a proverb illustration, the tendency is then to side-step the fantastic element in the image by redirecting our attention to its common-sense message; so the surreal element is recuperated — grounded — to the mundane world.[11] But Bruegel's own *Netherlandish Proverbs* (fig. 63) — or similar works by Frans Hogenberg (fig. 69) and others — show that there was no need to resort to surrealism in order to translate folkloric commonplaces into images. In fact, Bruegel used surreal imagery to give

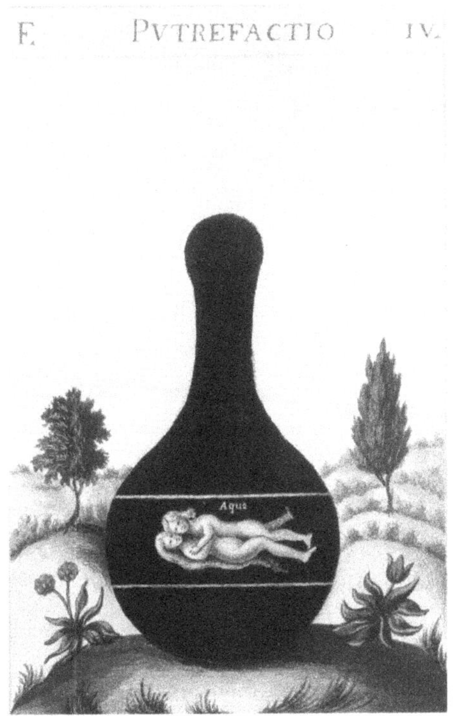

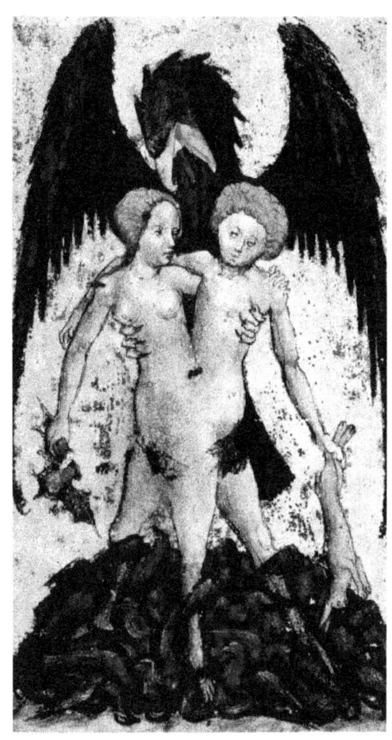

18 Anon, Putrefactio, *Petriosissimum Donum Dei*, Planche IV, Ms. 975, f.10r-26r, Bibliotheque nationale de France
19 Anon, Hermaphrodite with Eagle, *Aurora Consurgens*, Ms. Ferguson 6, Glasgow University Library, Glasgow

quite a different implication to such proverbs. His *Big Fish Eat Little Fish* (fig. 36) dramatised a commonplace drawn from nature by interpreting it in terms of the unreal and the nightmarish. Why did he do this? We must ask how, why and in what contexts, metamorphic imagery became associated with the psychological dimensions of fantasy and nightmare, rather than the simply demonic.

Ideas and beliefs about nightmares, dreams in general, and hybrid or metamorphic bodies, occur in many areas of Renaissance art and thought. Medieval dream theory was a hybrid blend of classical medicine and theology, achieving a new sphere of influence through print and translation in the sixteenth century. Though the basic categories by which dreams were understood hardly altered from the time of Chaucer through to the end of the thirteenth century, a sea-change in their interpretation does seem to occur in the wake of Ficino's thought, as the concept of melancholia was deepened and broadened.

Hybrid, metamorphic, or metamorphosing bodies also play key roles elsewhere in the classical corpus, in texts well-known throughout the Middle Ages, and others newly discovered in the fifteenth century. The sources divide roughly into literary (Ovid), philosophical (Plato), and scientific (Lucretius, Pliny). Ovid's *Metamorphoses* was one of the most beloved and most commented-on books of the Middle Ages. Plato's references to metamorphosis in man constituted a crucial source for the new Neo-Platonic psychology, pioneered, as we saw, by Marsilio Ficino et al in Italy. How do these discourses define these bodies?

In the visual arts, a creature with a metamorphic body is either a hybrid of several species, or is in the process of changing from one thing into another. The hybrid body itself is an ancient and disturbing image-type, with deep roots in Western culture. It transpires that the images are concerned with the ways in which people distinguish themselves from animals. The concept of metamorphosis itself, in particular of humans changing into beasts, is central to the imagery. In ancient and folk belief, human metamorphosis occupies a central religious position,[12] corresponding to doctrines of metempsychosis, the movement of souls between humans and animals. These seem to be theological, poetic, and mythic elaborations of the deeply-rooted "primitive" assumption that there is no hard and fast line between people and beasts, and that a "fundamental identity" exists between the two.[13] Variations of this idea persisted in the west under Christianity; early modern people did not hold undivided opinions on these subjects. Epistemologically, then, the metamorphic body — a visual embodiment of paradox[14] — marks points of contradiction, or slippage, between admissible, or orthodox, systems of explanation, and inadmissible, yet widely-held beliefs.

As developed in Pythagorean and Hermetic philosophical thought, the doctrine of metempsychosis lost its literal metamorphic character. Yet the idea of migrating souls remained attractive to thinkers in the latter half of the fifteenth century, who eagerly scrutinized and amalgamated all classical writings on the subject. Ficino was delighted by Plato's image of the soul travelling heavenwards in its Phraedran chariot. He devoted many pages of his commentaries on Plato to its discussion.[15] With Italian Neo-Platonism, classical ideas about metamorphosis came once more to the forefront of modern philosophy, in a new reinterpretation as metaphor. The concept of metamorphosis could be used to mediate between the old, hidden belief that humans and animals are in some sense interchangeable, and the Christian teaching that Man, made in God's image and uniquely possessed of an immortal soul, is fundamentally different from the beasts. In philosophy and rhetoric, the image of the metamorphic body signified something outside the natural order (*praeter naturam*);[16] but it could also be a sign of divine (or occult) intervention in nature: proof of an order beyond mere nature. This made it a fertile metaphor for depicting events and conditions conceived of as miraculous disruptions from the ordinary world.

In medieval visual culture, the metamorphic body remained alive and well, in the art of margins and edges. Its florescence in large-scale art from around 1500 on — in works from Venice, France, Northern Germany and the Low Countries — was closely involved with technical developments in illusionist painting. Leonardo advised the artist to construct a plausible fantastic beast by closely observing the parts of real animals (he recommends modelling the haunch of a dragon after that of a horse).[17] There were intimate links between the philosophical context of the imagery and its deployment in painting: the question of just what it was that metamorphic *diableries* were intended to represent.

Hybrid imagery represented an array of contexts, a scale on which an artist could compose, like a musician. Clearly, a thorough investigation into the history of metamorphs would have to cover an extremely wide field. Our interest here is in the new species of *diablerie*, as opposed to what might be termed traditional "nameable" hybrids — dragons, griffins, unicorns, centaurs, fauns, sphinxes, and so on — whose shapes were already fixed in texts and pictures. I will refer to the histories of these traditional creatures only where theories about their genesis shed light on the meaning of hybrids in general. I will look first at their philosophical aspects, around and after 1500, when the metamorphic body became a central metaphor in the psychological explorations of Pico della Mirandola and of Hieronymus Bosch, and examine how these first forays were absorbed and embedded into Renaissance culture over the next half-century. There are instances where some of the earlier Italian speculative thought has an unusually direct bearing on Bruegel's imagery (as in the *Fall of the Rebel Angels*; fig. 21), but I want to present this material less as Bruegel's "sources" than as examples indicative of the many-stranded traditions he had to hand; others could be added. The intention is to use the sixteenth century *universe of discourse* - that set of *authoritative texts which attract commentary*[18] — to evoke the movements of culture which shaped Bruegel's art.[19] The common library of the Renaissance is the first port of call.

Classical Sources and Renaissance Interpretations

Lucretius and Metamorphs as First Things

When looking for concrete descriptions of actual metamorphs, hybrid creatures that were said to exist or to have really existed, it is best to start with the works of the natural philosophers, and move from there to the interpretations of the "Platonic theologians," notably Ficino and his star pupil, Pico della Mirandola (1463-94). Though classical texts supplied many instances of beliefs in the actuality of hybrids, the most "objective" accounts occur in writings on natural history. Inherited classical ideas on natural history and geography were resistant to change, but, among the "new" classical authors in the sixteenth century, Lucretius became famous for his account of metamorphic creatures. Certain important classical assumptions about hybrids and metamorphs therefore emerge in his writing.

The lack of any guiding religious framework in Lucretius' vision of nature rendered his work scandalous in the eyes of the Church. The Venetian humanist-printer, Aldus Manutius (c 1449-1515), felt it necessary to apologize in his dedication for publishing the work of such a man as Lucretius, *who had written so much that was unchristian and untrue.*[20] Nevertheless, published he was. The first edition of the *De Rerum Natura* was made at Brescia in 1478. It was followed by a flood of Italian editions, including two from the Aldine press and one from Bologna. The latter was equipped with a huge commentary which undertook with gusto the task of integrating the Roman's uncompromisingly atheist vision within the more or less equally incommensurable framework of the Church's precepts and the received truths of medieval science. This commentary was reprinted in Paris as early as 1514. Lucretius spread rapidly via the main printing centres to northern Europe in the 1530s and 1540s. An edition appeared at Antwerp in 1566.

The attention paid to Lucretius' great didactic poem in part depended on the rise of secular education. As a contemporary of Cicero, Lucretius' prose style exemplified the kind of Latin most admired by Humanists. In terms of philosophical content, Lucretius' Epicureanism struck a familiar chord for those who had learned from Ficino to honor Plotinus. Lucretius' invocation of Venus against Mars[21] became famous, because it could be interpreted allegorically, as meaning that love is more powerful than strife, or, in a more elevated key, that the tempering power of beauty must supersede the strife which characterises contrary, i.e., disunified, elements in nature. Thus Italian Humanists deciphered (or enciphered) pieces of

Lucretius by way of their favourite rhetorical technique of *complicatio*: an *infolding* of the original image. Pico worked from similar passages in Plutarch and Plotinus to conclude that, *if Mars were always subordinated to Venus, that is, the contrariety of the component elements to their due proportion, nothing would ever perish*.[22] In this manner Lucretius quickly won a place in a range of Humanist projects. On the subject of metamorphs, paradoxically, he made them famous by decrying their probability. His cold common sense was applied first to the problem of their biology:

> You need not suppose, therefore, that there can ever be a centaur, compounded of man and draft horse, or a scylla, half sea monster, with a girdle of mad dogs, or any other such monstrous hybrid between species whose bodies are obviously incompatible. They do not match in their maturing, in gaining strength, or in losing it with advancing years... Their habits are discordant... Each species develops according to its own kind and they all guard their specific characters in obedience to the laws of nature.[23]

Lucretius' skepticism here clarifies a major point about metamorphic creatures and the beliefs they might incarnate. In this passage, Lucretius is talking about the present world. Under today's natural laws, he argues, hybrid species cannot exist. The very distant past, however, is a different matter. In the present state of the world, the poet likens the earth to a *woman worn out with age*. At the beginning of time, Lucretius' earth is fully magical, following a Greek tradition. The new earth was a fertile being who spontaneously gave birth to humans, plants, and animals. At this time, and only at this time, *the earth tried its hand at producing kinds of monsters, grotesque in build and appearance, hermaphrodites halfway between the sexes yet cut off from either; creatures bereft of feet or dispossessed of hands; dumb, mouthless brutes, or eyeless and blind, or disabled by the adhesion of their limbs to the trunk*. These sports of the creation could not survive down to the present day because they were incapable of reproduction: *Nature debarred them from increase*.[24] In other

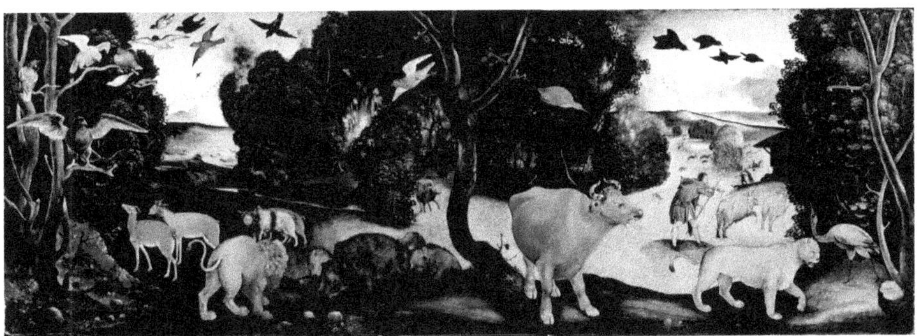

20 Piero di Cosimo, *Landscape with Forest Fire*, c 1505. Oil on wood, 71.2 x 202 cm. © Ashmolean Museum, Oxford. WA 1933.2\A420

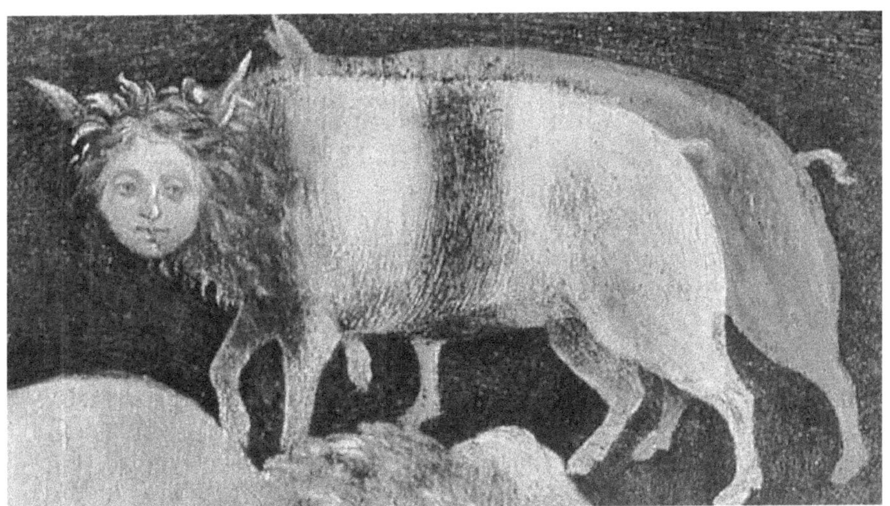

20a Piero di Cosimo, prehistoric hybrid creature, detail, *Landscape with Forest Fire*

words, the presence of metamorphic creatures marks an era when natural law is absent, and has not yet had time to work its effects.

As a "scientific" approach to visualizing human metamorphs, Lucretian metamorphs make their way into art in Piero di Cosimo's evolutionistic compositions; for example, in his *Landscape with Forest Fire*, at

Oxford (c 1505, fig. 20). This painting is a chapter in Piero's version of the prehistory of man. At the dawn of time, as Panofsky put it:

> the woods are still haunted by the strange creatures which resulted from the promiscuous mating of men and animals, for the sow with the face of a woman and the goat with the face of a man are... meant to bear witness to a very serious theory, contested and thereby effectively transmitted in no less than thirty-five lines of Lucretius.[25]

In Lucretius, metamorphic creatures are by definition supernatural, since they cannot exist naturally. There is a useful rhetorical term for this: they are *adynata*, or impossibilities. They are supernatural because they share by extension the supernatural quality characteristic of the time of Creation itself. More specifically, the hybrids characterise the uncontrolled aspect of raw Creation, since they run against natural law. With all this in mind, let us consider some cases of metamorphic First Things in paintings by Bosch and Bruegel.

Metamorphic First Things in Bosch's " Creation"

Bosch was very interested in First and Last Things. The metamorphic monsters in Hell scenes from his Last Judgements, his *Haywain*, and his *Garden of Earthly Delights* (fig. 17), are often thought to express *the medieval conception of hell as a state where the divinely ordained laws of nature have disintegrated into chaos*.[26] The presence of such creatures in Bosch's scenes of Creations has a similar Lucretian rationale. The overall formal development of metamorphic imagery in the famous *Garden of Delights* triptych makes clear the kinds of meaning present here. God presents Eve to Adam on the left wing triptych, where metamorphic beasts and normal animals appear together in a fertile landscape (fig. 17a). This landscape itself exhibits a metamorphic development over the triptych as a whole. At the right, a pink organic fountain is perched on a pile of *prima materia*; the latter is studded with test tubes and glowing jewels.

It is here as a symbol of the magical generative power of the earth during the first days of the world. From the pool which surrounds the fountain emerges a school of newt-like creatures – among them several bizarre metamorphs – which have spawned from the water (fig. 17b). More strange beasts, including a unicorn-headed fish, swim in the pool at Adam's feet. Next to the pool is another three-headed beast, this time bird-like.[27] Above, swarms of birds emerge from an oddly twisted mountain. Received classical ideas about the autochthonous origin of living things seems to lie behind both these conceptions.

This mountain and its blue counterpart to the right also have a metamorphic appearance. Like the fountain, they are hybrids, partly grown and partly built. Unlike the fountain, Bosch's phallic sculptural mountains are part of the earth. There is no source from which they grow (as the fountain "grows" from the *prima materia*), other than the magical earth itself. Bosch shows similar "designed" mountains on the outside of the triptych, in his depiction of the uninhabited earth before the creation of living things.

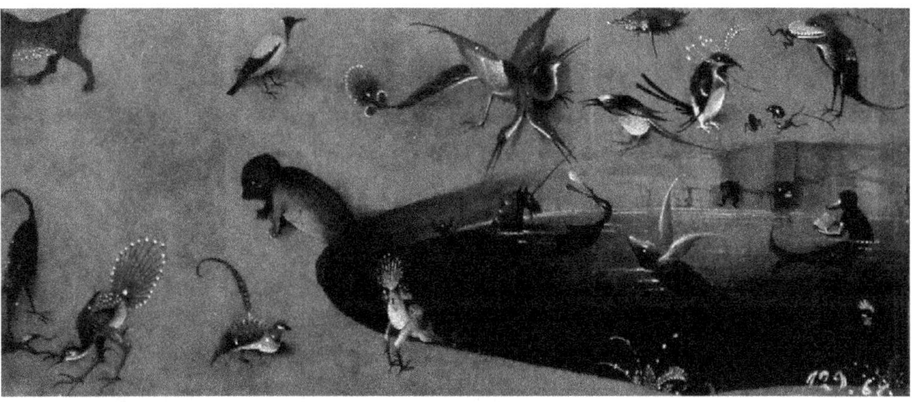

17b Hieronymus Bosch, newt-like metamorphs, detail, *Creation*, left inner wing, *The Garden of Earthly Delights*

For Bosch then, as for Lucretius, the newly created earth is conceived of as teeming with life, and at this moment metamorphic creatures naturally have their place in the context of the whole triptych.

The pink fountain and the mountains undergo a change from left to right. The fountain of the left wing is slender, stately, symmetrical, and closed upon itself like a bud. In the central panel, the equivalent pink formation has sprouted grotesquely. Where there was one, there are now two analogous structures. Similarly, the ominous promise of the strange blue mountains in the left wing seems to be fulfilled in the blue mountain-growing-orchid which sits in between the two pink structures in the centre panel. In the Adam and Eve panel, one of these mountains already spouts fire and impossibly long, slender tree branches. Another seems contained by a kind of cloak. In the central scene, these tokens of a coming florescence are fully developed. There are five large mountainous formations in the left wing, and five large mountainous structures in the middle panel. In the Adam and Eve panel, these are carefully distinguished from each other by color and position. The pink fountain is quite distinct from the yellow bird-producing mountain and from the three blue mountains in a row at the rear. In the centre picture, all of these original characteristics are grotesquely mixed and the mountains and fountains have become fully metamorphic. Bosch presents full-blown metamorphosis as an image of fertility, suited to the main action of the central panel, where common differences of scale and kind that normally keep humans and animals apart are deliberately eradicated.

A comparison of the animals and metamorphs in the Adam and Eve panel and in the central panel reveals a similar development. The animals on the left wing include several instances of hunters killing and eating their prey. Two of these are located to the left, below Adam, and to the right, below Eve. This is one of the points that serves to distinguish the fauna of the Garden of Eden from their human lords. None of the metamorphs in this part of the picture have a human aspect. In the centre panel, on the other hand, this clear distinction between humans and animals has been eroded. In the central parade of riders, certain humans bite into enormous fish, one of which is itself eating a fish. In the sky at the top left, a winged metamorph has captured as prey another smaller creature; the successful hunter is itself ridden by a human. Humans have now joined the animals in the pools of water which were previously the "breeding ground" for crawling things and metamorphs. New species of human metamorphs have appeared, notably merpeople. The birds have grown to an enormous size. Many of them feed humans as they would their own chicks, with berries from the beak.

Metamorphic imagery here embodies the procreative force of nature which was present in the beginning, and whose principal manifestation in humans since the Fall is lust. The specific form it is given dramatises this as a power of untrammeled growth. The metamorphs in the central panel show what happens when humanity gives itself wholly over to this force. The repercussions of this abandonment are given a cosmic dimension by their association with uncontrolled natural growth. To summarise, in this picture metamorphs are numbered among First Things, and they are connected with unsanctified procreation in nature, and thus with lust.

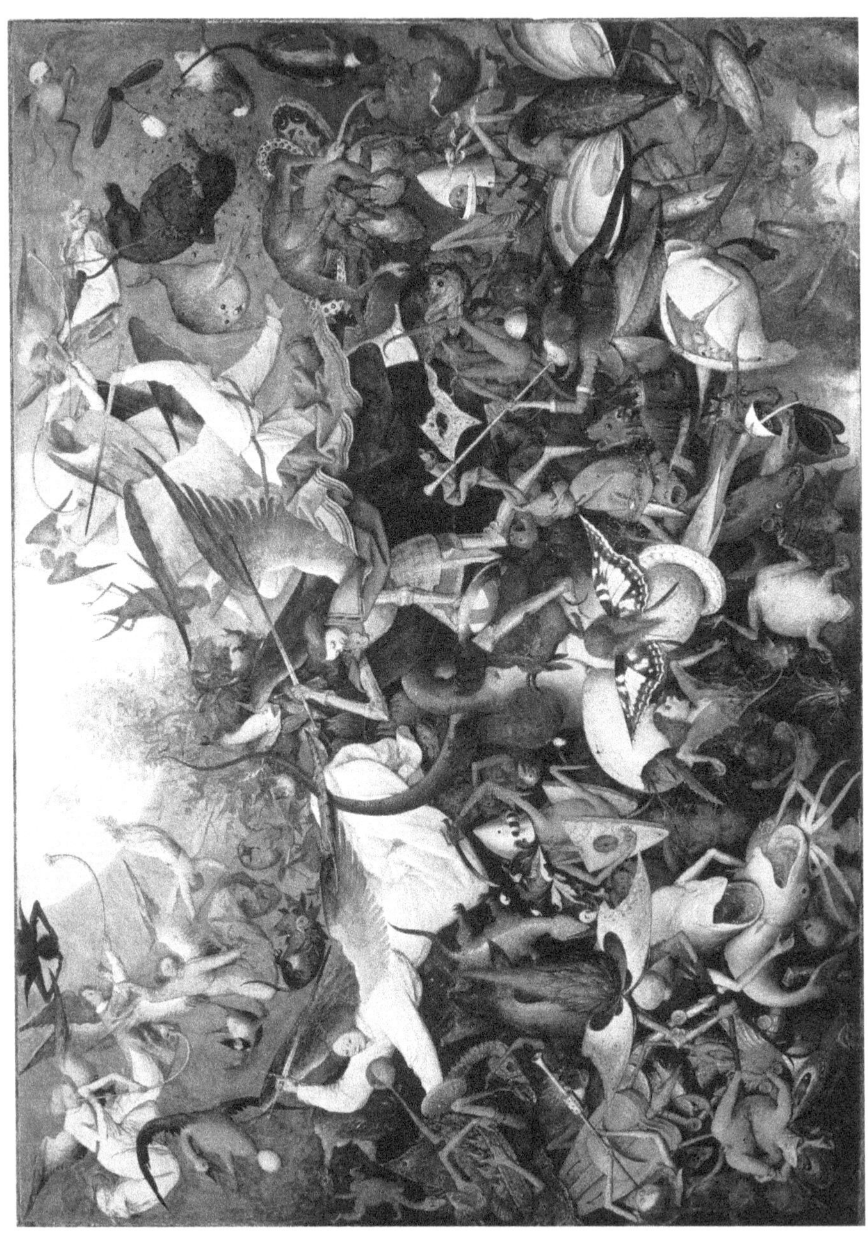

21 Pieter Bruegel, *Fall of the Rebel Angels*, c 1562. Oil on wood, 117 x 162 cm. Musées Royaux des Beaux-Arts, Brussels. Inv 584. Photo: Scala

Metamorphic First Things in Bruegel's "Fall of the Rebel Angels"

These connotations also inform Bruegel's version of metamorphic First Things, the *Fall of the Rebel Angels* (fig. 21). Here, the ideas that metamorph acquire their form both as beings of a newly-created earth, and as the proper denizens of a chaotic Hell, are brought together. The fall of Lucifer's angels historically precedes the creation of the earth. The rebel angels themselves are therefore among First Things. As soon as they fall, they take on monstrous aspects, the guises in which they will populate hell, the better to assist their master. From a very early date, medieval artists had felt it necessary to flesh out with pagan materials the slender data given in the Bible about the visual appearance of Hell. The tradition of filling in the gaps in scripture on the subject of First and Last Things from other sources, such as the Jewish legend of the rebel angels, came to a head in the latter half of the fifteenth century. In Italian circles, a great thirst was felt for more information about the beginning and end of the world. Piero di Cosimo's paintings of prehistoric times show one direction of these explorations in painting (cf. fig. 20);[28] Piero's work was described by Vasari, in an edition Bruegel could have read in 1559. At the same time, philosophers became interested in defining human nature with respect to the nature of angels. These researches, frequently based on clues in Platonic and hermetic texts, had by Bruegel's day become educated commonplaces, found in the "popular" works of Rabelais, Shakespeare and others.

What began as esoteric and heretical speculations had become far less radical by the mid-sixteenth century, when the varied forces of the Reformation presented more tangible threats to the established church. Bruegel's painting should be understood, I think, as a contribution to this by now respectable tradition of philosophic speculation. Its ironic humor can be explained as a result of its late position — parody even was now acceptable — but its content derives from a Christian Humanist tradition which may now be briefly traced.

Gianozzo Manetti (1396-1459) in the early 1450s wrote his discourse, *On the Dignity and Excellence of Man,* in reply to Innocent III's treatise on the miserable condition of mankind. Manetti's main theme is the uniqueness of human nature, the qualities of which are shared, he says, by no other of God's creatures, not even the angels.[29] In the following decades, another Florentine, Matteo Palmieri (1406-75), wrote a long heretical poem arguing *that man was the descendent of those archangels who remained neutral at the time of the rebellion, when Michael sided with God and Lucifer fell. In Man... the neutral archangels are given a second opportunity to choose their destiny.*[30]

At this date, then, it became possible to look for information about human nature through a reinterpretation of the first rebellion against God. Discontented with the idea that Adam was made out of clay, fifteenth-century commentators concentrated on the process whereby Adam was given a soul. Ficino found a more satisfactory account of *Genesis* in the texts of the *Corpus Hermeticum,* then thought to be of unimaginable antiquity, earlier than Moses. Ficino translated these works on the order of Cosimo di Medici before any of the previously unknown works of Plato which came into the possession of the Medici at the same time. One of these Hermetic books, the *Pimander,* described a tripartite Almighty easily reconcilable with the Holy Trinity. God the Father is called the *nous* in this text, which describes the creation of Man as follows:

> The *nous* gave birth to a man similar to himself, whom he loved as his own son. For Man was beautiful, reflecting the image of his Father: for it was truly his own form with which God fell in love, and he delivered to him all his works. Then ... Man also wanted to produce a work, and permission was granted to him by the Father. Having entered therefore into the demi-urgic sphere where he had to have full power, the governors [of the seven planets] were enamored of him, and each gave him a part of his own power.[31]

This passage describes Man as endowed with part of the same kind of power as that wielded by the great angels who control the seven planets in the hermetic cosmos. Like the legends of the rebel angels, and of Christ's Descent into Hell, Ficino read this account as supplementing rather than contradicting the Biblical version. Human nature is similarly linked with that of angels and demons in other passages of the *Corpus*. Thus, in the *Asclepius*:

> A great miracle is man, a being worthy of reverence and honor, because he enters into the nature of a god, as if he himself were a god, he is familiar with the race of demons, knowing that he issued from the same origin, he despises that part of his nature that is only human, for he has placed his hope in the divinity of his other part.[32]

By way of Ficino, hermetic ideas about human nature were absorbed into European thought. The hermetic view of man's angelic element percolated into Renaissance commonplace books and popular literature. So Rabelais has Pantagruel invoke it:

> You will be convinced by a common example... once our body is sleeping... the soul enjoys itself and revisits its own country, which is the heavens. There it receives intimations of its first and divine origins. There it contemplates that infinite, intellectual sphere... which sphere, according to the doctrine of Hermes Trismagistus, is God.[33]

Pantagruel talks also about the nature of dreaming, and we will have cause to return to this aspect of the passage later. His speech shows how questions about human nature had become woven into ideas about angels, fallen or otherwise. This development explains some of the novelties in Bruegel's *Fall of the Rebel Angels*, in particular, its treatment of metamorphic imagery. Some aspects of this picture are quite traditional. The long diminishing funnel of the angels falling in the distance from the light of heaven is seen in several works by Bosch (for example, in the Genesis panel of the Vienna *Last Judgement*, c 1506; fig. 24). The template for the good angels is taken from Jan van Eyck.[34]

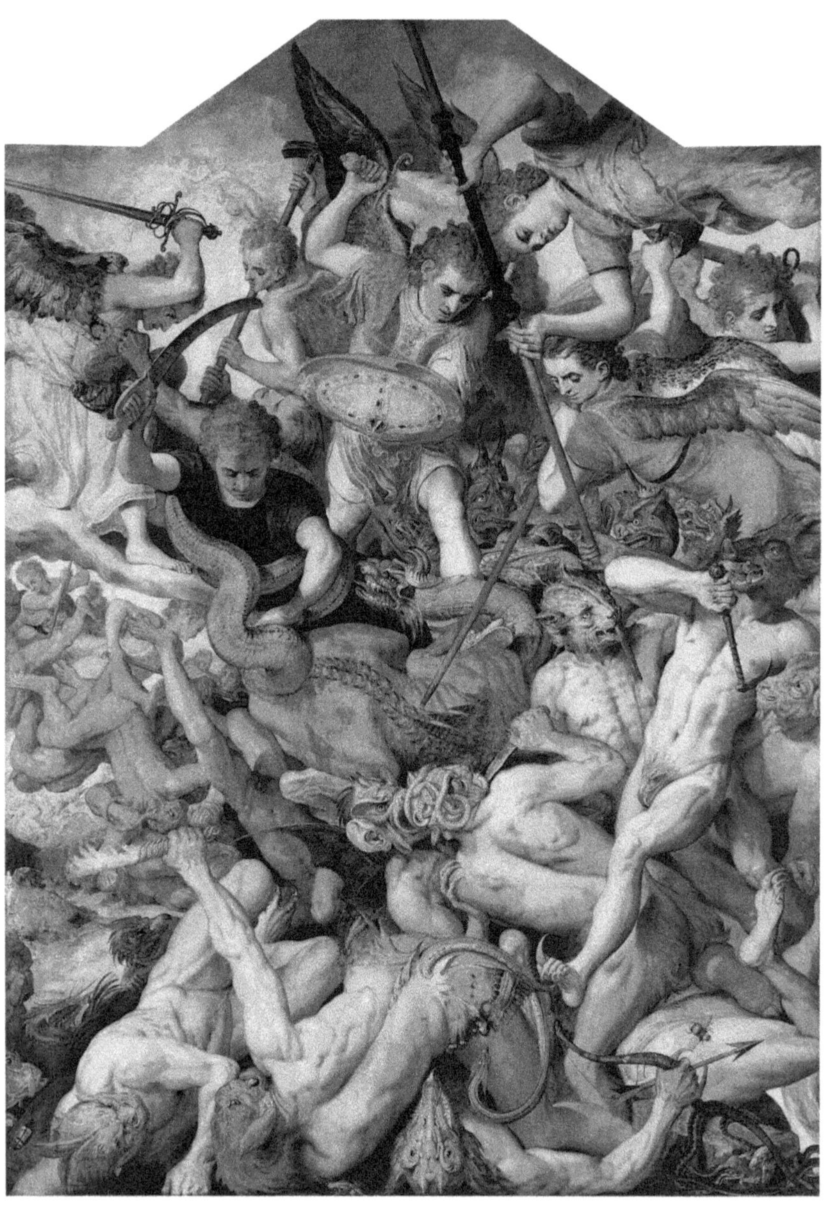

22 Frans Floris, *The Fall of the Rebellious Angels*, 1564. Oil on wood, 308 x 220 cm. Koninklijk Museum voor Schone Kunsten, KMSK Antwerp – Image courtesy of Reproductiefonds

However, the picture as a whole does not follow familiar or contemporaneous conceptions of this theme. Bruegel's departures from his models have been considered to be *fanciful and without specific meaning,* because the good angels seem merely to hold their swords in the poses of battle, rather than actually fighting their erstwhile colleagues, and because of the specific peculiarities of their hybrid bodies: *the animal form in the lower right-hand corner opens up its belly to reveal eggs inside. Such a figure is not fighting expulsion from Heaven.*[35] But Bruegel's innovations become meaningful when the significance of his decision to cast the rebel angels as metamorphs is recognised. For example, the creature opening its belly to reveal eggs (fig. 21a) is a reference to the procreative associations of the metamorphic body. In his choice of parts from which to make up these particular creatures, Bruegel draws a correspondence between the fall of the angels and the fall of humanity. He gives many of them human faces (fig. 21b).

This reverses the method followed for Last Judgements and Falls by earlier artists, including Bosch himself, and contemporaries such as Frans Floris (c1520-70), all of whom depicted rebel angels and devils in hell as having bestial heads on anthropomorphic bodies.[36] In his *Fall of the Rebellious Angels* (1554; fig. 22), Floris' rebel angels also have bestial extremities — one sports a hawk's head instead of genitalia, others have taloned hands — while their bodies as a whole conform to the Italianate conception of the human nude.

The difference in meaning between these two conceptions is more easily intuited visually than analyzed verbally. One effect is to bring the nature of the rebels closer to human nature, and thus to make the psychology of the Fall for the first time the pivot of the scene. By retaining the humanity of the head in several prominent metamorphosing figures, Bruegel is able to show the shock and dismay that these ex-angels feel as their own bodies change weirdly below their heads (fig 21b). Once this is recognized, we see that even the non-humanoid heads express these same

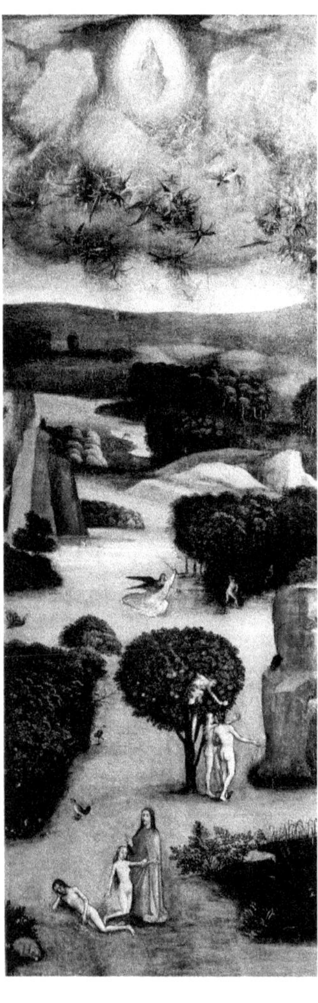

24 Hieronymus Bosch, *Fall of the Rebel Angels and The Creation*, left inner wing of *Last Judgement* triptych, c 1506. Oil on wood, 167.7 x 60 cm. Gemäldegalerie der Akademie der Bildenden Künste, Vienna

emotions. The metamorphosing bodies *themselves* represent the Fall. This is why the scene only superficially resembles a battle. The rebel angels here are presented as creatures caught up in their own metamorphoses. These have struck them with such terror as to deprive them of the will to fight back, as well as rendering them in many cases physically incapable of battle.

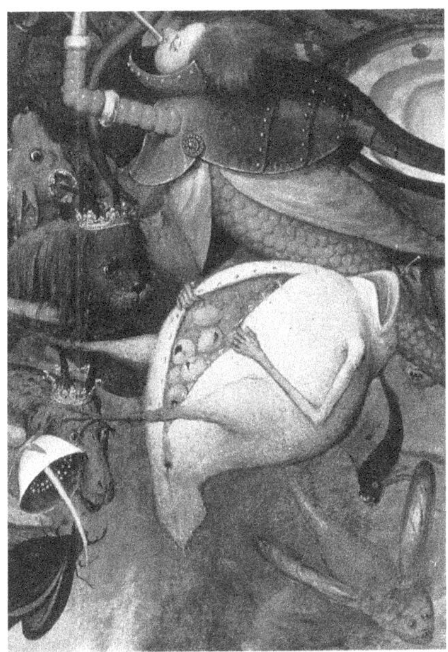
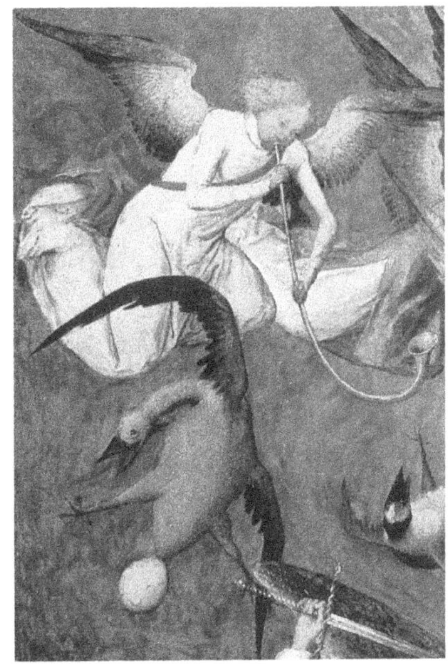

21a Pieter Bruegel, creature opening belly to reveal eggs, detail, *Fall of the Rebel Angels*
21d Pieter Bruegel, egg-laying goose-angel, detail, *Fall of the Rebel Angels*

The good angels need, therefore, only herd these monsters on their inevitable descent downwards. That the metamorphs are concerned in this picture with the changing nature of their bodies is made clear by several instances where Bruegel depicts individual creatures as engaged in attacks upon themselves.[37] Thus, in the bottom left-hand corner, a twisted metamorph grips its own rear limbs and bites at its leg. The beast which splits open its own belly also falls into this category. Similarly, near the top right-hand corner, two almost completely bestial metamorphs, one frog-like, the other dog-like, fall tangled together in an inextricable mass of limbs and tails, each biting and gripping the other's extremities (fig. 21c).

Only one of these creatures has a weapon to raise against St. Michael and his band. This is the figure in an armored helmet, its right arm partly

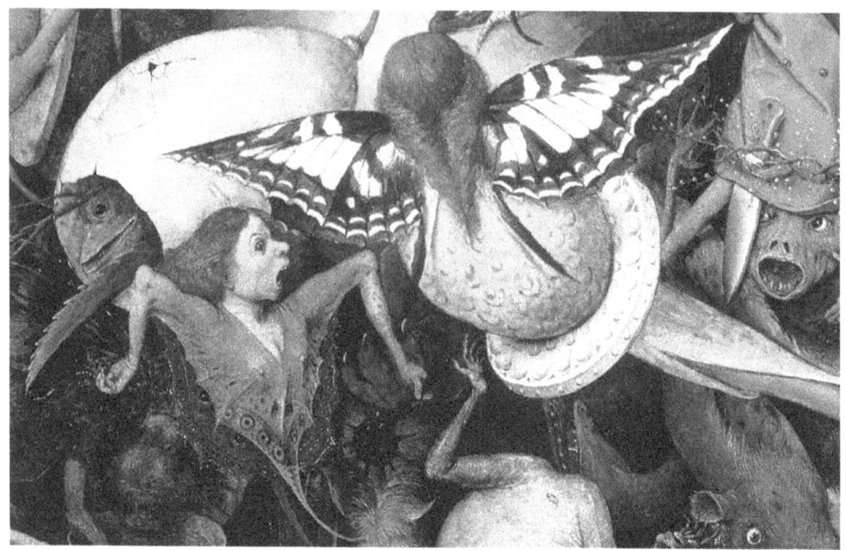

21b Pieter Bruegel, human-headed rebel angels, detail, *Fall of the Rebel Angels*

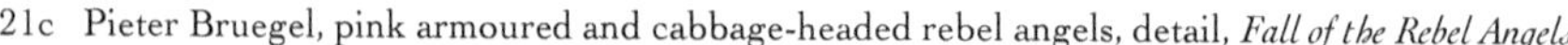

21c Pieter Bruegel, pink armoured and cabbage-headed rebel angels, detail, *Fall of the Rebel Angels*

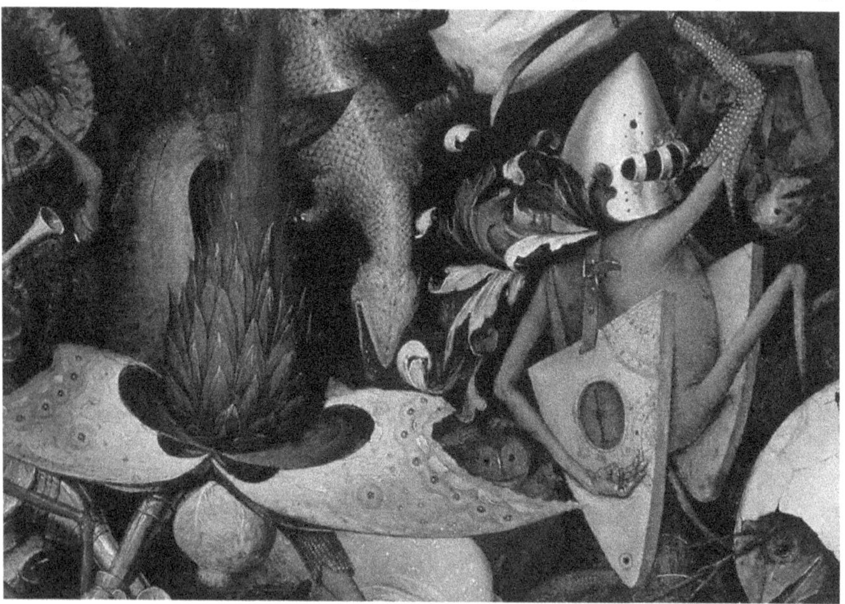

covered by chain mail. Again, this creature's effort appears both futile and undirected. In Bruegel's conception, the Fall is not a battle but a change of nature. Bruegel connects this change with ideas about human nature in the following ways. First, there are references to lust. Eggs abound in this picture. Starting at the top left-hand corner and moving down through a wide arc to finish at the top right-hand corner, we see first, a goose extruding an egg in an almost normal fashion except that here the egg seems to be stuck on to its parent (fig. 21d). Further down, the path of a white-clad angel is obstructed by a strange spindly appendage tipped with a sphere, which cracks open to reveal caviar-like eggs. Below this, a howling hybrid clutches to itself a basket filled with chicks. Moving down from this, near the bottom centre a beaked metamorph emerges from a huge egg tipped with a spike. Then there is the monster with the egg-filled belly (fig. 21a), and, at the top right, a dragonfly extrudes an egg in the same fashion as the goose in the opposite corner.

The rebel angels are therefore presented as becoming egg-layers in the moment of their transformation. There is an element of grotesque humor to this. The good angels are winged and, obviously, being immortals, do not procreate, let alone lay eggs. Many of the rebel angels are also winged, and Bruegel takes great delight in running metamorphic changes on these wings. Where Michael and his followers have wings modelled after those of birds, the rebels are given the wings of insects.[38] The goose at the top left-hand corner summarises this development in miniature (fig. 21d). Previously a heavenly winged creature, it has been metamorphosed as a punishment for its sin of disobedience into the body of an earthly bird. At the same time it is deprived of its angelic attribute; its angelic wings have mutated, moving up around its neck, and it is made to lay an egg, an act which confirms its new, low earthly and sexual nature.

In *Genesis*, the first human birth, that of Cain, is a consequence of original sin. God curses Eve for her disobedience by making her bear children in pain. Bruegel seems to have tailored his metamorphs in order to make this parallel more plain. By making them egg-layers, he underlined the bestial nature of procreation, and hence alluded to the associated vice of lust, which was thought to be in humans a peculiarly animal vice. In the print of *Luxuria* (fig. 15), the artist filled the foreground with groups of copulating animals and hybrids, while Luxuria herself consorts with a metamorph. In Mantegna's *Pallas Driving the Vices* (fig. 6), the main Vices are accompanied by a small flock of owl-faced, insect-winged cherubs.

The second allusion in this picture to the Fall of Man may be discerned by comparing the faces of the human-headed rebels. The most shocked and terrified faces are: those of the man's head at the bottom left corner underneath the fish-like monsters, his body completely invisible; the woman at bottom centre, in front of the monster coming out of the egg, whose lower body parts have vanished; and the two women's heads at the bottom right, with dishevelled hair and dragonfly wings (at corner and right of fig. 21a). Expressions of extreme emotion are in general rare in Netherlandish painting. A famous context in which they occur is the Fall of the Damned, in Last Judgement scenes by van der Weyden, Bouts, the van Eycks, et al. Prototypes for the faces of Bruegel's rebels exist in, for example, the far right wing of Rogier van der Weyden's *Last Judgement* polyptych (1446-52; fig. 23), where the faces of the damned are painted with extraordinary expressions of fear and horror. The resemblance to the heads of Bruegel's metamorphosing angels is pronounced.

Whether or not Rogier's painting was the actual source for these figures,[39] it is quite possible that these particular expressions, on their own, evoked the context of the Fall of the Damned for a contemporary viewer. This connotation would intensify the Humanist parallel between the state of the fallen angels and that of fallen humanity. The terror-struck heads represent "normal" or average human types, just as it was the bulk of humanity, the majority of "ordinary" people who were identified with the damned in earlier art. (Interestingly Bruegel's own *Last Judgement* (1558;

fig. 98)[40] is the first to reverse these proportions, making the saved outnumber the damned).

The other human heads depart from this norm in, as it were, higher and lower directions. An example of the "lowest" human type, its face and form degraded but still recognizably human (not, for instance, ape-like), can be found midway up the right side of the picture. This creature wears a metal helmet, placing it among the ranks of Bruegel's many armoured metamorphs. This sub-genre seems to have particularly attracted the artist, not least for its topical and satirical allusions;[41] several pieces of armour appear here among the rebel monsters. Another helmet wearer, left of centre, is the only one of the rebels still in possession of his weapon and apparently ready to use it, however aimlessly, in this last extremity. His skin is a bright rosy pink, possibly a reference to his choler, the humour linked with the vice of anger. To his left, is a butterfly-winged metamorph, whose right arm is also clad in armour and whose head has become a cabbage. Behind this, at bottom left, torsos of armour fall head-first, dragged down by their own weight. It is unclear what is inside them; one at least has no

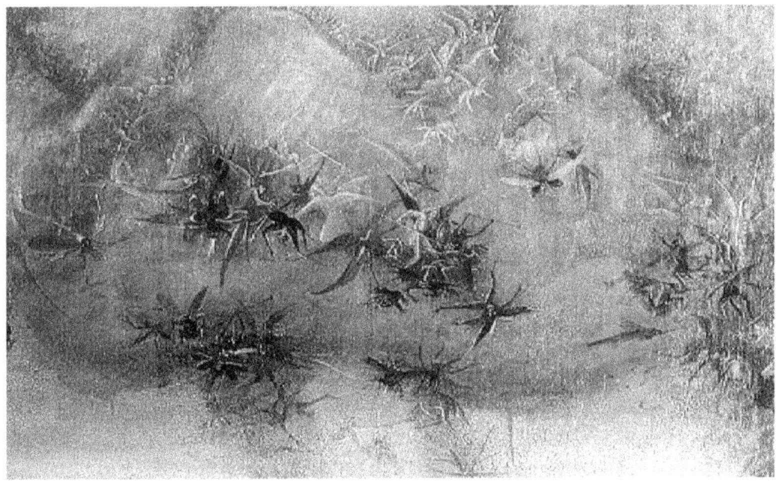

24a Hieronymus Bosch, *Fall of the Rebel Angels*, detail, left inner wing of *Last Judgement* triptych

legs. The helmet of the figure at the left, however, opens at the front to reveal a grotesque, pop-eyed face, heavily exaggerated. This figure also has thin, spindly arms, a device whereby many of the rebels, irrespective of the nature of their metamorphosis, show their kinship with the good angels.

The nature of the "highest" human types here is of interest. Consider the two rebel angels, who blow trumpets and retain the Eyckian physiognomies of the good angels. These are stylistically quite distinct from the facial types of the grotesque in the helmet, or of the "damned souls" (at bottom left and centre). However, at bottom right, there are two creatures whose distended human faces bear a family resemblance to the Eyckian angels. Transmogrified into dragonfly-like bodies, these two limbless metamorphs are plausible degradations of good angels. These faces, like the more "normal" humanoid heads, express horror and dismay at their fate (left corner and left of fig. 21a; cf. 21b).

The trumpet blowers, on the other hand, seem unaware of what is happening to them. The figure at the far left holds his trumpet across the body of a creature whose torso is a large stringed musical instrument. Musical instruments can signify the stirring of human passions; the trumpeter here does not seem to realise that the nature of his music has changed. Similarly, the lower body of the other trumpeter has become insectoid; still he holds and blows his instrument. Good and bad trumpets are subtly distinguished. The heavenly trumpeters blow unadorned, gently curved instruments. The rebels' trumpets are straight. One has a box wrapped around it; from the other depends a flag whose design is presumably the emblem of the rebellion. Both rebel trumpeters have closed eyes. Possibly this is why they have retained their angelic faces. They have not yet allowed themselves to see their change of nature, and so do not express knowledge of it.

However this may be, it is significant that Bruegel included a wide variety of humanoid heads among his rebel angels, and that these heads exhibit a spectrum of human types ranging from angelic to grotesque countenances. Speculations about the relationship between the nature of angels and human nature, by this date a commonplace idea, inform this conception. Bruegel interpreted this kinship visually with customary irony, weaving it in as one element among many to strengthen the parallel between the condition of the fallen angels and the condition of fallen humanity.

In his design, all the rebels are placed very close to the surface of the picture, in large scale. This flock of monsters is unified by their overlapping brightly colored parts; this arrangement also allows the viewer clearly to pick out the separate parts of each hybrid, and so to appreciate the nuances of their composition. That Bruegel did this to emphasise the "human element" of the Fall can be seen when this painting is compared to another treatment of the same subject, also using hybrids for the rebels. Bosch's *Fall of the Rebel Angels* occupies the top of the left wing of the Vienna *Last Judgement* (detail, fig. 24a). Many of the same constituents that Bruegel used are present. Both good and bad angels are winged: those of the good angels are bird-like; those of the rebel angels, bat-like or insectoid.

Most importantly, the rebels are hybrids, but we see this mainly by their silhouettes against the clouds. There is no hint of suffering analogous to that of post-lapserian humanity. Bosch's battle is a real one in which the rebels are resolutely pursued by the good angels. There is no sense here of actual battle being unnecessary because the rebels themselves have been overtaken and consumed by the changes in their nature. This is a psychological dimension which Bruegel's design opens up.

Our starting point for this analysis of Bruegel's *Rebel Angels* was Lucretius: the new classical authority for including metamorphic creatures among First Things. When Bruegel applied this idea to make a treatment of legendary Christian First Things, he moved the imagery of the metamorphic body in the direction of becoming a metaphor for human nature.[42] Let us now consider three further famous classical sources, all of which represent Man as, in various senses, a metamorphic creature. This idea appears in the writings of Pliny, Ovid, and Plato.

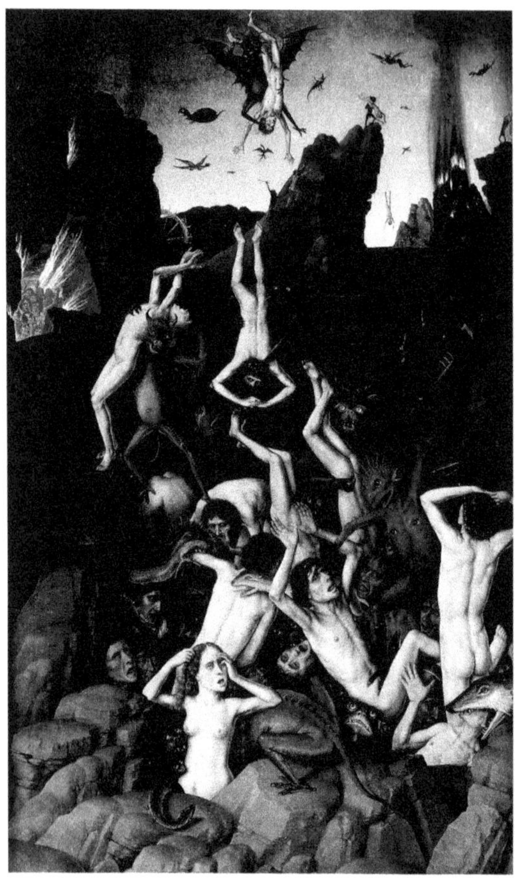

23 Rogier van der Weyden, *Fall of the Damned*, far right wing of *Last Judgement* polyptych, 1446-52. Oil on wood, 215 x 560 cm. Musée de l'Hôtel Dieu, Beaune

Pliny and the Variability of Man

Lucretius, it will be recalled, argued strongly against the belief that humans and animals could interbreed and produce mixed offspring. Still the idea persisted that this was possible, even if its subscribers, like Piero di Cosimo and Cima da Conegliano,[43] simultaneously followed Lucretius by situating such offspring in the distant past. A manuscript of the *De naturis rerum* illuminated in fifteenth-century Flanders contains miniatures which echo Sir John Mandeville's fantastic descriptions, showing hybrid humans, sciopodes, men with ten arms or no head.[44] Evidently, wonders on the fringes of the known world paralleled wonders from the mists of time. As Racine observed, *Geographical distance in some sense makes up for too great a proximity in time: for the people scarcely distinguishes between what is, if I may so put it, a thousand years away and that which is a thousand leagues away from them.*[45]

The *locus classicus* for hybrid tribes and their situation at the far edges of the world was Pliny's *Historia Naturalis*, newly edited by Erasmus, who also drew heavily on this work for his *Adages*.[46] Among the human races, Pliny included cyclops, hermaphrodites and a staggering list of hybrid peoples. Here is a selection from his Seventh Book, in the rich translation of Philemon Holland (1601):

> there is a kind of men with heads like dogs, clad all over with the skins of wild beasts, who in lieu of speech use to barke: armed they are and well appointed with sharpe and trenchant nailes... there is a kind of people named Monoscelli, that have but one leg apeece, but they are most nimble, and hop wonderous swiftly [they are] also called Sciopodes... some there bee without heads standing upon their necks, who carrie eies in their shoulders... the Choromandæ are a savage and wild people... hairie all over their bodies, eies they have red like the houlets, and toothed they be like dogs...
>
> Megasthenes is mine author, that among the Indian Nomades there is a kind of people, that in steed of noses have only two small holes, and after the manner of snakes... they crawle and creepe, and named theyare Syrictæ. In the utmost marches of India, Eastward, about the

source & head of the river Ganges, [the] Astomes… have no mouths: all hairie over the whole bodie… they live onely by the aire…

Duris maketh report, That certaine Indians engender with beasts, of which generation are bred certaine monstrous mungrels, halfe beasts and halfe men… there be certaine men with long shagged tailes… & some again that with their eares cover their whole bodie… [the] Menismini [dwell] from the Ocean sea twentie daies journey, live of the milk [of] beasts that we call Cynocephales, having heads and snouts like dogs… In the deserts of Affricke yee shall meet oftentimes with fairies, appearing in the shape of men and women, but they vanish soone away like fantasticall illusions.[47]

Deviations to the head, tails and claws recur in these descriptions; hairiness and lack of speech are repeatedly noted. Though efforts have been made to identify some of Pliny's less bizarre foreigners as species of apes, what is of interest here is the fact that such a range of creatures could be categorised as human tribes in the first place. This is further evidence for belief in a blurred border between men and beasts. Pliny's humans represent a "scientific" manifestation of this assumption. He has no problem with the possibility of interspecial progeny, and speaks of hybrid human tribes as though they existed in the present day. At the exotic fringes of human variability, human shaded into animal, and natural into supernatural, with no strict boundary between the two. Such attitudes persisted in Western culture. The sense of a "sliding scale" informs many classificatory schemes – from designs for suits of playing cards[48] to encyclopedia illustrations.

The huge popularity of the *History* speaks for itself: it was among the first books to be printed in Italy (1469), and more than eighty printed editions survive from the sixteenth century.[49] Though only four of his thirty-seven books touch on the subject, Pliny's strange tribes, often with original names intact, appear and reappear: in the fantasies of Sir John Mandeville, in bestiaries, even in eyewitness reports from the New World.[50] Book illustrators were particularly addicted to Pliny's creatures.[51] The staying power of Pliny's hybrid men depended also on their rare visual potential as

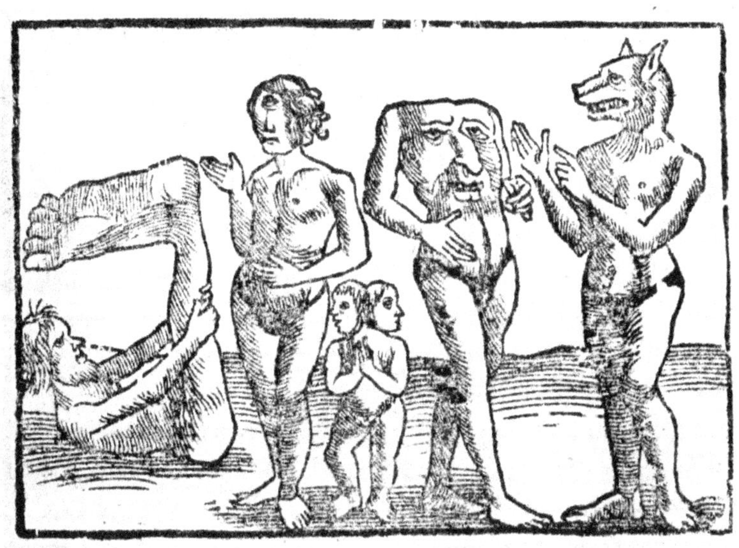

25 Anon, Pliny's human monsters, woodcut, from Sebastian Münster, *Cosmographia* (Basel, 1558) Staatsbibliothek Bamberg. Geogr. f 21

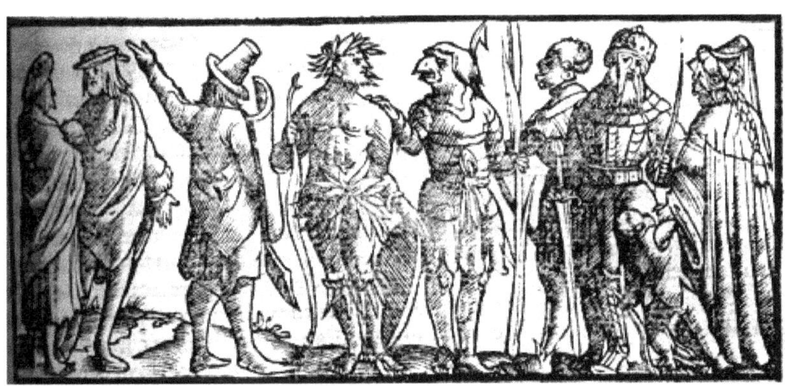

26 Anon, Barbarians, Savages and Monsters (The World's People), woodcut, from Sebastian Münster, *Cosmographia* (Basel, 1552), Biblioteca Lazzerini, Prato © Istituto Internazionale di Storia Economica e Sociale "F. Datini"

a template which could be embroidered and reinterpreted in many contexts. They furnished the imagination of the woodcutters responsible for illustrating Sebastian Münster's indispensible *Cosmographia* (first German edition, 1544; fig. 26). Here, *Barbarians, savages and monsters* (including a bird-headed man) were arrayed together as if in a continuum.[52] Compare a rendition of Pliny's original people, cut to the bare essentials, in a later edition of the same book (fig. 25). As a historian of anthropology commented: *These creatures haunted the minds of Europeans. They could not be exorcised, but appeared and reappeared for centuries, in the work of would-be scientists, in the sermons of the clergy, and in poetry and the drama.*[53]

Pliny's human menagerie — disseminated so widely in consciousness through editions of the *History* and through the manifold works of copyists, imitators and plagiarisers — has therefore a double relevance as a context for novel hybrids. On the one hand, it charts a horizontal dimension for the existence of metamorphic things, against Lucretius' vertical dimension: the edges of deep space, as opposed to the edges of deep time. On the other hand, the enormous popularity of the imagery suggests the strong roots of its conjecture: that humans and animals were miscible categories. On this issue, high philosophical mysticism and lived practical experience exhibited the same continuing fascination with human monsters, or monstrous humans. It was an inadmissable idea, rarely if ever stated outright, and contradicted by the Church's teaching about the unique situation and fate of the human soul. Catholic doctrine remains firm on the absence of the divine spark in animals. But Church and State found themselves involved in debates which turned on the presumption of human-animal identity well into the industrial era. How might a human cross the boundaries of nature in the present time? Was it possible for a person to become an animal, or vice-versa? These debates defined the "horizontal" limit of beliefs in human metamorphosis in the real world, and they were building to a climax in Bruegel's lifetime, most notably in the area of witchcraft.

Real and Unreal Metamorphoses: The Position of the Church

Apart from art and philosophy, issues of human-animal identity are visible elsewhere in popular culture: for instance, in the practice of beast trials. Both canon and secular law made provision for the prosecution of animals who committed criminal offenses. Ecclesiastical courts were involved in some of these trials because of the element of magic often associated with acts of malignance performed by animals. An egg-laying cockerel was put on trial for sorcery at Basel in 1474.[54] An edict of banishment was passed against a plague of caterpillars at Troyes in 1516.[55] A death sentence was passed against a French pig in 1494.[56] In the sixteenth century, a multitude of eels was put on trial and subsequently excommunicated from the Lake of Geneva.[57] In England, the last law which held animals rather than their owners responsible for crimes in this sense was repealed in 1846.[58]

The assumptions implicit in this area of jurisprudence became the subject of open scrutiny in the seventeenth century. So, for instance, Descartes' argument that an animal is more like a machine than a person was warmly welcomed by the Catholic church. The lawyer Gaspard Bailly employed this new conception of animals at a trial in Savoy in the latter half of the seventeenth century. Bailly pleaded that the town's case against his clients (assorted vermin) should be dismissed, *since it has been brought against beasts, [and] to commit a crime it is necessary to have the capacity of reasoning, which is not found in animals deprived of this faculty.*[59] Beast trials began to taper off as the seventeenth century took on board this novel line of reasoning.

Compare Bailly's argument with the case for the defense in the 1474 trial of the cock which laid an egg. The lawyer for the cock, *pleaded that there was no record of the devil ever having made a pact with an animal and that, in any case, the laying of an egg was an involuntary act.*[60] The fowl's defense rested on of the entire proceedings. The fifteenth-century lawyer lost his case because the rest of the court was perfectly willing to believe that a cockerel could be the grounds of insufficient evidence, not, as Bailly's did, on the impropriety a sorcerer in disguise. As was known in the Renaissance, animals also appeared in court in antiquity. The advocate Bailly cited several examples. The long history of this phenomenon demonstrates (among other things) the power and persistence of concepts of identity between human and beast. Catholic teaching mitigated against this, of course, on several different grounds. Actual sexual congress with animals was, for instance, strictly forbidden; metempsychosis was equally anathema. Christian souls after death were supposed to go straight into one or another of the supernatural zones under the jurisdiction of God or his deputy, The Devil. They could not be reborn in new bodies, animal or otherwise.

Similarly, church thinkers denied the possibility that humans could ever actually be changed into animals, even by The Devil. The Devil, it transpires, could only produce the *appearance* of such a metamorphosis. This distinction was to become hugely important for the development of theories of the imagination and the imaginary. Scholars had then to explain exactly what it was that The Devil could do within the brain, since no one questioned that such apparent transformations were indeed possible. At this point, metamorphic appearances, or fantasies, became linked for the first time to the physical theory of psychology. The accepted scholastic arguments on these subjects can be found conveniently summarized in the witch-hunters' manual, the notorious *Malleus Maleficarum* (c 1486).

These arguments more or less ingeniously try to combat what were clearly generally held beliefs about human-animal shape-shifting. Thus, on metamorphosis, *when the body of a man is changed into the body of a beast, or a dead body is brought to life, such things only seem to happen and are a glamour or illusion, or else the devil appears before men in an assumed body.*[61] The authors clarify this point with reference to the Aristotelian *organ of perception*. A person may only perceive a metamorphosis because The Devil is capable of tampering with human senses:

> The Devil does not, as has been shown, change the perceptive and imaginative powers by projecting himself into them, but by transmuting them... for he cannot of himself induce new appearances as has been said. But he changes them, by transmutation, that is, local motion. And this again he does, not by dividing the substance of the organ of perception since that would result in a sense of pain but by movement of the perceptions and humors.[62]

The Devil must, in other words, work with the material already in the skull. The odd (to our eyes) blend of supernatural and physical causes invoked to explain a mental event is a recurring feature of the literature on metamorphic imagery. As we will see later on, it appears in dream-theories, where metamorphic visions were also linked with a disorder of the humors.

Note the extreme complexity of this argument as it was used by the witch-hunters, and the way in which it attempted to resolve the conflicting epistemological states of The Devil, the mind and the fantasy. In practice, there was evidently no way of determining the difference between a "real" metamorphosis and a demonically-inspired appearance of metamorphosis, other than by holding to the article of faith which stated that it must be the latter. But such an argument, while having the advantage of explaining why other people cannot see a particular transformation, also had the crucial effect of rendering metamorphic visions private.

In the same *Question*, the authors referred to The Devil's capacity to create *imperfect creatures*, to explain the existence of hybrid beasts. They are the handiwork of devils: *It is certain that devils can make some imperfect creatures... The devils run throughout the world and collect various germs, and by using them can evolve various species.*[63] Such creatures are also made by witches: *When witches attempt to effect anything by the invocation of devils, they run about the world and bring the semen of those things which are in question and by its means, with the permission of God, they produce new species.*[64]

Two main points stand out from this which characterise official Christian thought on metamorphs and metamorphosis. First, on the subject of the natural history of metamorphs, the position is that hybrids are imperfect creatures whose conception is evil. The only humans who have anything to do with their production are witches, who are (novelly, at this date) officially devil-worshippers. Second, there is the absolute denial of the reality of metamorphosis. This was an important point. To deny that metamorphosis was a real phenomenon required medieval commentators, faced with the plethora of instances of metamorphosis in their inherited classical texts, to substitute non-literal interpretations for metamorphic changes.

One result of all this was to change the referents of metamorphosis in humans, away from visible changes in shape, commensurate with a fluid model of human and animal nature, towards interior, invisible changes in moral status, congruent with the official teachings of the church on human nature. This development was exemplified in the treatment of Ovid's *Metamorphoses*. This book is, of course, not concerned with the natural history of hybrid forms, but rather with the events leading up to complete magical shape changes in individuals.

Ovid and Mental Metamorphoses

The subject of reactions to Ovid's text may not appear to have much bearing on the meaning of the metamorphic body in Bruegel's art. But commentaries on Ovid played an important part in developing the idea that metamorphosis in humans is actually a metaphor for an interior, rather than exterior, shape change. The commentaries effectively psychologised Ovid. It is their *interpretatio christiani* of pagan figures which concerns us here.[65] There were two main ways of Christianising Ovid. The first, following early Christian precedent, was to set up a simple one-to-one equivalent, giving individual classical figures a Christian alter ego. Thus, Orpheus stood for Christ; Polyhymnia or Phaedra for the Virgin Mary; Hercules for Fortitude; and among the occupants of Hades, Sisyphus, Ixion, and Tantalus represented the three great sins, Pride, Avarice, and Lust.[66] Then there was also what we might call an overall cultural *interpretatio christiani*: a framework of Christian ideals within which the very act of reading Ovid was a transformative moral experience for the reader.[67]

Famously, in Ovid's tales, the shape-change comes to humans as a punishment for sexual trespass. This is the kind of metamorphosis which made Ovid's book notorious. In such stories, the gods themselves change shape in order to gain sexual access to specific humans. These changes are temporary illusions. The offspring of such unions are not often hybrid, though the manner of their birth may reflect the temporary shape of their divine parent (Castor and Pollux are born from an egg, because Jupiter lay with their mother disguised as a swan). However, when the humans in Ovid change shape, the change is permanent, and often tragic.

From 1100 onwards, Ovid rose to fame on the same wave of interest in romance that culminated in the Grail cycles and in the thirteenth century romantic epic of the *Roman de la Rose*.[68] The *Metamorphoses* was taken up by the leaders of the twelfth century secular education movement, who captured the attention of their (male) students with Ovid's racy stories. The architects of the "reader-oriented" *interpretatio christiani* understood that Ovid's "sexual" transformations could be accommodated if they were used to generate an analogous transformation in the person of the reader. The sensual components of the text were surrounded by an elaborate allegorical apparatus, which taught the student how to transform his own "base desires" into spiritual insights. Following the model of St. Augustine, each student would thus learn to channel sexual stimuli through allegory into spiritual reminders. Eventually this training would enable him, by a process of mental redirection, to use as fuel for spiritual thought the kind of real-life stimuli that might otherwise lead to sexual temptation. Reading the *Metamorphoses* in the context of a suitable moralizing apparatus would train the student to control his own arousal and redirect his emotion towards God.

To understand the implications of how and why this was thought to work, we must consider a complication of medieval thinking about sexuality. One aspect of the identity between human and beast was refined and given careful shape in scholastic thought: the equation of bodily passion with animality. The control of body by spirit was no mean goal at this period, since it was held that in the moment of orgasm, a human was given over wholly to his or her body. At this point a person was indistinguishable from a beast, the higher, conscious mind temporarily eradicated. Because it was believed also that what was erased, however briefly, could never be completely restored, it followed that the great danger of an active love life was the progressive loss of the mental faculties. Shakespeare expressed this old view of sexuality in the pun in his line, *the expense of spirit in a waste of shame* (Sonnets, 129.1), where *spirit* means both *seed* and *rational part of the soul*.

The idea of exploiting this principle in secular education lay behind efforts to adapt the *Metamorphoses* as a teaching tool.[69] It was felt that since sensory triggers were strongest and easiest to react to, they could and should be most profitably harnessed to inculcate correct Christian behavior patterns. This rationale for encasing Ovid in commentary was analogous to the famous justification for sacred images, whereby,

> *illiterati* [are] drawn away from their natural desires by the pictures, which are, by implication not only a 'feast for the eyes' but, because they include inscriptions, for the spirit also.[70]

Versions of the *Ovide Moralizé* were available in French and Latin from shortly after 1300, and editions were being printed in Bruges, Paris, and Venice by the end of the fifteenth century. All were equipped with lengthy commentaries which allegorized the transformations in a remarkably consistent way. Examples from two of these commentaries, the first written in the early 1340s, the second published in 1493, indicate their general strategy.

Pierre Bersuire, a friend of Petrarch's, wrote his *Ovidius Moralizatus* in Latin prose as the fifteenth book of a huge work, intended to be a moralised encyclopedia of all human knowledge. His Ovid, however, took on a life of its own with the invention of printing. Unlike its predecessors, Bersuire's Ovid was supplied with a mythographical introduction which explained the *dramatis personae* of the *Metamorphoses*. It contained convenient and complete moralisations of all the prominent members of the classical pantheon. For this reason, it was pirated and used as an introduction to other people's moralised Ovids (for instance, at Bruges in 1484 and again at Paris in 1493). Its history demonstrates the level of standardization that had been achieved in the work of interpreting Ovid. Thus Bersuire on the story of Jupiter and Io:

> Because Jupiter feared that Juno would discover him in his adultery with his lover Io, he put down a cloud cover so he would not be seen, and in addition changed Io into a beautiful heifer... Robbers seem to act in a similar way; for, when they fear that their secret deed will be known, they wait for a dark secret time and turn an innocent girl into a heifer, that is, into a wanton woman... Or say that Jupiter is the devil, who does not wish that Io, that is, the soul with which he fornicates by sin, be known or drawn back by Juno, that is by the Church, and so changes her into a heifer, that is, makes her a sinner and carnal and alien from all spirituality.[71]

Here, Io's change of shape into the likeness of a heifer is quite explicitly interpreted as signifying the transformation during sex of human into animal. This explanation was constantly invoked. In Bersuire's gloss on the story of Callisto, each element of Callisto's external transformation was given an interior meaning:

> She is changed from a woman into a bear because she loses her human shape, that is, her rational way of thinking and manner of acting, and takes on those of a bear, bestial and carnal. Then she acquires curved paws, that is, a twisted intellect and a perverse will; a hairy skin, that is, a vile and disreputable way of life; a terrifying voice, that is, shameful and dishonest speech.[72]

Bersuire concluded that: *When someone becomes a sinner, all good habits are changed in him. An example is Nebuchadnezzar, who was changed into a beast as Daniel 4 discloses: "You will be changed into another man."*[73] The passage in *Daniel* 4 is verse 16: *Let his mind be changed from a man's, and let a beast's mind be given to him*. Bersuire's quotation here shows that he interpreted this text, whose meaning in context is externally transformative (*let him be wet with the dew of heaven, let his lot be with the beasts in the grass of the earth*), to mean that Nebuchadnezzar is to be changed *internally* "into another man," that is, into the kind of man who is most like a beast. All the magical changes in Ovid were dealt with in this fashion, even where the story held no sexual component. Thus, for example, Bersuire's account of Cadmus and the dragon's teeth:

> It is said that from their teeth are grown soldiers, who slay one another because it often happens, when the teeth, that is, the slanderous words, of the impious are told to those whom they defamed that men take up arms... Ecclesiasticus 28:15: *The whispered and the double-tongued is accursed, for he has troubled the many who were at peace*.[74]

Here, the transformation of teeth into soldiers was rendered as the transformative, in this case evil, power of words.

The Gorgons, unsurprisingly, were singled out for discussion in terms which spelled out the steps a Christian man must take to avoid sexual temptation:

> Thus through women many men and animals, that is wise men and fools, are made into stones... But Perseus, the son of Jove, that is, a just man, the son of Christ... should not look at these women with pleasure, but flee their sight by avoiding the occasion of sin, and look at their form and status only in the shield of Pallas, that is in Scripture, which is the shield of wisdom.[75]

While on the subject of Medusa's metamorphic head, the author wished that:

> Would that all gorgons, that is all evil women, who fornicate with our Neptunes, that is, religious and ecclesiastics, in the temple of religion and of the church, or in homes which belong to the church, might be marked with such a sign, and be made to have snakes for hair.[76]

This is one of the very few occasions where Bersuire allowed himself to consider one of Ovid's shape-changings visually, expressing the hope that priests could see women who were inclined to sleep with them as gorgons. But he quickly concluded in his old style, *Or say that there was an evil woman who fornicated with someone. She had serpents, that is, different evils, for hair, fit for deceiving others and for attracting fine gifts.*[77]

A later commentary by Raphael Regius, published at Bevilacqua in 1493, followed the same method. For example, Daphne's transformation into a laurel, *shows that the girl who defended her virginity to the death is rewarded with an evergreen crown of chastity.*[78] Here Regius equated the transformation with death, according to Christian doctrine. Then he tried to replace the externally transformative relation between Daphne and the laurel tree with an internally additive one. Instead of Daphne becoming the laurel tree, the laurel becomes a possession or an attribute of Daphne, a testament to her moral worth. At the turn of the fifteenth century then, attempts were still being made, albeit weakly, to restrict the meanings of the transformations in Ovid's tales to those compatible with Christian orthodoxy, by insisting in exhaustive commentary that the transformations were really internal rather than external. Though Bersuire's text dates from 1340, it was considered worth printing complete as early as 1509.

Ovid first appeared at Antwerp in the *milieu* of the sixteenth-century *rederijkers* (or, rhetoricians). Chambers of *rederijkers*, like amateur dramatic societies, were attached to craft and militia guilds; they also constituted a type of religious confraternity. They wrote and produced vernacular poetic dramas on old and new themes for festivals and holidays. We will have cause to revisit the *rederijkers* and their doings in subsequent chapters: their productions formed an important parallel to contemporary painting, and one of the Antwerp chambers, the *Violieren*, was attached to Bruegel's Guild of St. Luke.[79] From the mid-1550s, a leading light of the *Violieren*, Cornelis van Ghistele (c. 1510-1573), was among those who translated parts of Virgil, Terence and Ovid into the vernacular. Of this project, Eringa commented:

> But these translators, insufficiently penetrated with the spirit of antiquity, over-assimilated the original texts into their own milieu; their need to moralise disfigured the classical works. Van Ghistele, in translating the *Metamorphoses*, preached the sanctity of marriage; his version of the *Héroïdes* was designed to make people flee from the seductive charms of Venus; in his hands the *Ars amatoria* became a crusade to purge impure vice from dishonest love.[80]

In other words, the *interpretatio christiani*, or something very like it, was still a force in these early Flemish versions of Ovid. At the same time, when another famous poet and *rederijker*, Matthijs de Casteleyn (1488-1550), used Ovidian motifs in his book on the art, *De Konst van Rethoriken* (Gand, 1555), he introduced a new element. The poet speaks of the laurel[81] which was Daphne as:

> Desen edelen Laurier al Goddelick bestoven / Mach niemant vulloven, als al vul secreten... den Laurier is vrij van allen venijne / Donder ende blixem mueghen ghenaken niet.[82]

> [This noble laurel, all covered with divinity / No one can praise it enough, since it is full of secrets... the laurel is free of all venom (spite) / Thunder and lightning cannot overwhelm it.]

This implication — that her metamorphosis is *covered with divinity* and *full of secrets* — invokes a different kind of *interpretatio*, shaped by Neo-Platonic ideas. The emphasis shifts, away from the view of the monster as marking a deviation from God's law, towards the notion that such impossible transformations were miraculous, sites of divine agency, evidence of occult intervention. This change was made possible by the determined deconstructive work of the commentators. By insisting on the allegorical reading of Ovid, they set the precedent for understanding metamorphosis as metaphor, and so opened the way for a quite different style of mystical interpretation.

The "deep structure" of metamorphic inventions always seems to involve some aspect of the identification of human and beast. Interpretative frameworks were devised to mediate and mitigate this assumption, in the moralisation of Ovid, as in legal theory and natural history. Ovid represents a complex intersection of several such frameworks, with unexpected long term consequences. The theological view that people become animals during sex and through sinful acts set up a structural resonance with Ovid's themes of shape-shifting and sexual trespass. Yet the effort to turn Ovidian transformations into Christian analogies meant that, in the long run, the idea of moral change in humans came to be deepened and enriched by its association with the visual imagery of metamorphosis. Metamorphosis and its associated images came increasingly to be used as metaphors for movements within the mind.

As we have seen, in the second half of the fifteenth century, the image of the metamorphic body began to appear in Italian Neo-Platonic speculations about human nature. Quattrocento Humanists turned attention away from the sexual lessons to be learned from controlling written metamorphoses, to the lessons about the soul and its qualities that could be found latent in images of bodies undergoing metamorphosis (*full of secrets*). They were interested not solely in metamorphosis itself, but in the exciting rhetorical and philosophical opportunities represented by a figure which contained two-forms-in-one.

One important reason for this must be mentioned here, although its scope and the exact mechanisms whereby it came about are difficult to pin down. This is the change in attitude toward sexuality. The priestly culture of the Middle Ages tried hard to control and harness sexuality, seen as the common means whereby people became brutes. At stake in these efforts was the well-being of the immortal soul. Whether or not the "bestial" view of sex was actually held by a majority of medieval people, this was the official philosophical and theological standpoint. At some point this orthodoxy altered. It becomes possible to speak, as Meiss does, of the *new and emotionally charged sphere of the erotic*[83] in the Renaissance. The popularity of metamorphosis as a means of envisaging mental events is related to this development. It is a manifestation of cultural change, like the flowering of the human nude in art:

> In the Middle Ages, to look upon a nude female body was regarded as sinful spying. The story of Susannah and the elders was first represented by symbols, and she was normally shown without clothes, in accordance with the biblical account, only after the establishment of a new attitude toward sexuality and the body in the Renaissance. In this change, ancient mythology played a fundamental role, not only taming the passions but sanctioning them.[84]

To this somewhat tantalising perception, we can add Jayne's evocative description of the philosophical climate of Florence, cradle of Neo-Platonism:

> We may imagine fifteenth century Florence as a city at the convergence of three love philosophies: from the East, the philosophy of Platonic love, a masculine and esoteric philosophy; from the West, the stream of Renaissance courtly love, traditions of romantic feminine personal love

> coming to Italy from Provence through Sicily; and, from the South, the stream of Christian love, intellectualized by St. Augustine and ritualized by the Roman Church.[85]

These impressions point to bend in the river of unconscious undercurrents motivating the conscious activities of the Florentines, as they endeavored, filled with the optimism of rediscovery, to wed Aristotle to Plato, and Plato to Christian teaching. In doing so, they supplemented the scholastic model of the mind with images drawn from Pythagorean thought, and so "covered" Daphne and her kin with mystery and divinity. The far-reaching changes that this brought about in the ways that people conceived of the experiences of mind and body can only be estimated. The Wittkowers argued that Ficino's work was responsible for a *veritable wave [of] melancholic behavior*[86] which swept across Europe in the sixteenth century. This followed a new awareness of the erotic, visible most noticeably in the arts, which spread a generation or so earlier in a similar fashion.

Can the Renaissance experience of sexuality be reconstructed? Psychoanalytic theory, following Freud's founding principles, seeks to explain the sexual "conditioning" of individuals, rather than cultures, by recovering events in family life, the traumatic condensation of images and feelings from childhood, etc. These conditions were quite different five or six hundred years ago, and in any case this data is irretrievable for any sixteenth-century individual. But with all due caution, we can maintain that desire was then, as now, the driving force of the unconscious. When philosophers, artists and poets became interested in the unconscious — the domain of dreams, divine illumination, and sin — it would be surprising if the imagery they used to describe its contents did not touch on desire and sexuality.

Among the best known of these explorations is Francesco Colonna's *Hypnerotomachia Poliphili* (Venice, 1499), wherein the dreaming narrator flouts Reason (Logistica) and follows Wish (Thelemia) in pursuit of the delights of Venus.[87] The striking woodcuts (figs. 27a-b) made for the first

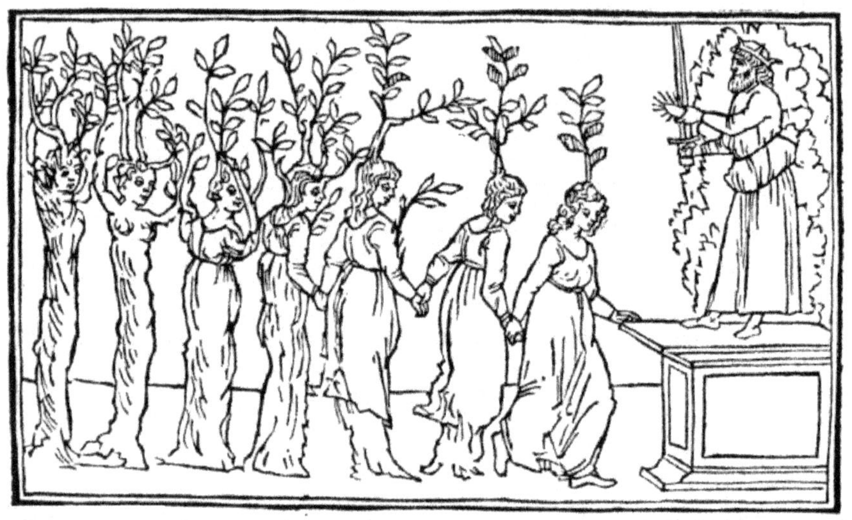

27a Anon, *Seven nymphs turn into trees*, woodcut, from Francesco Colonna, *Hypnerotomachia Poliphili* (Venice, 1499), Chapter 14: 174. Photo: Delft University of Technology and MIT Press, 1997

editions are noteworthy for their erotic content (and because they started a vogue for esoteric emblems). The narrator Poliphilo falls asleep, like Dante, in a dark wood, but his dream is a homage to pagan beauty and holy antiquity, filled with descriptions of ornate artworks and riddling symbols. At one point the narrator describes an excellent relief sculpted on the side of a marvellous vase. It depicts seven nymphs who slowly turn into trees, one by one, not to die or preserve their chastity, but to honour glorious Jupiter.[88] The woodcut of this scene (fig. 27a) omits the vase and depicts only the choreographic stages of the metamorphosis; a simpler precursor to the more complex, more tongue-in-cheek orchestration of Bruegel's good and bad angels.

Less than fifty years later, we find the topos of the dreaming, pagan lover in popular vernacular literature. The author of the *Antwerp Songbook* (1544) too complains, *Ick peynse om Venus discipline / die mi so late sandt dese sucht* [I dream under Venus's training / who sent me so lately this desire].[89] A new romantic element is expressed here, familiar to us, of which we catch only glimpses in the minds of people living before this time. This sea-change in attitude stems from the *convergence of three love philosophies*. In Ficino's philosophy, carnal love could for the first time be ascribed a mystical significance, and the transcendental could be sought in personal love for another individual. We can gauge the spread of this Neo-Platonic conflation of love for God and love for a human being by its popularity in art and poetry.

Among the poets, the Neo-Platonic content of Michelangelo's sonnets is perhaps the best-known; similar sentiments are found in the works of a younger writer who was Bruegel's exact contemporary, Gaspara Stampa (1523-54). Stampa wrote of her lover in these terms:

> I don't envy you in the least, holy angels, your so many glories and blessings, and those longings for what fully enjoyed is still desired, you always being in the presence of our exalted Lord. Because my joys are of such kind and so numerous as not to be encompassed by earthly hearts, while I have before me those kindly serene eyes of which I must needs write and sing always. And as you are wont to cull great refreshment and life from His face in heaven, so do I here below, from his infinite beauty. In this alone do you surpass my delight, that your glory is eternal and founded, and mine can speedily end.[90]

Her poems demonstrate the power of classical mythology as metaphor in this kind of exaltation of love. Thus the author calls *on the presence who makes the world pale and whiten with her sickle,*[91] (Diana, the moon goddess), to help her in her grief, and invokes the Lucretian trope of Love and Strife in her reproaches, *I have, however, read in antique pages that the great heroes did not scorn to follow Venus and Mars equally.*[92] Sometimes her metaphors take an explicitly Ovidian tone: *All that was lacking was for me then to have become lucky Alcmena, for whom the dawn delayed, to return so much longer than its wont.*[93] Or again, *Send back my heart, wicked tyrant, which you have and tear so wrongly, and do to it and me just what tigers and lions do to hinds.*[94] In these lines, pain is likened to a rending of the heart and a love relationship to the relation between animal prey and animal victim. The comparison is not moralising or derog-

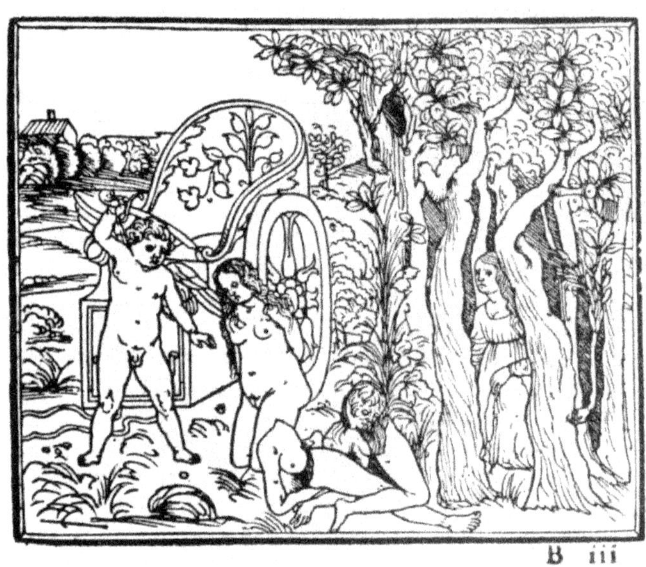

27b Anon, *Polia witnesses the massacre of two maidens by Eros*, woodcut, from Francesco Colonna, *Hypnerotomachia Poliphili* (Venice, 1499), Chapter 27: 401. Photo: Delft University of Technology and MIT Press, 1997

atory. Compare the episode in the *Hypnerotomachia*, where Polia runs away into the forest, and meets Eros whipping *two doleful maidens* harnessed to his cart; Eros then dismounts to stab and dismember them with his sword (fig. 27b).

As the poetry of de Casteleyn and others testifies, this mythologizing lyrical style is found all over Europe. The unfinished *magnum opus* of the Antwerp poet and town councillor Jan Van der Noot (1539-c. 1590), called *Olympias*, was an allegory describing a Neo-Platonic journey of the soul. A little later, Jean Baptista Houwaert (1533-1599), wrote his *Pegasides Pleyn* (1582-83; *The Palace of Maidens*), a long didactic poem entirely devoted to the varieties of earthly love. Both were strongly indebted to *Le Songe de Poliphile*, the French translation of the *Hypnerotomachia*.[95] The philosophy of Ficino and his school had an equally powerful distribution.[96] Vasari included him along with Dante, Petrarch, Bocaccio, Cavalcantes, and Politian in a stylized *Portrait of Six Italian Worthies*, subsequently published as an engraving by Cock at the Four Winds.[97]

Plato and Protean Man

In terms of the visual imagery of the metamorphic body, we can measure these changes by comparing two treatments of the most metamorphic classical figure mentioned in Ovid, Proteus, the shape-shifting prophet. Here is Bersuire on Proteus:

> Ovid says that in the home of the sun there was also a god called Proteus. He was called changeful because he was not of a set form, but quickly and unexpectedly changed himself into different shapes. In fact, there are many such proteuses in the home of the sun of justice, because in that place are depicted gods, that is, false and vain men like hypocrites, false friends, and flatterers who have a painted appearance, not a real existence. Such men can be called changeful gods because their shape or their goodness are not known... they [are] uncertain men, changeable and inconstant.[98]

For Bersuire, Proteus's changeful nature made him a figure of the kind of man who is untrustworthy because his true nature cannot be known. By the end of the fifteenth century, when the pagan myths had been transformed into a vehicle for philosophical reflection,[99] the image of Proteus, the "changeful god," instead expressed a central tenet of Neo-Platonism. Pico della Mirandola saw Proteus as an image of humanity's indeterminate nature: to be changeful and unknowable was no longer in itself a bad quality. Pico found in this indeterminancy Man's true glory. The essence of his interpretation is embedded in one of his Orphic *Conclusiones*: *He who cannot attract Pan approaches Proteus in vain.*[100] Pan and Proteus here stand for the two poles of the sensible universe, unity and multiplicity. Pan is equated with Plato's world soul, the One, or God. Proteus stands for the changing, shifting appearances of things. The whole *Conclusion* means that, without knowledge of the One, the universal unity, a seeker after truth cannot hope to understand the multiplicity of the sensible world.

It is one thing to employ Proteus as an emblem, as it were, of changeability itself. It is another thing to consider Proteus as a figure of human nature, to render human nature itself protean. Pico had classical authority for his development of the image in this direction. His most fully elaborated account occurs in his famous essay, *De hominis dignitate* (1486; *On the Dignity of Man*). There he pointed out that, according to Asclepius, Proteus had been used at Athens to represent "Man" *in the mysteries*, then enigmatically referring the reader to *those metamorphoses renowned among the Hebrews and the Pythagoreans*.[101] Asclepius, as Pico and his audience knew, was tutored by the centaur Chiron, so his wisdom itself had an esoteric and metamorphic source.[102] The figure of Proteus for Pico was much more than a simple metaphor. Pico invoked him as a concrete mystical image of *holy antiquity* — an image previously used for the same magical purpose as he intends. In Pico's treatment, the image of Proteus has something of the character of an incarnation. Proteus and his significance cannot be rendered precisely into words.

This kind of philosophical thinking was essentially religious. These Humanist philosophers were in search of new information about the natural history of the soul. They found it in classical sources that seemed at first to be both inside and outside the Christian framework. The most important of these "supplementary" sources, the writings around which the whole was centred, were, of course, those of Plato; but theirs was a Plato seen through the dark glass of the texts of the *Corpus Hermeticum*, as edited by Ficino. To understand Pico's interpretation of humanity as protean, as essentially metamorphic, we must consider how he and other thinkers read certain key Platonic texts as hinting at latent meaning in metamorphic imagery. Plato, for instance, uses visual metaphors to discuss the shape of the soul both in *The Republic* and in *Timaeus*. In Book 9 of *The Republic*, Plato describes how Socrates constructed a word-picture of the soul:

> Mold me then the shape of a multiform, many-headed monster with heads of tame and wild animals round him in a ring, all of which he has the power to change about or to make them all grow out of himself.[103]

Socrates explained that this model corresponds to the lawless desires of the (male) human mind. To this image of desire, he added a lion (temper), and a man (reason). He then invited his listeners to imagine them fused together and encased in a man's form. Up to this point, Socrates had been engaged in a discussion about the nature of human injustice, arguing that it stems from unbridled desires. He then concludes that: *We ought to do and say what will make our inside man completely master of the whole man, and give him charge over the many-headed monster.*[104]

In this passage, the many-headed monster which represents the unbridled passions is clearly malignant. But Man himself is also conceived of as a metamorphic creature: a combination of lion, man, and many-headed monster, contained in one skin. This image of human nature equally is not seen as admirable. It is rather presented as a formulation of a problem which must be solved. But for Pico, the metamorphic aspect of man is worthy of praise in itself. He asks, in his *Oration, who would not admire this, our chameleon?*[105] Pico found further mystical aspects of human metamorphosis discussed in Plato's *Timaeus*. This work had been known in Calcidius' partial translation (c 321) throughout the Middle Ages, and it was an important text for the Neo-Platonists of the twelfth-century, the School of Chartres. William of Conches (fl. 1120-54), for example, produced a commentary of *Timaeus*.[106] The whole text was now available, newly edited, translated and equipped with a commentary by Ficino. The *Timaeus* presents a systematic cosmology, the penultimate section of which covers the origins of women and of the lower animals. All of these, explains Plato, were originally men, who have assumed their present forms by a mixture of metamorphosis and rebirth: *The men of the first generation who lived cowardly or immoral lives [were] reborn in a second generation as women.*[107] This reads as straightforward metempsychosis, the transcendental side, as it were, of the metamorphic equation.

Then Plato switches tack and argues that people are also changed into animals as a punishment for their flaws not simply by rebirth: *Birds were produced by a process of transformation, growing feathers instead of hair, from harmless, empty-headed men.*[108] Here, Plato asserts a causal link between the appearance of the new outward transformation, and the nature of the defect in humanity which produced it. The mixture of internal and external factors in such transformations is strangely expressed by the case of the men who neglected philosophy. These people became four-footed beasts:

> Because they had ceased to use the circles in the head... their forelimbs and heads were drawn by natural affinity to the earth, and their forelimbs supported on it, while their skulls were elongated into various shapes as a result of the crushing of their circles through lack of use.[109]

The idea that the mental apparatus necessary for perceiving the universal is a physical attribute of the head is peculiarly Greek. From Aristotle, it made its way into Leonardo's thought (cf. his anatomical research on the *organ of common sense),*[110] ultimately fathering the pseudo-science of physiognomy. Plato's argument in the *Timaeus* is that people become beasts because they have allowed their powers of reason, based on geometry, to atrophy. This is expressed as an actual physical change, as a collapse of the *divine circle* inside the mind, visible from the outside in the flattened skulls of animals. But re-reading this, Pico followed the line of Bersuire and the authors of the *Malleus*. He firmly rearranged the elements of the metaphor, so that the actual transformation becomes inner, or behavioral, its visual counterpart supplied by the insight of the viewer. In other words, such a degraded metamorphosis in a fellow human being is visible only through that person's behavior. Thus, Pico thunderd in the *Oration*:

> For if you see one abandoned to his appetites, crawling on the ground, it is a plant and not a man you see. If you see one blinded by vain

> illusions, softened by their knowing allurement, delivered over to his senses, it is a beast, and not a man you see.[111]

He capped this with a quotation from Mohammed, *They who have deviated from divine law become beasts*.[112]

Plato's people change shape through a combination of stupidity and a kind of natural atrophy. Only in his last category of transformations is there a nuance of sin and hence of will, where souls described as *hopelessly steeped in error* are consigned as fish to the ocean depths. The conclusion is neutral: These are the principles on which living creatures change and have always changed into each other, the transformation depending on the loss or gain of understanding or folly.[113]

In this view, the transformative nature of Man is regarded as an evolutionary mechanism, in itself neither good nor evil. As well as the *Timaeus*, taken in the Neo-Platonic manner as a fully metaphorical and mystical text, Pico's concept of Man as chamelon was also informed by the speculations of Origen (c 185-254), most unorthodox of the Church fathers. One of Pico's more heretical *conclusiones* was the proposition that, *it is more reasonable to believe that Origen is saved than damned*. St Jerome complained that, in his *De Principiis*, Origen,

> argues at great length that an angel, a human soul, or a demon — he affirms that they share the same nature but are diverse in will — can become a beast through its great negligence or its folly, and that, rather than suffer the torments of punishments and the intense heat of fire, it may prefer to be an animal which lives in the sea or some other species of beast: thus we have to fear receiving not only the body of a quadruped but of a fish as well![114]

Origen understood metempsychosis as a Christian possibility. Pico again makes a virtue of the human potential for shape-changing:

> Man [is] not without reason, described sometimes by the name of *all flesh*, sometimes by that of *every-creature*, inasmuch as he himself molds,

> fashions, and changes himself into the form of all flesh and into the character of every creature. The Persian... writes that man has no semblance that is inborn and his very own... Why do we emphasise this?... to the end that, after we have been born to this condition, we can become what we will.[115]

The culmination of this passage is the idea that humans form their own shapes by an act of will. This is Pico's original recasting of the long tradition of human metamorphosis. It is his version of Proteus which we find transmitted into later vernacular culture; so, for instance, Rabelais presents the idea in a more accessible form, though with no loss of clarity:

> For as of old the great seer Proteus, while disguised and transformed into fire, water, a tiger, a dragon, and other strange shapes, could not foretell events to come, and therefore, in order to foretell them had to be restored to his own native shape, so man cannot receive the divine art of prophecy except when that part of him which is most divine - to wit his *Nous* or *Mens* — is quiet, tranquil, peaceable, and neither occupied nor distracted by extraneous passions.[116]

To assess the extent to which Neo-Platonic thought transformed the *changeable god* into a figure of Man, one need only compare this extract from Rabelais with the passage from Bersuire cited earlier. Rabelais's Proteus is far from being an emblem of an untrustworthy man. The wide dissemination of such mystical associations helps explain, for instance, why Humanist poets such as De Casteleyn would refer to the Daphne-laurel hybrid as *full of secrets*. This is the "Orphism" of Pico and his circle — the fully mysticised, Hermetic pole of Neo-Platonism. Wind analysed the taste which accompanied this Humanist mysticism, a fascination for classical hybrid figures as strange or stranger than Proteus. They cultivated a *spirit of sacred drolerie*:

> Whatever may be said against the divine hybrids, the curious crossbreeds that people the Orphic pantheon, they express the orphic spirit at its fullest, and it is remarkable with what persistence and

> shrewdness the Renaissance antiquarians justified a predilection for them... A secretive, esoteric tone attended all these mythological compounds, and often also a tone of mockery. Perhaps it is possible now to understand more clearly why the *hybrid gods*, who were at best a bypath of classical mythology (if not a remnant of a pre-classical phase), seemed so important to the Humanists of the Orphic persuasion. These gods seemed closer to the secret centre of myth than the plain gods, of well-defined character, who occupied the common highways. If they resembled monsters and abnormal portents, it was not because of a willful preference for the grotesque. The unusual subject demanded an unusual tone.... Like all valid symbols, the fabulous Orphic images reveal what they appear to conceal. Their meaning requires, to be properly expressed, a transcendent and hence implausible vocabulary which may produce laughter, as well as awe, and even a Christian kind of reverence. For it should be noticed that in composite gods the tension between chastity and passion, or penitence and pleasure, which is generally associated with the conflict between Christianity and paganism, was revealed as a phase of paganism itself.[117]

These observations acutely describe the typical bent of mind which directed Neo-Platonic antiquarian research. The Humanists approached mythological interpretation creatively, as a means of revealing hidden truths about human nature. As Wind so well recognised, the hybrid body is simultaneously horrible and funny. Metamorphic imagery has the potential to exploit such layers of doubleness: to express in one image the interrelatedness of opposed forces in human nature, the grotesque and the comic combined.

From all this, we can sum up some of the key associations which things metamorphic would have had for Renaissance artists, the friends and allies of Humanists and *redrijkers*. Metamorphic creatures are concerned with arguments about creation and appear in accounts of First Things (Lucretius, Plato). Some people are said to *be* or to become metamorphs (Pliny, Ovid). Outward metamorphosis is a metaphor for transformation of the spirit (Ovid, by way of Bersuire et al). Humans are capable of metamorphosis into higher and lower forms (Plato, Origen, by way of Pico). Pico was clear that such transformations were originated internally by free will, but ambiguous about whether the transformation is external or internal. It was this ambiguity which explains why, in representational art, metamorphic creatures came conventionally to represent inner states of humanity.

In painted or drawn images of metamorphic bodies, there can be no way of telling whether a given hybrid form is hybrid because it was born that way, or because it is in the process of changing from one form to another. In a sense, therefore, the metamorphic body substitutes its own *movement within the body*, a fluid change from one impossible body part to the next, for the protean movements of human nature as described by Pico. So, the specific forms of Bruegel's rebel angels refer to the condition of humanity, even as the presence of their general forms is justified by the traditional inclusion of hybrids among first things. The forms of hybrids in the *Vices* series also relate to the concept of *homo chameleon*. Dog-headed and bird-headed humans abound in these works. Each Vice is accompanied by suitably debased metamorphs, exemplars of the human capacity to metamorphose, in this case, downwards. All sinners are hybrids. Men's bodies devolve into impossible, monstrous forms.

There was a precedent in the conventions of *rederijker* theater for such a psychological reading of metamorphic creatures. The main action in these social satires developed around central (usually allegorical) personifications. But there were also other kinds of character, known as *sinnekens*:

> approximately persons symbolically representing evil forces or passions [who were] probably a development of the devils in the older mystery play. [W]hile not as a rule intervening in the action, [they] constitute a sort of perverse chorus. In frequent interludes they comment sarcastically, in extremely low, often obscene, language, on the course of events, consistently rejoicing in iniquity and sin, and bewailing any tendency towards improvement in human faith or morals.[118]

By 1550 if not before, the *sinnekens* had reached a more fully internalized form. In the romantic drama, *De Spiegel der Minnen* (*The Mirror of Love*), published by Coornhert in 1561:

> The perverse chorus of the *sinnekens* is here developed into a subtle device... besides commenting scurrilously on the action as it proceeds... presumably unobserved in their movements [they] whisper to Dierick and Katharina in turn all the suggestions through which their lower impulses hinder and finally wreck [their] fulfillment... these whispering devils are *their* devils.[119]

A Humanist painter, aware of the Neo-Platonic protean soul, might well dramatise this conception of humanity as tormented by *sinnekens*, in graphic terms unavailable to the theatre of the day. In his *Schilderboek* (1604), Van Mander used this exact term to describe the general style of Bruegel's art:

> He painted a picture in which Lent and Carnival are fighting, another where all kinds of remedies are used against death; and one with all kinds of children at games; and innumerable little *sinnekens* [*meer ontallijcke sinnekens*].[120]

What might *meer ontallijcke sinnekens* mean in this context? We come back to the issue of how Neo-Platonic formulations were expressed visually: the hybrid as an agenda in art. As we have seen, Pico's chameleon-man was a metaphor for the condition of the psyche. Although Pico's interpretation of the protean capacity of man was more internal and psychological than that of Plato, recall that he retained an element of mysticism and magic: Pico refused completely to metaphorise the figure of Proteus. There are passages in the *Oration* where he implies that shape changing in Man is something that could really happen: *[Man] himself molds, fashions and changes himself into the form of all flesh and into the character of every creature*. A delicate balance is struck here between external, visible changes (*the form of all flesh*), and internal, invisible changes (*the character of every creature*).

This issue had close parallels in later fifteenth- and early sixteenth-century painting, where, for example, the art of portraiture would be envisaged precisely as the difficulty of making the internal, animated part of the body legible on the external surface, which is all that can be painted. Leonardo wished to show the *movements of the mind* on the painted surface of his sitter's face. It follows that, even if Pico's chameleon-man were interpreted as a metaphor for changes in the psyche only, the way of representing this as an image would be as a metamorphic body.

These contexts suggest the importance of hybrid imagery as a means of making visible the invisible workings of the imagination. The desire to represent the inner world in visual terms led many artists and writers towards what Freud called that *royal road to the unconscious* — the realm of the dream. There are many clues which suggest that Renaissance antiquarian fascination with hybrid forms, inspired by Pico's Orphic Humanism, indeed shaped research into the visual representation of dreams in the sixteenth-century. In the 1560s, Annibal Caro (1507-66) was called in to advise in a professional capacity on the iconography of sleep, for a programme of paintings planned for the Camera dell' Aurora in Rome by Taddeo Zuccaro (1529-66). He was by then able to consult a range of mythographic manuals: Boccacio's *Geneologia de gli Dei* (Venice, 1527), for instance, cited Macrobius and Ovid; similar texts were tailored specifically for artists and patrons from the 1540s on.[121]

Bosch's trademark imagery was often described in general terms as dream-like.[122] In 1521, Marcantonio Michiel wrote in his journal that he had seen three works by Bosch in Cardinal Grimani's palace at Venice, one of which he denoted as a *tela delli sogni* (canvas of dreams).[123] Recall how, in 1572, shortly after Bruegel's death, the poet Lampsonius eulogised him as *this new Bosch who brings his master's ingenious dreams to life once more.*[124] More specialised writers made the same association; here we find some clear links between Neo-Platonic theories and Boschian surrealism. In a treatise on painting published in 1584, the artist and art theorist Giovanni Paolo Lomazzo (1538-1600) wrote of *Girolamo Boschi fiamengo, che nel rappresentare strane apparenze e spaventevoli et orridi sogni fu singolare e veramente divino* [who in the representation of strange apparitions and astonishing and horrible dreams was unique and truly divine].[125] In the 1560s, Lomazzo had himself researched and written a book on dreams: he found the sources for his *Libro dei sogni* in Hermetic philosophy and Neo-Platonic magic. He made extensive use of the encyclopedic *De occulta philosophia* (1533), by the German magus, Cornelius Agrippa of Nettesheim (1486-1535),[126] and quoted another famous doctor, sometime magus and student of dreams, Girolamo Cardano (Jerome Cardan; 1501-76).

The central Neo-Platonic text common to all these authors was an essay on dreams, *De insomniis*, by Synesius of Cyrene (c 373-414);[127] Ficino translated it into Latin in 1489, Lomazzo quoted from it, Cardan wrote a book about it, Adrien Turnebius published it (along with the rest of Synesius's *Opera*) in Paris in 1553. Ficino's translation turned this previously unknown treatise, by an obscure fourth-century philosopher into a new *locus classicus* for Humanist thought about dreaming. The importance of Synesius is that he exalted dreaming, on mystical grounds, as a creative labour, linked to the arts of representation:

> Anyone can see how great the work is, on attempting to fit language into visions, visions in which these things which are united in nature are separated, and things separated in nature are united... It is no mean

> achievement to pass on to another something of a strange nature that has stirred in one's own soul, for [by] this phantasy things which are expelled from the order of being, and things which never in any possible way existed, are brought instead into being — nay, even things which have not a nature capable of existence.[128]

Such a passage reads almost as a manifesto for Boschian surrealism. Synesius — a luke-warm Christian but enthusiastic Neo-Platonist — argued that dreaming involved the translation of private visions into the public world, creating entities which have not a nature capable of existence or expelled from the order of being. This "rhetoric" of dreams created novel impossibilities, which re-shuffle the categories of the world and point to a reality outside both nature and language. All this implies a web of links between Boschian fantasy, recognised as dream-like from one end of Europe to the other,[129] and contemporary esoteric thought about dreams.

The *Hypnerotomachia*, of course, begins with a dream, and its woodcuts draw on the taste for mythological hybrids with esoteric significance. From around 1500, Venetian artists were involved with exploring the classical iconography of sleep in other ways. Some print designs depict figures in sleep or reverie, attended by hybrids derived from Bosch. The first representation of a dream in Italian printmaking is Marcantonio Raimundi's beautiful *"Dream of Raphael"* (fig. 28).[130] The left foreground is occupied by two sleeping female nudes, a kind of *döppelganger*; they seem aspects of the same person. They sleep on the raised part of a river-bank, whose forms above them resemble clouds. At their feet are four small hybrid monsters, positioned on the shore, as if conjured from the water. Behind is a dark river, with peopled boats in the distance; behind this, a nocturnal city in flames, with silhouetted figures framed running or standing in the bright windows. This composition is echoed in Battista Dossi's later *"Night"* or *"The Dream"* (fig. 30; 1544), where a female figure, accompanied by owl and giant cock, sleeps in a night landscape, under a full moon, half-encircled by surreal creatures; in the background, another city blazes on the far side of a river.[131]

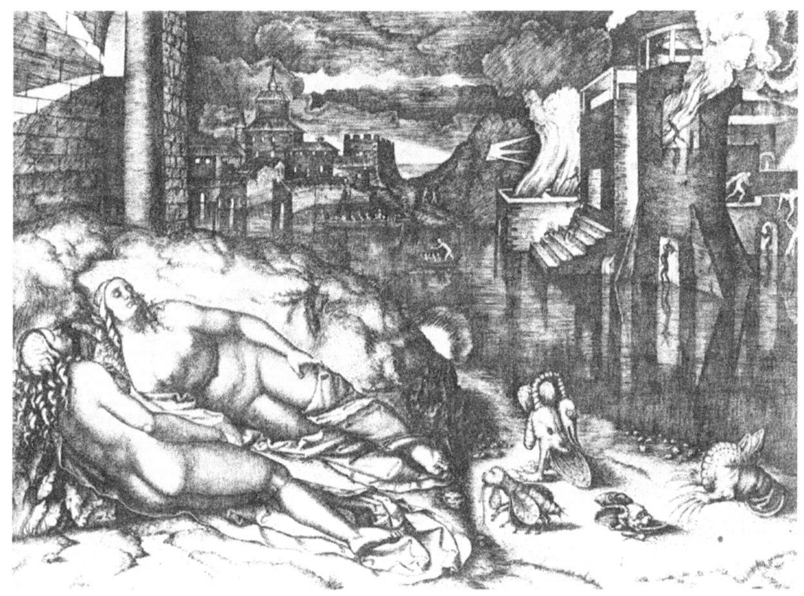

28 Marcantonio Raimondi, *The "Dream of Raphael"*, c. 1505. Engraving, 23.7 x 33.4 cm. Graphische Sammlung Albertina, Vienna

29 Guilio Campagnola, *The Astrologer*, 1509. Engraving, 99 x 152 mm. British Museum, London. 1845-8.25.771

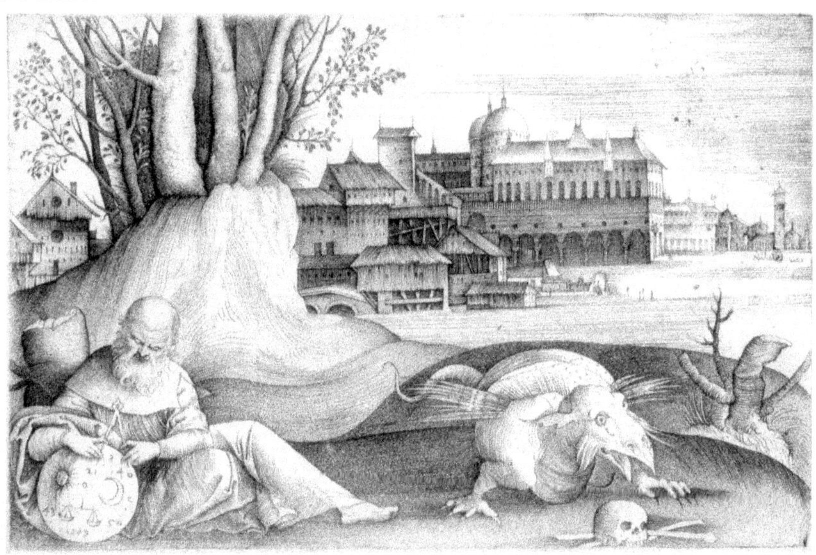

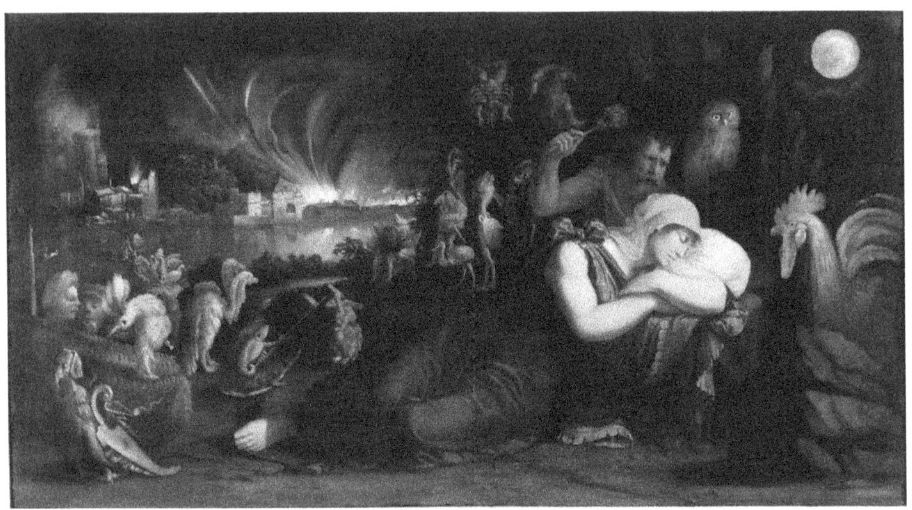

30 Battista Dossi, *"Night (The Dream)"*, 1544. Oil on canvas, 82 x 149.5cm. Gemäldegalerie Alte Meister, Staatliche Kunstsammlungen Dresden

In a design by Giulio Campagnola, an old philosopher holds compasses to a disk marked with the symbols of the sun and moon, the balances-sign of Libra, and other numbers (1509; fig. 29).[132] Next to him, almost as large, is a hybrid with something of the air of a mild dragon about it. This creature stands guard over a skull-and-cross-bones on the ground. The acquired title of this print, *The Astrologer*, does not explain all these elements. The philosopher's downcast gaze, rapt in his calculation, suggests a vision; his tools suggest he is measuring the movements of the spheres: for Neo-Platonists, the key to life before and after death, and a return to the soul's original home in the heavens, beyond the world of appearances. Compasses are an attribute of Dürer's *Melancholia I* (1514; fig. 5).

However, as the sign of Libra implies, this scene represents a balanced, and so higher, state of melancholia: the level of philosophical inspiration. Together, the philosopher, the hybrid beast and the skull convey a Synesian sense of *visions in which things united in nature are separated, and things separated in nature united*. The pose of head resting on hand, which Dürer's print made part of the new iconography of melancholy, was borr-

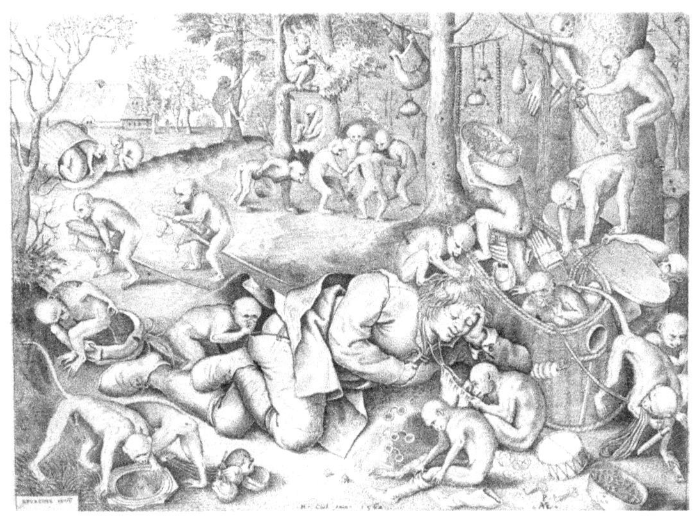

31 Pieter van der Heyden, after Pieter Bruegel, *The Pedlar Pillaged by Apes*, 1562. Engraving, 22.5 x 29 cm. Bibliothèque Royale Belgique, Brussels. S V 70758

-owed from an older tradition of representing dreams and visions. A popular subject of this kind was the Vision of Tondalus (fig. 47); the medieval monk Tondalus is shown in the foreground as a small figure with head on hand, while his famous vision of Hell, here expressed in Boschian motifs, fills the picture-space.[133]

In two designs, *The Pedlar Pillaged by Apes* (1562; fig. 31) and *The Land of Cockaigne* (fig. 65), Bruegel uses sleeping figures in similar ways, as if the rest of the scene is their fantasy, like a three-dimensional thought-bubble expanding out around them, through the magic of Renaissance illusionism, to make the impossible visible. The *Land of Cockaigne* (discussed in Chapter 3) depicts a popular, secular "vision": a dream of hungry folk. The subject of the Pedlar and the Apes also derives from a popular tradition, found first in Flemish manuscript illumination.[134] Bruegel's version significantly psychologises the theme. The small apes in the *Pedlar* act very like *sinnekens*. As the pedlar sleeps, his head on his hand, they rummage in his pack, string his goods from the trees and piss in his hat. They behave like bad children, turning everything into a game. Actual toys and games are prominent among their activities: two ride hobby-horses, others join hands in a dance, several have musical instruments, one tries on boots, another a pair of spectacles. Many of these cameos resemble details in *Children's Games*. Compositionally, the Pedlar's pack is his pillow; this open pack can be read as an extension of the top of his head. The little apes have literally taken the lid off him: removed the upper half of the pack and rolled it away into farthest extremity of the picture space (it appears in the distance at top-right). The apes are densest around the dreamer's head, they swarm inside and spring out of the pack. Most notably, one ape crouches fully on the back of the pedlar's head, its fingers twined in the sleeper's hair.

Bruegel used a similar compositional device in his print of the *Temptation of St. Anthony* (1556; fig. 32), his only design on this endlessly variable, quinessentially Boschian theme. Consider the "thought-bubble" aspect of the design. An infernal metamorphic scene rises in the background behind the small figure of the protagonist, who is folded into the right corner, eyes closed, back turned to the entire drama. This structure invites the viewer to interpret the background scene as occurring in the head of the dreamer.

Dream forms and novel hybrids come together in a different way in the work of François Desprez, whose book of caricatures, *Songes Drolatiques de Pantagruel*, was published at Paris in 1565 (figs. 33a-b). The title cashed in on the enormous success of Rabelais's great comedy; without having any connection with the matter of the text. Rather, the *Songes* is cleverly situated to appeal to several markets: the taste for Boschian fantasy, for Rabelaisian satire, and for the visual riddle, or rebus. Desprez's designs were certainly indebted to Boschian prints, if not to the works of Bruegel himself. The interesting point here is that the function of these images was precisely to reveal the inner, private selves of their subjects. As Adhémar comments:

> This album of 120 caricatures uses grotesque shapes as a means of ridiculing all the personages of the French court, who, while recognizable by their attributes, are at the same time transformed into a procession of monstrous animals.[135]

The existence of a work like the *Songes* demonstrates how well this psychological implication of the hybrid body was understood, in the mid-sixteenth century, by an artist and a public analogous to that of Bruegel.[136]

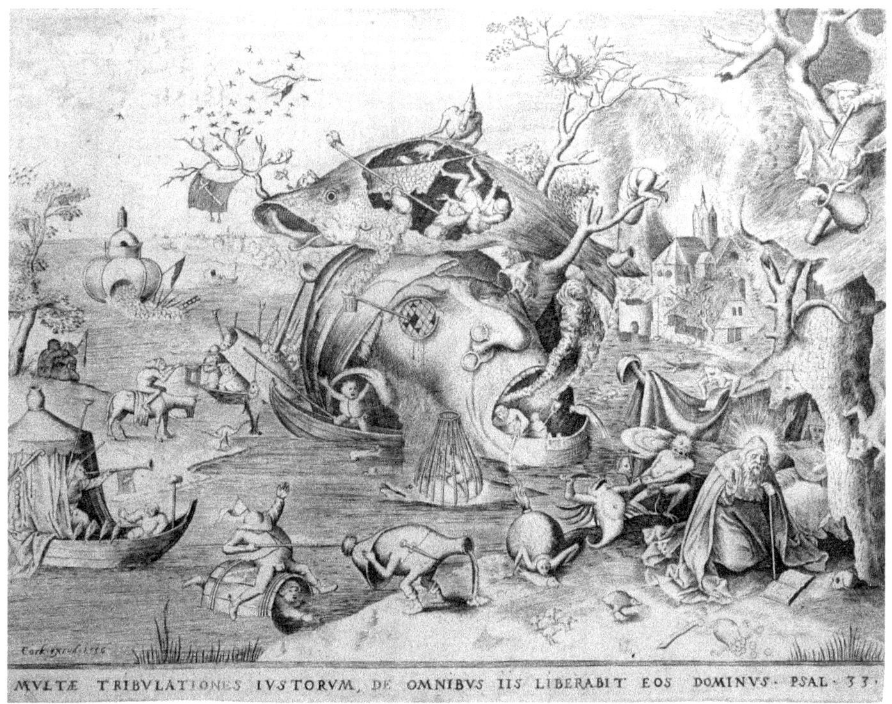

32 Pieter van der Heyden, after Pieter Bruegel, *The Temptation of St.Anthony*, 1556. Engraving, 24.5 x 32 cm. Bibliothèque Royale Belgique, Brussels. S I 7602

Besides the cues of composition, the nature of Bruegel's metamorphic imagery prompts a search for some explanation of its nightmarish quality. The source of this tone is not to be found solely in the Neo-Platonic texts. Pico's vision of Man as Metamorph is not, on its own, the stuff of nightmare. For Pico, the chameleon quality of Man stemmed from our kinship with angels: a mystic attribute of Man's highest self. This was the main point of the metaphor. However, because human nature is metamorphic, it could become debased through a failure (or an abeyance) of intention. It is here that Pico's thought (and Origen's) prefigures the stance of Bruegel's art: notions of a failure of intention or self-consciousness, the hybrid body as a metaphor for the human interior, the tone of nightmare. Together, these suggest common expressions of sixteenth-century conceptions of the unconscious. It is time to take a closer look at the institutions which dealt directly with these matters: dream theory, melancholia, and nightmares.

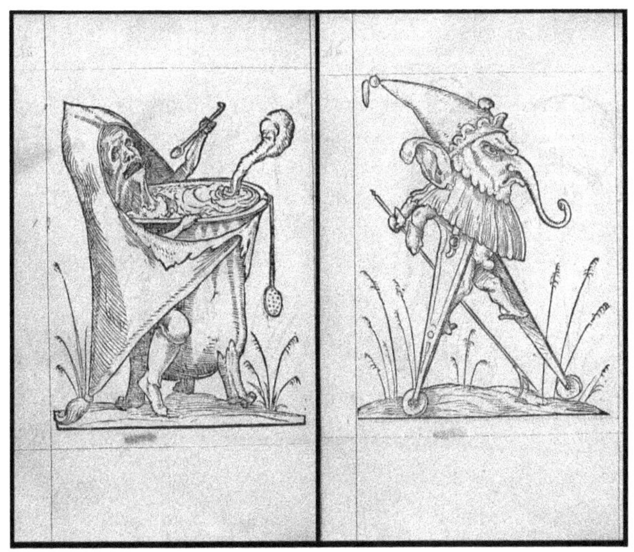

33a Francois Desprez, XLIV soup-spoon creature & XLVI wheel-feet man, from, *Les songes drolatiques de Pantagruel* (Paris, 1565). Photo: after Jules Morel (1869)

33b Francois Desprez, XCIII fish man & XCVI guitar man, *Les songes drolatiques de Pantagruel* (Paris, 1565). Photo: after Jules Morel (1869)

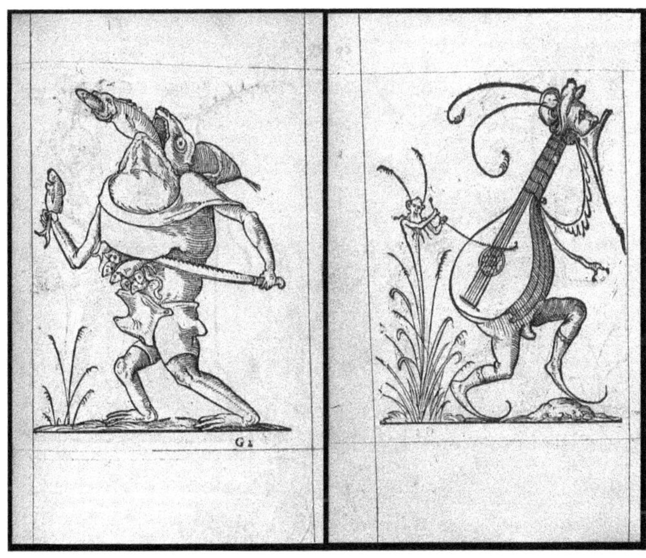

> As to the left shoulder of the chameleon, I should be quite ashamed to say to what monstrous purpose Democritus devotes it; how that dreams may be produced by the agency thereof, and transferred to any person we might think proper; how these dreams may be dispelled by the employment of the right foot of the said animal.
>
> Pliny, *Natural History*, xxviii

Dreams in the Middle Ages were conceived of and interpreted quite differently from the way they are now. Like inspiration, a dream worth paying attention to was thought of as originating outside the dreamer. Dreams were classified according to their origins. The most important dreams were of supernatural origin. This last is a medium we now find hard to take seriously, but in the highly-elaborated scheme of medieval dream lore, more than half of the categories are devoted to dreams caused by supernatural agencies. Only two kinds of dreams correspond to the modern idea that the source of dream images is to be found in the experience of the individual dreamer. Only in one class of dreams do we find metamorphic images presented as a disorder of the imagination.

These are fundamental differences between medieval and modern dream-cultures. This should not surprise us; it would be strange indeed if dreams had not changed in the interim. Before asking what late-medieval people thought it meant to imagine metamorphic things, it must be remembered that medieval and contemporary definitions of the difference between *real* and *imaginary* do not often coincide. In dream-lore, it was the supernatural dreams that were regarded as real, or true, and the personal dreams that were merely *imaginary*. The significance of metamorphic imagery in dreams depends on the categories of the system as a whole.

Scholastic dream theory has its roots in the late fourth century in the work of Ambrosius Theodosius Macrobius (395–423CE), famous throughout the Middle Ages mainly for one book, his *Commentary on Scipio's*

Dream.[137] This commentary was one of the most popular of all Classical texts, extant in about 150 manuscripts, and itself much-commented on. Macrobius in turn derived some of his material from ancient *Oneirocritica* by Artemidorus (Venice, 1518; Basel, 1539) and Astrampsychus. According to Macrobius there are five principal kinds of dreams:

Somnium
Visio
Oraculum
Insomnium
Phantasma

The first three are prophetic. The *somnium* provides prophecy or divine insight via obscure symbolism that requires interpretation. The *visio* is a straightforward view of things to come. In the *oraculum,* future events and advice on how to deal with them are revealed by a *parent or other sacred person*. The other two classes, says Macrobius, are *worthless* because they are *foolish and empty of meaning*. The *insomnium* is caused by anxiety or physical distress leading to the repetition in dreams of mundane personal vexations. The *phantasma,* or nightmare, occurs between waking and sleeping *in the first mist of sleep*. A variety of the *phantasma* is caused by the *ephialtes*, or *incubus*, a demon who presses upon people while they sleep.[138]

By the time of Chaucer (c 1343-1400), scholars had Christianised and distilled these classifications into three groups, organized by their causes.[139] Relying on the authorities of Aristotle, Galen and Augustine's psychology, a dream was initially determined by its interpreter to be one of three types:

somnium coeleste
somnium animale
somnium naturale

These classes translate as, respectively, *celestial, mental,* and *bodily* dreams. It is worth drawing attention to the shift implicit in this condensation.

Whereas Macrobius assigned supernatural content to three of his five categories, in the period just before the Renaissance, all celestial dreams were grouped together. Implicitly, the mind and body dreams were given more importance, since these categories now made up two out of three of the available classifications. It is the first of these types, the *somnium coeleste,* which has been dropped as an explanation in modern medical thought.

In this synthesis, the *somnium coeleste* subsumed the *somnium,* the *visio,* and the *oraculum,* all considered as dreams of celestial origin. Saints' dreams, for example, as they were written up in hagiographies, could be tailored to fit into this class. The purest *somnium coeleste* had the least visual content. In what was then thought to be a treatise by Augustine, a sub-category is discussed: the *visio intellectuale,* which occurs when God reveals divine mysteries directly to the *intellectus* (the faculty of mind superior to reason, capable of spiritual illumination).[140] In this case, no thought or imagery was involved in the individual's dream experience — the imagination was, as it were, sidestepped. This seems to have been an exclusively post-classical formulation. On the other hand, the *oraculum* version of the *somnium coeleste* continued to flourish in the form of dreams of the Virgin Mary and of the saints.[141]

The second and third classes of dreams, the *somnium animale* and the *somnium naturale,* came within the province of medicine. Here, for the first time, we find a dream ascribed to internal causes, in the private life and imagination of the individual. Although authors differ in detail, their consensus is quite clear. The *somnium animale* corresponded roughly to Macrobius' *insomnium.* According to Peter of Abano (1250-1316), it *springs from the great anxiety and perturbation of the waking mind.*[142] Chaucer followed this view (paraphrasing Homer), to produce his famous description of such dreams as stemming from individual preoccupations:

The wery hunter, slepinge in his bed
To wode ayein his mind goth anoon;
The juge dremeth how his plees ben sped

The carter dremeth how his cartes goon
The riche, of gold; the knight fight with his foon,
The sicke met he drinketh of the tonne;
The lover met he has his lady wonne
Parliament of Fowls, lines 99-109

Another variation on this took into account planetary influences, especially lunar influences. Astrologers tended to consider the *somnium animale* as midway between the *coeleste* and the *naturale* - having occult, but not divine, causes. This was position held, for instance, by Guido Bonatus (or Bonatti; fl 1233-77) and Abû l-Hasan 'Alî ibn Abî l-Rijâl (or Albohazen Haly; d. after 1037), whose authoritative books on astrology were given early printed editions and republished at Basel in the early 1550s.[143] Albohazen maintained that the *somnium animale* could be true or false, depending on the aspect of the planets. Arnaldus de Villanova (c. 1235-1313), on the other hand, considered that any dream caused by an external supernatural agency should be treated as a *somnium coeleste* of the Macrobian *somnium* type, that is, in need of expert interpretation. This interpretation, he continued, should be carried out by way of the twelve houses of the zodiac.[144] Here, we see a development of the *somnium animale* type going beyond the inevitable variations in category interpretation of individual authors. The astrological doctors thoroughly incorporated planetary influences into the principal classificatory schemes laid down by Macrobius and St. Augustine. The effect was to blur the distinction between divine and occult causes that Augustine had attempted to impose on his Classical sources. Therefore, in a sense, they renewed the original implication of these sources: for Macrobius, of course, and for Cicero, the divine and the occult had been one and the same.

In dream lore, efforts to include astrological causes meant in practice that the *somnium coeleste* could take on some of the attributes of the *somnium animale,* as Villanova suggested. At this juncture, medical theory shades into psychology. Renewed fifteenth-century interest in astrology meant that astrological medicine became psychological medicine, gaining in prestige and significance in accordance with Neo-Platonic reinterpretation of classical myth. Astrology can in fact be regarded as the experimental branch of Ficino's *Platonic theology*. As we saw in the discussion of Proteus, Rabelais makes an excellent barometer; showing how widely Neo-Platonic ideas were disseminated into vernacular culture. Rabelais has Pantagruel describe the soul's journey during sleep, when it enters the heavens which are its natural abode and walks among the stars. While it is there,

> it notes not only events in this lower world of motion, but also future happenings; and when it reports them to the body and, through the body's senses and organs communicates them to its friends, it is called vaticinal and prophetic. It is true that it does not report them as straightforwardly as it saw them, being prevented by the imperfection and frailty of the bodily senses; even as the moon, receiving her light from the sun, does not communicate it to us as clearly, purely, vividly, and ardently as she received it. Therefore, these somnial vaticinations require an interpreter... That is why Heraclitus said that dreams did not reveal anything to us, nor conceal anything from us, but that they gave us a sign and an indication of things to come.[145]

This lovely, though somewhat tongue-in-cheek, discourse on the nature of dreams demonstrates a characteristic sixteenth-century blend of Neo-Platonic ideas about the dreaming soul with more traditional models of dream interpretation. Later in the same chapter, Pantagruel gives advice which assumes knowledge of a basic principle of Ficino's astrological magic: that one may balance one's temperament by ingesting or surrounding oneself with, plants, animals, or objects under the governance of the planet whose attributes one wishes to acquire.[146] The object of balancing the inner humours according to planetary influences was, of course, to improve the mind spiritually and to have a happier life. This idea easily meshed with older, practical folklore on the best kind of diet or the best season of the year for receiving truthful, prophetic dreams.[147] Recipes and instructions of this kind appear in compendia of folk wisdom, such as the very popular *La*

Phisionomie des Songes et visions fantastiques by Jehan Thibault, the first edition of which came out at the end of the fifteenth century at Lyon. There seems to have been a Flemish translation in 1542 (as the *Grooten dubbelen Droomboek*); perhaps an outcome of Jehan's Antwerp connections.[148] Among the many *livres populaires* dispensing astrological and other sorts of information to sixteenth-century Netherlanders, dream-books of this kind were in great demand. In the non-scholarly medium of Rabelais' comic novel, all this information — Ficino's medicine and old wives' tales — is presented as continuous:

> No supper at all would be best [said Pantagruel] considering your good state and healthy constitution. An ancient prophet called Amphiaraus insisted that those who received his oracles and dreams should eat nothing all that day and drink no wine for three days previously. But we will not resort to so extreme and rigorous a regimen. I well believe that a man full of meat and overstuffed would have difficulty in gaining knowledge of spiritual matters. But I do not agree with those who believe that they can enter into deeper contemplation of celestial things after long and obstinate fasting. You will eat at supper [no] food which might trouble or darken your animal spirits, for... the spirit does not receive the shapes for divination by dreams if the body is disquieted and troubled by the vapors and fumes of meats previously eaten, and this on account of the indissoluble sympathy between the body and soul. You can eat some good... pears, one pippen, some plums from Tours, and a few cherries from my own orchard. Then you need not fear that your dreams will prove doubtful, fallacious, or suspicious, as some of the Peripatetics have declared them to be in autumn.[149]

The joke here is that Pantagruel is recommending to Panurge the fruits of Venus as the proper preparatory supper for a prophetic dream. According to the theory of the day, the consumption of venereal substances was highly unlikely to render the mind receptive to celestial influences. Later on, Panurge, who has followed Pantagruel's recommendations, dreams of his future wife. The humour of this passage depends on seeing

Pantagruel dress up some of these older ideas with new philosophical and mystic explanations.

A fourteenth-century *Book of Daniel* listed, for example, the bad days on which to have dreams. Among these are: forty dangerous days (*which the masters of the Greeks have tested by experiment*); *bromantic days*, falling during November and December; and *parentalic days*, from January to March. The anonymous author explains that *these are the days when the leaves fall from the trees*,[150] a phenomenon supposed to have a disturbing effect upon the clarity of dreams. Rabelais quotes this idea and its Greek origin, but he refers to it instead as *stated in mystical form by the ancient prophets and poets*.[151] In a similar vein, the authors of a popular compilation on *géomancie, physionomie et chyromancie* solemnly assured their readers that the material had been drawn from Plato, Ptolemy, "Albimaser", et al.[152]

By the sixteenth century, then, astrological and medical beliefs that had been around for centuries were being reinterpreted, their meanings and implications deepened by the practitioners of specifically Renaissance philosophies, Neo-Platonism and Hermeticism. Views about dreaming changed in emphasis accordingly. In particular, the *somnium animale*, or bodily dream became much more significant when Ficino recast the theory of planetary influences. Planetary influences, we recall, were thought of as divine, as manipulable through astrological magic, and as determining individual personality. In the *De Vita Triplici*, Ficino had re-assessed the whole field of medicine in relation to astrology. He believed the stars and planets determined a person's entire temperament: humours, preferred occupations and talents.[153] This view of the astral sciences gave a personal bent to the relationship between planetary influences and the individual. The crucial new tenet of Renaissance astrology was that, as Yates explained:

> there are no bad or unfortunate planets... aptitudes associated with the planets will become virtues in the person who develops the influence in a good way; if he receives them in a bad way, they will be vices.[154]

So Ficino, fusing Platonic inspiration with the "disease" of melancholia, adopted the desirable aspects of Saturn as its ruling planet and sank its lower associations (crippledom and miserliness). His ideas were popularised, for instance, by the Venetian architect and astrologer Francesco Giorgi (1466-1540), author of the hugely influential *De harmonia mundi* (Venice, 1525; Paris, 1545), copies of which abound in Renaissance libraries. One unexpected general consequence was to individualise dreaming and shift responsibility for its content on to the dreamer. If the meaning of a dream was unclear or occluded, this was no longer to be blamed on the inferior or malign nature of its occult origin, it was because the dreamer himself had not correctly balanced his bodily humors and accordingly, his state of mind. In the context of dream theory, the new principle effectively rendered the *somnium animale* into a type of *somnium coeleste*. In a manner which would have shocked St. Augustine, the magician Agrippa of Nettesheim, among others, recommended astrological magic to render the student receptive to a *somnium* of this new type, the content of which would be prophetic and divine:

> I call that a Dream here, which is caused by the Celestiall influences in the phantastick spirit, mind, or body, being all well disposed. The rule of interpreting this is found amongst Astrologers... These kind of Dreams come by use to divers men after a divers manner, and according to the divers quality, and dispositions of the phantastick spirit: wherefore there cannot be given one common rule to all for the interpretation of Dreams. But according to the opinion of Synesius... the memory is confirmed by [sense], and by keeping in memory... knowledge is obtained... After the same account you must conceive of Dreams.
>
> Whence Synesius commands that every one should observe his Dreams, and their events, and such like rules, viz. to commit to memory all things that are seen, and accidents that befall, as well in sleep, as in watching, and with a diligent observation consider with himself the rules by which these are to be examined, for by this means shall a Diviner be able by little, and little to interpret his Dreams, if so be nothing slip out of his memory. Now Dreams are more efficacious,

> when the Moon over-runs that Sign, which was in the ninth number of the Nativity, or revolution of that year, or in the ninth Sign from the Sign of perfection. For it is a most true, and certain divination, neither doth it proceed from nature or humane Arts, but from purified minds, by divine inspiration.[155]

Such preoccupations gave a different color to the third and lowest class of dreams in the medieval system, the *somnium naturale*. Under this heading we find for the first time dreams corresponding to the modern sense of *nightmare*. The preferred explanation for this kind of dream was, officially, purely physical, but marked by elements of paradox because older folk traditions (present also in classical texts) persisted in regarding the nightmare as a form of demonic visitation.[156] Medieval writers saw the *somnium naturale* as a symptom of bodily illness, caused by an imbalance of humours or complexions. The characteristics of the dream provided the physician with clues as to the nature of the disorder.[157] Thus Galen (c 129-200), whose textbooks remained authoritative for centuries, stated in his *De dignotione ex insomniis*:

> If anyone should see a fire in his dreams he is troubled by too much yellow bile; if he should see smoke, or a misty darkness or profound shadows, then by black bile.[158]

He wrote that sufferers from a *disturbed imagination* think they have no head, or see black men. His examples of those with an *afflicted understanding* included a man who threw glass vessels and a child out of a window. The sixteenth-century Italian doctor, Giovanni da Concorreggio explained this as a disorder of displaced categories of significance:

> because he did not know that the vessels were fragile and the child vulnerable and because he thought it correct and useful to throw such things out of the window as though they were harmful in the house.[159]

Archigenes of Apamea, writing under Trajan, thought that melancholics were liable to experience *fears, visions and true dreams*.[160] In serious cases, they were typically gripped by hallucinations, fear of demons, and *curious obsessions*, such as *the belief that one was an earthenware jar*.[161] This kind of diagnosis was cited by Augustine, Galen, Villanova, Rhazes, Peter of Abano, and Avicenna, all commenting on melancholia. Among other illnesses caused by humours and manifested in dreams, Avicenna, for instance, affirmed that:

> The principal signs of melancholia in the blood are these: fear without cause... dread... a kind of apprehension on account of things which are or are not... anxiety over that which is not ordinarily feared... some fear that the earth will open and swallow them... at other times, they imagine themselves being crowned kings, or transformed into wolves, or into demons, or birds, or even into artificial instruments or implements.[162]

Metamorphic imaginings therefore characterise the dreams of the melancholic. Melancholia was also firmly linked to nightmare: the old *phantasma* was a subspecies of the *somnium naturale*. Albohazen states that the melancholic man dreams *of dark places*, and that *he is being suffocated or oppressed by nightmares*.[163] Villanova maintains that *excessive black cholera causes dreams in which appear terrible monsters, apparitions, incubi and such*.[164] The oldest reference, from Macrobius, can now be seen to have a Synesian tone; his category of *phantasma* (nightmare) described how:

> [The dreamer] seems to see crowding in on him strangely moving or swimming forms, distorted in appearance and out of all natural proportions in size, or he may experience the rushing in of tumultuously whirling kaleidoscopically changing things, either delightful or disturbing.[165]

This notion of *kaleidoscopically changing things* is highly suggestive. This connects the metamorphic element in nightmare images with the use of metamorphic forms in Renaissance surrealism. Even the change in scale mentioned here became a characteristic visual device, used by Bosch and Bruegel, to evoking the dimension of the bad or hallucinatory dream.

The multiplicity of dreams was itself a very old idea. All dreams, in some ancient views, were peripatetic and populous. Hesiod spoke of a Tribe (or Host) of Dreams, *offspring of gloomy Night.*[166] In the fifth century, Herodotus had his wise Persian Artabanus speak of dreams both psychologically, as reflections of daytime concerns, and supernaturally, as *phantoms wandering among men*.[167] The Pythagorean Alexander Polyhistor wrote in the first century BC that,

> the whole air is full of souls, which are called *genii* or heroes, and it is these who send men dreams and signs of future disease and health, and not to men alone but to sheep and cattle also.[168]

As paraphrased by Diogenes Laertius, this philosophical characterisation of dreams found its way into the libraries of Italy and the North (editions printed in the 1470s at Rome, Venice and Nuremberg; then in 1533 at Basel, and in 1566, by Plantin at Antwerp). Synesius meditated on the same idea, and gave it a Neo-Platonic frame, thus Ficino and his followers would have known of the multiplicity of dreams. In literature, the *locus classicus* was Ovid's House of Sleep, where Morpheus himself lies, amidst the "throng of his thousand sons". There,

> on all sides lie empty dream-shapes, mimicking many forms, many as ears of grain in harvest time, as leaves upon the trees, as sands cast on the shore.[169]

Lucretius had another, more scientific, rationale for why hybrids are seen in dreams:

> many images of things are moving about in many ways and in all directions, very thin, which easily unite in the air when they meet, being like spider's web or gold leaf. [They] are much more thin in texture

> than those which take the eyes and assail the vision, since these penetrate through the interstices of the body, and awake the thin substance of the mind within, and assail the sense. Thus it is that we see centaurs and the frame of a Scylla... since images of all kinds are being carried about everywhere, [some] thrown off from [a] combination of these shapes. For certainly no image of a centaur comes from one living... but when the images of man and horse meet by accident, they easily adhere at once [on] account of their fine nature and thin texture. All other things of this class are made in the same way...
>
> [we see these things] when sleep has pervaded the limbs [because] the same images assail our minds as when we wake [and because] all our senses are obstructed and... unable to refute the false with the true.
>
> It sometimes happens again, that the image that follows up is not of the same kind, but what was before a woman seems to be changes to a man in our grasp; or that different shapes and ages [*aetas*] follow; but sleep and oblivion see to it that we do not wonder.[170]

The key aspects here are the multifariousness of the dream images, their link to the hybrid-patterns of mythology, their changeability, and their curious "thinness" — making it clear that they are not real. These ideas furnished a visual repertoire, capable of expressing Synesius' mandate, to visualise *things which have never existed, things which have not a nature capable of existing*.

We can now see how these materials came together in the evolution of the nightmare into the melancholic dream, and the melancholic dream into a visual (Synesian) rhetoric of the surreal. In medieval descriptions of standardised or "archetypal" nightmare imagery, the following points recur. Emotions of fear and dread express themselves visually in images of shifting appearances. The dreamer sees the world transformed, or imagines himself transformed. Weird visions, nightmares and melancholia are symptoms of the same pathology. These connections were the pivots for the fifteenth-century reassessment of the melancholic temperament.

In the latter half of the fifteenth century, just as the concept of the *somnium animale* came to incorporate some aspects of the *somnium coeleste*, so too did the *somnium naturale* move in the direction of the *somnium animale*. In old dream-lore, melancholia inspired nightmarish images; this kind of dream could have only medical diagnostic significance, because it was generated by purely physical causes. The medical and astrological authorities unanimously followed Macrobius on this point. However, the melancholic dream was also the only medieval type where metamorphic images were classified as a product of the private imagination. Only the images of the *somnium naturale* originated exclusively from within the individual. Nightmare imagery was seen as lacking meaning *because* of this; because it had no divine (that is, occult, external) propulsion. This component was added when melancholy became the conduit for heavenly inspiration in Ficino's philosophy, and the reigning humour of mental labour in Dürer's print. With the authority of Synesius, even *weird visions* could be understood as having a more positive connection with creativity. The metamorphic monsters of dreams could now appear next to philosophers, dreamers and other figures in the melancholic stance of head to hand.

This cultural wave-front drove the creation of *kaleidoscopic, out-of-proportion* images, traditionally associated with nightmare, newly associated with esoteric visions, understood as visually representing the movements of the mind. Some such development begins in the generation of Bosch. Where previous writers on nightmare had seen only unreality and disease, Bosch's nightmarish imagery delved into the diverse human capacities for passion, sin, and (alchemically) transcendence.

Metamorphic Psychology in Bosch's "Purgatory"

The triptych of *Earthly Delights* is a case in point of this novel Renaissance attitude; the "Purgatory" panel (fig. 17c) in particular depicts a multiplicity of possible ventures into the mind. Many are negative, showing people given over wholly to their bestial selves, as in the man consorting with a pig in ecclesiastical headdress in the lower right corner, the woman with a die on her head nearby, or, unforgettably, the gigantic pair of ears near the top of the panel, where brain, head, and face are replaced by a phallus-like knife signifying, presumably, lust and violence.[171] Other images are more ambiguous; for example, that of the man impaled on a harp. Bergman unravelled the thought here:

> In the midst of hell we see large musical instruments which presumably characterise different human attitudes to life: the bagpipes, like Pan's pipe, may symbolise sensuality, and the harp, like the lyre of Apollo and the angel's instruments, may stand for spirituality. A man in the posture of one crucified is transfixed by the strings of the harp... adjacent to this... on the sounding board is a gold-speckled and smoking toad transfixed by a spear.[172]

This last evokes a metaphor in a fifteenth-century *Vision* by the alchemist Canon Ripley, who described the *prima materia* substance as, *a toad that has been fed on grapes [which] bursts, and the venom trickling out of it [exudes] smoke and gilded vapor.*[173] This substance eventually becomes an elixir of life:

> The transfixed toad in Bosch's painting... constitutes an analogy to the pierced man on the harp... by means of a common alchemical symbol, the artist... reveals what is going to happen to the man — as in the toad's case, [his] prima materia nature will be transformed. This is to be interpreted as a change from the state of ignorance and sinfulness to a state of true insight.[174]

These alchemical symbols stand for invisible changes in the interior of the mind, beneath the surface of the sensible world. Elsewhere, the picture invites us quite literally to look below its surface, through the two holes which prominently open up in the black ground. Into one of these, humans fall, to be eaten by a bird-headed monster; they drop through a black bubble. Into the same hole, one man vomits while another defecates gold. This group as a whole draws an analogy between the purging of sin and a stage in the alchemical process where the participating minerals, thought of as organic, were "debased" into primeval, formless matter, the *prima materia* (compare fig. 18). The process of debasement, represented here as excretory, was also one of purification.

Above this, in an image clearer to our modern perceptions, a naked man propels himself over thin black ice on a gigantic skate (fig. 17d). At his left, a similar skater is half-submerged in a hole in the ice, while a bestial metamorph skates away in the opposite direction. Movements downwards, below the surface of the ground, appear privileged within the total structure of this panel. They refer to the common alchemical formula, VITRIOL:

> *Visita Interiora Terra Rectificando Invenies Occultum Lapidem* [visit the interior of the earth and by becoming purified you will find the hidden stone]. In religious alchemy, this was interpreted as a process taking place *inside* a person.[175]

The throne of the bird-headed eater (an allusion to Mercury) is firmly-mounted; in contrast to the nightmarish structures rising from the surface, with no means of redemptive descent. These are all depicted as unsteady, tottering, and filled with dramatic manifestations of sin.

At the top of the panel is a burning lake. People throw themselves into it at one end in a red light and emerge at the other into a whitish light. Small groups then seem to move towards the source of the light, an arch cut into a city wall. Though lakes of fire and brimstone are a feature of popular accounts of Hell, here the movement of bodies, and the change of colours, recalls the waters of burning punishment mentioned by the mystical alchemist, Zosimos (fl. c 300 CE). Into these the alchemical adept must plunge until he has been cleansed and purified, whereupon he may comprehend the Stone.[176] Zosimos dreams, and first questions the man he meets as to his identity:

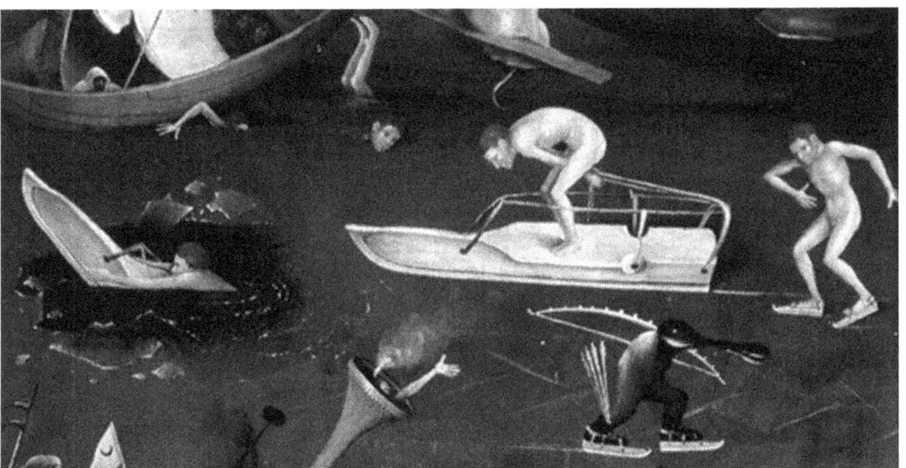

17d Hieronymus Bosch, skaters, detail, *Purgatory*, right inner wing, *The Garden of Earthly Delights*

He answered me in a weak voice, saying, "I am Ion, the priest of the sanctuary, and I have survived intolerable violence. For one came headlong in the morning, dismembering me with a sword, and tearing me asunder according to the rigor of harmony. And flaying my head with the sword which he held fast, he mingled my bones with my flesh and burned them in the fire of the treatment, until I learnt by the transformation of the body to become a spirit."

And while yet he spoke those words to me, and I forced him to speak of it, his eyes became as blood and he vomited up all his flesh. And I saw him as a mutilated little image of a man, tearing himself with his own teeth and falling away.

And being afraid I awoke and thought, "Is this not the situation of the waters?"... and I fell asleep anew. And I saw... water bubbling, and many people in it endlessly... I marveled at the boiling of the water and the men, burnt yet living. And he answered me saying, "It is the place of the exercise called preserving... For those men who wish to obtain virtue come hither and become spirits, fleeing from the body."[177]

He comes then to the *place of the punishments*, where the bodies of his guides are consumed by fire, boiled, dismembered, etc. Another priest explains that this is necessary, *to put blood into the bodies, to make clear the eyes, and to raise up the dead.*[178] In Bosch's panel, the alchemical-purgatorial scenery resembles that of Hell, but it stands nonetheless for interior torments through which the soul can become purified (see chapter 5). Thought of in this way, the nightmarish imagery simultaneously refers to the revelation of sin, the punishment for sin, and the process of purgation. Purgatory, in other words, can be understood as a place (or state) inside the self. The tenor of these ideas recalls the humanitarian heresy of Origen, who speculated that the purpose of the universe was to process every soul, through reincarnation, until Hell was empty.[179]

Metamorphic Psychology in Bruegel's "Temptation of St. Anthony"

From this fully mystical mobilisation of metamorphic imagery, Bruegel, with the increased detachment of the next generation but with no diminishment of essential seriousness, took a considerably less elevated view of human psychology. Bosch's visual inventions suggest a total disdain for matters of the flesh, together with transcendental hopes for the spirit: the opposite sides of the metamorphic body. In Bruegel, this equation was drastically readjusted. Their key differences of approach to metamorphic and nightmarish imagery can be seen in Bruegel's one variant on a trademark Boschian theme, the *Temptation of St. Anthony* (fig. 32). Like his *Vices* (fig. 9-15) series, and *Big Fish Eat Little Fish* (fig. 36), this is an early surreal composition, where Bruegel is still in the process of adapting the forms and conventions of the Boschian tradition.

The two most often represented encounters of the saint with diabolic forces were the saint lifted up into the air by devils, and temptation by a devil-queen (see e.g. fig. 16). These were late inventions for the legend of this saint, added by chapbook authors, working only a generation or so before Bosch, and elaborated by later painters.[180] Neither episode appears in the main texts for Anthony's life and works: a *Vita* by Athanasius (c 357 CE) and Jacob of Voragine's *Golden Legend* (c 1263). Athanasius' *Vita* was coloured by his Platonic training. He minimised the demonic encounters and emphasised the final journey of Anthony's soul through the celestial spheres. Athanasius reported illusions (vanishing beautiful bathers), but not the shapes of demons. The *Golden Legend* repeats all this and for good measure provides Anthony with more elaborate demonic illusions, copied from other Patristic models. Both writers describe the more dramatic of Anthony's temptations as imaginary; for example, Athanasius:

> The harassed Anthony suddenly sees the roof open and light stream in. The demons and the pain vanish. He understands that Christ has come to his rescue... On one occasion the hermit perceives how his spirit is rapt away, and he stands as an observer of himself. Angels lift him up towards heaven, but are checked by a flock of devils... On one occasion it happened that St. Anthony was spiritually absent from the body and beheld the whole world under him. He sees the earth covered by a grille, and asks how it is possible for anyone to slip through this. A voice answers, *Humility*.[181]

The hybrid monsters so characteristic of *Temptations* thus derive not from these texts, but, as we have seen, from the association of metamorphic imagery with visions. Bosch developed these clues in his various representations of Anthony as a melancholic beset by temptations within his mind. Bruegel also framed his version of the saint's temptation as an ordeal of the imagination. Like Bosch, he may have worked from specific passages in both sources. One of these relates St. Anthony's encounter with an archer, who draws his bow three times at Anthony's request. When the archer complains the bow may break, Anthony turns to his monks and makes the incident a moral homily on keeping spiritual zeal within one's own capacity.[182] Bruegel has an archer at top right corner, but he is wielding an unbreakable crossbow.

In Athanasius, a devil disguised as a queen urges Anthony's renunciation of the monkish life in favour of *an active life of loving service among his fellow men.*[183] The queen presents herself as engaged in works of charity on a massive scale; if Anthony will marry her, he can join her in these works. But Anthony will not deviate from his hermit's life. He is adamant that a monk must stick to his vocation: the *vita contempliva* of removal from the world. To a man who inquires of him how one may be saved, Anthony replies, *A monk who goes out into the world is like a fish on dry land.*[184]

This seems to be the source of the beached fish that is such a prominent feature of Bruegel's image. Why is it beached, however, on a gigantic head? In the same passage, Anthony concludes, *Through his solitary life a hermit escapes the temptation of hearing, sight, and speech, and has only to fight against his own heart.* The huge head in the centre of the picture thus relates to the temptations of hearing, sight, and speech, against which the person living in the world must struggle. Other grotesque disembodied heads of this kind appear in *Temptations* from workshops in Amsterdam and Antwerp between 1525 and 1550 (c.f. fig. 47),[185] but it was Bruegel's idea to enlarge the head to giant proportions and set it afloat. In two later painted *Temptations*, variations based on this design, the giant head has half the top of its skull sliced open by a gang of tiny metamorphs wielding a huge knife.[186]

The head is the seat of the senses, the media of temptation; but an inhabited head has further connotations. The body was often described as the house of the soul. An illustration in a book published by Plantin in 1601 (fig. 34) gives a surreal interpretation of this theme.[187] It shows the head of a man as a house, complete with hair and neck ruff. The caption, in Latin, Dutch and French, warns against the mortal danger of leaving one's senses open to temptation. Bruegel's head seems to have the same significance. One eye is represented literally as a window, with some diamond panes broken and a fiery lantern on a stick poking out through the hole. The

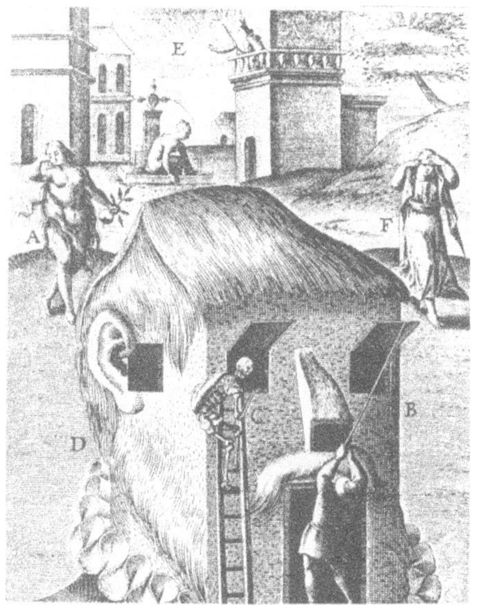

34 Theodore Galle, *The Mortal Danger of Leaving One's Senses Open to Temptation* (1601), from Jan David, *Veridicus Christianus* (Antwerp, 1606). Courtesy of Glasgow University Library

smoke from this torch, and the tongue-shaped smoke issuing from the open mouth, indicate a state of turmoil within. The head is threatened in various ways, apart from fire inside itself. Its other eye is pecked at by a hand-like appendage reaching down from a tree, itself growing on the head. Another attack is mounted by boat. Presumably in reaction to all this, a small figure emerges in a boat from the cave-like ear, his arms spread in a plea for help. He looks apparently for succor from the saint. Anthony, lost in contemplation, remains with his back turned to the head and its denizens.

This large head, of course, has no body. Barnouw suggested that the fish represents the Church and the head the State, both beset by corruption and decay,[188] and in fact the flag in front of the fish's mouth depicts a cross (clearer in the print than in the drawing), and two dangling seals of the kind used on papal bulls. This print is close in time to that of *Patience* (fig. 102), which includes bitter anticlerical images (see Chapter 5). Bruegel may already have inserted social satire into this *Temptation of St. Anthony*, in accordance with the general direction to which he turned metamorphic imagery in the late 1550s.[189] But whether fish and head have a satirical level of meaning or not, both are hollow receptacles for scenes of violence, and clearly the ensemble has been conceived of in psychological terms.

The many *sinnekens* whose bodies are displaced from their heads express rival modes of being to Anthony's effort to concentrate on his heart. For example, the creature above the saint, on the tree trunk, has a large head, no torso, and two limbs. This kind of hybrid is a *gryllus*, one of the few metamorphic bodies for which there is a name and a clear medieval line of descent.[190] It has a central position also in Bosch's Lisbon triptych *Temptations of St. Anthony*. Brion interpreted this creature as *a completely cerebral person, as he lacks a trunk, the site of the heart.*[191] According to Bergman,

> By representing him without a trunk, [Bosch] clearly demonstrates the man's lack of heart. Some may object that he lacks also other organs. One must assume, however, that the painter's symbolic idiom is restricted. Intellect and feeling have always been regarded as polarities, and it must be fundamental characteristics like these that the painter has wished to convey with corporal symbolism.[192]

Bruegel's *gryllus* has a scroll from which he reads. This refers to Anthony's temptation of the intellect: according to Athanasius, towards the end of the hermit's life, The Devil sent pagan scholars to assail his faith intellectually. The saint resisted their efforts to reduce questions of faith to the level of an intellectual dispute and defeated their shrewd words with the *wisdom of the cross*.[193] The theme of divided mind and body is represented by another motif, familiar from Bosch, and prominent here: the *jar-man*. Wertheim-Aymès argued that, in Bosch,

> various kinds of jars characteri[se] different spiritual states; an empty jar means that the "soul fluid" is dried up. A pot with a closed lid symbolizes the soul filled with divine substance.[194]

In Christian and Neo-Platonic mystic writings, the jar or pitcher is another metaphor for the body, the container of *spiritus*.[195] Bruegel's picture is filled with *sinnekens* whose bodies are hollow containers; like small deconstructions of the huge inhabited head. Such creatures also recall the medical stereotypes of nightmares, that someone suffering from a disturbed imagination thinks *he has no head*, or *believes that he is an earthenware jar*.[196] In the fore-ground, Bruegel's jar-man has its head concealed (indeed, visually replaced) by a large conical hat. From his hollow rear neck, fluid pours out. A figure astride a floating barrel jousts at this jar-man The barrel-rider also has a hat where his face should be, and a second figure crouches inside his barrel. The other notable context where a barrel rider appears in Bruegel is the figure of Prince Carnival (fig. 71), also an allegorical contest involving gluttony and abandonment to appetite. The fighting barrel-man and jar-man here are one end of a chain of cameos on the bank which lead towards the figure of Anthony.Other jars in the print have similar implications. A headless and armless figure on the tree protruding from the giant head has attached an empty jar. Another jug is hooked on a javelin inside the fish; the fiery smoke from the lantern below curls ominously around it. The figure bailing out the mouth of the giant head uses a jar. It may be attempting to save the head from foundering in the water; it may also be *expending spirit* — further draining the head of life-giving *soul fluid*. A figure inside a kind of lobster pot on the back of a fish, in between the jar-man and the gigantic head, may refer to the soul's imprisonment by the body; it may be a kind of parodic alchemical *athanor*, the crucible or container in which the soul is purified before reaching enlightenment.

The overall meaning is clear. Anthony's temptations are represented as to do with dangers lurking in the head. The head symbolises both the divorced of body and intellect, and the seat of the sensory temptations rejected by the hermit. Grotesque as the centrepiece is, elements of comedy are present. In the expression of the fisherman yelling for help, the parody of a joust between barrel-rider and jar-man, and the cameo behind the saint of the winged devil and legless, frog-like monster — there are indications of a kind of desperate exasperation on the part of the metamorphs against St. Anthony. The winged devil tugs at his reluctant comrade's arm, in an effort to bring him closer to the saint, though the frog-like one's legless anatomy makes it impossible for him to stand up straight or to take a step towards Anthony. This creature wields a knife in his right hand, but looks more likely to use it against himself than against Anthony. None of the other hybrids on Anthony's cut-off triangle of land seem particularly threatening. Some peer monkeyishly around the hollow tree, possibly another fake *athanor*, with lute player seated on a pig.[197] Where Bosch confers a mysterious and frightening aspect on his jar-man, Bruegel lightens the image by making the neck of his jar his rectum.

The difference in the style of conception between Bosch prototypes and Bruegel's comic recasting of them can be expressed psychoanalytically. Kris explains that,

> Whereas in dreams, owing to the operation of the primary process, thoughts undergo distortion until they become quite unrecognizable, in wit... the distortion is only carried through by half, and is subject to the ego's control; a thought is disguised rather than distorted, its distortion is pressed only so far as is consistent with its remaining intelligible to the first comer.[198]

The calm demeanor of Anthony in Bruegel's print, and the evident frustration and futility in the forms of his surrounding metamorphs, suggests that the saint's ego is more in control, less severely beleaguered by the representation of its baser selves, than, for example, Bosch's St. Anthony at Lisbon. The internal conflict, despite the fearsome central image, is tempered around its margins with playfulness. This quality, too, refers to the specific nature of Anthony's temptations in the "head of the world."

> The comic originates in the conflict between instinctual trends and the superego's repudiation of them... its position [is] midway between pleasure and unpleasure. These are the roots of its double-edged character... As its next relation in the household of man's mind, we may accept play... the play of adults which, like their comic invention, may be partially understood in terms of a "holiday from the superego."[199]

In a sense, Bruegel's picture presents the temptation of Anthony in these terms: as a conflict between instinctual trends and the superego's repudiation of them. The emphasis on bodily (rather than, say, astrological or alchemical) symbolism for the hybrid metamorphs exchanges the cosmic tone of Bosch for the comic. The imagery of nightmare is no longer presented as apocalyptic, in the sense that the Lisbon triptych likens the whole of Anthony's ordeals to the destiny of humanity since the Fall. Instead, dramas staged literally as conflicts of the body are grounded in the social world. The view of the unconscious that his metamorphic pictures present comes closer to modern clinical observations of the lack of affect, or dire triviality, characteristic of mental pathologies involving loss of control of the ego:

> In all these states... the world is taken apart, undermined, reduced to anarchy and chaos. There ceases to be any "centre" to the mind... The end point of such states is an unfathomable "silliness," an abyss of superficiality, in which all is ungrounded and afloat and comes apart.[200]

The religious meaning that Bosch manages to give to his hybrid denizens of Purgatory is thus side-stepped. In Bruegel's most horrible metamorphs (such as the castrating figure in *Luxuria*, fig. 15), the horror lies in self-mutilation rather than in mutilation by an outside (occult, or divine) agency. Since (as we saw in the *Malleus*), occult agencies, even demons, ultimately depend on God's authority, this "down-sizing" of the demonic in Bruegel represents an important shift. His concept of the infernal comes closer to that of Christopher Marlowe, thirty or so years later, giving Faust these answers when he questions Mephistopheles on the nature of Hell:

Faust	Where are you damned?
Meph.	In hell.
Faust	How comes it then that you art out of hell?
Meph.	Why this is hell, nor am I out of it.

I.iv. 80f

Meph.	Hell hath no limits, nor is circumscribed. In one self place, for where we are is hell. And where hell is there must we ever be.

Dr. Faustus, c. 1588-92, II.ii.121-3

Bruegel's metamorphic imagery is still founded on the esoteric structure of paradox, on the same Renaissance fascination with doubleness that Wind discerned in the Orphic monsters of the Humanists. But his inventions emphasise the ridiculous aspect of the human hybrid, and this entails a change in the moral weight of the imagery. The *spirit of sacred drollerie* mutates in his art into something more stoic and less sacred. How Bruegel derived comedy from this somewhat chilling view of the chameleon man, in his major metamorphic pictures, the *Dulle Griet* and its related prints, is the subject of the next chapter.

Notes to Chapter 1

[1] This chapter draws on materials in my PhD dissertation, *Dreams and Popular Beliefs in the Imagery of Pieter Bruegel the Elder* (Boston University, 1990).
[2] As is evident in G. Unverfehrt's study, *Hieronymous Bosch: die Rezeption seiner Kunst im frühen 16 Jahrhundert* (Berlin, 1980). Unverfehrt illustrates mainly anonymous works which stick remarkably to these few categories (151-186, 201-222); also popular are metamorphic versions of St. Christopher (187-200). M. Eemans, *La Peinture Flamande de la Renaissance* (Brussels, 1968), 8, lists known Southern Netherlandish followers of Bosch up to the time of Bruegel.
[3] See J. Koldeweij, P. Vandenbroeck & Bernard Vermet, eds, *Hieronymus Bosch: The Complete Paintings and Drawings* (Rotterdam; Ghent-Amsterdam, 2001); for a survey of earlier Bosch scholarship, J. Snyder, ed., *Bosch in Perspective* (Englewood Cliffs, N.J., 1973.
[4] See H. Lenneberg's article "Bosch's *Garden of Earthly Delights*, some musicological considerations and criticisms," *Gazette des Beaux Arts* 103 (1961), 135f. for arguments against the assumption that in the Renaissance musicians and the art of music had a bad reputation; though some aspects of music were still criticized (e.g., its use in the theater), the status of the art as a whole had never stood higher at this period.
[5] On the retorts specifically, L. Dixon, *Alchemical Imagery in Bosch's Garden of Delights Triptych* (Michigan, 1981), passim. On Bosch and alchemy in general, J. Van Lennep, *Art et Alchimie* (Brussels, 1966), ch. IX, 213-222.
[6] C. G. Jung, *Psychology and Alchemy*, and *Alchemical Studies*, volumes 12 and 13 respectively in the *Collected Works* (London, 1967-1972). For a fine summary of Jung's model, see B. J. T. Dobbs, *The Foundations of Newton's Alchemy, or "The Hunting of the Greene Lyon"* (Cambridge, 1975), 26-43.
[7] For a Bosch painting representing this theme in a relatively clear and uncomplicated way, see W. Fraenger's 1957 article ("Die Versuchungen des hl. Antonius von Hieronymous Bosch") on the small *Temptation of St. Anthony* in the Prado, reprinted in his *Hieronymous Bosch* (Dresden, 1975), 299-306.
[8] E. Panofsky, *Early Netherlandish Painting* (Cambridge, 1971), 1, 357,510-11; hereafter, *ENP*.
[9] J. Baltrusaitis, *Le Moyen-Age Fantastique* (Paris, 1955) observed that Anthony's aerial excursion has no direct model in the literary sources; M. Bergman, *Hieronymous Bosch and Alchemy* (Stockholm, 1979), 54.
[10] On the popularity of Prodigal Son motifs in the painting and pageantry of sixteenth century Antwerp, see W. S. Gibson, who points out that, "the terse bib-

lical parable has been transformed into an elaborate allegory of Everyman's progress through the world," in several Prodigal Son cycles of the earlier sixteenth century, "Artists and Rederijkers in the Age of Bruegel," *Art Bulletin* LXIII (September, 1981), 435ff. Cf. R. Helgerson, *The Elizabethan Prodigals* (Berkeley, 1977).

[11] Bergman, 31-35, sees many difficulties in D. Bax's attempts (*Hieronymous Bosch, his picture writing deciphered*, trans. M. A. Bax-Botha [Rotterdam,1979]) to link specific monsters in Bosch's Lisbon triptych of *St. Anthony* to proverbs about the evils of drink, incontinence, etc.

[12] Cf. the cult of the "hybrid" Pangolin among the Lele; a scaly ant-eater which is an anomaly in terms of the strict categories of edible and inedible animals; its corpse is treated "as a living chief" and surrounded by mysteries; M. Douglas, *Purity and Danger. An Analysis of the Concepts of Pollution and Taboo* (London, 1984), 168-69.

[13] This is the formulation in Ernest Jones, *Nightmares, Witches, and Devils* (New York, 1931), 68.

[14] Cf. R. Colie, *Paradoxia Epidemica: The Renaissance Tradition of Paradox* (Princeton, 1966).

[15] M. J. B. Allan has compiled Ficino's references to this image, published as *Marsiglio Ficino and the Phaedran Charioteer: Introduction, Texts, Translations* (Berkeley, 1981).

[16] For 16C definitions of monsters: I. Maclean, *The Renaissance Notion of Woman. A Study in the Fortunes of Scholasticism and Medical Science in European Intellectual Life* (Cambridge, 1980), 30, 103, n. 18. Cf. J. Céard, *La nature et les prodiges: l'insolite au 16e siècle, en France* (Geneva, 1977); K. Park and L. J. Daston, "Unnatural Conceptions: The Study of Monsters in Sixteenth- and Seventeenth-Century France and England," *Past and Present* 92 (1981), 20-54.

[17] Leonardo on "How to make an imaginary animal appear natural." in *The Notebooks of Leonardo da Vinci*, ed., trans. & intro. E. MacCurdy (New York, 1939), 890-1.

[18] Maclean, 2, applies this term to refer to certain agreed-upon scholarly generalisations:

> It is generally accepted that after the establishment of printing as a means of disseminating texts, and before the development of strong vernacular and national intellectual traditions, there was a "universe of discourse" expressed principally in Latin (but including also texts translated into various vernacular languages), which possessed common assumptions about academic disciplines. The temporal limits of this universe are not easily set, but they include the sixteenth century and

> the early part of the seventeenth. Its geographical boundaries encompass all European countries which received books published on matters of common academic interest and perhaps also produced them: principally Italy, France, Germany, Spain, Great Britain and the Low Countries. Common academic interests include theology, medicine, law and "practical philosophy" (ethics and politics)... All possess authoritative texts which attract commentary...

[19] The framework in this chapter is largely that of the history of ideas. Details of publication are given where needed to demonstrate a continuity or a novelty.

[20] G. D. Hadzitts, *Lucretius and his Influence* (New York, 1963), 269.

[21] Lucretius, *De naturis rerum*, Loeb trans. W. H. D. Rowse (1928), V. 890-924.

[22] E. Wind, *Pagan Mysteries in the Renaissance*, rev. ed. (New York, 1968),89, on Pico; 204ff. on Cusanus' *complicatio*.

[23] Lucretius, V, 890-924.

[24] Ibid., 838-50.

[25] E. Panofsky, *Studies in Iconology. Humanistic Themes in the Art of the Renaissance* (1939; New York, 1972), 55.

[26] W. S. Gibson, *Hieronymus Bosch* (Oxford, 1972), 60.

[27] Bosch's principle of mixing normal and fabulous animals together in this landscape is seen at its most lyrical in the group of deer and horses drinking at the central pool at the far right. Among them is a unicorn. Rabelais mentions that "the unicorn purified the water of pools and springs so [that] various animals could drink in safety after it." *Gargantua and Pantagruel*, trans. J.M. Cohen (1955), Book 5, 676.

[28] As discussed by Panofsky (1972), ch 2.

[29] The Church, not unnaturally, condemned Palmieri's heresy when his *Cittá di vita* was published posthumously (Basel, 1532). Book III, 173f, concludes with this passage:

> Nihil enim aliquid quicumque ei naturae, quam tam pulchram , tam ingeniosam et tam sapientem ac tam opulentam, tam dignam et tam potentem, postremo tam felicem et tam beatam constituerat, ad totam et undique absolutam perfectionem suam deesse putabatur, nisi ut ea per admixtionem cum ipsa divinitate, non solum coniuncta in illa Christi persona cum divina, sed etiam ut cum divina natura una et sola efficeretur, ac per hunc modum unica fact fuisse videretur. Quod neque angelis neque ulli aliae creaturae, nisi homini duntaxat, ad admirabilem quondam humanae naturae dignitatem, et ad incredibilem quoque eius ipsius excellentiam, datum, concessum at attributum esse novimus.

See I. Lavin, "On the Sources and Meaning of the Renaissance Portrait Bust," *Art Quarterly* XXXIII (1970), 222, n 38; for an illuminating discussion of the subject in relation to the concept of the *totus homo*, 213f.

[30] Lavin, 213. The *Cittá di Vita* was written in the 1450s and 1460s. On Palmieri's impact on cultural life, see M. Davies, *National Gallery Catalogues. The Earlier Italian Schools*, 2nd ed. (London,1961), 122-7.

[31] *The Corpus Hermeticum*, trans. A. J. Festugière (*La Revelation d'Hermes Trismegiste* v.1, [Paris, 1950]); P. J. French, *John Dee. The World of an Elizabethan Magus* (London, 1972), 73.

[32] Ibid., 64.

[33] Rabelais, 321.

[34] C. D. Cuttler, *Northern Painting. From Pucelle to Bruegel* (New York, 1968); he comments they are "elongated into a super-Gothicised slenderness," 476.

[35] Ibid.

[36] Frans Floris' *Last Judgement* (1565; Musées Royaux des Beaux-Arts, Brussels).

[37] These are reminiscent of the biting creatures interlaced together in Dark Age carvings from Northern Europe. Here, perhaps, as elsewhere, Bruegel shows his familiarity with manuscript painting traditions. Fierens, 10, briefly considers Celtic mss. antecedents for Flemish fantasy.

[38] Vaguely insectoid angels appear also in Bruegel's *The Last Judgement* print (1558; fig. 90).

[39] Bruegel used archaic Flemish models in a number of religious works, e.g., *The Procession to Calvary* (1564; Kunsthistorisches Museum Wien, Vienna) and the *Death of the Virgin* (1564; fig. 92).

[40] See Chapter 5.

[41] See Chapter Four, section 2; cf. also the Boschian satire on chivalry, fig. 55.

[42] Panofsky (1972), 55, n. 60, mentions an instance in early medieval art where a metamorphic menagerie appears in a representation of the Garden of Eden. None of its members, however, are human-headed.

[43] Cima da Conegliano attempted to give a "realistic" appearance to the classical satyrs in his *Procession of Silenus* by making the cast of their faces unmistakably Negroid; Panofsky (1972), 55, reads this as a more "scientific" reflection of Pliny's people.

[44] *De Naturis Rerum*, Bibliothèque de Bruges no. 411, described in P. Fierens, *Le Fantastique dans l'art flamand* (Brussels, 1947), 25.

[45] From Racine's second preface to *Bajazet*, trans. in P. Burke, *The Renaissance Sense of the Past* (New York, 1969), 6.

[46] See tabulation of classical sources for the *Adages* in M. M. Phillips, *The "Adages" of Erasmus. A Study with Translations* (Cambridge, 1964), 400.
[47] Pliny, *Historia Naturalis*, 7:2; Philemon Holland, translator (1601): *C. Plinius Secundus The Historie of the World*. Book VII, 152-191.
[48] See R. Bernheimer, *Wild Men in the Middle Ages. A Study in Art, Sentiment and Demonology* (Cambridge, 1952), 5-6, on suites of playing card designs which show a continuous progression between apes, wildmen, peasants and knights.
[49] G. Strauss, "A Sixteenth Century Encyclopaedia: Sebastian Munster's Cosmography and its Editions" in C. H. Carter, ed., *From the Renaissance to the Counter-reformation* (New York, 1965), 148; cf. E. W. Gudger, "Pliny's *Historia Naturalis*. The Most Popular Natural History Ever Published," *Isis*, 6 (1924), 269-81.
[50] M. Hodgen, *Early Anthropology in the Sixteenth and Seventeenth Centuries* (Philadelphia, 1964), 30-31, 33, 182-85, on eyewitness reports of New World hybrids.
[51] Fierens, 22-5.
[52] Hodgen, 127.
[53] Ibid., 35.
[54] E. Jones, *Nightmare, Witches, and Devils* (New York, 1931), 69.
[55] Ibid.
[56] E. P. Evans, *The Criminal Prosecution and Capital Punishment of Animals* (New York, 1906), 354-55.
[57] Evans, 287.
[58] Jones, ibid.
[59] Bailly's text was first printed at Lyons in 1668; reprinted in Evans, 287-306; his case illustrates the effects of Descartes' theory of mechanism, marking the formal beginning of the sharp modern demarcation between human and animal.
[60] Jones, ibid.
[61] Jakob Sprenger and Heinrich Kramer, *Malleus Maleficarum* (Speier, c 1486), Part I, Quaestion 10; trans. M. Summers (London, 1948), 64. For a summary of the work's influence, J. Klaits, *Servants of Satan* (Bloomington, 1985), 44-7.
[62] *Malleus*, ibid., 64-5. On the "organ of persuasion," cf. D. Summers, *The Judgement of Sense. Renaissance Naturalism and the Rise of Aesthetics* (Cambridge, 1987), 64.
[63] Ibid.
[64] Ibid.
[65] Much of the literature on commentaries to the *Metamorphoses* focusses on issues of classical survivals. The classic studies here are still J. Seznec, *The Survival of the*

Pagan Gods, trans. B. F. Sessions (New York, 1953), and E. Panofsky, *Renaissance and Renascences in Western Art* (2nd ed., New York, 1969), hereafter, *R&R*; see also L. Barkan, *The Gods Made Flesh. Metamorphosis and the Pursuit of Paganism* (New Haven, 1986), esp. ch. 3, 94-136, and bibliography, 306-17.

[66] Examples from Panofsky, R&R, 82-84, 92.

[67] For related issues, see M. Camille, "Seeing and Reading: Some Visual Implications of Medieval Literacy and Illiteracy," *Art History* 8(1) (1985), 26-49.

[68] Seznec, 90ff.

[69] Ibid., 51.

[70] Camille, 32.

[71] *Ovidius Moralizatus* (c 1342), trans. W. D. Reynolds, *The Ovidius Moralizatus of Pierre Bersuire; An Introduction and Translation* (Ph.D dissertation, University of Illinois at Urbana-Champaign, 1971), 142.

[72] Ibid., 162.

[73] Ibid.

[74] Ibid., 183.

[75] Ibid., 220.

[76] Ibid., 221.

[77] Ibid.

[78] M. Lowry, *The World of Aldus Manutius* (Ithaca, 1979), 45, n. 94.

[79] Gibson, "Artists and *Rederijkers*," 426, n. 4, lists authorities who have commented on "parallels in subject matter and thought between 16th century artists and rederijkers;" cf. the essays in J. Koopmans et al, eds, *Rhetoric-Rhétoriqueurs-Rederijkers* (Royal Netherlands Academy of Arts and Sciences: Amsterdam-Oxford, 1995), by R. L. Falkenburg, "Pieter Aertsen, Rhyparographer," 197-217; and by N. Serebrennikov, "'Dwelck den Mensche, aldermeest tot Consten verwect'. The Artist's Perspective," 219-246.

[80] "Mais ces traducteurs, insuffisamment penétrés de l'esprit de l'Antiquité, assimilent trop leurs originaux au milieu où ils vivent eux-mêmes; puis, le besoin de moraliser continue de défigurer les ouvrages classiques. Van Ghistele, en traduisent les *Métamorphoses*, prêche la sainteté du mariage, la version des *Héroïdes* est destinée à faire fuir les séductions de Vénus; celle de *l'Ars amatoria* a été enterprise pour exterminer le vice impur d'un amour déshonnête," S. Eringa, *La Renaissance et les rhétoriqueurs néerlandais* (Amsterdam, 1920), 3; my trans.

[81] Matthieu de Casteleyn, *Const van Rethoriken*, stanza 20; Eringa, 30.

[82] Ibid.

[83] M. Meiss, "Sleep in Venice. Ancient Myths and Renaissance Proclivities," *Proceedings of the American Philosophical Society* 110 (5) (1966), 359.
[84] Ibid.
[85] S. R. Jayne, "M. Ficino's Commentary on Plato's Symposium" *University of Missouri Studies* XIX (1944), 20.
[86] R. and M. Wittkower, *Born Under Satan. The Character and Conduct of Artists: A Documented History from Antiquity to the French Revolution* (New York-London, 1963), 104. The authors make it clear that they consider this phenomenon as a fashion, comparable to the "Angry Young Man" ethos of the 1950s.
[87] See G. D. Painter, *The Hypnerotomachia Poliphili of 1499: An Introduction on the Dream, the Dreamer, the Artist, and the Printer* (London, 1963), 4-7.
[88] Francesco Colonna, *Hypnerotomachia Poliphili: the strife of love in a dream*, trans. & intro. J. Godwin (New York, 1999), 174.
[89] *Antwerp Songbook* (Antwerp, 1544), no. XLIX (cf. also CVIII, CXXXIV); Eringa, 6.
[90] Gaspara Stampa (1523-54), Lyrics, trans. in G. Kay, ed., *The Penguin Book of Italian Verse* (Harmondsworth, 1965), 177.
[91] Ibid., 178.
[92] Ibid., 179.
[93] Ibid., 180.
[94] Ibid., 181.
[95] T. Weevers, *Poetry of the Netherlands In Its European Context* (London, 1960), 72; cf. 67.
[96] For Ficino's influence in the North, see, e.g., H. Haydn, *The Counter-Renaissance* (New York, 1950).
[97] According to T. Riggs, *Hieronymous Cock (1510-1570): Printer and Publisher at the Sign of the Four Winds* (New York, 1977), 361, this undated engraving is "based on a painting sold at Sotheby's, May 17, 1961, no. 34." Vasari's original 1544 painting was much copied, and this print was made after a copy; cf. L. De Pauw-De Veen, *Jérôme Cock, Editeur d'estampes et graveur 1507?-1570,* Exhibition catalogue, Bibliothèque Royale Albert 1er, Brussels, 1970, cat. no. 136, 55-6.
[98] According to T. Riggs, *Hieronymous Cock (1510-1570): Printer and Publisher at the Sign of the Four Winds* (New York, 1977), 361, this undated engraving is "based on a painting sold at Sotheby's, May 17, 1961, no. 34." Vasari's original 1544 painting was much copied, and this print was made after a copy; cf. L. De Pauw-De Veen, *Jérôme Cock, Editeur d'estampes et graveur 1507?-1570,* Exhibition catalogue, Bibliothèque Royale Albert 1er, Brussels, 1970, cat. no. 136, 55-6.
[99] See Wind, ch. XIII, 191ff; for the philosophical import given to classical myth generally, Seznec, 97ff.

[100] Pico, *De hominis dignitate*, 225-26, in *The Renaissance Philosophy of Man*, ed. and trans. E. Cassirer, P. O. Kristeller and J. H. Randall, Jr., (Chicago, 1948), 223-54.
[101] Ibid.
[102] H. P. Duerr, *Dreamtime: concerning the boundary between wilderness and civilization* (1978), trans. F. Goodman (Oxford, 1985), 270, n. 19.
[103] Plato, *The Republic*, trans. W. H. D. Rowse (New York, 1960), 389-390.
[104] Ibid.
[105] Pico, 225.
[106] For this background see J. C. M. van Winden, *Calcidius on Matter: His Doctrine and Sources; a Chapter in the History of Platonism*, trans. B. de Goede and S. J. P. van Dijk (Leiden, 1959); S. Gersh, *Middle Platonism and Neoplatonism: The Latin Tradition* (Notre Dame, IN, 1986), 421-492.
[107] Plato, *Timaeus and Critias*, trans. D. Lee (1965), 122.
[108] Ibid., 123.
[109] Ibid.
[110] See Summers, ch. 5, 71-109 on the common sense and 71-5 on Leonardo's *senso commune*, his studies of skulls, and the passage in his *Treatise on Painting*: "The eye that is called the window of the soul is the principal way whence the common sense may most copiously and magnificently consider the infinite works of nature."
[111] Pico, 226.
[112] Ibid.
[113] Plato, 123-4.
[114] St. Jerome, quoted in P. Cox, "Origen and the Bestial Soul. A Poetics of Nature," *Vigilae Christianae* 36 (1982), 115. On the revival of origin and his theories of metempsychosis, see D. P. Walker, *The Decline of Hell* (Chicago, 1964), 11-15 and passim.
[115] Pico, 226-27.
[116] Rabelais, 322.
[117] Wind, 199-200, 204.
[118] Weevers, 104.
[119] Ibid., 106.
[120] Karl van Mander, *Schilderboek* (Haarlem, 1604), 233. S. Hindman, "Pieter Bruegel's *Children's Games*, Folly and Chance," *Art Bulletin* LXIII (3) (September, 1981), 168, nn. 147-9, realised that C. Van der Waal's translation of this phrase as "innumerable little clever things" (in his *Dutch and Flemish Painters* [New York, 1936], 156) was too vague.
[121] Clare Robertson, "Annibal Caro as Iconographer: Sources and Methods,",*Journal of the Warburg and Courtauld Institutes* 45 (1982), 160-181. As Robertson points out, such elaborate programmes, involving a professional

iconographer (Caro was a poet, translator of the classics and secretary to Alessandro Farnese) are
only documented from the mid-sixteenth century; in other words, the fruitful collision of classical knowledge, patron and artist had by this date become fully formalised and had given rise to a new kind of professional expert. The cases of Mantegna, Bellini and Dürer (among others) can be cited to show that this kind of interchange existed well before the publication of works such as Vicenzo Cartari's *Le imagini con la spositione de i dei degli antici* (Venice, 1556), which should be seen as a response to developments in art, rather than as a trigger for them.

[122] See Milne (1990), ch. 1; W. S. Gibson, "Bosch's Dreams: A Response to the Art of Bosch in the Sixteenth Century," *Art Bulletin*, LXXIV (2) (June, 1992), 205-218.

[123] Michiel's tantalising remarks are analysed in F. Gandolfo, *Il "Dolce Tempo," Mistica, Ermetismo e Sogno nel Cinquecento* (Rome, 1978), 84; cf. C. de Tolnay, *Hieronymous Bosch* (Baden-Baden, 1966), 353; J. Fletcher, "Marcantoni Michiel: his friends and his collection," *Burlington Magazine* 123 (1981), 453-67.

[124] See Introduction for Bruegel as a Second Bosch; Domenicus Lampsonius, *Les Effigies des peintres célèbrés des Pays-Bas* (1572), ed. J. Puraye (Liège, 1956), 61, no. 19.

[125] *Trattato dell' arte della pittura* (1584), in his *Scritti sulle arte*, ed. R. P. Ciardi (Florence, 1973-4), v. 2, 305; John Florio's Italian-English dictionary translates *spaventevoli* as *terrible, frightfull, dreadfull, astonishing* (London, 1611).

[126] On Henry Cornelius Agrippa, see C. G. Nauert, *Agrippa and the Crisis of Renaissance Thought* (Urbana, IL., 1965).

[127] The *Libro dei sogni* is reproduced in the *Scritti sulle arti* (as in n. 122 above), v.1, 1-240. See Ciardi's *Introduction,* xxxvi ff, lxxxi-lxxxii, for probable date of composition and sources, especially the use made of Agrippa of Nettesheim. As Gandolfo (288) notes, Cardan is directly quoted, e.g. on 194. On Lomazzo, see R. Klein, "*I sette governatori dell' arte* secondo Lomazzo," in *La Forma e l'intelligibile* (Turin, 1975), 178-199.

[128] *The Essays and Hymns of Synesius of Cyrene, including the Address to the Emperor Arcadius and the Political Speeches*, trans. w. intro and notes, A. Fitzgerald (London, 1930), 355.

[129] On Bosch's reputation in Italy (though not in esoteric circles), see B. Aikema, "Hieronymus Bosch and Italy?," in J. Koldeweij and B. Vermet, eds, *Hieronymus Bosch. New Insights into His Life and Work* (Rotterdam, 2001), 25-31.

[130] On sleep and Venetian humanist art, see Meiss, 348-382; Maria Ruvoldt, *The Italian Renaissance Imagery of Inspiration: Metaphors of Sex, Sleep, and Dream* (Cambridge, 2004), 122-140, relates the work to Ficino and Neo-Platonism and lists Italian prototypes for sleeping nudes.

[131] The connection between these images, and their links to Bosch, was first proposed by Guy de Tervarent, "Instances of Flemish Influence in Italian Art," *Burlington Magazine* 85 (1944), 290-4; see also Gibson (1992).
[132] See G. F. Hartlaub, "Giorgione im graphischen Nachbild," *Pantheon* XVIII (2) (1960), 76-85; also Gandolfo, 77-112.
[133] For more on this work, see Chapter 2.
[134] H. W. Janson, *Apes and Ape Lore in the Middle Ages and the Renaissance* (London, 1952), 216-25, fig. 13-14, pl. XL-XLIII; see Michel Weemans, "Herri met de Bles's sleeping peddler: an exegetical and anthropomorphic landscape," *Art Bulletin*, LXXXVIII (3), Sept, 2006, 459-482. An early 17C panel shows a young dreamer like Bruegel's pedlar leaning on a large sphere while troop of costumed apes dance around him. According to Janson,"the symbolic sphere is instability;" 216. A similar sphere appears in Michelangelo's much-copied drawing, *The Dream*, discussed by M. Zehnpfennig, *Traum und Vision in Darstellungen des 16. und 17. Jahrhunderts* (Hanover, 1979), 31-91; the meaning seems to be similar to that of Fortuna's sphere. In 1981 the painting was in the collection of D. Richardson, Cambridge, Mass.; Janson, 169, says it is "of uncertain date and provenance but reflects a Flemish prototype of the very early seventeenth century, probably a print."
[135] J. Adhémar, "French Caricatures of the Sixteenth Century," *Graphis* 10 (54) (1954), 343, discussing Francois Desprez's book; cf. the facsimile edition, F. Desprez, *Les songes drolatiques de Pantagruel, ou son contenues 120 figures de l'invention de Maitre Francois Rabelais; copiees en fac-simile par Jules Morel sur l'edition de 1565, pour la recreation des bons esprits, avec un texte explicatif et des notes par Le Grand Jacques (pseud)* (Paris, 1869).
[136] For more on Bruegel's satires, see Chapter 2.
[137] *Ambrosii Theodosii Macrobii Commentarii in Somnium Scipionis*, ed. Jacob Willis (Leipzig 1970); *Macrobius, Commentary on the Dream of Scipio*, trans. W. H. Stahl, *Records of Civilization, Sources and Studies*, XLVIII (New York-London, 1952).
[138] Macrobius, *Commentary on Scipio's Dream*, bk. 1, ch. 3; trans. W. H. Stahl (New York, 1952), 87-92. For data on the etymology of *ephialtes* and other early European names, W. H. Roscher (1900), "Ephialtes: A pathological-mythological Treatise on the Nightmare in classical antiquity," trans. A. V. O'Brien, included in J. Hillman, *Pan and the Nightmare* (Irving, TX, 1979), 45-57.
[139] W. C. Curry, *Chaucer and the Medieval Sciences* (rev. ed. New York, 1960), 207ff, to whom I am indebted for many references here. J. Le Goff, *The Medieval Imagination*, trans. A. Goldhammer (Chicago, 1988), devotes two essays to dreams: one on the Christian patristic interpretative tradition, before and after Macrobius, the other on a thirteenth-century German epic. In the Middle Ages, Augustine was thought to have commented on Macrobius's ideas about nightmare in the famous treatise *De Spiritu et Anima*, ch. 25, now not accepted as authentic.

[140] On the *visio intellectuale*, see Augustine, *De Spiritu et Anima* (attributed), ch. 24-25; *Liber de Divinatione Daemonun*, ch. 5; and *De Genesi ad Literam*, bk. 12, ch. 7; cf. also Thomas Aquinas, *Quaestio XII*, art. xiii, in *Opera*, vol. 7. Cf. Le Goff, 193-229 (esp. 202, 214-8 on Augustine) discusses the Christianisation of dream theory.
[141] Le Goff, ibid., 204-5, 227f., Bede's *Ecclesiastical History*, and in a more sophisticated way, Jacob Voragine's *Golden Legend* are full of dream encounters with deceased saints.
[142] Peter of Abano, quoting Avicenna (*Compendium de Anima*, bk. 4, printed at Venice in 1546) in his *Liber Conciliator differentiarum philosopherum precipuegne medicorum appelatus*, CLVII, fol. 202.
[143] Guido Bonatus, *Liber astronomicus, decem continens tractatus astronomie*, publ. Erhard Ratdolt, Augsburg, 1491; Venice, 1506 (by Aldus Manutius); Basel, 1550; later Basel editions (1533, 1551) by M. Pruckner follow the Aldine text; Albohazen Haly, *Praeclarissimus liber completus in judiciis astrorum* ("The very famous complete book on the judgment of the stars"), trans. Erhard Ratdolt (Venice, 1485); reprinted as *De iudiciis astrorum* Basel, 1551.
[144] *Expositiones visionum quae fiunt in somnia* (1524), 625f.; especially ch. 4. This work was printed among Arnold's *Complete Works*, but it is in fact by William of Aragon, as L. Thorndike has shown, *A History of Magic and Experimental Science*, (New York, 1924), vol. 2, ch. 50, 302. Editions of Arnaldus's *Opera* were printed at Lyon in 1504 and 1532, at Basel in 1585, at Frankfurt in 1603, and at Lyon in 1686.
[145] Rabelais (c. 1542), bk. 3, ch. 13, 321.
[146] *Marsiglio Ficino: The Book of Life. A Translation by Charles Boer of "Liber de Vita" (or De Vita Triplici)* (Irving, TX., 1980), 86-183.
[147] So Vincent de Beauvais says that "Dreams are diversified... in accordance with the seasons; in spring and autumn they are particularly confused, disordered and false," in his thirteenth-century encyclopedia, the *Speculum Naturale*, bk. 26, ch. 1; see Curry, 211; Thorndike, v. 2, ch. 56.
[148] Jean Thibault was a printer at Antwerp in 1519 but seems to have left that city under a cloud; we next hear of him in 1530 when Agrippa of Nettesheim wrote an invective against the physicians of Antwerp on his behalf. Cf. Thorndike, v. 6, 478. On *La Physiognomie* as the source of the *Grooten dubbelen Droomboek* and on the general popularity of dreambooks, see E. H. Van Heurck, *Les Livres Populaires Flamands* (Antwerp, 1931), 142-4.
[149] Rabelais, 322-23.
[150] Thorndike, v. 2, 296.
[151] Rabelais, 323.
[152] Van Heurck, 143-4. This astrological work, a kind of annotated *Kalendrier des Bergers*, was published at Antwerp in 1554.
[153] R. and M. Wittkower, 103.

[154] F. Yates, *The Occult Philosophy in the Elizabethan Age* (London, 1983), 33-34.
[155] Heinrich Cornelius Agrippa, *De Occulta Philosophia*, Bk. 1, part 3, ch 59, Of Divination by Dreams; cf. Bk 3., part 4, ch. 51, Of Prophetic Dreams; also C. G. Nauert, *Agrippa and the Crisis of Renaissance Thought* (Urbana, 1965), 287-88.
[156] On the demonic idea of the nightmare, see Thorndike, v. 2, 299; Roscher; Jones, ch. II, III; on folk dreams, see 165, 265 below. The thirteenth century scholarly author cited by Thorndike explains that what vulgar folk think of as a demon sitting on the sleeper is really "a feeling of suffocation produced by blood-pressure near the heart." This eminently rational idea was jettisoned late in the fifteenth century by the authors of the *Malleus Maleficarum*, 109-14, who popularized the image of the witch copulating with an *incubus*. The latter thereby took on far more fearsome dimensions than it had previously possessed; sixteenth-century witch trial records and witch hunter's manuals are full of the natural history of the species. Cf. J. Klaits, 24; Jones, 89. This development is one more instance of the new interest in manifestations of the unconscious, since, as Jones' analysis makes clear, *incubi* appear in the context of sexual dreams.
[157] Galen says, "A dream indicates to us the condition of the body." *De dignotione ex insomniis* in his *Opera*, 4:213 (Venice, 1609); quoted in Curry, 205.
[158] Ibid., 223.
[159] Giovanni da Concorreggio, after Galen, *Practica nova* (Pavia, 1509), fol. 15v.
[160] R. Klibansky, E. Panofsky, F. Saxl, *Saturn and Melancholy* (London, 1964), 47.
[161] Ibid.
[162] Avicenna, *Compendium de anima* (Venice, 1546), bk. 3, ch. 18; Klibansky et al, 222.
[163] Klibansky et al, 223.
[164] A. de Villanova, *Opera Omnia* (Basel, 1524) pt. 1, ch. 4.
[165] Macrobius, bk. 1, ch. 3.
[166] Hesiod, *Theogony*, 200-225; Loeb trans. G. W. Most (2007), v. 1.
[167] Herodotus, *Histories*, 7.16b; Loeb trans. A. D. Godley (1922), v. 7.
[168] In Diogenes Laertes, *Lives of the Philosophers*, 8.32; Loeb trans. R. D. Hicks (1925), v. 2.
[169] Ovid, *Metamorphoses*, XI, 613-5; Loeb trans. F. J. Miller (1916), v. 2.
[170] Lucretius, *De naturis rerum*, IV. 724-744; 757-764; 818-822.
[171] For folklore examples of the penis as a dagger in dreams, see S. Freud and D. E. Oppenheim, *Dreams in Folklore* trans. from the MS of 1911 by B. L. Pacella (New York, 1958), 30-36.
[172] Bergman, 76.
[173] Ibid.
[174] Ibid, 76-77. However, R. Vervoort argues that the toad in Bosch is simply a symbol for the demonic, one of Satan's creatures: "The Pestilent Toad. The

Significance of the Toad in the Works of Bosch," in J. Koldeweij and B. Vermet (2001), 145-151.
[175] Ibid, 63.
[176] Zosimos's vision is translated and interpreted in C. Jung's *Alchemical Studies, Collected Works*, v.13, 57ff; also in F. S. Taylor, *The Alchemists* (London, 1951), 61.
[177] Taylor, 61.
[178] Ibid., 62-3.
[179] For Erasmus and Origen, see W. J. Bouwsma, *Concordia Mundi: The Career and Thought of Guillaume Postel (1510-1581)* (Cambridge, Mass., 1957), 112ff.
[180] The Bible itself is reticent on the visual characteristics of Hell and its devils: the forms of its demons and angels are rarely defined - they are simply messengers or spirits. Monstrous forms are rather confined to formal dreams and visions; thus Ezekiel and Daniel see hybrid supernatural bodies. Therefore, if a representation of the religious hero's adventures in a given text were the main aim of artworks employing Boschian imagery, then one could still point here to some connection between metamorphic creatures and certain canonical dreams and visions.
[181] Athanasius's *Vita*, trans. Bergman, 16-19.
[182] Ibid., 18.
[183] Ibid.
[184] Ibid.
[185] Unverfehrt reproduces several such *Temptations* (figs 140, 147-9); the ones he ascribes to Antwerp shops are: figure 140, cat. no. 98, c. 1525-30, whereabouts unknown, showing a moderately outsized human head with gaping mouth, embedded in the earth like a Hell-mouth, javelins protruding from eyes and nostrils; figure 149, cat. no. 135, c. 1540-50, where a decapitated head, resembling that of John the Baptist, again moderately outsized, dangles from a metamorphic tree. This print was in the possession of the Hallsborough Gallery, London, in 1970. I have not been able to obtain photographs of these works. The Jan Mandyn reproduced here is listed as a *Temptation of Anthony* but may actually be a *St. Christopher*. For reasons which remain unclear, the subject of Christopher as well as that of Anthony attracted Boschian imagery at this period. The explanation perhaps lies in a perceived connection between the image of Christopher carrying the Christ-child across the river, and the image of the river crossing as a metaphor for the soul's pilgrimage through life. The metamorphic components of these pictures would then, as for Anthony, represent temptations of the passions, and in general, of earthly existence.
[186] Ibid, 181f. As Unverfehrt argues, figures 137 and 138, cat. no. 139, in unknown collections, are two painted variants from around 1560 of a design based on Bruegel's print.

[187] Jan David, *Veridicus Christianae* (Antwerp, 1601). Our illustration comes from the 1606 ed., which used the same plates.
[188] A. J. Barnouw, *The Fantasy of Pieter Brueghel* (New York, 1947), 72.
[189] Some details are cryptic, such as the menacing bubble-like boat disgorging an army into water in the background; Barnouw sees this as an emblem of the Turkish threat to Christendom, ibid, 72.
[190] Around 1560, Felipe de Guevara referred to Bosch as a painter of *grilli* in his *Commentaries on Painting* (trans. Snyder, 28-30); *grillo* means 'cricket' and, by extraction, a metamorphic conceit. The name *gryllus* is usually applied, however, to figures lacking a trunk which follow the prototype on Raoul Aubry's pseudo-antique seal from the 1320s. See Baltrusaitis, 44f.
[191] M. Brion, *Bosch* (Paris, 1938), 48.
[192] Bergman, 33.
[193] Ibid., 17.
[194] C. Wertheim-Aymès, *Hieronymous Bosch. Eine Einführung in seine geheime Symbolik* (Berlin, 1957), 25f.
[195] Cf. Bergman, 125, n. 93.
[196] Klibansky et. al., 47.
[197] Barnouw, however, sees this lute player as King David "playing his harp in the depth of the hollow trunk," and connects this with the figure of the archer: "search then in the Psalms for the man with the crossbow. And indeed in the eleventh Psalm you will find, 'Lo, the wicked bend their bow, they make ready their arrow upon the string that they may privily shoot at the upright in heart.'" (ibid., 7). The reference to the Psalms is attractive but it is hard to see what King David could be doing in this hollow tree. Elsewhere in Bruegel the context of stringed instruments is negative; for instance a lute hangs above the barber's shop in *Superbia* (fig. 10).
[198] E. Kris, *Psychoanalytic Explorations in Art* (New York, 1952), 180.
[199] Ibid., 182.
[200] O. Sacks, *The Man Who Mistook His Wife for a Hat and Other Clinical Tales* (New York, 1985), 113; à propos of the case histories he gives, 97-120.

2 *Dulle Griet*

> A stranger in her own home, where she finds everything in disarray, she has lost rudder and mast, and is forced to float in strange worlds, times, and spaces, on the waves of her creative imagination.
>
> J. C. Reil (1803)[1]

Introduction
The Problem of the Painting's Subject

One of Bruegel's most famous and most baffling "metamorphic" pictures is the painting known as *Dulle Griet* (c. 1562; fig. 35). This is an extraordinarily complex work; a comic masterpiece whose comedy has dated almost beyond the point of recovery. It is simultaneously the place where Bruegel presents himself most explicitly as a *Second Bosch*, and where he distinguishes himself most clearly from the earlier artist (and his school) in tone and subject. The nightmarish aspects of this work were conceived of as social rather than spiritual. The figure of the central giant on the roof is like a wicked parody of the melancholic giant face with its broken-eggshell skull that stares out of Bosch's inner purgatory (fig. 17c).

There are many topical allusions in the work — to lost clichés, proverbs, town customs — and these are not, naturally, straight-faced allusions. Bruegel gave this material his own twists and made it serve his own satirical ends through the plastic, nightmarish potential of the metamorphic imagery. The picture when new was a bravura piece of convoluted rhetorical humour, a close pictorial equivalent to the highly ornate (and topical) poetic dramas produced by Bruegel's *rederijker* colleagues within St. Luke's. Though no detailed contemporary description of the *Dulle Griet* survives, the critical literature on the painting has established the name and character of its protagonist, and its roots in folk-

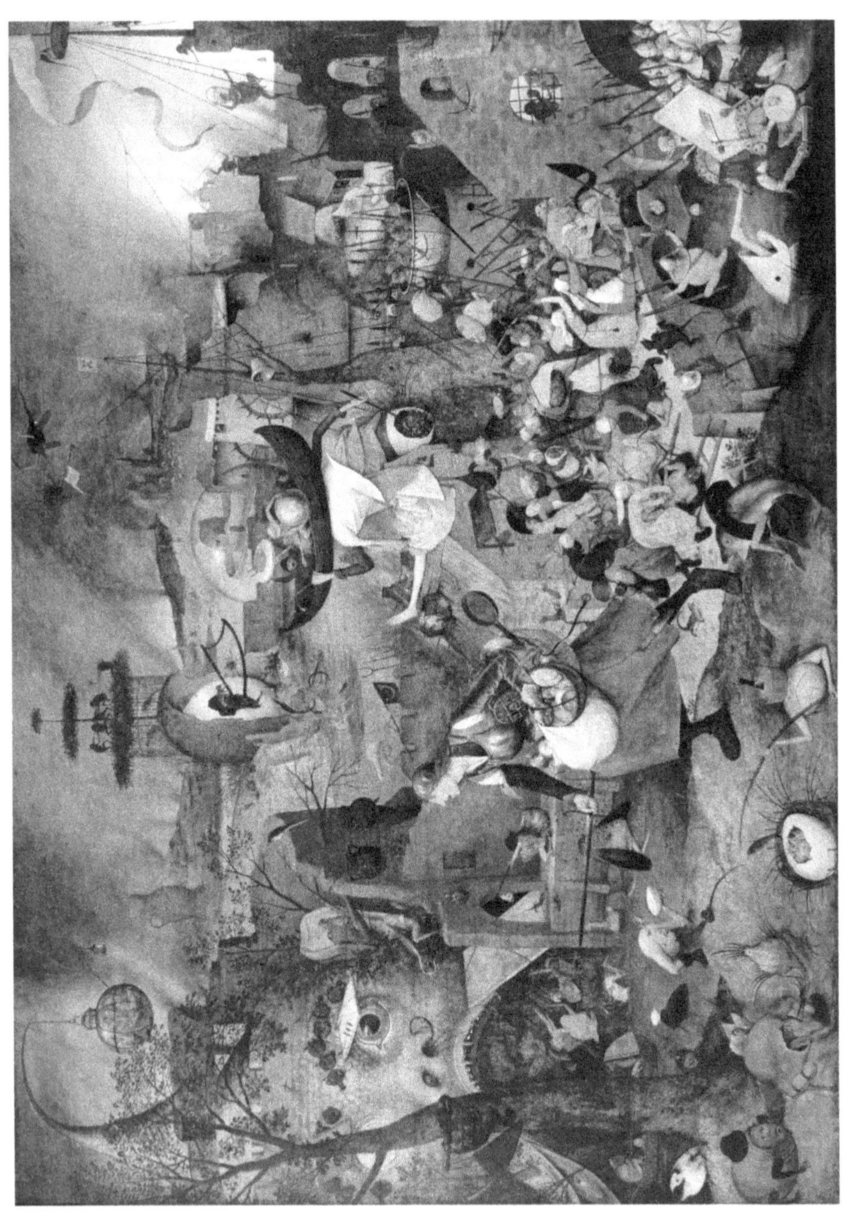

35 Pieter Bruegel, *Dulle Griet*, c 1562, Oil on wood, 117 x 162 cm. Musée Mayer van den Bergh, Antwerp. Photo: Scala

lore. This evidence can be used in various ways to interpret the painting.

The *Dulle Griet* was among works from a private Stockholm collection, sent to a sale at Cologne in 1894. There it was described as: *Höllenbruegel, Phantastische Darstellung, Landschaft mit einer grossen Menge Spukgestalten.*[2] Fritz Meyer van den Bergh bought it and suggested that the subject represented might be the *Dulle Griet* mentioned by Van Mander.[3] In his *Schilderboek* (1604), the latter used an old proverb to talk of a painting by the elder Bruegel:

> *een dulle Griet, die een roof voor de Helle doet / die seer verbijstert siet / en vree[m]t op zijn schots toeghemaeckt is*
>
> [a Dulle Griet, who robs in front of hell, wears a vacant stare and is *cruel* or *strangely* and weirdly dressed] [4]

Van Mander thought this work belonged to the then Emperor, Rudolf II; though he himself never saw the Imperial collections at Prague, the painter Bartolomeus Spranger could have been his informant.[5] The writer of a Prague inventory in 1621 described (from memory): *ein Daffel mit Feuerbrunst, dorbey die Furia mit underschidlichen Monstern*; [6] this has often been taken to refer to the *Dulle Griet.* The picture may have returned to the Netherlands in the seventeenth century, where two painters' inventories mention its subject. An Antwerp artist (d 1642) owned a work, *daer de Dulle Griet den rooff uut die hel haelt*; this is the same proverbial metaphor as that used by van Mander. In 1674, another artist possessed *een Boose Griet van Bruegel* (an Angry Meg by Bruegel) at Amsterdam. [7]

Concentrating on Van Mander's laconic synopsis, the folklorist Jan Grauls discovered that the expression *to rob in front of hell* referred to foolhardy behavior, by women who fear neither hell nor The Devil. *Dulle Griet* seems to have been a folk synonym for *virago* or *bitch.* The phrase, *she could plunder in front of hell and return unscathed,* appears in a collection of proverbs published at Kampen in 1551.[8] In 1561, a team of *rederijkers* referred in one of their farces to, *Griet die den roof haelt voorde helle* (Griet who fetches the loot from Hell), as the kind of woman whom only a fool would send to market.[9]

Turning his attention to the folkloric context of this *Angry Meg*, Grauls uncovered a wide range of tales, jokes and ballads about various Flemish Margarets current in Bruegel's time. A Griet may be a domineering wife who gets the better of her husband. The old tale of the *Battle of the Breeches* presents the figure of the wife who fights her husband over who should get to wear the trousers. Popular from the thirteenth century on, this scene became the subject of popular prints around 1500 (fig. 46, 47); by the seventeenth century, it evolved into a broadsheet story of Jan de Wasscher and his domineering wife, Griet.[10] Another Griet may be a fearsome old crone, capable of taking on The Devil himself in a fight; German woodcuts exist depicting such bouts.[11] In the southern Netherlands and Germany, a *Boose* (black or angry) Griet was a sinister witch-figure, a creature of the night, a type of *revenant*. At times, these various stock characters were conflated with elements from the legend of St. Margaret of Antioch, patron of midwives, whose chief exploit involved outfacing a (demonic) dragon. This informs the relationship in Bruegel's painting between the giant figure of Griet and the group of women behind her, overcoming small devils. This scene would then illustrate a cluster of proverbs, all linked thematically to the Griet complex, to do with women overcoming devils (*she could tie the devil to a pillow*), looting in front of hell, and generally behaving excessively.[12] It is quite certain from these researches that Bruegel's painting deals with folkloric material.

Despite this illumination of the central group, the painting's complexity elicits the universal sense that more remains to be said.[13] Most analyses start by proposing alternative identifications of the Griet figure as the picture's protagonist. Efforts have been made to see her as an allegorical figure: a personification of greed, anger, heresy, or Two-Sided Fortune. Her appearance has been diagnosed as schizophrenic, or as that of a latter-day bacchante.[14] The common focus on Griet means the rest of the painting is often seen as "background" and tends to receive less attention. Many scholars seem to think that the reference to *looting before hell* in Van Mander sufficiently explains the nightmarish landscape of the *Griet*;[15] while authors writing in the 1930s and 1940s saw in this panorama presentiments of war and chaos, linked to the coming turmoil of the Duke of Alva and the Spanish Fury.[16] This landscape and its bizarre denizens repays a closer, more specific kind of analysis, starting from the potential meanings outlined so far for imagery involving metamorphic bodies. The *conflagration*, the *various monsters*, and the *great host of ghosts* mentioned in the Prague and Cologne texts form what Bruegel evidently felt was a fitting context for his particular *Griet*. Given the multi-faceted, polysemous body of lore about St. Griet, Boose Griet et al., clearly, it is the context of each case that defines the nature and significance of any particular Griet.

Griet's activity in the picture is connected to the proverb, *she could plunder in front of Hell and return unscathed*, but Griet herself cannot be a simple illustration of this saying. If the contents of her basket are regarded as *plunder*, why do they include a frying-pan and a belt? This Griet and her loot are also moving towards, not away from, the Hell-mouth. Finally, the strange details of her clothing are not accounted for by any of the Griet proverbs. A generally warlike stance, and a usurpation of male clothing (armour, sword) come from elsewhere in the associated folk lore. Here already we have a composite, creative use of stock images.

This creativity is a standard feature of Bruegel's pictorial treatment of proverbs, a point that is particularly important in the *Dulle Griet*. Proverbs are used within the painting to comment — often ironically — on adjacent images. This point is clearer if we compare the *Griet* to other proverb-based works by Bruegel. Bruegel generally preferred to render a single proverb into a visual image of great economy, using just one or two figures. One monumental composition, with many cameos, explores one basic proverb: *Big Fish Eat Little Fish* (1559; fig. 36).[17] There are points of similarity between this and the *Dulle Griet.* The print presents a concise image rippling out from its inspiring proverb through composition and design; the painting similarly unfolds outwards from the figure of Griet. The print seems — at first glance — as remarkably comprehensible as the *Dulle Griet* is mysterious. Yet in both cases, the relation between image and proverb (more accurately, *proverbial phrase*[18]) is not straightforward. Bruegel could have illustrated the "action" of *Big Fish Eat Little Fish* a good deal more simply — as he did two years later in his *Netherlandish Proverbs* (fig. 63) — by depicting two fish in a river. One of Desprez's figures (fig. 33b) shows a possible metamorphic treatment of similar proverbial content, minus the cosmological dimension. To illustrate this proverb, it was not necessary to enlarge a fish to nightmarish size, beach it in a panoramic landscape, have men clamber over it and cut into it with weapons, place monsters in the background, and reiterate the thematic action to the level of universal cannibalism. The artistic reasons for doing this are evident. This treatment gives a chilling social dimension to the proverb; chilling because it denatures a natural metaphor for human rapaciousness. We can expect the proverbial references in the *Griet* to be predicated on pictorial ironies of equal complexity.[19]

Thus, if Van Mander's proverb is the "subject" of the *Dulle Griet,* there are clearly other, larger, thematic concerns infused into this treatment. The ferocious-women proverbs, like the other identifiable proverbs in the painting, are starting points for reconstructing these themes. A full interpretation must account for the presence together of the painting's key motifs: the Hell-mouth, the figure of Griet, her companion oversized figure with the ship on its head, the crowd of women, the town setting, the nightmarish landscape behind them, and the rich metamorphic imagery which binds the whole together. These diverse elements can be seen to knit together coherently, if we look at them in terms of the common contexts established so far for the creation of novel metamorphic imagery.

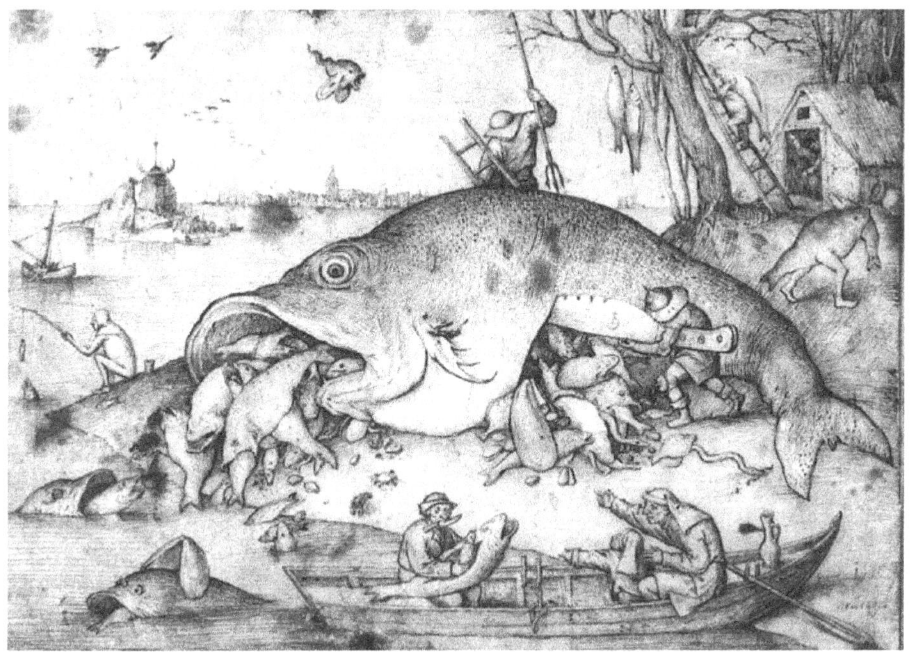

36 Pieter Bruegel, *Big Fish Eat Little Fish*, 1556. Pen, brush, gray and black ink on paper. 21.6 x 30.7 cm. Graphisches Sammlung Albertina, Vienna

If metamorphic imagery expresses psychology in Bruegel's surreal imagery, then the fantastic world which Griet inhabits must equally reference sixteenth-century articulations about dreams and the unconscious. I previously sketched two of the most general of these articulations: dreams and inspiration seen as a conduit of divine knowledge, and dreams as a sewer of bestiality, sin and diseased imaginings. Other articulations now come into play: folk or popular understandings of the domain of dreams. Compared to the fears and hopes of consciously systematic thinkers, folk thought is morally neutral.[20] Common assumptions about dreams surface as metaphor and anecdote. Certain motifs appear both in the context of dreams and of festivals. For example, the place where dreams happens is often spoken of as a spirit-world; at the same time, at certain seasons of the year, the gates of the spirit-world were open to witches, *night-riders* and other favoured mortals.

The common folk culture of dreams and carnivals conceived of both as partly magical and partly pragmatic. In a dream, one might meet ghosts or witches; one might also receive information about lost objects or treasure, or perform symbolic actions thought to have a real effect on the coming harvest. Carnival celebrated a moment of the year when normal social relations were suspended. During this period, "out of time" mummers might dress as devils, ghosts or women; they could also express practical communal grievances — by producing a satire against taxes, or an anti-clerical float (see Chapter Four). These shared features of folk dream-lore and festivals can best be described by the term *dreamtime*: the twilit counterpart to the already thoroughly demonised daylit world of most sixteenth-century people.[21]

From one point of view, a seamless conjunction between the supernatural and the matter-of-fact is the hallmark of folk articulations of the conscious-unconscious interface. Specific images in the *Dulle Griet* show that this is the mode of thought on which Bruegel drew for its inventions. The picture is a carnivalesque satire, mixing images from contemporary city customs and concerns with associations from popular and elite dream-lore. The satire is given a penetrating Humanist treatment, which takes it well beyond the range of a contemporary Carnival play or *rederijker* drama. One testament to this is the inclusion of literary, non-folk forms of imagery, such as alchemical and chivalric references. Cast in such ways, as in the *Big Fish*, the "local matter" is given cosmological dimensions.

Yet, an understanding of its deeper themes must, I think, begin with its local form and subject. The *Dulle Griet* may be thought of as essentially combining two things. On the one hand, it is a *rederijker*-like elaboration of the Dumb Griet folk-figure: a creature diminished to a comic villain in jokes and prints about the wife and the breeches, or grown to a bogeyman in stories of maddened hags, half-witted and possessed of visions. On the other

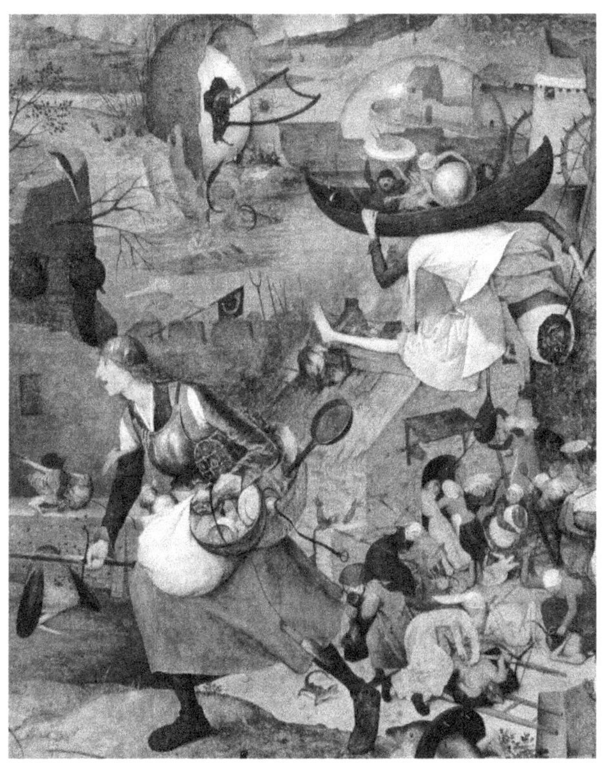

35a Pieter Bruegel, Griet and Dukatenscheisser, detail, *Dulle Griet*

hand, the work is a sort of caricature on the state of Antwerp, to be captioned perhaps with a version of a proverb: *Lady Antwerp loots before hell.* The two outsize figures in the painting thus correspond to the Giant and the Maid of Antwerp, two contemporary city symbols.

This Maid, her characteristic red sleeves inverted, is cast as a Dulle Griet (fig. 35a), prepared for battle against an unclear enemy, her desperate gaze obscured by a veil. Her accoutrements, and, in more complicated ways, her entourage, represent folkloric references. Her basket, for example, contains a frying-pan: an attribute of "loose" carnivalesque wives. It refers to her domain in the kitchen, the power-base for old wives' kitchen-magic. The casket and treasure testify to greed; also to half-witch status. Women subject to seasonal visions claimed to have visited heaven or hell and found there lost treasures; village witches were routinely enlisted in treasure hunts. Meanwhile, the city's Giant is shown as a monstrous *Dukatenscheisser* (excretor of ducats); he is also accoutred as a folk-witch and burdened with signs relating to false money. An outsized cauldron strengthens this idea; the avaricious suffer in cauldrons in painted Antwerp hells, and coiners of false money were ordinarily boiled in oil or water according to Antwerp law. The cauldron in the painting is a refuge for half-human thieves. These are the core aspects of Bruegel's elaborate visual joke: the central matter of the *Dulle Griet*.

The sections that follow offer evidence for these various identifications piece by piece. To prepare the ground, I must first clear away some issues and objections arising from previous interpretations. Three short discussions therefore preface the exposition of subject-matter: the first (and briefest), on the work's complexity; the second, on its status as a comedy; the third — in a slightly different vein — on misogynist views and misogynist rhetoric as a context for the *Dulle Griet*.

The Nature of its Design

The summary above of the *Dulle Griet* as a sort of political caricature is bald indeed compared to the richness of the painting itself. The deepening and merging of this drama with the elements of evil dreams transforms it into a vision of a modern, psychological hell. Its dominant images have a common source in the dream-time, or folk-consciousness, already fracturing in Bruegel's time, which shaped the thinking (to a greater or lesser extent) of everyone alive in 1562. The mise-en-scène of the *Griet* is a universe of the imagination. This quality differentiates it sharply from other "political" caricatures of the period — popular prints, book-illustrations, printed satires — which also employed complex, fantastical imagery.

What did these caricatures look like? We have already seen Desprez's lampoons of the French court. One gets a better sense of the extremes of the popular imaginary from what it was possible to show in anonymous Reformation broadsheets. Intended for a largely illiterate public, these might show devils defecating priests, the papal cart as a Carnival float, or a clerical banquet (of corpses) occurring inside the mouth of a grotesque she-devil; the detailed cooking scene in fig. 37 is particularly reminiscent of Bosch.[22] Less vicious but equally intricate broadsheet images could represent, for instance, distortions of the papal arms, with the keys shattered or replaced by thieves' jemmies, a hanged pope equated with Judas, a hand shown gripping a moneybag stuffed with royal crowns and surmounted with a cardinal's hat. Such material issued in floods from German and Netherlandish print-shops.[23]

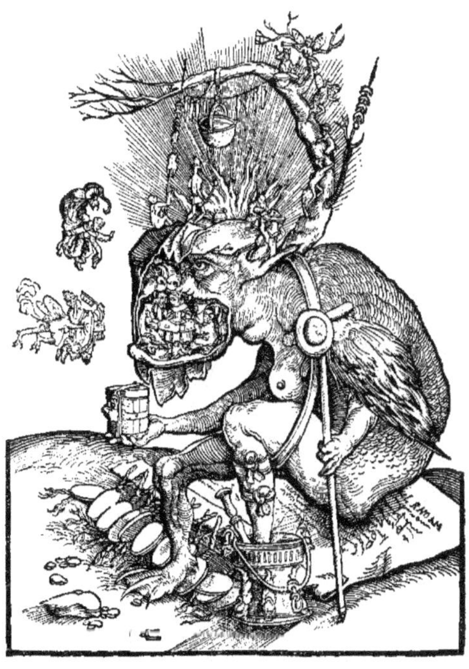

37 Anon, *Devourers of the Dead in the Jaws of Hell*, Dahlem, Coburg, c 1530. Engraving, 31.6 x 24.2 cm. Germanisches National Museum, Nuremberg

The visual traditions used in the prints, forty years before Bruegel's *Griet*, were used to express political opinions broader than those of the Reformed party, as a series of Antwerp ordinances, from 1514 on, banning *the mocking of princes* obliquely testifies. Henry VIII and Anne Boleyn were made the subject of satirical *images and pictures in cloth*, apparently in rebus-form, set up for sale at a local Bourse by a *naughty person of Antwerp*. Henry, of course, was a famously unsuccessful husband; it is worth noting that his marital woes laid him open to lampooning by Antwerp songsters as *abused by diabolic illusions*.[24]

Political fantasy in turn derived from broader traditions of visual fantasy. The merchants, craftsmen and printers of the sixteenth-century, like their fifteenth-century aristocratic predecessors, relished visual riddles of all kinds. Italian merchants would bet on who could first find Herri met de Bles's trademark owl, hidden in obscure corners of his paintings. By Bruegel's day, every print shop had its emblem, usually a punning play on the owner's name or the name of the shop. Bruegel put one of Cock's trade signs on an empty box in his *Elck* drawing. The most famous of these printers' marks was a form of hieroglyph — the dolphin and anchor of Aldus Manutius, the Venetian Humanist publisher. Antwerp painters and thinkers shared the passion for such hieroglyphs, really decodable composite emblems. Joachim Beuckelaer (c. 1535-74), for instance, an artist whose interests in subject matter were close to those of Bruegel, included hieroglyphic messages in the background of two market scenes from the early 1560s. He derived their forms from Francesco Colonna's mystic dream romance, the *Hypnerotomachia Poliphili*, a work whose impact we have already seen in Flemish poetry. The appetite for riddles and *rebus* symbols of this kind was marked by a tide of of emblem books flowing from the presses from 1554 onwards (such as Paradin's *Devises Héroiques*, published by Plantin in 1561).[25] A final example in this area from a circle close to Bruegel is the elegant pictorial tribute (fig. 38) paid to Abraham Ortelius by Joris Hoefnagel (1542-1600). The miniature has a hieroglyphic composition: an owl standing on a globe on a book. Two branches hung with tiny shells sprout from the globe (in a Boschian touch) while the owl clutches a caduceus, the rod of which is a painter's brush.[26]

To familiarity with the *rebus* as a mode of thought may be added the taste for satirical drama. In *rederijker* plays, contemporary problems were the dominant subjects. Religious, political, and social questions were usually allegorised, often by inventing novel personifications. One such drama, written between 1534 and 1546, describes the plight of *Amsterdam, a sick woman*. Among the cast can be found *Folk, a common burgess*, *More Than One, an artisan*, and *So Much, a rich man*. Backing them up were two more abstract figures, Hypocrisy and Tyranny.[27] The use of *sinnekens* as a perverse chorus in these plays parallels the relationship between the giant figures and painted details of the *Griet*. Such lengthy allegories — leavened by farce — commanded large audiences who seem to have appreciated linguistic flamboyance quite as much as controversy of plot. These forms illustrate the kind of visual culture that informed Bruegel's *Griet*.

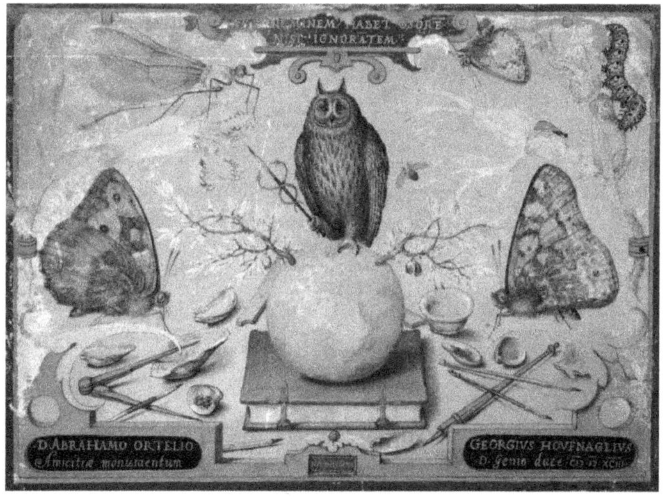

38 Joris Hoefnagel, *Emblematic Composition in Honor of Abraham Ortelius*, 1593, Stedelijk Prentenkabinet, Antwerp. Museum Plantin-Moretus/Prentenkabinet, Antwerpen: Collection Printroom. Photo: Peter Maes

Bruegel's fellow citizens, evidently, delighted in intricate pictorial enigmas, which could be mystical or parodic in tone. Viewed as an allegorical caricature, the painting is commensurate with such models and such an audience: educated merchants and artisans.

However, the *Griet*, – to a much greater extent than a *rebus*, a *rederijker* drama, or a propaganda print – resists efforts to unravel it in the form of a hortatory message. The picture does not have a single linear narrative. It is more like the tableau of a dream representation, gathering and merging many associations from folkloric and other sources. In a sense, it is akin to what modern political cartoonists do in modern newspapers, using a folk image to make an instantly recognisable point; as in this early twentieth-century satire on capitalism (fig. 39). But the reflexive use of folklore around 1562 was a more formidable undertaking.

Bruegel's creative use of folk images in the *Dulle Griet* occurred at a time when the existential status of these images was problematic. The play between real and unreal in the picture is significant: is a Hell-mouth real? is a *Dukatenscheisser*? The reality or otherwise of dream-time phenomena were explosively open issues, as the craze for witch-trials in the last decades of the century makes clear. The *Griet* was composed before this final crystallisation of Inquisition and witch-hunt, and before the fall of Antwerp itself from economic hegemony. Thus, Bruegel could make the loose, transitional status from belief to fiction of certain folk images (particularly to do with women) the entry point for his own exploration of how and why folk-jokes were transforming into real-world nightmares. From his characteristic stance of detachment, he could use the medium of Boschian surrealism to refer to popular beliefs without endorsing them. To contend that Bruegel really did undertake, within the terms of his own culture, an ethnographic investigation of this kind, leads us first to the issues of its tone and content. Is the picture a comedy? Is its meaning misogynist?

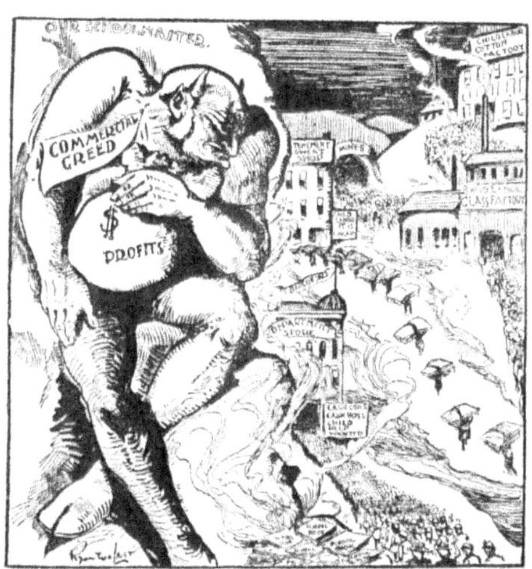

39 Ryan Walker, *Commercial Greed*, from his "The Social Hell" in *Shadows* 2 (Oct. 1902), Missouri. Courtesy of the Trustees of the Boston Public Library

The Comic in the Nightmare

I suggested earlier that psychoanalytic theory supports an interpretation of Bruegel's metamorphic art as a redirection of transcendental nightmare towards comedy. The perception that the joke and the dream bear a family resemblance to each other is, of course, Freud's. The effect of comedy can be analysed as an operation of the unexpected and the recognisable, similar to that whereby the unconscious mind produces dreams. Freud saw the deep structure of dreams and of wit as essentially similar, though, he argued, *wit [is] a consummately social product [where] dreams are a consummately asocial one.* [28]

Bruegel's art was remembered after his death as primarily comic, according to a key passage in Van Mander's biography:

> He practiced a good deal in the manner of Jeroon van den Bosch, and made many similar weird scenes and drolleries. For this reason, he was often called Pierre den Droll. Indeed, there are very few works from his hand that the beholder can look at seriously without laughing. However stiff, serious, and morose one may be, one cannot help laughing or smiling.[29]

Was the *Dulle Griet,* then, thought of as a comic picture? Looking at it today, we are unlikely to find it funny. Grotesque, weird, terrifying even, but not funny. Why is this?

Two observations from Ernst Kris's *Psychology of Caricature* are helpful here. The first is the (more or less obvious) observation that comedy dates: *Achievements in comic expression age very quickly.*[30] Kris then analyses the reasons for this:

> We know that every period and class of society and quite a number of local communities have their own peculiar forms of the comic, which often differ widely from one another and are not readily amenable to a change of climate... the comic in its tendentious forms cannot really find a mark where indifference prevails; the kind of disparagement which it allows us to infer, however, rather suggests that it can scarcely make the eternally forbidden its object (if it does, it is wont to produce a painful effect), but that this [i.e., its object], must be found in something which is even now held in esteem.[31]

This seems conclusive: laughter is a release of anxiety, and we no longer share many of the same anxieties as sixteenth-century people. Can we deduce from this that the *Griet* may have been considered comic in Bruegel's day because the subject matter did address common anxieties? Candidates for these anxieties are not hard to identify. Griet herself is a middle-aged shrew, out of (male) control, like the hoard of unruly, looting women beside her. "Marginal" women — including midwives and beggars — were beginning to be persecuted as witches around the time that Bruegel ainted this picture. Women of this type evidently represented a source of anxiety, to put it no higher, from the viewpoint of those who accused, judged, and burnt them.[32] These dramatically misogynist attitudes are well-documented;

and it is clear that changes in belief-systems motivating and legitimising this behaviour must have been widespread and elaborately developed well before 1600. Although, as we will see, views on this subject among educated male writers could differ widely, it is likely that some of the imagery in Bruegel's *Griet* did indeed represent anxieties shared by a substantial number of sixteenth-century men.

The question then becomes, did the picture succeeded in giving a comic release to these anxieties? I would argue that comic release may have been blocked as a possible response to the *Dulle Griet,* as it is blocked for us today, due to what Kris calls the *painful effect* which results from choosing a *forbidden* subject as the object of comedy. There are, he says, *cases in which the comic intention fails of its purpose... very often [this] gives rise to feelings of discomfort instead of pleasure, and this experience may be either painful or uncanny in tone.*[33] This *failure* occurs when the recipient *recognises the aggression behind its comic disguise*. The comic, then, may slide into the uncanny or the painful, and the transition from one to the other is accompanied by a recognition of disguised aggression. In the *Dulle Griet,* Bruegel shows himself to be a master of this un-guising elision, from pleasure to discomfort.

The next question to ask, then, is to do with Bruegel's specific audience: what would a sixteenth-century art patron find funny? Can we piece together a rough picture of educated urban attitudes? Miedema argued against the idea that Bruegel's paintings of peasants and their feasts are sympathetic or celebratory,[34] concluding, devastatingly, that the only possible response that merchant patrons could have had to Bruegel's depictions of weddings, *kermis* dances, and yokels asleep in the sun would have been loud, derogatory bellylaughs. Scenes of peasants behaving like fools, or innocuously celebrating a fair or festival, might then be analysed as having anxiety-release comic effect rooted in historical context. Depictions of harmless peasants might assuage repressed fears, associated with uneasy collective memories of the peasant risings in the first half of the century.[35]

Bruegel's *Dulle Griet,* in comparison, encompasses a range of tonal shifts from the comic to the uncanny. There are examples of aggression concealed from, or acceptable to the viewer, and examples of unmasked, or unacceptable, aggression. Judging from the reactions of modern viewers to this picture, those aspects of the work which are plainly (in our terms) "impossible" are the ones now found least disturbing (the seated giant, or the Hell-mouth). The less fantastic events in the background — the naked people on the island and the gibbet — are more horrifying to modern eyes. Sixteenth-century male viewers may have found the rebellious women simply "impossible" (cf. the discussion of the *World-Upside-Down* in Chapter Three), and therefore funny. Or their behavior could even have looked realistic, in contrast to that of Griet herself, since it evoked *what everybody knows* of rowdy female behaviour in real life and folk-custom.

Whatever the nuances here, broadly-speaking, the tone of the *Griet* moves from a largely comic foreground to a markedly uncomic background. As the eye moves further back into the right half of the picture (the space at the left, by contrast, is flattened and impenetrable), there is an unmistakable, overall shift from the comic to the uncanny: from the particular (or proverbial), to the cosmological (or nightmarish).

As Meijer noted, elsewhere in Bruegel's oeuvre, comic groups are designed to be read as examples of sin: *Van Mander stresses the comic character of some of the accessory scenes in Bruegel's Christ Carrying the Cross... We may suggest that Bruegel opposes these comic lowlife scenes to Christ's sacrifice and that here the comic may stand for the sinful; sinful mankind in a sinful world.*[36] This insight can be applied to the *Griet*. The "comedy" (however mixed) of the foreground is put in a dramatic relation to the scenes of horror along the horizon, where natural cataclysms — waterspouts, fires, etc. — may also underline a message of punishment for sin.

I am suggesting that the cosmic perspective implied by these shifts of tone is an important key to understanding Bruegel's vision here; quite commensurate with a folkloric interpretation. The painting can be thought of as exploring certain contemporary cultural developments by expanding and elaborating on the comic metaphor of the "unbalanced" woman. It could still be argued that the picture is primarily "about" sixteenth-century fears of women, and that the cosmic setting here simply serves to show the depth of this unease on the part of men like Bruegel. Let us take a closer look, then, at the evidence for the painting as a statement of misogyny.

Misogyny and Satire

When Walter Gibson first proposed a connection between Bruegel's *Dulle Griet* and sixteenth-century misogyny,[37] he presented as evidence contemporary male reactions to the phenomenon of female heads of state: *when the Dulle Griet was painted, the Netherlands, France, England, and Scotland were all governed by women. This unusual conjunction of women rulers occasioned numerous treatises arguing against their right and ability to govern.*[38] Gibson pointed to two public figures in particular with views on this subject. The first was John Knox (c. 1514-72), whose masterpiece of vituperative rhetoric, *The First Blast of the Trumpet Against the Monstrous Regiment of Women,* was published in 1558. His choice of metaphor is instructive:

> No women raised aloft in authority will be able to resist the feeling of pride, and he who judgeth it a monster in nature that a woman shall exercise weapons must judge it a monster of monsters that a woman shall be exalted above a whole realm and nation.

The other figure Gibson cited as sharing Knox's opinion was the political theorist Jean Bodin (1530-96).[39] Bodin was indeed from one point of view, a *distinguished French jurist*; but he was also the future author of *De la Demonmanie des Sorciers* (1580), an insanely thorough tome on witches and witchcraft, written for convenient use at the witch-trials then getting underway in France. How representative of public opinion were the opinions of these men? Bodin's book
became a veritable manual for the worst misogynist excesses.[40] Knox was motivated by radical Calvinism of a particularly virulent character. The excessive rhetorical language of Knox's pamphlet might also be accounted

for as a piece of *realpolitik*, whose ultimate goal was not simply to classify women as monsters but specifically to dislodge the Catholic Queen of Scots and replace her with a protestant theocracy, along the lines of Geneva.

It may also be pointed out, not irrelevantly, that both Knox and Bodin appear to have been singularly humourless individuals, whereas Bruegel, if we are to believe van Mander, was a famous comedian. I think Gibson's main insight is correct: misogynist fears are indeed *given concrete expression in the figures of Dulle Griet and her horde*. Common expressions of misogyny provide the sources for some of the painting's imagery, but this does not mean that the painting can be regarded as a misogynist statement, in the same way as Knox and Bodin's writings.[41] The picture itself is not an expression *of* contemporary misogynist attitudes; it is rather an *exploration* of such expressions, in terms of their novel potential for surreal and uncanny effects.

There is no question that the belief that women were inferior to men was regarded as a fact in Bruegel's lifetime. This belief was not seriously challenged during the Renaissance. Maclean concluded:

> there is less change in the notion of women throughout the Renaissance than intellectual ferment and empirical inquiry of various kinds might lead one to expect. [But] at the end of the Renaissance, there is a greater discrepancy between social realities and the current notion of women than at the beginning.[42]

Suppose then, that, in the possible spectrum of (male) Renaissance attitudes to women, Knox and Bodin stand at one end as radical conservatives. What might the rest of the spectrum look like, the novel, or "progressive" counterpart of the conservatives? The answer here is unexpected. The range of possible views does not run so much from *anti-feminist* to *feminist*, but from the earnestly fanatical to the flippant. Much as Erasmus opposed Luther's profound righteousness with civility and wit, so novel thinking on the subject of women investigated the gap between theory and reality by means of paradox and satire.

Liberal attention took this form because certain fundamental assumptions in medicine and theology, which underpinned the ideology of inferiority, remained unassailable directly. This was due to the unchallengeable position of matrimony:

> The influence on thought of the institution of marriage may be said to prevent fundamental changes in the notion of women during the Renaissance. Matrimony is a divine, natural, and social institution in the eyes of Renaissance thinkers: any alternative is theologically contentious, and requires a new vision of the mental and physical predisposition of the sexes... Even if the injustice of certain aspects of the institution is recognised, the status quo is still generally defended in the name of religious orthodoxy or a conservatism based on the belief that change in itself is bad.... [The] influence is even apparent in medicine, whence comes its "natural" justification.[43]

On this basis, in popular culture, the rebellious wife, *she who wears the trousers*, took her place as an image of the *World-Turned-Upside-Down*. Bruegel's Griet is, among other things, a figure of this type.

Cultural conservatism, anchored by the God-given hierarchy of marriage, also held sway in medicine, including dream-theory. However, the sea-change in erotic and philosophic attitudes did have some impact on the standing of women:

> [Of] the new philosophies which emerge in the Renaissance, Neo-Platonism is influential in the promotion of new ideas on woman in two domains: the theory of love and politics.... The passage of *The Republic* in which Socrates argues that women should be allowed to participate in the running of the state is widely known and quoted, and opposed to the Aristotelian view.[44]

Some currents of taste, then, in important domains of life, worked to turn the strictures of arch-misogynists like Knox and Bodin in a different direction. Novel Renaissance speculations on female nature, because of the paradoxes involved, preferred the forms of satire. This tendency culminated in, for example, such ponderous jokes as the widely reprinted anonymous Latin tract, *Disputatio nova contra mulieres, qua probatur eas homines non esse* (A new argument against women: do they have souls and are they human beings) (Frankfurt, 1595). What can be deduced about mental attitudes and habits of thought from this new genre?

> We encounter [the] Renaissance intellectual joke — *woman is not a human being* — in three contexts: theology, medicine, and law.... In each case it seems that the satire is directed against an object other than woman... In each case the effect of the joke is to reinforce the contrary opposition: woman is a human being... it may be that [woman] is particularly well suited to be [a] vehicle [for satire], as it will be evident to those to whom the satire is addressed that there is a discrepancy between what she is and what she is said to be according to traditional authorities. One way of escaping from the infrastructure of scholastic thought would thus appear to be by the use of humour. This explain[s] why contemporary thinkers take texts seriously which are clearly signposted as flippant, or which actually advertise their flippancy[45]

It seems that the more visible the discrepancy became between the inherited view and knowledge of actual women, the more likely it was that the mismatch would attract attention as a subject for satire: *Neo-Platonism and neo-Stoicism, albeit widely celebrated and influential, do not altogether liberate Renaissance thought about woman from its scholastic axes. This is more effectively done by thinkers such as Parcelsus or Postel, who attempt to discard not only scholastic method but also its language; and by those who employ intellectual satire to this end.*[46] Bruegel's *Griet* has an affinity with this intellectual attitude.

The *Disputatio nova* marks one extreme to which this tendency could be taken in the field of theology. Scaliger's *Exercitationes de Subtilitate* (1557) is the equivalent in medicine. Beliefs about the make-up of female humours are an important factor: they supported the view that women were less mentally stable, and more liable to diseased melancholic visions, than men. The Aristotelian Scaliger, in his tract, contradicts at one point the doctrine derived from Aristotle which holds that the male is hotter (and therefore nobler and better) than the female. Scaliger argues instead that man and woman are of equal temperature and that the apparent difference of hotness between them stems from the fact that woman is more humid than man. Scaliger here was deliberately joking; but the joke back-fired. His "refutation" of Aristotelian misogynist science came to be widely quoted, by serious doctors and feminists; a measure of the changed times.[47] In the case of Agrippa's *Declamation of the Nobility and Excellence of the Female Sex* (1529), the humourous tone of this attitude was clearer. Maclean comments:

> Agrippa... admits that, in declamations of the sort he wrote in favor of woman, there are many invalid arguments and jests... [But] the humour may indicate the impossibility of discussing in serious terms the proposition of woman's equality, and therefore represents a strategy of discourse which is subversive in intention.[48]

Even in academic discourse, then, distanced by its Latin from the consciousness of most ordinary Europeans, the other side of the misogynist coin turns out to be humour. Bruegel's interest in comedy and paradox is well-attested. Everything we know of his art up to the point of the *Griet* places him in the ranks of these intellectual satirists, who continued to debate the problems posed by women's nature in terms of deliberate rhetorical excess throughout the century. Popular and official attitudes were alike in maintaining both views of women — joking and slanderous — simultaneously.

The aggression inherent in these dual approaches is particularly visible in imagery surrounding the figure of the rebellious wife, a comic challenge to the incontestable lynchpin institution of matrimony. As beliefs about female mental instability became enshrined in medicine and law, the same basic patriarchal codes were structured also in folk-culture There we find the whole set of Renaissance paradoxes about female nature — woman/human/not-human/super-human — given concrete, colourful and visible forms. The original context for any kind of Griet figure was, as

Grauls discovered, folkloric. The paradoxical and dramatic qualities of folk misogynist expression in themselves go far towards explaining why Bruegel would associate this material with the half-world of dreams. The dominant wife is a comic motif and also an image of the World-Turned-Upside-Down. Bruegel brought to the "Quarrel" on woman's nature an artist's eye for the visual, ethnographic curiosity, and encyclopedic knowledge of folkloric images and customs. Seen as a contribution to the satirical work on women's nature, his *Griet* is a kind of map of beliefs about uppity women and the men who fear them.

Dreams, Witches, and the Women of the *Dulle Griet*
The Evidence of Folklore

In 1911, Freud summarised the results of his research with Oppenheim on dreams and folklore:

> Oppenheim in his studies of folklore has made two observations with regard to the dreams narrated there which seem to him worth communicating. Firstly, that the symbolism employed in these dreams coincides completely with that accepted by psychoanalysis, and secondly, that a number of these dreams are understood by the common people in the same way as they would be interpreted by psychoanalysis — that is, not as premonitions about a still unrevealed future, but as the fulfillment of wishes, the satisfaction of needs which arise during the state of sleep. Certain [of] these, usually indecent dreams [are] told as comic anecdotes.[49]

The view of the "common people" that dreams *satisfy needs which arise in sleep* thus tallies with the characteristics of the *somnium naturale,* discussed earlier. In dream theory — and in theories about women's nature — popular and elite accounts of the same phenomena informed each other. This mutual exchange can be seen at work in sixteenth-century writings about witches.

Both the witchcraft texts and Bruegel's picture present a rich interchange of ideas about dreams, women and witches. All manner of information can be recovered about the fantasies of witches and accusers, their preferred imagery, their reworking of old folk beliefs and practices.

Bruegel painted his *Dulle Griet* at a time when the old, more or less neutral concept of the witch, a loose folkloric assemblage of attributes and stories, was beginning to undergo demonisation. Like everyone else in the early 1560s, Bruegel would have had conflicting mental pictures, both of the older traditional image of a witch and of her new, deadlier sister being assembled in the wings. In his own work, the older set of representations can seen giving way to the new. His *Witch of Malleghem* (1559; fig. 40) parodies a village witch, a harmless charlatan passing herself off as a healer. While only fools are taken in, ominous signs appear at the edges of her activity – notably the giant broken egg dribbling little stones (of folly), on the ground next to coins tipped from a purse. In Bruegel's *St. James and the Magician Hermogenes* (1565; fig. 41), the iconography of the sabbat-flying witch, complete with satanic steed and broomstick, is fully formed. The scene includes a prominent cauldron in the background, emitting a smoke filled with hallucinations. Between these two images, around 1562, Bruegel devised the *Dulle Griet*. Griet and her fellow giant have attributes characteristic of the older folkloric kind of witch, while the phantasmogoria around them reflects the newer beliefs.

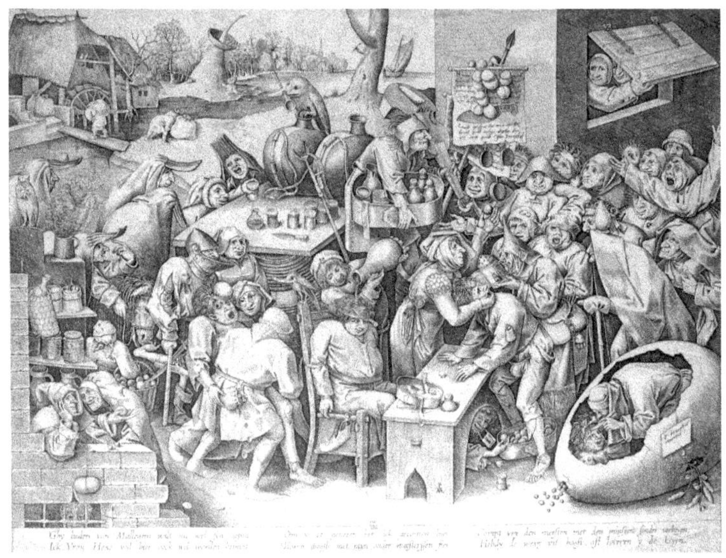

40 Pieter van der Heyden, after Pieter Bruegel, *The Witch of Malleghem* 1559. Engraving, 35.5 x 48 cm. Bibliothèque Royale Belgique, Brussels. S 11 19162

41 Pieter van der Heyden, after Pieter Bruegel, *St. James and the Magician Hermogenes* 1565. Engraving, 22.2. x 29 cm. Bibliothèque Royale Belgique, Brussels. S1 7614

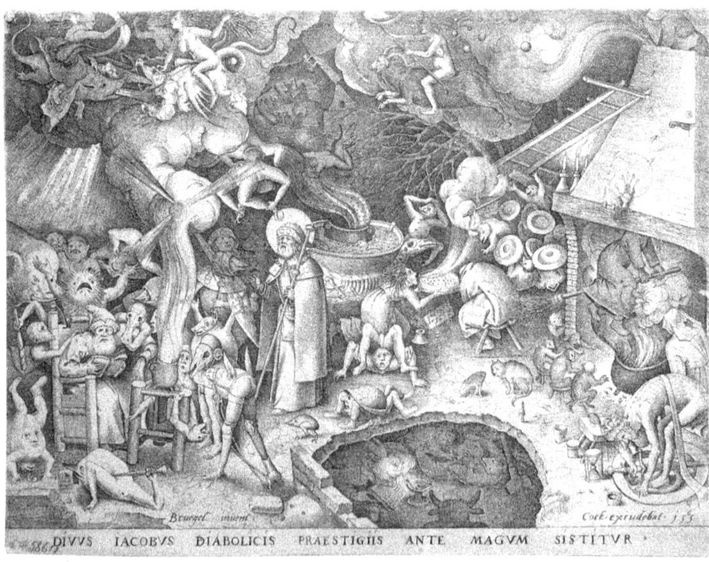

If the painting is seen as emerging at a point of cultural transition between two *mentalités*, this explains much about its apparent difficulty of interpretation. History made of it an uneasy *suture*; an image from an envelope of time whose double-vision was soon to pass. Something of this sense is expressed in the unique construction of the picture's space. The artist Leonard Rosoman, looking on the scene with a painter's eye, made a sketch of the essential planes and platforms in and around the figure of Griet, shorn of their swarming personages (fig. 42).[50] The result looks very much like a stage set. The sketch shows how the fragmented buildings, walls, and ruins extend from the Hell-mouth at the left through to the red and black silhouettes at the top right, forming an unbroken barrier separating Griet from the more open landscape at the rear. Consider how Griet is placed spatially in this setting. Like the pilgrim who opens Bosch's *Haywain* triptych (c. 1510; Prado, Madrid), both are represented as being in transition by the device of the bridge: Bosch's pilgrim is about to cross a

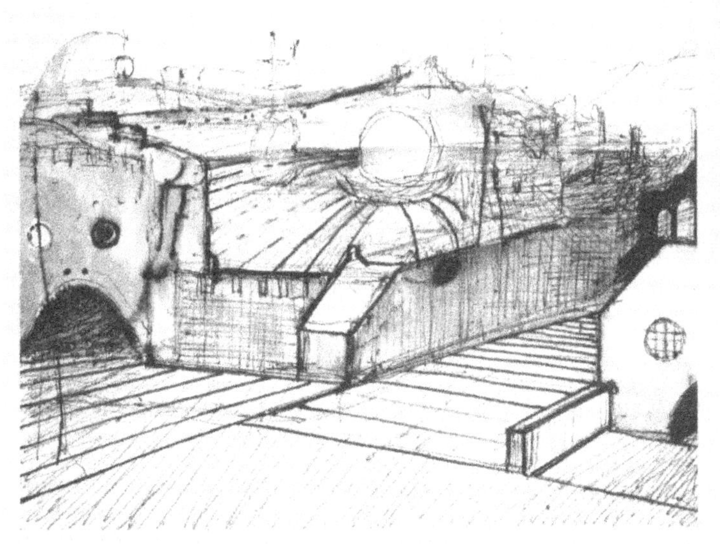

42 Leonard Rosoman, *Plan of Dulle Griet*. Pen on paper. Photo: after Rosoman (1969)

bridge, leaving behind him the scenes of murder and robbery in the landscape; Griet is shown as having just stepped over the bridge in her painting. The pilgrim travels through a sinful earthly world, on his way to a higher spiritual state. Griet turns her back on a distorted town and crosses into a kind of twilight wilderness.

Griet's position in terms of the bridge is significant. A witch in folk tradition was someone who existed on the boundary between civilisation and wilderness, like the contortionist peering at us from between his legs, on the boundary wall of the *Griet* (fig. 35a). Such a creature inhabits two worlds:

> As late as the middle ages, the witch was still the *hagazussa*, a being that sat on the *hag*, the fence or hedge which passed behind the gardens and separated the village from the wilderness. She was a being who participated in both worlds.[51]

It is interesting in this context that the metaphor of the fence as a boundary between sacred and secular space appears in the proverb, *hij smit zijn kap over de haag* (*he throws his cowl over the hedge*; number 56 in Bruegel's *Proverbs*; fig. 63a); referring to an individual leaving a religious or monastic order for the secular world.

A *hagazussa* was traditionally identified by reversals in dress. Bruegel's Griet has sleeves of two different colors; she also wears a breastplate and a helmet. Her hair is flowing; in the sixteenth century, *the loose hair of the witches is mentioned with increasing frequency*.[52] As well as casting her as a cross-dresser, Griet's armour and sword call to mind the psychic battles practiced by a fascinating group of folk "witches" from the Friuli in Italy, who called themselves the *benandanti* (good walkers). The *benandanti* were a kind of sect or club whose self-perceived function was to *go forth at night*, at certain seasons of the year, while their bodies lay sleeping, ritually to battle witches and thereby secure the harvest. Their existence came to the attention of the Inquisition, as so into the historical record, in a series of trials beginning in the 1570s. Ginzburg argued that their beliefs represent an isolated remnant of a once widespread pre-Christian cult.[53] However this might be, the trial records reveal much about the mental world of these people and their beliefs concerning themselves and their military but benign mission. The "confessions" of the *benandanti* clearly incorporate material drawn from more widespread groups of beliefs concerning "night travels" as journeys to the spirit-world. Accounts of night travellers recur in Northern European sources, sometimes associated, like the *benandanti,* with the seasons of the Ember days.[54] Female night travellers were classed as inhabitants of the twilit world:

> Very early, women undertaking *night travels* and fence demons are mentioned in the same breath. In a poem probably composed at the beginning of the fourteenth century in Ghent, there is talk of *fence demons, travelling women, spirit children, belief in spirits, hobgoblins, elves, goblins and mares*.[55]

In a collection of sermons published at Strasbourg in 1516, Geiler von Kaisersberg wrote of witches and other night-walkers. He described *women who during the ember days fell into swoons which rendered them insensible to pricks or scoldings. When they revived, they related what they had seen, declaring that they had been in heaven, and spoke of stolen or hidden objects*.[56] Insensibility to pricks, it may be noted, were shortly to become an attribute of the witch's *devil's mark*.

An earlier account, independent of Geiler, confirms the existence of these beliefs and adds some details. At the beginning of the fifteenth century, the Dominican J. Nider compiled a list of types of sinners who had contravened the first commandment through superstition. Counted among them were women who *during the ember days, out of their senses, boasted of having seen the souls in Purgatory and of many other fantasies*. When these women awoke, *they related extraordinary things about souls in Purgatory or in Hell, about stolen or lost objects, and so forth*.[57] Nider's book as a whole was printed at Basel in 1481, a good example of the admixture of sermons and sensationalism that form the bulk of early printed literature. These particular passages were considered worth republishing in a treatise on superstitions published at Rome in 1559 by Martin d'Arles, and were still being quoted in their entirety in seventeenth-century manuals on witchcraft.[58] The key points here are the references linking trance or dream-states to hunts for stolen or lost objects in purgatory or hell. Griet in Bruegel's painting now has several attributes which link her to the stories of *good women who go forth at night*. Under her arm and around her waist, she carries baskets and a sack filled with what is generally described as her *loot*. It looks as if two aspects of the old stories connected with Ember days and night-walkers have been amalgamated here.

In ordinary life, people looking for treasure or for lost or stolen goods would commonly enlist the help of a local *cunning person*, or village witch. Techniques for such searches survive in Brabant folklore and are recorded for other Flemish and northern French provinces.[59] In England, the pursuit of treasure-caches — assumed to be scattered under barrows or ruined castles, and guarded, more than likely, by an evil spirit — had become a recognisable craze by mid-century. Magical treasure-seeking was legislated against as both sorcerous and fraudulent, while, according to Thomas, *excavation in the hope of quick riches was so common that "hill-digger" had become a recognised term of abuse for a man on the make*.[60] Such tales provided an explanation for unusual upward social mobility, thus, *whole families were rumoured to owe their rise to lucky finds with the ploughshare or spade*.[61] Thomas argue that the peasant concept of *limited good* is illuminating here. A society holding this assumption thinks of the supply of *good* — good fortune, goods, wealth, luck, etc. — as limited. Since it is not believed possible that everyone can be equally fortunate (in this world at least), it follows that one man's misfortune means another's good luck; thus, finding treasure is like coming across a cache of pre-existing *good*.[62] All this shows how amenably a complex of magical beliefs about treasure could be updated to fit the aspirations of early modern entrepreneurs. Treasure-seeking was a focus of desire; and for this reason, a prominent motif in peasant dream-anecdotes, as we will see shortly. This is the knot of themes — magic, money-fever and fraud — which informs the *Griet*.

In Bruegel's painting, Griet's treasure is a focal point in several ways. Considered as an attribute of Griet, it identifies her as a *night-walker*. Other aspects of her plunder qualify her character further. Most of the obviously valuable objects are held inside an upturned cooking-pot or helmet (fig. 35a). Behind this, she carries a shopping-basket with a protruding frying-pan. The frying-pan appears as a piece of carnivalesque headgear in the *Carnival and Lent* (fig. 71), and also in the bag of a woman in the crowd at the *Sermon of John the Baptist* (1566; fig. 95). Here it links Griet to the sphere of kitchen-magic, the focal point for old wives' lore, and the *milieu* of the crowd of small housewives. The flapping belt is probably a reference to Griet's intemperance,[63] a quality further alluded to in her hastily-stuffed apron and dangling heavy knife. Everyone carried a knife, an iron-clad stick or even a sword in Bruegel's time. The French expression *aller en Flandre sans couteau* (going to Flanders without a knife) signified an unthinkable situation literally and metaphorically.[64] Griet's knife and sword make her ludicrously over-armed and ready for violence.

Knives, rods, and swords appear behind Griet, in the rough-and-tumble on the opposite bank. Griet's emblematic possessions are thus also scattered among the *mêlee* of women, their impact diffused and subtly adapted to the more normal appearance of the housewives. Some of the women are armed with hatchets and farm implements. One woman in a dark dress fights a duck-billed monster with a long rod. While the *benandanti* claimed to fight witches with fennel stalks, a similar cult in Livonia, *battled the devil and witches, striking them with long iron rods*.[65] To the left, another woman gathers in her arms objects similar to the "stolen" goods which Griet holds. This figure has its eyes covered — as are Griet's — by an upended kitchen pot. Depicting figures who blindly persist in senseless their actions was a favorite joke of Bruegel's. The woman blinded by a pot deftly echoes both the contents of Griet's basket and the shape of the giant pot to the right.

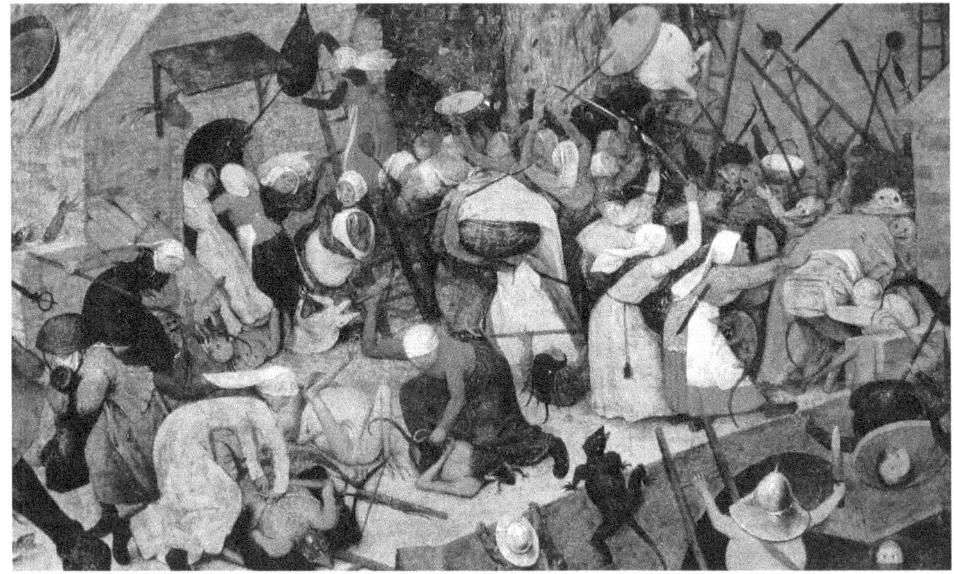

35b Pieter Bruegel, horde of women, detail, *Dulle Griet*

Imagery drawn from a particularly rich, surreal folk metaphor pervades this whole small group behind Griet. Underscoring the theme of Griet's fearlessness in looting at the gates of Hell, close by her, two or three women are prominently engaged in *tying the Devil to a pillow* (fig. 35b). They illustrate a Brabant proverb group, referring to a type of reckless and foolhardy woman, vituperative enough to confront The Devil himself and come off better from the encounter. Visually and metaphorically, the pillow aspect of the proverb alludes to female power in the domain of the bedroom, as well as the kitchen. The proverb thus condenses *woman, power* and *bed*; it simultaneously connotes illicit sexuality (a domain where the male is supposed to be dominant), childbirth (a female domain resented and feared by men), and, of course, dreams. The connection of female power with dreams is itself complex. As well as the kitchen, the principal domestic arena of female magic was the bed-chamber; since the care of infants was also a female domain, women were "in charge" of children's dreams. experience, as well as through the more formal collective magic of night-walkers. Psychoanalytically, women shape the dreams and nightmares of men and children: ordinary mothers also figures as witches. In the later Middle Ages, the visual type of a woman armed with a household tool, winning a fight in the presence of, or against, a demon, can be found manifested in many different forms. One of these became the now familiar grouping of witch, broomstick, and familiar. An early subject of this kind can be found carved on a stall at Corbeil near Paris (fig. 43). According to Wright, *it represents a woman who must by her occupation be a witch, for she has so far got the mastery of the demon that she is sawing off his head with a very uncomfortable looking instrument.*[66] Her malign expression might well lead one to take her for an illustration of a housewife from a French proverb of the same flavor as *tying the devil to a pillow*. Wright's assumption that she is a witch because she is getting the better of a demon shows how easily the stock proverbial figure and the figure of the witch can be converged. The housewife-as-witch motif appears also in a carving at Winchester, where a woman is shown working at her distaff while seated on the back of an enormous cat (fig. 44).

The next step in demonising this association of ideas can be seen in a print (fig. 45), often ascribed to Israel van Meckenem the Younger (c. 1445-1503). It shows a version of the *Battle of the Breeches*, the venerable popular theme of combat between husband and wife. This motif was evidently akin to the housewife-tool-devil type; and like that *topos*, late medieval examples display a much greater degree of variability than the sixteenth century ones. There are *fabliau* versions where the husband wins; more often the wife is the victor. From the mid-sixteenth-century on the scene was standardised and adopted for *World-Turned-Upside-Down* broadsheets.[67] There is no question that the two motifs are represented together in the Van Meckenem print, and that this convergence has resulted in a more negative, more

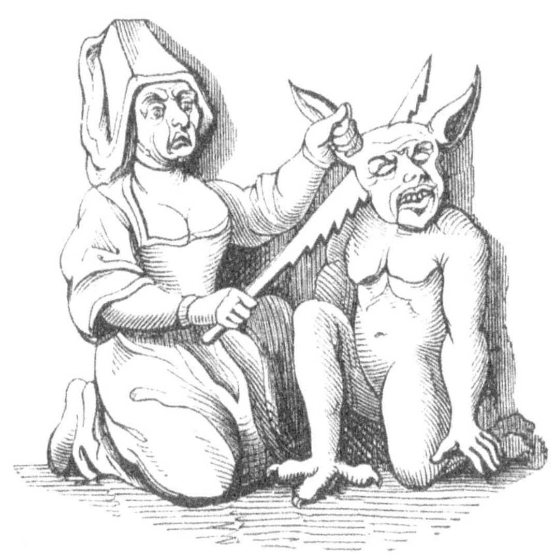

43 Anon, *housewife, demon and saw*, drawing of a stall carving at Corbeil, Paris. Photo: after Wright (1865)

44 Anon, *housewife and cat*, drawing of a stall carving at Corbeil, Paris. Photo: after Wright (1865)

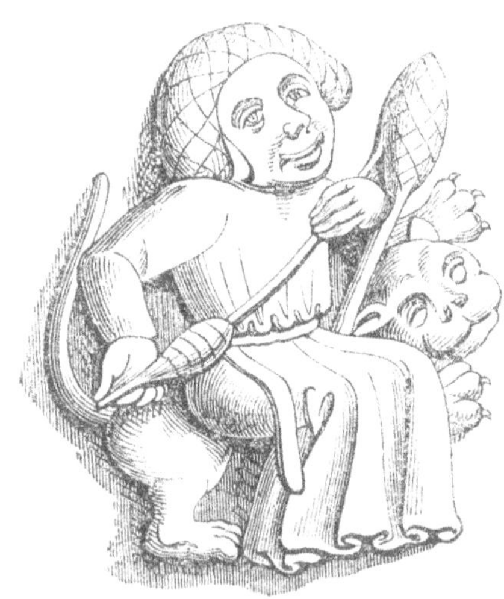

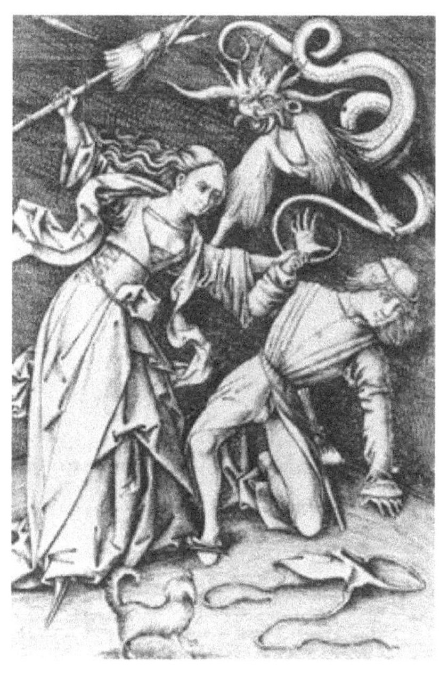

45 Israel van Meckenem the Younger, *Battle of the Breeches*, early sixteenth century. Engraving. Berlin, Kupferstichkabinett. Photo: Maeterlinck (1902)

46 Anon, *The Battle of the Breeches*, 1555, Netherlandish, mid-sixteenth century. Woodcut with stencilled watercolour, Rijksmuseum, Amsterdam

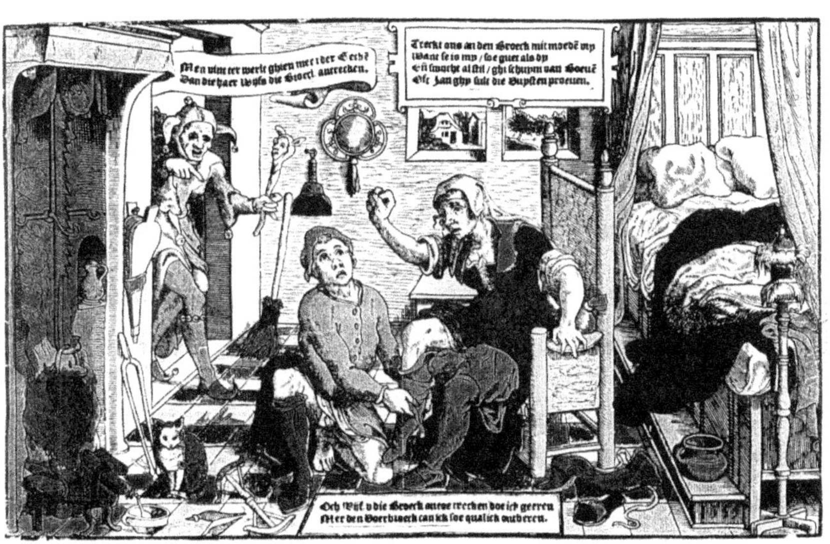

dream-like image. The sought-after breeches are visible on the floor in front of the couple. The woman holds the man by the arm and pushes him to the ground. In her other hand she holds an inverted broomstick. Behind her looms a devilish monster, one arm (or tentacle) stretching out towards the broomstick. The design presciently and succinctly deepens fears about witches by relating them to male fears about rebellious or domineering women. Recall the kinds of paranoia expressed in the *Malleus Maleficarum*, whose authors, for instance, thought it necessary to prescribe *Remedies... for those who by Prestigitatory Art have lost their Virile Members or have seemingly been transformed into the shapes of Beasts*[68]

All these images connect devils and unruly women in various ways. The potential range of different themes and moods in this genre is important, because the *Breeches* motif as a whole has been widely accepted as a close parallel to the *Dulle Griet*.[69] Most *Battle of the Breeches* prints have no demonic overtones (fig. 46, c. 1550, is typical). They are generally taken to bear witness to a tradition of boisterous half-joking misogyny. The later progeny of the genre (including all seventeenth-century examples) are broadly comic.[70] In the latter, the wife is invariably named Griet, her husband Jan, and the action unfolds in a comic-book grid, a marriage-turned-upside-down.

To understand how differently Bruegel shapes this material returns the discussion to the issues of tone as a means of subverting sixteenth-century misogyny, and its straight-jacket focus on matrimony. As comedy, the *Battle of the Breeches* is a carnivalesque metaphor more deeply rooted in institutional misogyny, in the public life of the town, than its sister folk tradition of the housewife besting a devil with a domestic object. Consider a non-comic context for the breeches motif, bearing in mind the unshakeable status of marriage as a barrier to reform. In Antwerp, a certain detail in the form of punishment for female capital offenders is striking. Men and women were sentenced to die in different ways, as was usual at this period. The prison accounts for 1552 reveal an order for a supply of breeches for condemned women. Another record clarifies this. A chronicler notes that, as a departure from usual practice, after the execution of three Anabaptist women on the 6th of July, 1557:

> their bodies were not put into sacks *or covered with the breeches used on such occasions* but that in order to shame them they were thrown naked into the Scheldt.[71] [emphasis added]

This practice seems to offer a kind of macabre official parallel to the popular scenarios studied by Natalie Zemon Davis, where men wore women's clothes in carnivalesque protests. This sort of transvestite demonstration shows how folk practice could employ the paradoxes of learned discourse. Thus the garb of woman, who was *not a human being* equally in the tongue-and-cheek world of the satirists and in political reality, was used to present the cases of men who felt themselves similarly victimised.[72]

The appearance of a demonic familiar in the Battle of the Breeches print certainly marks a shift in direction of this complex of motifs, but the configuration of elements within the motif was evidently still malleable in Bruegel's time. Muchembled described the polysemous character of early modern folkloric material in his discussion of sixteenth-century peasant magic:

> In other regions the general signs of good and bad fortune differ from or even contradict the examples we have chosen here, and relatively seldom are animals and things connected with one quality alone, diabolical or beneficent... Signs did not have fixed meanings in peasant thought because the forces that they helped to interpret were themselves not fixed. Every detail was important to interpretation: time, place, and circumstances colored positively or negatively what seems to us to be the same phenomenon.[73]

Bruegel used all the elements of the Battle of the Breeches motif in the *Dulle Griet* — dominant housewives, breeches, kitchen-magic, even the demon — and his arrangement changed their significance entirely. At the right side of

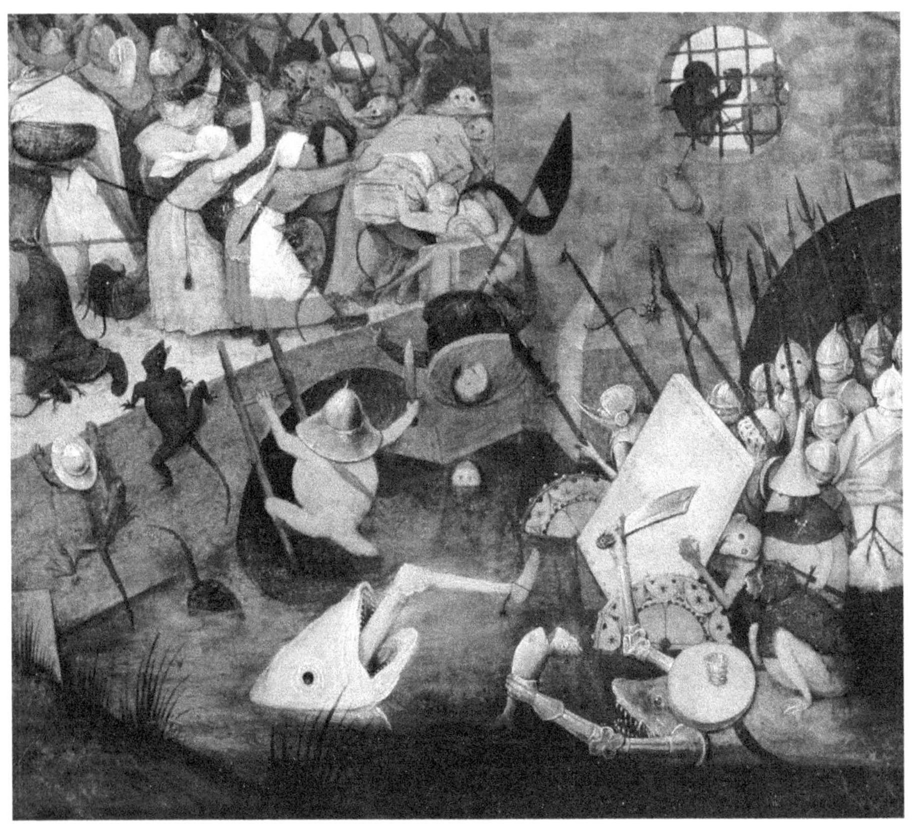

35c Pieter Bruegel, woman pulling breeches off man and army in the water, detail, *Dulle Griet*

the bridge, next to the wall, where monkeys toast each other behind a barred window, a woman is engaged in pulling the clothes off the back of a bent-over male figure (fig. 35b). The woman seems oblivious of the little devil that has leapt on her and is clinging to her apron. This is a sly joke drawn from the same sources as the earlier print of the battling wife and her demon, but totally different in effect.

Context redefines the meaning of the motif here, the context of the *Dulle Griet*. In the panorama of the whole painting, female stubbornness is made to look pointless or misdirected. What good does it do to *tie the devil to a pillow*, or insist on wearing the trousers, when the world itself is disintegrating? The *Battle of the Breeches* is not, in this context, evil or demonic. The Brabant proverb of the woman who can tie up a devil was used to deplore analogous behaviour, particularly by a wife to a husband. It could also be colored with a certain respect for such strong-mindedness, similar to the respect expressed by neighbors of benign night-riders. [74] Apart from real latter-day cults like the *benandanti*, stories abound in European folklore of the resourceful peasant who is able to out-bargain The Devil or to get the better of him by means of a trick. Bruegel's small devils are unintimidating and easily overcome by their determined foes. The kind of devil who can be tied to a pillow by an ordinary housewife is not closely related to the Satan of Christian cosmology.

The woman pulling the breeches has a further "microcosmic" compositional context of her own. Her cameo is the unsteady centre of a carefully orchestrated composition filling the lower right corner. Her diagonal divides the crowd of rampaging women on one side, and the horde of armed men in the water below. The women reverse their normal behavior by running wild on top of the arched bridge; the men conversely, though armed to the teeth, take refuge under an arch. The women demonstrate an unsettling masculine fearlessness by tying devils to pillows; the men under the arch seem noticeably reluctant to display the same qualities. Bruegel used a series of surreal vignettes visually to sew together the edges of the groups of men and women (fig. 35c). These "edge-images" dramatise the psychological dimension of the conflict between the two in a manner quite different from, say, the Van Meckenem print's demonisation of the wife. The women pulling the breeches from the man's back also conceal his head — and eyes. Below them, a spindly-legged man falls backwards, headfirst into the water. Below him, the eyes of another man, submerged up to his nose, peer from the water. These three figures enact a transformative sequences, a dream-logic. First, the man whose rear end is exposed, head and eyes hidden in the folds of his garment; then the falling man, whose head has been thrust through a platter (this odd collar serves to demarcate his head from his body); finally the half-hidden head, with only the eyes visible.

This ensemble in turn is balanced to the left and below by further metamorphic sequences. Left of the platter-man, a small bloated mannikin – knife in hand, nude apart from a huge helmet (concealing and exaggerating the head) – leads a half-hearted assault on the bridge. Two figures echo his effort, diminishing in size as they approach the space where the women are tying the devils; they are in fact going to be next in line to be tied up. Below, in the dark right corner, misogynist fears shape the forms of the least human hybrids: a fish-head swallowing an armoured leg; a fish-monster performing a gruesome symbolic castration. All this takes longer to recount than to see: what we see is a set of metamorphic ripples, moving out in ever more fantastic stages, between the bridge and the water.

The other "macroscopic" compositional context for the women is of course Griet, whose huge foot links her body to the group on the bridge. Her right leg is unnaturally elongated, the better to connect her to the *mêlée* of women; the meaning of the two is thus bound together. Bruegel thus relates Griet, an image of the night-walking folk-witch, "going forth" among evil spirits in her mind, to the metaphor of a woman capable of trapping a devil. The cameos depicting the latter, in the scenes closest to Griet, present cases writ small of the former: folk beliefs pressed into novel arrangements as part of a modern comedy. The women in turn contextualise this Griet as a figure seen from the perspective of the satirist.

It is typical of Bruegel that, with his keen eye for the visual roles expressed in popular culture, he should have taken Dulle Griet, a figure whose appearance was as shadowy and unfixed as, for example, that of Mother Goose or Greasy Joan, and equipped her with a suite of novel but recognisable folk appurtenances: martial references to night- riders, loose hair, reversed clothing, stolen goods which ember dreamers "brought back" with them. He followed a similar procedure when he conceived of Prince

Carnival as a butcher. But for Griet's identity in the "comedy," and for her topical association with the behaviour of these women as a metaphor for modern life, we must consider the latter's character also in terms of an organised, costumed charade; that is, in terms of the carnivalesque.

The Evidence of Carnival

The behavior of the rioting women is drawn in part from a widespread festival during which women reversed their role in the life of the town by holding revels in the street and breaking into stores. In the Netherlands, there were several regional holidays of this kind. At Brussels, January 19th was *Vrowkens-Avond*, or *Vrouwenavond*. At Bruges, the Saturday before Mardi Gras was *Vrowkens zaterdag*, or Women's Saturday. Writing in 1870, the folklorist Otto de Reinsberg-Düringsfeld commented that,

> In Brabant, until fifty years ago, women and men masked as women assembled in the hills [on February 23rd] to light bonfires; there they danced and sang burlesque songs. This was a kind of carnival farce, which, one is told, had as its object to *chasser le "méchant semeur."*[75]

In Germany and parts of France the fête was known as *women's Thursday*, or *Old Woman's Shrovetide*:[76]

> Thursday was also the favorite day for the flight of the witches and that of the *benandanti*.... It was the day on which the women could cut loose against the men. A report about a "women's day" in Alsace records that the women met in the market wearing masks and every baker and innkeeper had to give them a loaf of bread and some wine. From the community they received twelve guilders... With that, they bought a large billy-goat and decorated it; one of the women put bells on it. With a band of musicians they went to the dairy, where they had to be given butter. They ate on the highway, baked small cakes, and forced the travellers to dance with them around the billy-goat. The men had to

hide until the evening. They rioted in the streets and broke the windows. This was on the 24th of February, 1681.[77]

Basel women, storming through the streets, created a scandal at Carnival time in 1418. According to an eyewitness, *So old hags and married women behave as if they were children, and an honest man cannot pass through a street for they will attack him and want to have intercourse with him.*[78] Such *women's days* seem to have been held especially during feasts involving delivery and midwives.

St. Margaret of Antioch, whose legend Grauls linked to that of other Griets, was a patron of midwives, and also victor over a dragon. Midwives as a group later became prime targets for accusations of witchcraft.[79] During the Thirty Years War nearly all the midwives of the city of Cologne were executed as witches. The accounts of women's carnivals portray them as unruly and riotous — a recurrent nuisance, if not an actual threat, to the established order of life:

> According to the reports of Danish women's guilds [of midwives], their members behaved in quite an unrestrained fashion after delivery. They broke into houses to rob meat, eggs, and bread. In the streets they made kindling of the wagons and took liberties with the men. Married women passing by had their bonnets knocked off. This was also a custom at the Cologne 'women's carnival' on Thursday before Shrovetide.[80]

Since midwives were identified with such festivals, memories of their behavior (and that of other women) on these occasions certainly informed the later idea of the witches' Sabbat. Bruegel's contemporaries were capable of drawing the same conclusion, with one interesting difference. They ascribed the Sabbat's existence to the *imaginations* of the women involved. The magician Cardan published as his opinion at Basel in 1559, that:

> Without a doubt these things took their start from the old orgies where the women behaved in a wild and senseless manner in public. When this

> was forbidden by law, they gathered in secret. When this was also forbidden, *they assembled only in thought*. [my emphasis] [81]

There are several points here pertinent to the imagery of the *Dulle Griet*. As women's festivals became identified with the activities of witches, this was linked in the minds of educated writers to the moment when the location of these activities changed from the physical to the psychological, from a riot in the streets to a riot in the mind. Cardan was not alone in arguing that the doings of witches were imaginary. Johann Weyer (c. 1515-88), a Lutheran doctor to a German ducal court on the lower Rhine, became famous for his book *De praestigiis daemonum* (On the Tricks of Devils), which ran through many editions and translations after its first appearance at Basel in 1563.[82] Today Weyer is (justly) best known for his opposition to the burning of witches. Weyer himself summed up his view simply in a letter attached to the Frankfort edition of his book: *Our witches have been corrupted in their fantasy by the devil, and imagine often that they have done evil things that didn't even happen.*[83] Weyer writes here from his own experience as a physician. A witch, by his definition, was someone prey to infernal fantasies, a victim whose melancholia was taken advantage of by The Devil. He devoted Chapter 7 of the third book of the *De Praestigiis Daemonum* to case histories of melancholics. These were intended to prove the depraved imagination associated with the disease, as Baxter explained:

> Weyer's case for distinguishing between witches who are female and *used by* the devil and magicians who are male and *use* the devil, is that women are subject to melancholy vapors on which the devil imprints fantasies, thereby persuading them of entirely imaginary phenomena. [84]

Agrippa and Cardan also agreed that witches are melancholic, and hence subject to visions. [85]

Bruegel too was working with this material, as it was beginning to surface in the public world of books and prints, but before its several ingredients set hard in the new *idée fixe* of the witches Sabbat. Memories of women's festivals were still quite clear. Behind the women fighting devils, Bruegel placed women breaking into a house to rob, not gold or treasures, but ordinary foodstuffs. One holds a sack, its mouth filled with loaves of bread. Quite specific references to the *old orgies* which by this date occurred *only in thought* appear to have been assembled here. In later works on witchcraft, the Sabbat could be likened to *a bustling market scene*. Thus Pierre de Lancre, an exact contemporary of Bruegel — whose two hundred-page account quickly became "authoritative"[86] — described a 1610 Sabbat:

> *Le Sabbat est comme une foire de marchands meslez, furieux et transportez, q'arrivent de toutes parts. Une recontre et meslanges de cent mille subjects soudain et transitoires, nouveaux à la verité, mais d'une nouveauté effroyable qui offence l'oeil.*[87]

Even for those firmly convinced of the Sabbat's new and diabolic character, this visualisation persisted, an echo of the original setting of women's festivals. Bruegel's ensemble of Griet and the women on the bridge was composed out of at least three different kinds of folk beliefs and customs, often found associated with Carnival or expressed in terms of the carnivalesque. Later distorted and fused into the imagery of the Sabbat, at this date they were still relatively discrete elements: ember dreamers and treasure-hunters; night-riders and those who battle evil spirits in their dreams; women who "turn the world upside down" in ritualised rebellion at certain seasons of the year. Bruegel gave these images a modern cast, most obviously by providing them with an infernal context.

In as far as the mere fact of grouping these diverse activities together is significant, he contributed to the processes of fusion completed in the next generation. Ember dreamers and night-riders accomplished their characteristic activities at night, during sleep, whereas unruly women had only recently been consigned to the sphere of dreams, and treasure-seekers were still very much operating in the real world. It is also interesting that the dangerousness of his pack of night-walkers still hovers at the level of proverbial expression (albeit with clear psychological meaning), whereas the dangerousness of Griet as leader of the festive women has been increased. Griet carries a sword, and the ripples of imagery concentrated in the corner of dark water make unmistakable play with fears of castration. Such fears seem to lie at the heart of the new attitude to witches, and explains much about the significance of their translocation into the place of dreams. Recall the kinds of paranoia expressed in the scenarios of the *Malleus Maleficarum,* whose authors, for instance, thought it necessary to prescribe *Remedies... for those who by Prestigitatory Art have lost their Virile Members or have seemingly been transformed into the shapes of Beasts*[88]

The collective male nightmare of the Sabbat was created in part by translating the traditional activities and imagery of uppity women and village witchcraft from the sphere of carnival to the sphere of dreams. The shift from day to night changed their meaning: they became uncanny and frightening rather than comic. The Sabbat was a bent mirror into which inchoate male fears and desires could be projected and returned in the shape of nightmares. The most notable dream-change of this kind is the feat of condensation and displacement represented by the second giant in the painting: the creature on the roof.

The *Dukatenscheisser* of the *Dulle Griet*
Excrement and Money in Dreams

The custom of reversing norms for ritual reasons is at work in the costume of the gross being who occupies the centre of the picture: perched on the burning roof of the town, facing into the surreal background, he/she holds the ship of the world on his back and spoons silver money from his broken-eggshell rear. This figure is a good deal less human than Griet. Its impossibly elongated leg, stretched out along the roof, can be connected to its body only by passing through the gable of the building. As far as one can tell from the stubble on its chin, its face is male. Yet it wears a female garment, a reversal which balances and matches the reversal of Griet in armour. As Duerr explained:

> To make clear that the witch was not a being of the "inside," that she had at least one foot "outside," beyond culture, a reversal of the ordinary has been used since ancient times. Thus in the Vatnsdaela saga, we are told about the old witch Ljot: *She had pulled her clothes over her head, stepping backward with her head stuck between her legs, and the glance from her eyes was not good to see.*[89]

Like Ljot, Bruegel's ship-man is more obviously malign in appearance than is Griet. In meaning and design he is a foil and balance to Griet. Rosoman considered this figure to be more strategically important to the overall design than the figure of Griet herself, in that it is just possible to imagine the painting "holding together" if Griet were removed, and impossible without the giant:

> the position of the house and the figure act as a kind of keystone to practically everything else; strong movements radiate from this point in all directions. Secondly the figure is *balanced* on the roof and the ship is *balanced* on the shoulders and this itself creates a focus... Thirdly, there is the important element of scale and the creation of a link with Meg herself: they are both about the same size. Fourthly, the actual position in depth. Most of the movement in the painting is from side to side but the skinny leg of the Monster points away from us towards the background and the posterior is thrust forward towards the foreground, creating a strong movement from front to back.[90]

This configuration is the first aspect of the *Dulle Griet* we have looked at to suggest the structure of a composite emblem, similar to the visual riddles so popular among Antwerp Humanists. Like Hoefnagel's tribute to Ortelius (fig. 38), it is a kind of visual rebus. It points the way, as it were, towards the more clearly emblematic, though no less bizarre, broken-egg construction that lies beyond the town wall. Leaving aside for the moment the significance of the ship-scene on its back, let us concentrate first on one striking aspect of this latter-day Ljot: the silver money (now tarnished to black) which fills its rear. From this we can christen the monster: it is a type of *Dukatenscheisser*, a figure known in Germanic folklore (literally, an excretor of ducats).[91]

In terms of the composition, the *Dukatenscheisser*, Griet, and the crowd of women are visually and thematically connected. A small woman reaches up to rifle the giant's purse; a long thin hand stretches out of the window above to douse her from a jug. As the giant spoons, the woman below holds up a bowl to catch the falling feces-coin. These elements are thus related structurally and symbolically in a kind of thesis and antithesis; the same actions of theft and dousing in the first are balanced by more fantastic symbolic equivalents in the second.

Bruegel's *Dukatenscheisser* derives its general shape from Bosch. It bears a family resemblance to the "alchemical man" — the giant deconstructed figure at the heart of the *Purgatory* panel in the *Garden of Earthly Delights* (fig. 17c). Images analogous in certain respects to this figure, using the motifs of cauldron and money pouring from a giant body, can be found in paintings by followers of Bosch working at Antwerp in the 1520s and 1530s. One design exists in a number of variants: a surreal rendering of the Vision of Tondalus.[92] As Tondalus sleeps, we see behind him a dream of hell. At the centre of this design (fig. 47), coins drip from a giant's nose onto the heads of people half-submerged in an outsized barrel. The nose's vast face is empty and mask-like, like the head in Bruegel's *St Anthony* (fig. 32).

Though Bruegel's monster is part of a complex, more emblematic kind of image, the Great Nose of the *Visio Tondalus* suggests a common thematic structure: both figurations involve body-contents, money, and Hell as a dream destination. Early psychoanalysts discovered that gold and excrement were symbolic equivalents, in both popular and elite culture. Freud and Oppenheim conducted their research into structures of this kind

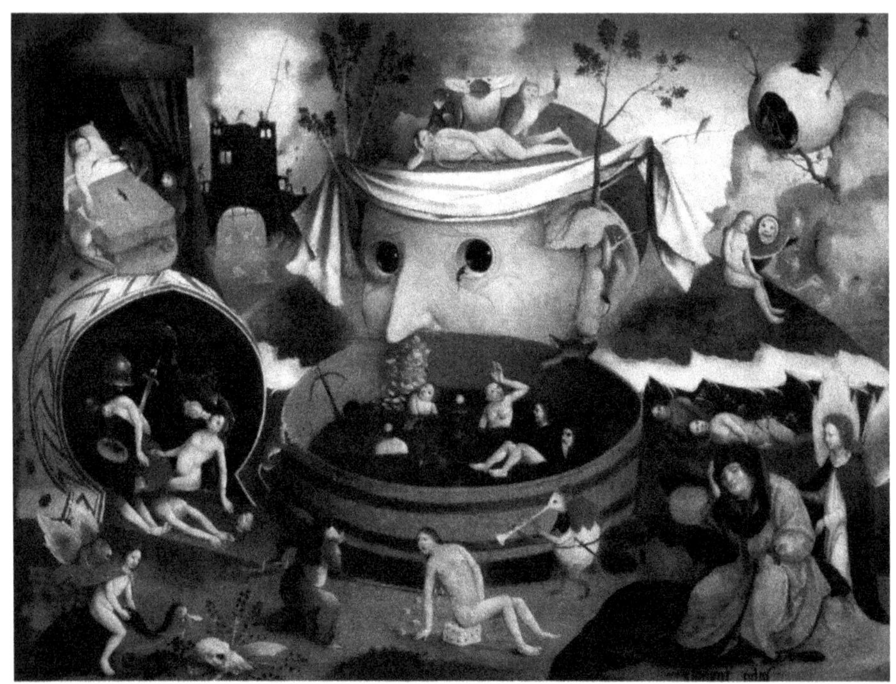

47 Anon, The Vision of Tondalus, Antwerp workshop, c 1530. Oil on Panel. 54 x 72 cm. Fundación Lázaro Galdiano, Madrid. Inv 2892

in folklore at a time when it was still possible to study peasant oral culture at first hand. They concluded that:

> In dreams in folklore, gold is seen in the most unambiguous way to be a symbol of feces. If the sleeper feels a need to defecate, he dreams of gold, of treasure. The disguise in the dream... is designed to mislead him into satisfying his need in bed... The dream — as though by means of endopsychic perception — states outright even if in a reversed form that gold is a sign or a symbol for feces.[93]

Variants on these dream-tales are recorded in the folklore of many regions. In all of them, unmasking the connection between treasure and excrement is the invariable end of the story, when the dreamer wakes up and finds that he has defecated in the wrong place. The dream-tale very often takes the form of a joke, of which the "revelation" is the punch-line. A significant number include an encounter with The Devil, or a visit to an afterworld. These supernatural encounters or journeys introduce the situation in which the transmuted defecation will take place.

A story related by the Humanist scholar Poggio Bracciolini (1380-1459) in his hugely popular *Facetiae* illustrates the formula at its simplest:

> My neighbor once dreamt that the devil had led him to a field to dig for gold, but he found none. Then the devil said, *It is there for sure, only you cannot dig it up now. But take note of the place, so that you may recognise it again by yourself.* When the man asked that the place should be made recognisable by some sign, the devil suggested, *Just shit on it. Then it will not occur to anybody that there is gold lying hidden here, and you will be able to recognise the exact place.* The man did so, then immediately awoke and felt that he had done a great heap in his bed.... Thus his dream gold was turned to filth.[94]

The Devil appears in this context as a representative of the spirit-world. In other folk dream-tales reported by Freud and Oppenheim, all of which have a comic punch-line similar to this, the spirit world is equated with the world of sleep. For instance, the dreamer may visit Heaven, a very superficially Christianised spirit world. In one such *indecent anecdote,* which Freud and Oppenheim describe as *extraordinarily widespread in Europe,*[95] the dreamer reaches Paradise, where he sees oil lamps hanging. When the oil burns out in a particular lamp, a human dies; an essentially pagan idea with roots in Norse legend.

In another tale-type, the peasant originally set out for Heaven because *he had heard that wheat in Heaven was standing at a high price.*[96] Therefore he harnesses his cart, whips up his horses, and drives to Heaven. The spirit world here is an adjacent region, to which the peasant can travel, undertaking a dream journey with orthodox transport. This presents an attitude to dream-time geography akin to that of the *benandanti,* who battled their foes in dreams over familiar country. In another story, once the peasant has arrived in Heaven, St. Peter must turn the dreamer into a spider, so that he may "excrete" his own escape route, descending back to the earth on the silk emanating from his body.[97] Notice that the structure of this tale presents a folk equivalent in miniature to the principle governing the metamorphosing *Rebel Angels* (fig. 21); the sign of the rebels' mortality was their capacity to procreate, the reason the peasant gives for wanting to leave Heaven is to be with his wife and children.

In the dream anecdotes dealing specifically with treasure and excrement, the dreamer's guide to the gold is as likely to be one of the spirits of the dead as The Devil.[98] The world of the dead appears as a neutral spirit world, a world very much like our own, where the dreamer finds it plausible that he can discover gold:

> We observe that those defecation dreams which are concerned with treasure contain little or no fear of death, whereas the others in which the relation to death is expressed directly (dreams of an assumption to Heaven) disregard treasure and motivate the defecation in other ways.[99]

The spirits one meets in these dreams are, of course, not entirely neutral, because the end result of their counsel is to trick the dreamer into defecating where the imaginary gold should be. The important point is that this is viewed without exception as a comic resolution. The equivalence between money and excrement is relatively free of anxiety in these stories; the effect of their surrealism is comic, not uncanny.

Turning back to Bruegel's image, to the giant *Dukatenscheisser* at the centre of the *Griet*, it is clear that comic resolution is suspended here. The folk dreams represent the transmutation of money into excrement as a trick set in the spirit-world, the consequences of which (defecation in the wrong place) are funny. This folk formulation seems to be the seed from which Bruegel developed this particular image, just as he condensed the tales of women's festivals and *hagazussas* with proverbial lore to create his particular marauding women. However, in the case of the giant, the seed material has been elaborated in an extraordinary fashion, and its simple coarse humour completely altered. What do these elaborate alterations mean, and why were they elaborated precisely in this way, at this time? Bruegel's weird *Dukatenscheisser*, with its ship-artefact and its peasant's ladle, fits Kris's sense of a *joke gone wrong*; its tone verges on the uncanny, which is to say that it evokes the presence of *aggression behind the disguise*. Understanding the complexity of this figure, with its props, its clashes of tone and rhetorical density, is the key to the picture. A collision seems to be occurring here between Bruegel's folkloric sources and other forces shaping conscious and unconscious collective attitudes.

The Psychology of Money and the Marketplace in Sixteenth Century Antwerp

> Money cannot bring happiness, because happiness is the fulfillment of infantile wishes and money is not the object of infantile wishes.[100]

This famous conclusion came from Freud's discovery that money is the symbolic equivalent of feces, or body contents in general. Freud found that in the mind of the very young infant, feces is a highly prized substance. When this valuation is repressed by upbringing, the substance is denigrated, then in adult life references to it are restricted to the spheres of insults or jokes:

> The most important residue of this former esteem is, however, that all the interest which the child has had in feces is transferred in the adult onto another material, which he learns in life to set above almost everything else — gold.[101]

Freud drew this insight from his examination of patients suffering from anal neuroses. The nature of these afflictions, of course, vary widely depending on the life history of the individual victim. The relationship between money and neurosis is also dependent upon historical circumstance.[102] The philosopher Georg Simmel expressed this idea in social terms:

> If the character of money as an ultimate purpose oversteps that intensity for an individual in which it is the appropriate expression of the economic culture of his circle, then greed and avarice emerge. I specifically wish to emphasise the dependence of these concepts on the current specific economic conditions, because the same degree of passion in acquiring and holding onto money may be quite normal for the particular importance of money in one context but may belong to the hypertrophied categories in another. Generally speaking, the threshold for the beginning of a real greed for money will be relatively high in a developed and lively money economy, but relatively low at primitive economic levels, whereas the reverse is true for avarice. Whoever is considered thrifty and reasonable in spending money under restricted circumstances little affected by the money economy, will appear to be avaricious under conditions of a quick turnover and easy money.[103]

These points are crucial. First, that money has been clinically demonstrated to be at the root of a certain kind of neurosis. Second, that avarice and greed — the two main malignant behavior patterns recognised in late medieval Europe — depend for their visibility on the status of the money market at any given period. "Money diseases" vary with the vitality or otherwise of the money market; to speak only of greed and avarice as if they were fixed entities assumes a relatively static conception of what money itself really is. The psychoanalyst Joel Kovel extended this observation to hold that all kinds of "money diseases" — that is, money-linked anal neuroses — change in character and virulence with the nature of the economic culture in which the patient lives.

Kovel's work considers the psychological syndromes that present themselves to view when changes occur in the concept of money *per se*; when it ceases to be a material thing and becomes the invisible medium of credit, when it is less present in the world as sensual heavy gold than it is as a series of abstract digits. The imagery in which this kind of "social" neur-

expresses itself bears a remarkable resemblance to Bruegel's concept of the giant. Writing in 1981, Kovel described the case history of one of his patients, a New York banker, as follows:

> Though he was unable to enjoy commodities or even to much use them, he was fiendishly interested in money for its own sake, i.e., as part of himself. Its accumulation warmed him and its expenditure chilled him. Nor did this occur metaphorically, so to speak, but was accompanied by direct bodily sensations. In sessions when Curtis talked of money, its passage through his hands or the relations at work through which it was made, sensations in his groin or neck or rectum — stabbing pains or moments of flushing — would occur. Sometimes he felt as if a warm fluid were incontinently running down his legs, at other times as though his insides would rise through his gorge and choke him. To say that Curtis was fiendishly interested in money is not an idle comment. As the analysis proceeded, we learned that for him, to be declining in wealth was to open the portals of his body, especially his anus, to demons. These were variously described, usually as powerful men who resembled people in real life; at times they had a purely fantastic aspect. They would come for him, nail him to a rack, pull his insides out to extract the precious stuff.[104]

The specific imagery of this fantasy is suggestive. Evidently, connections between money, excrement, bodily deformation and demons are phenomena conceived of visually and sensually under certain conditions. The details of this modern fantasy provide another term against which to measure the distance between the way in which these connections are shown in the folk dreams and in the figure of Bruegel's giant. The banker's experience surely must count as symptomatic of fully-fledged neurosis. The graphic intensity of its imagery makes the *Dukatenscheisser* look almost tame by comparison. Yet, in comparison to the relative simplicity with which the same elements are interwoven in the peasant tales, it is, I think, possible to see that Bruegel's visualisation takes these elements and brings them closer to the condition of Kovel's banker. The relation between money and excrement in his image has more in common with the role money plays in the mind of a modern neurotic businessman than it does with the relatively anxiety-free peasant dreams.

The position of Bruegel's invention here on this scale from the comic to the neurotic is borne out in part by the earlier analysis of the comic status of the *Dulle Griet* as a whole. I suggested then that the *Griet* presents a range of shifts in tone from the comic to the uncanny or nightmarish. The image of the *Dukatenscheisser* hovers on this borderline between the comic and the uncanny. Its closest relation to nightmare is the way in which the equivalence between money and feces present in the folk dreams has now become an identity. Treasure is the feces of this monster, just as for Kovel's patient money was experienced as a bodily part of himself. Bruegel's nightmarish image represents a kind of midpoint in the development of money-related images in the unconscious. Economic developments during Bruegel's lifetime support this hypothesis.

The relationship between money inside and outside the mind appears to turn around the increasing number of ways in which money *ceases* to supply the same affective satisfactions as its infantile equivalent. For example, Kovel connected the imagery of the banker's neurosis to the way in which money is disembodied in late capitalist society: *The money that characterises capitalism — and that Curtis labors to "make" is nothing but pure exchangability: quantity itself without any occluding quality. The sensuous character of money is ultimately a burden to capitalism, which insists on an ever-widening abstraction of the world.*[105] He continued:

> None [of my patients], to my knowledge, treat money as a purely abstract medium of exchange. As far as the capitalist society goes in the direction of abstraction, so do its individuals go to negate that direction... Excrement... as the most sensuously real production of the human body links the infantile life of power with money, the sign of adult power and the most desenuously real production of the human mind.[106]

Kovel, not unnaturally, is angered by the psychological results that this engenders, but the core of his argument is that the more abstract the money system becomes, the more sensuously real become the unconscious configurations of money in the minds of his patients. To phrase the matter as neutrally as possible, it is clear that any system of money is a mental abstraction invented by human minds. It is also clear that such a system, once invented, itself operates upon the minds of people living in it and with it. It then seems probable that, as a money system grows in complexity and reaches higher levels of abstraction, so too the position of money in men's minds and in their dreams will become increasingly complicated and elaborated.

Examples of this process can be found associated with earlier and later changes in the money system. A revealing story is told of Peter Damian (c. 1007-72), a famous hermit who was offered a gift of silver by an abbot. He tried unsuccessfully to turn it down, then became troubled by his acceptance: *At night, when he was trying to recite psalms, his head swarmed with dizziness, and his intestines seemed to undulate with a swarm of vermin.* Peter then returned the silver. Lester Little interpreted the tale historically:

> In this very personal experience [we] see Peter Damian's definitive rejection of gift-economy behavior in connection with the religious life, behavior that he had interpreted not in its own terms but in terms of the commercial environment in which he had grown up, studied, and taught.[107]

In this case, a nightmare linking treasure and bodily contents occurs at a transition point between the old "gift-economy" of the early monastic orders and the new commercial economy of the towns, where silver is seen as money, not as treasure. When Peter later became Cardinal Bishop of Ostia, his policy was to translate his church's accumulated treasure into the local economy as money.

The imagery of popular prints shows further stages in the trajectory

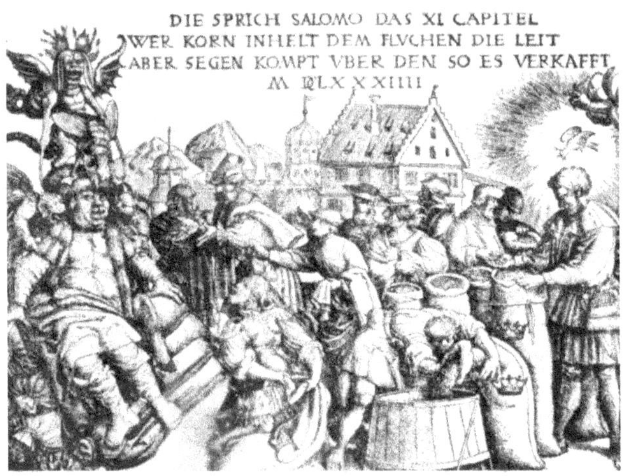

48 Anon, *Merchant with Moneybags and Demon*, German (?), 1574. Engraving Bibliothèque Nationale, Paris. Photo: after Jeannin (1957)

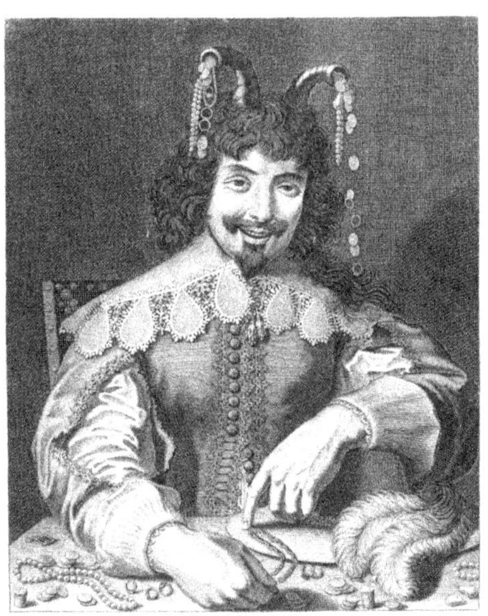

49 François Langlois ("Chiartres"), *Le Cornard Contant*, early 17C. Engraving, 31 x 22 cm. Harvard University, Baker Library

of the metaphor after Bruegel. A German print from 1574 bears an Old Testament inscription, a favourite Lutheran quotation: *Thus spake Solomon, He that withholdeth corn, the people shall curse him, blessings shall be upon the head of him that selleth it* (*Proverbs*, 11.26). The picture translates this injunction against miserly hoarding into modern terms (fig. 48).[108] As a visualisation, the tableau is dominated by a grotesquely fat merchant, with the townspeople in supplication behind him. Pictorially, this figure is part of a pyramid of bulging sacks. While halos grace the heads of his open handed colleagues, the curse on the fat merchant is given literal form; a monstrous hybrid demon crowns his head and smaller ones attend his shoulders.

In a more secular vein, a French print, *Le Cornard Contant* from the early seventeenth century (fig. 49), depicts a *happy cuckold,* who does not care about losing his honour, because he has *horns of plenty* which make him very happy.[109] This smiling cuckold wears horns festooned with bells and beads; from the mouth of each horn dribbles a stream of coins. This invention is thus explicitly presented as a visualisation of misplaced or displaced desire.

These examples suggest that the original metaphorical equation of gold and body-contents became the subject of surreal elaboration in the course of the sixteenth century, and that Bruegel's work with the imagery was part of this wider development. The general stimulus for this change was undoubtedly the mercantile transformation of sixteenth-century culture, in which Antwerp played a precocious and extraordinary role. This was, after all, the city which Ehrenberg described as:

> a trading centre such as the world had never seen before or since; for never since has there been a market which concentrated to such a degree the trade of all the important commercial nations of the world.[110]

The mechanisms by which this splendour was achieved indicate the key changes of culture and experience at issue here. Van der Wee's study of the growth of the Antwerp market concluded that the amazing success of the

Antwerp merchants in the middle of the century can be ascribed largely to the boom in implementing new forms of credit:

> In these circumstances, the massive participation of the ordinary merchant in long-distance trade would have been impossible without credit. Bonds to bearer circulated ever more quickly and safely and reduced metallic payments to a minimum. The wider use of the bill of exchange circulating from hand to hand made it possible also to mobilise capital for distant transactions.[111]

At Antwerp, the main innovation lay in the new use of letters obligatory. These had always been a means of postponing payment; now by making them payable to bearers, *they began to pass from hand to hand, as a form of fiduciary money, until the point was frequently reached when the original debtor received his own letter as a credit from another party.*[112]

The widespread use of such bonds was also an adaptation to fluctuations in availability and value of metallic currency. By mid-century, Antwerp depended on shipments of precious metals from the New World via Spain. In 1553, Thomas Gresham wrote to London:

> Here is no kind of gold stirring, which is the strangest matter that ever was seen upon the Bourse of Antwerp, having no other payment but silver Spanish reals; as for angels and sovereigns here is none to be gotten, for that the exchange is so high.[113]

Other developments combined to further the abstraction of the money system which the shift to credit represented, while at the same time increased risks created an atmosphere of high anxiety. Thus in 1543 Charles V approved the practice of lending at interest. According to Guicciardini, lending at interest together with "exchange arbitrage" were the main activities at the Antwerp Bourse by the 1560s.[114]

The Bourse was no sober club; incidents of violence were not unknown and the new building (1531) itself was plagued by vandals and graffiti writers.[115] It was also a centre for gossip and scandal of all kinds. *He that will believe every nue that is blasted in Flanders amongst merchants shall have a mad head,* commented Stephen Vaughan to Cromwell in a dispatch in 1535.[116] Prior to the sixteenth-century boom, the financial structure of Antwerp was relatively primitive. There had been no precedent in local customary law or in surviving Roman private law for the transferability of debts.[117] This in part explains the extraordinary atmosphere at the Bourse:

> The financial structure of the first half of the sixteenth century was so deeply embedded in medieval tradition that exchange activities were completely dominated by 'gambling and chance.' Betting and lotteries were everyday affairs. People betted on everything, on the return of ships from the East or West Indies, on the next journey by Philip II to the Netherlands, on the armistice between the King and the rebels, and even on the sex of unborn children or the date of the death of certain people. These bets were often linked with commercial contracts.[118]

Jeannin discusses a contract from 1534, whose validity depended on the buyer marrying a nun or the daughter of a nun within a set time; also a macabre case of life-insurance fraud (apparently very common at Antwerp) from 1566. He summarises that:

> la bizarrerie de telles conventions... constituent une forme archaïque, dont moins abstraite, de la speculation qui consiste a vendre des marchandise au pris qu'elles atteindront à une date ultérieure... Le pari ici porte sur la conjuncture, non plus sur la réalisation d'un eventement fortuit, différence importante; mais dans le deux cas le pari participe de la même psychologie... n'est-ce pas la même chance qui distribue les gains en affaires et au jeu? La réussite pourtant est plus sûre si l'on aide la chance: fraude au jeu, habileté en affaires... *Loterie tromperie,* note en souscrivent un Anversois; il souscrit néanmoins.[119]

While the Antwerp economy underwent a series of visible booms and depressions (famine and a wave of bankruptcies in 1556-7),[120] following the Peace of Cateau-Cambrésis, the Bourse was back in business.

Bruegel's working life was bound up in these developments in practical and psychological ways. In 1540, the Guild of St. Luke moved its headquarters to the new Bourse. By 1560, it had expanded to include a large number of luxury crafts supported by the international marketplace. In addition to painters, illuminators, sculptors and printers, there were now mirror makers, gold beaters, makers of artistic buttons, embroiderers, harpsichord and organ builders, etc., etc. The fortunes of the guild depended increasingly on the augmented economy generated at the Bourse.[121] Whereas in the fifteenth century *the urban authorities still took measures to forbid or at least limit sale "on the tally"*, by the sixteenth century, everybody in Antwerp, including the guilds and corporations, *bought increasingly retail and soon almost all on credit.*[122] Using information from the accounts of the Church of Our Lady in Antwerp, van der Wee explains that:

> The sixteenth century saw an enormous expansion of consumption credit not only in the commercial but in the private sphere. Institutions asked longer and longer credit. They bought less in the markets and more from local retailers. Whereas the churches, for example, had the habit of buying wine in large quantities on the market, the tally came to be used more and more in the sixteenth century. Accounts were sometimes settled only after a period of two years. For the ordinary man, the tally of the bakers and innkeepers had become the normal way to buy on credit.[123]

Money-transactions swiftly replaced barter in other areas of life; in the rules governing discipline within print shops, for example. A set of regulations for 1555-6 from Plantin's shop, the Golden Compasses, shows that employees had to atone for breaches of the rules by presenting jugs of ale in various numbers. For apprentices, corporal punishments could be meted out. The older men could also be physically punished for grave sins, such as dropping valuable typefaces, or they could choose to pay a fine instead. In the next surviving set of records, from 1563, all the fines are expressed in money.[124] Though regulation sheets have not survived, similar rules were doubtless in force at the Four Winds, since both establishments came under the aegis of the Guild of St. Luke's. The shift from barter to money, from corporal punishment or jugs of ale to monetary fines changed the culture of the craft workplace, making it less physical and more impersonal; a direct example of qualitative change in Bruegel's *milieu*.

The social ramifications are clear: money became the common measure for the assignment of values in more and more aspects of life. Agnew analysed the psychological impact of this in terms of consumption:

> Money... makes it possible to divide the act of exchange of real goods between two dates... By thus extending the moment and the distance of exchange, money undermines the immediate bilateral negotiation of direct barter, while simultaneously underwriting a prolonged multilateral competition among buyers and sellers. Money thus seems to bear within itself the seed of capitalism... Money's capacity to defer or postpone consumption [was] limited during the Middle Ages [in ways] not recognized until the late fifteenth century nor fully remedied until the late seventeenth century.[125]

In other words, money splits the original exchange of goods into two *mutually indifferent acts*, and as such makes it possible to defer the conclusion (even, one might say, the consummation) of the transaction almost indefinitely. This what made Max Weber call money *the most abstract and impersonal element that exists in personal life*. Money, in Little's formulation, is what makes dealings between strangers in an urban society possible.[126]

The sudden expansion in and elaboration of the uses of money had psychological implications and consequences. The system of money engenders an attitude of delayed consumption which fits the general profile of anal neurosis:

> within the context of the expanded commerce of the sixteenth and seventeenth centuries... money now appeared to be a source of productive possibilities, not just a protection against them. The desire for liquidity thereby... suggested a simultaneous readiness and reluctance to transact — a threshold moment of indecision in the cycle

of exchange, a moment frozen in the money form itself.[127]

Agnew implies here that the new liquidity — more precisely, the new *desirability* of liquidity — resulted in the adoption of a permanent, speculative mercantile attitude towards the world. The "threshold experience" of the marketplace thus was simultaneously internalised and turned outwards once more, to judge the world and its contents by the new yardstick of exchangability.

With this psychological and economic background in mind, the significance of the staging in the *Griet* becomes clearer. The middle ground of the painting is an infernal city, dominated by the Hell-mouth and by the figure of the money-spooning giant. This monstrous *Dukatenscheisser* is filled with the silver money, the standard coinage of Flanders. Formally, he is tied to the image of the town in the painting; enveloped in the building where the looting is going on. He functions, in fact, as a kind of town sign.

Both giant figures have symbolic associations with the town of Antwerp, as Sullivan realised:

> Two civic symbols are prominent features of... Antwerp's pageantry at this time — the beautiful young Maid of Antwerp (who traditionally wore rich red sleeves, and the Antwerp Giant (an effigy so large it would not fit through the city gates). The Antwerp Giant, who always wore a helmet and breastplate, had been designed for the city of 1534 by Bruegel's master Pieter Coecke.[128]

This type of processional civic giant was new in the sixteenth century. Town giants were larger-than-life portable sulptures, designed to show off civic authority. They grew out of the genre of the festival Triumph, expanding on (and in some cases inventing wholesale) regional popular traditions about giants as legendary inhabitants of Northern Europe. The character of Coecke's giant, Druon Antigonus, was taken from just such an old foundation myth.[129] The city fathers of British, Flemish and northern French towns seem to have used these figures to simultaneously cow and impress their citizens.[130] George Puttenham wrote sardonically of:

> these midsommer pageants in London, where, to make the people wonder, are set forth great and vglie Gyants marching as if they were alive, and armed at all points, but within they are stuffed full of brown paper and tow, which the shrewd boyes underpeering do guilefully discover and turne to a great derision.[131]

Appreciating the artifice of these monsters was more than half the point; this may have encouraged Bruegel aptly to stuff his deformed civic Giant with silver coins. A penchant around the middle of the century for bestowing brides on these giants is also suggestive. At Louvain, the new wife of the giant was named Megara in 1521.[132] The Maid and the Giant of Antwerp appeared together in a tableau presented at an Antwerp *ommegang* of 1561.[133]

Sullivan argued that these two images in the *Griet* are subsumed into an allegory of Madness; I think the imagery can be interpreted more specifically than this. Bruegel has cast the Maid of Antwerp as a Dulle Griet, a *hagazussa*, the epitome of the women run amok in their dream-time. His *Dukatenscheisser* is an even more perverse version of the Antwerp Giant. The reversal of attributes in this couple — like the reversals in their dress — is a mark of the ominous night-world they inhabit. Both figures then evoke Antwerp, though the money-giant seems to embody more specifically what is wrong with the life of the town in the manner of his deformation.

The house on which the giant sits has a burning straw roof, dramatising the instability of its position. Next to the fire and the giant's foot, a small man protrudes through a hole in the roof. He scrapes a kettle with a knife (figure 35a). This image represents the proverb *hij wil altijde het onderste uit de kan halen* — the English equivalent is the expression *to scrape the pot* — referring to people who want more than is reasonable.[134] The small scene stands in relation to the giant as the proverb *she could tie the devil to a pillow* stands to Griet; it operates as a sort of simpler introduction to the more complex image.

Maeterlinck suggested that an idiom *Geldschijten*, to defecate gold, might have been in existence around this time.[135] Dundes and Stibbe traced an expression *poeprijk*, literally *shit-rich* (cf. English *filthy rich*)[136] These associations support a reading of the images around the *Dukatenscheisser* as references to contemporary "money-diseases". They all evoke a complex of ideas and experiences to do with money, excrement, greed and the *bizarreries* of consumption. The clever satire of these scenes works by simplifying and abstracting recognisable elements from the simultaneously archaic and modern Antwerp marketplace. In as far as these scenes involve a denunciation of *Avaritia*, the concept they convey of this has less in common with medieval depictions than with the updated, adaptable Vices that populated the *rederijker* stage.

That said, certainly some ideas stemming from the old personification of Avarice, its images and attributes, inform Bruegel's thought here. Perceptions of Avarice, as Simmel noted, are contingent on circumstance, and vary from age to age. During the thirteenth century, a broad shift of this kind occurred. Avarice began to rival Pride for the position of the chief vice in religious thought,[137] a development linked to the rise of towns and the formation of an urban, mercantile society based on money: *If pride was the greatest vice of those who held power in precommercial society, then avarice held a corresponding place in connection with the rich people of commercial society.*[138] The change in the status of avarice was a sign of an increasing ambivalence towards money and a growing tendency to visualise money as *filthy and disgusting waste.*[139]

Two centuries before the *Griet*, the imagery of money-madness was already proliferating in these lurid directions. An early fourteenth-century Flemish manuscript shows on one page an ape defecating coins which are caught in a bowl (fig. 50a). On another page, an attenuated hybrid creature — growing out of the capital *I* of *Imagis* (fig. 50b) — also excretes coins into a bowl held by an ape. These images represent early visual examples of what was to become a fixed piece of visual rhetoric: an early seventeenth-century print depicts an ass defecating coins, as peasants, merchants and aristicrats alike hurry to catch them in a bowl.[140]

As images condensing defecation, bestial appetite and money, the manuscript apes are ancestors of Bruegel's surreal central giant, and also of his apes. In manuscript tradition, the ape stands for the fleshly, physical aspects of mankind; in Bruegel's *Pedlar Pillaged by Apes* (fig. 31), the apes work as *sinnekens*. In the *Griet*, they carry both roles. Apes and monkeys gambol and snake their tails in every corner of the scene; theirs are among the many pairs of peering eyes which look sidelong at the viewer from behind a tree, an arch or a shield.[141]

Over the course of the sixteenth-century, the gold-body-waste tradition was developed in many ways, and these can be understood as responses to the novel social and psychological effects as money-based culture became the dominant norm. Bruegel's earlier images of avarice and money-diseases show how he responded to the subject in the years before he commenced the *Dulle Griet*; what he took from the older visual culture of money, and how he re-invented this imagery to fit the contemporary situation.

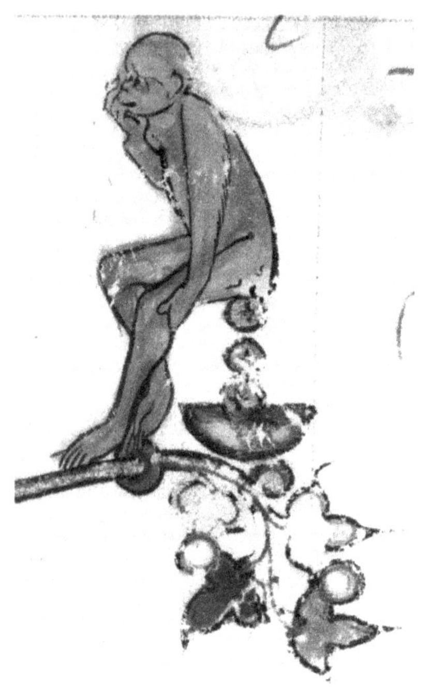

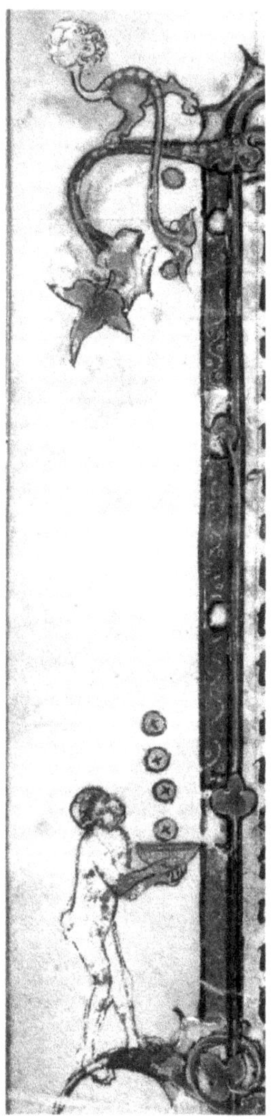

50a *Ape Defecating Coins*, Breviary, use of Saint-Pierre of Blandigny, Ghent, first quarter of fourteenth century. British Museum, London, Add. 29253, f. 410^{V}. Photo: © BM Images

50b *Monster Defecating Coins*, Breviary, use of Saint-Pierre of Blandigny, Ghent, first quarter of fourteenth century. British Museum, London, Add. 29253, f. 41^{V}. Photo: © BM Images

Avarice and Men as Containers of Money

Bruegel created his image of the *Dukatenscheisser* after making several previous works which comment on the social and psychological consequences of money and urban life. Three of these works by or associated with our artist speak eloquently of his interest in, and strong views about, the theme of money. First, there is Bruegel's own depiction of *Avaritia* (1556; fig. 10). Recall that Bruegel chose to start his series of the Seven Sins with this particular Vice. The design contains a number of visual inventions reprised in the *Griet*: a broken egg-like vessel filled with money; two anal hybrids in the lower right corner; the naked couple with a hybrid companion; the crossbowmen (here also competing for money); the purse-cutter; the cauldron in a hollow tree.

Lady Avarice herself Bruegel represented traditionally, as a seated woman, a treasure chest beside her. She wears the kind of fifteenth-century headdress whose horns, contemporary moralists asserted, were the hideout of devils. The horns of the Happy Cuckold, overflowing with money (fig. 49), represent a late example of this tradition. In the middle ground of the *Griet*, a figure with the same distinctive headdress as Lady Avarice presides at a picnic in the corner of the huge broken egg-harp emblem. This scene, not least on account of the contrast of scale, evokes other surreal picnics inside grotesque heads or bodies. The idea originated probably with Bosch himself (there is one in the *Purgatory* panel of the *Garden of Earthly Delights*; fig. 17c); the device became a favourite template for scurrilous Reformation prints (figs. 37, 104). By the date of the *Griet*, the visual combination of old woman with picnic would also have had a whiff of the sabbat about it.

In terms of the surreal imagery, the most striking overlaps between the denizens of *Avaritia* and those of the *Griet* occur in figures depicting the over-valuation of money through monstrous distortions of body and appetite. Prominent in *Avaritia* is the nude male figure being cut in half by a gigantic pair of scissors; this detail is echoed in the *Dulle Griet* by the group in the water underneath the Hell-mouth, where a nude human is bisected by a scissor-like beak. In the foreground of *Avaritia,* a long-beaked bird pokes at an anus and the constipated body of a *gryllus* sags like a purse. Both have equivalents in the foreground of the painting, in figures to the left of Griet.

Bruegel's metamorphic structures are allied loosely to emblem-book designs, and it is tempting to view Avarice's picnic in the *Griet* as a clue to the meaning of the whole edifice in which she sits. A contemporary mode of painterly thought in the Netherlands composed by placing the "real subject" of the picture in small-scale in the background, so that it was at first sight eclipsed by apparently incidental genre or still-life scenes. Bruegel's own *Christ Carrying the Cross* (1564; Kunsthistorisches Museum, Vienna) "hides" the figure of Christ himself in the crowd in this way. The miniature picnic of Avarice in the middle-ground of the *Dulle Griet* may be a device of this kind. Whatever the spatial position and scale of Dame Avarice, the consequences of her rule are legible both in Bruegel's print and in his painting. The metamorphic "consequences" of money-madness, outlined in the foreground of the print, are pushed further, folded in on themselves, to produce new levels of complexity in the *Griet*. The "excess" at the heart of the *Griet*"s surrealism is a rhetorical elaboration of visual ideas in the earlier work.

Our second Bruegelian work related to money comes from a series of proverb illustrations, engraved by Jean Wierix (1549-1618), around 1568. The picture is known as *The Man With the Sack of Gold and His Flatterers* (fig. 51). The mystery surrounding the execution of this series makes it hard to assign this design definitely to Bruegel, but stylistically it must be of his circle.[142] It shows a giant crouching figure with a square-shaped opening cut into his rear. Through this opening, a group of men crawl. The giant holds under one arm a long sack of money from which gold coins fall to the ground. The bag is drawn in such a way, however, that its opening can be read graphically as the cuff of his sleeve. The money thus seems to fall out of his arm through his fingers to the ground.

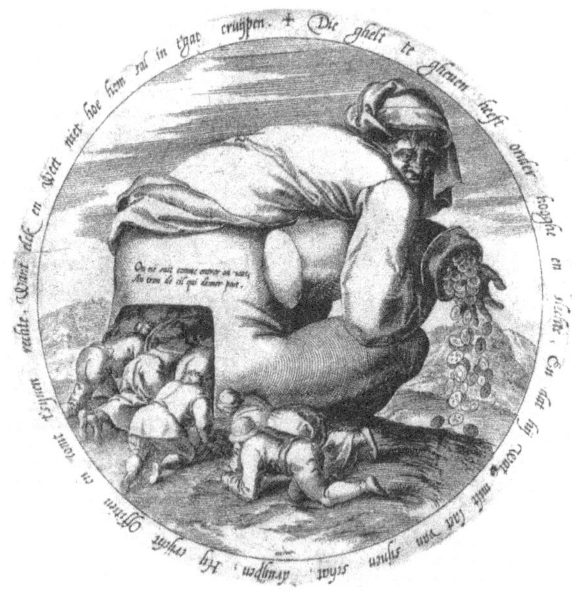

51 Jan Wierix, after Pieter Bruegel, *The Man with the Moneybag and His Flatterers*, c.1568, from *Emblemata Secularia* by J.-Th. de Bry. Photo: after Lebeer

The print bears a French text engraved on the figure of the man himself, and a Flemish text around the circular perimeter of the print:

> *Die ghelt te gheuen heeft ander hooghe en slechte, En dat hij wat milt laet van sijnen schat, druijpen, Hy crijcht offitien en comt t'synen rechte, Want elck en weet niet hoe hem sal in t'gat cruijpen*
>
> [He who has money to spend among the great and the small, and lets it run lavishly through his fingers, gets offices and all that he wants, for they all scramble to creep into his hole].

The French is more succinct: *On ne sais comme entrer on veut / Au trou de cil qui donner peut* [why crawl up his arse when he opens his purse]. The relationship between gold and body contents is configured slightly differently here than it is in the giant of the *Griet*, but the elements are the same. In the one, men crawl into a grossly enlarged anal entrance in order to receive money; in the other, money is spooned out from the same place to be caught below.

The third work is Bruegel's famous *The Battle of the Money-banks and Strongboxes* (fig. 52), plausibly dated by Würtenberger to 1558.[143] Bruegel devised a battle between animated "piggy-banks" and reinforced treasure chests. The banks and boxes have armoured legs and arms. Some also have heads; most do not. In the left foreground, the only round money-bank with a human head attached is also the only one with an ordinary opening, like a jug or vessel. Its confederates are closed shapes, broken here and there by the weapons of their enemies to show gold coins leaking out from inside. At the left, one has a human head stuffed around with coins.

Again, the body contents of these weird beings are, obviously, money. The general meaning of this picture is immediately evident. It is usually taken as a satirical attack on war and on the wealth necessary to finance campaigns. Schama has described it as an *image of capitalism as all-out war*.[144] The subject was topical, since, as any urban Fleming would know, a major cause of the worsening relations between the Netherlandish cities and the imperial government was the imposition of extraordinary taxes to pay for the imperial wars. In his last decades as emperor, Charles V did little else but seek revenues to pursue his campaigns, while Phillip's even more relentless imprecations were particularly focused on Antwerp.

If this print was, as seems likely, designed in 1558, then it dates from the year before the Peace of Cateau-Cambrésis, when Philip was forcing loans from his merchants to pay his troops.[145] The depiction of the two forces as armoured men evokes knightly wars. The armour makes a more specific allusion to sin. A giant knightly helmet is featured in a print satirising chivalry (fig. 53), apparently an invention by Bosch.[146] Pride was the sin of the mighty and the Fall of Pride was customarily depicted as a knight in armour falling off his horse.[147] The idea of an evil knight as Pride

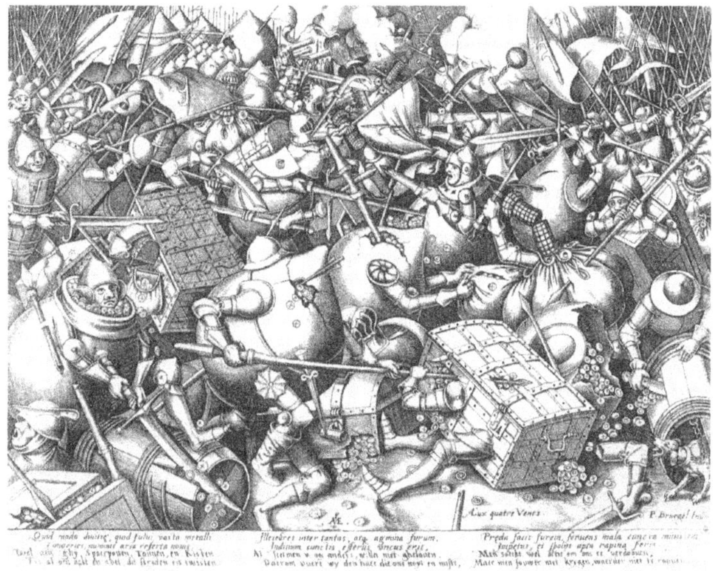

52 Pieter van der Heyden, after Pieter Bruegel, *The Battle between the Moneybanks and the Strongboxes*, c 1558. Engraving, 23.7 x 30.4 cm. Bibliothèque Royale Belgique, Brussels. S 11135114

53 After Bosch (?), *Satire on Chivalry*, Engraving. Bibliothèque Royale Belgique, Brussels. S 11 31203 f res

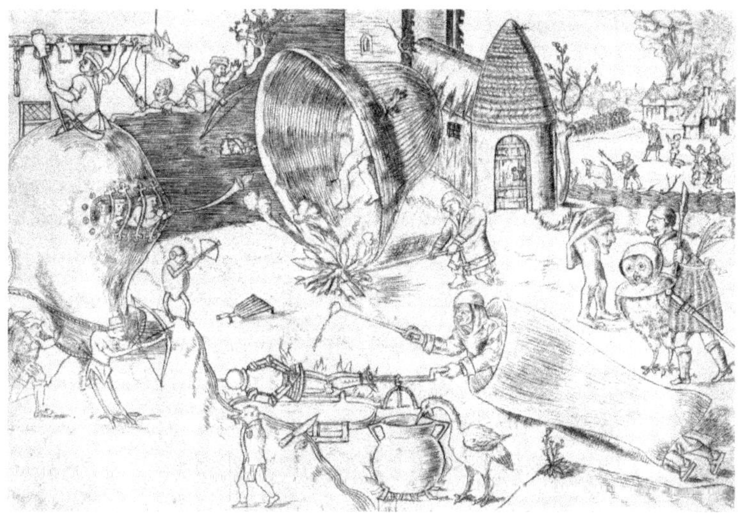

invites us to see present in this battle the two chief vices, Pride and Avarice, and the deadly consequence of their marriage, war.

Several of Bruegel's contemporaries also explored the themes of excess wealth and its attendant evils. A lockable treasure-chest — overflowing with bonds, money-bags, goblets, etc — fills the foreground of a *Kitchen Scene with Christ in the House of Martha and Mary* by Pieter Aertsen (1552; Kunsthistorisches Museum, Vienna). There it functions as an allegory against materialism (the domain of Martha versus that of Mary),[148] somewhat more pointedly than the more common wealth of food. The Humanist Dirck Coornhert (1522-1590), and the painter, Maarten van Heemskerck (1498–1574), also produced works on the evils of money around the time that Bruegel made his *Battle of the Moneyboxes* print. In each case, their strictures were couched in the language of allegorical humanism. Coornhert published several works in 1550 about riches and righteous living. In his *Roerspel der Kettersche Werelt*:

> Everyman is dressed as a rich merchant and is converted by Money to the belief that physical and spiritual salvation can be acquired by riches. Falsehood then instructs him that the ways to win it are (naturally) through deceit, usury, and theft.[149]

Van Heemskerck's *Divitum Misera Sors* (*The Unhappy Lot of the Rich*, 1563) similarly represented the personified miseries deriving from money arranged as an allegorical float. The series of six prints were all engraved by Philip Galle (1537-1612), Bruegel's best collaborator. Plate Four (fig. 54) shows Queen Money's cart drawn by Danger and Fear, while Robbery hides in her cloak. They are followed by Folly, Envy, Theft and the Entire Populace. Van Heemskerck's designs for the great procession of floats through the city of Antwerp in 1561 used eight allegorical Triumphs to represent the cycle of human troubles. The Triumph of Wealth came before those of Pride, Envy, and War:

> Th[is] triumphal car featured Opulentia riding Fame, accompanied by all the usual undesirable traits associated with her victory. Her charioteer was Guile, her steeds Fraud and Rapine, her attendants Usury, Betrayal, and Lust.[150]

This illuminates the professional hinterland of Bruegel's decisions in the *Griet*. Bruegel could easily have used the same system of personifications. Instead, he dramatised his similar set of abstractions in a completely different manner.

The interest of Bruegel's visual thought lies in the forms he invented to embody these themes. Closer to Bruegel's thought is an *Allegorical Hunt of Money*, another engraving by Galle, after Johannes Stradanus (1536–1605), published at Antwerp in 1578 (fig. 55), The personifications are given more dynamic relationships; three figures, supported by their hounds, hunt Lady Money, while Lady Justice is trodden underfoot. The peasant's hounds are Frugality, Industry and Labor; Lady Prodigality has Rapine and Chance, Lady Avarice has Usury and Fraud. A rhetorical tendency to brachiate and elaborate is in evidence here. The device of the hounds allows for elegant proliferation, so the lesser corroborative abstractions are both literally tied to, and ripple out from, their central figurations. This resembles the strategies of the *Griet*. Formally also, in terms of composition and action, the visual idea of this print has marked similarities with the *Griet*: large-scale personifications, engaged in desperate action, with a varied panoramic landscape filling the frame. The reduced composition with a smaller number of bigger-scale figures is, the direction which Bruegel himself helped set for painting at the end of the 1560s. The print's wild Lady Prodigality could be a daughter of Dulle Griet.

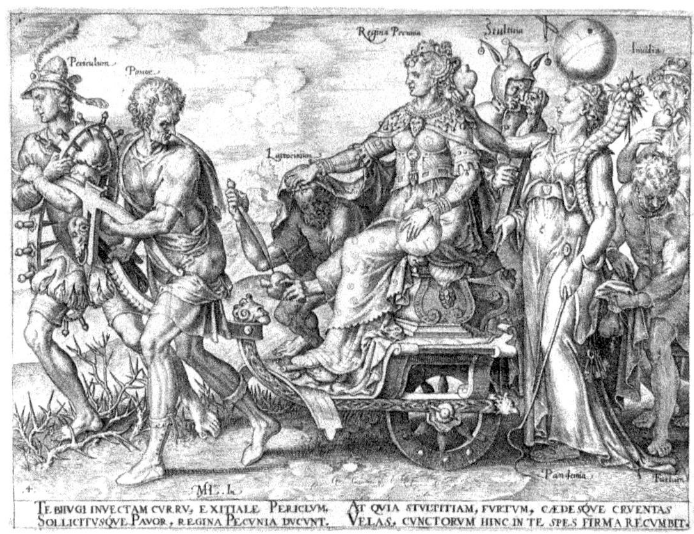

54 Philip Galle, after Maarten van Heemskerck, *Divitum Misera Sors* (The Unhappy Lot of the Rich; Plate 4 of 6), Antwerp, 1563. Engraving, 17 x 23cm. Museum Boijmans van Beuningen, Rotterdam

55 Philip Galle, after Johannes Stradanus, *Money pursued with hounds by Prodigality, Avarice, and a peasant,* Antwerp, 1578. Engraving, 21.7 x 24 cm. Baker Library, Harvard University

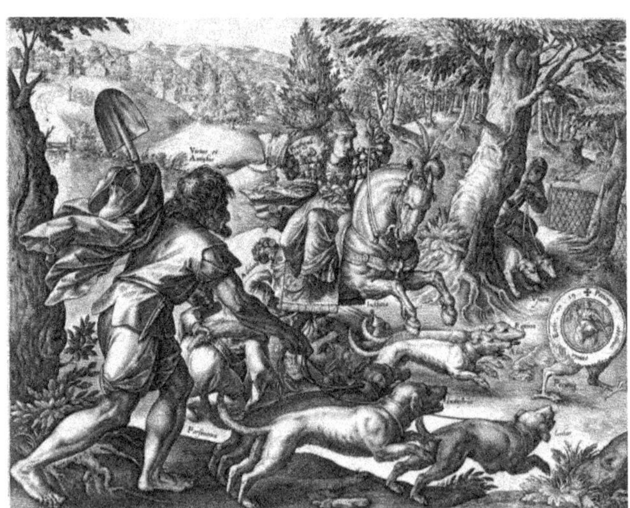

The main differences are therefore equally telling. Compared to his contemporaries, Bruegel creates more different kinds of *sinnekins* by developing his corroborative abstractions from folk-characters and folk-language, and from the metamorphic hybrid tradition; his genius for panorama enabled him to manage vast crowds of such figures. The resulting surrealism is so striking as to make Bruegel's visual ideas appear sharply distinguished from those of his contemporaries.

Consider the complexity even of the apparently rather simple animated money-men in the *Battle of the Money-banks and Strongboxes* (fig. 52). These money-bank and treasure-chest men are usually described as humanised inanimate objects, as though they are dead receptacles, which have weirdly come to life and sprouted limbs. They are, in a sense, a new kind of jar-man, last seen in the *Temptation of Anthony* (fig. 32). Equally, it is possible to construe them as men who have become dehumanized; they have devolved, in a Pico-esque way. The fighting money-banks invite us to read them as men whose bodies have become carapaces of constipated wealth; the strong-boxes are people imprisoned in their own treasure chests, locked in for life. All march under the carnivalesque banner of the hook or barb.

Besides these two main types, there are also purse-men and barrel-knights. The prevalent type is the pear-shaped money-bank. The range of forms among these implies a metamorphic progression. At the centre of the picture, slightly to the top right, is a fat knight, whose swollen ceramic torso logically derives from his helmeted head and armoured collar and arms. The left corner holds a similar knight, with a similar collar. But here, the collar is extended, and the gap between neck and head stuffed with coins; as if the head was about to sink into and be swallowed up by the body, drowned in coins. In the central group, the final stage in this metamorphosis has occurred. Two headless bank-men blindly fight on. Their bodies, like those of the chest-men, are completely without openings, other than those caused by the weapons of their enemies. One of these headless figures still has its armoured hat, perched incongruously on the surface of the carapace which its owner has become.

The dehumanization process owes part of its success to the ingenious choice of armour, itself a form of chilling encasement. Between the cap-like helmet and the fully visored helmet the human face disappears. A visored helmet is a deadly kind of mask, a fully inhuman form of head. The Boschian giant helmet (fig. 53) is like the huge "empty" heads in *St Anthony* and some of the *Vices* prints. Bruegel found the image a fruitful one. He used it again in the *Fall of the Rebel Angels* (fig. 21) and in the *Griet*. The metal helmet, like the metal-clad arm, was a ready-made image for something that is simultaneously animate and inanimate. Bruegel took full advantage of this quality in the *Battle of the Strongboxes*; he used the image also for some of the most dream-like details of the *Dulle Griet*.

In the dark right corner of the *Griet*, a large fish-monster, equipped with two mailed arms, chops in half a phallic-looking object (fig. 35c). In almost the same position, in the *Battle* print, a severed mailed arm clutches its sword. Above the castrating fish-monster in the *Griet*, the group of men huddled in the shadow of an arch are also helmeted. As in the images of the money-bank-people in their various stages of enclosure, one of the *Griet* armoured men has a helmet that seems to have grown round his head and replaces his face.

The print of the *Money-banks and Strongboxes* thus presents several visual parallels to the *Dulle Griet*. The most important among these is the *reductio ad absurdum* of the equivalence between gold and bodily contents. The print explores the position of money by turning people into money receptacles and having them fight viciously with each other. To represent this, the artist uses the imagery of external transformation as a means of showing an inner transformation. The protean potential of the body is applied here not to an allegorical myth, as, for example, that of the rebel angels, but to a disturbing development in the modern secular world.

The *Dulle Griet,* I now suggest, is the artist's widest statement of this kind. The man with the moneybag and his flatterers, and constipated, reasonless, headless bank-man stuffed with money, are both in their ways prototypes for the giant *Dukatenscheisser* at the centre of the *Dulle Griet*. The idea that this figure acts as a kind of town sign with its connections to avarice, to anal psychology, and to the increasing complexity of money and credit in Antwerp itself, becomes more credible in the light of these other works on very similar themes from Bruegel's pen and Bruegel's circle. Let us now consider in more detail how this *Dukatenscheisser* is situated in the painting as a whole: its urban setting, its relation to the Hell-mouth and to the landscape in the background.

The Hell-mouth
Hell in Dreams and Satires

The Hell-mouth is the most clearly infernal aspect of the *Dulle Griet* and it has led many writers, following van Mander's somewhat vague suggestion, to conclude that the scene is taking place "in Hell." However, by the middle of the sixteenth century a hell-setting need not denote either a religious motive for the artist or a fear-stricken response from the audience. The secularism of this particular hell has been at least tacitly acknowledged by most commentators, and this feature deserves further exploration. What were the contemporary secularised contexts in which hell, the Hell-mouth, and its variants could appear?

The Hell-mouth as a visual device had been to a large extent demystified by the later Middle Ages. Most people would have been familiar with the Hell-mouth as a stage prop, the background for the most popular part of the seasonal mystery plays, the comic *diablerie* of the late medieval theatre. By the second half of the fifteenth century, "domestic" scenes in Hell, involving much comic banter between many named devils and increasingly elaborate special effects, had become the rule rather than the exception. The Hell-mouth for the passion play at Metz was described in 1437 as follows: *The mouth and the entrance to hell of this play was very well done; by the use of a machine, it opened and closed by itself as the devils wanted to enter or leave.*[151] In the Parisian theatre, a historian notes that

> even though there were no purely comic versions of the infernal visit, the burlesque element and the *diablerie* must have influenced the public view of Hell in a sense contrary to the Church's eschatological teachings. Instead of folk leaving such spectacles with their faith confirmed and their terror of hell increased, they were more likely to laugh at the antics of the demons and discuss among themselves which was the best clown.[152]

The Hell-mouth was the *pièce de résistance* of the marketplace theatre, where increasingly sophisticated urban audiences assessed elaborate Hell-mouths with a connoisseur's eye. These special effects could be mentally dissociated from the plays and compared to one another without reference to their original symbolic meaning.

Outside the theatre, the attributes of Hell were so well known that writers of romances used them freely as clichés of peril. As Owen puts it, *The hero, or some other person, has to visit a place of great danger [and] so, to emphasise the perils of the locality, the author gives it infernal characteristics, yet without pretending that this is the true Hell.*[153] The stories of King Arthur and his knights, for instance, taken for their own first by Burgundian courtiers, then by Flemish merchants in the later fifteenth century, frequently included visits to infernal castles, bridges, or caverns. The wheel and cauldron of Hell are familiar from the descriptions of these medieval visitors. Such old chronicles and romances poured from the Antwerp printing presses throughout the sixteenth century.[154] One of these well known geographical "hells" was St. Patrick's Purgatory in Ireland. Flemish and Spanish knights were among those who published accounts of their adventures in these caverns; these tales were speedily translated into several languages and were famous long before the advent of printing.[155] Just as peasants could dream of driving their carts to Heaven, so could the heroes of romance visit Hell, or somewhere very like it, and return to tell the tale.

Secularised and even comic hells appear also in medieval parodies of such romances.[156] Even the more rambunctious late medieval examples are not heretical in tone, though they may steer close to blasphemy. In the mid-thirteenth century song of *St. Peter and the Minstrel*, Peter enters Hell with dice and gaming board in hand in order to gamble with the minstrel for the souls under his temporary charge. To make of Peter a trickster-hero might appear sacrilegious, but Christian dogma was not the point here — the intended effect was comic.[157]

Satirical journeys to Hell were often couched in the form of a dream, a point of great interest here, in the search for ancestors of the *Dulle Griet*. Dante's great poem formed a powerful precedent here: the *Inferno* (c. 1308) starts with the narrator entering the dark wood in a dream-like state:

> *I'non so ben ridir com'iov'entrai*
> *Tant'era pien di sonno in su quel punto*
>
> [I cannot well repeat how there I entered,
> So full was I of slumber at the moment]
> *Inferno* 1. 10-11

By populating his circles with contemporaries, Dante strengthened people's ability to visualise modern kinds of Hell; in a general sense, his vision informed all later concepts of satirical hells.[158] The dream-frame was already in use as a vehicle for social commentary, starting apparently in the twelfth century with Raoul de Houdenc's anti-clerical *Songe d'Enfer*. This features a banquet in Hell. The tablecloths are made of the skins of usurers, and the company samples the grilled tongues of false advocates and other choice dishes.[159] In the mid-fourteenth century, the Flemish poet Jehan de le Mote wrote his *Dream of Hell and of Paradise*, wherein the poet in his sleep meets Murder, who undertakes to guide him to Hell.[160] The dream journey to Hell was much copied. Similar works went immediately into print in the late fifteenth century, appealing to a taste for the fantastic and dealing with attractively radical subjects.[161]

The satirical format was employed, for example, by the author of the *Il Sogno dil Caravia*, published at Venice in 1541.[162] Caravia meets in a dream his old friend the celebrated buffoon Zampolo, who has just died. In Hell, Zampolo's clowning has won him friends among the devils. He meets there another dead buffoon, who makes a long speech in praise of Luther. This is followed by a carnivalesque dance in front of Beelzebub's tribunal and more anticlerical conversation.[163] Popular and accessible works of this sort mixed the carnivalesque with the infernal to achieve satirical ends; they found new audiences of literate artisans and craftsmen.[164] The fact that these infernal interludes are frequently located in dreams is also significant, like Heaven in the peasants' stories. On the folk level, as in the story about St. Peter and the minstrel, Hell was part of the twilit world where one could discover treasure, battle witches, or encounter the souls of the dead. This is the kind of folk Hell unruly women were thought to have retreated.

In the hands of its most illustrious practitioners, the dream format could become much more than a convention of romance. From the *Roman de la Rose*, to the *Hypnerotomachia Poliphili*, to *A Midsummer Night's Dream*, the context of the dream was used to license somewhat explosive subject matter; pagan, radical or frankly erotic material. The *Hypnerotomachia* was available in French at least by 1546; its illustrations were being imitated by Antwerp artists — including Aertsen — in the 1550s. The license of the dream operated in Caravia's *Sogno*, allowing risky pro-Reform opinions to be placed in the mouths of devils or dead clowns, all safely encased in dream unreality. The themes of the *Griet* appear to be quite as controversial as these, touching as they do on deeply felt ambivalences about money, women, castration fears, etc. Bruegel may well have stressed the elements of pure nightmare in his design in order to take advantage of the license traditionally given by the frame of the dream.

Bruegel's Hell-mouths

The use of the Hell-mouth as a piece of dream scaffolding shows how far the dissociation of infernal elements from their religious contexts could go before and during the time-frame of Bruegel's art. This progressive "uncoupling" of the Hell-mouth image from uncomfortable questions of actual damnation is marked in several ways. There is the general acceptance of Hell (or a more vaguely infernal city) as one among several stock fantastic stops in travellers' tales. There is the Hell-mouth as the *pièce de résistance* of marketplace theatre: an entertaining special effect to be admired and criticised as pure technique. Klein discerned a quality of artificiality in Bruegel's earliest Hell-mouth, in his *Last Judgement* print (1558; fig. 98):

> It does not seem likely that print purchasers in Bruegel's day were severely shocked or depressed by such presentations... as this engraving offers. They were quite familiar with "morality" plays, passions and masques in which Hell, damnation, the Day of Judgement, and the Devil himself were all sources of slapstick and gross guffaws... At each carnival or kermess, stage directors and designers did their utmost to create Hell-mouth settings more gruesome and teeth-chattering than anything previously achieved. The more horrendous and convincing the better... [This was] normal if not actually essential for any popular passion play during the Middle Ages and long afterward.[165]

Barnouw went so far as to suggest that Bruegel himself may have designed Hell-mouth settings for passion plays and moralities.[166] The Hell-mouth in the *Dulle Griet* does have a pronounced theatrical quality in keeping with the stage-like setting of the architecture. The Hell-mouth in Bruegel's *Last Judgement* is considerably nastier in character, but at the same time it has an air of shorthand about it. It is used almost as a convenient *sign* for Hell, a sign detached somewhat from the main subject of the print. The *Last Judgement* was traditionally an opportunity for *diablerie*; here this is notable by its absence: Bruegel plays down the deterrent traditionally provided in the shape of infernal tortures. The separation of the good and evil dead, for the first and only time in sixteenth-century iconography[167] does not take place directly below Christ. Christ himself is depicted very close to the earth, above a few resurrected souls (two women and a man), who lift their arms towards him.[168] The saved (also, I think, uniquely) visually outnumber the damned; the latter enter the Hell-mouth already packed into a boat. This juxtaposition of Hell-mouth and ship motif appears again in the *Dulle Griet*; it evokes the familiar metaphor of the Ship of Life, here come to a sticky end. Otherwise the fate of the damned is hardly depicted, just as the artist would later exclude the Judgement from the *Triumph of Death* (c. 1566; fig. 89).

This print was published in the same year as the artist's *Vices*, which also feature Hell-mouths of various kinds. Bruegel evidently found devising psychological Hells for the theme of human vice more interesting than literal Hells. Two unmistakable versions of Hell-mouths appear in the Vices series, one in *Pride* (fig. 9) and another in *Envy* (fig. 12). In addition, some of the animated buildings in the *Vices* suggest Hell-mouths by a judicious placement of windows and doors. The huge disembodied heads scattered through the series suggest Bruegel was developing the notion of giant heads in more psychological directions.

The *Descent into Limbo* (fig. 91), from around 1561, includes a Hell-mouth as part of a full-scale literal Hell. This design owes much to mystery plays of the Harrowing of Hell; the original theatrical context for the Hell-mouth-as-stage-prop. A certain theatricality can be seen in the overlapping flat forms which make up the right-hand side of the print. There are also comic elements. Satan himself, visible through the smashed skull of the Hell-mouth, is hardly a fearsome figure. His air of comic vexation recalls the domestic buffoonery in Satan's household before the actual arrival of Christ in the Easter plays. In a similar spirit, the head of the Hell-mouth has the tonsure of a monk. The creatures in the foreground are the predecessors of Bruegel's metamorphosing rebel angels, occupied by problems with their own bodies or made relatively harmless by lack of arms, head, etc. Thus even in this relatively orthodox use of the Hell-mouth, Bruegel instills comic, theatrical, and psychological elements.

Evidently the idea of the Hell-mouth lent itself to a wide range of variations. The artificial appearance of Bruegel's Hell-mouths, and their adaptations as part of the landscapes of Vice, show an interest in stretching and developing this image to gain satirical effects and describe inner hells. Only one of the image's many uses in his oeuvre is as an identifying feature of Hell itself. Elsewhere, the Hell-mouth is as likely to be abstracted into an animated house or metamorphosed into an inhabited head. Working from the various pictorial traditions of the head as the house of the soul, Bruegel's giant heads are images of madness; in his repertoire of surreal imagery, the Hell-mouth is one among many motifs of this kind. A *built-head* for instance, appears in the *Dulle Griet,* above the Hell-mouth proper; as if implying that this Hell-mouth itself is going mad.

There are analogous giant heads elsewhere in secular culture. The first book of *Gargantua and Pantagruel* describes a world inside the giant Pantagruel's mouth.[169] Rabelais developed the idea from antique and late medieval travellers' tales; the episode also draws slyly on accounts of the New World. The narrator enters the mouth, travels among the mountains of the teeth, visits the great cities of Larynx and Pharynx, and discovers a town where one can earn money by sleeping. The basic image of a grotesquely huge inhabited mouth comes from the Chapbook of the Giant Gargantua, a folk product in circulation long before Rabelais worked his Shakespearean transformations on the theme in 1534.[170] Here, without any infernal connotations at all, yet clearly surreal, we have a popular parallel to the fantasy of the Hell-mouth, abroad decades before Bruegel created his variations.

Finally, a more consciously philosophical example of a dreamlike hellmouth, in the remarkable Mannerist park near Bomarzo in the region of

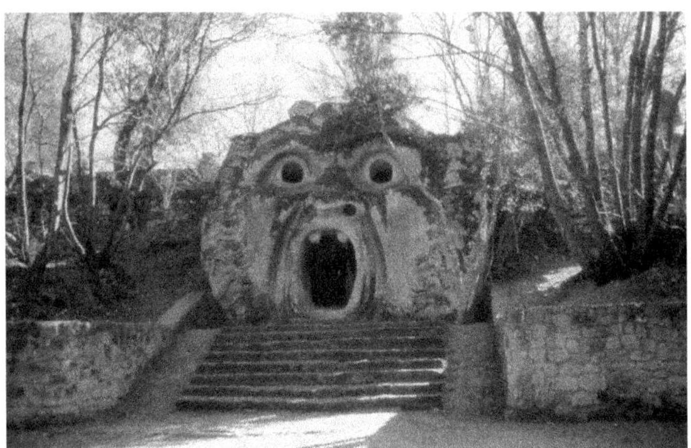

56 View of the Hell-mouth, Bomarzo, Viterbo. Park begun c 1564. Photo: Stefano Colonna (2003)

the Hypnerotomachia and its many imitations, and possibly had in mind some of the themes from Tasso's epic poem Amadigi (1560).[171] At Bomarzo, the upper jaw of the Hell-mouth carries an inscription punning on Dante: lasciate ogni pensiero o voi ch'intrate, which can be rendered as: Let all thoughts go flying away, you who enter here.[172] The difference between this injunction to visitors and that of Dante's famous entrance to hell (lasciate ogni speranza...), exemplifies the new kind of dream-like meanings that a Hell-mouth might have in this period. Ironically enough, Orsini was taken prisoner in the Flanders campaign of 1553, and took up his project again on his release two years later. One imagines the two great fantasists, Bruegel and Orsini, crossing paths on their respective ways to and from Italy. It is suggestive in any case that a carved Hell-mouth should be part of the program for this aristocratic park, taking its place naturally among other purely fantastic and pagan giant garden sculptures: a huge double-tailed mermaid, a dragon, outsize urns and miniature temples. By the end of the century, the Hell-mouth had became a popular design for grand fantastical chimney breasts and fireplaces.

This final conceit can be seen as marking a point of no return in the dissociation of the Hell-mouth from its original context as a religious representation. Belief in hell did in fact decline in the century after Bruegel.[173] The Neo-Platonist revival of Origen — who had argued that Hell was a place where reincarnated souls could be purified over many lifetimes — is another indication that the concept of hell, never very clearly defined in the Bible, had become more fluid and amenable to reshaping in the sixteenth century.[174] As we will see in Chapter 5, by Bruegel's time, Purgatory had taken over many of the principal descriptive marks of hell: in one sense, this was a victory for Origen. For our present purposes, it is important simply to show that Bruegel had a certain amount of freedom to identify aspects of hell with aspects of contemporary life.

In the first half of the sixteenth century, it seems, people became interested in the Hell-mouth as an image in its own right. Once this separation had begun, the image was found to fit in very well with the peculiarly concrete quality of early modern ideas about psychology. The idea of the gaping mouth as a doorway, with windows as eyes, had an obvious relation to theories about what went on in the head. The image of a gigantic head growing out of the ground quickly came to signify the fantastic or the supernatural, the arena of nightmare.

By around 1562, the date of this painting, Bruegel had made two compositions which used the Hell-mouth in a relatively orthodox manner (*Last Judgement, Christ in Limbo*), and two others where the image appears as a type of psychological metaphor (*Pride, Envy*). In addition, several of the other *Vices* and the *Temptation of St. Anthony* show Bruegel in the late 1550s exploring imagery related in form to the Hell-mouth — gigantic heads, house faces, etc. As we have seen, this imagery was psychological in meaning. The absence of a sacred protagonist in the *Dulle Griet* suggests that the *Griet*'s Hell-mouth also carried a psychological significance in Bruegel's modern satire.

I have dealt at some length with the history of the Hell-mouth in order to show that a psychological interpretation of its imagery is supported both by contemporary sources and by the artist's own earlier works. The

Griet shares the dissociation of infernal things from serious religious life (*la vie serieuse*), the comic or satirical effects that this could generate, and, most importantly, the frame of the dream. All these contexts suggest some answers to the question of what the Hell-mouth connotes in the *Dulle Griet* as a whole. To address this issue, we must return, from a somewhat different angle, to the subject of money and its psychological association with different parts of the body.

The Hell-mouth, Avarice, and Consumption

The invention of the *Griet* Hell-mouth was informed by some very old and widespread psychological metaphors. The characteristic combination of disembodied mouth, anality, and a symbolic identity between precious metal and faeces, can be found in other cultures possessing an exchange system based on precious metals. Anthropological and folklore studies over the last eighty years bear out this statement; starting with the work of the early psychological anthropologists, Lincoln and Ròheim, who sought to confirm the universality or otherwise of Freud's theory of the unconscious by studying non-Western cultures.[175]

The best parallel for early modern Europe is provided by the settled hunter-gatherer societies of the Northwest American coast. Among these peoples, the metal concerned was more often copper than gold. They thought in terms of treasure: precious metals had pivotal symbolic and economic significance in elaborate systems of gift-exchange. The Kwakiutl, for example, developed the institution of potlatch, where treasuries of artefacts including priceless copper objects were ceremonially destroyed to enhance the owner's status.[176] The lore associated with copper in this region provides a kind of "objective correlative" to the psychological configuration treasure-body-orifice-excrement. Northwest Coast folklore includes a figure named Wealthwoman who can be made to defecate four gold balls. Among the Tagish, *if a man hears how Wealth Woman's baby cries, he should strip him off clothes and metal ornaments, throw urine at the Woman, take her baby; she scratches him with her golden nails, defecates four gold colored balls; when he gives her the baby back and fulfills necessary rituals (to fast, bathe four days, etc.), balls become pure gold.*[177]

Like Europeans, the Kwakiutl speak of the body as the *house of the soul*. According to Curtius, *in the fantastically figurative thought of the Kwakiutl, the house is represented as a face with the door a great mouth, ready to swallow the guests of the master.*[178] And again, *the door of the house is often described as the mouth of an animal or a monster.*[179] Conceptions of a monstrous mouth are linked to a supernatural figure, whose excrement is a precious metal. Anality, as a cultural characteristic or theme, may also have something to do with the *fantastically figurative* nature of this thought. Aspects of this imagery — the figure of Wealth Woman, the monstrous mouth — parallel the connections in sixteenth-century thought which Bruegel made manifest in the *Dulle Griet*.

This evidence suggests that the psychological equation between gold and excrement is so deeply embedded in human culture as to be of great antiquity. Equally clearly, it can manifests itself in metaphor, image and dream in a wide range of tones and on many different levels. In relation to anal themes in the *Netherlandish Proverbs*, Dundes and Stibbe comment that: *even if one were inclined to see an anal erotic component... the question would remain whether it was a reflection of Bruegel's own personality or whether it was rather a characteristic of Dutch or Flemish "national character."*[180] The proverb and folk metaphors, after all, were not invented by Bruegel. On the other hand, it was he who selected the specific examples to be included in the painting. Dundes speculated that the Dutch may share the marked anality that characterises German culture.[181] In a flawed but fascinating study, Freud was surely correct to intuit that a predilection for *fantastic formations* in Leonardo's art was connected with a deflection of the artist's sexuality in infancy: for the adult, desire subsequently took the form of inexhaustible curiosity.[182] In view of Bruegel's similar penchant for the encyclopaedic, one might speculate that a similar deflection, involving an anal displacement, may have shaped his outlook.

It is, of course, more relevant (and practicable) to show the evidence of such a displacement on the level of collective, rather than personal psychology, and consider the changes in tone and metaphor across the whole society of which Bruegel was a member. In the West, people seem to have begun to consider the equation between gold and excrement as horrible instead of comic, and to envisage the transformation of one into the other as something occurring internally, around the time of the first commercial revolution (950-1350).[183] This changeover took further centuries to become a Europe-wide ruling habit of mind, and it happened in a staggered way, gaining ground at different times in different places.[184] As the number of individuals living in towns rose, the size of the towns themselves increased, the exchange of goods became a matter of *mutually indifferent acts*, and the alienating effects of money became stronger and more visible. As we saw, when Bruegel was a young man, money was replacing barter and tithes in the rural economy and in traditional areas of urban life.[185] At the same time, the financial activities of Antwerp generated a revolution in banking practices, the most widespread of which was the extension of credit for ordinary commodity purchases. By mid-century, the experience of paranoia and other alienating effects of the boom-and-bust culture centred on the Antwerp Bourse was hand-in-hand with the progressive elaboration of images associated with money and faeces. The giant *Dukatenscheisser* in the *Griet* was one such response.

Consider the Hell-mouth's relationship to this image: a Hell-mouth is a disembodied head, a mouth without an exit to dispose of that which it receives. This configuration was an old attribute of avarice. On the cathedrals at Vézelay and Autun:

> Avarice is a wretched little figure, shown squatting. His vast mouth is open wide, and in each fist he grasps a bulging sack of coins. He consists mainly of alimentary canal, open at the receiving end and closed at the other. The decaying matter is stored not in his intestines so much as in those moneybags.[186]

Similarly, Innocent III (1198-1216) compared the avaricious man to Hell, *because both eat but do not digest, both receive but do not give back*.[187] Thus the Hell-mouth could be explicitly likened to the mouth of the avaricious man, and the likeness lay in their common lack of a digestive system. They are mouths without anuses, unable to expel what they take into their bodies. That this image of the gaping mouth was felt to be an apt way of depicting avarice shows again the depth of the equation between money and body contents and the ways in which a "money-disease" could be represented visually as an anal dysfunction.

This metaphor could be honed to represent specific monetary sins with astonishing precision. In Canto XXX of the *Inferno,* Dante describes the fate of Master Adam, a notorious counterfeiter who was burned in 1281:

> I saw one shaped like a lute, if only he had been cut short at the groin, from the part where a man is forked. The heavy dropsy which dispairs the members by ill disposal of the humours [*l'umor che mal connerte*], so that the face does not answer to the belly [*che'l viso non risponde a la ventraia*], made him hold his lips apart.[188]

The skinny limbs and hugely inflated belly of this figure were signs of a disease of the digestive process (dropsy). In Aristotelian physiology, dropsy was a neat parallel to Adam's particular species of fraud, the adulteration of pure gold with dross during coining. The stages of coining could be likened to cooking, just as the body's digestion *cooks* food.[189] Even today, we might refer to a latter-day Master Adam as someone who *cooked the books*. Counterfeiting could thus be represented as a disease of the body politic's digestive system:

> Dante distinguishes Adam and his fellow Maleboge by [a] special association of fraud with the bells.... As the belly of Hell, the Maleboge [are] dysfunctional; they do not nourish, they poison the body of which they are a part and they represent perhaps the most gigantic case of constipation on record. References to food, to cooking... to excretion and excrement are legion.[190]

It is worth noting the compact ease and brevity with which the thirteenth-century poet makes use of these bodily metaphors. To translate thought and word into present-day terms gives both an air of laboriousness quite foreign to the original late medieval audience, which delighted in ringing the changes on old, complex but commonplace tropes.

Familiarity with the basic metaphors likening monetary sins and infernal constipation makes it possible to judge more nicely a poet's — or artist's — novel contribution. The notions of digestion gone wrong, of evil cooking and of fraud as disorder lay equally readily to hand in early modern thinking. Behind Bruegel's *Dukatenscheisser* one may sense a reworking of elements often found, for instance, in stock formulations of Avarice such as this one from Alain of Lille (1128-1202): *The rich man, shipwrecked in the deep sea of riches, with burning hydroptic thirst, thirsts for wealth.*[191] The Hell-mouth and the *Dukatenscheisser* came together out of a venerable set of *topoi* often used to comment on the abuses of money.

The Hell-mouth is not the only element of the *Dulle Griet* drawn from popular accounts of Hell. Behind the crowd of women, to the right of the *Dukatenscheisser,* the space in the "town square" is filled by a kind of cauldron. Immediately behind this, an oblong pool holds three heads and a skull immersed up to the nose in the murky liquid. The cauldron has an obvious association with cooking; it also has a venerable popular tradition as part of the furniture of hell. In a *Kalendrier des Bergers*, for instance, the Seven Deadly Sins are given various different punishments:

> There are huge millwheels turning rapidly, and the crowd are attached to them by fiery hooks. The envious are immersed to the navel in a river of ice, and are lashed by a biting wind... The avaricious are plunged to

> the neck in cauldrons of boiling oil and metals. In a valley there is a foul river and a table heaped with filth is set upon its bank. Here the gluttonous are fed with reptiles and the water of the river. The lustful are sunk in pits full of fire and sulphur.[192]

Different texts match tortures and vices differently;[193] in the early Flemish version of the *Vision of Tondalus* (Antwerp 1482; 1515), the avaricious are devoured instead by a monstrous beast. In Antwerp, the existence of a special statute for counterfeiters may have strengthened the idea of an infernal cauldron for the avaricious: *In July 1489 a Westphalian [was] boiled alive in a brewer's vat near the Mint for making false money. He suffered in water, but oil was the usual medium on such occasions.*[194] Antwerp Hell panels regularly connected monetary sin with torture by pot or cauldron. One design we have already touched on: the versions of the giant nose dripping coins from around 1530 (fig. 47). Another panel, from around 1520, is a direct copy of the small corner *tondo* from Bosch's *Tabletop of the Vices* in the Prado (fig. 7).[195] The cauldron, set over hot coals, is clearly labeled *Avaricia*.

These associations in the giant cauldron of the *Griet*, where a small horde of figures take refuge, with an implication of the frying-pan and the fire. To this grossly enlarged bowl, mounted high on a tower above street level, a couple of hybrids ascend by ladder. One carries a heavy sack; the other a circular tray from which glasses are falling. They seem to be fleeing from the women below. As with the Hell-mouth, the traditional function of the cauldron is subverted; here it is a last resort where beleaguered metamorphs huddle. This horde of little hybrid men, bound together under the sign of the cook-pot, inside a vast cook-pot, evidently allude to perverted appetite.[196] The pleasures of the table are certainly turned inside out in the *Griet*, which abounds in instances of abnormal consumption. Apart from the overtly anal imagery in some of the monsters, references to eating and drinking include Dame Avarice's picnic underneath the monstrous egg-harp, and the ubiquitous drinking vessels that mark the eyebrows of the hell-face, and appear toppling from trays in the hands of monkeys and metamorphs.

The sign of the cook-pot runs through the whole of this, evoking an atmosphere which steers the mood of the painting from the infernal to the carnivalesque. The ladle held by the *Dukatenscheisser*, for example, is used in a carnival custom. Sullivan thought the presence of the drinking vessels referred to the bacchanal aspect of carnival, arguing that Griet and her marauding women should be identified as a type of bacchante. Carnivals were by definition a time to over-indulge in food and drink, and were indeed described as bacchanals by some disapproving contemporary commentators (as we will see later on).[197] Glasses and tankards could as easily refer to Antwerp, that city of many breweries and more taverns. By 1567, beer and wine excises formed the town's main source of revenue.[198] One must imagine the vast quantities customarily consumed at any street festival, and the sight of this drunken crowd, when the newly-invented Giants of urban folklore would be wheeled down narrow streets amidst throngs of revellers. This sense of excess consumption, consumption to the point of madness, is condensed into the surreal imagery of money and anality and rampaging appetites at the heart of the painting.

Kovel's psychoanalytic research in this context enables us to understand better what any of this might have to do with how *imagery* develops in the collective unconscious; specifically, how visualisations of money change. It is naturally difficult to obtain confirmation for the sixteenth century of the sorts of traumatic conglomerations within individual psyches proposed by Freud, Jones, Kovel and subsequent researchers. However, following Kovel, sites for these conglomerations can be found in the visual history of collectivities — in cultural history as a whole. Bruegel's imagery, I suggest, is evidence of a traumatic development in *mentalité* of this kind (see Introduction).

The evidence presented so far points to a *non-cognitive* cultural evolution of imagery associated with money, originating several hundred years before Bruegel, erupting into *cognitive* culture in the sixteenth century. Such crises are *over-determined*: a Freudian term for a phenomenon with an over-sufficiency of causes. Like a world war, a revolution, or the Reformation itself, these are mass-events with multiple causes and deep roots in the past. They "acquire momentum" over centuries, until their potential energy for change is capable of being triggered by a handful of events, which then in retrospect appear inevitable. In the case of the Reformation, a key trigger is often identified as Luther's gauntlet thrown to to the Papacy: the famous Ninety-five Theses which he nailed to the door of the Castle Church in Wittenberg on October 31, 1517, thus opening the controversy on indulgences for public debate. In the case of money as a site of collective psychic trauma, the dramatic ascendency of the Antwerp Bourse is a similarly visible trigger, though many contributing factors are subsumed in such an event.

In any case, what such triggers "really" do is mark a qualitative change in the position of the issues in people's minds: the subject moves from being an unspoken or non-cognitive aspect of public culture, to being a cognitive, debatable issue. Among other things, this means the area of discontent or dissent becomes capable of being cognitively manipulated by people trained to think in terms of images: it invites new representations. That money was more or less demonised during this period seems beyond dispute; at the same time, a prerequisite for such a demonisation would appear to be an increasing consciousness of its effects on people's minds.

A main objective in this part of my argument will be fulfilled if the shift in attention can simply be shown to have occurred. Were sixteenth-century people demonstrably more interested than their predecessors in representations of money, and in representing perverted behaviour motivated by money? We can cite here the common interests of the late Renaissance playwrights, from Shakespeare and Jonson to Molière, in the dramatic potential of the miser as a central character. Evidently, associative chains informing this representation had been moving in this direction for centuries; one result was the relatively novel stereotype of the old Jewish moneylender as an unnatural, Machiavellian figure, operating behind the scenes, a focus for demonic forces. This character is an example of how a traditional personified Vice from the mystery plays was likely to be updated, resulting in an unexpected deepening of the illusion of real psychology.

With this in mind, we can see an earlier step in the same direction in the casting of the *rederijker* morality play about Amsterdam: *Folk, a common burgess, More Than One, an artisan,* and *So Much, a rich man.* A dramatic interaction among these three figures might indeed be a way of describing the "money-plot" of the *Dulle Griet,* despite the different surreal and folk embodiments of Bruegel's abstractions. Psychological dimensions immediately arise. Is *So Much* a Vice? Is he necessarily doomed? Will he mend his ways and "solve" the problem of his desires, expressed in his over-valuation of wealth? The fascination of Marlowe's Faust or Shakespeare's Shylock as characters lies in the fact that the outcome of these issues is uncertain. This uncertainty opens a space into which both audience and author project their own fears; it simultaneously generates a sense of depth and creates a focus of horrified desire. The situation encouraged further representation of hallucinatory or paranoid flights of fancy, in novel forms such as the introspective monologue, and in denser plot structures, turning on secrecy and disclosure, revelation and confession. Such structures underpin and motivate the characters and plots of Hamlet, Macbeth and Lear, all of whom are represented as inwardly tormented; all of whom talk of their dreams.

Issues of distinguishing between the real and the unreal were intrinsic to this evolution. The character-type of the miser was developed as part of a century-long wave of interest in introspection. As the *sinnekins* of the previous generation moved inside the head, the *personae* of the new theatre were represented as having warring thoughts; they became victims of desires they should not fulfil.

As we have seen, Bruegel found "money-madness" an apt subject for surreal fantasy. The *Griet* is his densest exploration of money-diseases, addressing their qualities of hallucination and distortion, the fascination they hold as foci for excessive and forbidden desires, as places of fear and deficit. In visual and symbolic terms, the images of the Hell-mouth and the cauldron are counter-parts to the giant on the roof. Both carry a whole skein of connotations — secular, sacred, comic, nightmarish — drawing together the themes of money, digestion, fraud and folk-magic. Early modern people, more familiar than ourselves with scatological imagery of all kinds, would perceive the perversity of the two separated giant orifices and grasp the connection with the distorted digestion that was the mark of avarice. Consciously or subliminally, this association furnished Bruegel with a formal means of visualising the general structure of his fantasy.

Sinnekins, thesis and antithesis

These formal resonances are best understood by examining the complex visual orchestration of the *Griet* as a whole image. The picture borrows its basic composition from Bruegel's own *Vice* series; however the genre of the *Griet* more closely resembles a *psychomachia*[199]: a kind of allegorical war inside the head. Bruegel precisely composed his minor monsters as a means of dramatising such a struggle, spilling out to shape a panoramic landscape. As he did with the forms of the rebel angels, Bruegel created novel hybrids whose bodies exemplify common themes, in this case, anality, excess and bad digestion. Hybrids and non-hybrids are linked variations whose formal relations to each other evoke the dream-processes of condensation and displacement. Guided by this kind of dream-logic, the surreal vocabulary of the *Griet* expands the ramifications of its subject well beyond the normal range of lampoons of thievery and fraud.

Anal or digestive deformation is one of these common principles of design linking the smallest metamorphs to the larger. When Griet steps

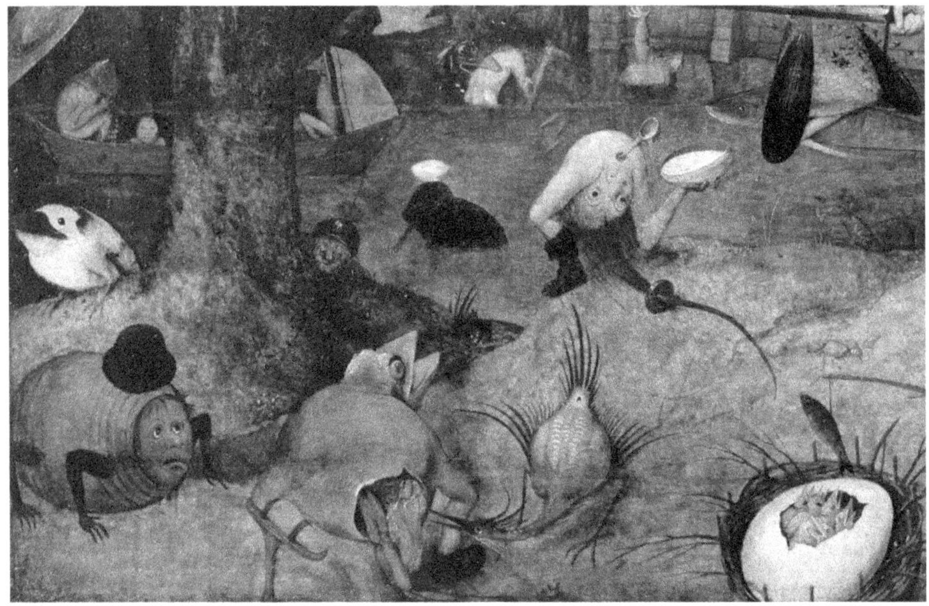

35d Pieter Bruegel, anus-gryllus in foreground, detail, *Dulle Griet*

away from the central activity on the bridge, the territory that she enters is inhabited by little metamorphs, representing perversions of food and eating (fig. 35d). Like painted *sinnekins*, they comment on the thematic action. The figure to Griet's immediate left, for instance, is a *gryllus* whose mouth is also its anus. A spoon juts out from its single orifice, and with its single arm it holds a bowl of soup or porridge. The chances of a creature so constituted actually being able to eat are small; this recalls the impossible digestion of the cathedral *Avaritia*.

Moving counterclockwise round the promontory there is also a barrel-man, then a bird-creature with a broken-eggshell rear, one of whose legs is a stump bound to a crutch. Another spiky long-beaked bird pokes at the contents falling out of this creature's body. To the right of this, a small round neckless creature wears a porkpie as a hat with a knife stuck in it. He is fishing with a rod baited itself with a fish, over a huge egg inside a basket, broken to reveal the chicks inside. In the water, fish or fish-like monsters eat men (fig. 35d). The inventions of the foreground strip thus suggest proverbial imagery transmuted through condensation and displacement *(all the chicks in one basket, big fish eat little fish)*. Compared to the earlier print (fig. 36), humans and fish in the *Griet* have more drastically shuffled roles and body parts.

The forms of these little images echo the perverse digestion linking the Hell-mouth with the money-spooning giant. Others appear governed by the rules of controlled inversion characteristic of Carnival: *animal eats human, to go fishing for birds*. They are grotesque relatives of World-Turned-Upside-Down imagery (cf. fig. 107, and discussion in Chapter Three). In the *Griet*, more or less recognisable reversals and inversions in the foreground serve as a kind of introduction for the images on the other side of the town-wall. The small-scale cameos, on the promontory and in the water around Meg, are legible as isolated, broken-down examples of the more elaborate imagery woven more densely together around the giant.

If your gaze arrives at these creatures starting from the centre of the picture, the semicircular foreground fringe of small monster – extending from the Hell-mouth in front of Griet, to the dark circular arches in the bottom right corner – appears as a kind of ripple, or fallout, from the central disturbance focused on the figure of the ship-giant. If your eye then follows the creatures back from the foreground into the centre, these cameos work as *sinnekin*s to prefigure in miniature larger aspects of the design. For example, staring wildly out of the arched doorway where women rob beneath the giant, the open fish-mouth with a spear stuck in it echoes and adapts the meaning of the head of a fish eating an armoured leg (fig. 35c). The broken egg with the young birds in it relates to the emblematic invention of the broken egg with the harp, the monkey-serpent, and the topiary dance floor that looms in the middle distance. It is possible to regard the painting's grand gigantic themes — Hell-mouth, *Dukatenscheisser* and cauldron — as nightmarish extrapolations of the small upside-down figure with its mouth-anus, its spoon, and its bowl (fig. 35d). A similar analogy exists between the small bird-monster with its broken rear, gawking nervously at Griet in the foreground, and the *Dukatenscheisser*.

In the middle ground, the larger counterparts of these *sinnekins* are made comparatively more horrible, principally by the addition of human features and by change in scale. Remember here that *things out of all proportion* were one of the hallmarks of nightmare according to Macrobius. One senses a progressive movement in the *Griet*, whereby its elements are first stated in small cameos, greatly magnified and elaborated in the middle ground, simplified and concentrated once more in the background.

Bruegel excelled at this kind of harmonic resonance, evident in the geometric formal patterns which help hold together the apparent chaos of the design. This is a design held together by disks; artfully presented as nests, eggs, pans, globes, windows, trays, etc. Repeated shapes and motifs create a progression backwards into space, while a rhythm of voids and solids unifies the design horizontally. Round hollows are balanced by spheres, archways echo each other. The crystal ball of the ship on the giant's back fits neatly into the void of cauldron or Hell-mouth. The gold sphere being rolled out of the ship above the giant's shoulders seems designed to fill the cavity from which he spoons his silver. Griet's frying-pan is formally equivalent to the dark disk and handle formed by the giant's rear cavity in conjunction with his spoon. The Hell-mouth is part of the pattern of disc/holes that lends irony to the work — the "same" form to be read as concave, convex, flat or hollow — like the *Dukatenscheisser*'s egg-shell rear, the broken-egg-emblem, Griet's frying pan.

If the scene as a whole is a *tour-de-force* of (very Netherlandish) technical mastery, the forms of the *dramatis personae* and of the "furniture" represent an exercise in visual condensation and displacement as a mode of analysis. Like the antithetically pairing of Hell-mouth and *Dukatenscheisser*, formal and functional visual wit is a linking device throughout the picture.

At each stage in the *Dulle Griet,* small motifs are linked to larger ones by the judicious repetition and development of common elements. Thus for instance, the man having his clothes pulled over his head echoes this characteristic of the ship-bearing giant. This parallelism of small and large recalls the famous Humanist theory that microcosm reflects macrocosm and vice versa.[200] In terms of content and design, this is an important principle in Bruegel's painting. The artist unifies his many disparate pieces of lore, observation, tradition, and experience by imposing upon them a system of internal visual references.

The Ship Images
Ship allegories and carnival ships

The principle of microcosm and macrocosm determines the development of the last of the painting's great themes to be discussed. This is the image of the Ship of the World, placed at the centre of the design, mounted on the shoulders of the *Dukatenscheisser*. The imagery of sea voyages was, of course, topical and familiar in the age of navigation. The ship as a metaphor for life was an old *topos*, initially associated with the passage in *Luke* 5:3 (*And he entered into one of the ships [and] prayed him that he would be thrust out a little from the land. And he sat down and taught the people out of the ship*). Scribner untangled the first radiation around 1500 of the motif into Christian allegory:

> The ark of Noah as a prefiguration of the church... contributed to the connotations of this image, by the late fifteenth century, it was a standard topos for the church. It became more explicitly so with the development of the ship of St. Ursula into a representation of the Papal church.... The perils of sea travel in that age added another connotation, the precarious and dangerous nature of ship voyages... a further influence on this metaphor [was] the perilous sea voyages undertaken by those on pilgrimage to the Holy Land.[201]

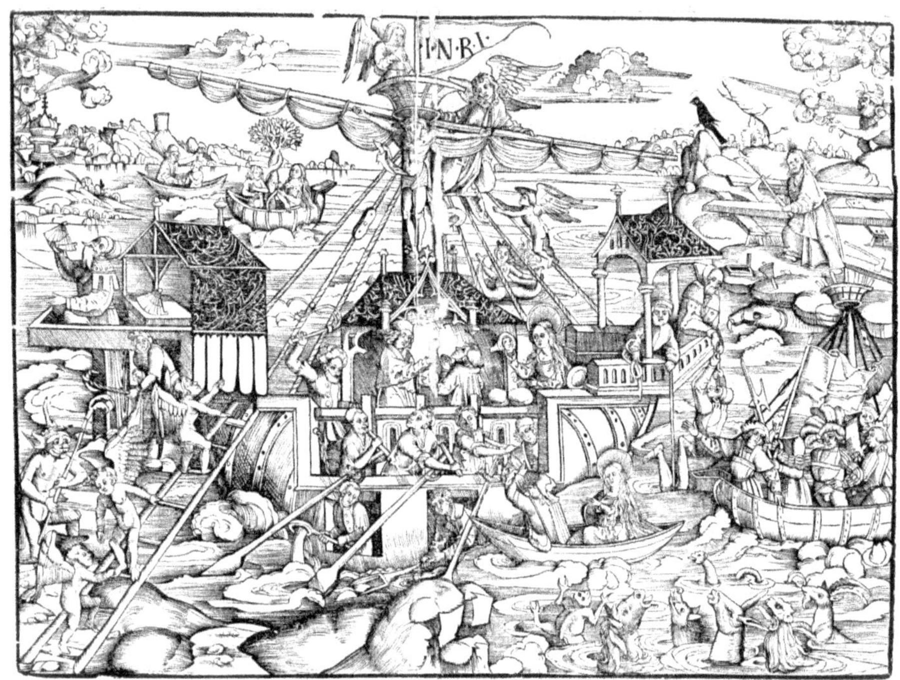

57 Anon, *The Ship of Salvation*, 1512, Germanisches Nationalmuseum, Nuremberg

On the eve of the Reformation, there was a market among the print-buying public for more elaborate religious allegories, including ship-allegories. In one woodcut of this type, showing a *Ship of Salvation* (c. 1512; fig. 57), the design is packed with symbolic detail: the whole world and much of the Bible is in this ship and its attendant flotilla. Monsters occupy the sea at bottom left. Lest anything should be unclear, the identifications are painstakingly spelled out in the accompanying text:

> This ship sails the sea of the world, in which lurk the numerous monsters of vice. These often overturn or swamp the ship, but the sailor can bail out the water with confession. Faith [is] the compass; the rudder is God's commands and precepts; the mast is Christ's cross; the sails are laid on with free will, but not in every wind, only in the fair

wind of piety. There is the anchor of hope... the ship's hands are the holy angels who take good care for the barque.[202]

By the second half of the sixteenth century, these ideas had been adapted for Protestant propaganda prints, such as *The Ship of the Papal Church* (fig. 106; Chapter 5). This central stem of allegories likening the Church to a Ship, or the course of a human life to a sea voyage, branched out in secular directions also over the course of the century. The Humanist Sebastian Brant (1457-1521) developed the famous image of the ship of fools, in his best-selling satirical poem of that name, *Das Narrenschiff* (Basel, 1494).[203] The scholar Brant was naturally versed in previous uses of ship-metaphor; in Chapter 103, for instance, he compares St. Peter's barque to the ship of the Anti-Christ; this became a favourite subject in Reformation prints (see e.g. fig. 106).[204] In terms of its illustrations and translations as well as its development of images and ideas, the trajectory of this book illuminates much about the mental world of Bruegel and his audience.

Das Narrenschiff first of all set a new bar for instilling layers of complexity and erudition into a popular work. Written in German and copiously illustrated with woodcuts showing fools engaged in every walk of life (figs. 58 a-c), some of which have been attributed to the young Dürer,[205] the work won mass audiences in the sixteenth century and could be enjoyed on many levels. Latin, French and English translations proliferated. The first Flemish translation appeared at Paris in 1500, to be reprinted at Brussels in 1548.[206] Numerous imitators followed suit, producing dozens of poems and satirical novels about ships of foolish priests or foolish women.

There were in fact more references to the ship motif in the Dutch editions than in the German original. This is because the specific conceit of a ship of fools seems to have occurred to Brant halfway through the writing

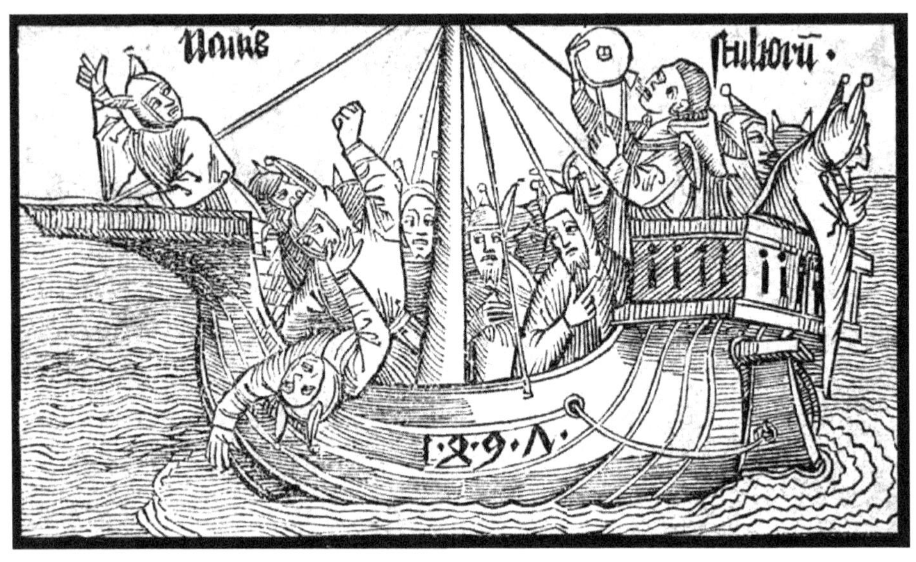
Nauis
stultorū

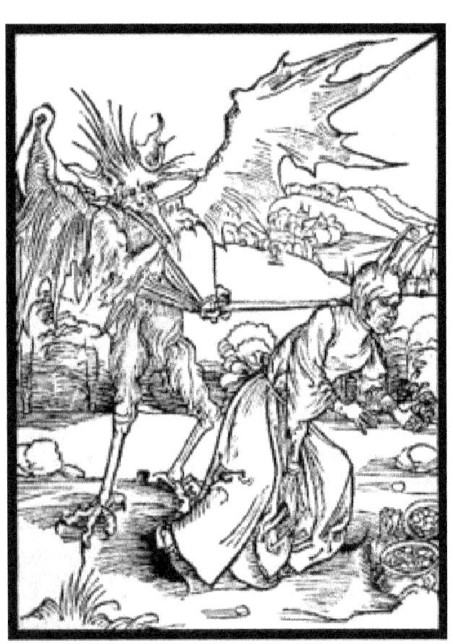

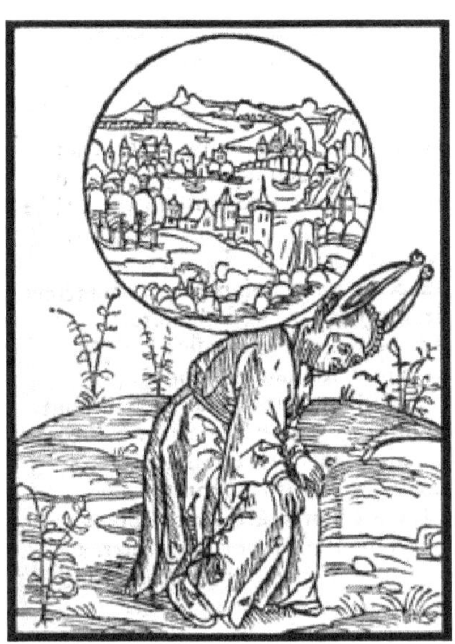

Figures for preceding page:

58a (top) Anon, Frontispiece (1494); woodcut from Sebastian Brant, *Stultifera Navis* (Basel, 1497). Photo © 2000, University of Houston Libraries

58b (bottom left) Attributed to Albrecht Dürer, *XX Of Finding Treasure* (1494); woodcut from Sebastian Brant, *Stultifera Navis* (Basel, 1497). Photo © 2000, University of Houston Libraries

58c (bottom right) Attributed to the Master Haintz-Nar, *XXIV Of Too Much Care* (1494); woodcut from Sebastian Brant, *Stultifera Navis* (Basel, 1497). Photo © 2000, University of Houston Libraries

to this new idea. Brant's Latin translator, Jacob Locher (1471-1528), did what he could to correct the imbalance by inserting extra references to the ship (more than 30 of them) in the first half of the work.[207] The Dutch and Flemish translations relied heavily on Locher's edition, *Stultifera Navis* (1497), and so the idea of the ship was given greater prominence than it had in the original.

Two images suffice to give a sense of how the visual vocabulary of the *Narrenschiff* contributed to the movements in representation we have been discussing: the currents of thought and taste out of which Bruegel wove his *Griet*. Supernatural imagery is almost entirely lacking in these pictures. One exception is *Of Finding Treasure* (Ch. XX; fig. 58b), attributed to Dürer, where an unusually monstrous demon appears behind a treasure-hunting fool, as it does in the Van Meckenem *Battle of the Breeches* (fig. 45). More simply, the fool who has the world on his shoulders in *Of Too Much Care* (XXIV; fig. 58c) carries a world crammed with a detailed landscape, in contrast to the plain world on which he stands. The bubble of Bruegel's world-ship is similarly a packed sphere which also acts as a lens, so the moated house in the distance bears down on the heads of the ship's frenetic inhabitants.

Brant did not invent the notion of a ship of fools; it was a motif whose time had come, first recorded in a German sermon from the 1460s or '70s, as a variation on St. Ursula's ship as the Church.[208] The idea of creating a parody of Ursula's ship occurred to Hieronymus Bosch at almost exactly

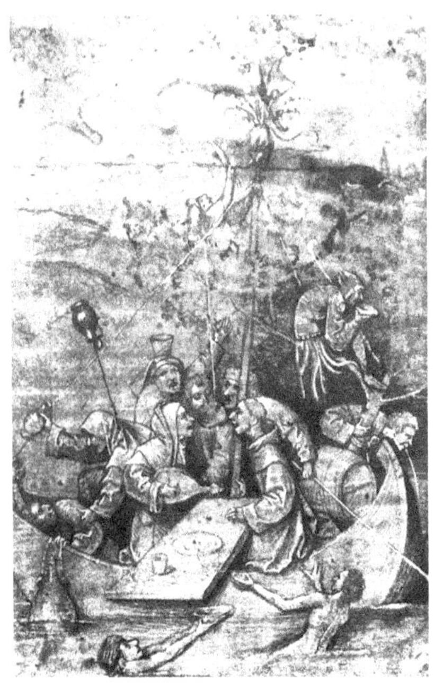

59 Hieronymus Bosch, *The Ship of Fools*, c. 1495-1500. Brush and pen on paper, 25.6 x 16.6 cm. Département des artes graphiques, Musée du Louvre, Paris. Inv :3714. Photo: RMN \ © Jean-Gilles Berizzi

the same time as it did to Brant. His design for a Ship of Fools (c. 1490-1500; fig. 59) used carnivalesque fantasy to express an anti-clerical satire. A music-making nun and monk occupy the centre of the ship; a fool sits pensively in the rigging, half the crew is in the water. The mood is dream-like: the deliberate detail of silent painted singers emphasises a sense of removal. The mast is a tree, like the Tree in Adam and Eve's boat at the top right of the *Ship of Salvation* (fig. 57). This tree, however, is stripped of its lower branches, leaving a tuft at the top: it is a "may-tree" of the kind planted in front of young unmarried women's houses, as part of the St. John's Day midsummer festivities.[209] Ships were also a common component of carnival processions, and the illustrations of Brant's book were shaped by this association with images of ships of carnival fools familiar to the poet's Europe-wide audience (fig. 58a). Figures dressed as fools ride the rigging of a wheeled ship-cart in a manuscript miniature, depicting a carnival pageant held at Nuremberg in 1506.[210] A figure in a monk's habit sits in the hold, with a beer mug in one hand and a sausage in the other. The monk and crew in Bosch's boat also have a barrel on board. In the *Griet*, the occupants of the world-ship wave a roast fowl.

Bosch's *Ship of Fools* refers both to a carnival ship and to the degenerate condition of the ship of the church; it merges religious and folk visual traditions to create a sophisticated parody, in a manner ancestral to that of the *Griet*. In each case, the choice and placement of details determine how the image is to be interpreted. In this sense, Muchembled's analysis of the interpretation of peasant oral culture applies equally to other kinds of early modern culture, and especially to visual culture: *relatively seldom are animals and things connected with one quality alone, diabolical or beneficent... Signs did not have fixed meanings... because the forces that they helped to interpret were themselves not fixed. Every detail was important to interpretation: time, place, and circumstances colored positively or negatively what seems to us to be the same phenomenon.*[211]

To take a small example, drinking vessels appear in both the Nuremberg pageant depiction and the Bosch design. In the first, they function both as a general attribute of carnival, and as a more particular attribute of a traditional folk joke-figure, the fat friar. In the second, cherries are shown next to the tankard on the table — cherries rather than the carnivalesque sausage or porkpie — indicating the sin of lust. Juxtaposition with cherries, reinforced by the lusty may-tree, pushes the meaning of the cup (and the whole) scene towards identification as a depiction of sinful gluttony and folly.

In the wider context of carnival, as the Bosch painting testifies, the image of a ship with a tree-mast itself evokes older and more mythic dimensions of folk custom and ritual. Strands of folkloric and pagan traditions were knotted together in festival imagery, including some very ancient connotations of the ship image, most notably the idea that the *door to the underworld* is opened during the revels. Ritual ships appeared in carnivals in classical antiquity. During one festival,

> Dionysius, the *great loosener*... rolled through the streets and alleys of Athens, seated on his ship-cart. The cart was drawn by two satyrs, and the god was accompanied by the souls of the dead, who on this day arrived from the swamps of Lerna, the door to the underworld, to visit the mortals.[212]

At the other end of the pagan era, as late as the eleventh century, the Norsemen carried visual constellations with similar ritual associations into European culture. Scandinavian rock art contains the earliest representation of a ship with a tree for a mast, bearing four musicians who play the *lure* (a bronze wind instrument shaped like an ox horn).[213]

Dream-like associations of this kind inform details of Bruegel's design. At the far left of the *Griet*, several odd musical instruments hang from the tree or have part of the tree growing through them. The contortionist on the boundary wall – a pared-down *hagazussa* – carries a banner depicting a curling horn. The epithet describing Bacchus as the *great loosener* is suggestive: the *Dukatenscheisser* could be considered as a humourous, punningly perverted rendering of this title.

Classical carnival practices were well-known in the sixteenth century. Locher, translating Brant's strictures on carnival fools, transposed the whole sense of the passage into classical terms: *The limbs of the Druids are moved by holy emotion to celebrate the wild feasts of Cybele... The bacchantes celebrate their orgies and this foolish crew commemorates the bad shades of the dead.*[214] Sullivan's theory, that Bruegel's women could be thought of as latter-day bacchantes, rests on associations of this kind.

However, the strongest meaning of the carnivalesque ship-cart, a ship on wheels, is as an image of reversal. Its appearance in the streets of a city signifies that suspension of natural order which is at the heart of carnival: *When a ship rolls on land, all matters are turned upside down.*[215] A ship-cart was central to the shadowy cult of Nerthus, which flourished among the early Germanic tribes.[216] The monk Rudolfus witnessed a manifestation of this cult in 1133:

> A wooden ship on wheels traveled from Corneli Müonster to Tongern and Looz via Aachen and Maastricht, where it was fitted out with sails and mast. Wherever the ship halted, the women were overcome by wild ecstasy. Half naked or clad in a short shift, their hair loose, they danced around the ship.[217]

Rudolfus strongly hints that orgies took place around the ship after nightfall, but modesty and shame, he tells us, prevent him from going into details. The ship's course after Looz is uncertain; one tradition maintained that its final destination was the Scheldte at Antwerp.[218] Rudolfus' report illuminates a folk association between the idea of an reversed ship and unruly female behavior.

Authorities differ as to the origin of these ship rites. According to Rudwin, German women danced *in a devilish way around the ship-cart* on Old Women's Shrovetide.[219] The ship does seem to have held a special place in Netherlandish carnivals. The *Blauwe Schute* (*Blue Boat*) was the name of a carnival society or guild of *bambocheurs,* who acquired their charter at Antwerp for the carnival of 1413. According to Minnaert, they *parodied the church and society and conducted their sports especially on the days of carnival.*[220] Jacob van Oestvoren wrote a long poem, also called *Die Blauwe Schute,* to commemorate the founding of this *joyous company*; his work remained very popular through the next century.[221] Bruegel, of course, placed the carnival side of his painting of Carnival and Lent under the Sign of the Blue Boat (see fig. 71). Knowledge of folklore, sign, guild and poem connects the out-of-place ship to the context of carnivalesque revelry.

Clearly, then, several kinds of meanings and combinations of meanings had accrued to the ship motif by the time of the *Griet*'s creation. The genre of religious allegory takes the ship image from St. Ursula's ship to the Ship of the Church and the Ship of Life. Classical texts characterise the ship-on-land as a sign of revelry and drunkenness, of the World-Turned-Upside-Down and the opening of doors to the spirit world. The venerable tradition of the carnival ship similarly signified the entrance into a liminal time where the natural order was reversed or temporarily suspend-

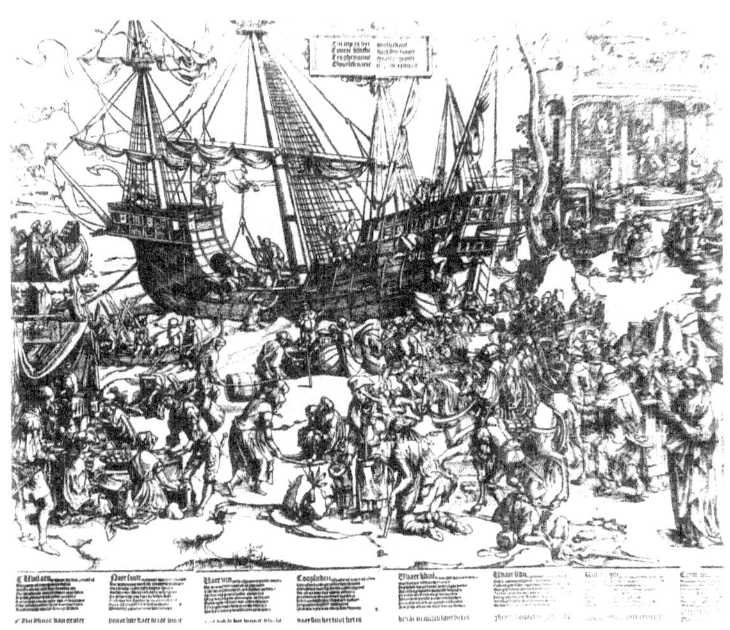

60 Jan Wellens de Cock, *The Ship of St. Renuyt* (The Ship of Mismanagement), c. 1520-30. ©Ashmolean Museum, Oxford. WA 1863.3088

ed. By the later fifteenth century, we see Brant and Bosch turning the basic *topos* of the carnivaleque ship to satirical purposes, anticlerical or universal; this satirical tone is also an aspect of real carnival ship-floats (as at Nuremberg). By the 1520s and 1530s, aspects of the carnivalesque and the religious traditions were regularly combined in Reformation propaganda prints, such as the frenetically metamorphic *Ship of the Papal Church* (fig. 106). An example of the genres combined is *The Ship of St. Renuyt* (or *The Ship of Mismanagement*), ascribed to Jan Wellens de Cock (Amsterdam, c. 1520-30; fig. 60).[222] Renuyt was a popular Dutch pseudo-saint, the patron of drinkers. His name is a play on words meaning *cleaned-out* or *broke* (*rein* and *ute*). A tablet at top centre names the scene: Renuyt and his ne'er-do-well followers are preparing to set out on a dubious pilgrimage.

By the time of Bruegel's *Griet,* the Christian roots of ship-symbolism had transmogrified in this way into discourses of fantasy, philosophy and secular allegory. These streams of ship-symbolism roughly map the ways in which images of ships function in the foreground, the middle ground, and the background of the *Dulle Griet*. Layers of meaning are evoked from different contexts within the painting, linked by threads of thesis and antithesis to the surrounding imagery. The connotations attached to each image change according to the immediate context, shifting as the eye moves around the painting, producing a controlled yet open and apparently limitless phantasmagoric pattern. These techniques of visual orchestration demonstrate, Bruegel's mastery of condensation and displacement.[223] To follow each of the referents here — proverbial, folkloric, classical, mythological, alchemical — is like attempting to track a series of ripples extending far into the artist's culture, demanding a kind of cultural *ekphrasis* (description of painting in words), which does not do justice to the elegance and simultaneity of Bruegel's visual forms.

It is the interrelationships of all these visual vocabularies, shaped into chains of composite images, which "condense" in this proto-Freudian way the themes of the *Dulle Griet*. Bruegel's inventiveness on this level required no greater erudition than that of his allegorising peers such as van Heemskerck and Aerlsen. He based his phantasmagoric effects — his surrealism — on contemporary psychological metaphors, available in contemporary metaphysics. These interlocking vocabularies are visible most clearly in the four distinct levels — separated/nested, condensed/displaced — for which Bruegel uses ship tales, lore and traditions in the *Griet*.

The Ship of Fools

The foreground boat is at the bottom left corner, in front of the Hell-mouth and behind the tree. (fig. 35d) In this image, I think we may perceive a Bruegelian interpretation of the ship of fools. This vessel relates visually to the odd army in the opposite corner. (fig. 35c) The crouched, pale figure at the left end of the boat, head concealed by a conical helmet, is the twin of the small figure who storms the women's bridge with his ladder. The boat floats on the same murky moat characterised here, as at the right, by images of devourment and castration. The beleaguered horde in the Hell-mouth parallels the beleaguered army cowering under the bridge. The giant beaked waterbird bisecting its nude victim parallels the actions of the fish-monsters on the other side of the bridge.

The theme of cowardly, inactive males is carried through these two corner-scenes. The giant winged beehive is probably an emblem of timorousness; it appears, for instance, in the Boschian print parodying chivalry (fig. 53). On the wall above this beehive, a figure with the body of a knight's helmet tries to raise the drawbridge, apparently to protect the Hell-mouth and its denizens from the marauding women. A giant helmet of this type appears in the chivalry satire, where, like Bruegel's cauldron, it is a refuge for a host of metamorphs. These details suggest that the meaning of the left-hand scene in the water matches that of its counterpart on the right.

Yet clearly, a sea-change has come over the creatures at the left. They are less human than their counterparts. There are almost no recognisable humans among them, and the few that are left have no clothes and weapons. The small reptilian metamorph in between the devouring beak and the beehive raises its arm in a gesture that echoes the raised armoured arms of the group in the right-hand corner; evidently to save itself from drowning. This detail also contains a perspectival joke, in that — regarded in terms of adjacent two-dimensional forms — the grasping hand of the metamorph looks as if it is trying futilely to grasp Meg's sword.

Among these altered forms, the edge and purpose of their violence removed, the boat and its occupants float; reminiscent of the boat of the dead man in *Invidia* (fig. 12) or the deserted boat in *Desidia* (fig. 13).[224] Its inhabitants are hiding, like the figure of a helmet-capped man below, who peers from the cover of the tree. The two most human figures at the left show no consciousness of the nightmarish cameos occurring all around them. All appear to have withdrawn from the fray.

The ship of fools, as we have seen, owes something to both the religious and the carnivalesque traditions. It is the best known example of the designs that could be obtained by crossing and inverting the fertile traditions of ship images. The notion of a sinful or insane life's voyage is a parodic inversion, for instance, of the notion of the Ship of the True Believer. Bruegel had at his disposal this array of meanings, but in his image he pared away any carnivalesque element to their basic absurdity, to create a darker, more chilling ship of fools, closer to the world of madness.

The World Ship

In the centre of the painting, Bruegel filled the ship on the giant's back with the large bubble of glass that stands for the world. This bubble fully encases the ship's occupants. These figures and their props must represent the contents of this particular world, and, by extension, the contents also of the world of the picture. Bruegel's world-ship image contains four small figures, dwarfed in a very large globe (fig. 35e). They certainly refer in some sense to greed, but the whole represents more than a simple emblem of gluttony. It is informed also by the later Renaissance passion for punning emblems, where many referents could be woven into a single composite image: a different kind of "polysemous" riddling.

Let us start by considering the proverbial contexts and forms of the image. This ship-world could be an imaginative development of one of the proverbs that Bruegel depicted in the *Netherlandish Proverbs* (1559; fig. 63): *men moet zich Krommen, Wil men door de wereld Kommen* (one must bend/crawl/squirm) if one wants to get through the world; i.e., to succeed in mundane affairs).[225] A hooded figure is half encased in the globe of the world, here given a cross at its top (a common attribute). The position of the cross shows that the world has been turned on its side, as the figure enters it. The lower half of the man crawling into the globe is half undressed. In addition, he wears a shoe on his right foot but none on the left; a kind of shin-guard or splint on the right leg, and again none on the left.[226] Dundes and Stibbe suggested that the brace refers to another proverb using the same verb, *krommen: Bij Krommen leert men hinken* (by bending one learns to limp), implying *that the pleasures of living can produce permanent impairment*.[227] Bruegel's image thus combined two proverbs with contradictory senses, a device he employed often in the *Netherlandish Proverbs* (a subject examined in more detail in Chapter 3).[228] The clothed/unclothed dichotomy may present a similar paradox to do with the nature of the man who bends. To have clothing undone or falling off below the waist is the mark of a fool.[229] In the *Proverbs*, at the top right, Bruegel depicted the *fool who gets all the best cards* with his lower clothing undone in this way, sitting above the sign of the world turned upside down. To crawl or squirm through the world, then, may seem to be the act of a sensible man; it shows at the same time a split self and a misplaced focus of desire.

The cross of the world in the *Proverbs* scene overlaps the foot of the man from the proverb to the right: a young man in expensive garments who *spins the world on his thumb*; as in the American saying, *the whole world in his hand*. The Flemish proverb does not necessarily refer to wealth, merely to an individual *who has everything under control*.[230] Bruegel depicts this figure as rich and fortunate, with a *feather in his cap* (the sense of this is identical in English). He also gave this man markedly pointed shoes; in Netherlandish tradition, the pointier the shoe, the wealthier the wearer.

The two-fold proverb cameos in the *Griet* flank the giant-and-the-ship-of-the-world; they act as microcosms of the elements of the more complex composite image. The *Dukatenscheisser* holds the world on his shoulders, as the fortunate man balances it on his thumb. The smaller, open-mouthed, hooded face staring out from the glass "world" is like the man in the globe in the *Proverbs*. The sense in that proverb of movement *through* the emblem of the world is displaced and inverted into the visual idea of the nude, hatted figure heaving a ball of gold over the side of the ship. The sense of these figures and their props can be thus be read as a set of distilled, inverted proverbial actions.

An explanation of the contents of Bruegel's world-ship, based on the analogies with the *Proverbs*, might run something like this. There are two kinds of materials inside the globe: the roast bird and the solid gold sphere, making it evidently a worldly world. Inside the ship, one figure attempts to make off with a sphere of treasure and roll it over the side of the ship, where it will fall, like the money from the giant's rear, on to the crowd below. Two other figures, all mouth and teeth, brandish the roast fowl; another figure stares off blankly to the right. The ship is a satire on consumption, linking thievery, the surreal detail of a ball of gold the size of the world, with hybrids as degenerate men, enslaved to greed.

In the context of other aspects of the painting, several sorts of reference to consumption, money and dreams are attached directly or indirectly to the world-ship. One is its relation to the stage-setting to its right. Another is its position as part of a pattern of alchemical symbolism in the painting. No doubt other "compass-bearings" for the ship-motif could be teased out — other frames within the painting unravel further threads of meaning. A few such analyses will demonstrate how the image works as a pivot, around which the complex meanings of the *Dulle Griet* turn.

One "frame" may be construed by taking this ship of the world primarily itself as an toy-artefact — a sort of prop — and by asking what such symbolic ships meant in urban life. By the mid-sixteenth century appeared as devices in many kinds of theatrical contexts. Like the Hell-mouth, the wheeled ship spread out from its original home as part of carnival-theatre, and the change in use seems also motivated by a novel appreciation of the image's formal potential:

> The mechanical aspects of the wheeled ship were so attractive that every opportunity to exploit them was utilized. We find practicable

> ships and hobby ships in the mysteries and passion plays, where movement from one *mansion* to another was sometimes carried out by *ship*. The ship appeared... in triumphs and pageants with captain and crew and in allegorical spectacle and as stage property in the festivals of the guilds.[231]

Again, as in the case of the Hell-mouth, the effect of de-contextualisation was to surrealise the image further. A manuscript illustration shows the theatre at Valenciennes, near the Flemish border, during the 1547 performance of a Passion play; its high viewpoint shows ingenious machines (levers, wheels, etc.) controlling the Hell-mouth. In front, a small ship floats on an artificial pool.[232] Ship motifs, as we have seen, could have religious, parodic or playful significance. Its appearance, during the most notoriously carnivalesque scenes of the passion play, signals a noteworthy conjunction of secular and comic genres.

There are a number of references to the theatre in the *Dulle Griet*. The most direct is the presence of a literal theatre, to the right of the Ship-*Dukatenscheisser*; drawing a familiar comparison between the artifice of the theatre and that of the marketplace.[233] This stage, a metaphor for the social world, is empty; as if all the action we see is going on back-stage, or has erupted off-stage. The space between the ship-man and the stage is filled by the murky pool with the people immersed in it. Adding these submerged people between the *Dukatenscheisser* and the stage further elaborates (or condenses) Bruegel's idea.[234] On a subliminal level, the placement of the heads in the mire between the *Dukatenscheisser* and the stage resonates with older meanings of *obscenum*, or *obscene*: that which stood outside of the sacred space of the *scenum* in the classical theatre.[235] Legends about the stage as a portal to the other world were part of the folklore of the medieval and early modern theatre, particularly in plays involving hell.[236] The reference would be clear in the minds of Bruegel's Latin-literate audience, who were also, we recall, inveterate punners.

The image of human heads immured in filth has a place in the pattern of dream-logic that links money-faeces with the disembodied head of hell.

Another cave mouth (apparently filled with treasure) opens to the side of the stage, underlining the visual pun between the obscene, money, and hell. As part of this configuration, the Ship of the World on the giant's back diminishes to the level of a stage property, a special effect. Just as the stage in the painting is surrounded with muck and hoarded-up money, so the bubble of the world's boat is gripped by the embodiment of a new kind of obscenity.

From the perspective of alchemical symbolism, several otherwise inexplicable elements in the painting fall into visually meaningful patterns centred on the ship. Van Lennep first argued that the ship could be read as an alchemical symbol, and that the painting as a whole might have two levels of meaning, one for the adept or alchemically knowledgeable person, another for the less knowledgeable.[237] This raised some inevitable questions. How much alchemical knowledge would be required to read the painting in this way? Who had this knowledge and how widespread could it have been? Would Bruegel, his patrons, or anyone in similar circles, have been sufficiently alchemically knowledgeable to understand this "adept" level?

As in the case of Bosch, such questions have meant that research on potential alchemical meanings focussed on trying to establish personal specialist knowledge on the part of the artist. The results for Bosch have been inconclusive,[238] and for Bruegel even more so, since there is no evidence for Bruegel's private interests other than his art itself. But the problem is to some extent an artefact, caused by mistaken assumptions. To start with, there was no such thing as a systematic symbolism of alchemy; the phrase endows the field of alchemical illustration (or visual culture), with a rigour it was far from possessing in Bruegel's time. The kind of surreal alchemical imagery which calls to mind the work of Bosch or Bruegel was a relatively new genre, introduced in the late fourteenth and fifteenth centuries.[239] Prior to that era, there was a very restricted tradition of visual illustration or illumination in alchemical manuscript production, which tended to rely on diagrams and a few image-types depicting apparatus.[240]

Much richer manuscript production began to flourish around the time of Bosch. Such denser illustrations are best seen as products of the same cultural turn that produced surreal Renaissance art. The imagery produced by this flowering of alchemical illustration resembles sixteenth-century surreal inventions in art, because both are constructed from the same cultural "tool-box" and because they share a purpose: the representation of dream-states and fantasy. They are all aesthetic inventions, shaped by and emanating from the same sets of interests and habits of mind.

The alchemical material, like novel mythological hybrid gods, or the rhetorical figures of the emblem books, crystallised into orthodox manuals towards 1600, but at mid-century this standardisation was far from being achieved.[241] Since there were few medieval precedents for a visual culture of alchemy, Renaissance alchemical illustrators found themselves either translating verbal images and metaphors literally, with surreal results, or drawing on the same focal points and frames of reference which shaped the production of dream-like metamorphic imagery elsewhere in their visual culture. Such commonality as can be found between the alchemical imagery and the surreal can therefore be ascribed to deeply–rooted common cultural frameworks.

Consider, for example, the formal structure of the picture-riddles made for the *Aurora consurgens* (early 16C; figs. 19 and 61), famous for its astonishingly surreal illustrations. Compare the "monkey-harp" structure in the *Griet* with this "monkey-violin" picture from the *Aurora consurgens* (fig 61). In the latter, an ape (no tail) plays a lobster violin using a wavy blue snake for a bow, framed on a background of brilliant red. One leg is a sheaf of corn, burning at the foot, the other leg terminates in a hoof resting on the mouth of a skull; effectively a third leg is formed by the tail end of a large blue fish. This choice and combination of elements is very close in character to Bruegel's. The images in the oldest and richest copy date from the 1420s.[242] Obrist commented:

> The early fifteenth-century Aurora consurgens marks a further step in the elaboration of pictorial metaphors combined with glass vessels. On a purely pictorial level [the] inventive and high-quality artist developed a core of recurrent alchemical metaphors that relate to human and animal procreation, the dismemberment of bodies (symbolizing calcinations and putrefaction).... In and around glass vessels, the artist metaphorically depicted stages of operation relating to the alchemical art of transformation as well as cosmological and philosophical principles of the art, such as *two are one* and *nature vanquishes nature*. Two or more principal metaphors are frequently combined within a single picture, reflecting the increasing use of chains of metaphors.[243]

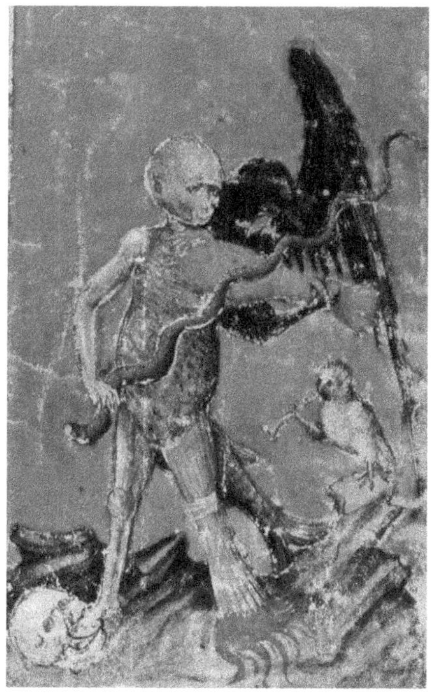

61 Anon, *Ape playing lobster violin, Aurora Consurgens*, Ms. Ferguson 6, Glasgow University Library. Courtesy Glasgow University Library

Some points emerge here about the formal devices and visual rhetoric used to construct these pictures. Condensation and displacement are again the preferred techniques. Two or more *principal metaphors* are fused or spliced into one image; often framed by or set *in and around glass vessels*. The same substance, in two different states, is represented as two unrelated motifs: *the eagle and the dragon [respectively] denote mercury as a volatile and as a solidified substance*; making possible a sense of collapsed or suspended time. Note also the preference for paradoxes and *chains of metaphors*. The preferred medium for these transformations is the human or animal body: so procreation and dismemberment become visual ways of conjoining and ramifying the human figure. In other words, these images achieve their surreal effect by the same rhetorical rules or processes that characterise both dream-imagery and Renaissance surreal inventions.

Van Lennep argued that the *Griet's* world-ship resembles a kind of *athanor*, the closed chamber or oven in which the glass alchemical vessel is placed. Many alchemical treatises and manuscripts show this chamber as a kind of *inhabited sphere*. In addition, the *image of the chicken is frequently employed by alchemists who moreover designate the crucible by the expression "chicken's nest."*[244] Alchemical references in the *Griet*, then, might connect the globe (or *chicken's nest*), the ship (or *athanor*), and the egg (or philosopher's stone). Two pairs of smaller glass globes — one in the prow of the ship, one wedged between the giant's leg and the roof — could refer to alchemical vessels. The creature carrying on his shoulders this *vessel containing the chicken's nest* would then be actually in the process of laying a big, half-broken egg, as opposed to being a hybrid with an eggshell rear.

The huge egg-structure with the monkey and the harp in the landscape, wedged into a cranny between city wall, cliff and water, may indeed be read as a kind of *athanor*; a hatching of the large single egg in the nest at Griet's feet. But what kind of *athanor* might the ship be? The stuff that the Giant spoons out of the egg is silver. There is the detail of the small woman robbing the giant's purse and being doused; one of Bruegel's many pairings of a larger and a smaller version of the same action. In every other context we have looked at, the significance of these things appearing together is unquestionably negative.

Interpretations based on alchemical correspondences next bring into play the difference between true and false alchemy. Serious alchemists may have thought of the philosopher's stone as a metaphor for Christ, but alchemists themselves were popularly seen as would-be gold-makers, self-deluded, if not actually frauds. False alchemists were legislated against, along with other people who took money for magic, because they generally demanded gold in order to make it grow. The things that emerge from Bruegel's eggs are like parodies of the serious alchemical book illustrations reproduced in Van Lennep and Obrist: black money, a monkey-serpent, a

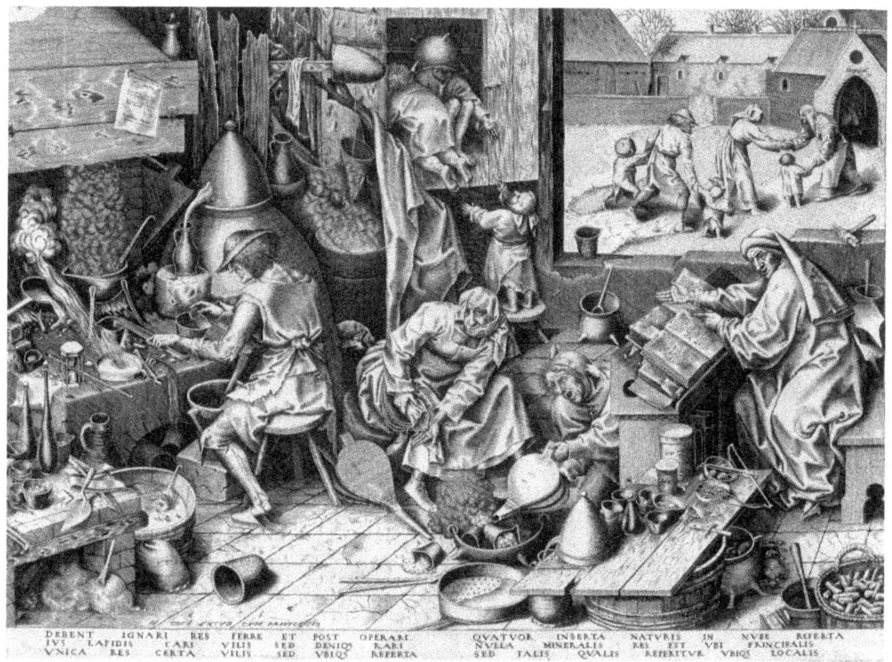

62 Philip Galle, after Pieter Bruegel, *The Alchemist*, 1558. Engraving, 32 x 44 cm. © bpk/Kupferstich Kabinet, Staatliche Museen zu Berlin. Inv 45-1964. Photo: Jörg P.Anders

spider whose web is a harp, a scrawny clutch of birds. The broken nutshell-broken egg complex seems rather an emblem of corrupted enlightenment.

In 1558, Bruegel produced a comic design related to this subject, *The Alchemist* (fig. 62). The scene is divided into two zones. In the foreground, the deluded alchemist pours all his energy and resources into his futile quest for gold, at the expense of his own welfare and that of his family. In the background, the alchemist, having lost everything, changes his way of life and turns to the mercy of Christ, the true philosopher's stone. Evidently, this print is another Bruegelian comment on money-madness in contemporary life. But the vocabulary of the Latin inscription explains this in vocabulary familiar from religious alchemy.[245] This indicates general knowledge of the distinction between alchemy as a charlatan's procedure motivated by profit and alchemy as a path to God. Agrippa of Nettesheim denounced false alchemy in these words:

> Das Goldmachen ... ist fürwahr eine recht schöne Erfindung und ein artiger unstrafbarer Betrug, dessen Vanität und Eitelkeit gar leicht sich herfür tut, indem es dasjenige verspricht was die Natur Keineswegs leiden noch erreichen Kann.[246]

The deceptive associations of fraud with gold — things which are not as they appear, or as they are said to be — are thus again the main point here. Towards the end of the century, alchemy became a natural metaphor for the entrepreneurial doings of the merchants in the marketplace. As possessors of gold and manipulators of the occult forces of credit, merchants were popularly depicted as in league with demonic forces (fig. 48). By 1593, Thomas Nashe could comment:

> He that buyes must sell, shrewd Alcumists there are risen vp, that will pick a merchandise out of euery thing, and not spare to set vp theyr shops of buying and selling even in the Temple.[247]

These connotations resonate in the themes of the *Griet*: alchemy gone astray, alchemical imagery as a screen for profitable fraud, whose false *athanors*, like those of Bosch, generate only mis-births. Bruegel found this another apposite frame of reference for the transitional imagery, half-comic, half-nightmarish, of the middle-ground of the *Griet*; here, instead of procreation and dismemberment, excretion is the mark of transmutation.

Regarded from this perspective, the figure inside the world-ship, with his arms around the gold, ball looks as if he is trying to steal the yolk of the world-egg (a kind of secular philosopher's stone). He is like a bird-nester, attempting to make off with the egg itself. The image of the chicken, whose presence in philosophical manuscript illustrations denotes both the function of the athanor as a *nest* for the stone and, incipiently, the egg itself, is here represented as a roast dinner; alchemy reduced to a species of cooking.

Some aspects of the monkey-egg construction, such as the harp with the spider, secularise Bosch's images of true transmutation. Bosch's followers often imitated his famous creation of the man impaled on harp strings (fig. 17c). Harbison mentions their tendency to view Bosch's inventions *in terms of motif, rather than of spirit*, and there is a sense in which this is indeed what Bruegel does: to substitute a spider in the harp reworks the Boschian motif in an entirely satirical spirit.[248] Further details here refer to a kind of perverted alchemy. Growing from the casing of the broken-egg-form is something which could be a parodic version of the philosopher's tree. On the middle platform formed by its branches, ape-like figures, one horned, dance in a circle. They seem to stand here, as elsewhere in the painting, for the material, desire-driven aspect of Man. They dance on a cage above two imprisoned deer — deer were a common alchemical symbol for *spiritus*[249] — this may represent an ascendency of apes over the house of the spirit. Like the *Aurora consurgens* ape, the hybrid imagery represents a chaotic, metamorphic state; a state of flux.

If the monkey-egg-motif is a kind of symbolic extrapolation of the ship-world-*athanor*, the tenor of this extrapolation is to redirect references to gold and gain into the rhetorical vocabulary of false alchemy. The same elements appear here, cast in more surreal terms, producing an effect that is more enigmatic and thus more sinister. The allegorical Dame Avarice, if such she be, shrinks to become a detached small element of the whole ensemble. The ape-serpent coiling itself round the mad artifice of the broken egg is linked visually, by the curl of its tail, to the naked couple on a rock in the water, itself an allusion to the story of Eden and the human Fall.

Formally these two miniature cameos — naked-couple/Adam-and-Eve, and Old-Woman/Dame-Avarice/Picnic/Sabbat — act as outriders to the main structure. Each group represents the animal desires so fantastically tied up and elaborated in the monkey-harp/egg. If we consider the two groups in relationship to the contortionist on the bridge, extending in a line from the view through his legs, it becomes clear that the distances and degrees of similitude among the three are nicely calculated. They line up precisely as a chain of increasing *complicatio*: a) sexual desire, the original sin, b) its progeny, avarice, in the shadow of c) an insane, diseased alchemical structure, redolent of more complex kinds of money-disease, whose snake-tail tendrils out towards "Adam and Eve." This is the arrangement "framed" from the anchor of the contortionist's legs. As a *hagazussa* peering into the spirit-realm, this may represent what he sees staring out of the picture, into the world of the viewer, or how he perceives the picture's own world.

The meaning of the egg-harp structure as a whole thus has many levels. As a visual riddle, or emblem, the meaning decodes as the victory of bestial man over spiritual man. As a visual device, it establishes a net of surreal kinships and hierarchies, through chains of increasingly condensed and displaced elements.

The central world-ship, then, is among other things, a clue or key to the parodic use of alchemical metaphors in the *Griet*. These range from the comic (the hybrid fishing for chicks) to the horribly fascinating (the harp-egg), yet embody a common theme. The alchemical dimension links the ensemble of the ship-man more clearly with the concerns of the rest of the painting. Taken as a whole, the *Dukatenschiesser*-world-ship is a *tour-de-force* condensation, uniting these concerns. Like a huge wobbly prop from a carnival drama which has got wholly out of hand, it is uneasily balanced between the empty stage and the Hell-mouth, embodying themes of urban chaos and disorder. As an alchemical joke, like the carnival and proverbial references, it dissects surreal and perverted money-madness.

These contexts blur into one another. The ship is lodged on the giant's shoulders, no longer a mode of transport but a thing transported, as in the Reversed World of float and broadside. The creature it rides on is a transvestite dream-time denizen, its inside half-inverted. This land-locked ship is actually surrounded with painted water, another of Bruegel's vertiginous visual jokes, like the frying pan and the giant's oriface. Perspective and placement compel the viewer to "see double," in order to read the sense in which the ship is in its natural element.

Formally, the Ship of the World unites three distinct planes of the painting. The top of the globe shows, as if through a lens, a deserted house, surrounded by a moat from the barren landscape stretching to the horizon. The odd, moated house is thus also "inside" the ship. Beyond this deserted outpost lie bleaker events, outside the comforting theatricality of happenings in the town. The context of dreams as well as carnival is a necessary framework for understanding the dark panorama which appears in the horizon zone, above the Ship of the World.

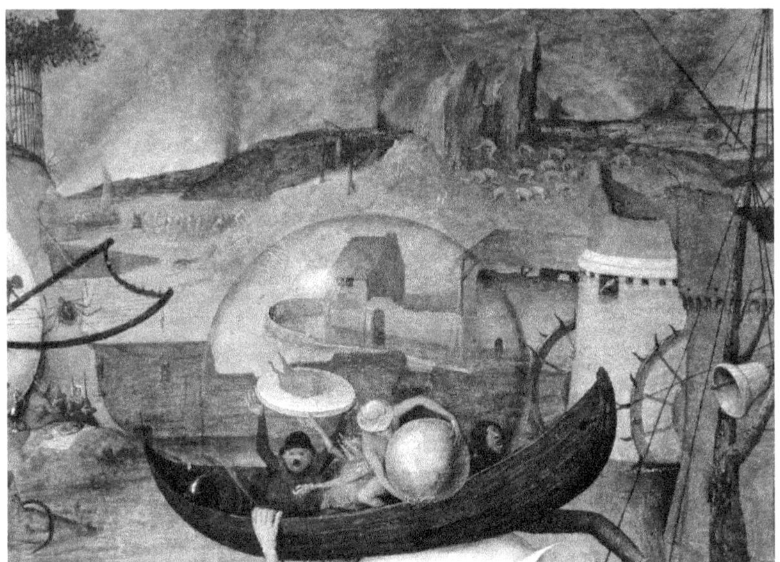

35e Pieter Bruegel, world-ship, detail, *Dulle Griet*

Allegorical ships were thought of as engaged in journeys: the voyage of the church on the world's sea or the voyage of the soul through life. There are two ships on the dark sea in the distant background of the *Griet* (fig. 35e above; 35f, p. 296 below) a boat, top-left of the egg construction; a ship with a single sail, above the harp, close to shore. On the shore is a group of naked people. A darker figure waves its arms in the air between them and the sailing boat. Below these, a single man leads or has his hand bitten by a dog. A naked band of humans clambers up over some rocks to the right. Further right, the eye comes to a gallows with a hanging corpse; another naked group ascends jagged rocks; others grovel on the ground beneath them. At the extreme right, slightly above the crawling people, a shadowy giant figure faces out to sea, his back to the viewer.

We need to consider this panorama in its separate stages to see how these stages are linked or otherwise inform each other. Are the two boats part of the same company? Have the people on the beach disembarked from the sailing boat? Are they on their way to join the others who crawl in the lee of the mountain? Is the figure in black, between the people and the boat, giving chase or running from the boat? These images do not resolve into a recognisable text-based narrative, any more than do the other parts of the *Dulle Griet*, but this is not to say they have no cultural or literary frames of reference. These motifs and scenarios bear family resemblances to matter from dreams and legends; they occur as stock ingredients of popular descriptions of infernal journeys, travellers' tales and spirit-worlds. The contexts given to these ingredients in imaginative literature allows us to discover what connotations they might have in common.

The first literary frame of reference to come to mind is the Bible: the figures climbing the rocky outcrop evoke the Deluge; the huge shadowy man, *Genesis* 6:1-6, which describes how, before the Flood, the sons of God united with the daughters of men to produce a race of giants. Such connotations inevitably colour any configuration of naked people, dark waters and giants, even in the absence of more specific attributes, such as an ark, or God in the sky.

A sea voyage to an island of the damned evokes the *Voyage of St. Brendan*, an Irish epic made into a Flemish poem in the twelfth century. Like the better-known *Travels of Sir John Mandeville*, this work became popular with Flemish illuminators in the thirteenth and fourteenth centuries and went into print in the 1470s. Brendan and his companions sail looking for the earthly paradise. This is one of the islands they visit:

> One day the wind drives their vessel towards a rugged and barren island, covered with slag and full of smithies. The saint expresses his fear of this place, from which comes the thunderous sound of hammers beating upon anvils, and he asks God for deliverance. One of the inhabitants of the island emerges. He is shaggy, fiery, and dark in appearance, and when he sees the pilgrims he returns into his forge. Brendan orders his crew to try to flee the island; but the *barbarian* runs

> to the shore bearing a huge blazing mass of slag.... He hurls it at the vessel, but misses; and the sea boils where it falls, and smoke rises as if from an oven. As the voyagers withdraw, all the inhabitants of the isle rush to the shore and cast similar masses at the ship and even at each other, then return to their forges and light them, so that the island looks like a globe of fire. The sea boils like a pot, and even when the fleeing pilgrims can no longer see the island, they can hear the wailing of its inhabitants and smell the stench of the place. Then St. Brendan tells his companions that they have been close to Hell.[250]

Though the denizens of Bruegel's isle do not otherwise resemble those of Brendan's, aspects of the background panorama evoke this *mise-en-scène*: the great columns of smoke and fire and (possibly) the shaggy, dark barbarian.

It was customary for the dead to be shown naked in Flemish art, (cf. fig. 23) and a naked crowd in general evoked one of the infernal regions. An episode from another *livre populaire* of the day, describes a scene in St. Patrick's Purgatory close in spirit to the pitiful scene at the back of the *Griet*:

> The hero is then taken to a mountain, where there is a vast number of naked people crouching on tiptoe. They are facing the north, and look like people awaiting death. [The knight] Owen... wonders at their pitiful attitude; and he is being threatened with the same fate when a mighty wind from the north seizes the wretches and casts them, together with the knight and his attendant demons, into a stinking, icy river. As they try to climb out, other demons are waiting to push them back with iron hooks.[251]

The *mis-en-scène* in the *Griet* kindles memories of this kind of scenario, while still resisting resolution as a recognisable region of Hell. Bruegel's group are not suffering typical infernal torments; the dark figure on the beach and the giant are not depicted as torturers. Nothing identifies the island as a place of active supernatural punishment along the lines of Brendan's island of damned smiths or Owen's devil-guarded mountain. These omissions are significant.

The work that comes closest to these scenes in the *Griet* is Bruegel's own, later, *Triumph of Death* (fig. 89). In the top right area of this painting, a boat sinks in the sea to the right of a jar-like tower, with a rudimentary face, on a small island. A man falls from the wreck into the water, while a band of skeletons wave from the tower. The implication is that this shipwreck was caused by the armies of the dead. To the right of this scene, further down, a naked man is attacked by two dogs. Behind the dogs walks a skeletal huntsman carrying his human prey on a stick. The man attacked by a hound could be a World-Turned-Upside-Down motif; the man and dog in the *Dulle Griet* have something of this quality. Parts of Bruegel's background panorama clearly draw on *topoi* which occur also in legendary tales. But as a whole, the imagery is used without the contexts and conventions which narrativise these *topoi* in the legends.

This may seem a rather circumlocuitous way of concluding that the background scenes of the *Dulle Griet* are "fanciful" — a word often used for visual inventions which demonstrate this kind of resistance to narrative interpretation. When no specific identifications can be made with literary precedents, this strategy of last resort manages to imply at the same time that the imagery is not worthy of much attention and that there is nothing unprecedented about it. It achieves this by employing the rhetorical device of claiming the imagery was created by the artist giving free rein to his imagination. But "fanciful" — or "full of fancies" — in the context of art, must be taken to indicate an artfully structured set of choices, extracted from an equally structured repertoire of possibilities. The artist's imagination indeed travels freely, but only within and through the institutions and categories of the personal imagination; the imagination can only be inscribed through culture.

Thus, as we have seen, the motifs and the rhetorical techniques of Bruegel's imagery were informed by his common mental worlds of popular and elite fantasy. This continues to be the case, even when his art represents parts of these motifs and pieces of rhetoric abstract form the narrative frameworks to which they are conventionally attached in literary or artistic contexts. The result is a massive increase in the affect carried by the imagery. When slotted into the familiar story-type of the infernal journey or the magical voyage, these same "infernal" part-motifs — the naked crowd, the shipwreck, the great column of smoke, the shadowy giant — are provided with an explanatory framework — or narrative — which to some extent defangs, or earths, the horror of the image for the audience. Such elements, as Bruegel evidently realised, can work as interchangeable set-pieces in such narrative frameworks. But outside such a framework, the images become detached from the possibility of narrative resolution. A greater degree of mystery is automatically attached to them by the viewer; they become more eerie and puzzling. This dissociation from narrative is also a way of evoking the world of dreams. The background scenes introduce a completely different approach to representing the dream-state than that induced by the foreground landscapes of proliferating metamorphs.

Nightmares, Folktales and Giants

The twilit world of dreams and folklore has been invoked throughout this chapter as an essential context with which to make sense of the events and personages of the *Dulle Griet*. In discussing the painting's tone, I referred to the *Griet's* background as *fully nightmarish*. I now suggest that these background scenes draw power from that part of culture where nightmares and folktales overlap. Formal parallels between the two are clearest in the area of childhood nightmares, when templates provided by nursery rhymes and fairy tales have the strongest impression on the dreamer's visual vocabulary and grammar.[252]

Comparing children's dreams with folktales, Sutton-Smith concluded by commenting: *What is perhaps most noteworthy about the tales is that they seem an extraordinary complement to the dreams.*[253] In Bruegel's culture, themes taken from folk literature and dreams had much in common. Parallels between childhood dream material, analogous folktales, and the nightmare panorama of the *Griet* demonstrate the psychological astuteness of Bruegel's imagery. Contemporary applications of the theory of humours to children's dreams are of interest here. The Flemish physician Cornelius Roelans (1450-1525) wrote a book *On Diseases of Infants* (c. 1500). In a list of fifty-two kinds of illness, he ranked *dreams terrifying them* ninth. Around 1544, Dr. Thomas Phaer (1510-60) observed, in his *Boke of Chyldren*, that,

> oftentimes it happeneth that the child is afraid in ye sleepe and somtymes waketh sodainly, and sterteth, somtyme shriketh and trembleth, which effect commeth of the arysing of stynkying vapours out of ye stomacke into the fantasye.[254]

Physicians saw such dreams as a form of *somnium naturale*. It will be recalled that the *somnium naturale* was thought to derive from purely physical imbalances of humours; this included children's dreams, which were not ascribed supernatural significance. Notice the important role of the stomach, from whence *aryse stynkying vapours*, as the cause of nightmares; notable given that so many of the nightmarish images in the *Griet* turn around digestive perversions.

For more information about the typical content of childish nightmares and their connections to folkloric imagery, we can turn to modern analyses. In the course of a discussion of the nature of the fantastic, the folklorist Dundes commented:

> A psychoanalytically oriented folklorist might realize that giants are... infantile projections of parents. An infant does not necessarily see itself as small in comparison to adults, but in the infant's view adults, especially parents, are simply larger versions of the same kind of being that the infant is.[255]

What applies to giants in folklore may reasonably apply to giants in dreams. An unconscious identification of giant figures with parents accounts in part for the chilling effect of Bruegel's shadowy giant who turns his back on the naked people crawling by the rock. Its presence increases the sense of abandonment and threat in this scene. According to Sutton-Smith, in both nightmares and folktales,

> there is a moratorium on ethical and religious concerns. The dreams provide what [Vladimir] Propp might call a lack, or deficiency, *a sudden emergence of misfortune*, and the folktales provide a response.[256]

Such a moratorium is, I think, to be seen in the absence of demons or of recognisably infernal mechanisms of punishment in the Bruegelian imagery. There is no teleological mechanism to explain suffering on the island, just as there is none for suffering in a nightmare.

In folktales involving a monster, a giant, a witch, or other malignant enemy (e.g., Little Red Riding Hood, Hansel and Gretel, Jack and the Beanstalk) the protagonist always overcomes the villain. In the dreams of five-year-old children, the opposite is true:

> While the subject is in the dream on all occasions... the predominant counter-actor is a monster figure in seventeen out of twenty dreams (lion, ghost, tiger, witch, animal, murderer, monster). Where sex is attributed to these figures, females predominate over males, seven to two. In fifteen out of twenty dreams the dreamer is the passive recipient of another's actions. The monster chases, captures, bites, hurts, scares, and injures the dreamer bodily. In only five out of twenty dreams does the dreamer counteract.[257]

This suggests that the main significant difference between a typical childhood nightmare and a typical folktale is the hopeless end of the nightmare for the protagonist.[258] In the scene on the island, folktale elements such as the ship and the giant appear, and the fate of the humans is, apparently, hopeless.

The lack of a narrative resolution itself is an attribute of nightmare. In folktales, the protagonists may be frightened by *a sudden emergence of misfortune*, but the crisis always finds them prepared to act; with native cunning or magical assistance, they respond to the threat. In this double sense, a folktale is *a response* to the *deficiency* — experienced as helplessness — inherent in elementary nightmares. In nightmares, there is no such response. The dreamer cannot act. Sutton-Smith comments:

> The fact that most dreamers report being scared and yet do not do anything suggests a predominantly *freezing* reaction to fear, which is also the most familiar elementary fear response reported in animal and human literature... In all of these forms, as used by children at the age of five, the *flight syndrome* is the key imaginative structure. Furthermore, it is pre-dialectical. It is possible to envisage defeat and failure without adequate counterbalance, although in fully developed folktales there is usually such redress.[259]

In the painting, the people on the beach scramble up the slope to the right; around the central outcrop, two people continue this movement by climbing the rock. These are examples of flight as a nightmarish *resolution*. It may be permissible to consider the whole panorama according to the *key imaginative structure* of flight. The logical breaks in the panorama then work like the transitions in a dream. Reading from left to right, boats flee from the events in the foreground towards the beach. Next people are chased onto, or marooned on, or simply appear on the beach. They move inland. There is a gallows with a rotting corpse. Then there is the rock, futile climbing and groveling, the giant in the distance. Flight ends here, where there is nowhere else to go.

The enigmatic imagery of these background scenes pictorially echoes and restates elements of the carnivalesque foreground and emblematic middle-ground. Thus the theme of partial immersion or burial links the figures in the lake by the stage, and the figure whose head and arms emerge from the earth, to the left of the egg-harp structure; like intermediate stages in an *explicatio* whose end-point is the crowd on the island. Another chain is provided by the careful positioning of naked figures leading back into depth. In the foreground, in front of the Hell-mouth, one is eaten by a beaked monster. In the middle-ground, our old friend the spindly-limbed contortionist balances on the wall that connects Hell-mouth to town, and divides town and wilderness.

As we have seen, this figure is liminal in several ways: a mooning fence-demon, peering through his legs. As a knot of paradox, contortion and reversal, he ushers the viewer into the intensified inverted symbolism of the compound beyond the town, with its false *athanor* and imprisoned *spiritus*. His anatomically impossible stance relates him to the hybrid figures on the near side of the wall; his nudity connects him to the "Adam and Eve" figures behind him. These figures are in turn related to the crowd beneath the rock, by virtue of their nakedness and their position on an island. In the context of the ape-serpent, they allude to the Fall, just as the group on the island more distantly alludes to the Deluge and the corruption of humanity that caused it.

The quality of these background scenes is thus nightmarish in quite specific ways. The fate of the naked people, as Bruegel's adult audience, staring in fascination, would undoubtedly have been aware, is the loss of what made them, in Renaissance terms, essentially human. Recall Pico's words: *For if you see one abandoned to his appetites, crawling on the ground, it is a plant and not a man you see*. Or Plato's argument that people became four-footed beasts because they had stopped thinking of abstract (that is, divine) matters.[260] The limbs of some of the people on the island are buried in the ground. Another has a buried head. Whether this mimics animal or vegetable behavior, evidently humanity's chameleon-like nature has here plummeted to its lowest level. In this most metamorphic of paintings, this culmination is depicted visually as behavioral.

Thomas Nashe (1567-1601), writing late in the century, expressed his view of the nightmare as the rational mind tormented by its own desires:

> When Night in her rustie dungeon hath imprisoned our ey-sight, and that we are shut separatly in our chambers from resort, the divell keepeth his audit in our sin-guilty consciences, no sense but surrenders to our memorie a true bill of parcels of his detestable impietis. The table of our host is turned to an index of iniquities, and all our thoughts are nothing but texts to condemn us. The rest we take in our beds in such another kind of rest as the weerie traveller taketh in the coole soft grass in summer, who thinking there to lye at ease... layeth his fainting head unawares on a loathsome nest of snakes.[261]

It is clear by now that the whole of the *Griet*'s action can be regarded as expressed in relation to dreams: dream-beliefs, dream-reversals, dream-anxieties. The forms of the imagery as much as its themes evoke the kinds of concerns and fears expected to preoccupy the unconscious in the sixteenth century. The fantastic chords of the *Griet* touch on fears of dismemberment, of burial, of attack through the body's orifices. Chains of images connected by these themes hold together the main planes of the picture. Each variation is linked to the others by relationships of visual telescoping, expansion, inversion and displacement. They progressively erode the uneasy barriers, felt as permeable and fragile, between the dreams and the supernatural, wilderness and civilisation.

Bruegel's ship variations exploit the dream-like potential of the motif and its traditions: the passive, static ship of fools, the precariously balanced ship of the world, and the two far-off ships sailing to a mindless destination. These appear almost literal conceptions, however, compared to the most phantasmogoric ship-image of the painting, and its most striking example of inversion.

Beside the *Dukatenscheisser*, as Rosoman noticed: *Bruegel has placed a kind of signpost... in the form of a tree which grows into a ship's mast with rigging and a crow's nest and a tolling bell.*[262] Seeking the rest of this vessel, at the far right, we see another mast growing from the silhouetted monkeys' tower. A pair of simian hybrids ascend to its crow's nest by rope-ladder. A huge snaking banner, a plumbline held by a monkey, and the long whip of a bird's tail counterpoint the linear rhythm of these ropes. As in a ship's rigging, the ropes are strategically placed to anchor the masts to parts of the town. From the central tree-mast, a rope-ladder runs down into the mire beside the theatre. Another rope, the handle of the bell, is pulled on by an occupant of the cauldron. A line depending from just below the crow's nest at the far right splits into two halfway between the two masts. The higher line leads to the flag at the top of the tree-mast. The lower, however, actually passes through a hole in the keel of the world-ship, like a jib rope holding it to the larger mast.

The town itself is metamorphosing into a ship. The world-ship is dwarfed by this half-realised town-ship, all but surrounded by its moat. The ship within the ship represents a kind of imploded metonymic figure, where the whole stands for a part of the same whole. The town-ship encompasses the central world of the painting, among whose contents is the ship of the world. Inversion seems too simple and broad a term for the spatial and symbolic transformations at work here; one is reminded of the mathematics of the Möbius Strip or the Klein bottle, represented in terms of variations in metamorphic fantasy

This huge ship-image also signifies a journey into the twilight realm of dreams and witches. Its form indicates the sense of vertigo associated with this world. Its components appear in other expressions of the themes of the *Griet*. Thus a seventeenth-century Dutchman described women who *forget themselves in brandywine and other strong drinks and go around all day thoroughly polluted*, using the old metaphor *met een nat zeyl* (three sheets to the wind).[263] In London, on the question of whether or not witches really fly, Thomas Fuller (1608-61) wrote that:

> These with Drake sail around the world, but it is on an ocean of their own phancies, and in a ship of the same.... They boast of brave banquets they have been at, but they would be very lean should they eat no other meat.[264]

The "orgy" of Fuller's harmless, deluded witches centres on the consumption of meat and drink; so the association veered eventually back towards its folkloric roots, and away from the full-blown concept of the Sabbat.

These examples use the same metaphorical models as the *Griet* to represent flights of the imagination. All make it clear that those who embark on such trips — alleged witches and others — are not really going anywhere. Bruegel's ships are becalmed, raised out of water, landlocked or engaged in a fruitless flight. Like the "pilgrimage" embarked on by the layabout followers of St. Renuyt, the journeys in the *Griet* have no destination.

Conclusion

The painting unites elements familiar in a number of fields considerably more interrelated in the sixteenth century than I have perforce made them appear. I suggested earlier that Bruegel's depiction of Griet and the women draws on the elements and associations which characterised popular magical beliefs, just before they underwent the demonisation which led to the witch-hunts. In Bruegel's time, it was possible to view witches' gatherings as carnivalesque. When every ordinary housewife was more or less versed in charms and popular lore, the difference between housewife and witch (or wise-woman) was one of degree, not of kind.[265] Griet's reversed clothes and martial breastplate link her to folk-magic; her frying-pan to the kitchen. She is a figure of the headstrong women writ large. This character was proverbially represented as having some folk-witch characteristics, like one who could tussle with The Devil. At the same time, public opinion was shifting to the point where a woman capable of analogous victories against her husband was more and more likely to be credited with unseen demonic help. The expanding definition of witches was also seen in the transmutation of female carnival clubs into sabbats. What once happened in the streets now occurred *only in thought*.

The new role of the imagination was a crucial factor in these developments. As philosophical culture redrew the contours of the male imagination, this triggered a corresponding interest on the part of men in the female imagination. This male picture of the female mind was constituted from a variety of sources. It was demonstrably an important factor in a general demonisation of the spirit world, gathering pace from c. 1500 on, and itself a contributory cause of the Reformation. Sixteenth-century Inquisitors concocted their tests and testimonies in a strange feedback relationship with folkloric customs, beliefs and practices. Since they regarded witchcraft exclusively as a form of satanism, they were often surprised by the notions expressed in their victims' evidence, which had nothing to say about Satan, and plenty to say about night-walking, treasure-hunting séances, encounters with ghosts, and women getting the better of devils and imps. They interpreted that evidence in the light of male fears about what went on in women's minds, and projected the results, strongly coloured as diabolical, back into the social world. The myth of the sabbat, for example, expressed a mass of assumptions about the depraved aspects of the dreaming mind, impacted with their own educated dread of sexuality. At the same time, received wisdom on such topics as women's rapacious appetites, their poorly adjusted humours and propensity for irrationality, were focussed and shuffled back into the mix, to produce a new vision of female madness as dangerous and demonic.

Bruegel's *Dulle Griet* belongs both to the satirical tradition which refused to take these ideas too seriously, and to the deepened view of madness and nightmare developing in Renaissance culture, ultimately indebted to Neo-Platonism. Applied to the marginal scapegoats of the witch-hunts, increased fear of female irrationality helped cast such women as human vessels for demonic influences. In Bruegel's hands, however, the perception of mad women as dangerous was raw material from which to build a grand choleric and melancholic setting for a fantasia on money-madness.

Enlightened opinion on the subject of witches regarded them as the victims of diseased imaginations, the prey of their own fevered desires. In the same spirit, Bruegel implied that Griet, like the city as a whole, deludedly seeks treasure in evil dreams. The shared madness of consumption — shown in terms of bodily deformation — is what qualifies her imagination as diseased and brings the unfocused stare to her face. That her quest is a delusion — that what she "sees" is unreal — is indicated also by the transparent veil over her eyes.[266] This Griet is one among many pursuers of *phancies* in the picture.

The central scenes in the *Griet* rely for their effect on processes of catharis, which externalise and thus relieve anxiety. Neurotic phenomena in the sixteenth century appeared in supernatural guise, as reversals of the natural order of things, or as Nashe's nightmarish *reductio ad absurdum* of waking desires. Bruegel envisaged the secret alchemy of money twisting minds in terms of a world-ship wobbling on the back of a giant *Dukatenscheisser*, on a burning hovel in the town centre. As for the town metamorphosing into a ship, among the many devices of inversion and reversal in the painting, this is the instance where Bruegel most clearly depicted people living within their own delusion. The small women engage in their carnivalesque bacchanal apparently unaware that their own condition of being *three sheets to the wind* is shaping the entire town. Bruegel's pictorial dream logic constructs a fantasy of the urban mental world as a species of infernal dream, paving the way towards a conclusion coincident with a famous Neo-Platonic tenet. The idiom of representing the world of the mind as metamorphic derives from the same philosophic source.

The design as a whole gains credibility and form from the recognisable proverbs, superstitions, satirical prints and broadsheets, etc. out of which it was built. Topical jokes about the condition of Antwerp use traditions of civic allegory and alchemical imagery to make their points. Any visitor to Antwerp would be familiar with the imagery used in the seasonal processions to represent the city; the imagery of alchemy constitutes an only slightly more abstruse level of meaning. The creator of the *Griet* proves himself to have been at home in many different aspects of his culture; conversely, the *Dulle Griet* itself testifies to the sense in which these different fields were indeed experienced as the same culture.

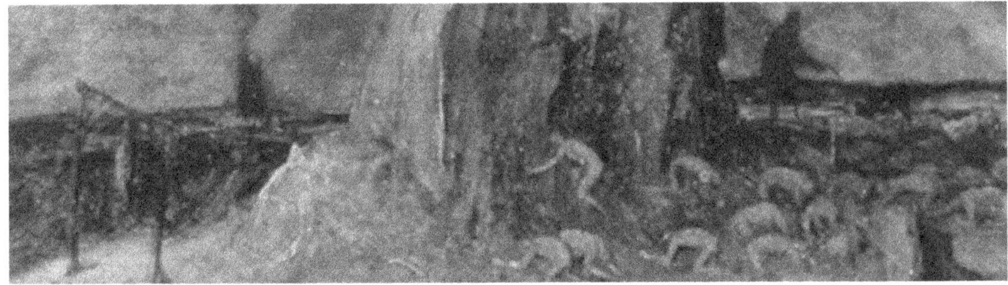

35f Pieter Bruegel, crowd in background, detail, *Dulle Griet*

Notes to Chapter 2

[1] In *Rhapsodien über die Anwendung der psychischen curmethode auf Geisteszerruttungen* (Halle, 1983); H. P. Duerr, *Dreamtime: Concerning the Boundary Between Wilderness and Civilisation*, trans. F. Goodman (Oxford, 1985), 199, n. 66.
[2] See J. De Coo, *Museum Mayer van den Bergh, Catalogus I* (Antwerp, 1966), 30.
[3] In a letter of 1894 to H. Hymans: J. De Coo, "Forschungen zu Bruegels *Dulle Griet*," *Pantheon* XVIII (1960), 180.
[4] For the full text of this passage, see R. Marijnissen and M. Seidel, *Bruegel* (Stuttgart, 1969; New York, 1984), 556, n. 10. For discussion of the variant wording of *vreemt* and *vreet* (depending on the different texts of the 1604 and 1618 editions of the *Schilderboek*), see Jan Grauls, *Volkstaal en Volksleven in het werk von Pieter Breugel* (Antwerp-Amsterdam, 1957), 48; cf. De Coo (1966), 31; also Karl van Mander, *Dutch and Flemish Painters*, trans. C. van de Wall (New York, 1936), 155. Subsequent references to Van Mander are to this edition; Marijnissen and Seidel hereafter will be shortened to Marijnissen.
[5] Van Mander knew Spranger well both before and after his time in Prague, as his life of that artist testifies, ibid, 309-29, esp. 323-9.
[6] On the inventories, De Coo (1966), 30; idem (1960), 234-5; see also P. Bianconi, *The Complete Paintings of Bruegel*, intro. by R. Hughes, notes and catalogue by P. Bianconi (New York, 1967), 97, 114-5. Many works by Bruegel in the Rudolfine Collections had already left Prague by this date.
[7] In De Coo (1960), 235; cf. idem (1966), 33.
[8] See, for example, W. S. Gibson, *Bruegel* (Oxford, 1977), 102-8.
[9] Marijnissen and Seidel, 56, n. 9.
[10] Cf. E. van Heurck and G. J. Boekenoogen, *L'Imagerie Populaire des Pays-Bas Belgique-Hollande* (Paris, 1930), 27, 104; a seventeenth-century broadsheet is illustrated by them and discussed in Grauls, 27-8. On the later development of this form, see M. de Meyer, *De Volks-en Kinderprent in de Nederlanden van de 15e tot de 20e* (Antwerp-Amsterdam, 1962), 495-9.
[11] Gibson (1977), 105, figure 71, illustrates one such woodcut.
[12] Grauls, 14-5, on St. Griet and midwives; 6-13 and passim, on the conflation of legends; 19ff., 35-8, on *Dulle* and *Zwarte* Griets; 22-3 and passim, on Griet proverbs.
[13] De Coo (1966), 33-5, lists more than seventy studies on the painting before 1966.
[14] Griet is described as a witch by L. Rosoman, *Leonard Rosoman, A.R.A., on Bruegel's "Mad Meg'* (London, 1969); as Greed or Anger by M. Sullivan, "Madness and Folly: Pieter Bruegel the Elder's *Dulle Griet*," *Art Bulletin* LIX(1) (1977), 55-66; as a Nordic giantess by P. Minnaert, "Essai de l'interpretation de la *Dulle Griet* de P. Bruegel" *Apollo: chronique des beaux-arts* Brussels, (May 1943), 8-10. R. Delevoy follows Grauls in seeing the woman next to Griet as St. Margaret of Antioch overcoming the devil, *Bruegel* (Geneva, 1959), 70-5. R. Graziani, "Pieter Bruegel's

Dulle Griet and Dante," *Burlington Magazine* CXV (1973), 209f, thinks Griet represents Two-Sided Fortune; F. Panse and H. J. Schmidt, *Pieter Bruegels Dulle Griet: Bildnis einer psychisch Kranken* (Berlin, 1967), 22-25, find her clinically schizophrenic; J. D. Bangs, "Pieter Bruegel and History," *Art Bulletin* LX(4), (1978), 704-5, connects her with contemporary heresy trials.

[15] The exception is Graziani, who thinks this architecture owes some of its details to passages in Dante's *Inferno*.

[16] E.g. for Minnaert she is the *spirit of violence*. See Grauls, 56-61, on these older studies.

[17] H. A. Klein, following Barnouw, points out that the picture contains references to other kindred "fishy" proverbs; thus the fish in the tree *hang by their own gills*, i.e. they are caught by their own weakness, or hoist by their own petard; *Graphic Worlds of Pieter Bruegel the Elder* (New York, 1963), 138.

[18] See A. Dundes and C. A. Stibbe, "The Art of Mixing Metaphors. A Folkloristic Interpretation of the *Netherlandish Proverbs* by Pieter Bruegel the Elder," *Folklore Fellows Communications*, no. 230 (Helsinki 1981), 11.

[19] Some of Bruegel's proverbial ironies are: *The Blind Leading the Blind*, where a joke is given monumental scale; *The Netherlandish Proverbs*, which is full of referential sabotage (see Chapter Three); the *Bird Nester*, where irony seems inherent in the proverb; the *Fall of Icarus*, where, as De Tolnay pointed out, *not a plough stops when a man dies*.

[20] I.e., these folk dreams are not fitted into the Christian framework of divine inspiration (as are those of Ficino and Agrippa), or satanic temptation (as described in the *Malleus*); if the devil appears, he is seen as a trickster.

[21] This is a main tenet of Duerr's study. See also K. M. Briggs, *Pale Hecate's Team* (London, 1962), Appendix 3, "Some Illustrations of Magical Beliefs," 240-63, and R. Muchembled, *Popular Culture and Elite Culture in France 1400-1750*, trans. L. Cochrane (Baton Rouge-London, 1985), ch. 1 and 2. On Flemish magic and supernatural stories, see A. van Gennep, *Le Folklore de la Flandre et du Hainaut Francais (Département du Nord)* (Paris, 1935), v. 2. 563-650, 670-81.

[22] R. S. Scribner, *For the Sake of Simple Folk: Popular Propaganda for the German Reformation* (Cambridge, 1981), 89-91, for the *she-devil* print; much of this imagery was scatological; Scribner discusses many similar works: *The Origin of the Monks* (c. 1545), where devils defecate priests (ibid, 86, figure 63); cf. his comment on a print depicting peasants farting at a pope holding a Bull: *The emission of the bull is answered by the emission of wind, a piece of grotesque realism worthy of Rabelais*, ibid, 82.

[23] Scribner, 89, figure 66, illustrates a parodic papal cart which he thinks is Dutch. The Antwerp printer and *rederijker* Jacob van Liesvelt, later executed for heresy, published an illustrated vernacular Bible in 1542; one of his woodcuts showed the devil as a monk; see J. Wegg, *Antwerp, 1477-1559* (London, 1916), 202.

[24] Wegg (1916): for the ordinances from 1514 and 1540 (126; 272); the elusive *naughty person* (210) and the diabolical lampoons (210). Henry's agents in Antwerp provided much useful information on this kind of popular demonstration.
[25] Early in the century, Italians would bet on who could first find Herri met de Bles' trademark owl, hidden in obscure corners of his paintings; Wegg (1916), 238-9; for more on strange betting practices in Antwerp, see section 5B below. Cock's motto was a pun on his own name and that of his wife. Beuckelaer's mottos appear on painted obelisks in two different *Market Scenes with Ecce Homo*. They have been interpreted as *a warning to the city magistrate, addressed to him by the patron of the work, possibly a member of the city council, a council which believed that peace should be maintained but that the Inquisition should not be given a free hand*, K. P. F. Moxey, *Aertsen, Beuckelaer and Secular Painting in the Reformation* (New York-London, 1977), 87. Moxey doubts this, due to the vagueness of the deciphered message; he illustrates a copy of the 1561 painting, formerly in the Germanisches Museum, Nuremberg (figure 22), and the 1565 work in the Nationalmuseum, Stockholm (figure 23); discusses the issue of Flemish hierogylphs surrounding these and other works in the context of emblem book production, 78-87. The first emblem book to appear at Antwerp was La Perriere's *Théatre des bons engins*, translated into Flemish in 1554. Plantin later published imitative works by the humanists Sambucus (1564) and Junius (1565).
[26] See comments and description by Frans Baudouin in *Antwerp's Golden Age. The Metropolis of the West in the Sixteenth and Seventeenth Centuries*, exhibition catalogue by the City of Antwerp and the Smithsonian Institute, Washington (Antwerp, 1973), no. 21, 47.
[27] *Een Spul van Sinnen van den Siecke Stadt*, in T. Weevers, *Poetry of the Netherlands in its European Context* (London, 1960), 104. All writers agree on the persistence of "late medieval" forms and topical subjects in *rederijker* plays, though stiffer censorship seems to have encouraged incipiant efforts towards more classical themes after mid-century; see essays by M. Spies and H. Pleij in J. Koopmans et al, eds, *Rhetoric-Rhétoriqueurs-Rederijkers* (Amsterdam-Oxford, 1995), 117-22, 157-74; cf. S. Eringa, *La Renaissance et les Rhétoriqueurs néerlandais* (Amsterdam, 1920); W. S. Gibson, "Artists and *Rederijkers* in the Age of Bruegel," *Art Bulletin* LXIII (3) (September, 1981), 430- 3; Weevers, 67-72, 102-19.
[28] S. Freud, *Wit and Its Relation to the Unconscious* (1905), trans. A. A. Brill (London, 1922).
[29] Van Mander, 153.
[30] In E. Kris, "The Psychology of Caricature," (1935), in his *Psychoanalytic Explorations in Art* (London, 1953), 176.
[31] Ibid, 185-86.

[32] J. Klaits, *Servants of Satan* (Bloomington, 1985), ch. 4: "Classic Witches, the Beggar and the Midwife," 86-103. It is notable that Margaret of Antioch was a patron saint of midwives; cf. Grauls, 70-6.
[33] Kris, 181f.
[34] H. Miedema, "Realism and Comic Mode: The Peasant," *Simiolus* IX(4) 1977), 205 - 219; cf. discussion in Chapter Four, n. 147, below.
[35] For a late sixteenth-century case study, among whose contributing factors was the governing classes' fear of rebellious peasants, see E. Leroy Ladurie, *Carnival at Romans*, trans. M. Feeney (New York, 1979).
[36] B. Meijer, "From Leonardo to Bruegel: Comic Art in Sixteenth-century Europe," *Word and Image* (Proceedings of the First International Conference on Word and Image) (4), no. 1, January-March 1988, 408. See also, on the subject of the comic as sinful, R. Falkenburg, *Joachim Patinir: Landscape as an Image of the Pilgrimage of Life*, trans. M. Hoyle (Amsterdam-Philadelphia, 1985).
[37] W. S. Gibson, "Bruegel, Dulle Griet, and Sexist Politics in the Sixteenth-century," in O. von Simson and M. Winner, ed., *Pieter Bruegel und seine Welt* (Berlin, 1979), 9-16. This expands on his comments about the picture in Gibson (1977), 102-8.
[38] Gibson (1977), 108.
[39] Ibid.
[40] On Bodin's career as a misogynist, see H. R. Trevor-Roper, *The European Witchcraze and Other Essays* (New York, 1969), 122, and, more radically, M. Daly, *Gyn/Ecology* (Boston, 1978), 182f.
[41] Gibson concludes the views of Knox and Bodin show that *it would have been natural for Bruegel and his contemporaries to ascribe the ills of their time to the malice and ineptitude of female rule,* (1977), 108.
[42] I. Maclean, *The Renaissance Notion of Woman: A Study in the Fortunes of Scholasticism and Medical Science in European Intellectual Life* (Cambridge, 1980), 1.
[43] Ibid, 84-85.
[44] Ibid, 85.
[45] Ibid.
[46] Ibid.
[47] Ibid, 86.
[48] Ibid, 91.
[49] S. Freud and D. E. Oppenheim, *Dreams in Folklore*, trans. from the ms. of 1911 by B. L. Pacella (New York, 1958), 25.
[50] Drawing after Rosoman, 18.
[51] Duerr, 46; Dundes and Stibbe, 39.
[52] Ibid, 57.

[53] On origins of tales of night riders, see C. Ginzburg, *The Night Battles: Witchcraft and Agrarian Cults in the Sixteenth and Seventeenth Centuries*, trans. J. and A. Tedeschi (Harmondsworth, 1985), 40-50; on a Livonian counterpart to the *benandanti*, 28-32; on the cult of Diana and the Wild Hunt, 40-51; on a similar Tyrolese cult, 57-8; cf. Duerr, 232-33, n. 28, on the good reputation of these last *percht* members among their neighbors.

[54] J. C. J. Metford's *Dictionary of Christian Lore and Legend* (London, 1983) gives this entry for *Ember days*: Fast days *about* or *around* (old English *ymbren*) four seasons of the Christian year: the third week in Advent; the first in Lent; the octave [i.e., eight days] of Pentecost; and the week after the third Sunday of September. Clergy are ordained at these seasons. In other words, Ember days fall (as one might expect) around the winter solstice, the spring festival, the summer solstice, and Hallowe'en. Cf. Ginzburg (1985), 183, n. 35; these were also the seasons of *benandanti* activities.

[55] Ibid, 155, n. 49. For the poem, see J. Franck, "Geschichtes des Wortes *Hexe*," in J. Hansen, ed., *Quellen und Untersuchungen zur Geschichte des Hexenwahns* (Bonn, 1901), 636; for a description of the origins of tales of night riders, see Ginzburg (1985), 40-50.

[56] *Die Emeis, Dis ist das Buch von der Omeissen... von dem Hochgelerten doctor Ioannes Geiler von Kaissersperg* (Strasbourg, 1516), ff. XLIIv-XLIIr; passages on popular superstitions collected in *Zur Geschichte des Volks-Aberglaubens im Anfange des XVI. Jahrhunderts. Aus der Emeis von Dr. Ioannes Geiler von Kaiserburg*, ed. A. Stobwer, 2nd ed. (Basel, 1985); this excerpt cited in Ginzburg (1985), 44.

[57] *Praeceptorium divinae legis* (Basel, 1481), preceptum I, cap. X and XI (9.X), quoted in Ginzburg (1985), 43.

[58] Ibid, 8, n. 32.

[59] Van Heurck, 140-1, describes as *fréquement reimprimés*, popular books, *plein de conjurations... pour decouvrir des trésors, se faire aimer d'amour et même "pour faire danser devant soi une personne nue."* Techniques for locating subterranean or buried treasure imply a form of dowsing: *à Avesnes... on alla chercher le "tourneur de baguette et de clé"... pour trouver un trésor*, says Van Gennep, v. 2, 598. Flemish treasures were often thought of as guarded by a demon, or by an animal made of gold; ibid, 690-4. As Van Gennep points out, popular sorcery was transmitted orally and therefore has few printed sixteenth century sources. Towards the end of the century, Flemish translations appeared of such works as the *Duivelgeese*, and the chapbook of *Faust* (1592). To these may be added popular compedia like *Den Sack der Consten*, with its recipes for baldness, love potions, etc. (see Chapter Three, section 4, below). It is worth noting that the walloon name given to books of this type was *agrâfa*, or *agrippa*, after Agrippa of Nettesheim, the doyen of Renaissance magical writers; ibid, 597-8.

[60] Thomas, 234-5. Treasure-seeking was legislated against in line with other enactments against witchcraft. In England in 1542, the use of magic to recover stolen goods or to seek hidden treasure was made a felony; in 1563, the penalty (death) was reduced somewhat, only to be re-enforced in 1604.

[61] Ibid.

[62] Cf. G. M. Foster, "Peasant society and the image of the limited good," *American Anthropologist* LXVII (1965), 307-8.

[63] C. G. Stridbeck discusses the belt as an attribute of Bruegel's *Temperance* (figure 60), *Bruegelstudien* (Stolkholm, 1956), 163f.; linking it to metaphors about control of the *zone below the belt*. Its meaning here, flapping wildly from Griet's basket, would thus be the opposite. Compare the metaphor Brant uses in his *Ship of Fools*, of an *unbelted fool*; several of Bruegel's fools are in this kind of disarray, notably the *fool who gets the cards*, in the *Netherlandish Proverbs* (see Chapter 3, fig. 63a; no. 25).

[64] The expression, *aller en Flandre sans couteau*, appears in print in a book by Henri Estienne in 1579; its realism is attested to by periodic efforts to curb knife fights and routine convictions. See Muchembled, 118.

[65] From the transcript of a trial for lycanthropy in 1692; reprinted in part in the appendix of O. Hofler, *Kultische Geheimbunde der Germanen* (Frankfurt-am-Main, 1934), 345-57; trans. Ginzburg (1985), 29.

[66] Sir Thomas Wright (1865), *A History of Caricature and Grotesque in Literature and Art (New York, 1968)*, 131 and figure 84.

[67] Wright discusses: the cat-rider with her distaff, 120; the tradition of the battling husband and wife, 124-30; the *fabliau* versions of the motif, 125-28. For the married couple with monster, see L. Maeterlinck, "La genre satirique dans la peinture flamande," *Mémoires Couronneés et Autres Mémoires, L'Academie Royale des Sciences, des Lettres et des Beaux-Arts de Belgique,* LXII (4) (March 1902-January 1903), 198-99 [hereafter, Maeterlinck (1902)]. Gibson (1977), 104-5, figs. 70 and 71, illustrates another anonymous Flemish print of the Battle for the Breeches from c. 1560. Cf. the interesting account of lewd women in G. R. Quaife, *Wanton Wenches and Wayward Wives, Peasants and Illicit Sex in Early Seventeenth Century England* (New Brunswick, NJ, 1979), ch. 7, 165f.

[68] *Malleus Maleficarum*, Part II, qn. 2, ch. 4; trans. M. Summers (London, 1948), 173-4.

[69] The relevance of the *Battle of the Breeches* for Bruegel's Griet was first noted by Gibson (1977).

[70] Cf. discussion in Van Heurck and Boekenoogen (1930), 35, 104; also De Meyer, 496-99, figs. 151, 152.

[71] *Het Bloedig Toneel*, II, 185; Wegg (1916), 316; the prison account records are given on 207. Infractions of the Placards of 1529 and 1531 (against protestant books and pictures, blasphemy and iconoclasm) involved burning or decapitation for men and

burial alive for women. This last was also the standard penalty for a wife who murdered her husband - indirect conformation of Maclean's analysis of the central status of marriage. While ancient privilege required that men be executed *under the blue sky* at Antwerp, by fire or sword, female heretics were generally drowned in tubs in the Steen, the bodies then placed in sacks and thrown quietly in the river; op. cit., 76, 190, 193-4, 316-7.

[72] N. Z. Davis, "Women on Top," ch. 5 of her *Society and Culture in Early Modern France* (Stanford, 1975), 124-42. At Antwerp during the crisis of 1542, the authorities expressed fears of *traitors in women's clothes*. Wegg (1916), 221.

[73] Muchembled, 80.

[74] See n. 56 above.

[75] Otto de Reinsberg-Düringsfeld, *Traditions et Légendes de la Belgique* (Brussels, 1870), v.1, 143.

[76] Ibid, v.1 65, 115; Sullivan (1977), 63, related the "devilish" dancing of Bruegel's women to Old Women's Shrovetide. The main point of her argument was, however, that these women are "bacchantes" and that here they act as a kind of classical reference. I think that the folkloric origin of this image does not require a classical gloss, but see nn. 188-9 and n. 202 below.

[77] Document in A. Becker, *Frauenrechtliches in Brauch und Sitte* (Kaiserslautern, 1913), 27; Duerr, 225-6, n. 6.

[78] In R. Grether, "Frauen an der Basler Fastnacht," *Schwiezer Volkskunde* (1972), 2; Duerr, 195.

[79] See references in 16 and 34, above; also T. R. Forbes, "Midwifery and Witchcraft," *Journal of the History of Medicine* 17 (1962), 264-83; and essays in *The Midwife and the Witch*, ed. T. R. Forbes (New Haven, 1966).

[80] Duerr, 24.

[81] H. Cardan, *Offenbarung der Natur* (Basel, 1559), DCXLV; Duerr, 226, n. 6.

[82] There was, for example, a French translation by Jacques Grevin in 1567.

[83] J. Weyer, *De Praestigiis Daemonum* (Frankfort, 1586), 491-9; trans. R. M. Kingdon, ed., *Transition and Revolution* (Minneapolis, 1974), 222.

[84] C. Baxter, "Johann Weyer's *De Praestigiis Daemonum*: Unsystematic Psychopathology," in S. Anglo, ed., *The Damned Art: Essays in the Literature of Witchcraft* (London, 1977), 61-2.

[85] Baxter, 73-4, n. 17.

[86] See account of its history in M. M. McGowan, "*Pierre de Lancre's Tableau de l'Inconstance des Mauvais Anges et Demons*: The Sabbat Sansationalised," in S. Anglo, ed., 182-3.

[87] P. de Lancre, *Le Tableau de l'Inconstance des Mauvais Anges et Demons* (Paris, 1612), 119; in McGowan, 1.

[88] *Malleus Maleficarum*, Part II, qn. 2, ch. 4; trans. M. Summers (London, 1948), 173-4.
[89] Duerr, 46.
[90] Rosoman, 24.
[91] According to K. Spalding, *An Historical Dictionary of German Figurative Usage* (Oxford, 1960), 501, the notion of a *mannikin that excretes ducats* goes back at least as far as the seventeenth century. In 1908, Freud wrote that, *everyone is familiar with the figure of the "excreter of ducats"* - but as A. Dundes, *Life is Like a Chicken Coop Ladder: A Portrait of German Culture Through Folklore* (New York, 1984), 80, shows, this seems to be a peculiarly Germanic configuration. Dundes, ibid, 81, figure 9, illustrates a modern candy *Dukatenscheisser* of the kind still sold in German sweet shops.
[92] See Unverfehrt , cat. nos. 83, 84, figs. 223, 224.
[93] Freud and Oppenheim, 37.
[94] Poggio, *Facetiae*, No. 130; composed c1451, first edition (?) Rome, c1470; many subsequent reprinting throughout sixteenth century; Freud and Oppenheim, 38.
[95] Freud and Oppenheim, 56-7. The story of the *Light of Life* ends as follows: the man is shown his oil-lamp and that of his wife. There is far more oil in his wife's lamp than there is in his own. While St. Peter's back is turned, the man sticks his finger in his wife's lamp and begins trying to transfer some of her oil to his own lamp, thinking to prolong his life. At this point he is awakened by a buffet from his wife, beside him in the bed. He has been sticking his finger in her vagina.
[96] Ibid, 46.
[97] Ibid, 44-5.
[98] Ibid, 40-2; Freud's explanation of the devil's presence in dreams of this type is given on 39.
[99] Ibid, 55.
[100] Freud's dictum is quoted in J. Kovel, *The Age of Desire* (New York, 1981), 39. It is worth noting Kovel's statement (45) that *Freud's discovery... has been confirmed endless times in clinical experience*.
[101] Freud and Oppenheim, 37. The classic statement of this transference and its effects is Freud's 1908 essay, "Character and Anal Eroticism," in his *Collected Papers*, v. 2 (New York, 1959), 45-50. Cf. also E. Jones, "Anal-Erotic Character Traits" in *Papers on Psychoanalysis* (Boston, 1961), 413-37; and the remarks in S. Freud, *The Interpretation of Dreams*, The Standard Edition, ed. J. Strachey et al., IV (London 1953), 200; for useful subsequent bibliography up to 1977, see L. K. Little, *Religious Poverty and the Profit Economy in Medieval Europe* (Ithaca, 1978), 227-28, n. 86; and up to 1984, cf. Dundes (1984), 80-4.
[102] Key works here are M. Schneider, *Neurosis and Civilisation*, trans. M. Roloff (New York, 1975); R. Lichtman, *The Production of Desire* (New York, 1983); cf. bibliography in Kovel, 270-276.

[103] G. Simmel, *The Philosophy of Money*, trans. T. Bottomore and D. Frisby (London-Henley-Boston, 1978), 238.

[104] Kovel, 43-44.

[105] Ibid, 53.

[106] Ibid, 57.

[107] Little (1978), 73; for the words ascribed to Peter, 235-36, n. 11.

[108] *DIE SPRICH SALOMO DAS XL CAPITEL WER KORN INHELT DEM FLUCHEN DIE LEIT ABER SEGEN KOMPT VBER DEN SO ES VERKAFFT*. Luther's *Sendbrief vom Dolmetschen* (1530) opens with this quotation, used in defence of translation. The print is probably German; illustrated in Jeannin, 70.

[109] This print by F. L. D. Ciartres, or François Langlois (1589-1647) may have been published as part of the engraver's series, *Oiseaux et Grotesques*.

[110] R. Ehrenberg, *Capital and Finance in the Age of the Renaissance* (London, 1928), 234.

[111] H. van der Wee, *The Growth of the Antwerp Market and the European Economy, Fourteenth-Sixteenth Centuries* (The Hague, 1963), v. 2, 322.

[112] J. N. Ball, *Merchants and Merchandise. The Expansion of Trade in Europe, 1500-1623* (New York, 1977), 65. Of course, credit practices similar to those which made the Bourse's hegemony possible had been in theory available since the late thirteenth and fourteenth centuries; these are documented for Italian banking companies, particularly in Genoa; ibid, 60-5. On the application of these techniques on a hitherto unprecedented scale see H. van der Wee, "Anvers et les innovations de la technique financière aux XVIe et XVIIe siècles," *Annales: Economie, Société, Civilisation* XXII (1967), 1067-89.

[113] Ball, 54-60, explains further: *Constantly changing relative values in intrinsic terms of gold and silver coins of various denominations and dates of issue theoretically demanded an equally constant review of their values in terms of the money of account In practice these readjustments were delayed... in the sixteenth century the trend was towards the appreciation of silver in terms of gold, later followed by the reverse... governments did not adjust the value of coins together* .

[114] On respect for canon law and changes in behaviour following the lifting of the ban, Van der Wee (1963), 352-53: *Lending at interest had been prohibited by the Pope since 1312. In the intervening period, although some businessmen continued to charge interest in secret still, the prohibitive law of the Church was formally respected to a surprising degree. Once given Imperial sanction, however, the merchant bankers in Antwerp and elsewhere in the empire made lending at interest the second basis of their financial activity. Interest payments could be regarded as a form of investment*. See also B. Gordon, *Economic Analysis Before Adam Smith: Hesiod to Lessius* (London, 1975), ch. 7, 8, 9; esp. 244f. On Lessius and the development of interest theory as stimulated by the example of Antwerp. J-C. Agnew, *Worlds Apart: The Market and the Theater in Anglo-American Through, 1550-1750* (Cambridge, 1986), 45, states that, starting in the sixteenth century *ecclesiastical*

authors such as Cajetan, Summerhart, and Lessius began to embrace a definition of interest as the opportunity or displacement cost of sums available not just for settlement but for investment. See also J. T. Noonan, Jr., *The Scholastic Analysis of Usury* (Cambridge, MA, 1957), 53-57, 110-12, 139-51, 251-55; and Gordon, 160-79. The doings of the Bourse are described by L. Guicciardini, in the Antwerp chapter of his *Descrittione di tutte i Paesi Bassi* (Antwerp, 1567); 147-48 in the Dutch edition used by van der Wee. cf. I. Wallerstein, *The Modern World System: Capitalist Agriculture and the Origins of the European World Economy in the Sixteenth Century* (New York, 1974), passim.

[115] A murder occurred by the Bourse in 1555; Wegg (1916), 254-5, gives details and describes incidents of vandalism and graffiti.

[116] Ibid, 211.

[117] Ball, 65-6.

[118] Van der Wee (1963), 364-36

[119] Jean Paul Clebert (Pierre Jeannin), *Les Marchands au XVIe siecle* (Paris, 1957), 128. Jeannin discusses other bizarre clauses (128-31) - reminiscent of *The Merchant of Venice* - of the proliferation of lotteries among the speculators, of newly-born children concealed in efforts to defraud bettors on their sex, etc.

[120] Van der Wee (1963), 219 - 22. Cf. the references in the note on famine, Chapter 3, 465, n. 43 below.

[121] See Z. Z. Filipczak, *Picturing Art in Antwerp 1550-1700* (Princeton, 1987), 12-14; Van der Wee (1963), 226.

[122] Van der Wee (1963), 334-35

[123] Ibid, 324

[124] L. Voët, *The Golden Compasses: A History and Evaluation of the Printing and Publishing Activities of the Officina Plantiniana at Antwerp* (Amsterdam 1969), 357-58. Cf. the corroborative findings of M. G. Davies, *The Enforcement of Engish Apprenticeship: A Study of Applied Mercantilism, 1563-1642* (Cambridge, Mass., 1956).

[125] Agnew, 43-4. The original insight is, naturally, in K. Marx, *Grundrisse*, trans. M. Nicolaus (New York, 1973), 148-49. For a non-Marxist critique coming to very nearly the same analysis of the displacement function in money, see G. L. S. Shackle, *Epistemics and Economics: A Critique of Economic Doctrines* (Cambridge, 1972), 359-61.

[126] M. Weber, "Religious Rejections of the World and Their Directions," in *From Max Weber: Essays in Sociology*, ed. and trans. H. H. Gerth and C. W. Mills (New York, 1958), 331; Little (1978), 33.

[127] Agnew, 46. Cf. Gordon, 195-204; Noonan, 109-28, 184-89, 249-67, 328-31, 349-52, 367-68.

[128] Sullivan, 64. Cf. J. Wegg, *The Decline of Antwerp Under Philip of Spain* (London, 1924), 143-257, 309; S. Williams and J. Jacquot, "Ommegangs Anversois du temps

de Bruegel et de van Heemskerk," in *Les Fêtes de la Renaissance*, v. 2 (Paris, 1957), 361.

[129] Druon Antigonus lived in a castle on the site of Antwerp, tossing the severed hands of seafarers who refused to pay his tax into the Scheldt. The Roman, Silvius Brabo, killed him, cut off one of his hands and threw it (*handwerpen*) into the river.

[130] This is the interpretation proposed by W. Stevens, *Giants in Those Days: folklore, ancient history and nationalism* (Lincoln, NE, 1989), who briefly discusses Antwerp. Van Gennep, v.1, 154-9 discusses giant processions and distinguishes them clearly from older forms of seasonal celebration. The first record of this event in Antwerp is from 1470 and concerns two giants, Antigonus and Goliath. It was evidently at a later date, with Coeck's commission, that Antigon became a city emblem. In Brabant in general there are no medieval giants and most of them appear in the first half of the sixteenth century or much later. See ibid, 156-7 on Antwerp, Brussels and Brabant.

[131] G. Puttenham, *The Arte of English Poesie* (London, 1589); see M. D. Bristol, *Carnival and Theater. Plebian Culture and the Structure of Authority in Renaissance England* (New York-London, 1985), 66. Bristol suggests that by Puttenham's day the giants were figures of fun.

[132] The Giant of Brussels received a spouse in 1549, that of Louvain in 1521. How the Giant of Nivelles was married is told in a long poem by the Abbe Renard; van Gennep, v.1, 158-9.

[133] Williams and Jacquot, ibid.

[134] Sullivan, 62, n. 45. It is conceivably relevant here that the house of the treasurer of Antwerp was known as the 'House of The Big Fool.' Bruegel's master, Pieter Coecke painted murals there in 1544. Cf. Wegg (1916), 233.

[135] L. Maeterlinck, "Nederlandsche Spreekworden," *Vlaamse Academie voor Taal en Letterkunde*, 55 (1903), 109 - 29; Dundes and Stibbe, 37-8.

[136] Dundes and Stibbe, 38.

[137] My argument here is drawn from L. K. Little's excellent article, "Pride Goes Before Avarice: Social Change and the Vices in Latin Christendom," *The American Historical Review*, 76 (February 1971), 16-49.

[138] Ibid, 38 and n. 89, where the complex question of identifying the main contemporary critics of avarice by social class is discussed; cf. M. Schapiro, "The Sculpture of Souillac," in W. R. W. Koehler, ed., *Medieval Studies in Memory of A. Kingsley Porter* (Cambridge, Mass., 1939), v.2, 383; J. Le Goff, *La Civilisation de L'Occident Medieval* (Paris, 1964), 309-13.

[139] Little (1971), 38.

[140] Anon, *Der Bruder Esel mit dem Gelt*, etching and engraving, possibly German, early17C, Baker Library, Harvard University, CA g3 xx.

[141] It is hard to gauge the precise significance of the apes in this context. According to H. W. Janson, *Apes and Ape Lore in the Middle Ages and the Renaissance* (London, 1952), 164, 188, n. 11; 190, n. 33, apes in general are *extraordinarily numerous* in Flemish manuscript art of this period. They may appear in these two examples as a means of suggesting the foul nature of money, since apes were traditionally *viles et despectos* among animals. Apes, along with owls and toads, enjoy this description in the earliest printed edition of the *Dialogus creatorum*, published at Antwerp in 1491 by Gerardus Leeu (Janson, 183, figure 8 shows the relevant woodcut). C. Nordenfalk observed that, *the foul money of gothic marginalia presents a sharp contrast with the precious royal and imperial coins that decorate the borders of Carolingian and Ottonian books of the Gospels*, in Little (1971), 38, n. 88. Apes and commerce are linked in a couple of cases where sixteenth-century goldsmiths and pedlars chose *singerie* designs for their guild signs (Janson, 190-1, for the goldsmiths of Colmar, c.1582; ibid, 221-2, pl. XLIIIa, for the pedlars of Bern, c. 1500). To understand the prevalence of mischievous apes in the townscape of the *Dulle Griet*, these associations are of some interest. It seems that the Flemish were quick to proceed from the medieval use of the ape as a metaphor for physical, sensuous man to a more modern use of apes as a metaphor for society. Although the full-blown singeries of roccoco interiors occur in France, *the pictorial motif of costumed simians parodying human actions undoubtedly came from Flanders* (Janson, 191, n. 43). Midway between the apes' enigmatic shadowing of the human action in the *Dulle Griet* and the plainer satires of Teniers et al. is the work of the engraver Pieter van der Borcht (1540-1608) who *devoted an elaborate series of prints to [this] theme, including most of the subjects previously developed in Gothic drôlerie: a naval battle, the siege of a castle, a hunt, a kitchen scene, an alchemist's workshop, a quack selling medicines, a school, a barbershop... a village dance... a skating party, and a group of popular games* (ibid, 168-69; 190, n. 39). The similarity of these subjects to those chosen and popularised by Bruegel is worth noting.

[142] See L. Lebeer, *Catalogue raisonné des estampes de Pierre Bruegel L'Ancien.* Bibliothèque Royale Albert Ier (Brussels, 1969), 155-58.

[143] F. Würtenberger, *Pieter Bruegel der Ältere und die deutsche Kunst* (Wiesbaden, 1957), 78-80. T. A. Riggs, "Bruegel and his Publisher," in O. von Simson and M. Winner, ed., *Pieter Bruegel und seine Welt*, (Berlin, 1979), 168-69, concurs in pointing out that the *Money-Banks* design, though published posthumously, is, *analogous in subject, format, and handling to prints published by Cock much earlier*, naming *Elck* (1558-59) and the *Fat* and *Lean Kitchens* (1563; our fig. 66 and 67).

[144] S. Schama, *The Embarrassment of Riches, An Interpretation of Dutch Culture in the Golden Age* (New York, 1987), 329.

[145] See, for example, the account of Charles V's finances in S. Ozment, *The Age of Reform, 1250-1550.* (New Haven, 1980), 254-60; H. Trevor-Roper, *Princes and Artists: Patronage and Ideology at Four Hapsburg Courts, 1517-1633* (New York, 1976), 11-46.
[146] Discussed in Maeterlinck (1902), 227-28.
[147] See Little (1971), 31-35.
[148] Aertsen's treasure as an allegory of materialism is discussed in Moxey, 40-1, 47.
[149] Schama, 327.
[150] D. Bax, *Hieronymous Bosch, His Picture-Writing Deciphered*, trans. M. Bax Botha (Rotterdam, 1979), 217-19.
[151] Duerr, 273, n. 26. On the Hell-mouth in general see D. C. Stuart, "The Stage Setting of Hell and the Iconography of the Middle Ages," *Romanic Review*, IV (1913), 330-42; O. Driesen, *Der Ursprung des Harlekin* (Berlin, 1904), 72; G. Cohen, *Histoire de la mise en scène dans le théâtre religieux francais du moyen âge* (Paris, 1926), 95; D. D. R. Owen, *The Vision of Hell* (Edinburgh, 1970), 224-52; G. D. Schmidt, *The Iconography of the Mouth of Hell, Eighth-Century Britain to the Fifteenth Century* (Selinsgrove-London, 1995), 165-82.
[152] Owen (1970), 243.
[153] Ibid, 195, 199, n. 49.
[154] E.g., in the works of Chrétien de Troyes, author of the *Conte du Graal* and the *Lancelot* (c. 1170); ed. F. Lecoy, *5* (Paris, 1972); see also D. D. R. Owen, *The Evolution of the Grail Legend* (Edinburgh, 1968). The late fifteenth-century "bourgeois" taste for Arthurian and chivalric wall decorations is discussed in E. Panofsky, *Early Netherlandish Painting* (New York, 1971), v.1, 68, 386, n.2.
[155] Owen (1970), 217 (the Sire de Beaujeu in the first half of the fourteenth century); 218-20 (Ramon de Ferelhos in 1397-98).
[156] Ibid, 207-11; see also P. Lehmann, *Die Parodie in Mittelalter* (Munich, 1922), passim.
[157] Owen (1970), 206-9, explains this *fabliau* as a parody of the Harrowing of Hell.
[158] The evidence for Bruegel's access to an actual edition of the *Divine Comedy* in a language he could read is not strong - a French translation may have been available around 1500 but this was of the *Inferno* only and hardly circulated; cf. C. Morel, *Les plus anciennes traductions francaises de la Divine Comedie* (Paris, 1897); and discussion in Owen (1970), 169-170. The Dantëesque idea of putting representations of contemporaries in a depiction of Hell was employed by Michaelangelo in the Sistine *Last Judgement,* which Bruegel could have seen in Rome in 1552.
[159] *Le Songe d'Enfer suivi de la Voie de Paradis, poèms du XIIIe siècle,* ed. P. Lebesque (La Rochelle, 1908); discussed in H. R. Jauss, "Form und Auffassung der Allegorie in der Tradition der *Psychomachia,*" in *Medium Aevum Vivum: Festschrift für Walther Bulst* (Heidelberg, 1960), 191ff.; see Owen (1970), 158-9.

[160] *La Voie d'Enfer et de Paradis*, ed. Sister M. A. Pety (Washington, D.C., 1940). This particular work, interestingly, was commissioned by a royal goldsmith, Simon de Lille. Avarice has an especially prominent place in Jehan's Hell.

[161] Owen (1970), 169.

[162] The *Sogno dil Caravia*, for instance, was owned by the Friuli miller Domenico Scandella (c. 1532-99), who also owned copies of *Sir John Mandeville*, Bocaccio's *Decamaron* (unexpurgated), and a version of the *Golden Legend*, among other books; C. Ginzburg, *The Cheese and the Worms, The Cosmos of a Sixteenth-century Miller*, trans. J. and A. Tedeschi (London, 1980).

[163] Ginzburg (1980), 23-6.

[164] The best known examples of this are the popular prints and broadsheets of the Reformation, so ably described by R. W. Scribner (see n. 22 above). Yet, as Scribner recognised, the flood of pro-Lutheran, anti-papal material was itself based on earlier carnivalesque and parodic satirical forms. For this reason, I resist the temptation to list the many striking uses of infernal imagery in Reformation satire: the latter should properly be seen as a subgenre representing one particular development of the main tradition, while the *Dulle Griet* takes a different direction.

[165] Klein, ibid.

[166] A. Barnouw, quoted in Klein, 288.

[167] Ibid, 241.

[168] C. Harbison, *The Last Judgement in Sixteenth Century Northern Europe: A Study of the Relation Between Art and the Reformation* (New York, 1976), points out that this work reveals a sympathy with spiritualist Christianity of the sort promoted by the Familists or by Coonhert's disciples, 240-42; see Chapter 5 below.

[169] This scene comes in the book Rabelais wrote first (Book 2), of *Gargantua and Pantagruel*, trans J. M. Cohen (London, 1955), 2, ch. 32, 272-5.

[170] The scene in the mouth occurs in the book Rabelais wrote first (Book 2); for the reference to the New World, ibid, 273; on Rabelais, the chapbook, travellers' tales and the New World, see E. Auerbach, *Mimesis* (Princeton, 1953), 266-7.

[171] On Bomarzo, see J. Darnall and M. S. Weil, "Il sacro bosco di Bormarzo: Its Sixteenth-Century Literary and Antiquarian Context," *Journal of Garden History* 4 (1984), 1-94; also J. Theurillat, *Les Mystères de Bomarzo et des Jardins Symboliques de la Renaissance* (Geneva-Paris, 1973), 16, 110; A. P. de Mandiargues, *Die Monstren von Bomarzo* (Hamburg, 1969), 82; on Tasso and Bomarzo, G. R. Hocke, *Labyrinthe de l'art fantastique*, trans. C. Heim (Paris, 1967), 92-5.

[172] Theurillat, 6; Duerr, 63.

[173] See D. P. Walker, *The Decline of Hell; seventeenth-century discussions of eternal torment*. (London, 1964).

[174] See W. J. Bouwsma, *Concordia Mundi: The Career and Thought of Guillaume Postel, 1510-1581* (Cambridge, MA, 1957), esp. ch. 4.

[175] Lincoln, 107-8, lists examples from Papua, Siam, Tangier, China, England, Ancient Egypt; also sayings current among the Ashanti, the Naga and the Sinhalese; J. Campbell, *The Masks of God: Primitive Mythology*, rev. ed. (Harmondsworth, 1987), 173-6, relates a version of a ritual collected in West Ceram which he believes to date from the Near Eastern Neolithic era.
[176] A. Dundes, "Heads or Tails: A Psychoanalytic Study of Potlach," in *Parsing through Customs, Essays by a Freudian Folklorist* (Madison-London, 1987), 54; cf. This study demonstrates the anal structure behind the Northwest American custom of potlatch, a form of male competition turning around the ceremonial breaking and exchange of wealth, frequently in the form of expensive copper dishes. Though Dundes does not cite this source, his conclusions about the metaphorical psychology common to the Kwakiutl and related tribes are borne out by the earlier Kwakiutl dream material presented in Lincoln 297-321, particularly nos. 23, 31, 46, 57.
[177] C. McClellan, "Wealth Woman and Frogs among the Tagish Indians," *Anthropos* 58 (1963), 123. cf. also A. Cameron, *Daughters of Copper Woman* (Vancouver, 1981), 45; F. Boas, *The Religion of the Kwakiutl Indians* (New York, 1930), II, 75, 81, 88, 91. Boas speculated also on the similarity of the Kwakiutl words for *mouth* and *anus*, as Dundes, 60, notes.
[178] E. S. Curtis, *The North American Indian* (Norwood, MA, 1915), v. 10, 8, n 264, in Dundes (1987), 62-3. The *house of the soul* metaphor is described by I. Goldman, *The Mouth of Heaven: An Introduction to Kwakiutl Religious Thought* (New York, 1975), 64. Among the Tlingit, a related tribe, a dead person must rest at the back of the house and the corpse is eventually removed through the back wall, or hoisted out through the smoke-hole; in other words, the dead exit through the house's symbolic anus. See Chapter Five for a related custom in Northern Europe.
[179] F. Boas, "Kwakiutl Culture as Reflected in Mythology," *Memoirs of the American Folklore Society* 28 (New York, 1935), 2.
[180] Dundes and Stibbe, 68-9, on the anal proverbs.
[181] Dundes (1984), 8-9.
[182] S. Freud, *Leonardo da Vinci, A Study in Psychosexuality*, trans. A. A. Brill (New York, 1916, 1947), esp. 97-107.
[183] R. Lopez, *The Commercial Revolution of the Middle Ages*, 950-1350 (Cambridge, 1976).
[184] Little (1978), 83, 96. Thus for instance the eleventh- and twelfth- century religious leaders who started movements based on poverty all grew up in precociously commercial cities. By Bruegel's time in the Netherlands, agriculture was wholly mercantile; Van der Wee, *Antwerp Market* v.2, 209-12, 330.
[185] Agnew, 40-8.

[186] Little (1971), 37; cf. D. Grivot and G. Zarnecki, *Gislebertus, Sculptor of Autun* (London, 1961), pl. 19; also F. Salet, *La Madelaine de Vézelay* (Melun, 1948), pl. 31.
[187] *De miseria humane conditionis*, 2.14; ed. M. Maccarone (Lucca, 1955), 49-50, in Little (1971), 378.
[188] Dante, *Inferno*, Canto XXX, lines 49-56; R. Durling in his "Deceit and Digestion in the Belly of Hell," in S. Greenblatt, ed, *Allegory and Representation* (Baltimore-London, 1981), 67
[189] Durling, 67-72, cites sources for this passage (and for other references to digestion in Dante) from Aristotle, Albertus Magnus, Avicenna etc. Dropsy was believed to occur during the "second digestion" (there were thought to be four), when the liver fails to convert chyle to blood and instead produces an indigestible watery humour (*acqua marcia*) that swells the stomach. Coining too occurs in stages, and Adam adulterated the second stage of coining; 89, nn. 27-9; 90, n. 3
[190] Ibid, 63.
[191] Alain of Lille, in his *De plantu Naturae*; Durling, 67.
[192] A printed copy of the popular *Compost et Kalendrier des Bergers* is extant from 1493 and there were many later editions. This extract is from Owen (1970), 245-46.
[193] In the *Passion de Sainte-Geneviève*, in A. Jubinal, ed., *Mystères inédits du quinzième siècle*, v. 2 (Paris, 1837), 171-74; cf. Owen (1970), 250 n. 36, 252 nn. 68-9.
[194] Wegg (1916), 78.
[195] See Unverfehrt on *Visio Tondali* paintings by Followers of Bosch, 221ff. An English cauldron from c.1200 is illustrated in Owen (1970), pl. 6, opposite 229. A Flemish infernal cauldron is depicted in a thirteenth-century manuscript of the *Miroir du Monde*, illustrated in Maeterlinck (1902), figure 74, opposite 86.
[196] There may be an allusion here also to stereotypes about the greedy side of the Netherlandish national character. In the Adages, for example, Erasmus describes his countrymen in this way: *[they] have no cardinal vices except, perhaps, an addiction to the pleasures of the table*; Barnouw, 52.
[197] On the custom of collecting money from bystanders with a ladle during a carnival procession, illustrated in a Boschian grisaille (pl. 14 in J. De Coo, *Museum Mayer van den Bergh, Catalogus I* [Antwerp, 1960]), see Sullivan, 61; on bacchanal references at the time of the *Dulle Griet*, ibid, 65.
[198] On the many Breweries of Antwerp, Wegg (1916), 231, 267-8, 270. Guicciardini is his source for the excise revenues, 307. Most of the printers' shops were on Brewers' Street, which had at least six operational brewery-taverns by 1550. These seem to have been a perpetual source of litigation and brawls.
[199] A *Psychomachia* is a type of allegory popular in the Middle Ages, a battle between personified abstractions, such as virtues and vices; see n. 159.
[200] For a convenient account of the concept of macrocosm and microcosm in Renaissance philosophy, see J. B. Bamborough, *The Little World of Man* (London,

1952); deeper ramifications explored in D. P. Walker, *Spiritual and Demonic Magic from Ficino to Campanella* (London, 1958).

[201] Scribner (1981), 108. On ship imagery, see also E. Kirschbaum, *Lexikon der christlichen Ikonographie* (Freiburg, 1968), v. 4, 61-7; E. M. Vetter, "Sant peters schifflin," *Kunst in Hessen und am Mittelrhein* 9 (1969), 7-23.

[202] Scribner, ibid.

[203] See S. Brant, *The Ship of Fools*, trans. W. Gilles, with the original woodcuts (London, 1971).

[204] Scribner, 109.

[205] Johann Bergmann von Olpe printed the first edition and the first Latin edition at Basel in 1494 and 1497 respectively. All these woodcuts can be viewed online courtesy of the University of Houston Libraries (http://infolib.uh.edu/sca/).

[206] On the translations, see *The Ship of Fools by Sebastian Brant, Translated into Rhyming Couplets with Introduction and Commentary* by E. H. Zeydel (New York, 1944), 28, 31; A. Pompen, *The English Versions of the Ship of Fools* (New York, 1925; repr. 1967), 8; 19, n. 2. Wright (218) mentions a Dutch translation from 1519, but I have found no verification so far of this.

[207] Pompen, 299.

[208] In a sermon by Adolph Spamer dating from the 1460s or 1470s; Zeydel, 13f.

[209] The tree in the Louvre painting has been altered; its original may-tree shape is preserved however in the preparatory drawing for the work, here, fig. 59.

[210] S. L. Sumberg, *The Nuremberg Schembart Carnival* (New York, 1941), 148-49.

[211] Muchembled, 80.

[212] Ibid, 24.

[213] Duerr, 199, n. 67.

[214] Brant added a chapter on Shrovetide fools only in the second German edition (110b). The difference between the local and topical references in the German and the classical transpositions in the Latin is extremely marked, as Pompen shows, 252-55.

[215] Duerr, 24.

[216] Zeydel, 11-12.

[217] Summarised in Duerr, 25; the 1133 procession is discussed as a Nerthus cult survival by M. J. Rudwin, *The Origin of the German Carnival Comedy* (New York, 1920), 10f.; cf. also Sumberg, 39, n. 77.

[218] See Duerr, 198.

[219] Rudwin, 42.

[220] The activities of the *bambocheurs* are described by P. Minnaert, "A propos de Carnaval et Carême par Bruegel," *Apollo* (Brussels, May 1943); their charter by D.

M. Enklaar, "De Blauwe Schuit," *Tijdschrift voor Geschiedenis* XLVIII (1933); both quoted in P. Fierens, *Le Fantastique dans L'Art Flamand* (Brussels, 1947), 54-5.

[221] See Zeydel, 12; Pompen, 298.

[222] The latter are discussed in Scribner, 106-115.

[223] See Introduction; for a shorter account of the condensation process in dreams and in the unconscious, see Freud's 1901 essay, *On Dreams*, trans. J. Strachey (New York, 1952), 41-50, 111-2.

[224] Ships and boats appear in four Vices: *Sloth, Anger, Envy*, and *Gluttony*.

[225] See Dundes and Stibbe, 62-3; also Marijnissen, 40, 92-3.

[226] These asymmetries in leg-wear and body clothing remain enigmatic. In the older view of melancholia, its ruling humour, Saturn was often depicted as a cripple. The association occurs elsewhere in Bruegel's *Proverbs*, cf. the image of the man beating his head against the wall; Dundes and Stibbe, 61-2 n. 105; Marijnissen, 40, n. 8.

[227] This proverb is discussed in P. J. Harrebomée's collection, *Spreekwordenboek der Nederlandsche Taal* (Utrecht, 1858-70), v. I, 451; Dundes and Stibbe, 63.

[228] This point is one of the major insights to emerge from the study of the painting by Dundes and Stibbe; see Chapter 3 on the *Proverbs*.

[229] Brant speaks of fools *belted not with decency* (ch. 72; Zeydel, 238); Holbein the Younger's *Fool with Death* (Lyons, 1545) shows the fool with loosened lower clothing; a fool of this kind also bares himself in Bruegel's *Feast of Fools* (here, fig. 73) as Sullivan, 62, points out.

[230] Cf figure 23a; this discussion is drawn from Dundes and Stibbe, 63-4.

[231] Sumberg, 149; mechanical ships appear for instance in the *spyl und scheff am aschermittwoch* of the Fishmongers' Pageant of 1616, ibid, n. 100. The use of such contraptions was not limited to courtly circles.

[232] Discussed in Maeterlinck, 94.

[233] This image had become a self-conscious metaphor by the middle of the sixteenth century; see Agnew, ch 1-3.

[234] Later authors regarded immersion (in varying degrees) as a suitable punishment for different kinds of sins. Dante, for instance, cast those who *blacken in the mire* and sob underneath the water as practitioners of anger and sloth. In the third century *Vision of Paul* (available in various vernaculars from the twelfth century on), for instance, the sinful are immersed in water to different degrees according to their deserts. This text stands at the beginning of the tradition of descriptions of hell. Later, the immersed damned were usually equipped with more dramatic liquids: freezing infernal rivers or pits of flaming metal. See Owen (1970), 4 (on Paul); 53, 86 (on other immersions). For Dante's immersions, *Inferno*, Canto VII, lines 110-130.

[235] Personal communication, 1990, L. Dunton-Downer, Department of Comparative Literature, Harvard University, from her research on the concept of obscenity in medieval Latin, French and English literature.

[236] R. Warning, *Funktion und Struktur* (Munich, 1974); Duerr, 273, n. 26, sees *pagan traces in the custom of leaving the centre of the stage "free"* ; participants in the Passion Play at Alsfeld believed that broaching this space meant that one *had to go to hell with the devils* (ibid). Tales abound about the risk run by those who impersonated demons on the stage; either the impersonation would become real or its enactment would summon genuine devils; ibid, 236-7, n. 38; see W-E. Peuckert, "Der Schodüvelstein" in W. Lang, ed., *Von fremden Völkern und Kulturen* (Düsseldorf, 1955), 129.

[237] J. van Lennep, *Art et Alchemie. Étude de L'Iconographie Hermétique et de ses Influences* (Brussels, 1966), 223-4. Subsequent references are to this account, a fertile source of suggestions, although frustratingly brief.

[238] On Bosch and alchemy, see L. Dixon, *Alchemical Imagery in Bosch's Garden of Delights Triptych* (UMI Research Press, Ann Arbor MI, 1981), Van Lennep (1966), ch. IX, 213-222, M. Bergman, *Hieronymus Bosch and alchemy: a study on the St. Anthony triptych* (Stockholm, 1979).

[239] B. Obrist, *Les débuts de l'imagerie alchimique, XIV-Ve siècles* (Paris, 1982), 119ff, 188-213.

[240] B. Obrist, "Visualization in Medieval Alchemy," *HYLE - International Journal for Philosophy of Chemistry,* 9 (2), (2003), 131-170, concludes, *the transition [to] pictorial representation took place [in] alchemical documents dating from the second half of the fourteenth century... Only toward the end of the Middle Ages, a somewhat codified pictorial tradition emerged out of very diverse tendencies in visualization.*

[241] Ibid: *alchemy was unique in continually adopting various cosmological models and philosophical theories for justifying artificial transformation of substances and in abandoning them again as quickly. Theory and practice, especially in its innovative aspect, never complemented one another for any length of time.* Cf essays and literature in C. Meinel, ed., *Die Alchemie in der europäischen Kultur- und Wissenschaftsgesichte* (Wiesbaden, 1986); J.C. Margolin and S. Matton, eds., *Alchimie et philosophie à la Renaissance. Actes du colloque international de Tours* (Paris, 1993).

[242] Versions of the *Aurora consurgens* containing a set of between 36 and 38 water colour illustrations: Glasgow University Library, Ferguson 6; Zurich Zentralbibliothek, Rhenoviensis 172; Leiden, Vossiani Chemici F. 29; Paris, Bibliotheque Nationale, Parisinus Latinus 14006; Prague, Universitni Knihovna, VI. Fd. 26; Prague, Chapitre Métropolitain, 1663. O. LXXIX; Berlin, Staatsbibliothek Preussischer Kulturbesitz, Germ. qu. 848. Our figs. 19 and 61 come from the Glasgow MS. Nine illustrations can be seen at www.alchemywebsite.com

[243] Obrist (2003), ibid.
[244] Van Lennep (1966), 224.
[245] P. Dreyer, "Bruegel's *Alchimist* von 1558; Versuch einer Deutung *ad sensum mysticum*," *Jahrbuch der Berliner Museen* XIX (1977), 69-113. The text refers to the Ignari, who are urged to locate and "work" on the Stone which is Christ.
[246] In ch. 90 of this *Die Eitelkeit und Unsicherheit der Wissenschaften* (On the Vanity and Uncertainty of the Sciences), in C. de Tolnay, *The Drawings of Pieter Bruegel the Elder* (New York, 1952), 72; c.f Würtenberger, 70.
[247] In his *Christ Teares over Ierusalem* (1593), reprinted in the *Works of Thomas Nashe*, ed. R. B. McKerrow (London, 1904-10), v. 2, 105.
[248] For instance, in a panel apparently depicting Purgatory, now at Bruges in the Groeninge Museum; illustrated in W. S. Gibson, *Hieronymous Bosch* (Oxford, 1972), figure 148, who calls it a workshop production. Cf. Harbison, 200-2.
[249] Cf. Bergman, 84.
[250] This is a summary version from Owen (1970), 23; on the earliest mss., 22; see Fierens, 24f. on the story's popularity with Flemish illustrators.
[251] Ibid, 43.
[252] Starting with Freud, psychoanalysts finding parallel materials in folklore include O. Rank, *The Myth of the Birth of the Hero* (New York, 1959); E. Jones, *Nightmare, Witches, and Devils* (New York, 1931); cf B. Bettelheim, *The Uses of Enchantment: The Meaning and Importance of Fairy Tales* (New York, 1977). For anthropological work along these lines, see studies by Lincoln and Roheim previously cited; for the historian's perspective, two older classic articles: H. Frankfort, "The Archetype in Analytical Psychology and the History of Religion," *Journal of the Warburg and Courtauld Institutes* XXI (July-December, 1958), 166-78; J. Bialostocki, "Encompassing Themes and Archetypal Images," *Arte Lombarda* X (1965), 275-84. These both acknowledge the depth and power of Jung's thought while explaining that the fluctuating meanings of Jung's term *archetype* makes it a difficult tool for the historian's task of analysing specifics. Folklorists explaining their material psychoanalytically include P. de Carvalho-Neto, *Folklore and Psychoanalysis* (Miami, 1972) and A. Dundes, "The Psychoanalytic Study of Folklore," *Annals of Scholarship* 3(3) (1985), 1-42.
[253] B. Sutton-Smith, "The Expressive Profile," in A. Paredes and R. Bauman, eds., *Towards New Perspectives in Folklore* (Austin and London, 1972), 85.
[254] For Roelans ,J. Mack, *Nightmares and Human Conflicts* (Boston, 1970), 4-5; for Phaer, R. Bowers and T. Phayer, *Thomas Phaer and the Boke of Chyldren (1544)*, Medieval & Renaissance Texts & Studies, v. 201 (March 1999).
[255] Dundes (1987), x.
[256] Sutton-Smith, ibid. The reference is to V. Propp's "Morphology of the Folktale," *International Journal of American Linguistics*, 24 (1958), 1-135.; for definitions of

motifs and tale-types, Introduction, A. Aarne and S. Thompson, *The Types of the Folktale: A Classification and Bibliography*, 2nd ed. rev. (Helsinki, 1961).

[257] Sutton-Smith, 82.

[258] The predominance of threatening female characters in the folktales just mentioned (stepmother and witch in *Hansel and Gretel*; mother and giant's wife/mother in *Jack and the Beanstalk*) correlates well with the ratio for the nightmares.

[259] Sutton-Smith, 83, 87.

[260] See Chapter One, n. 111

[261] Thomas Nashe, *The Terrors of the Night* (1594), in *Works* v.1, 345.

[262] Rosoman, 20.

[263] Hieronymous Sweerts, in a diatribe derived from the Battle of the Breeches tradition, De Tien Vermakelij-kheden des Houwelyks (Amsterdam, 1684), 156; in Schama, 453; for an analysis of the genre, ibid, 448- 54.

[264] T. Fuller, *The Holy State, the Profane State* (1642; London, 1952), 353; cf K. M. Briggs, *Pale Hecate's Team* (London, 1962), 43.

[265] See the persuasive account of popular sorcery in Muchembled, 79-92; For more on this subject, see Chapter Three. On differences between folk and satanic witches, Ginzburg (1985), 188, n. 33.

[266] On the delusory meaning of the gossamer veil, see comments by L. Steinberg, *The Sexuality of Christ in Renaissance Art and in Modern Oblivion* (New York, 1983), Excursus XX, 147-8.

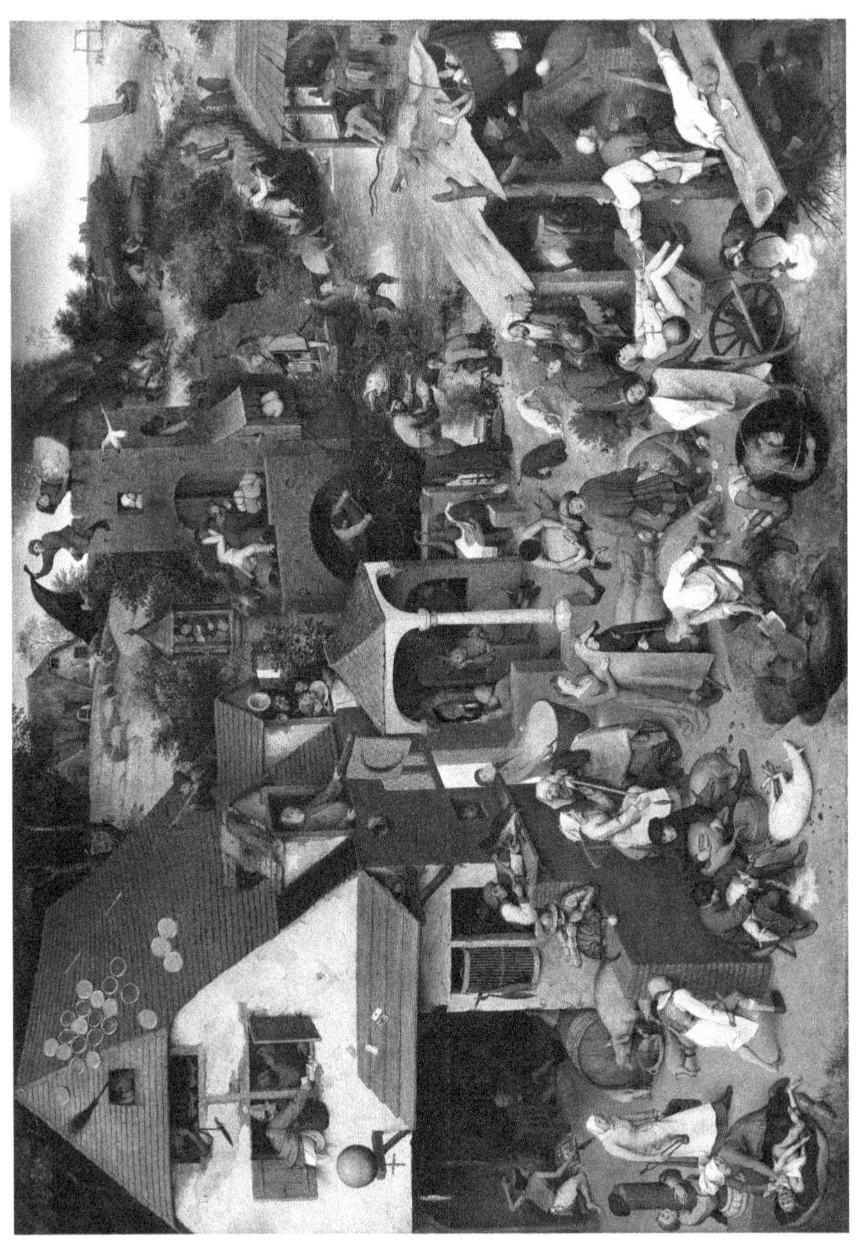

63 Pieter Bruegel, *The Netherlandish Proverbs*, 1559. Oil on panel, 117 x 163 cm. © BPK/Gemäldegalerie, Staatliche Museen zu Berlin. Inv 1720. Photo: Jörg P. Anders

3 Luilekkerland

Introduction

The *Netherlandish Proverbs* (1559; fig. 63), the *Battle Between Carnival and Lent* (1559; fig. 71), and the *Children's Games* (1560; fig. 3) are traditionally known as Bruegel's *theatrum mundi* pictures. To this group might be added also *The Triumph of Death* (c. 1566; fig. 89). The *theatrum* epithet was given to spectacles, as well as atlases, encyclopedias, *kunstkammern* and other classification schemes. The later Renaissance produced dozens of theatres: *of botany, of chemistry, of celestial wisdom, of universal nature, of peace, of consumption, [of] politics, of poetry*. Abraham Ortelius's *Theatrum Orbis Terrarum* (in preparation by 1564, published 1570), referred to maps and geographical essays; *Inscriptiones vel tituli Theatri Amplissimi* by the Antwerp doctor, Samuel Quicchelberg's (1529-67), referred to systems of memory and knowledge governing the Perfect Museum: Elias Ashmole's *Theatrum Chemicum Brittanicum* (c. 1652), to alchemical and hermetic poetry.[1]

Bruegel's *theatrum* works are all large-scale panels, crowded with small figures, whose underlying patterns are perceived as if from above. A high horizon and high viewpoint creates the effect of a tilted panorama; the distance between spectator and protagonists also represents a distance in knowledge. This composition has a number of visual precursors. The high horizon and panoramic landscape format is a characteristic of the early sixteenth-century *weltlandschaft* (Patinir, Herri met de Bles et al).[2] Popular prints and broadsheets often reduced or dispensed with landscape and spatial conventions, the better to fit in more graphic content; high horizons were preferred for this reason (cf. figs. 37, 57, 60). Tapestry design also avoided deep recession in favour of "stacked" allegorical and all-over decorative field; and at least one known tapestry prefigures a *theatrum mundi* work, the *Proverbs* fragment in the Gardner Museum at Boston.[3] However, the single most important contemporary parallel for this group of works is the most modern of all: the new visual genres of maps and map-like views.

In its first century, cartography covered a wide spectrum of visual culture, everything from military maps to mystical cosmography. At the Sign of the Four Winds, Hieronymus Cock published a range of "flat" maps, aerial views and topographic prints halfway between the two throughout the 1550s. These depicted recent battles and sieges conducted by imperial forces, as well as scenes of famous cities such as Lyon, Florence, or Antwerp herself.[4] Cock's *Map of Piedmont* (1552; fig. 4) shows the typical combination of flat plan for coasts and rivers and perspectival detail for mountains and forests. Bruegel's own early works – the landscape prints (fig. 1) and painted *View of Naples with Sea Battle* (c. 1558)[5] – demonstrate his interest in this model.

As well as portable prints, a vogue for large wall-maps, backed with linen and painted in vivid watercolors, was in full swing around 1550.[6] The liking for this form of decoration evolved from the earlier taste for the *weltlandschaft*; the mercantile internationalism of Netherlandish patrons evidently played a part here. Though few examples have survived and none have their colors intact, at the time they were a cheaper substitute for the rich effect of tapestries, like paintings on linen.[7] One castle in South Holland had 50 wall-maps in 1560; *they decorated in great numbers the palatial homes of wealthy Europeans... the Emperor Charles V and other princes had apartments entirely filled with maps*.[8] It was as an illuminator of such maps that Abraham Ortelius (1527-1598) was entered in the rolls of St. Luke in 1547.[9]

Ortelius called his atlas, the first in the world, the *Theatrum Orbis Terrarum*: The Theatre of the Globe of the World. The book was a unique combination of maps and text, and the *theatrum* element in the title applied to both. The geographical text, referred to by the author's friends as his *essays*, included many Humanistic reflections on the relations between ancient and modern geography.[10] Ortelius even added two fantastic topographical prints (*La Vallée de Tempé* and *Daphnaé, le Faubourg d'Antioch*) to a later enlarged *Theatrum*; demonstrating the wide latitude given to cosmography at this time. In its discursiveness, his *Theatrum* was not unlike Guicciardini's best-selling work of geography, *Descrittione di tutti Paesi Bassi* (1567), the first parts of which were written around 1560.[11] When Ortelius finally published, the whole work, and especially the text, met with a chorus of praise.[12] The kind of descriptive analysis at which he excelled is paralleled by Bruegel's ambitious panoramas of the same date.

The "cartographical" aspects of Bruegel's works rest in their "cosmographical" concerns — somewhere between the scope of Ortelius and Guiccardini. Here is the mode of thought that led Ortelius to elegize Bruegel as one who *painted well the things that cannot be painted.... In all his works there is always more thought than painting,*[13] and, perhaps, the effect on Ortelius of a Bruegelian interest in mapping the things that cannot be mapped. In Bruegel's designs, as in a map, only the spectator, privileged, detached and elevated, can see the whole of the activity and comprehend its meaning.

This combination of inclusiveness and detachment is an important common feature of the *theatro mundi* paintings. These paintings deal with large communal concerns: ordinary speech, calendars, childhood, carnivals and feasts. Let us begin by considering the implications of the detached stance Bruegel built in to his treatment of these themes. I will begin with the work where Bruegel might be expected to deal with the popular culture of his day most directly, the *Netherlandish Proverbs* of 1559. The way will then be open to consider Bruegel's pictures of carnival and the carnivalesque (Chapter 4).

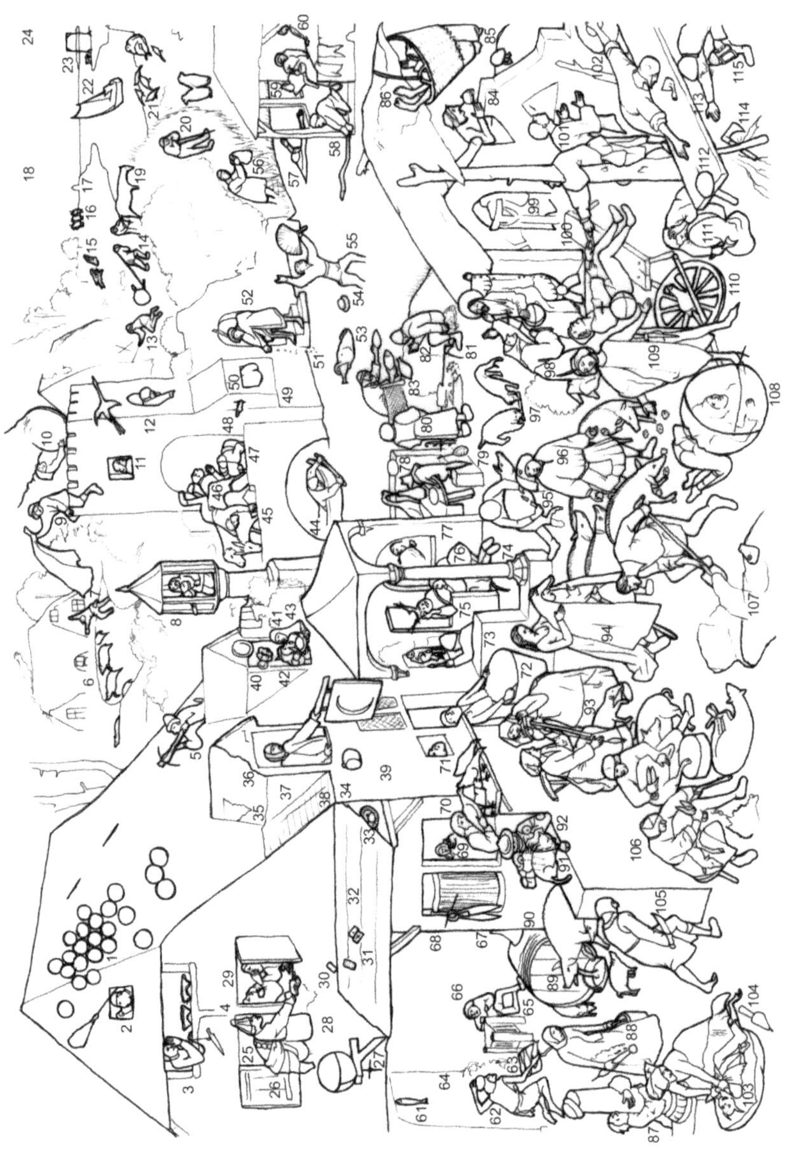

63a Pieter Bruegel, *The Netherlandish Proverbs*, 1559, diagram after A. Dundes and C. Stibbes (1981). Image: Julian Hodges (2007)

1. *Daar zijn de daken met vlaaden gedekt* There the roofs are tiled with tarts
2. *Daar steekt de bezem uit / Onder de bezem getrouwd* There the broom sticks out / Married under the broom
3. *Hij ziet door de vingers* He looks through his fingers
4. *Te patijnen staan* To stand with one's clogs on
5. *De eene pijl na de andere verschieten* To send one arrow after another
6. *De varkens lopen los in 't koren* The pigs run loose in the wheat
7. *Hij loopt of hij het vuur in zijn aars (broek of gat of lijf) had* He moves along as if his arse (backside or body were on fire)
8. *Hij speelt op de kaak / Hij zit in de viool* He plays on the pillory/ he sits in the fiddle (jail)
9. *Hij hangt de huik naar de wind* He lets his cloak go with the wind
10. *Hij want pluimen in de wind* Pours feathers into the wind
11. *Zij kijkt naar de ooievaar* She watches the stork
12. *Hij slaat twee vliegen in één klap* He hits two flies with one blow
13. *Als het huis brandt, warmt men zich bij de kolen* When the house is burning, one can warm oneself from the coals
14. *Hij sleept het blok* He drags the block (unhappy in love)
15. *Angst en vreese doen den oude loopen* Terror & fear make the old run
16. *Als de ene blinde de andere leidt, vallen ze beiden in de gracht* If the blind lead the blind, both fall in the ditch)
17. *De reize is nog niet gedaan, al ziet men kerk en toren staan* The journey is not yet over, though one can see the church & belfry (spires)
18. *Iemand in 't zonnetje zetten* Put someone in the sun
19. *Paardenkeutels zijn geen vijgen* Horse manure is not figs
20. *Hij ziet de beeren dansen* He sees the bears dancing (he's hungry)
21. *Er zijn om ganzen te hoeden* He's there to tend the geese (useless action)
22. *Een oogje in 't zeil houden* Keeping an eye on the sail
23. *Hij beschijt de galg* He shits on the gallows
24. *De kraaien moeten op aas loeren* The crows must await carrion [like vultures]
25. *Onder het mes zitten* Sitting under the knife
26. *Hij beschijt de geheele wereld* He shits on the whole world
27. *De verkeerde wereld* Topsyturvy world
28. *De gek krijgt de kaart* The fool gets the card
29. *Zij hebben elkander bij de neus* They have one another by the nose
30. *De teerlingen zijn gevallen* The dice have fallen
31. *'t is naar het vallen van de kaart* It depends on the fall of the cards
32. *Een knip oog* A snip-eye (wink)
33. *Een nestei* A nest egg
34. *Daar zijn latten aan het dak* There are laths on the roof (eavesdroppers)
35. *Hij heeft een gat in zijn dak* He has a hole in his roof
36. *Een oud dak heeft veel hermakens van doen* An old roof needs much repair
37. *Hij heeft tandpijn achter zijn oren* He has a toothache behind his ears (acts in deceptive fashion)
38. *Hij pist tegen de maan* He pisses at the moon
39. Daar hangt de pot uit There hangs a pot outside
40. *Ongelijke schotels maken scheele oogen* Different size platters make crossed eyes
41. *Twee zotten onder éénen kaproen* Two fools under one hood
42. *Den gek scheren* Shaving the fool (mocking someone)
43. *Het groit het venster uit* It grows out the window (cannot be kept secret)
44. *Hij vist achter het net* He fishes behind the net (he's too late)
45. *Hij springt (of valt) van de os op de ezel* He jumps (or falls) from the ox onto the ass
46. *Hij kust het ringetje van de deur* He kisses the ring on the door (shows too much respect)
47. *Hij veegt zijn gat aan de poort* He wipes his arse on the door
48. *Iemand het gat van de deur wijzen* Pointing at (or out) the hole in the door
49. *Twee schijten door één gat* Two shit through one hole
50. *Dat hangt als een kakhuis over eene gracht* That hangs (out) like a shithouse over a canal
51. *Hij gooit zijn geld in het water* He throws his money in the water
52. *Een gescheurde muur is haast afgebroken* A broken wall is almost torn down
53. *Grote vissen eten de kleine* Big fish eat little fish
54. *Hij kan het hoofd niet boven water houden* (He can't keep his head above water
55. *Hij kan de zon niet in het water zien schijnen* He can't stand to see the sun shining in water
56. *Hij smijt kap over de haag* He throws his cowl over the hedge
57. *Hij zwemt tegen de stroom op* He swims against the tide/ keeps his head above water
58. *Een aal bij de staart hebben* To have an eel by the tail
59. *De kruik gaat zo lang te water, tot zij breekt* The pitcher goes to the water (well) until it breaks
60. *Het is goed riemen snijden uit een andermans leer* It's good strap-cutting from another man's leather
61. *Iedere haring moet aan zijn eigen kieuwen hangen* Every herring must hang by its own gills
62. *Hij heeft de koek op t' hoofd* He has the cake on his head
63. *Zijn haring braadt hier niet* His herring won't cook here
64. *Wat kan de rook het hangijzer doen?* What can the smoke do to the pothook?
65. *Tussen twee stoelen in de as zitten (of vallen)* Sits (falling) between two chairs in the ashes
66. *De hond is in der saapraden* The dog is in the cupboard (finishing his master's food)
67. *Daar hangt de schaar uit* There the scissors hang outside (an expensive place)
68. *Lichtekooi* A light cage (whore's bed)
69. *Altijd op een been knagen* Always chewing on one bone
70. *De hennetaster* The hen toucher (woman chaser)
71. *Met twee monden spreken* Speaks with two mouths
72. *Hij draagt de dag met manden uit* He carries the day (light) out in baskets
73. Voor de duivel een kaars aansteken Lights a candle for the devil
74. *Een geveinsde kerkpilaar* A feigned church pillar (religious hypocrite)
75. Bij de duivel te biecht gaan Confess to the devil
76. *De oorblazer* The earblower (a malicious gossip)
77. *De vos en de kraan hebben elkaar te gast* The fox & the crane entertain each other
78. *Hij staat in 't krijt* It's written in chalk (owes money)
79. *Het is zoo ondugt als een schuimspaan* Hold water like a skimmer
80. *Het is gezond in 't vuur te pissen* Healthy to piss in the fire
81. *Daar is geen spit mee te wenden* There's no way to turn a spit with him
82. *Hij zit op hete kolen* Sits on hot coals
83. *Hij vangt den eenen visch den anderen* Catches one fish with another
84. *Zij raapt het kippenei, en laat het ganzen ei loopen* She picks up the chicken egg, & lets the goose egg walk
85. *Hij valt door de mand* He falls through the basket (caught in his own deceit)
86. *Een wit voetje hebben bij iemand* To have a white foot (with someone)
87. Een pilaarbijter Pillar biter (religious hypocrite)
88. *Zij draagt water in de eene, en vuur in de andere hand* She carries water in one hand & fire in the other
89. *Het varken trekt de tap uit* The pig removes the spigot
90. *Men zal het hem met een' trechter ingieten* (One pours it into him with a funnel)
91. *De kat de bel aanbinden* Bell the cat
92. *Hij is tot op de tanden gewapened* Armed to the teeth
93. *De een rokkent wat de ander spint* One provides distaff for what the other spins
94. *Zij hangt gar man de blauwe huik om* She hangs the blue cloak on her husband
95. *Het varken is door de buik gestoken* Pig is stuck through the belly
96. *Rozen voor de varkens strooien* Cast roses before swine
97. *Twee honden, aan één been, komen zelden overeen* Two dogs on one bone seldom agree
98. *Hij wil onzen Heer een' vlassen baard aandoen* He wants to put a flaxen beard on our Lord (false piety)
99. *Hij zit in zijn eigen licht* He sits in his own light
100. *Aan het langste (of kortste) eind trekken* Pull for the longest (or shortest) piece
101. *Hij gaapt tegen de oven* He tries to outgape the oven
102. De paal is door den oven gestoken The pole has been stuck through the oven
103. *Zij zou de duivel op het (een) kussen binden* She would bind the devil himself to a pillow
104. *Alwaar het spinrok dwingt het zwaard, Daar staat het kwalijk met den waard* Where the distaff rules the sword, it goes ill with the manor's lord
105. *Men kan met het hoofd niet door den muur loopen* One cannot walk headfirst through a wall
106. *De een scheert de schapen, de ander de varkens* One shears the sheep, the other the pigs
107. *Als 't kalf verdronken is, dempt men de put* Fills the well after the calf has drowned
108. *Men moet zich krommen, Wil men door de wereld kommen* One must bend if one wants to get through the world
109. *Hij draait de wereld op zijn duim* He spins the world on his thumb
110. *Een stok in het wiel steken* To put a stick in the wheel
111. *Die zijne pap gestort heeft, kan niet alles weder oprapen* He who has spilled his porridge cannot pick it up again
112. *Hij weet nauwelijks van het eene brood tot het andere te geraken* He can hardly reach from one bread to the other
113. *Een barkje zonder steel* Hoe without a handle
114. *De bijl ligt alree aan de wortel* The axe already lies at the roots
115. *Hij zoek het bijltje* He looks for the axe

The World-Turned-Upside-Down

The *Proverbs* painting draws on the tradition of the World-Turned-Upside-Down, a new combination of old folk-motifs that had appeared just after mid-century.[14] The inn at the left-hand side of the painting has as its sign an inverted globe. Thus the whole action of the *Proverbs* takes place under the aegis of the Upside-Down World. The humourous effect of all these proverbs acted out *en masse* does indeed resemble the absurdity evoked by the visual reversal of accepted norms. Bruyn suggested that, though the inn sign represents the *inverted* world, the action of the painting is better described as a representation of the *perverse* world (*verkeerde wereld* as opposed to *omgekeerd wereld*).[15] The phrase is used in the caption to a similar proverb composition from around 1580.[16] Bruegel's painting may thus have been recognisable to his original audience as a variation on the theme of *De verkeerde wereld*.

The difference in meaning is subtle but important. To consider the Perverse World as a subject for painting is to undertake an illustration of the ways in which, or through which, it becomes perverse. Bruegel does this by exaggerating the surreal potential of visualised proverbs, and linking them thematically, as he did in the *Griet*, through chains of visual resemblances and inversions. As a set theme in which to do this, the Perverse rather than the Inverse world allowed much scope for invention.

However, in the popular broadsheets and songs where these themes were manifested, images from the perverse world and from the inverted world tended to intermingle.[17] Both Bruegel's painting and the genre of reversed world broadsheets are products of the same currents of taste, incarnated in visual culture shortly after the middle of the sixteenth century.[18] By examining the sources and roots of the popular material, we can start to piece together what attracted Bruegel and his contemporaries to this kind of subject at this time.

The broadsheets depict, in a continuous strip or series of boxes, this kind of motif: *Mice eat cats. A wolf watches over sheep; they devour him. Children spank parents. The father, not the mother, wipes a baby's bottom. The cart goes before the horse.... The king goes on foot.... The fisherman gets caught.... The goose puts the cook in a pot.... A wheelbarrow stows a sack on a man's back.*[19] Kunzle analyzed the structure and classificatory schemes involved in these motifs:

> The principle of inversion is that there are two parties, the one dominant, the other dominated, whose roles, in some action typifying their relationship, are simply reversed. In all these groups the inversion is hierarchical, involving a power relationship, except in the fourth, where elements, usually air and water, are treated as *opposite but equal* and switched around in respect to the creatures normally associated with them. The last three groups, which are the least important numerically, belong essentially to a tradition ... of pure nonsense and fantasy. [These groups] tend to fuse insofar as the hierarchical principle is often added to the element reversal, so that the fish in the air catches the bird in the sea. The only kind of element reversal not involving animals is a cosmic one, which is appropriately present in the majority of world upside down prints and indeed acts as a kind of frontispiece or motto for the theme as a whole: earth and city above, sky and stars below. There are also a few insignificant topical reversals within inversions. Thus the city in the sky may itself appear upside down as may the mill to which the ass drives the miller.[20]

Thus the broadsheets contain little scenes depicting reversals of familiar hierarchical relationships. Reversals of natural relationships (predator and prey) are mixed together with reversals of social custom (father cleans baby). Scattered in with these are other kinds of reversals, some of which do not involve a dominant/dominated relation; others do not seem to be reversals at all. Kunzle calls them *pure nonsense*: a castle in the air turns upside down, a flying fish catches a swimming bird.

Reversed world motifs have parallels in the *adynata*, or *impossibilia*, of classical and medieval literature. As a rhetorical device, *adynata* achieve their effect by reversing or denying some natural law. Frequently the speaker wishes to evoke an apocalyptic context. What has happened, the implication goes, is so unthinkable that the end of the world must be at hand.

Thus when the Greek poet Archilochus witnessed the eclipse of the sun in 648 BC, he could only think that now that the sun had been darkened, nothing else was impossible: *Nothing would surprise me now, not even if the beasts on land were to eat the food of dolphins, and dolphins that of the beasts on land.*[21] In a more personal sense, when one of Virgil's shepherds is disappointed in love, he expresses himself in terms of the end of the world: *May the wolf now of his own will flee from the sheep. May the oak now bear golden apples. May the owl vie in song with the swan.*[22]

In classical *adynata*, both hierarchical reversals and "nonsensical" reversals are figures of impossibility. They characterise a state of affairs which can only exist at the beginning or end of time. Virgil used the device to convey the atmosphere of the Golden Age, deep in the mythic past, where natural enemies live at peace with each other and the lion lies down with the lamb (cf. *Isaiah*, 11:6-8). These utopian examples are represented in the scattering of purely nonsensical scenes in the reversed world broadsheets,[23] and something of their apocalyptic tone persisted infusing the general concept of reversed worlds. These *adynata* resurface notably in the work of Bosch, as Kunzle noted:

> certain ancient and medieval *adynata* are transformed and elaborated in Bosch, who inverts the normal process by which humans hunt down, cook, invest and excrete animal prey; and [in] the theme of *the revenge of the Animals on the hunter* [in] the work of sixteenth-century graphic artists. The reversal of a human-object relationship, also a feature of the World Upside Down print, occurs in Bosch.[24]

So Bosch, for example, represents *Ira* as a man with a chair on his head, in the *Seven Deadly Sins* tabletop (c. 1500-25; fig. 7). The appeal of the *topos* for Bosch is interesting. His art, like that of the World-Upside-Down prints, manifests a new concentration on *adynata* concerned with reversals in human society. The broadsheets also show more interest in domestic animals and man-made objects than natural ones: *Statistically speaking, exchanges in character between animals (cat eaten by mice) or man and animals (farmer roasted by turkey) are far more frequent than changes in natural order, or what culture perceived as natural.*[25]

The point of such reversals in the broadsheets is ambiguous. To modern eyes, the images showing reversals of power relationships inevitably look, at least incipiently, political. Kunzle links them to the "revolutionary" ideas behind the peasant uprisings of the early sixteenth century.[26] However, the imagery in context has a different emphasis. It is more likely that the ideological effect leans in the opposite direction. To depict role-reversals through actions which typify fundamental social relationships – between master and servant, goose and cook, husband and wife, human and chair – draws attention to the immutability of the action itself. This underwrites, rather than challenges, the primacy of hierarchies.

Other categories of relationship in the broadsheets similarly reinforce the status quo; the "social" scenes are further contextualised by the "natural" ones which appear alongside. So, reversals within human society are tacitly likened to reversals in the animal kingdom, or to reversals between tools and their users. Just as it is unthinkable that the mice should eat the cat, the format of the prints encourages the belief that it is equally unthinkable that a servant should command a master, or a wife beat her husband. Looking at these pictures, the given order of the world asserts itself and gains renewed coherence. At the same time, rebellious desires may be accommodated in this safe "impossible" framework, rather as the framework of the dream made it possible to get away with topical satire. In the images taken singly, there is a sneaking satisfaction in watching the mighty fall; the King walking, and the peasant riding for a change. In this sense, reversal imagery gives an outlet to the dissatisfactions inherent to a society where everybody is born into an allotted place. The surrounding prints quickly contextualise such sympathies, assuring us that pigs will fly before changes of this kind can come about. The meaning of specific treatments of the World-Turned-Upside-Down may vary, but they all have the same broad function: to channel potentially rebellious imaginings into the structure of therapeutic reversal.[27]

"Cosmic" reversals therefore retained a place in the reversed world broadsheets, where they worked as signs of the dream-like on a number of different levels. The spectacle of fish nesting in trees, or ships sailing on dry land, is a nonsensical displacement which has little to do with models of dominance and whose effect is either comic or poetic. These are *opposite but equal* scenarios which do *not* involve hierarchic reversal. Cosmic reversal imagery was also proverbial, the matter of ordinary speech. Thus the maid and the trooper in the ballad converse:

O when will we two meet again?
Or when will you marry me?
When cockle-shells grow silver bells
I winna longer tarry.[28]

In the next verse, the response is *When frost and sno' shall warm us al'* and so on.[29] These images appear together with servant-master/cat-mouse reversals in the printed grid of the World-Upside-Down, because they emanate from a wider folkloric context where these elements are bound together.

This common context includes a group of folktales where the Upside-Down World is represented as a kind of Never-Never Land. The Nuremberg poet and playwright, Hans Sachs wrote a successful version of *Das Schlaraffenland* (1530), based on older German materials. His text, in rhyming couplets, included pure nonsense memorates such as this, *A village sat in a peasant, who liked to drink spoons with milk.... His corner had four houses ... his kitchen stood in the middle of the hearth.*[30] Where the broadsheet imagery presents, or reinforces, a hierarchical, vertical view of the world and society, the reversed world potential in folklore is far more diverse. Cosmic reversals can move, as it were, in several different directions, inwards, outwards and horizontally as well as up and down. The topsy-turvy land in folklore, like heaven and hell in the peasant dream anecdotes, is represented as a place in the world, a country one can travel to. The stories told about such lands were often framed as travellers' tales; they occupy the most frankly fantastic extreme of that thoroughly fantastic genre. At the same time, in the sixteenth century, aspects of these tales could be coloured with the same kind of controlled political suggestiveness Kunzle sees in the broadsheets. Bruegel depicted two of these strange places, *Malleghem* and *Cockaigne*.

Cockaigne and Utopian Fantasies

Reversed world images also occur in fabulous countries specially constituted for the purpose. The German *Schlaraffenland*, the Dutch *Luilekkerland*, the English Cloud-Cuckooland, or the universal Land of Cockaigne, are in turn related to the genre of tales told about a town of fools, the town being always located some distance away. Nonsensical stories illustrate the stupidity of the wise men of the English Gotham, the townspeople of Flemish Malleghem (literally, *Suckersville*), presented as firmly under the thumb of their witch in Bruegel's 1559 print (fig. 40) or the citizens of German Schildburg.[31] Schildburg, although inhabited by Germans, was a town *in Misnopotamia, beyond Utopia, in the Kingdom of Kalecut*.[32] In the tale of Schlaraffenland collected by the Brothers Grimm, the hero's journey first takes him to Rome, which he sees suspended on silk threads. Then, *he sees a young ass with a silver snout which is pursuing two hares, a linden tree on which hot pancakes grow, crows which mow hay, gnats which build bridges ... cows baking bread, and infants ... consoling their mothers*.[33]

By the end of the seventeenth century, people were making maps of Schlaraffenland and its neighbouring provinces. Johann Baptist Homann published his *Accurata Utopiae Tabula* at Nuremberg (1716; fig. 64), to illustrate an older satire by Johann Andreas Schnebelin (d. 1706).[34] As well as Schlaraffenland itself, this map depicts a whole continent of imaginary countries: *Mammonia*, the *Republic of Veneria*; *Bibonia* (Land of Booze), the

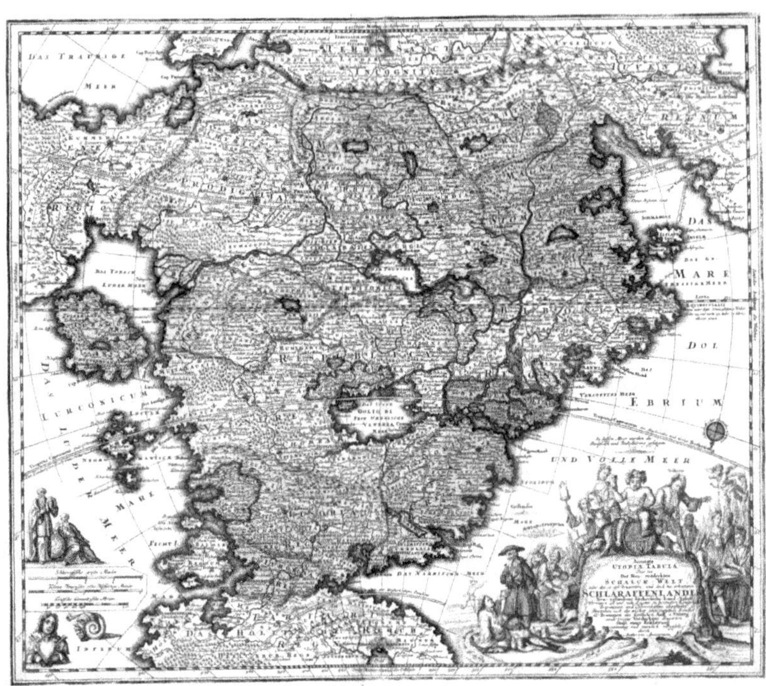

64 Johann Baptist Homann, *Accurata Utopiae Tabula...* (Nuremburg, 1716). with accompanying book by Johann Andreas Schnebelin. Universitätsbibliothek, Karl-Franzens-Universität, Graz

Magni Stomachi Imperium (Great Empire of the Stomach), the Kingdom of Fools and the Island of Tobacco, among others. Each Vice has its territory.

To the west lies the Kingdom of Youth, to the east, that of Old Age; a region in the north is labelled *Terra Sancta Incognita* (unknown country of the pious). The cartouche (fig. 64a) is adorned with a veritable montage of contemporary dreams and desires, a pyramid composed of revellers, a treasure chest, lords and ladies playing cards, a cupid aiming at them, all crowned by the presiding figure of Bacchus riding on a barrel.

The traditional Land of Cockaigne[35] was invariably given a distant and rural setting. Sixteenth-century versions of the Land of Cockaigne fed into accounts of the New World and *vice versa*;[36] the tradition furnished the

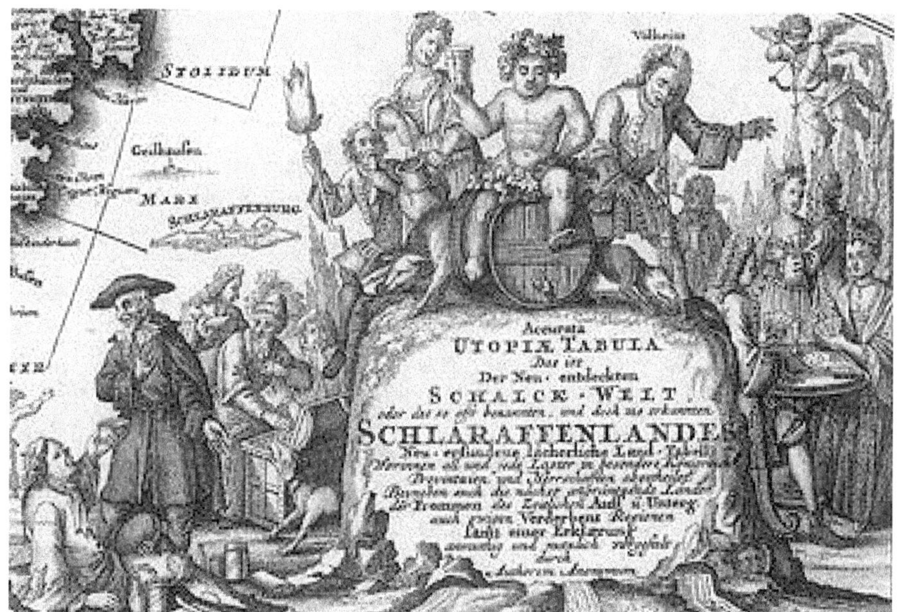

64a Johann Baptist Homann, Cartouche, detail, *Accurata Utopiae Tabula...*

models for "eye-witness" narratives of the wonders of America. As Montaigne commented, *Human eyes cannot perceive things but in the shape that they know them by.*[37] The testaments of sixteenth-century explorers were already halfway to myth, dwelling as they did on the carefree nudity of these far-off islanders, the amazing fertility of their lands, and their lack of hierarchical government.[38] One of the many versions published in the middle of the sixteenth century states that the land of plenty has been discovered in the New World. The description is a mixture of nonsense and reversed elements:

> A mountain of grated cheese is seen standing alone in the middle of the plain... a river of milk gushes forth from a cave ... the king of the place is called Bugalosso. They have made him king because he is the laziest. Like a haystack he is big and fat ... and from his arse, manna comes forth, and when he spits, out come marzipans. Instead of lice he has fish in his head.[39]

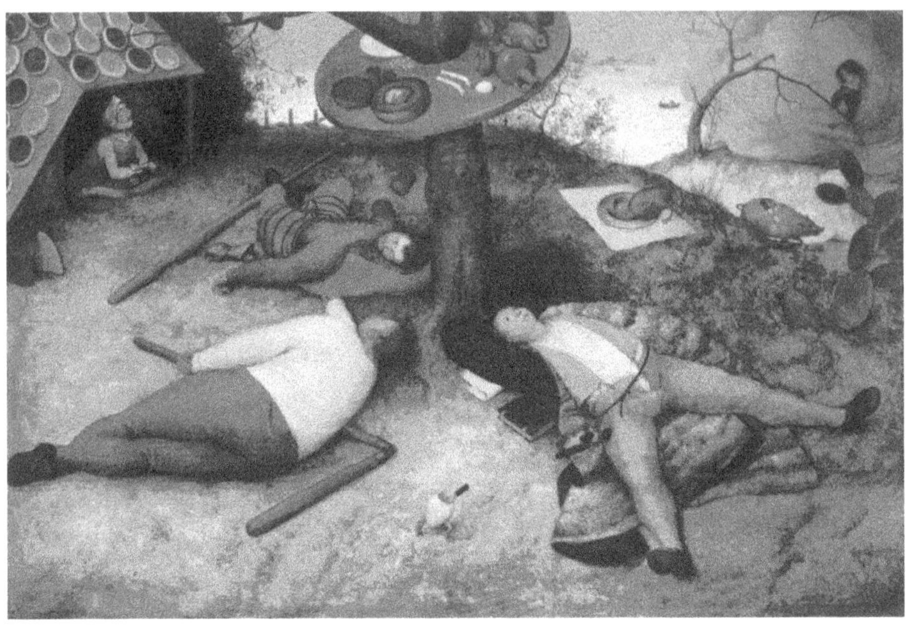

65 Pieter Bruegel, *Land of Cockaigne*, 1566. Oil on panel. © Bayerische Staatsgemäldesammlungen, Alte Pinakothek, Munich / Kunstdia-archiv ARTOTHEK, Weilheim. Inv. 8940

The poem ends with the standard mocking formula: *Who wants to travel there, I shall tell him the way. Go embark at the port of the simpleton, and then navigate through the sea of lies. Whosoever arrives is king over every dolt.*[40]

In Bruegel's *Land of Cockaigne* (1567; fig. 65), the newcomer at the top right corner has crossed the sea in order to get there.[41] He emerges through a hole in what looks like a dense cloud barrier, but is in fact porridge. The cactus below the man falling gently from his entry-hole may suggest the New World. The painting contains no strictly hierarchic reversals. Its inversions are all of the "nonsensical" type already encountered. The tree grows cups and comes equipped with a loaded table; both egg and pig carry, stuck inside them, the implements with which they are to be eaten; the fowl, ready-plucked, lays itself on the plate; a roast bird flies into the knight's open mouth.[42]

Other details (like the porridge barrier) were taken directly from the Dutch text of 1546 (itself based on Hans Sachs' 1530 poem), which mentions fences made of sausages and houses roofed with pancakes and tarts.[43] Here, Cockaigne may be found:

> *recht in't Northommelen, dwars op de depe syde na by de galghe, drie mielen door lange nachten*
>
> [to the right, to Northommelen, on the bias towards the deep side near the gallows, through the long night for a distance of three miles][44]

These are joking directions, but the implication of references to the gallows and the long night is that one must die to go there. This itself invokes certain peasant ideas about paradise and the spirit-world; recall the peasant who heard that Heaven was paying good prices for wheat.[45]

By depicting this fantasy land, Bruegel both entered into and disparaged a sharply-felt dream of his countrymen; an old collective dream which was also a barometer of tensions in collective experience. His painting is double-edged, like the legend itself in its sixteenth-century incarnations. There is little doubt that the theme of the Land of Cockaigne has its origins in wish fulfillment; it is a collective dream about universal objects of desire, whose sole narrative is the satisfaction of appetite. As an open-ended repertoire of set-piece images, the formula of describing an edible land lent itself to infinite chains of rhetorical elaboration. An anonymous Dutch poetic fragment on Cockaigne seems to have drawn for inspiration on the spectacle of *Great wealth, such as may have been displayed at the courts of Brabant and Flanders after 1435.* The poet *admits at the outset that half of Cockaigne is better than all Spain and the other half is even better than Betowen* [i.e., Batavia, the Netherlands]. After revelling in elaborate accounts of edible houses, the author concludes that such a dreamland is needed to make life bearable (*om dat lef mede ton draghen*).[46]

For Muchembled, the fat sleepers of Bruegel's Cockaigne *are above all*

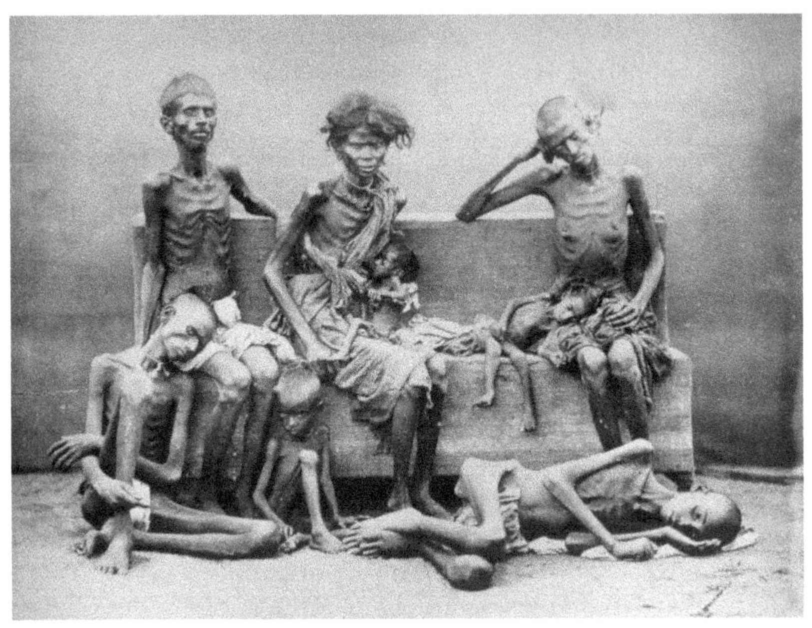

68 Willoughby Wallace Hooper, Madras Famine, c. 1877-1878, Album print, private collection. Photo: Vidya Dehejia

dream figures peopling the fantasies of undernourished men.[47] Pointing to the regular food shortages and famines that plagued the rural population even in prosperous Flanders and Brabant, Muchembled argued that Bosch's ectomorphs are closer to the real shape of the average countryman at mid-century than Bruegel's rotund peasants: *In all probability [hunger] created a sharp contrast between two types of human being: the robust bodies of the nobles ... opposing the fragile silhouettes of the human animals that haunted the countryside.*[48]

Data from the early seventeenth century shows that levels of mortality among European adults resembled those of late nineteenth-century India during the Madras famine (1877; fig. 68). According to Thomas, *About one harvest in six seems to have been a total failure ... it was rare but certainly not unknown for men to die in the streets from starvation or exposure... The dietary deficiencies of the lower classes reflected not so much ignorance as simple poverty.*[49] Such statistics give some support to Muchembled's contention about the visual appearance of the people. If true, this piece of evidence would also lend support to the theory that Bruegel's famously well-fed peasants were idealised, rather than realistic, figures, like the plump denizens of his *Cockaigne*. The rotund shapes of Bruegel's peasants at weddings and dances should accordingly be read as inventions, designed to populate a nostalgic and idealised vision of the rural past (see Chapter 3). In pictures where the figures are noticeably scrawnier, this would imply that the figures are correspondingly less idealised; as is the case, for instance, with the crowds in the *Procession to Calvary* (1564; Kunsthistorisches Museum, Vienna).

It is possible therefore that the exaggeration in Bruegel's pair of prints, the *The Fat Kitchen* and *The Lean Kitchen*, from 1563 (figs. 66, 67) is not as pronounced as it appears to modern eyes. The gesture of cannibalistic intent at the door of the *Lean Kitchen* — is the fat man trying to get out? Are they pulling him in? — makes a blackly humourous reference to the ultimate recourse in times of famine. In Ireland in 1588-9, *one did eate another for hunger*, according to one chronicler.[50] Though stories of this kind are folklore as well as folk history, in many regions the tension between the haves and have-nots was all too plainly identifiable as the tension between the lean and the fat. The 1563 prints are also known as the *Poor* and *Rich Kitchens*. These pictures hark back to decisions Bruegel made four years earlier, when composing his picture of *Carnival and Lent*; where a conflict between fat and thin is the central dramatic action (see Chapter 3). A design by Bruegel or his immediate circle depicts this clash more drastically. Three heads are depicted: two thin and female, one of which bites the cheek of the fat male one (fig. 87). The *Rich* and *Poor Kitchens* meet, their conflict simplified and honed into one image. This "Carnival and Lent" though visceral and disturbing, still conveys an emblematic quality.

The strongest element separating the myth of the Land of Cockaigne from other topsy-turvy nonsensical places is its preoccupation with food. The Land of Cockaigne can be thought of as a dream generated by lean people of a land where everyone is fat. The depiction of excessively thin and

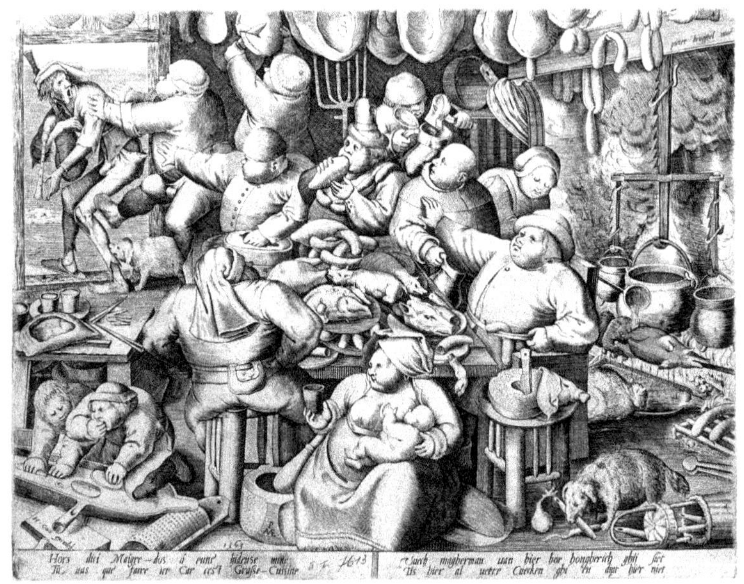

66 Pieter van der Heyden, after Pieter Bruegel, *The Fat Kitchen*, 1563. Engraving, 22.4 x 29 cm. Bibliothèque Royale Belgique, Brussels. S I 7613

67 Pieter van der Heyden, after Pieter Bruegel, *The Lean Kitchen*, 1563. Engraving, 22.4 x 29 cm. Bibliothèque Royale Belgique, Brussels. S IV 12746

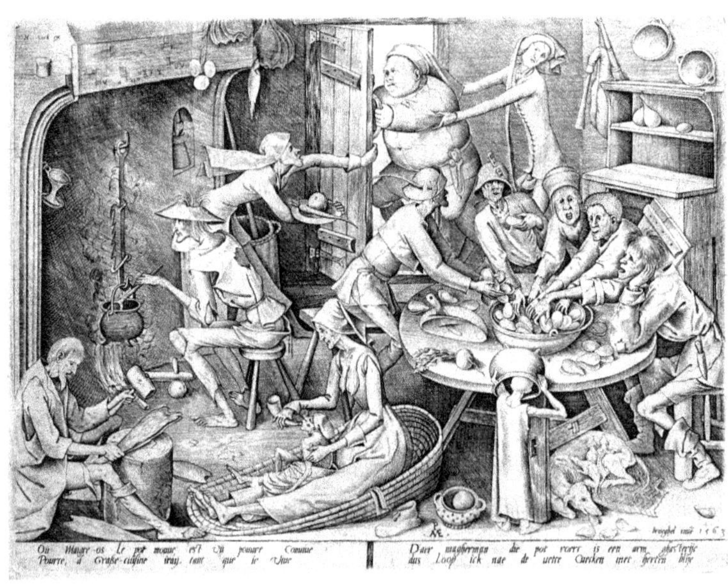

excessively fat human figures must also be understood in the metamorphic sense also: as a means of making visible that which is within. On one level, lean figures embody hunger; the imagery of food can be understood as a displacement focus for hunger/appetite, a pretext for the real object of unconscious desire. As Pleij commented, *The dream of food spontaneously offering itself is part of the yearning for Paradise Lost.*[51] For many, the myth allowed the vicarious appeasement of appetite within a safely fantastic framework. In this the dream of Cockaigne, like the dominance reversals of the broadsheets, worked as a social placebo.

Despite its broadly palliative format, the imagery in the individual scenes of the broadsheets could hit nerves of inequity. The Land of Cockaigne also had its subversive implications. The *Schlaraffenland* stories were the popular utopias of the late medieval period. Because food is everywhere, no one has to work, and, implicitly, the given hierarchy of society dissolves. In sixteenth-century versions, these ramifications[52] become more explicit:

> Everyone has what he wants in every way, and who should ever dare speak about working, they would hang him... There are no peasants or villeins in that place. Everyone is rich. Everyone has what his heart desires. Because tabletops are laden with goods ... neither fields nor land are divided. There is an abundance of things for everyone, and so the place is totally free.[53]

An analogous satirical spin was given to tales of Cockaigne in the mouth of Shakespeare's character, Jack Cade:

> There shall be in England seven half-penny loaves sold for a penny. The three hooped post shall have ten hoops, and I will make it felony to drink small beer. All the realm shall be in common and in Cheapside shall my palfrey to grass. And when I am king ... there shall be no money. All shall eat and drink on my score and I will apparel them all in one livery, that they may agree like brothers, and worship me their lord.
>
> *Henry VI* (1598) IV, ii, 70-82

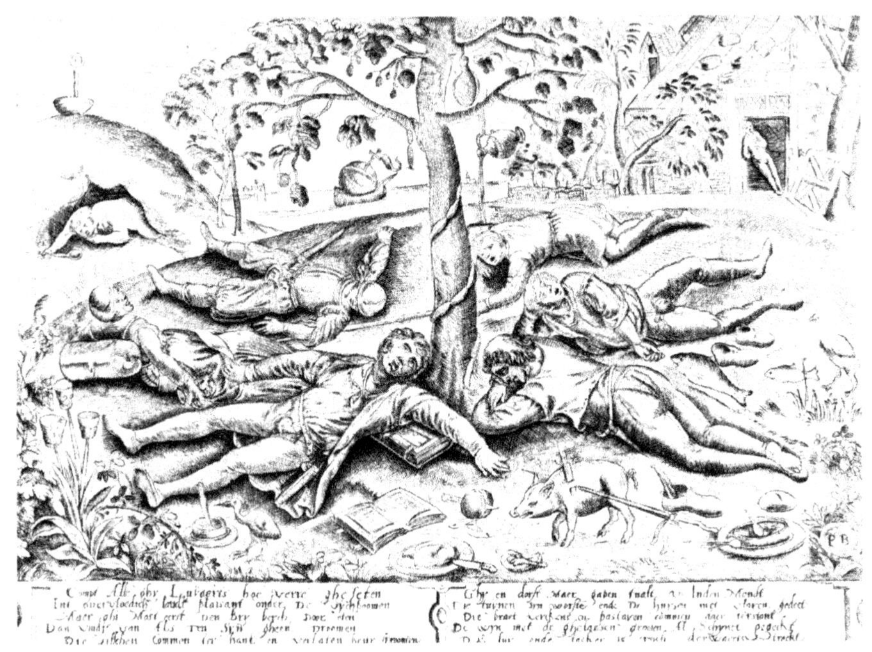

69 Pieter Baltens, *Gluttony* (or, *The Land of Cockaigne*), c 1565. Engraving, 22.3 x 30.5 cm. © Cleveland Museum of Art, Gift of Fitzroy Carrington. Inv. 1925.598

Turning to Bruegel's painting with these complex constituents of the legend in mind, it is clear that this vision of Cockaigne has contemporary social connotations as well as archaic ones. A print by the Antwerp artist Pieter Baltens (1527-84), probably made around 1560, is the main source for Bruegel's image.[54] It shows men of different walks of life lying like spokes around a central tree (fig. 69). The differences between the two designs are significant. Baltens included several details from elsewhere in the popular repertoire, such as the Ship of the World in the background at top left. He tipped the subject towards the theme of sin by winding a string of sausages round his tree-trunk, like the snake in Eden. The image as a whole thus becomes "about" gluttony. Bruegel, on the other hand, streamlined the group of personages and omitted any direct reference to sin. His tree has two breast-like boles on it; a more subtle allusion to desire and appetite.

In his painting, the recumbents are reduced in number. This is a compositional improvement; it also means that the people around the tree are more definitely characterised as three classes of men. They represent a soldier, a peasant, and a cleric; possibly intended to represent a Humanist, this figure gazes up at the sky while the other two sleep. The three are visually equal, as suggested in the legend. This point is often noted. Less attention has been given to the presence of the knight; in this land of plenty, he is lodged differently and separately from the others, mocking the utopic dream of Cockaigne as a place where *there are no peasants or villeins*, and *neither fields nor land are divided*.

When versions of the lore and literature of Cockaigne went into print, the material went into flux, undergoing further updating and reframing to reflect contemporary concerns. In line with the general effort to "reform" popular culture, the printed Dutch versions of *Luilekkerland* tried to moralise the stories and turn them into warnings about gluttony, rather as Baltens did in his print. This development was common to all the European printed versions. It is almost as if the authors felt their all but narrativeless, nonsense-motif material would signify nothing on its own, without this frame; while at the same time they consciously thought of their task in terms of giving the tradition the right kind of moral spin.

In the case of one translation, we have a textual history which enables us to gauge the kind of shifts that could occur in a single such redaction. The author of the 1546 Dutch prose text, living in Antwerp, worked directly from the Hans Sachs German version of the *Land of Cockaigne*. He markedly increased the number of references to money in the Sachs text, and added whole passages about financial transactions of every description, including fines and whores. *Earning while you sleep* had always been a Luilekkerland topos, despite the contradiction of having or needing money in a world where everything is free. The desire for cash, as well as food and drink, infiltrated the Cockaigne dream-world as the market economy became dominant; by the fifteenth century, the trees of the Netherlandish Luilekkerland grew money as well as pies and sausages. But the number of financial references in the 1546 text went well beyond anything seen before. Where Sachs had mentions of how one could earn half-a-crown for breaking wind and a sovereign for an extra loud fart, the Antwerp writer took these as his cue to insert lengthy descriptions of rewards for debtors and loan defaulters:

> People who gamble away all their money are immediately given twice as much in return. Those who are heavily in debt and make no attempt at repayment are banished to a remote corner [and] condemned to eat nothing but roast chicken and white bread... After a year these debtors are free to return from their "prison" and are then absolved of their debts ... they [can] return to the landlord [they had] during their year of exile who will direct them to a couple of trees on which enough money grows to settle their debts [and] resume their profligate lives.[55]

As Pleij remarks, *Time and again [the adapter] loses sight of the prototype by letting the age-old dream of Cockaigne become enmeshed in a series of obsessions typical of the urban culture of late-medieval and early-modern times*.[56]

While we have seen plenty of evidence that Bruegel was well aware of these obsessions in his society, he had already dealt with these subjects in the set of works culminating in the *Dulle Griet* (c. 1562; fig. 35). His *Land of Cockaigne* is not about these problems at all. By the late 1560s Bruegel was treating popular subject matter with greater economy and restraint; even, one might say, treating it more seriously. He moves away from deploying his crowds, to preferring two or three simplified monumental figures as protagonists. In the legends, *Luilekkerland* is crammed with marvels. In the painting, these are reduced to the bare minimum. The focus is on the wheel of dreamers, and the sense of their profound slumber, their bodies weighted to the earth, linked by the gaze of the clerk to the sky. Bruegel's version of the legend is up-to-date in that it satirises the more modern, proto-political emphasis on *Luilekkerland* as a place of social equality. But it is also deliberately archaic, choosing to envisage an older kind of wish-land, focussed solely on food rather than money. This preference for the archaic is our first clear indication of an antiquarian and even nostalgic bent to the painter's interest in folkloric materials.

The Netherlandish Proverbs

No such *gravitas* informs Bruegel's earlier essay in the imagery of the reversed world, the effervescent *Netherlandish Proverbs* (1559; fig. 63). This lighthearted work represents a radical modern approach to a hoary subject. Viewed as an example of an inverted world, the main joke of the *Proverbs* is the new use it finds for the governing principles of *Schlaraffenland* and its lore.

To understand the radical nature of the painting, we can start by thinking once more about the question of distance in the nonsense-tales. It will be remembered that the reversed world is always elsewhere. One must travel in these tales, in order to reach the woods where fish nest in trees or the village filled with foolish inhabitants.

The folklorist Martti Haavio noticed that many of these stories are formally travellers' tales in which the speaker is implicitly a member of the same group as his audience. Thus, a Finnish song *The Wonders of Häme,* begins with the chorus, *Wondrous things I saw in Häme / Pigs were kneading, cows were baking*. A traveller who visits the topsy-turvy village of Näri exclaims on his return, *Wonders, oh wonders, what wonders I have seen!*[57] Haavio therefore argued that the basic premise of the Upside-Down-World was the contrast between the normal order of the traveller and his audience of neighbors, and the wondrous oddities of life as it is lived far away:

> We are therefore dealing with a critical attitude towards unfamiliar conditions and customs, a critique which is expressed in terms of hyperbole and which is marred by prejudice. The narrator's examples are driven to the most remote extremes.... The entire theme of the upside-down world [is an] example of what modern sociology calls the out-group attitude.... [This] consists of deriding and disdaining the con-

ditions which prevail in another group and of stressing the excellence of the conditions which prevail in one's own group. The comparison with the miserable conditions prevailing elsewhere serves to strengthen the conviction that the norms at home are the only ones which deserve full approval. The poems and tales quoted are a clear expression of such ethnocentrism.[58]

Though classifiable into different forms and types, the rich variety of the lore of *Schlaraffenland*, Misnopotamia, et al. would have been experienced as a range of overlapping options in popular and traditional culture.[59] The composers of World-Upside-Down broadsheets chose to select mainly reversals, and to set them in non-specific locales. Bruegel found contradictions and *impossibilia* in folk metaphors which were neither *adynata* nor role reversals; by rendering these contradictions visible, he made traditional wisdom the source of nonsense.

Every commentator realises that it is the panoramic orchestration of the painting, invisibly deploying the technical skills of modern art, that lends Bruegel's *Proverbs* its rare enchantment. The improbabilities of the proverbs are anchored and unified by the realistic town and landscape. The light falling upon this village square comes from the left, while the sun itself is shown at the right, rising or setting over the sea. This sign of cosmic reversal is integrated naturalistically into the landscape, like the "disguised symbolism" characteristic of Renaissance Flemish painting in the previous century.[60] The buildings in the painting are topographically odd, but rendered as plausible three-dimensional forms. The pink arches of the strange pavilion pink arches sprout incongruously from the inn. Each doorway, arch or window frames a proverbial scene or two, and the regular forms of the architecture organize these scenes into readily legible cameos.

An essential part of the humour of the *Netherlandish Proverbs* thus lies in the fact that Bruegel chose to populate his Perverted World with illustrations of the proverbs of his own country. Others before him had produced illustrations of animated proverbs. Around 1550, the old topos of

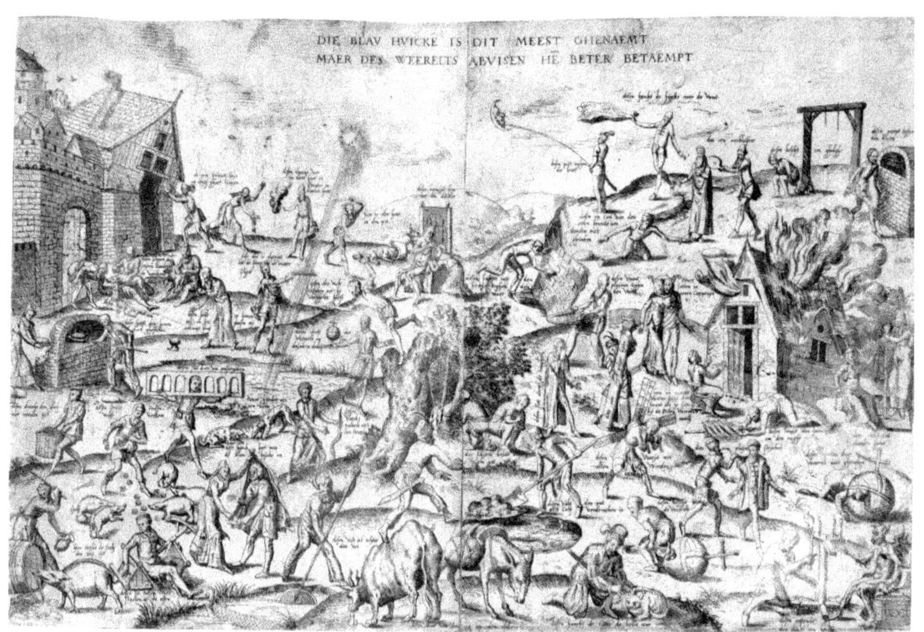

70 Franz Hogenberg, *De Blauwe Huyck* (The Blue Cloak), c 1558. Engraving. Bibliothèque Royale Belgique, Brussels. F 16039 plano R.58b

the mad, upside-down village[61] was made the basis for a print titled *Sloth Village*, a frame for a suite of figures personifying proverbs about laziness. This represents an effort to graft the nonsense village onto the vogue for proverbial lore and anchor the meanings of both within an unambiguously moralising frame. About a year before Bruegel, the painter and engraver Frans Hogenberg (c. 1540-90) made an ambitious print of proverb-figures dotted around the landscape just outside a town: *De Blauwe Huyck* (*The Blue Cloak*) (fig. 70). The print carries as its subtitle, *The Follies of the World*. This work is often cited as a direct source for Bruegel's image: it collects forty separate proverbs, and it singles out as the key-note the blue-cloak proverb of the title, an idea copied by Bruegel.

Though a lesser artist, Hogenberg made a number of engravings after Bruegel and shared his interest in, and talent for, finding visual subjects in popular traditions (cf. fig. 86, Chapter 4). Bruegel's *Proverbs* is the first panel painting to take this subject as its theme. Once again, a movement of subject-matter into the elite medium of panel painting indicates a demographic shift in its audience; different kinds of people are now interested in it. As in *Sloth Village*, a frame for a suite of figures personifying proverbs about laziness, and to a certain extent in *De Blauwe Huyck*, Bruegel sets his proverbs in a topsy-turvy village, with a landscape background. The key differences between his treatment and the print-designs of his predecessors and contemporaries rest in the way he makes his proverbs express the particular nonsense genre of his village. It is the surreal potential of the material which interested Bruegel: the opportunity to tease out the wonderful peculiarities of individual proverbs and make them comment on each other.

This subversion of proverbial material was also a hit at the prevailing rhetoric of contemporary proverb anthologies (paremiologies), literary and visual. The painting takes an implicit stance towards this genre, its motivation, contents and typical structure.

Proverbs, Printing and Paremiologies

The *Netherlandish Proverbs* invites comparison with other paremiologies of the day. As a paremiology itself, the content of the painting has been extensively studied.[62] Scholars have identified all but a few of the proverbs or, more precisely, proverbial phrases,[63] which the picture illustrates. They have speculated also on the meaning of the proverbs taken as a group.[64] As a genre, the florescence of encyclopedic proverb collections begins with the tremendous success of the *Adages* of Erasmus at the start of the sixteenth century.[65] A Flemish proverb tapestry showing some of the same proverbs that Bruegel depicts is a contemporary of the *Adages*, predating the painting by almost fifty years.[66] A written collection made at the end of the fifteenth century lists 803 Dutch proverbs.[67]

Looking broadly at the phenomena, some general motives and causes can be discerned. Some proverb compilers were doubtless inspired by the example of Erasmus' *Adages* to do the same for their own native tongues. People developed interests in the vernacular as an object of study, and in regional description generally. Literate Europeans in the mid-sixteenth century were curious about the traditions and customs of their own regions; the books of Guicciardini and Ortelius are among the more famous of a flood of such works. One of the first folklorish compendia, the volume of old wives' lore known as the *Livre des Quenouilles* (the *Book of the Distaffs*) or the *Evangiles des Femmes* (Bruges c.1475) went through nine editions before 1600.[68]

Collections made after the Reformation was underway have a newly polemical character. An important aim for the reform-minded was to provide morally improving reading matter; recall how the *rederijkers* bowdlerised Ovid for this purpose. This was the goal of a Protestant writer such as Sebastian Franck (1499-1543), whose *Sprichwörter* of 1541 was designed as source of *exempla*, in the medieval sense, for the new reading public. Franck's compilation *reveals a thoroughly conservative outlook and an often Machiavellian cynicism with repeated condemnations of social mobility and the aspirations of the poor... One may suspect that the proverb in general... became at this time a major means of moral indoctrination of the lower classes.* [69] In the long perspective, moralising or expurgated proverb collections of this kind were part of the campaign to purify popular culture, in this case popular speech, and repress its wilder elements. This was done in the name of civility and Christianity and, less attractively, in the interests of continued and enhanced control by administrators.[70] This repression, or cultural reformation was a major shaping force in sixteenth-century society; certainly it shaped Bruegel's attitudes to carnivalesque and folkloric culture.

However, the vogue for paremiologies itself is a complex phenomenon, with ramifications beyond the immediate agendas of the Reformation, cultural or otherwise. As well as being a depiction of the Inverted World, and of a nonsense world, Bruegel's *Proverbs* is a paremiology of the vernacular tongue. This particular genre has a surprising specific historical context: it arises as a cultural response to printing. The advent of mass-produced books meant that the vast body of dicta that had previously passed from mouth to mouth was among the first matter to be recorded (at first relatively haphazardly) in book form. In a study of Renaissance encyclopedic works, Ong explained the value carried by the commonplace tradition:

> The management of commonplace material has a long and complex history.... The source of the tradition [is] ultimately ... primitive oral culture... Memorable sayings from this culture and in an oral culture, expression, and thought as well, not mnemonically patterned for recall to all intents and purposes do not exist from simple turns of expression, epithets, and anecdotes to highly sophisticated aphorisms, gnomes, apophthegms, moralistic fables, and brilliant paradoxes, are woven from the ancient oral store into early writing, which in its most artistic forms continues the oral practice of reiterating and embellishing the already known. In this morass of commonly shared mnemonically structured knowledge there is [no] answer to the question, *Who first said...?* Everybody is quoting everybody else, and has been for tens of thousands of years before the written records began, on purpose and with a feeling of achievement.[71]

People who had never participated in literacy before formed the bulk of the market for the new books. But the manuscript culture of the Middle Ages similarly prized *florilegia*, collections of common knowledge, and reproduced these in large numbers. Their contents *were often presented as "sayings" or orally conveyed narrative and were intended to be recycled through the oral world.*[72] Such anthologies were the cornerstone of education for many centuries. Since Latin was spoken in clerical, diplomatic and academic circles, its mastery demanded the artificial cultivation of ordinary conversational expressions. The expansion of education under the Reformation thus fed the rising demand for commonplace books, which tumbled from the presses in huge numbers.

In elegance and erudition, Erasmus's *Adages* are at the top end of this genre. Humbler compilations such as Ravisius Textor's *Officina* and *Epitheta*, reprinted many times and in copious quantities, filled the schoolrooms and libraries of Europe from 1530 on. These works were used, as is now known, by almost every literary figure of the day, from Rabelais to Shakespeare.[73] The habit of their use assisted in that exuberant piling-on of images,[74] frequently proverbial, which is characteristic of sixteenth-century writing.

The flowering of vernacular paremiologies was a byproduct of the shift from a predominantly oral culture to a predominantly literate one, and printing was the catalyst for this shift. The obvious first step (though actually the last step) in this transition was to record in the new medium *what everybody knows*. On the transitory nature of vernacular paremiologies, writing in 1977, Ong commented:

> Modern cultures emerging from orality into prints and into electronic culture at a rate hundreds of times faster than Europe's and with full consciousness, impossible in early Europe, of the evolution being undergone, are manifesting the same passion as that of the European Renaissance for collecting in print the proverbs and other formulaic sayings on which the earlier oral cultures always relied. Thus, for example, at Onitsha, Nigerian printers have been flooding the popular market with printed collections of proverbial materials....
>
> Like their Renaissance counterparts, producers and users of these popular collections in Nigeria appear unaware that print makes cultivation of proverbs outmoded or even counter-productive, though Nigerian scholars are often exquisitely aware of this fact, as their Renaissance counterparts were not. The novels of Chinua Achebe and of other African writers, counterpoint proverbial materials against growing technological developments, with great literary success.[75]

Printing affected the compilers' attitude to the compilations in other ways. It was in this context that alert moralists like Franck, viewing with disapproval the first compilations of such homespun material, saw a golden opportunity to alter *what everybody knows* for the better. To be fair, Franck and his ilk saw themselves as faced with a torrent of superstitious nonsense. The printing of *what everybody knows* typically meant the production of catch-all works like the *Livre de Quenoilles*, or *Den Sack der Consten*, first published at Antwerp around 1528. It was never out of print for the next century, until it was finally banned by the Antwerp censors in 1621. This is a compendium drawn, as the authors proudly claim in the title, from Latin, Italian, French and German texts. From its pages the reader can discover:

> Remedies against drunkeness, the retention of urine, insomnia, the plague, against flies in meat, sorcery, how to dye hair yellow, clarify wine, test to see if a young girl is a virgin, how to tell if a sick person will recover or not... how to catch fish at night, how to live a long time, how to assure peace in a troubled home, why a horse won't go up a street, how to make your face younger, how to tell the sex of an unborn child.[76]

According to Van Heurck, the book attracted censure because it was specifically addressed *aux jeunes gens, aux jeunes filles de quelque état, qualité où condition qu' ils soient* (young people and young women of any degree). To these the author reveals, among much else:

> why women in summer and men in winter are more inclined to games of love, why men with long hair are more passionate, why a pregnant woman has a big appetite, and how prolonged celibacy engenders a horrible headache and other ills.[77]

One must quote at some length here to demonstrate the most striking characteristic of all these compilations, apart from the rambunctious content: the chaotic ordering of their material. When the printed book was a new medium, it took some time for authors and publishers to develop *visual knowledge retrieval systems*. No one had yet devised logical ways of organising data compilations on the page and within the book — such as indices, tables of content, alphabetical ordering — so that a particular subject could be easily found by eye.

There was equally no attempt to arrange subject matter by sense in these works.[78] Reading through *Den Sack der Consten*, or the *Book of Distaffs* or Textor's *Officina*, the unconscious humour of their juxtapositions is striking. Erasmus made the point, with a different emphasis, in an introduction to the *Adages*:

> I saw that it would be possible to arrange the book in some sort of order, if one followed a scheme of like and unlike, agreement and contradiction, introduced a good many sub-titles and classed each proverb in its place. However, I intentionally avoided this, partly because of a feeling that in a miscellany like this it was better not to have an order, partly because I saw that if I arranged all remarks of the same nature in the same class, the resultant monotony would produce such boredom for the reader as to sicken him (and make him say, *Twice-cooked cabbage is poison*, and *Corinthus son of Jove is in the book*.)[79]

These contexts shed some light on aspects of Bruegel's painting. The artist's relish in chaotic commonplaces can be seen as a more zestful extension of Erasmus's tongue-in-cheek praise of disorder. Bruegel's arrangement of proverbs and folk sayings, not by sense, but by their visual components, is a pictorial equivalent to the encyclopedic jumble of printed collections. The idea of creating visual nonsensical links among the chaotic elements of a paremiology is interwoven with the context of analogous organisational problems and solutions present in the printer's milieu around this time.

As an artist, the problem of organisation naturally struck Bruegel in terms of visual composition. In painting, as opposed to text, materials must be arranged for simultaneous "reading" as a whole image, within (and against) which hierarchies of importance subsequently must be marked, through conventions of scale, relative positions, colour etc. The main challenge for the picture-maker thus lies in making visible relationships among simultaneous elements. Bruegel had considerable experience already in solving issues of what we might call visual information display. His *Virtues* series, in the same year as the *Proverbs*, presented similar kinds of difficulty: the organisation of a wealth of separate pointed enactments on a unified page (see discussion of *Temperance*, fig. 78, Chapter Four).

The subject-matter of the *Proverbs* led Bruegel to a radically naughty solution. He discovered he could produce a kind of unified visual arrangement based on the subjection of his linguistic materials to terms of nonsense. Their sense had to become "non-sense" in order that the presiding "sense" in which the picture is to be read should be visual. The painting is therefore held together by its visual web of resemblances, repetitions, inversions, reversals, etc. — we recall the similar use of such formal chains in the *Dulle Griet*. In the *Proverbs*, because of its subject matter, this subversion of linguistic meaning arguably constitutes a lampoon on didactic paremiologies. This style of humour is commensurate with the interest Bruegel was to show in parodying the emblematic thought of his contemporaries in the *Griet* a few years later. Recognised by Erasmus with irony, the largely unconscious humour of solemnly didactic compilers and paremiologists was unmercifully exploited as an organising principle in the zany, artful juxtapositions of the *Proverbs*.

To understand this artfulness in the painting, one must compare the meaning of the original phrase with the ways in which that meaning is altered by the other images around it. This herculean task has been all but accomplished by Dundes and Stibbe's excellent study,[80] though they stop short of a cultural reading of the picture.

Commonplace Wisdom Perverted in the *Proverbs*

Research on the original proverbs reveals quite precise changes in the cultural hinterland of commonplace wisdom. To say that proverbs and folk sayings are commonplaces means that what they express is both common experience and cliché; more subtly, this means they embody common "philosophy" or common interpretations of experience. What assumptions about the world, then, were embodied both in proverbial idiom itself, and in Bruegel's treatment of it?

As protagonists of proverbial sayings, the inhabitants of Bruegel's painting can be usefully regarded as *artificial persons*;[81] Everyman or Everywoman multiplied many times. In this sense, the painting does not illustrate a specific class of society (as in the *Land of Cockaigne*); all ranks and occupations are represented: rich and poor, labourer and priest, farmer, fisherman, soldier, etc. What is represented in its perverted form here is the adult world of common speech, a point supported by the fact that there are no children in the work. Though there are very few (seven) women represented, those in the foreground play an important role in the painting. At the centre stands the woman with the blue cloak who traditionally gives the painting one of its names.[82] The two old women to the left of her are gossips representing the proverb *one provides distaff for what the other spins*;[83] they may also make a sardonic reference to the old wives whose "wisdom" was represented by the enormously popular *Book of the Distaffs*.

What exactly did this wisdom consist of? The views expressed in popular culture were and are innately conservative.[84] This is largely due to conditions of production in oral cultures; novel opinions and turns of phrase are by definition not proverbial. Radically oral cultures treat change with caution, because it threatens the knowledge-base which is both their collective memory and their symbolic capital. Peasants tended to believe, with some reason, that no change was good change. The rebellious peasants of 1525 saw themselves as protesting against innovations which curbed traditional freedoms. Out of the famous Twelve Articles of Memmingen, eight specifically demanded the retraction of new violations by landowners of customary rights and laws.[85] The peasant leaders understood their demands as supported by the new religion, which seemed to promise the aid of "divine justice" in redressing their wrongs. A foreign merchant, writing from Antwerp a few months after the beginning of the revolt, told his brother that the peasants were acting in the name of Lutheranism, which *advocated a return to the days when fields were without boundaries and individuals had no rights to property*.[86] The keystone idea of a *return* had its roots in a belief in the cyclical nature of time to be found also in more cultivated circles at this date. The word *revolution* originally carried this sense of the wheel of time come full circle, as well as the notion of the World-Turned-Upside-Down. In the case of peasant revolts, the longed-for return was fatefully and tragically sabotaged by the disturbance created in trying to bring it about.

In the decades following the revolts, contemporaries viewed the peasantry with a novel sense of its potential power, and wondered what kept it in its place. Etienne de la Boétie (1530-63) argued that peasants were bound only by *la servitude voluntaire*, and he urged them to rethink their position in a startlingly passionate discourse. De la Boétie likened the peasantry to a body, which could at any time overthrow its tyrannous head; he urged this body to feel the strength of its limbs. The same trope was used by Shakespeare in *Coriolanus* (1608; I. i. 55-127), where the extended metaphor of the body's lower parts rebelling against the head was treated as an instance of impossible reversal.[87]

Like marriage, the social hierarchy at this date was believed to be God-ordained and so not open to criticism. However, the experience of the peasant wars had evidently made this less clearly inevitable by the middle of the century. In 1550, Thomas Wilson argued that overwhelming persuasion was necessary to underwrite the ordering of society:

> for what man I pray you, beeing better able to maintaine himself by valiante courage than by living in base subjection would ... live like an vnderling: if be reason he were not perswaded that it behoueth euery man to live in his own vocation.[88]

Both Wilson and de la Boétie recognised that it was cultural rather than divine forces — dumb acceptance, enlightened persuasion — the world-view, in short, of the peasant — which kept him in his place. Proverbial habits of thought certainly assisted here.

Within this larger political context, people in the lower strata of society, in the towns as much as in the country, did indeed perceive the social world in terms of hierarchies, but these were not simple vertical power structures but networks of affiliations, resemblances, and mobile oppositions, extending through the natural world. People and nature were joined in an interlocking web of invisible relations and magical similitudes. One such "invisible" line we have met already, the *haag* (fence); recall how the levels of this demarcation were revealed in the proverb *Hij kap over de haag* (*he throws his cowl over the hedge*), i.e. he leaves the priesthood. In Bruegel's rendering of this proverb (*Proverbs*, fig. 63; top right), the figure places his cowl on the fence rather than throwing it over; in other words he is depicted as poised halfway in a proverbial action which is firmly binary; rather as if Caesar was to be shown hovering over the Rubicon.

The original proverb provides a glimpse of how divisions between sacred and secular zones were anchored in real-life geography. The *haag* and its ilk were part of a supernatural *habitus* covering all of life.[89] In its midst, along with nature, was the given social hierarchy. The world as a whole was thought of as charged with signs, indicating good or ill fortune, and full of hidden influences, which had to be averted, neutralized, or harnessed. Traditional sayings and beliefs reflect this sense of connectivity. Among much else, the *Book of Distaffs* and similar manuals told the reader how to interpret such signs and what to do about them. *A man on horseback who meets a woman spinning must turn back and take another road, unless the woman hides her distaff in her lap or behind her.* A bird flapping over the house means illness or recovery, depending on its species and the day of its flight. Many bats flying around a house mean that someone will soon set fire to it.[90] The cult of the saints was deeply intertwined with this belief system, as Franck complained in 1534: *who can describe this buffoonery in all its detail? There is no misfortune need or disease that does not have a specific saint for it... For fire, flood, confinement, toothache, the falling sickness and every evil they have not only specific spells but specific saints.*[91]

The body and its products were especially magical, and also vulnerable to contamination: *Crumbs must not be left overnight on a tablecloth, for mice will eat them, and the teeth of the person who uses the cloth the next day will blacken and rot.*[92] It was widely believed that almost anything a pregnant woman encountered would influence the shape, disposition, or sex of her child. As Muchembled explains:

> Popular culture envisions the body not as an independent system gifted with a vital equilibrium, but as part of a whole that is the visible and invisible world. All is in all, and reacts upon all.... The basic idea of this logic is that like either attracts like, or provokes its antithesis.... This principle [is] the "primitive" way of introducing order into the physical world by interconnecting everything. Thus the human body is sensitive to dangers and is in itself dangerous, both for its own possessor and for others. In certain particular instances illness and death, sexuality and excretion, pregnancy and childbirth, the human body is particularly open to contact with the *exterior* by either receiving something from it or providing something to it.[93]

Body products were thought of as imbued with the mysterious vital powers of the body's interior. Urine and excrement in particular belonged to the powerful *zone below the belt*, as the great Russian scholar of the carnivalesque, Mikhail Bakhtin, observed. Urine was, for example, a key ingredient in folk medicine. The acts of producing both kinds of bodily waste are famously fertile sources of folk metaphors.[94] In many cases, Bruegel made use of the extra denotive power this rich vocabulary supplies. The *Netherlandish Proverbs* includes ten explicitly scatological metaphors and several more with the same kind of overtones. Referring to the numbers in the diagram (fig. 63a), the explicit metaphors are:

7 *Hij loopt of hij het vuur in zijn aars.*
He [moves as if he] has fire in his ass.

23 *Hij beschijt de galg.*
He shits on the gallows.

26 *Hij beschijt de gheele wereld.*
He shits on the whole world.

38 *Hij pist tegen de maan.*
He pisses at the moon.

This may also stand for:
Hij pist buiten den pot.
He pisses outside the pot (i.e. he misses the mark).

39 *Daar hangt de pot uit.*
There hangs the [chamber] pot outside. (In other versions of the *Proverbs*, the chamber pot is full.)

47 *Hij veegt zijn gat aan de poort.*
He wipes his ass on the door.

49 *Twee schijten door een gat.*
Two shit through one hole.

50 *Dat hangt als een kakhuis over eene gracht.*
That hangs [stands out] like a shithouse over a canal.

80 *Het is gezond in 't vuur te pissen.*
It's healthy to piss in the fire.

The implicit ones are:

48 *Iemand het gat van de deur wijzen*
To show him the hole in the door.
Dundes and Stibbe suggest that Bruegel has made this proverb into a scatological pun by the gestures of the actors

85 *Hij valt door de mand.*
The man falling through the basket is *cocking a snook* (for the obscene significance of this gesture, see discussion of *Feast of Fools*, Chapter 4)

105 *Hij loopt met zijn hoofd tegen den muur.*
In several copies of the *Proverbs* by Pieter the Younger, the "empty space" under the man *banging his head on the wall* is occupied by a hat with faeces in it. This could be a pun on the double meaning of the word *droll*, which was also Pieter the Elder's nickname; a strange way of tipping one's hat, perhaps. Alternatively, the two images together, read like an acrostic, could refer to the proverb: *Hij doet slecht, die zich in zijn' hoed laat kakken, maar nog slechter, die hem op zijn hoofd zet* (He does badly who lets others shit in his hat, but even worse off is he who puts it on his head).

As well as enacting this playful deconstruction of the magical body, the painted Everymen incarnating these proverbs subvert, comment on, or plainly contradict the messages of their originals; everyone is crossed or paired with proverbs of opposing sense. Some proverbial expressions are themselves based on doubleness: *two fools under one hood* gaze from an inn window; *two shit from one hole* into the river; a woman carrying both fire and water embodies doubleness in another sense.[95] More complex are those where Bruegel condenses two opposing meanings into the same image. Thus, *two fools under one hood* refers to two people who agree on absolutely everything; in Bruegel's image, one face is comic and the other tragic.[96] More commonly, a single figure illustrates more than one metaphor. Frequently, the result is a series of paradoxes. Bruegel appears to have especially delighted in using this technique to reverse the meaning of identical acts or similar binary relations in adjacent scenes. The effects can be seen in his treatment of the scatological metaphors already mentioned.

For example, above the inn sign of the World-Turned-Upside-Down the fool is *getting all the best cards*, that is, he is being favored by Fortune. At the same time, he is *sitting under the knife*, similar to *being under the gun* in modern idiom. The same fool is also one who *shits on the whole world*, and thereby expresses contempt for the current state of things. Fortune and misfortune are thereby balanced in a stalemate. The joke is underlined by the scene in the room behind the fool, where the expression *to take someone by the nose* (to take advantage of someone) is depicted in its variant, *to have each other by the nose*.[97] The final twist in this cluster of images is that the world being shunned in such an earthy fashion by the fool is, of course, not the natural order which the globe would normally symbolize but the Upside-Down world.

Moving round the side of the building, the globe inn sign is matched by the sign of the sickle moon, against which an individual urinates. While *to shit on the whole world* is an act of contempt, *to piss at the moon* is an impossible act, signifying futility. Again, this man standing at the window dramatizes oddly opposing meanings. He *has a toothache behind his ears* (i.e., he is acting in a deceptive fashion). But he urinates on the painted sign of the moon, not at the moon itself, thus turning an impossible act into a possible one. He also appears to be deliberately *pissing outside the pot* in that he ignores the chamberpot hanging outside the window (he is breaking the rules).[98] The pot is itself a proverbial pot which *hangs outside* to denote an inn. Using a chamberpot instead of a jug for this purpose is *an illustration of the topsy-turvy world* [in] *that a vessel used for the elimination of body fluids is in opposition with a jug signifying the incorporation of some form of liquid refreshment. As the world is turned upside down, so is the normal sequence of drinking and urinating.*[99]

The same sort of wit governs the juxtaposition of images on the waterbank to the right of the inn. Moving from left to right, in close succession, we see first an illustration of the fox and the crane inviting each other to dinner. This is a tale of reciprocal trickery, since neither can eat out of the other's choice of dish: *Binary oppositions in the tale include bird versus animal and vertical deep vessel versus horizontal flat plate.*[100] Leaning against the bench where the fox sits is a sieve illustrating the proverb *it holds water like a skimmer*, in other words, not at all. Metaphorically, this refers to a sponger, specifically someone who arrives at dinner in hope of a free meal. To the right of the skimmer stands a man illustrating the belief that *it is healthy to piss in the fire*. To his right, a helmeted man *sits on hot coals*, a metaphor for impatience or nervousness.

Taking these four proverbial images as a sequence, the witty association of forms and meanings between them becomes evident.[101] The joke in the fable of the crane and the fox turns around the difference between two containers. The skimmer is also a sort of container; its connection to the urinating man depends, as Dundes and Stibbe note, on a change in the meaning of not holding water:

> *It holds water like a skimmer* means that it doesn't hold water at all. The failure to hold water in this context is a negative attribute: [whereas for the man] the failure to hold water is considered a positive attribute letting water (urine) go is healthy.[102]

Lastly, this group of images presents two quite different relations between men and fire. In the first, the fire is an exterior thing, which the urinating man can control. In the second, the fire is a metaphor for an internal state, and as such it could be said to control (or burn) the man.

A final example shows Bruegel's mastery of and delight in paradox in the *Proverbs*. The image of the man *falling through a basket*, about halfway down the painting's right side, represents a proverb describing someone who has been caught in his own deceit. An English equivalent would be, *hoist with his own petard*. In a more general related phase, *to get the basket* could mean to be rejected in love or to fail a test.[103] In a late sixteenth-century print showing a *Parody of Courtship*, a blindfolded man and woman pick their mates out of an enormous basket.[104] Here, the man falling through the basket has met with some misfortune, whether by his own fault or not. At the same time, Bruegel has given him a white foot:

> A person with a white foot is a person in favor, a person about whom nothing negative is allowed to be said. A person falling through a basket is a person out of favor. Perhaps it is the knowledge that one has a white foot that enables one to give the Shanghai gesture of defiance, even while falling through a basket.[105]

And indeed, the protagonist of this paradox is *cocking a snook*, like (or even at) his opposite number, who looks from the window just above the fool and the globe of the reversed world. The basket-foot image is a more concise, concentrated version of the elements surrounding the fool. The same set of paradoxes have been tightened.

All this serves, I think, to demonstrate Bruegel's singular attitude towards his proverbial material. None of the other proverb paintings, tapestries, or designs that have so far been uncovered demonstrate anything like this creative duplicity, if one may use the word positively. The best parallel for the kind of rhetorical structuring and inventiveness Bruegel directs towards his proverb can be found in the intricate punning emblems beloved by painters, printers and humanists at this time (see Chapter Two).

Although never applied before to the subject of vernacular language, there are then formal parallels in Humanist art for the kind of visual riddling at work in the painting. Bruegel plays with metaphor in the *Proverbs*, artfully contriving dense permutations of visual and semantic correspondences in a sort of *tour de force* orchestration of punning.

In this way, the painting deviates substantially from its closest immediate contemporary, Hogenberg's grand double-plate proverbs print, *The Blue Cloak* (fig. 70). The inscription on the Hogenberg print varies with different impressions; the most common version runs: *This representation has been called the blue cloak, but it might better be called the follies of the world.* As a framing convention, and general interpretative discourse, as we have seen, the condemnation of folly clearly flourished in Bruegel's society. Hogenberg, Van Heemskerck, Coornhert et al consciously embraced and worked within this discourse, and they certainly perceived their efforts as a contribution to the reform of public life and morals.[106]

Can we assume this was also Bruegel's motivation? Were this motivation to be granted, what would be the consequences for our understanding of the art? If we try to gloss Bruegel's *Proverbs* as a diatribe against *the follies of the world*, we risk effectively collapsing all the precise tensions of likeness and unlikeness, of reversals and balanced contradictions, which give the painting its peculiar character. It may be helpful here to return to the issue of *visual knowledge retrieval systems*, or the lack of them, at this period. It is instructive to set the blanket claims encyclopedists and compendia-compilers made for their own work against the structure and import of what they actually did. For instance, Zwinger's purported goal, in his *Theatrum humanae vitae*, was to treat universal history in terms of the good and evil of mankind. By this,

> he appears to mean in fact a large proportion of everything that has ever happened, since there is little in the world which cannot be related directly or deviously to man, for his good or evil... various sections of his work treat good and bad things of the soul, of the body, good and bad chance occurrences... money, refinement... religious and secular

justice, mechanical skills (in artists, workmen, craftsmen)... his exempla include items such as an account of a betting system to recruit oarsmen for galleys...[107]

A discrepancy appears between the rhetoric of moral purpose (itself rooted in commonplace tradition) – appeal to which is used to knit together a Theatrum or an Anatomy – and the substantive content of the actual works, which can vary wildly in sense and seriousness. The rhetoric of Folly is such a broad stream in sixteenth-century discourse, invoked so often and across such a diverse set of works, as to be less than helpful in distinguishing qualitative differences of approach within the topic. Where Bruegel's art is concerned, his interest in Folly has more specific and deeper foci: the absence, perversion, or inversion of reason. It is not "Folly" in the moralists' sense that interests Bruegel, but madness (in the *Griet*), or non-sense (in the *Proverbs*).

The *Proverbs* is an investigation, then, into the nature of sense, nonsense, and metaphor. The painting visually represents proverbial metaphors as microcosms of the wider world of folk nonsense. The man carrying out the daylight under the sign of the moon is a figure one might meet in Gotham or Malleghem. As Dundes and Stibbe comment:

> [There] is a whole host of folk tales and other folkloristic forms which play upon a fool's literal understanding or misunderstanding of a traditional metaphor ... translating verbal metaphors into pictorial form necessarily involves a literalization process.... All folk metaphors depend for their meaning upon the ability to move from the initial literal image to a metaphorical one. Bruegel in this painting has reversed the direction insofar as he has moved from a metaphorical starting point to a literal depiction of the image. The literalization of metaphor can constitute a ritual reversal, and in this sense, the entire painting represents a scene of countless reversals.[108]

This analysis supports the interpretation advanced by Snow of the "central" proverb in the painting, that of the blue cloak:

> It is especially misleading to assert without qualification that blue is the color of deception and folly. To the degree that it does possess iconographic meaning independent of the context in which it appears, just the reverse is true. Blue is the color of the Virgin (as we can see from her blue cowl in Bruegel's own *Adoration of the Magi*), and it will always connote hope, truth, or faith in a signifying context unless special circumstances subvert its usual associations. In late medieval and early Renaissance love poetry, blue is the color of fidelity.... One suspects in fact that these positive connotations are still operative in the negative meaning that has parasitically subsumed them in the proverb.... Being covered with a blue cloth seems to have become a metaphor for deception or the state of being deceived precisely because *blue connotes truth so emphatically* even in the proverb, that is, blue really signifies not deception per se but the false appearance of truth and fidelity.[109]

The blue cloak, like the fool with the cards or the man and the basket, should also be seen in relation to the metaphors around it, which reinforce its different aspects. The blue cloak signifies that adultery has already taken place, and that there is therefore no point in *filling in the well where the calf drowned*, as the old man is doing in front of the couple. *Roses before swine* wryly comments on the difference between the young wife in the red dress and her elderly husband. The woman is of course placed behind the husband, so he cannot see what she is doing. Behind her, in turn, are the old gossips.[110] Visually and semantically, the cloak is a focal point from which ripples of related meanings emanate in the central square of the picture.

It is, in other words, the structure of meaning in the metaphor which qualifies the blue cloak for its central position in Bruegel's picture. The image is there not to supply a keynote of folly and deception, but because the *manner* of its meaning — to deceive with an appearance of fidelity — is a ready-made instance of the visual subversion of original meanings in this painting. A sixteenth-century audience would have understood both the significance of the cloak and why it meant what it did. Thus Rabelais teases his readers when he wants to use blue to stand for Heaven: *he knows in advance they will all insist it signifies steadfastness.*[111] The colour of fidelity, turned into a cloak of concealment, is the key to the contextual way in which meaning is deviated and comedy generated in the *Netherlandish Proverbs*.

Bruegel's View on the Commonplace Tradition

The "injunctiveness" of the proverb is then not the point of Bruegel's interest in these folk phrases, since the advice value of individual proverbs is everywhere subverted. This subversion sharply distinguishes the *Netherlandish Proverbs* from other paremiologies of the day. How does the artist's attitude to his popular material compare with that of a didactic paremiologist, such as Franck?[112] Many of Bruegel's contemporaries would have seen proverbs as essentially moral *exempla*, and assumed that the point of illustrating or arranging them in compendia was didactic. What this stance has in common with Bruegel's art is that both put their peasant subject matter at a distance. Let us consider how the detachment evinced in the *Proverbs* towards the norms of popular culture fits in the range of attitudes possible among the educated.

Franck's detachment, for example, is that of a prescriptive urban reformer, to be measured by his selection of proverbs praising the status quo: *hunger costs little, anger much, poverty is good for all things, too much justice is injustice, each should behave according to his rank*, and *God helps the strongest.*[113] Bruegel's detachment is pictorial. His painting invites the viewer to occupy an intellectual stance towards the proverbial material; a position of consciousness firmly demarcated from its half-conscious function as a web of similitudes in popular usage. His painted *Proverbs* is like an analytic key to the workings of this web. Seeking precedents for this stance among recorded attitudes, it is clear that, while very many educated people lived and thought, unreflectively, within the web, some were drawn to tabulate its adages, others to study its arcana. Speaking of educated interest in folk thought in the sixteenth century, Thomas comments:

> The intellectual magician [was] stimulated by the activities of the cunning man into a search for the occult influences which he believed must have underlain them. The period saw a serious attempt to study long-established folk procedures with a view to discovering the principles on which they rested [resulting in] attempt[s] to rationalise magical recipes which had no intellectual basis at all.[114]

At the same time, as early as 1433, an ironical attitude to such superstitions was cultivated in the towns. An anonymous cleric's parody of a folk medicine recipe recommends taking *the bile and entrails of a magnet, the lungs of a piece of marble, the nose of a stone pillar ... blood from sand,* all to be ground, cooked, and cooled in various impossible receptacles, then:

> *At Vespers when you are in bed, covered with burning heat or straw to keep you from the rain that follows the midnight wind ... drink it in one breath; and know that if you do this you will find yourself, if you are not lost, healthy ... which was tried one candle-less night, in a dream; and we know not by whom; and was given without worse exchange, in the month of August, Christmas Day, in the morning of nones, three hours after twilight, by a lusty, merry fellow.*[115]

Notable here is the Never-Never Land ending, familiar from the Cockaigne texts. Bruegel's orchestration through semantic subversion, under the rubric of a nonsense world, represents a unique use of satirical traditions of this kind.

The range of means available to reflect on folk culture covers the same spectrum as those used to comment on female nature: straight denunciation and satire. An understanding of the marked difference between the two is necessary to appreciate both the *Proverbs* and Bruegel's scenes of carnival and feast days. Snow argued that a critical method *concerned mainly with correlated similarities* is unhelpful in understanding Bruegel's art because:

> The act of painting was for Bruegel, a rethinking and often a refusal of his culture's attitudes, not an automatic mirroring of them, and ... those attitudes were at any rate such conglomerates of warring differences that they cannot serve as "given" points of reference with which to stabilize his meanings. It may in fact be more fruitful to regard Bruegel's work as a perspective from which to make sense of the ambiguities of its historical context. The paintings, at least, suggest that this is how he himself regarded his enterprise.[116]

This seems to me especially true with regard to Bruegel's essays in popular culture. This outline has not by any means exhausted the interpretative possibilities of *Luilekkerland*, but in terms of carnivals and dreams, some broad conclusions are now possible. In the *Land of Cockaigne*, carnivalesque imagery and dream are unambiguously joined; at the same time, all nonsense, reversed, perverted and topsy-turvy lands are types of dream- or spirit-lands. The *Fat* and *Lean Kitchens* can also be regarded as linking carnival feasting and lenten starvation to the surreal exaggeration of the dream. The *Proverbs* itself is an analysis of folk-culture that also renders it surreal. The painting could well be described in Snow's phrase, as representing *conglomerates of warring differences*. The hundred cameos of the *Proverbs* make explicit levels of contradiction implicit in commonplace expression, by realising the latent surrealism of proverbial phrasing. Condensation and displacement are precisely the processes employed. Some distance down this path lies Freud's interest in how proverbial associations and "ready-made" metaphors from popular tradition continued to populate his patients' dreams. Freud noted in 1913,

> how great an influence folktales have upon the mental life [of] children. In some people a recollection of their favourite tales takes the place of their own childhood memories: they have made the tales into screen-memories.[117]

The imagery and discourse of folk nonsense acts as a collective dream-scape in a number of different senses. Like *Cockaigne* itself, the Topsy-Turvy world is quite literally a collective dream-tradition: a tradition of semantic games which determine the boundaries of what all agree is sense. Proverbial expression uses these same sense-nonsense rules to represent sane versus insane behaviour. Striking metaphors and modes of expression in popular discourse have long roots in oral culture; in elite culture, they recur in the precepts of Classical memory systems for rhetoricians, where colourful and unusual images were advised as easiest to remember. The context of the "visual information retrieval system." In his *theatrum* work, the *Inscriptiones* of 1565, the Antwerp doctor Samuel Quicchelberg (1529-1567) argued that a visual model of the world (a collection where the cosmos was represented by objects) would have to express all the correspondences, similitudes and resemblances possible among its elements.[118] The mental stance inherent in such a proposition is not dissimilar to Bruegel's. We will find the same interest in *conglomerates of warring differences*, and the *ambiguities of historical context* in the next series of images to be discussed, Bruegel's scenes of feasts and carnivals.

Notes to Chapter 3

[1] W. J. Ong says he has *accumulated a collection of several dozen such titles*; "Commonplace rhapsody: Ravisius Textor, Zwinger and Shakespeare," in R. R. Bolgar, ed., *Classical Influences on European Culture, A. D. 1500-1700* (Cambridge,1976), 114, n. 4. On *theatrum* spectacles and pageants, R. Bernheimer, "Theatrum Mundi," *Art Bulletin* XXXVIII (1956), 225-47. As early as 1560-1, Jean Bodin planned a "synthetic philosophy of the universe," finally published as *Le Theatre de la Nature Universelle*; on this idea see H. Haydn, *The Counter-Renaissance* (New York, 1950), 197. On the idea of the *kunstkammer*, see E. Scheicher, *Die Kunst- und Wunderkammern der Hapsburger* (Vienna, 1979); on Quicchelberg, E. M. Hajos, "The concept of an engravings collection in the year 1565; Quicchelberg, Inscriptiones vel Tituli Theatri Amplissimi," *Art Bulletin* XL (1958), 151-6.

[2] For the critical history of this word and the works it has been applied to, see R. Falkenburg, *Joachim Patinir. Landscape as an image of the Pilgrimage of Life*, trans. M. Hoyle (Amsterdam-Philadelphia, 1988), 66-72.

[3] Described by E. S. Siple, "A Flemish Proverb Tapestry in Boston," *Burlington Magazine* LXIII (1933), 23ff.

[4] On Cock's topographic prints, see T. A. Riggs, Hieronymous Cock (1510-1570): *Printmaker and Publisher in Antwerp at the Sign of the Four Winds* (New York, 1977), 280-8, 379-83. The Four Winds sold prints of the Sieges of Parma (1551), of Sienna (1555) and of Ostia (1555), and Views of Lyons, Florence, Antwerp etc. See also Chapter Four, "The Mapping Impulse in Dutch Art," in S. Alpers, *The Art of Describing. Dutch Art in the Seventeenth Century* (Chicago, 1983), 119-68.

[5] In the Galleria Doria, Rome; puffs of smoke can be seen near the ships.

[6] Koeman, 24.

[7] On substitutes for tapestry, see G. Gluck, "Die Darstellung des Karnevals und der Fasten von Bosch und Bruegel," *Gedenkboek A. Vermeylen* (Antwerp, 1932), 264.

[8] Koeman, ibid.; c.f, L. Voet, *The Golden Compasses* (Amsterdam, 1969), II, 242-3; who explains why these maps, though less expensive than tapestries or murals, were still by no means cheap.

[9] The information that follows is drawn from L. Wauwermans (1895), *Historie de l'ecole cartographique belge et anversoise du XVI siecle* (Amsterdam, 1964), 112-7, and C. Koeman, *The History of Abraham Ortelius and his "Theatrum Orbis Terrarum"* (Lausanne, 1964), 11-21 both of whom give copious extracts from the Ortelius family documents, letters, and other sources. The sparse, but important, evidence linking Bruegel and, more securely, Plantin to Ortelius via professions of friendship is given in A. E. Popham, "Pieter Bruegel and Abraham Ortelius," *Burlington Magazine* LIX (1931), 184-8, and M. Rooses, "Ortelius et Plantin," *Bulletin de la Societé de Geographie d'Anvers* 5 (1880), 350-356. This is by now so well known that there seems little point in presenting it again; interesting also is R. Boumans, "The

Religious Views of Abraham Ortelius," *Journal of the Warburg and Courtauld Institutes* 17 (1954), 374-7; now see also A. Hamilton, *The Family of Love* (Cambridge, 1981), ch. 4 (65-82) on the Antwerp Humanists.

[10] Koeman, 25.

[11] J. Wegg, *Antwerp, 1477-1559* (London, 1916), 323

[12] Koeman, ibid.

[13] *Multa pinxit, hic Bruegelius, quae pingi non possunt guod Plinius de Appelle. In omnibus eius operibus intelligitur plus semper quam pingitur,* from Ortelius's *Album Amicorum*, after 1550 (MS. Pembroke College, Cambridge).; C. De Tolnay, *Pierre Bruegel L'Ancien* (Brussels, 1935), 61.

[14] See D. Kunzle, "Bruegel's Proverb paintings and the World Turned Upside Down," *Art Bulletin* LIX (2) (1977), 197, n. 1, for a comprehensive list of authorities connecting the tradition and the painting up to that date, starting with De Tolnay, 21. Kunzle's own article was reworked as "World Upside Down: the iconography of a European Broadsheet Type," in B. Babcock, ed., *The Reversible World: symbolic inversion in art and society* (Ithaca, 1977), 39-94 [hereafter referred to respectively as Kunzle (1977a) and (1977b)]. See also J. Bruyn's criticism of Kunzle's analysis: letter in *Art Bulletin* XL(4) (December 1978), 741-2; and Kunzle's reply in the same issue. The World-Turned-Upside-Down is structurally very similar to the world of carnival; each may be analysed anthropologically in terms of the other, cf. E. Le Roy Ladurie, *Carnival at Romans*, trans. M. Feeney (New York, 1979), 191f and passim. Folk Upside-Down motifs are treated in M. Haavio, "The Upside Down World," *Studia Fennica* 8 (1959), 209-21; for their uses in carnivalesque popular prints in the service of the Reformation see ch. 6 of R. W. Scribner, *For the Sake of Simple Folk. Popular Propaganda for the German Reformation* (Cambridge, 1981), 148-189.

[15] Bruyn, 741-2.

[16] L. Lebeer, "De Blauwe Huyck," *Gentsche Bijdragen, Tot de Kunstgeschiedenis* VI (1939-40), (Amsterdam, 1941), 161-229; cf. M. De Meyer, "*De Blauwe Huyck*. La Cape Bleue de Jean van Doetinchem, datée 1577," *Proverbium* 16 (1971), 564-575.

[17] Of course sixteenth-century people did not consider this material in terms of rigid iconological categories but it does seem, as Bruyn points out, that there were two fairly distinct forms which later intermingled. On the relative "looseness" of iconological and emblematic images in the Netherlands at a later date, see Alpers, 229-33; on the development of the World Upside Down after Bruegel's period, see W. A. Coupe, *The German Illustrated Broadsheet in the Seventeenth Century* (Baden-Baden, 1966), I, 197-223.

[18] Kunzle (1977a), 198.

[19] Ladurie, 191.

[20] Kunzle (1977b), 41-2.

[21] Quoted in Haavio, 210. E.R. Curtius identified this as the earliest extant example of *adynata* in the Western tradition in his *European Literature in the Latin Middle Ages*, trans. W. R. Trask (London, 1953), 94-104.
[22] Curtius, 95.
[23] Kunzle (1977b), 60.
[24] Kunzle (1977a), 198, n. 1.
[25] Ladurie, loc. cit.
[26] Kunzle (1977b), 61-4; however, this is a misleadingly oversimplified summary of the peasant wars, e.g.: *Some peasant leaders quite seriously demanded that all ranks among men be abolished forever*, 64. Such a demand, unrelated to (for instance) radical reformed beliefs in the imminence of Christ's Second Coming, was highly atypical of the peasant leaders' stated aims. See e.g. S. Ozment, *The Age of Reform, 1250-1550* (New Haven, 1980), 272-89, esp. nn. 61, 63, 66-75; documents in G. Strauss, ed., *Manifestations of Discontent in Germany on the Eve of the Reformation* (Bloomington, 1971), 144- 69; for millenarian revolts, N. Cohn, *The Pursuit of the Millenium*, rev. ed. (New York, 1970) ch. 11-13, esp. 252-61.
[27] H. Grant, "The World Upside Down," in R. C. Jones, ed., *Studies in Spanish Literature of the Golden Age, Presented to Edward M. Wilson* (London, 1973), 113, opts for this "safety-value" theory, while Kunzle does not (see note 26 above). The explanation, I think, has a validity in the narrower field of broadsheets that becomes more strained when applied to carnivals and other festive protests (see Chapter Four).
[28] From F.J. Child, *English and Scottish Popular Ballads* V, 173, n. 299; quoted in Grant, 10.
[29] Ibid.
[30] Kunzle (1977b), 78. This is Aarne-Thompson type 1930, in their index of folktale motifs, A. Aarne and S. Thompson, *The Types of the Folktale: A Classification and Bibliography*, 2nd rev. ed. (Helsinki, 1961). See E. M. Ackermann, *"Das Schlaraffenland" in German Literature and Folksongs. Social Aspects of an Earthly Paradise, with an Inquiry into its History in European Literature* (Chicago, 1944), ch. 1-3, esp. 42-9 on sixteenth-century examples; also 51-5 on the Dutch versions; these texts reprinted 151-3, 162. See also Haavio, 212, on Schlaraffenlands as a type of Never-Never Land; and in general on the world wide distribution of the theme, 210-3. Many of these tales refer to linguistic but "non-visual" and therefore unpaintable reversals or nonsenses.
[31] On Gotham and Schildburg, see T. Wright (1865), *A History of Caricature and of the Grotesque in Art and Literature*, ed. F. K. Barasch (New York, 1968), 232-6; on Mallegham, H. A. Klein, *Graphic Worlds of Pieter Bruegel the Elder* (New York, 1963), 167.
[32] Wright, 232.

[33] Haavio, 212.

[34] *Accurata utopiae tabula, das ist der neu-entdeckten schalck-welt oder des so offt benannten, und doch nie erkannten schlaraffenlandes neu-erfundene lächerliche land-tabell... durch authorem anonymum*, published by Johann Baptist Homann, Nuremburg, 1716, with accompanying book by Johann Andreas Schnebelin (d. 1706); see Dieter Richter, *Schlaraffenland. Geschichte einer populären Phantasie*. (Cologne, 1984).The Homann 1716 version of the Schlaraffenland map is online at the Universitätsbibliothek, Karl-Franzens-Universität, Graz, http://ub.uni-graz.at/sosa/karten/schlaraffia.html. This same map was later published in atlases and other books; e.g., a Seutter atlas at the Royal Library, Stockholm.

[35] See n. 30 above. On the Dutch sixteenth-century examples of this theme, see H. Pleij, *Dreaming of Cockaigne: medieval fantasies of the perfect life*, trans. D. Webb (New York, 2001), Part 2, 33-86. Still fundamental are: L. Lebeer, "Le Pays de Cocagne (Het Luilekkerland)," in *Miscellanea Erwin Panofsky* (Brussels, 1955), 199-214; P. Burke, *Popular Culture in Early Modern Europe* (New York, 1978), 82-4, 190; C. Ginzburg, *The Cheese and the Worms: The cosmos of a sixteenth-century miller*, trans. J. and A. Tedeschi (London, 1980), 81-6, 162-4; more generally, see F. Graus, "Social Utopias in the Middle Ages," *Past and Present* 38 (December, 1967), 3-19, and the classic study by G. Boas (1948), *Essays on primitivism and related ideas in the Middle Ages* (New York, 1978).

[36] Ginzburg, loc. cit.

[37] M. Hodgen, *Early Anthropology in the Sixteenth and Seventeenth Centuries* (Philadelphia, 1964), 192; cf. 193-4.

[38] For these accounts, ibid, 167, 182-4.

[39] Quoted in Ginzburg, 83.

[40] Ibid., 84.

[41] On the painting, with many illustrations of its fifteenth- and sixteenth-century precedents (especially prints), Lebeer (1941), 161-229; on the subject in popular prints, M. De Meyer, *De Volks- en Kinderprent in de Nederlanden, van de 15e tot de 20e* (Antwerp-Amsterdam, 1942), 432-40; the earliest version of the World-Upside-Down seems to be an Amsterdam picture sheet from c. 1580 (cf. Ackerman, 55, n. 2).

[42] This detail is now almost completed abraded in the painting itself but it can be seen in early photographs: e.g. P. Bianconi, *The Complete Paintings of Bruegel* (New York, 1967), no. 47, 108.

[43] This text is a prose version after Hans Sachs, reproduced in Ackerman, 162-5, who discusses its history, 54-5.

[44] Ackermann, 54.

[45] See H. R. Patch, *The Other World according to Descriptions in Medieval Literature* (Cambridge, Mass., 1950).

[46] Ackermann, 53, 153.
[47] R. Muchembled, *Popular and Elite Culture in France, 1400-1500,* trans. L. Cochrane (Baton Rouge, 1985), 17.
[48] Ibid., 16-17; on famine and high grain prices in 1557, see C. Verlinden et al., "Price and Wage Movements in Belgium in the Sixteenth Century," in P. Burke, ed., *Economy and Society in Early Modern Europe. Essays from "Annales"* (New York, 1972), 73f.; on the impact of death and famine in general, see the chapter, "The Centuries of Hunger" in R. Tannahill's *Flesh and Blood* (New York, 1975), 35-55, esp. 47f.
[49] K. Thomas, *Religion and the Decline of Magic* (New York, 1971), 5-6.
[50] Cited in Tannahill, 103-7, esp. 106. One of the stories reported by Tannahill was told to me as a child, with the names and century of the event changed.
[51] Pleij, 142.
[52] E.g. Ginzburg, 82-4; Ackerman reproduces a Flemish "Weaver's Song" of Cockaigne, recorded in the nineteenth century, called The Land of Wealth, 166-7. This is of some interest because weavers as a group had a long history as a spearhead of sedition and social change. The attribution of the Land of Wealth to a Weaver is perhaps ironical; a comment on the Utopian impossibility of the radicalism associated with the group. Possibly songs of this kind reflect the urban craftsmen's radicalisation of a folk idea. Social factors loom large among the regional variations that shaped the different tones of sixteenth-century Reversed Worlds. The popularity of the broadsheets in Germany reflects increased social tension in the years following the Peasant Wars. Bruegel and his public did not live under such harsh feudalism.
[53] *Capitolo, qual narra tutto l'essere d'un mondo nuovo, trovato nel mar Oceano* (Modena, c. 1550); Ginzburg, 83-4.
[54] The Baltens print has been viewed both as a predecessor and as an imitator of Bruegel's *Cockaigne*; L. Lebeer (1955), 204-14; most authorities now agree it predates Bruegel's image by about seven years; N. M., Orenstein, ed., *Pieter Bruegel the Elder: Drawings and Prints*, exh. cat. Museum Boijmans Van Beuningen-Metropolitan Museum of Art (Rotterdam-New York, 2001), 256-257; on the print tradition used by Baltens, see R. H Frank, "An Interpretation of *Land of Cockaigne* (1567) by Pieter Bruegel the Elder," *Sixteenth Century Journal* XXII (2) (1991), 303-8.
[55] Pleij, 84. Pleij, 81-5, discusses the case of Text G, which he reproduces entire, 438-42.
[56] Ibid., 83.
[57] Haavio, 210.
[58] Ibid., 213. Cf. Muchembled's comments on the prevalence of xenophobic attitudes in the sixteenth-century, 125-6.

[59] On modes of folk-composition see Burke, *Popular Culture*, 113-48, esp. 136f.
[60] On which see L. Benjamin, "Disguised Symbolism Exposed and the History of Early Netherlandish Painting," *Studies in Iconography* 2 (1976), 11-24.
[61] Hogenberg's *Blue Cloak* and the *Sloth Village* prints are discussed in W. S. Gibson, *Pieter Bruegel* (Oxford, 1977), 65-71; cf. Lebeer, "De Blauwe Huyck," 182f. Bruegel takes 40 of Hogenberg's proverbs and adds 67 of his own.
[62] A full list would be huge; for works up to 1930, see the bibliography in E. Michel, *Bruegel* (Paris, 1930); then the bibliography of "Proverb Interpretations" in R. Delevoy, *Bruegel* (Geneva, 1959), 138-9; literature cited in A. Dundes and C. Stibbe, "The Art of Mixing Metaphors. A Folkloristic Interpretation of Pieter Bruegel the Elder's *Netherlandish Proverbs*," *F.F.Communications*, no. 230 (Helsinki, 1981), 70-1. In discussing the *Proverbs*, the diagram in our fig. 63a is based on their numbering scheme.
[63] See A. Taylor, "Proverbial Phrases not Proverbs, in Breughel's Painting," *Proverbium* 3 (1965), 57f.
[64] E.g. Gibson, 65-6; representative is F. Grossman, *The Paintings of Bruegel* (London, 1955), who divided the *Proverbs* into two groups: *First, those that show the absurdity of human behaviour, common sense upside down... But as prudence is a virtue, folly can be a sin. And so the second type illustrates proverbial sayings characterizing wicked and sinful behaviour*, 191.
[65] Erasmus produced six revisions of his first edition (1500), which itself went through twenty-seven reprints. On the *Adages* and its publishing history, see the introduction in M. Phillips, *The "Adages" of Erasmus. A study with translations* (Cambridge, 1964), x-xi; and, more broadly, the essay on "Proverbial Wisdom and Popular Errors," ch. 8 in N. Z. Davis, *Society and Culture in Early Modern France* (Stanford, 1975). Among those who have compared contemporary paremiologies with Bruegel's painting are: W. Fraenger, *Der Bauern-Bruegel und das deutsche Sprichwort* (Munich, 1923), on Rabelais's courtyard full of proverbs from 1564; C. G. Stridbeck, *Bruegelstudien. Untersuchungen zu den ikonologischen Problemen bei Pieter Bruegel d. A. sowie dessen Beziehungen zum niederlandischen Romanismus* (Stockholm, 1956), 172-3; 180-2 on Erasmus and Sebastian Franck; also, Kunzle (1977b), 72-7, on the proverb generally and idem., (1977a), 199-202, on Franck and attitudes to peasants.
[66] Siple, 27-8.
[67] *Proverbia Communia* (Delft, c.1495), ed. with commentary by R. Jente (Bloomington, 1947).
[68] For this work, see Muchembled, 70-1.
[69] Kunzle (1977a), 199, thereby concludes that the painting defines *proverbial folly as the particular province of the peasant*, loc. cit. This is not far from the more traditional conclusions of Grossman (see n. 64 above).

[70] This thesis, as expounded by e.g. Muchembled and Burke, is now a commonplace of the history of popular culture, though opinions differ on whether or not the ends justified the means. Famous studies taking opposite viewpoints are N. Elias's *The Civilising Process: the History of Manners* (New York, 1969) and M. Foucault's *Discipline and Punish. The Birth of the Prison*, trans. A. Sheridan (New York, 1979).
[71] Ong, 102.
[72] Ibid., 103. Ong's argument informs this next part of the discussion.
[73] On Rabelais, see, for instance, M. Screech, "Commonplaces of law, proverbial wisdom and philosophy: their importance in Renaissance scholarship (Rabelais, Joachim du Bellay, Montaigne)," in R. R. Bolgar, ed., *Classical Influences on European Culture* (Cambridge, 1976), 127-34; on Shakespeare, see T. W. Baldwin's mammoth *William Shakespeare's Small Latin and Lesse Greeke* (Urbana, 1944), esp. I, p. 714; II, 366, 414-16, 455, 506, where, as Ong notes (121, n. 2), the poet's direct use of Textor's book, or one like it, may be traced.
[74] F. P. Wilson, "The Proverbial Wisdom of Shakespeare," in W. Mieder and A. Dundes, ed., *The Wisdom of Many. Essays on the Proverb* (New York, 1981), 174-89, gives instances of "clustering" proverbs, especially in Shakespeare's early writing, and links it to the boom of vernacular proverb books from around 1546.
[75] Ong, 108, n. 1; E. Obiechena, *An African Popular Literature: A Study of Onitsha Market Pamphlets* (Cambridge, 1973); B. Lindfors, "Perverted Proverbs in Nigerian Chapbooks," *Proverbium* XV (1970), 62 (482)-71 (487). On printing in general, E. Eisenstein's main points can be found in her "The Advent of Printing and the Protestant Revolt: A New Approach to the Disruption of Western Christendom," in R. M. Kingdon, ed., *Transition and Revoulution. Problems and Issues of European Renaissance and Reformation History* (Minneapolis, 1978).
[76] *Den Sack der Consten, Wien Latine, Italianschel, Fransche, duytsche ghecopuleert, Om te vermaken die beswaerde sinnen. Ende voor hem dye gheerne wat nyeus hooren* (Antwerp, 1528), trans. E. H. van Heurck, *Les Livres Populaires Flamands* (Antwerp, 1931), 118-9.
[77] Ibid., 120.
[78] Ong, 104-5, 109-11, 117; extraordinary lists of contiguous subjects from Textor and Theodore Zwinger (the Basel encyclopedist, 1533-88) can be found on 99-100, 113.
[79] In Phillips, 202.
[80] See n. 62 above.
[81] As usefully defined in J-C. Agnew, *Worlds Apart: The Market and the Theater in Anglo-American Thought, 1550-1750* (Cambridge, 1986).
[82] The structural resemblance of the woman in the blue cloak to the persons of the *Vices* and *Virtues* is striking; they are also alike in that her significance is in a sense the pivot of the painting.

[83] Dundes and Stibbe, no. 93, 5.
[84] As Burke for example argues, 173-7.
[85] See texts in Strauss (as for n. above). I quote from Ozment's survey, 272f.: *Peasant demands had traditionally centred on hard economic and political issues and were argued on the basis of ancient or customary law and natural human rights... Changes in the exercise of lordship... gave birth to the Twelve Articles."*
[86] Quoted in Wegg, 160.
[87] Etienne de la Boétie, *De la servitude voluntaire* (c. 1552-3); *The Politics of Obedience: The Discourse of Voluntary Servitude*, trans. H. Kurz, intro. M. Rothbard (1975; Montreal-New York-London, 1997). In his essay *On Friendship*, Montaigne lied about his deceased friend's age in order to make this highly seditious essay seem the work of a very young man, and hence more forgivable.
[88] Thomas Wilson, *The Arte of Rhetoric* (London, 1550), in S. Greenblatt, "Murdering Peasants: Status, Genre, and the Representation of Rebellion," *Representations* 1 (February, 1983), 28-9, n. 32.
[89] On the *haag* proverb, Dundes and Stibbe, no. 56, 39. On the connections between supernatural and natural worlds and their invocations, see M. Douglas, *Purity and Danger. An Analysis of the Concepts of Pollution and Taboo* (London, 1966), 58-93; Thomas, 25-50; Muchembled, 81-4.
[90] The *Book of Distaffs*, Day III, no. 5; Day V, nos. 4, 20; Muchembled, 73.
[91] Sebastian Franck, *Weltbuch* (Augsburg, 1534), 134b, in M. Baxandall, *The Limewood Sculptors of Renaissance Germany* (New Haven, 1980), 55-6.
[92] Muchembled, 81.
[93] Ibid., 71-2.
[94] M. Bakhtin, *Rabelais and his World*, trans. H. Iswolsky (Cambridge, Mass., 1968), 148, 175, 356, 369-436.
[95] Ibid., no. 41 (Two in one hood), no. 49 (Two in one hole), no. 88 (carrying fire and water).
[96] Ibid., no. 41; this analysis is taken from Dundes and Stibbe, 33.
[97] Ibid., no. 28 (Fool gets the cards), no. 25 (shits on the world), no. 26 (has him by the nose); a variant of this last (they have each other by the nose is present also in the *Feast of Fools* print.
[98] Ibid., no. 38 (pissing at the moon and outside the pot); no. 37 (toothache behind the ears).
[99] Ibid., no. 39, 32.
[100] Ibid., no. 77, 49; the fable of the fox and the crane is in Aesop; cf. Aarne-Thompson tale-type no. 60.
[101] Ibid., no. 79 (like a skimmer), no. 80 (healthy to piss in the fire), no. 82 (sits on hot coals).
[102] Ibid., 50.

[103] Ibid., no. 85, 51-2.
[104] *Parody of Courtship*, late sixteenth century, in the Bibliotheque Royale, Brussels; illustrated as fig. 30 in S. Hindman, "Pieter Bruegel, *Children's Games*, Folly, and Chance," *Art Bulletin* LXIII (3) (September, 1981), 467. Hindman tentatively assigns it to Pieter van der Borscht IV.
[105] Dundes and Stibbe, 16-7; 52-3 n. 86; cf. Marijnissen, 41, n. 39.; A. Taylor, "The Shanghai gesture," *F.F.Communications*, no. 166 (Helsinki, 1956), 10, 59, discusses Bruegel's print of the Feast of Fools as the earliest example of this gesture he could find.
[106] Hindman, 447ff., summarises the salient points that underpin the theories about Folly in this and other works.
[107] Ong, 113.
[108] Dundes and Stibbe, 67-8; referring to Stith-Thompson folk-motifs, J2470, J2490.
[109] E. Snow, "'Meaning' in *Children's Games*: On the Limitations of an Iconographical Approach to Bruegel," *Representations* 2 (Spring, 1983), 44-5.
[110] Dundes and Stibbe, no. 94 (the blue cloak); with additional bibliography on the colour blue given on p. 56; no. 96 (roses before swine); no. 107 (filling the well when the calf has drowned).
[111] Paraphrased slightly from Snow, 44; he is referring to *Gargantua and Pantagruel*, Book I, ch.9, "Gargantua's Colours and Livery;" cf. also ch. 10, "Concerning the significance of the Colours White and Blue."
[112] Bruegel has often been compared to Humanist moralists; Coornhert and Sebastian Franck are invoked frequently in Stridbeck; for on misleading analogies with later emblematists like Pieter Roemer Visscher and Jacob Katz, with a critique of Stridbeck, see Snow, 36ff.
[113] Kunzle (1977a), 199, n. 6.
[114] Thomas, 229; on the general prevalence of belief in magical healing, 178-211.
[115] Muchembled, 156-7.
[116] Snow, 53.
[117] S. Freud, 'The Occurrence in Dreams of Material from Fairy-tales' (1913), in *Zeitschrift*, I (1913); trans. J. Strachey (1925); *Collected Papers* IV (London, 1948), 236-43.
[118] Hajos, 151-6; on early modern theories of similitude, see J. C. Westerhoff, "A World of Signs: Baroque Pansemioticism, the Polyhistor and the Early Modern Wunderkammer," *Journal of the History of Ideas* 62 (4) (October 2001), 633-650.

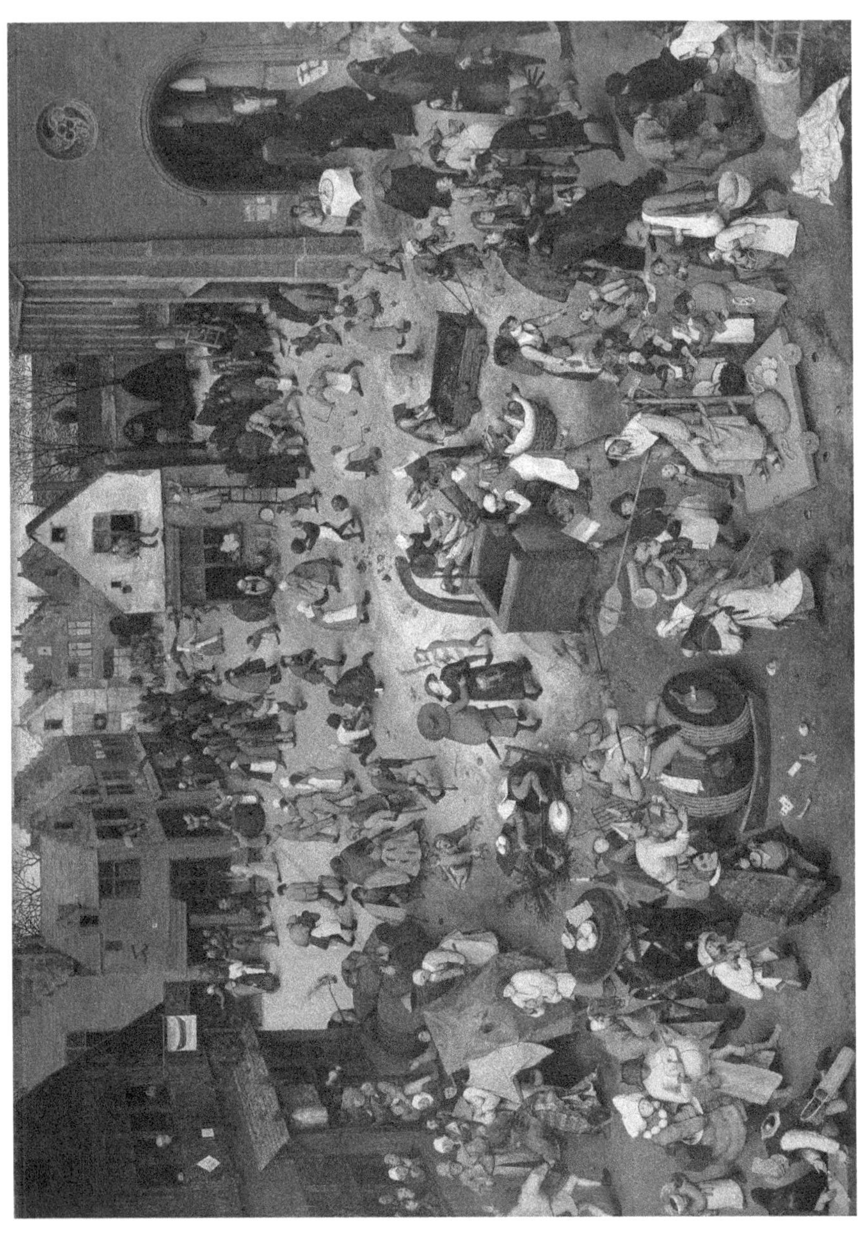

71 Pieter Bruegel, *The Battle Between Carnival and Lent*, 1559. Oil on panel, 118 x 164.5 cm. Kunsthistorisches Museum Wien oder KHM, Vienna. Inv GG 1016

4 Forms of Carnival and the Carnivalesque

Introduction

In 1559, Bruegel made a *theatrum mundi* picture depicting a *Battle Between Carnival and Lent* (fig. 71), set in a village square. The painting is thronged with figures acting out traditional feast-day customs, rather like the characters in the *Netherlandish Proverbs*. The subject of festivals and carnivalesque imagery evidently fascinated Bruegel. By the mid-60s, he had developed two distinct modes for addressing this theme: "ethnography" and fantasy. In terms of fantasy, he worked carnivalesque material into the surrealism of [the] *Dulle Griet* (1562), and continued to develop the material in this surreal direction in a number of later prints. The *Proverbs* in the same year (1559) as the *Carnival and Lent* could be said to combine the two approaches in a "one-off" solution. But the "ethnographic" approach came first: Bruegel was studying folk customs along with folk language, and he evolved his ideas about the phantasmogoric potential of carnivalesque imagery after undertaking these studies. Like the *Proverbs*, the *Carnival and Lent* seems delightfully observational; it is frequently cited as an authoritative source for historians of folk and popular culture. However, Bruegel was studying a moving object. Arguments about carnival traditions and customs were the focus of massive cultural and political debate, acted out in the streets, law-courts and printing houses throughout the century. Why exactly this aspect of culture was singled out for this kind of attention at this time and place is the subject of this chapter. The narratives of Bruegel's *Carnival and Lent* present a complex meditation on these debates, and this meditation is the best starting point to see why the "ethnographic" approach moved in the direction of fantasy, and how Carnival came to be represented in terms of bad dreams.

A Note on Carnival

The institution of Carnival and the quality of the carnivalesque have, since Bakhtin's analysis of Rabelais,[1] been recognised as key characteristics of popular culture in the early modern period. But the application of these terms to the practice and meaning of festivals in the regions of Renaissance Europe raises certain problems. In tribal cultures, Carnival is fully magical, and, one might say, fully religious. In northern Europe, the main carnivalesque feasts could and did coincide with religious anniversaries such as Christmas, but carnivalesque activities were marginal to the official Christian meaning of these occasions, as educated commentators and idealistic clergymen regularly pointed out throughout the Middle Ages. Sometimes the carnivalesque fête was adjacent in time to a religious feast — thus Carnival proper came before Easter. Sometimes the religious feast gave little more than its name to an essentially pagan revel — thus the summer revels of St. John's Eve in Flanders or Midsummer's Night in Britain. In the case of the Flemish *kermis* (or *kermess*; literally, *kerk-mis*, or *church mass*), a celebration of the "birthday" of the local church which came to have both Christian and carnivalesque components.

The tension between religious and secular feasts was made explicit by the rise of a powerful lobby in the second half of the fifteenth century which, one hundred years later, had won many influential people to the belief that religious festivals should be purged of their carnivalesque components and that the more purely carnivalesque fetes were pagan and irreligious practices which should be actively discouraged, if not banned altogether. We have already touched on some aspects of this phenomenon, to which Peter Burke gave the name of the *Triumph of Lent*.[2] Different festivals came under this kind of attack and underwent changes in form in different countries at different times. The Feast of Fools was among the first to succumb; this feast celebrated no Christian anniversary and its relation to official religious meanings was exclusively parodic.[3] In addition, during

Bruegel's lifetime the theatre fully separated from its original context as part of carnivalesque celebrations to become an independent institution.

All the elements of the Triumph of Lent were manifest in the visual and political culture of mid-sixteenth century Antwerp. The situation there was exacerbated by increasing tension between the Flemings and their Imperial governors and by the controversies of the Reformation. Festival clubs became fora for dissent, initially by protesting government efforts to silence or control their traditional activities. Dissent, moreover, was often expressed in carnivalesque imagery and style; the battles of the Reformation were waged as much with paper as with weapons.[4] Ballads, broadsheets and popular prints typically appropriated the familiar formulae of Carnival to score sectarian points.[5] The forces of Lent, the party of cultural reform, took over much carnivalesque material for their own, at the same time toning it down considerably and decrying the excesses of the original festivals.

It seems best to approach the significance of Bruegel's paintings and prints of festivities by first exploring this landscape of Carnival and the carnivalesque, to reconstruct how these festivals were produced and experienced in and around Antwerp at this time. In this way, some surprising facts come to light about Bruegel's use of this material. For Bruegel omits as much as he represents. He is far from being a transparent recorder of the scenes around him, and his ideas concerning the significance to be drawn from feasts are, once more, tangentially removed both from those who disapproved of, and those who desired to purify, popular fêtes.

"Primitive" Carnival

Modern understanding of the institution of Carnival comes initially from anthropology. "Primitive" festivals are intimately connected with time. They mark the passage of the year, and time itself, during such passages, is different from ordinary time. The anthropologist Edmund Leach described the structure of the festival in terms of Van Gennep's analyses of rites of passage.[6] Leach proposed a pendulum view of the flow of time in traditional and festive cultures. Time, he says, flows normally during the year up to the time of the festival, then runs briefly in reverse. When the festival concludes, time returns to its normal flow. The first stage of the festival separates it from normally experienced time; the second, or *liminary* phase, when time runs backwards, is marked by role reversal. The third and last phase of reintegration moves forward into profane or ordinary time:

> there is an explicit connection between this three-part time flow and Carnival themes... there are also three types of ritual behavior encountered on festive occasions: masquerade, role reversal, formalities. The *masquerade* is a striking expression of the breaking away from ordinary or profane time, the entrance into fictive or sacred time. Rites of role reversal signal that the transition period has begun, indicate that the human group serving as the societal base for the festivities is momentarily turned upside down... This is the divine instant of communication between the revelers. The group is "fused" in a mutual state of role reversal. *Formalities*, finally... coincide with the entrance into Phase C, the repressive, or... *redressive* stage. The emphatic accentuation of normative dress... in effect signifies the act of compulsory return to the rules governing ordinary time... [there is an] alternating swing between life and death (from the beginning to the end of the year), then from death to life (during the brief moment of resurrection provided by Carnival).[7]

In the "primitive" or fully magical Carnival, then, the period of altered time is characterised by reversals and inversions, and by rituals which include the donning of special costumes. What purposes did these festivals serve? Van Gennep thought they were essentially rites of passage: the passage from one season to another in terms of the cycle of the year, or in terms of human life-stages. So rites of passage mark the transition from winter to spring, or the passage of an age group through puberty to full adulthood, or both together. Thus: *When women in certain parts of Africa usurped the clothing, weapons, or tasks of the "superior" males and behave in lewd ways... these rituals are intended to increase the chance for a good harvest, or to turn aside an impending natural catastrophe.*[8] Such rites can take many forms, such as symbolic funerals, or the likening of a male initiate to a menstruating woman.[9] The argument goes that such transitional stages are *highly dangerous to society. The disaggregation of established values they involved could easily be followed by a destructive dissolution of those values.*[10] For this reason, they are ritualised and controlled by society, through initiation ceremonies or carnivals.

The second great argument about Carnival addresses the issue of its "function." Like the imagery of a World-Upside-Down broadsheet, carnivalesque festivals can be regarded as a sort of safety valve for the society and the individual:

> Rites and ceremonies of reversal are ultimately sources of order and stability in hierarchical society. They can clarify the structure by the process of reversing it. They can provide an expression of and a safety valve for conflicts within the system. They can correct and relieve the system when it has become authoritarian. But, so it is argued, they do not question the basic order of the society itself. They can renew the system but they cannot change it.[11]

Turner expressed the subjective aspect of this: *All social classification of living humans means existential deprivation for those classified, and the resulting loss and frustration are compensated for by symbols of reversal such as... transvestitism and clowning.*[12]

Role reversals therefore express in costume and mask either a release of dangerous antisocial feelings or psychological compensation for the normal disadvantaged status of the actor. Ideally, as Van Gennep, Gluckman, and Turner follow Durkheim in believing, the function of Carnival as a religious ritual is strongly reconciliatory.[13] Since all rituals are based on common social goals, a society participating in rituals of this kind is in fact continuously reintegrating itself. Functionalist models in general can be criticised for assuming an overly static, conservative view of society as constituted of "mechanisms" for the maintenance of the status quo. However, in the case of Carnival, the functionalist tendency to downplay the importance of change may be countered by taking seriously the dangers of the changes at the festival's heart, as do contemporary tribal peoples, and, in a slightly different sense, as did late medieval people.

Turner makes an important point about the tensions inherent in a highly divisive society which require such dramatic reintegrations on a regular basis. Remember that Bruegel's society was also held together through general belief in a "web" of supernatural connections running through the world, a world teaming with spirits who controlled illness, misfortune, and crop failure. This magical attitude towards the natural and social universes is, as Mary Douglas pointed out, by late modern standards, the source and product of a paranoic mindset.[14] When anything can be a sign (or omen), the life-world becomes charged with potential significance. Among tribal peoples, with tenuous control over their immediate physical environment, the sense of being constantly threatened is a part of life. This too is magically combated and given expression at Carnival time, when not only social but natural categories may be reversed or switched. Thus humans dress as animals, or in suits of leaves, like the European Wild Man.[15]

"Primitive" Carnival could thus also be regarded as a formalised recognition of the fact that society itself is a fragile and fluid phenomenon, capable of disintegration and requiring to be periodically remade. Anthropological research on carnivalesque ritual illuminates the new signifying potential imparted to traditional feasts as religious and political institutions became fluid in the course of the sixteenth century. Among the many differences between primitive and early modern carnivals, the persistence of certain components is striking. The individual's experience of the festival as *compensatory*, the relation to seasonal time, the forms of masquerade, the involvement of age sets or youth-groups; all these classic aspects of the "primitive" model are found in carnivals and carnivalesque festivals in the first half of the sixteenth century. The magnification and elaboration of carnivalesque forms and images from the common store at this period paved the way for further dissociation of, and new uses for, the material altogether. By the end of the century, carnivalesque imagery had undergone strange mutations *en route* from festival practice to fantasy. Bruegel's art was a central arena of this transition.

Early Modern Carnivals

> The square... of the *common people*, the square of bazaars, puppet theatres, taverns, that is, the square of European cities in the thirteenth, fourteenth, and subsequent centuries... in earlier times itself constituted a state... it constituted the entire state apparatus with all its official organs. It was the highest court, the whole of science, the whole of art. The entire people participated in it.[16]

In the northern British Isles and in the Netherlands, the full range of Carnival activities was split between the December-February festivities and the summer carnivals of May Day and St. John's Eve:

> Carnival did not have the same importance all over Europe. It was strong in the Mediterranean area... and at its weakest in the North... probably because the weather discouraged an elaborate street festival at this time of year. Where Carnival was weak, and even in some places where it was lively, other festivals performed its functions and shared its characteristics... elementary *particles* of ritual wandered from one festival to another. Most obviously *carnivalesque* were a number of feast days which fell in December, January and February... the Carnival period in its widest sense.[17]

I am therefore using the term *Carnival* (capitalised), in its broadest sense, as a catch-all term for the shared characteristics of the winter and summer festivals, where the structure and imagery of reversal was a main ingredient. Bruegel, living in Brabant, would have experienced Carnival in terms of several discrete festivals during the year. So what were these festivals like, how were they organised, and what meanings did they convey?

The most far-reaching difference between Carnival in the context of tribal and early agrarian societies and Carnival in the society of Bruegel's generation, or that of his parents and grandparents, was the element of choice. Because Carnival for early modern Europeans was no longer part of *la vie sérieuse* (the serious, spiritual life),[18] each individual could in theory control his or her level of participation in the event. In this sense, the sixteenth and the twenty-first centuries are similar:

> Option is dominant – people do not have to act invertedly; some people, but not all people, choose to act invertedly at Carnival, which unlike a tribal ritual can be attended or avoided, performed or merely watched... For it is a genre of leisure enjoyment, not an obligatory ritual. It is play, not work.[19]

For Gluckman's student Turner, this change alone was sufficient to justify two different terms for the central festival moment of "self-forgetfulness." Turner suggested we should reserve the word *liminal* for *ritual proper,* and apply a derivative term, *liminoid,* to the corresponding quality invoked through *modern symbolic inversions and expressions of disorder.*[20] Large consequences follow from this development. First, notice that the emerging category of the liminoid is an aesthetic and psychological quality. Second, the replacement of the liminal with the liminoid signals a diminishment in the "seriousness" of Carnival. This means a weakening of the ritual controls which limit the disorder of Carnival and protect the status quo from the impact of its reversal. The liminoid event differs from liminal Carnival in these key respects:

> [These] symbolic genres... play with the factors of culture... just as tribesmen do when they make masks, disguise as monsters, combine many disparate ritual symbols, or invert or parody profane reality. But they do this in a far more complicated way, multiplying genres of

artistic and popular entertainment and, within each allowing authors, dramatists, painters, sculptors, musicians, folk-singers, and others lavish scope to generate not only weird forms but also models highly critical of the status quo.[21]

This analysis closely corresponds to Bakhtin's vision of Carnival in the time of Rabelais as a *second life* or *second culture* of the people.[22] Turner suggested that the more liminoid the festival, the more it becomes a sort of forum for the *conscious* expression of dissent. Its function as a safety valve is eroded. Early modern festivals were midway between the archaic tribal form and contemporary multiplicity; recorded Renaissance carnivals manifest a mixture of the old and the new, the liminal and the liminoid, the collectively non-cognitive and the consciously topical.[23] Following Bakhtin, this proto-political aspect of Carnival has aroused much scholarly interest, prompting the view that early modern carnivalesque imagery and performance were becoming vehicles for social and change.[24]

However, it is equally important not to underrate the power of non-cognitive components. These were unreflective, in that they were not reflected on by the individuals involved — who carried on "doing what had always been done" — and collective, in that non-cognitive thought itself changes as a result of changing common experience. Early modern non-cognitive culture — as we have seen — expressed itself in many areas of life now considered the province of the unconscious: sexuality, demons, food fantasies, spirit worlds etc. This was the culture which, during Carnival, could be projected outward again as grotesque or reversed images, whose style of distortion resembled dreams. Increasing fascination with, and conscious awareness of, these components explains the presence of much that is blasphemous and obscene in the imagery of Renaissance carnivals. The Reformation itself released a torrent of such imagery. As deep-seated institutions were overturned by deep-seated grievances, so the imagery of Carnival became the imagery of polemic, and society itself could indeed seem fragile and fluid. This also meant that non-cognitive beliefs underwent cognitive recognition. The capacity of Bruegel and other artists to manipulate carnivalesque material in art appears to be predicated on "re-cognitions" of this kind. On a more general level, heightened awareness of shifts in consciousness and consensus explains the strength of acts of authoritative repression. As the cultural playing-fields shifted, we can assume also that increasing numbers of individuals felt that "coming out" of Carnival was tantamount to enforcing a personal repression of desire.

In terms of the form and function of imagery, early modern carnivals contained both "fixed" reconciliatory elements (the oldest, relatively unchanging plays and costumes), and a more flexible tradition of improvising inversions and reversals from topical material. In a "fixed" play such as *Orson and Valentine* (fig. 74), about a wild man and his brother,[25] the protagonists carried traditional carnivalesque meanings with a set ending. In a carnivalesque folk punishment such as the charivari, the victim was placed on an ass, then led through the streets while serenaded by *rough music* (made with kitchen utensils etc.).[26] In this case, the form remains fixed; the identity of the protagonist and the nature of the "crime" were mobile elements.

Quite different in conception were the various *ommegangen*: religious processions, city anniversaries, state occasions, and often all three combined.[27] These were really modern urban festivals, full of new inventions (like the Giant Antigonus) and Humanist allegories. Yet, they had carnivalesque accretions; the media of float and *rederijker* drama were similar; while the content presented was novel, the playwrights worked with some traditional costumes and characters, particularly in their farces.[28] The Feast of the Circumcision in February was an important *ommegang,* which coincided with Carnival.[29]

Rederijker productions for these festivals could certainly involve social comment in the modern sense, but it seems that this was the aspect of the carnivalesque that least interested Bruegel as an artist. *Rederijker* activities appear in his works as an attribute of virtue (as in *Temperantia*, fig. 78) or as a manifestation of old traditions (such as the *Feast of Fools*, fig. 76) in new forms; like *old wine in new bottles*. As in his interest in children's games and proverbial metaphors, it was the traditional and "incidental" aspects of Carnival — the "fixed" old plays and customs — which first caught Bruegel's attention as an ethnographer. As the 1560s progressed, he became more drawn to the surrealist potential of masks and guising, feast and fast — the less clearly content-filled "marginal" ingredients of the carnivalesque.

One important factor here was the odd paradoxical relationship between the magical elements in secular festivals and in Christian custom and ritual. "Elective affinities" between the two were manifested clearly during Carnival, and this became a source of acute anxiety in the decades leading up to and following the Reformation. Early modern carnivals were inherently unstable to begin with, because of their uneasy relations with the official religion and its tenets, but also because carnivalesque inversions or parodies were of necessity drawn from the given categories of the normal world. Disturbances in these inevitably surfaced through the sounding board of the festival, to be commented on in carnivalesque imagery.

The festivals were thus barometers of social change in more senses than one. The choice of materials to be inverted or "switched" and the manner in which these switches are presented reveals information about the condition of society. More specifically, the strength of the authorities' reactions to particular parodies reveals the vulnerability of the parodied institutions. And it is not just parodies — criticisms of government — that aroused violent opposition to Carnival; masks, fancy dress and feasting also came under attack. To pose the question of why apparently neutral — or at least non-propagandistic — forms should be worth banning involves considering evidence about the non-cognitive aspects of Carnival. These aspects inform several works by Bruegel where the artist explores degrees of rationality and irrationality in terms of controlled and uncontrolled carnivalesque forms: *Temperance* (1560; fig. 78), the *Feast of Fools* (1559; fig. 76), and the *Fall of the Magician Hermogenes* (1565; fig. 77).

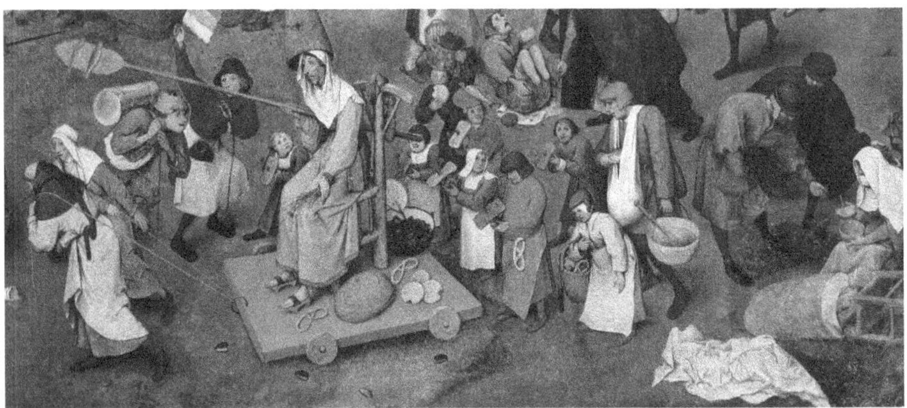

71a Pieter Bruegel, monk and nun, Lady Lent, almsgivers, detail, *Battle Between Carnival and Lent*

In Bruegel's *Battle between Carnival and Lent* (fig. 71a), there are three figures in clerical costume. The man at the left, dressed as a priest, is a carnival mummer, there to officiate at the wedding of the *Dirty Bride*. He walks alongside the other performers of this old Carnival play, next to the Inn of the Blue Boat in the wake of Prince Carnival. The status of Prince Carnival and Lady Lent, like that of the *monk* and *nun* who pull Lent's platform, is less clear. This ambiguity derives from the deliberate conflation, basic to the humour of the painting, between the allegorical personifications of art, and the enacted *personae* of the festival. Whether they are players or personifications, the meeting between the figures of Carnival and Lent has the same significance: a representation of one sort of festive time giving way to another. But the figures of the monk and the nun remain ambiguous in a different sense. They are either genuine members of the church, present attributes of Lent, or they are mock clergy, pulling a mummer dressed as Lent, in a carnivalesque mock tournament.

This doubleness of meaning reflects and comments on a real discomfort. It seems that from the mid-fifteenth century onwards, the civil authorities found it increasingly difficult to distinguish between the old festive practice of mock ritual and mockery of ritual. Mock baptisms, mock tournaments, mock weddings, mock coronations: all of these were a traditional part of Carnival, which in some larger towns would be organised by mock abbeys, whose head sometimes had the title of Abbott.[30] Folk art represented this as a World-Turned-Upside-Down theme; thus a parade of animals, including a fox in a surplice, hold a mock-funeral procession for the hunter they have just caught (fig. 107). But in the sixteenth century, authoritative opinion turned firmly against mock-church ritual during Carnival:

> During the 15th century, parodies of the clergy [were] frequent in Carnival celebrations, especially through dressing up as monks and nuns in Carnival processions. In Cologne in 1441, a mock reliquary was carried through the streets, accompanied by a Carnival puppet with an asperger and banner, in mockery of a religious procession. In Frankfort in 1467 17 citizens were punished for parodying a religious procession. In Augsburg in 1503 several youths carried around a goat lying on a cushion bedecked with ribbons, which was baptised by a mock priest. Such parodies were usually regarded with good humour by authority, although the more blatant cases of irreverence were punished. Towards the end of the 15th century, however, there was an increase in prohibitions of Carnival mummers wearing monks' and nuns' costumes, of mockery of church customs, and of wearing masks during Carnival.[31]

Both parodies and prohibitions multiplied during the Reformation. In Zwickau, in 1525, there was a mock hunt of monks and nuns through the streets lasting two days. That same year, the citizens of Naumberg held a Carnival procession with a mock pope, cardinals, and bishops, *while figures dressed as monks and nuns danced merrily*.[32] The tone of such demonstrations was most virulent in towns which were later to accept the Reformation, but they occurred elsewhere also. At the carnivalesque festival in Goslar in February 1530, the people sang that *the cathedral is a whorehouse*, and then staged a mock Palm procession with a mock emperor on an ass and a mock

Pope on a sow.[33] A similar spirit imbues Bruegel's use of a charivari procession — here a punishment for sexual transgressions — in his print of *Luxuria* (fig. 15). Humans and hybrids mix indiscriminately behind the offender. The procession is led by a bagpipe player in a monk's habit.[34]

This imagery is connected in part to traditional rituals of rebellion. In as far as the priesthood constituted a genuine landed class at this time, its parodies in folk discourse can be interpreted as efforts to express discontent by symbolically overturning authority.[35] This is commensurable with the Bakhtinian view that carnivalesque *mockery, mimicry, and parody of official life, culture and ceremonies seeks to overturn the official world by exposing it to ridicule. The process is twofold: exposure of the official world, and robbing it of its dignity.*[36] The power of the clergy could be attacked through the demystification of its rituals.

Such explanations assume that the impetus for increasing performance of carnivalesque mock ritual was more or less consciously political. Certainly, disputes over the machinery of sanctity were central to the struggles of the Reformation. But early modern Christian ritual was also an efficacious religion, in Durkheim's sense of the word. It is anachronistic to assume that the sole purpose of the Church's rituals was to support the power of the Church. The majority of the population may well have perceived Church ritual as a form of magic;[37] nevertheless it was viewed as an effective and benign magic. It follows from this that different kinds of religious parodies, in the context of Carnival, reveal different levels at which the communal consensus that produces effective ritual had been disrupted. So, for instance, the increasing popularity of mock baptism performances, of the kind previously cited, in the liminoid time of Carnival, is a symptom of disturbance in the assumptions and beliefs underlying baptism itself. Since a good deal is known about the history of this particular ritual, we can test that hypothesis against the wider history of baptism in this period.

Baptism was the principal rite of passage by which parents enrolled their child into church and community.[38] The strength of collective investment in this custom can be seen in the ferocity with which Anabaptism was crushed in Germany and the Netherlands. Anabaptists challenged the principles of customary infant baptism on the grounds used so often by Luther: that it lacked biblical foundation. In 1525, the Swiss authorities responsible for charging the first Anabaptists in Zurich executed them on the grounds that they were a menace to the community; by their own lights, their analysis was quite correct. By 1529, opposition to Anabaptism had reached hysterical proportions; Charles V responded by reviving an ancient Justinian law against re-baptism, making it a capital offence throughout the empire.[39] The Council of Trent issued stringent regulations to ensure that newborn children should be baptised as quickly as possible.

The power ascribed to the rite can be gauged by the way the consequences of its omission were imagined. Theologically, unbaptised souls could not be saved; dead newborns were condemned to Limbo because they had not been shriven of original sin. In folk belief, the dead souls of unbaptised children were an especially feared species of *revenant* (a returning spirit, or ghost). They were thought, for instance, to follow in the train of the Wild Hunt (see Chapter 5). In Duerr's words, *unbaptised children had no normal status, they belonged neither to the realm of the dead nor to that of the living... [they were] always potentially "lost"... Baptism therefore was of the utmost urgency.* Since children born dead could not be baptised, every imaginable resort was used to create an illusion of life in the still-born (warming the body by the fire, blowing air into the lungs).[40] It is notable that Luther, while admitting the lack of clear biblical precedent, retained the custom for reasons of social cohesion.

The appearance of mock-baptisms then, in the collective world of Carnival imagery, is not surprising. The satirical use of this mock-rite — by selecting, for instance, a goat as its subject — shows that the imagined community to which the rite gave passage was now more doubtful. In a divided Christendom, there was no longer one automatic sense of community. By applying baptism to an animal, the meaning for humans is thrown into doubt and its effect is reversed.

Increasingly, and with good reason, the authorities feared anything that smacked of an inversion or reversal of church ritual. Such demonstrations manifested themselves most visibly in the context of carnival, where the half-submerged, shared structures of people's minds were expressed in collective imagery. Fears of this kind eventually engendered the ultimate such inversion, the powerful myth of the Black Mass, a dire imagining taking shape in the minds of late sixteenth-century Inquisitors.[41] As we saw in Chapter 2, the imagery of the Sabbat was created in this way, from distorted memories of women's festivals.[42]

The fight against mock-ritual, and against Carnival as a whole, can be seen in the long term as part of a growing tide of opinion against the *second culture*. Prohibitions on mock-ritual provide information about the standing of the Church, because mock ritual is dependent for its impact on real ritual. It was therefore only going to be perceived as funny, tolerated in a good-humoured fashion by the guardians of the *status quo*, as long as the status and power of the real ritual that it is based on remained inviolate. It must be thoroughly understood that there will be a *return to formalities* after Carnival. In the groundswell of religious disillusion formalised most completely in the Reformation, such a return to efficacious, revitalised ritual was by no means clear.

Turning back to the painting, the level of mockery of the clergy in the *Carnival and Lent* can be gauged more closely. Mock ritual is involved in that a mummer-priest is present to perform a mock marriage ceremony in a carnival play. The wedding itself is a form of humourous inversion, a parody of a traditional prosperous Flemish wedding featuring a "dirty bride" and her lumpish groom. Though the actors perform in the street and are shown as part of carnival's train, they are part of a separate entertainment. The fine line separating a Carnival mock-priest from an

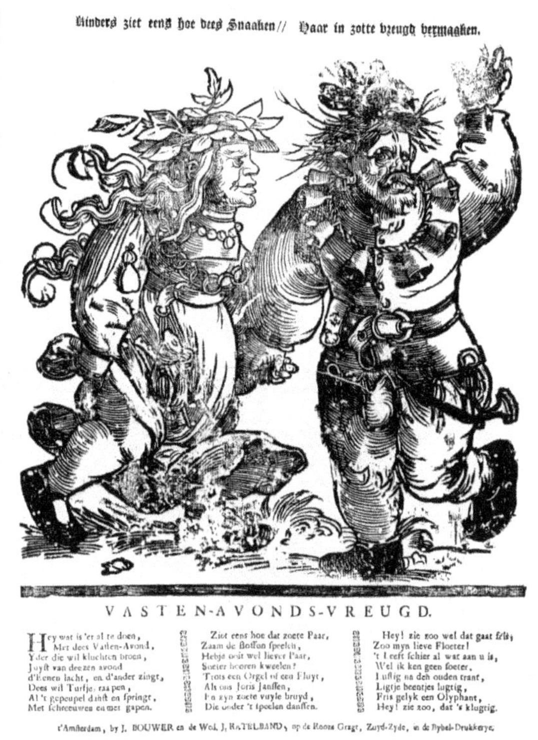

72 Anon, *De "Vuile Bruid"* (*The Dirty Bride*), Flemish. Sixteenth-century woodcut on later broadsheet. Rijksprentenkabinet, Rijksmuseum, Amsterdam. Afb. 172. Coll. v. Kuyk

actor playing a priest in a Carnival play is further emphasised by the actor's whited face.[43]

The Dirty Bride and her mate were the subject of at least one popular print (fig. 72), where they are seen dancing together, the bride crowned with leaves, their clothes dotted with bells and carnival favors.[44] By contrast, Bruegel's woodcut explicitly presents the subject as a theatrical performance (fig. 73). This scene is almost identical to its equivalent in the *Carnival and Lent*: the same rickety tent, the same costume for the bride, the same number of mummers. In carnivalesque fashion, the bride wears a

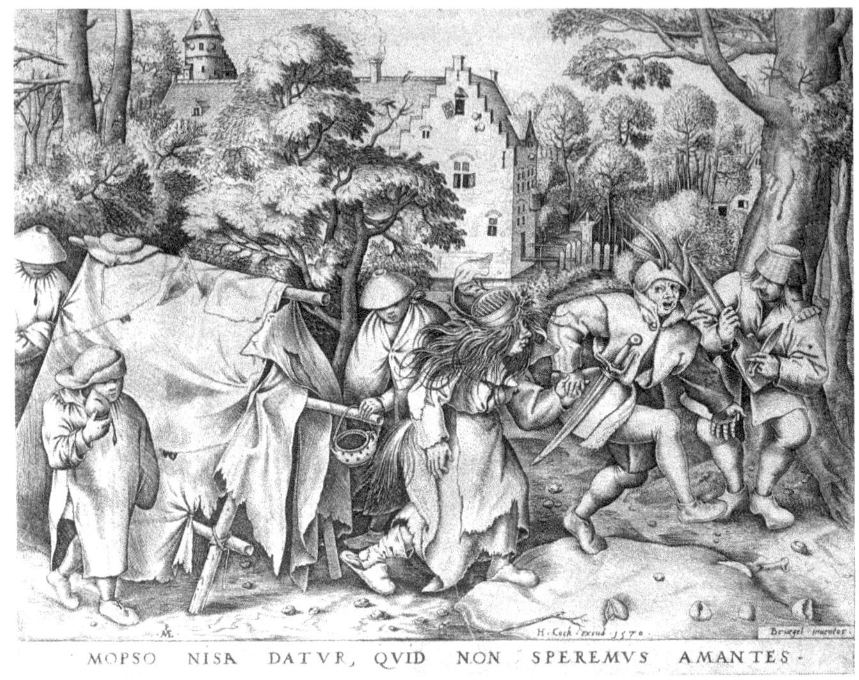

73 Pieter van der Heyden, after Pieter Bruegel, *The Dirty Bride*, designed c 1566, published 1570. Woodcut, 22.2 x 28.9 cm. Bibliothèque Royale Belgique, Brussels. SI 8723

colander instead of a crown, and the musician, complete with false nose, holds a paddle and a knife for his instrument. Other actors wear the bowl-like hats and improvised cloaks that characterise several of Bruegel's mummers. A figure in this costume appears next to the tent in the painted version.

Figures dressed in this style appear in Bruegel's two depictions of the masquerade of *Orson and Valentine*: in the painting of *Carnival and Lent* and in the 1566 woodcut (fig. 74). In the print, mummers hold out collection boxes to the audience at the windows. In the *Carnival and Lent* another such mummer appears, with a whitened face. In the *Dirty Bride*, the odd hatched effect on the faces of the two-hatted mummers may represent makeup; it may also represent the thin netting worn over the face by mummers in imitation of the shrouds of the dead. The boy by the tent carries a small

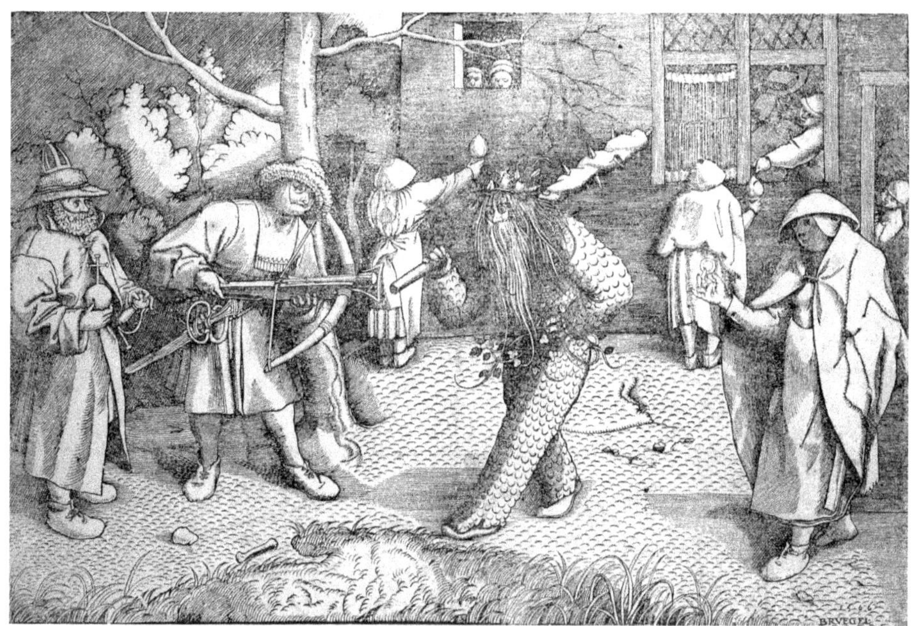

74 Anon, after Pieter Bruegel, *The Masquerade of Orson and Valentine*, 1566. Woodcut, 27.4 x 41 cm. Bibliothèque Royale Belgique, Brussels. S 11 24127

collection box (the distinctive shape of this piggybank is familiar from the *Moneybanks and Strongboxes*, fig. 52). Bruegel thus makes it quite clear that his mock priest in the painting is in carnival costume.[45]

While the ambiguity of Lent's team is in the *Carnival and Lent* is important, when this is placed in the context of other church parodies, simply dressing up as a monk or a nun by this time counted as very gentle mockery. Clerical costume were a customary part of carnivalesque processions, in keeping with the marked late-medieval tradition of anti-clerical humour, but, as we have seen, by this date parodies of the rituals of their real-life equivalents had come to appear dangerous. The appearance of these figures in the *Carnival and Lent* is therefore carefully handled. The butt of the joke in the play of the *Dirty Bride* is the inverted character of the couple themselves, not the priest, and in any case he is safely identified as a mummer by his white face. Similarly, the monk and the nun are given a *bona fide* allegorical role as attributes of Lent, while of course reminding everyone who saw the painting of the traditional presence of the mock-clergy in Carnival.

The Triumph of Lent

Why did people oppose Carnival? Over the long term, one must concur with Scribner's observation that Carnival was suppressed,

> because it... seeks to expose and degrade the values and style of official culture, to submit it to observability... A primary characteristic of a power elite is its relative degree of secrecy. The reduction of observability of those holding power enables them to plan and follow out strategies for preserving it... Carnival was [a] popular form of observability. The demystification of church ritual is only the best known of this aspect of Carnival. The forms of chivalry, of civic justice, and of government itself could also be stripped of their numinous associations and made objects of ridicule.[46]

Such procedures became increasingly intolerable, for what are now obvious reasons. In a sense, the debate was openly conducted in these terms, as a struggle for power. Prohibitions on Carnival in a number of specific instances were a means of maintaining political control and civic order, as, for example, the many edicts against carrying arms during festival suggest.[47] The rationale for festivals as providing a safety valve for potential unrest was consciously acknowledged. A group of French clerics defended the Feast of Fools in 1444 in these words: *We do these things in jest and not in earnest, as the ancient custom is, so that once a year the foolishness innate in us can come out and evaporate. Don't wineskins and barrels burst very often if the airhole is not opened from time to time? We too are old barrels.*[48] It was always recognised that the barrels might explode rather than simply let out air. Major festivals were the occasions of some famous riots. In the city of Basel, a massacre which took place on Shrove Tuesday 1376 was long remembered as a *Böse*

Fastnacht (Evil Carnival). Protestant and Catholic civic authorities came to be on the alert for such outbreaks.

Far from endorsing Carnival because they had abolished Lent, Protestant town councils acted as promptly as anybody else if it looked as if the imagery of a particular festival had adopted an incendiary flavor. In Nuremberg in 1539, the Carnival, which had been banned entirely during the years 1525 to 1538, featured a satirical float directed against a prominent Lutheran preacher. The man complained to the town council, who had the Carnival organisers arrested and the Carnival immediately prohibited again.[49]

In addition to governmental opposition, there were other forces working against Carnival in the name of order. Most sixteenth-century people would have agreed with the words Shakespeare gives to Ulysses: *Take but degree away, untune that string / and hark, what discord follows.*[50] The Upside-Down dimension of the imagery now also might appear too inflammatory. This suggests that aspects of secular hierarchy were also now perceived to be under threat. The desire to "purify" popular culture was initially indeed less prescriptive than proscriptive. The sixteenth-century *Triumph of Lent* was the start of a cultural Reformation, the most drastic aspects of which can be seen in the culture of Puritans in the following century.[51] Civic Humanists, moralists, preachers, artists and playwrights from both sides of the confessional boundary were among these secular crusaders. They were motivated in general by a kind of moralising zeal, and a newly perceived necessity to protect the sacred from the profane:

> The reformers objected in particular to certain forms of popular religion such as miracle and mystery plays, popular sermons, and, above all, religious festivals such as saint's days and pilgrimages. They also objected to a good many items of secular popular culture.[52]

The list given in the English Puritan Philip Stubbes' *Anatomie of Abuses* (1583) includes many subjects depicted by Bruegel: cards, charlatans, dancing, dicing, fairs, magic, masks, minstrels, taverns. Because so many of these items could be found in combination at Carnival, *it is no surprise to find the reformers concentrating their attack at this point. In addition, they banned or burned books, smashed images, closed theatres, chopped down maypoles, and disbanded abbeys of misrule.*[53] Erasmus, for example, generalised *à propos* of a Carnival that he witnessed at Siena in 1509:

> In the first place, Carnival is unchristian because it contains traces of ancient paganism. In the second place, it is unchristian because on this occasion the people overindulges in license.[54]

The two grim reforming Sebastians, Brant and Franck, shared this view of Carnival as a survival of ancient Saturnalia.[55] Stridbeck worked from documented opinions of this kind to conclude that, towards the end of the Middle Ages, *the religious festivals tended to degenerate. Their religious character retired into the background, and they became primarily an excuse for loose living and orgies of eating and drinking.*[56] Huizinga described views of this kind around 1400:

> the most sacred festivals, even Christmas night, says [Jean-Chartier de] Gerson, are passed in debauchery, playing at cards, swearing, and blaspheming. When the people are admonished, they plead the example of the nobility and the clergy, who behave in like manner with impunity. Vigils likewise, says Clemanges, are kept with lascivious songs and dances, even in church; priests set the example by dicing as they watch... In the accounts of Strasbourg, we find a yearly gift of 1100 litres of wine granted by the council to those who "watched in prayer" in church during the night of St. Adolphus.[57]

But, he went on to comment, *At the end of the 14th century, people took the increasingly irreverence to be an evil of recent date, which indeed is a common phenomenon at all times.*[58] Carnival celebrations in the sixteenth century were probably not any more degenerate or debauched than at any other time. Rather, festivals continued to channel in popular forms the same public matters which concerned educated writers. The upheavals of the Reformation and of the peasants' revolt instilled new tensions and drama in the concrete shapes of Carnival parades.

If festivals had always been *one of the principal means employed by society to draw its collective bonds closer, to feel united,*[59] the manner of their expression can be read as a barometer for shifting collective desires and fears in the participants. Such a change seems to underlie the growing wave of prohibitions against the wearing of masks during Carnival.[60] The phrasing of this particular legislation reveals a new psychological concern propelling the forces of Lent. In the first half of the fifteenth century, an ordinance was passed in Lucerne against people who *masked their faces and ran around in the manner of devils or billygoats*.[61] In late fifteenth-century Germany, there was a *swelling chorus* of laws against masking *in the interests of good order*.[62] Around 1566, the city of Lyons threatened excommunication to anyone *performing in the churches plays, tragedies, farces, and putting on ridiculous spectacles with masks, arms, and drums* on the Feast of the Innocents and other feast days.[63] In 1586, a Zurich citizen wrote angrily that,

> wanton youths put on devil's costumes or shrouds and scare people, for simple folk may think that it is the evil spirit or some other monster that appeared to them in human shape.[64]

By 1601, the same legislators were still thundering against,

> all those who celebrate that feast [and] betray themselves in their external shape and clothing... they do not serve God, but rather Satan, in that they run around in devil's garments and looking like devils.[65]

What kind of masks are they talking about here? Early modern nomenclature is often unclear, but a shift in the usage of masks seems to have occurred around 1500. This significance of this change can be expressed in terms of the modern distinction in meaning between *guising* and *disguising*. A chronicler at the English court relates how, in 1513,

On the day of the Epiphany, at night, the King, with xi other, were disguised after the manner of Italy, called a masque, a thinge not seen afore in England. They were appareled in garments long and broad, wrought all with gold, with visors and caps of gold, and after the banket doen, these maskers came in with six gentlemen disguised in silk bearing staff torches and desired the ladies to dance. Some were content, and some that knew the fashion of it refused, because it was not a thing commonly seen. And after they danced and commoned together, as the fashion of the masque is, they took their leave and departed, and so did the queen and all the ladies.[66]

This *thing not seen afore* was in all probability an Italian domino-mask.[67] While the new type of mask by no means superseded the older forms, in the long run its introduction was a watershed. Masks were tools by which an individual steps outside of his or her everyday self and into a fictional time. They evolved for use in ritual; in Europe, for the religious theatre of the Greeks. The Romans considered the wearer of a mask (*larvatus*) to be possessed by the spirits of the dead (*larvae*).[68]

Some of these connotations continued in Carnival, where a mask could be part of a role reversal or other traditional costume. But whereas the person masked as part of a carnivalesque impersonation was provided by the specificity of the *guise* with a kind of script for his or her subsequent actions, the person in a plain domino has no such guidelines. Domino-wearers would experience the degree of license always granted by the mask mediated through no assumed identity and no script other than their own desires. A libidinous quality in the domino is hinted at in the account of its English debut, and in later Netherlandish prints showing amorous couples feasting with masqueraders. A design by Joos van Winghe (fig. 75) shows a *Night Banquet* where the entertainment is in the form of *rough music*, as for the Dirty Bride's wedding. The "musicians" and some of the guests wear dominos.

Psychologically, by cloaking the face, the mask cloaks also those restrictions, which the individual normally imposes on his or her self. Confessed "witches" of the later sixteenth century reported that they always

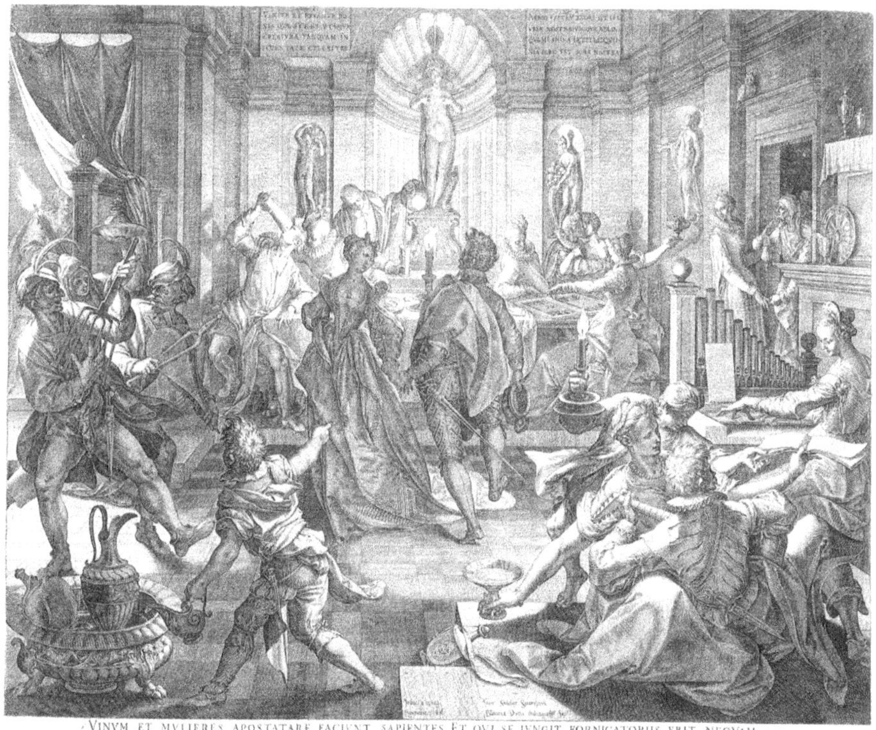

75 Jan Sadeler I, after Joos Van Winghe, *Night Banquet with Masqueraders*, 1591. Engraving. 37.9 x 45.1 cm. Rijksprentenkabinet, Rijksmuseum, Amsterdam. Inv RP-P-OB-7500wore

masks at their sabbats.[69] Early in the century, the Italian poet Mantuanus (1447-1516) understood this new dimension of the mask when he described Carnival as the time when:

> *Per fora per vicos it personata libido*
> *Et censore carens subit omnia tecta voluptas*
>
> [Desire in his mask goes through the squares and streets / And in the absence of the censor / Pleasure enters under every roof.][70]

In the absence of the censor had a scale of meanings for privately and publicly masked people in sixteenth-century Carnival, running from the personal to the political. First, there was the release from the individual's own "censorship" of the self. Notice here the predilection for "demonic" disguises, a term that evidently covered a wide field. Among the *Perchten*, or Austrian wise-folk (a less-undercover version of the *benandanti*), *If a man was killed wearing the Percht's devil mask, he could not be buried in the cemetery.*[71] According to one of Locher's inserts for the Latin *Ship of Fools*,

> Rumor has it that once a masked man was killed and the devil straightaway carried off him and his mask to hell; and rightfully so, for he whose image he bore might justly claim his own.[72]

Second, masks and guises enabled the community as a whole to express views on subjects which would be normally undiscussable. In a Carnival procession in Madrid in 1637, one figure, who seemed to be skinned, carried the inscription: *the excise, the sales tax and the tax on stamped paper have fleeced me.*[73] These subjects could be relatively innocent, for example, the ritual harassment of the unmarried or the twice-married, or more serious:

> The violence, like the sex, was more or less sublimated into ritual. Verbal aggression was licensed at this season; maskers were allowed to insult individuals and to criticize the authorities. This was the time to accuse your neighbor of being cuckolded or beaten by his wife.[74]

Against this, however, official censorship was a strong force, and Carnival satires were less and less free from interference. In Rouen in 1541, an Abbott of Misrule was *arrested by the sergeants right off his festive float... because it attacked the city fathers too sharply.*[75] Masks had another, pragmatic purpose of concealing an offender's identity from the authorities. Of course, they could also be used as a cover for more run-of-the-mill lawlessness; Plantin was attacked by masked men in Antwerp during the Carnival of 1554.[76] All these uses of masks shaded into one another.

Bruegel's demonic carnivalesque imagery reflects these contemporary ideas about the mask's effect on the individual, when *Desire in his mask goes through the squares and streets*. The plain mask released license, or, as we would now say, the masked individual was given over in a controlled way to the desires of his or her unconscious. If we recall what the sixteenth century thought the unconscious consisted of, the presence of masked figures in Bruegel's scenes of vice and sin becomes legible. These figures are not simply emblems of deceit. Their masked faces illustrate the (demonic) absence of reason.

Most horrible are those figures where the mask seems to have become fused with the face, or where there is no face at all under the mask; I think here of certain figures in the *Dulle Griet* (fig. 35c), of the sinister appearance of the masquerader at Carnival's right in the *Carnival and Lent* (fig. 71a), and of the masked skeleton who ushers us into the *Triumph of Death* (fig. 89c). Mask-like faces in the *Seven Vices* carry a similar message.

The head of a suit of armor is also a form of mask: a sub-genre represented many times in Bruegel's works. Such heads can often be interpreted as satirical references to knighthood and chivalry. What makes these images parodic is their carnivalesque component. Bruegel's armoured heads appear in the midst of metamorphic imagery denoting madness, chaos, or bestiality (e.g., *Fall of the Rebel Angels*, fig. 21c; the *Fall of the Magician Hermogenes*, fig. 77; *Dulle Griet*, fig. 35c), and in his formal hell-scenes (*Christ in Limbo*, fig. 91; *Last Judgement*, fig. 98). Bruegel's masked figures thus represent a redirection of parodic traditions native to Carnival, towards the exploration of license — or desire. The generally negative association of masks with vicious excess broadly follows from the same association of ideas that led legislatures unanimously to prohibit masking.

From the authorities' point of view, the fear of lawless desires unleashed in the citizenry was quite sufficient a rationale for banning masks. Certain cities had been trying to abolish carnivalesque activities for longer than others. Lille first tried to prohibit the summer festival of St. John's Eve, with its bonfires, dances, plays and games, in 1382. The proclamation's lack of impact may be judged by the number of its reiterations: in 1397, in 1428, in 1483, in 1514, in 1520, in 1544, in 1552, in 1559, in 1573, in 1585, and in 1601.[77] In other words, while the magistracy of Lille only issued two such prohibitions in the fifteenth century, it issued seven in the sixteenth, and by the middle of the century the frequency had risen to one every seven or eight years. The battle to suppress Carnival was particularly successful in Flanders and northern France,[78] where the size and number of towns in that region had led to the evolution of strong civic organisations.

The widespread sense of the mask as threatening suggests an underlying connection between the imagery of Carnival and the imagery of dreams. Historians of early modern carnivals have tended to analyse what might be termed their "manifest content" — their conscious message. This focuses attention on the most organised, most structured aspects of the festivals: plays, mock rituals, inversions and costumes. In a sense, this emphasis agrees with the sixteenth century's own usage of *disorder*. In a festive context, *disorder* could refer to anything from mockery of the mighty (remember the *naughty person* of Antwerp lampooning King Henry, and the Abbot of Misrule arrested at Rouen), scurrilous inversion (the Madrileños protesting their taxes) or the reversed institutions of Carnival (Lords of Misrule, Abbots of Unreason, Princes of Fools). These phenomena all derive their sense from the official order of things, albeit an order momentarily turned upside down, or inside out.[79]

However *disorder* in the modern understanding of the word also had its place in Carnival. Carnivalesque behaviour was driven by latent, unconscious components: it was an opportunity to enact illicit deeds. As we will see, this sense of Carnival as a forum for the irrational directly informed some aspects of Bruegel's surreal imagery; indirectly, it explains his evolution of this imagery as a response to the psychological reclassification of the carnivalesque.

Rederijkers and Fools

In Antwerp, Brabant, and the southern Netherlands generally, Carnival and carnivalesque activities underwent a series of reorganisations in the late fifteenth century. In the long term, these changes were indeed drastic, part of a kind of Triumph of Lent. Carnival in its original wild form was all but eradicated. In Antwerp, with the blessing of the authorities, *omegangen* commemorating civic anniversaries and religious feasts became the main seasonal festivals.[80] Thus the *omegang* featuring Druon and Antigonus was first recorded in 1470,[81] that of St. George's Day celebrated the Victory of Kloppersdyke in 1485[82] (hence the involvement of the archers' guilds, as we will see shortly). The *rederijkers* took to organising the parades for the Feasts of the Circumcision (Trinity Sunday) and of the Assumption (12th August).[83] The first was originally the greater,[84] and close in time to Shrovetide; the second grew in importance in tandem with the late fifteenth-century cult of the Virgin, who was also the patron of Antwerp.[85]

Within these modern frameworks, the forces of Carnival were re-channeled and suppressed. Their elements were redistributed; some functions imagery and style were taken over by other institutions, other aspects were deleted or "went underground." During the sixteenth century, the new forms — and the new containers for the old forms — of the carnivalesque still retained their old significance as the *second life* of the people. But the sense of who "the people" were and how they could be characterised shifted profoundly.

The most dramatic of these shifts had a political dimension. In the case of the Netherlanders, the events of the 1570s and 1580s were to prove that "the people" were increasingly aware of themselves as a distinguishable nation. Carnivalesque institutions played an important role here; and their emerging role as a crypto-nationalist focus was recognised in Bruegel's designs for kermess celebrations: in the *Kermis of St. George's Day* (1559; fig. 79) and the *Kermess at Hoboken* (c. 1560; fig. 80a-b).

At the same time, on a psychological level, the climate of the Triumph of Lent equally informed Bruegel's exploration of imagery linking carnivalesque forms with lechery and mental chaos; in the *Feast of Fools* (1559, fig. 76) and the *Fall of the Magician* (1564, publ. 1565; fig. 77). The common aspects of these apparently very different prints come into view when we consider the disposition of the forces of Carnival and Lent within an institution intertwined with Bruegel's professional world: that of the *rederijkers*. Many ambiguities characterise the *rederijkers'* relation to carnivalesque feasts.

When we first had occasion to discuss the *rederijkers*, it was in the context of their moralising approach to the classics. We then encountered their allegorical dramas with novel personified characters in the context of the *Dulle Griet*. In Netherlandish cities, the *rederijker* chambers were attached to guilds; the *violieren*, or gillyflowers, chamber to the Guild of St. Luke's. Their dramas were therefore run by the same classes who produced official Carnival performances. Urban *rederijker* performances themselves derived, like most medieval drama, from feast-day *histoires*, or mummeries; these had always been a traditional part of kermess and fair-day festivities in the countryside.[86] *Rederijkers* wrote plays and designed pageants which could resemble Carnival processions; one such incorporated the figures of *the Giant of Antwerp and the Maid of Antwerp, accompanied by the river god, Scaldis, and flanked by Mercury and Copia.*[87] The Assumption procession of 1563[88] borrowed its theme, the character of Elck (Everyman), from the native medieval drama (incidentally, the oldest secular drama in Europe).[89]

Rederijkers used a carnivalesque format, the float, for their presentations. Van Vaernewyck refers in 1568 to *rederijker* shows occurring *up sleden*.[90] This tradition was early criticised as frivolous: *Tableaux, both pantomimic and dramatic, were presented on sleighs in Belgium in the fifteenth century. It was not long before the preachers were inveighing against these vehicles of pleasure and condemning the sleighs to be publicly burnt.*[91] However, as we saw in the case of Ovid, the main conscious thrust of *rederijker* dramas was the dissemination of morality and high culture.[92] Like the *Elcke* procession, these were essentially morality plays or parades in which the names of the Vices and Virtues were brought up to date. Among the novel Vices were Lord Profit, Earthly Desire, Troubled Times, and Obstinate Heart. Novel Virtues included Extract from the Scriptures, Willing Labour, and Upright Simple Faith, as well as the more familiar personages of Hope and Faith, etc.

Cultural reform for some *rederijkers* was a conscious aim. Cornelis van Ghistele, the factor of the Goud Bloem chamber at Antwerp, explained that he translated classical works into the vernacular, *to give the common man something better to read than books about Eilenspiegel's tricks and suchlike knavery.*[93] Till Eulenspiegel (Howleglass) was a famous trickster. His tales were told in a popular chapbook, placed on the Antwerp index of forbidden books in 1570. An extract from this work illustrates the populist "knavery" of these tales. Thus Eulenspiegel explains to a Bishop how matters stand with the people:

> Your Grace, the spectacle-maker's craft is dying out, and may become completely extinct, because nowadays you and the other great men of the world... the Pope and all the rest of them — Cardinals, Bishops, Emperors, Kings, Dukes, Judges, city fathers, governors — God save us! — look through your fingers [i.e., connive at wrongdoing], and refuse to distinguish right from wrong for the sake of the bribes this brings you. In earlier times those gentlemen diligently studied the law so that they would know to whom... justice was to be dispensed. And in those days there was a great demand for eyeglasses, so we did good business. And the priests used to study much more than they do now, so we used to sell plenty of eyeglasses to them too. But today, they often recite their hourly prayers by rote, and it can happen that they don't open a book in three weeks. So our trade is dying out. And this failing is so widespread throughout the land that our peasants are learning to look through their fingers too.[94]

The *rederijkers* also produced comedies of peasant life. These, like their "higher" dramas, frequently treated the most serious issues of the day: the threats of impending war, food shortages, inflation, and of course, the matters of the Reformation, which Luther and his followers had thrown open to public debate.[95] In this way *rederijker* drama took over an old function of Carnival, as a forum for expressing community concerns. This was now done in a literate manner, through new plays using Humanist allegory, written for specific occasions; not in the way of parody and inversion. This was an important change: a movement from oral to literate forms and habits of mind. At the same time, some aspects of the new civic festive imagery became more fixed. Unlike a Carnival figure, Pieter van Aelst's *ommegang* Giant was carefully preserved from year to year, so its theme of civic unity became a recurring seasonal motif. This was imagery commissioned and brought out by the government, instead of rising, as it were, out of the concerns and through the initiative of less civic-minded people.

A striking "Lenten" aspect of the *rederijker* dramas was their separatist attitude to the *zone below the belt,* the focus of carnivalesque attention to the material body and its orifaces, according to Bakhtin.[96] References to copulation, gestation, ingestion, digestion and defecation — central to carnivalesque representation — were increasingly to be expunged from polite or literate discourse. As Montaigne commented in 1575,

> what has rendered the act of generation, an act so natural, so necessary, and so just, a thing not to be spoken of without blushing and to be excluded from all serious and regular discourse? We boldly pronounce, *kill, rob, betray,* but the other we dare only to mutter between the teeth. Is it to say, the less we expend in words, we may pay so much the more in thinking? For it is certain that the words least in use, most seldom written, and best kept in, are the best and most generally known; no age, no manners, are ignorant of them, no more than the word bread: they imprint themselves in every one, without being expressed, without voice... the sex that most practices it, is bound to say least of it. 'Tis an act that we have placed in the franchise of silence, from which to take it

is a crime.[97]

Bruegel's design for his *Feast of Fools* comments sardonically on this phenomenon in mid-transition. During the sixteenth century, the Feast of Fools underwent an archetypical Lenten re-invention as a civic feast. This venerable holiday was originally a kind of ecclesiastical Carnival celebrated in the cathedral chapters of the southern Netherlands during the dead of winter. In different regions, it was held during the twelve days of Christmas, on Epiphany, or on the Feast of the Circumcision.[98] The extraordinary behavior of priests in this festival constitutes a truly carnivalesque role reversal. In the middle of the fifteenth century, Paris theologians described it as follows:

> Priests and clerks may be seen wearing masks and monstrous visages at the hours of office. They dance in the choir dressed as women, panderers, or minstrels. They sing wanton songs. They eat black puddings at the horn of the altar while the celebrant is saying Mass. They play at dice there. They cense with stinking smoke from the soles of old shoes. They run and leap through the church... [and] they drive about the town in shabby traps and carts and rouse the laughter of their fellows and the bystanders in infamous performances with indecent gestures and verses scurrilous and unchaste.[99]

The geographical boundaries where the Feast of Fools flourished followed more or less the contours of the old duchy of Burgundy. Around 1442, in a book entitled *Le Champion des Dames*, the poet Martin Franc recommends his noble patron to *go to the fetes of Tournai... There you will see ten thousand people more than in Torfolz Forest who serve in the halls and throughout the city your God, the Prince of Fools*.[100] The peculiarly ecclesiastical character of the Feast led to a series of condemnations by the Council of Basel in 1435 and by the theologians of the Sorbonne in 1445.[101] As Moxey noted, *This however did not result in its demise. As a result of a process that is still little understood, the dramatic festivals associated with the Feast of Fools at Lille and in several other French cities were divorced from their religious context and became the sole responsibility of secular rhetorical societies.*[102] This process remains shadowy but may now be traced a little more precisely.

Like primitive or magical Carnival, the original Feast of Fools took place at the dead time of the year, as did the fertility rites of peasant societies. Its inversions and role reversals involved genuinely sacred objects and sacred officials. This seems to have been its most objectionable aspect to its critics. The main protagonists of the Feast of Fools were unmarried male juveniles, the young clerics and novices of the chapters.[103] This age group, it will be remembered, plays a prominent role in primitive Carnival. Youth age groups also existed in the countryside of early modern Europe, where young unmarried men banded together into *kingdoms* or *abbeys* of *jeunesse*.[104] It seems clear that *similar institutions survived in the cities, although profoundly modified in their structure and their functions to imitate other corps confraternities and trade guilds in particular.*[105] Apart from these religious and craft rôles, Davis suggested that urban organisations of young men had an *ornamental function* at this period, and that the increasing complexity of such groups can be correlated to the inclusion of adult members, which was in turn a response to the early modern phenomenon of delayed marriage.[106] Muchembled adds that, *above all, these organisations were structured according to the military model furnished by the companies of archers and cannoneers that existed in every city.*[107]

Taken as a whole, as a set of inherited, evolving categories likely to be adapted differently from city to city, it is clear that a *youth society,* in the broadest sense of the word, could well take upon itself the duties of a Carnival society, or might imitate a company of archers, or might form a special club within a guild. St. Lieven's Guild, for instance, was a fools' association with *considerable political influence in Ghent. [It] organised nightly processions during the height of the Middle Ages, where its members, the woestards, plundered and robbed.*[108] Organisations fitting these descriptions, albeit considerably toned down, also existed in sixteenth-century Antwerp.

The Company of the Blue Boat was made up of young people who invented and performed parodies on Carnival days.[109] The motto of the *Violieren* was *By friendship united*.[110] A new chapter of *rederijkers* was formed in 1510; the members called themselves *The Unvalued*.[111] Around 1540, the Hansa merchants complained (not for the first time) of Antwerp's plague of turbulent youths.[112] Of course there are misleading indications of this kind also; the Young Guild of Crossbowmen, like the other militia, was open to well-born men between the ages of 20 and 60.[113] But a common thread can be found of organisations of young men adapting archaic institutions to the new demands of the sixteenth-century cities, fulfilling and elaborating their *ornamental function*, and in the process keeping more or less continent (at least in theory).

This explains why a secularised Feast of Fools should have been inherited by Carnival societies or *joyous companies* in Paris and elsewhere in France, but by *rederijkers* in Brabant and the southern Netherlands. The *joyous companies* who organised the Feast of Fools around Valenciennes *were in fact guilds or bodies specialized in the preparation of festivities*.[114] In Antwerp, the *rederijkers* were entrusted as a body with preparing the *Joyous Entry* of the future Philip II into the city in 1549. The grand feast of *rederijker* fools organised by the Antwerp artist Jan Walravens at Brussels in 1551 was not dissimilar in format from the gathering of French and Flemish fools that took place in Valenciennes in 1548.[115]

Both the similarities and the differences between the *rederijker* Festival of Fools and the old ecclesiastical Festival of Fools are relevant to Bruegel's print from 1559 (fig. 76). The first major difference is costume. It is known that *each Kamer [chamber] had its own fool, or jester to enliven its meetings*.[116] These fools, interestingly, had adopted costumes patterned on those worn by court fools. A *rederijker* fool dressed in this way peers round the back cloth of the *rederijker* stage in Bruegel's engraving of *Temperance*, designed in 1560 (fig. 78). Evidently this was also the costume worn by all the fools who gathered at Brussels in 1551.[117] It is therefore probable that the *Feast of Fools* engraving represents a gathering of *rederijker* fools.

A notable point about this design is the effect produced by so many figures in motley. In the ecclesiastical Feast of Fools, *the costumes worn by participants [were] highly varied and quite fantastic... men... dressed as women and animal disguises were common.*[118] The standardisation of costume in the print has an effect analogous to that of the domino, or plain mask. Deprived even of the usual singularity of their motley, which is now multiple and uniform, and without the diversity or specificity of cues for behavior provided by transvestite or animal *personae,* each fool must express his folly solely through gesture or action. Moxey recognised the importance of gesture in this print, and gave an excellent enumeration of its use as an expressive code:

> One of the most prominent [actions]... is the *fig* gesture made by the fool standing in the foreground who hold an owl on his left arm. This gesture... possesses an obscene significance derived from its being a visual metaphor of the sex act... This fool [is] associated with an owl... While the owl was known as a general symbol of evil, it was sometimes used to refer to the specific sin of lust. Both gesture and bird therefore serve to define this fool as lustful and suggestive... The violin attached to the fool's belt may... be a reference to the secondary significance of the Flemish word *vedelen, to fiddle,* meaning *to make love.* Just as prominent... is the *nose thumbing* action of the fool on his left... Other gestures... are the *moon casting* gesture of the fool to the left of the nose-pulling couple and the *mouth-stretching* gesture of one of the fools on the upper left. The former has an obviously offensive meaning meant to conjure up images of defecation and excrement, while the latter seems to have had a derogatory significance.[119]

The common meaning of these gestures (and the attributes of violin and owl) becomes clearer when the significance of the *nose-thumbing* or *shanghai* gesture is recognized.[120] The Dutch expressions for this are: *hij trekt een' langen neus* (he pulls [or makes] a long nose), and *een (langen) neus krijgen (of halen)* (to receive the long nose). There are two possible reasons why

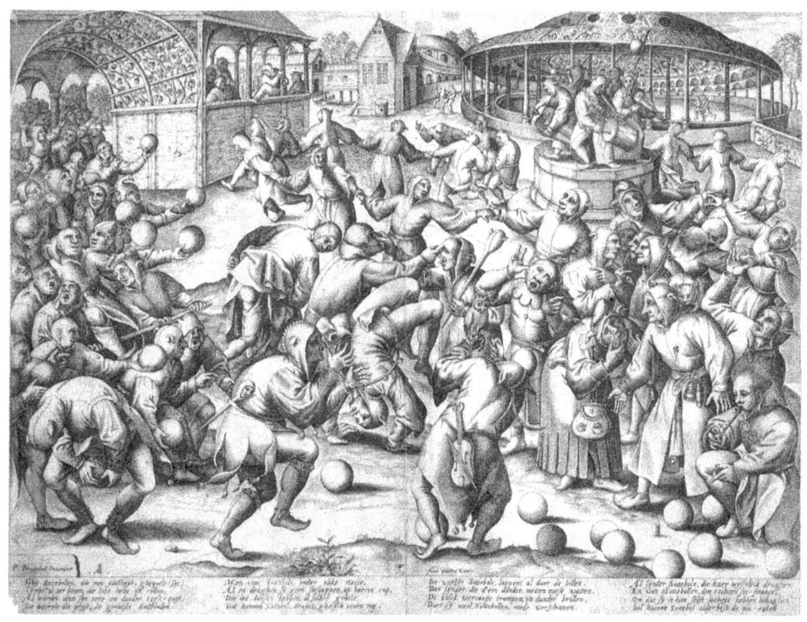

76 Pieter van der Heyden, after Pieter Bruegel, *The Feast of Fools*, 1559. Engraving, 32.5 x 43.7 cm. Bibliothèque Royale Belgique, Brussels. S II 113002, plano

pulling a long nose should be regarded as insulting. Both depend on identifying the long nose as a symbolic phallus. The question then becomes,

> why would anyone, that is, any male, be insulted if he were told he had a long phallus? ... irony is the clue. A person is being mockingly told, *what a long penis you have, and you are still powerless*, or *get me with that long penis of yours if you can*, with the clear implication that the person will be unable to do so. Of course, it is also possible that the *long nose* belongs to the maker of the gesture, in which the case the meaning might simply be that the person being insulted is also being symbolically assaulted. This would be similar to the meaning of another common gesture, namely the *digitus impudicus* or *digitus infamis*, better known in English as *the finger*.[121]

The fools in the foreground, then, manifest lewdness and give themselves over to their lowest impulses in what was now seen as the characteristic manner of Carnival.

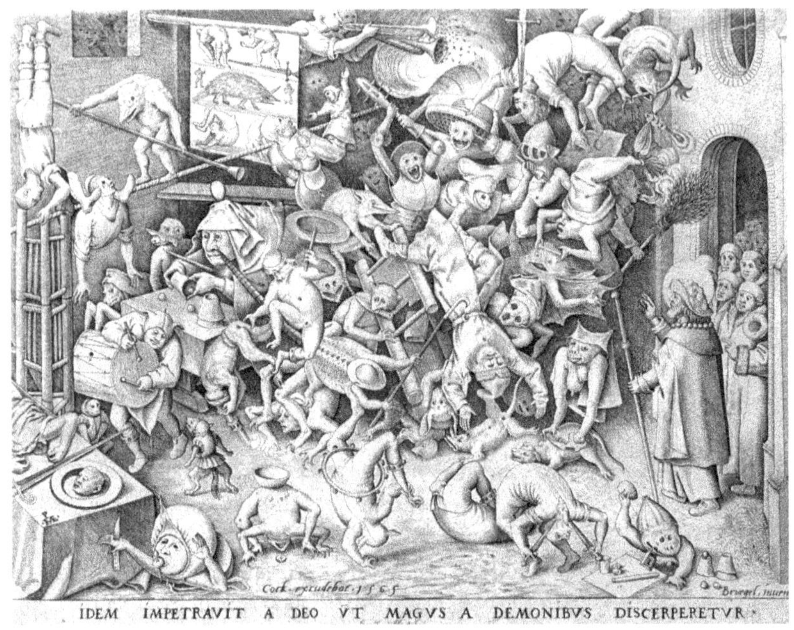

77 Pieter van der Heyden, after Pieter Bruegel, *The Fall of the Magician*, 1565. Engraving, 22.2 x 28.8 cm. Bibliothèque Royale Belgique, Brussels. S I 7615

Connections between Carnival and the free rein of mindless impulse are made explicit also in the *Fall of the Magician Hermogenes* (fig. 77).[122] The ostensible subject of this print is the story from the *Golden Legend* of how St. James beat the pagan wizard Hermogenes in a contest of magic. Its companion print, *St. James and the Magician Hermogenes* (1565; fig. 41), depicts an earlier stage in the same narrative; as we saw in Chapter 2, this is the work where Bruegel made his first depiction of the new kind of hallucinatory witch. Both scenes are dominated by demons. Little monstrous hybrids crowd the picture space. The rationale for their presence in each scene is that they are Hermogenes' helper spirits, but, as with *St. Anthony*, this is a kind of pretext. This world-filling aspect of the imagery diverts the "subject" away from the text entirely and invites its own interpretation.

The choice of this scene itself represents a particular selection by Bruegel; in other versions of the legend, Hermogenes dies by plummeting to the earth (no longer held up by his demons) or is converted to Christianity.[123] First there is the question of the demonic crowd's relationship to the text. As in the case of Anthony's temptation, a psychological element inherent in the legend permits (or invites) expansion in this direction. In Bruegel's *Fall of Hermogenes*, the magician's struggle with his demons is the core action. James is sidelined, standing with a few onlookers. Hermogenes is shown caught in the act of being overwhelmed by his erstwhile helpers. Upside-down in his chair, he is not immediately distinguishable from the hybrid crowd knitted thickly around him. At the same time, the viewer also is overwhelmed, since the demons are pushed up towards the picture surface by a drastically tilted perspective. As in the *Rebel Angels* (fig. 21), the creatures fill the frame; but where the angels seemed to float, arrayed for inspection, the sharp angle here precipitates a tide of mad mannikins towards the viewer. Spatial perspective is negated at the heart of the print by an explosive pyramid of fighting figures.

Bruegel then found in the potential of the legend materials to construct a novel motif: a thick, interlaced knot of demons around a fallen flyer tied upside down to a chair. From this central knot, ripples of fantastic figures invade the rest of the picture space. Bruegel makes this mass movement the centre of visual attention, the pictorial focus. Though the general effect is Boschian, in fact Bruegel re-invented the visual detail of the hybrid imagery for this work in a remarkably novel style. Acrobats and Carnival fools appear among the nightmarish metamorphic bodies of the magician's rioting former servants. One fool in motley apes the acrobats; another plays his drum, watched (or aped) by two small creatures in human costume.

This carnival imagery is expanded and elaborated along grotesque and nightmarish axes. The unfixed, fluid elements of Carnival are used as templates for specific aspects of the writhing crowd of part-men. Conversely the same elements, shorn of narrative context, reflect a dark, twisted light back on their sources, tilting the view of what carnivalesque might mean, to represent it as a kind of negative, violent nonsense. This Carnival is pregnant with psychological metaphors. Prominent in this imagery are dangerous tricks where sword-points aim at the head. One such trick has evidently "gone wrong" at the bottom right, resulting in a decapitation. Swords and knives in general are natural phallic symbols; it is notable how many of these metamorphic bodies lack nose or phallus. One creature has a knife cutting into its muzzle; another holds one in its beak; another ball-like metamorph has both tongue and hand skewered. The sword is most dramatically used here as a means of divorcing head from body, or the illusory appearance of such a divorce.

The disembodied head on the platter here recalls the head in the *Temptation of St. Anthony* (fig. 32), and some of its implications are the same. In this print, visual similitudes hold together the design, as in the *Dulle Griet* (fig. 35), made a few years earlier. Carnivalesque imagery connects the impossible "head-trick" with the conjuror's games played by the large monster under the side-show sign. More games surround the small capped *gryllus* below St. James. At the edge of the sign, his head fully encased by its corner, and formally "cut off" through the neck by a pole, a bald man stares at the glove puppet on his hand, and the puppet seems more alive than he is. In the dark behind them, ghostly eyes and faces can be seen looking on. At the right hand edge of the throng, above James, a woman breathing smoke emerges holding up her broom; below her a much less human female grips a dog-like creature, like an evil transformation of the woman tying a devil to a pillow. Performing acrobats surround all this. In the original drawing, the onlookers behind James have serious faces; in the print they were altered to appear amused.

The scene depends for its effect on the parallels drawn between the inward imagery of madness and the outward forms of carnival. For instance, at the top right, the acrobat with the sword at his throat reprises the form of the hybrid to the right. The visual correspondence between the two is matched by a correspondence in meaning. It is no accident that the forms of the carnivalesque favoured here involve illusion, trickery and contortion. The presence of the conjurors is plainly connected with the profession of the print's protagonist; the magician's tricks have gone wrong and his worst dreams come true. Bruegel's imagery envisages violent emotion run rampant, in terms of the least rational, most bodily aspects of carnival.

These associations illuminate the earlier *Feast of Fools* print. While the *Fall of the Magician* treats its carnivalesque unconscious as evil and nightmarish, the choreography of bodies with which this is expressed is the same on many counts as the symbolic body language of the fools. The presence of the nose gestures requires no further comment. The contorted acrobatic postures of the fools in the foreground are repeated in the later print, even down to the hand-standing fool, encircled by a tambourine, who occupies the centre foreground in both prints. In both, a set of contorted bodies in the foreground looks like an unreadable line of human hieroglyphs. In the earlier design, the upside-down fool with the tambourine faces the viewer; in the *Fall of the Magician* its back is turned: a detail which nicely epitomises the escalating trajectory of irrationality between the two designs.

The obscene gestures of the fools in Bruegel's *Feast of Fools*, with their gaping mouths, their punning fiddles, and their collective motley, still express the carnivalesque *zone below the belt* which the organisation of *rederijkers* had inherited from the older, wilder Feast of Fools. But by the 1560s, this kind of expression had been safely cordoned off into this more discreet, separate institution. The *mise-en-scène* of the print is a "bowling green" where every fool has his ball in hand. This broadly hints at the sexual basis of the foolery, and shows that foolery is occurring, like a game, within certain limits of place and degree:

> It has long been recognized that the game of bowls played by the fools in the foreground was a pun on the word *sottebollen*, which [may be] translated as *numbskulls*. The Flemish word *sot* means *fool* while *bol* can mean either *ball* or *head*. *Sottebollen* can therefore just as easily mean *foolish heads* as it can *foolish balls*. The shorn heads of the fools and the bowls with which they play serve to illustrate and equate the two senses of the word *bol*.[124]

The other sense of the word *bol* hardly needs to be spelled out. One typical kind of Bruegelian hybrid was formed by placing the head where the genitals should be, or by conflating mouth and anus, and so creating a ball-like body (e.g. fig. 35d). Though the *Feast of Fools* uses a different style of surrealism, the bowls of the fools here are indeed in one sense also their balls: a transformation of body-parts through displacement and disguise, rather than condensation.

The background of the print bears witness to the double character of the contemporary Feast of Fools. In the middle ground, a line of dancing fools leads the eye back into the distance. They perform one of the earliest and simplest peasant dances; their demeanour considerably less rambunctious than that of their fellows in the foreground. The serpentine line of their dance echoes the mannerist curves of the trellised pergolas on either side. These structures evoke pleasure pavilions in private parks and gardens — and perhaps also in the walled gardens of the guilds — such as the one depicted in Bruegel's drawing for *Spring* (1565; fig. 83). The culminating performances of the Antwerp *landjuweel* of 1561 were given outside the city walls, and hence called the *haagspel* (*hedge-* or *fence-play*).[125] Bruegel's gathering of *rederijker* fools on the contrary happens in a piece of tamed, walled nature. These refined arches and "pleasure domes" match the degree of civility provided by the auspices of the *rederijkers*.

A good part of the artist's interest here is concentrated on the rhetoric, as it were, of gesture and body language. The germ of his idea evidently came from the paradoxes involved in a collection of craftsmen and artisans donning motley in order to license their expression of what could no longer be voiced openly. It is difficult to tell whether or not citizens who performed as *rederijker* fools also performed in "straight" roles.[126] In any case, the division between skill in speechmaking and skill at physical buffoonery is striking. The separation of these elements was no more than fifty years old at the time when this picture was made.

There is one final cultural strand running through these elements. This is the mysterious figure of *Vice*, who appears in the English equivalent of the *rederijker sotteries*. He is sometimes explained as *the summation of the seven deadly sins* and he is always *a riotous buffoon*.[127] The costume of motley and cap and bells is described as a *vice's coat* in a description of the train of a Lord of Misrule in the 1550s.[128] A fool's coat was by this date a badge of license for liminoid humour, more or less completely dissociated from a carnivalesque context.[129]

Fool and Vice converged into the coat of motley, as hinted at by Ben Jonson (1572-1637). In his satirical play *The Devil is an Ass* (1616), Jonson has Satan accuse his sprite of being out of date, since the year is now:

> *six hundred and sixteen*
> *Had it been five hundred, though some sixty*
> *Above; that's fifty years agone, and six*
> *When every great man had his vice stand by him*
> *in his long coat shaking his wooden dagger [but]*
> *there are other things that are receiv'd now on earth for vices*
> *Stranger and newer and chang'd every hour.*[130]

The *Fall of the Magician* and the *Feast of Fools* make visible such changes in attitude, as the carnivalesque started to be regarded simply as vicious.

Lodovico Guicciardini describes *kermissen* that lasted eight full days, attracting people from up to forty miles away. The saint of the church whose anniversary was being celebrated would be given a procession with floats and mummers' plays on the first day. Among the feasting, games and sporting events that would follow, there were also exercises of rhetoric. According to Guicciardini: *These were the amusements that everyone liked best… but the censors accused them of accustoming the people to speak senselessly on the capital points of religion, affairs of state, and particularly on the sovereign's responsibilities.*[131]

During such *kermissen*, the fraternities of archers, crossbowmen, and cannoneers, also held competitions. A clergyman complained in 1587 that: *The custom is that every year the man who shoots down the wooden parrot or bird affixed to the top of the stick during the entire year is king or leader of the brotherhood.*[132] Chambers of *rederijkers* and Guilds of archers thus both played leading roles in the sixteenth-century *kermis*. The activities of these two groups, it seems, embodied many of the old functions of carnival as a *second life of the people.* They are depicted in this way in Bruegel's two *kermis* prints, the *Kermis of St. George* (fig. 79) and the *Kermis at Hoboken* (fig. 80).

Debate about these pictures has been framed in terms of deciphering their stance towards *kermissen* specifically and peasant feasting generally. Carroll argued that *kermis* prints as a genre demonstrate a positive attitude towards the peasantry and their feasts, linked to a growing sense of national identity.[133] In this view, the *rederijkers* and the militia companies, variously linked together by the middle of the sixteenth century, channelled nascent nationalist ideas into *kermis* fairs and other traditional celebrations.

Whatever their origins, both organisations had some of the characteristics of the youth societies, which flourished in Northern European cities between the fifteenth and seventeenth centuries. The *rederijkers*, Gibson tells us, *flourished from the fifteenth through the seventeenth centuries and in some cases even later, but it was the sixteenth century that saw the climax of their prestige and influence.*[134] Youth groups had the traditional charge of providing social comment and entertainment on rural feast days; recalling the daring performances of *rederijkers* at rural *kermissen*. The *rederijkers* of the cities, better educated and with broader concerns and goals, maintained some apparently archaic but still significant symbolic links to the militia companies.

For example, the periodic contests between different chambers of rhetoricians were called *landjuwelen*. The Antwerp *rederijkers* hosted a national *landjuweel* in 1561.[135] This name means literally *jewel of the land*: that is, an adornment of the land by holding a competition-cum-fair on it. It originally referred to old secular festivals centred around archery contests. Archery itself was a loaded subject in the sixteenth century, largely because the bow and arrow was the weapon of the peasant, made famous by the legendary prowess of the longbowmen at Agincourt. In the fifteenth century, the skill of the Swiss in the use of this weapon became equally famous. To *turn Swiss* was a slang term, meaning to emulate the successful revolt of the Swiss against Hapsburg rule.[136]

Even before the Great Peasant War of 1525, the uncanny marksmanship of peasant archers seems to have inspired fear in the other weapon-wielding classes.[137] The *Malleus Maleficarum* mentions only one form of male witchcraft, the wizardry of archers.[138] The Netherlandish *landjuwelen* in Bruegel's day had substituted a battle of words for a battle of arrows; but something of these proto-republican associations remained attached to their activities. The form of the *sottie* or *sotterie* which the *rederijkers* had made their own was also a descendent of carnival. In these plays *a genuine fool or dervés* was accustomed, *to shoot his wit in showers of arrowy satire on mankind.*[139]

The activities were linked in other contexts. Bruegel's print of *Temperantia* (1560; fig. 78), one of his *Virtues* series, shows a *rederijker* performance in progress on the stage at the top left. Opposite it, two crossbowmen shoot at a high target on a pole, evidently the traditional

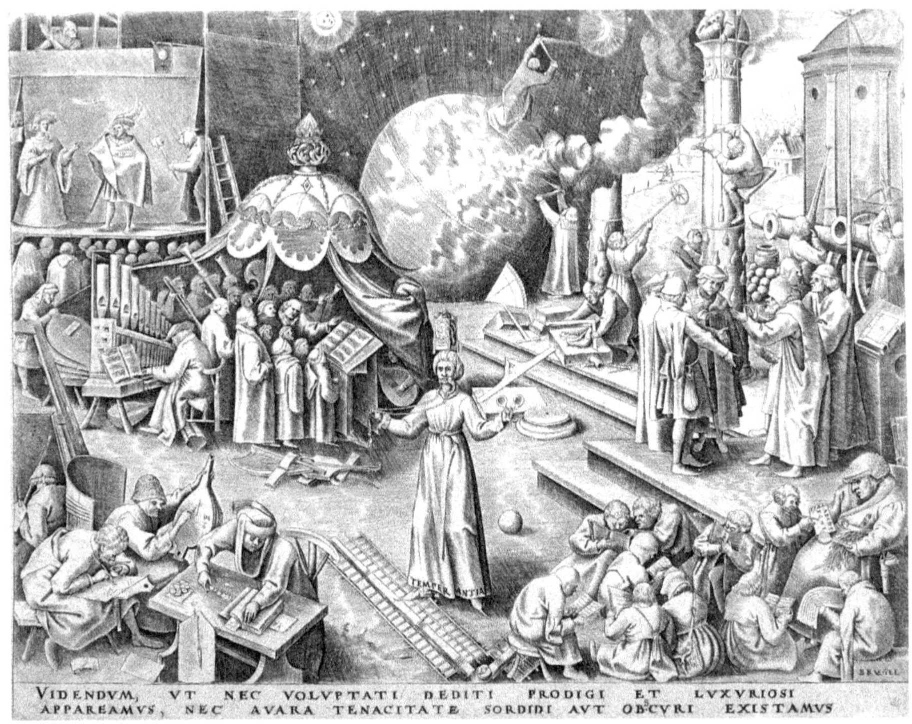

78 Philip Galle, after Pieter Bruegel, *Temperantia*, 1560. Engraving, 22.5 x 29.5 cm. Bibliothèque Royale Belgique, Brussels S I 7599

parrot. Behind them are two cannons with a pile of cannonballs next to them. In this design, as has often been noted, Lady Temperance herself is represented by the seven liberal arts.[140]

But it seems a little strained to consider the crossbowmen and the cannons as present here only to signify *ballistics, the bellicose branch of geometry*; they personify the institution of the militia, and its traditions of feast-day contests.[141] This *Temperantia* stands under a clock, still a rare device in the sixteenth century.[142] The live snake knotted around her waist symbolises her mastery over the *zone below the belt*; her bit and bridle carry a similar message.[143] The *rederijker* fool, and perhaps the game of the bowmen, represent approved methods of rechannelling the forces *below the belt*. Painting and sculpture, steadily rising in status, are also included as attributes of Measure, as is the art of the *rederijkers*. The members of St. Luke's qualify as practitioners of temperance on account of their craft, and their extracurricular activities as *rederijkers*.

Including the archers in this design, whatever irony may be involved, at least indicates parity of status and kind between their activity and that of the *rederijkers*. A play written in 1556, and performed again to celebrate the Peace of Cateau-Cambrésis in 1559, the year before the drawing for this print, underlined the important position of the archers' guilds.[144] One of the novel *rederijker* personifications in this play, representing largely *all the happy spirits of the arts*, makes his appearance last (i.e. in the position of honor). Distributed over his person are the attributes of *music, rhetoric, all target games, and fencing*. He then declares:

> My heart is burning! Who could regret that? How happily people should now shoot with crossbows at the parrot according to ancient custom, or at targets, each according to his desire. How should the longbowmen pierce the bull's eye. It is amusing to watch whether standing or sitting. All can see the skill of the rich shooting with the poor. How should the arquebusiers shoot? How should others fence for prizes, here within or outside the city? There the wine tavern keepers rejoice too. Let all spirits celebrate the truce. Let there be sizzling and brewing, it does not harm. Let people cook pies and pancakes so that their aromas fill the air. The rhetoricians should perform wonders in rhetoric to the sound of joyous music in every district. Who would complain about that![145]

Quite a few could complain, and here a great range of levels and motives becomes apparent, on which the forces of Lent (in Burke's sense) could be manifested. Charles V started issuing edicts against peasant feasts and *kermissen* in 1531. This and subsequent similar pieces of legislation can be understood as a purely political move, part of the efforts of the Spanish government to reassert its control over the Netherlands. In this light, Carroll argued that the first Netherlandish *kermis* prints, appearing from

1549 on, were a response to the worsening political situation, since the shooting guilds who were so often associated with the *kermissen* of their patron saint were in fact incipiently political organisations.

In support of this, there is a statement by an apologist of the revolt in 1574:

> For who does not know that the provinces of these Netherlands have always derived the greatest benefit from each other. Has this union not been the origin of the old custom they have always observed, of assembling towns and provinces for the meetings of archers and crossbowmen and bearers of other old-fashioned arms, which they call the *landjuweel*. Why else have the towns and provinces always met for public repasts and plays by order of the authorities unless it were to demonstrate the great unity of these provinces, as Greece showed her unity in the meeting of the Olympic Games.[146]

The predilection of Netherlandish artists and their audiences around this time for pictures showing *the prominent role of shooting guilds in provincial life*, therefore starts to look like a patriotic response to the alienating actions of Charles. The Emperor did not stop at censorship and the prosecution of heresy: *In 1553, Charles V started stationing Spanish troops in the Netherlands. In 1555, bypassing the local citizens' militia, he moved ten companies of German footsoldiers into Antwerp and conducted public torture and executions in the wake of local rioting over the beer tax.*[147]

Certainly the rise of the prints and the increase in repression were connected. Peter van der Borcht's *Feast Day of St. George* seems to have been the first of these prints to show the activities of the shooting guild members, whose feast day this was, in the background of his design. The date of the print coincides with the arrival of the first Spanish soldiers. Bruegel's *Kermis of St. George* (1560; fig. 79) made some years later, around 1560, gives the activities of the shooting guilds a bigger place. Archery contests were also an important part of the opening ceremonies of Carnival. They were

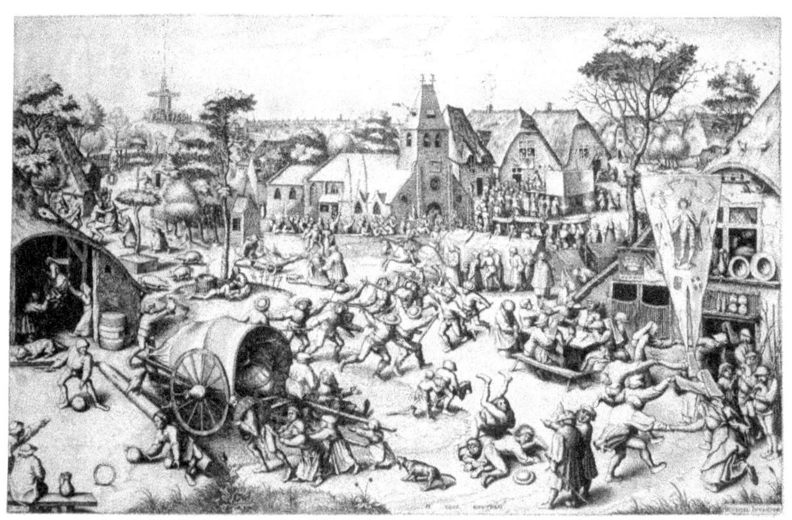

79 Johannes and Lucas van Doetecum, after Pieter Bruegel, *The Kermis of St. George's Day*, c 1560. Engraving, 33.2 x 52.3 cm. Bibliothèque Royale Belgique, Brussels. S II 48461 plano rés

used to select a Carnival king or a master of ceremonies.[148] We see one taking place in the background of Bruegel's *St. George's Day* print. In the foreground is the banner of the saint. On it, the saint himself is equipped with bow and arrow, and flanked by two pairs of crossed arrows. Though elsewhere George was usually depicted as a knight and the knightly weapon was the sword, the arrows on these banners refer to the role of the guild in the Battle of Kloppersdyke:

> the armed guilds and other Antwerpers went out on St. George's Day (23rd of April, 1485)... and the victors returned home with... pieces of the boom [the enemy's wooden barrier over the Scheldt], which they brought, as tradition says Brabo brought the hand of Antigonus, to show the citizens that the Scheldt was free again, and they rejoiced, says Molinet, as much over these fragments as if they had been holy relics. To show the town's gratitude... a procession was held and the statue of St. George carried through the streets, and it was decreed that it should be so each year on St. George's Day to commemorate the event.[149]

This was in fact the last battle to be fought by Antwerp's citizen militia, and they received substantial assistance from Maximilian's troops, but it was a famous victory. In the middle ground of the print the actor playing George in a mock battle against a wheeled dragon, is indeed dressed as a knight in armor on horseback and equipped with a lance. On the shooters' guild banner, a legend above the saint's head says, in Dutch, *Let the peasants hold their kermis.*

The significance of this motto has been the subject of some controversy.[150] It is very close (*Laet de Boeren haer kermis houuen*) to the last line of an inscription on a 1559 village *kermis* print attributed to Pieter van der Borcht, whose full text runs as follows:

> *De dronckarts verblijen hem in sulken feest(e)*
> *Kijven en vichten en dronken drincken als beeste(n)*
> *Te kermissen te ghaenne tsij mans oft vrouwen*
> *Daer om(m)e laet de boeren haer kermissen houwen.*
>
> [Drunkards rejoice in feasts
> Arguing and fighting and drinking themselves drunk as beasts
> They must go to *kermissen*, be they men or women,
> Therefore let the peasants have their *kermissen*][151]

Obviously, taken out of the context of the rest of the verse, the motto on the flag means exactly the opposite. However, the same lines, slightly varied, appear also as the inscription at the foot of Bruegel's *Kermis at Hoboken* (fig. 80 a-b):

> *Die boeren verblijen hun in sulken feesten*
> *Te dansen springhen en droncken drincken als beesten*
> *Sij moeten die kermissen onder houwen*
> *Al souwen sij vasten en steruen van kauwen.*
>
> [The peasants delight in such feasts
> As long as they could have their *kermissen*
> They would go without food or die of cold
> To dance, caper and get bestially drunken][152]

These verses seem unambiguous moral denunciations of feasting. However, in Bruegel's prints, the only words of the verses that can be ascribed with any certainty to Bruegel himself are those directly in his design for the St George's Day print: *Let the peasants hold their kermis*. It seems to have been standard practice at the Four Winds and elsewhere to "cover" satirical prints with a moralistic caption; this particular print was in fact published by one of Hieronymus Cock's competitors, Bartholomeus de Momper. Given the eagle eyes of the Imperial Censors, the inclusion of such captions may have been merely pragmatic. Penalties for flouting the law could be draconian; the *rederijker* and bookseller Frans Fraet was beheaded in 1558. If the short motto in the banner was perceived as too laudatory of peasant disobedience (that is, viewed as contravening the Placards regulating feasts), the print-makers could always point to its longer context in the moralising verse.

The best point in favour of Carroll's argument is that a purchaser, reading the *Hoboken* caption and looking at the picture, would be unable to see any instances of the bad consequences itemised. The vomiting and fighting figures so prominent in the Van der Borcht are pointedly absent in the Bruegels; a couple of figures fight in the left rear ground of the *St. George's Day*, but this is minimal compared to the full-scale riot depicted by the other artist.[153]

The captions therefore do not settle the question of whether the overall visual message of the prints was anti-feasting or incipiently patriotic. The real problem may lie with our modern assumption that these are indeed two contradictory things. This is anachronistic. A derogatory attitude to drinking peasants co-existed quite easily in the sixteenth-century mind with a reliance on the same peasants to uphold customary freedoms (as did the archers). This attitude is seen in Shakespeare, whose low-life characters are held up to ridicule, yet display yeoman mettle on the battlefield. Bruegel's selection of this subject, and the prominence he gives the archers, contribute to the new genre of *kermis* prints. But the general tenor of his *kermis* designs is to direct the viewer's attention as much towards the older ethnographic

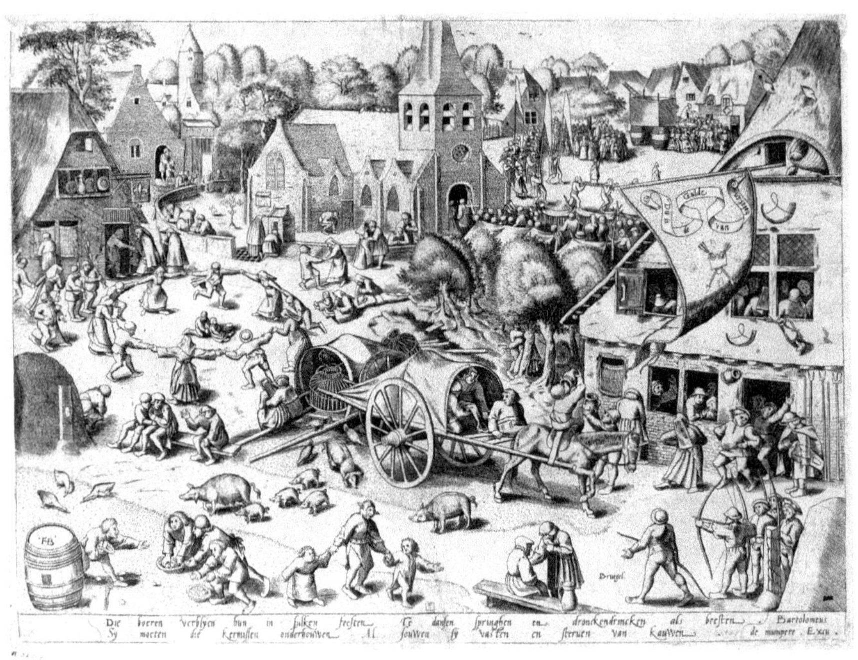

80 a. Frans Hogenberg, after Pieter Bruegel, *The Kermis at Hoboken*, 1559. Engraving, 29.8 x 40.8 cm. Bibliothèque Royale Belgique, Brussels. S II 31207

aspects of *kermis* as to its topical significance. The shooting guilds, after all, presented traditional plays and entertainments such as the staged fight between George and the dragon. Their feast days were associated with satirical *rederijker* performances and with archery competitions where one could *see the skill of the rich shooting with the poor*. In these ways, shooters' guild feasts and *kermissen* maintained the structures of old Carnival.

That this was in fact the main "expressive purpose" of the subject for Bruegel[154] is evidenced in the design for the *Kermis at Hoboken* (fig. 80a); the more so because the drawing for the latter survives (fig 80b). As usual, a certain power imparted by precise formal relationships in the design is lost in the abstraction that is the engraving. The Feast of St. George had an

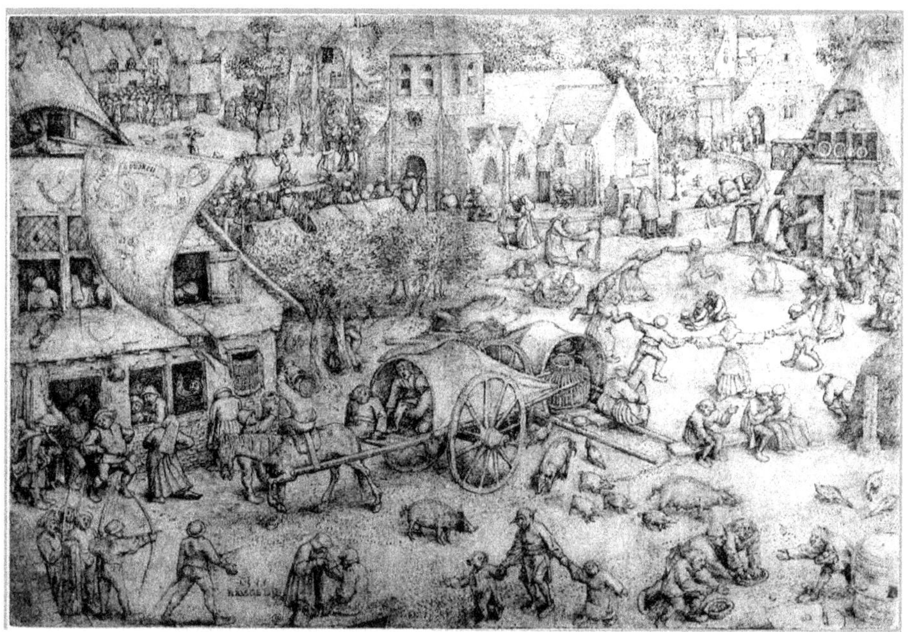

80 b Pieter Bruegel, *The Kermis at Hoboken*, 1559. Pen and brown ink on paper, 26.5 x 39.4 cm. Courtauld Institute of Art Gallery, London

obvious connection to the shooting guilds. This particular *kermis* at Hoboken probably also represents an archer's guild festival traditionally held on the second day of Pentecost (i.e., Whit Monday).[155] The subject and year of this work leads us back to the complex forces working against the carnivalesque in this period.

Recall that Charles V had tried with no success to restrict feasts and *kermissen* of this kind to one day's duration,[156] motivated by political and religious factors. He introduced the Inquisition and censorship to combat the Protestant heresy, which had already cost him substantial losses in Germany. In the meantime, urged by cultural reformers to "purify" popular festive practices, local authorities backed up the imperial edicts against *kermissen* with their own legislation. Hoboken came under the jurisdiction of the synod of Cambrai, which in 1550 issued restrictions directly aimed at profane celebrations of sacred holidays.[157] In 1559, the town changed ownership, and Philip II issued new regulations to forbid the sale of alcohol on feast days during mass and sermons. Among other things, he reiterated Charles V's earlier injunctions against a duration of more than one day for *kermissen*.

This was the context within which Bruegel made his *Hoboken* design, the year after Charles' death and Philip's succession. Hand's analysis brings out the complexity of the drawing:

> The seemingly random placement of figures is actually a carefully composed group of linking configurations, which directs the viewer's glance diagonally across the surface... The wagon with its boisterous occupants is parallel to and juxtaposed to the solemn procession entering the church; in the same manner, the circle of men and women dancing is contrasted to the circular wall that surrounds the church. The [design] is thus divided into two zones, one religious and dignified, the other robustly profane.[158]

But, effectively, Bruegel's composition also marries the main "zones" of the religious and the profane in the picture. Once this dichotomy as an organising principle has been pointed out, one sees how these categories are interrelated by a myriad of small details (fig. 80b). Beyond the procession entering the church is another parallel procession, headed by figures carrying devotional images of saints. Behind them come the archers, all shouldering crossbows, with their banners. The presence of sacred images in this procession refers to the guild's other identity as a religious confraternity. The archers in the foreground perform profane competition, the archers in the background perform the religious side of their activities. The behavior of the people in these two processions underlines this antithesis.

The people entering the church in the drawing carry no cross (this was added to the print). Several of them stop to look at the procession of archers as it goes by. A man kneels next to one of the banner bearers, in homage to the devotional images and banners (another detail missing from the print). In keeping with the mixed character of this procession, its diagonal is in parallel with the movement into the church, while the curve of the parading archers echoes both the curve of the church wall and the *sarabande* dance in the middle ground.

The churchyard itself is the focus of another series of juxtapositions. Some locals are depicted lolling over the wall, watching other activities. One figure, head covered as if in penitence, stands with a kneeling companion, evidently engaged in some form of observance at a small memorial chapel built into the church wall. To their right, a man defecates against the side of the church. Another figure in a similar position can be seen just behind the target in the foreground. These have been explained as a punning reference to a scabrous nickname for the inhabitants of Hoboken.[159] The figure relieving himself by the church forms an antithesis with the devotional couple at his left.

Another antithesis is given by the different degrees of respect shown towards the profane and sacred activities of the archers. Their religious activities, central to this particular *kermis*, are treated with dignity and seriousness in the background of the print. Meanwhile in the foreground, the shooting contest is disrupted by a family of pigs wandering into the line of fire. One of the leading bowmen expostulates with the people in the wagon (the owners of the pigs?).

The diagonal path for this shooting game augments the other diagonals which, as Hand noted, serve to demarcate religious and profane spaces. Just as these "lines" are everywhere crossed, symbolically or literally, in the design as a whole, so too the lines of the archers' target space are also breached, and the result is, of course, humour.

This drawing, then, explores ways in which the order of the game or the order of the ritual are continually liable to be broken into, to become irregular in the middle, and to reassert itself once more. People in a church procession turn aside to look at the events going on around them, sheep graze on the green as the images of the saints are carried past (they too are removed from the print), and pigs get in the way of an archery contest. An ironic detachment is at work here, similar to that of the *Netherlandish Proverbs* (fig. 63), which delights in drawing gently satirical parallels between the rituals and rules of religious and secular "games."

Where might this almost anthropological detachment find support in the spectrum of contemporary mental attitudes towards sacred and profane feasts? Ortelius, Plantin and others were among the adherents in Antwerp of the group who called themselves the Family of Love.[160] Like Erasmus, the Family were political and religious eirenicists, preaching conciliation and unity in the strife of the Reformation.[161] They held that the outward forms of religion were less important than the spirit of the worship. Thus Ortelius succinctly defined Christianity as the *religion by which all good men were tied to one another*. This religion, *is not to know, say, or do this or that, but to be it. The latter is of few, but the former is of many, both bad and good*.[162] The Reformation forced people on all sides to think of the forms of religion comparatively.[163] This development was a *sine qua non* of popular visual propaganda (cf. figs. 37, 57, 106).

Late medieval hellfire preachers had always raged against the "vanities" of secular festive forms. This imagery was radicalised and redirected into the charge of *mummery*, which the Reform party persistently levelled at the Catholic church from the 1520s on. Devout Christians, alleged the pamphleteers, would not be fooled *like young children with carnival masks and straw dolls*, since Luther has exposed the Pope and *torn from him his mummery mask with which he has fooled and deceived the whole world*.[164] The consequences of the massive jolt which the Reformation gave the world of ritual are discussed further in the next chapter.

For the moment, even if the Lutheran view is taken as a radical extreme (which it was not), a wide middle ground occupied the territory between these extremes. By 1560, there were people who thought that the traditional forms of the Catholic religion needed to be purged of contaminating mummery. There were also people who alleged that the forms of the church had become so corrupt that they were now indistinguishable from mummery. Despite confessional differences, both positions supported the cultural Triumph of Lent. The intellectual position of the *Kermis at Hoboken* is equidistant from these poles of opinion: it offers a point of view wherein similarities between the forms of religious and secular feasting become visible.

The compositional structure of Bruegel's *Hoboken* drawing thus defines an eirenicist position on this debate as clearly as the eliptical comments of Ortelius and other Friends. While the forces of Lent bore down against *kermissen* during this time, the focus of their attack was precisely that intermingling of sacred and profane which Bruegel so deliberately presents as an artistic unity. The most unattractive aspects of secular peasant feasts, such as vomiting or fighting, are equally excluded altogether from his major work on this subject, the painting of *Carnival and Lent*.[165]

The Battle Between Carnival and Lent

This vision of secular and sacred customs as forming a unified whole is the basis for Bruegel's grand *Battle Between Carnival and Lent* (fig. 71), created at about the same time as the *kermis* designs in 1559. The print designs have a rural setting, evoking the traditional roots of shooting guilds, *rederijker* performances, dances and processions. The *Carnival and Lent* is set in a city square and explores the complexities and contradictions of festival at a higher level of abstraction.

In the course of making these concerns into a large-scale oil painting, Bruegel found ways to philosophise the play between sacred and profane present in the *Hoboken* drawing. He fused together two older visual schemes: the cycle of seasonal feasts, and an allegorical "combat" between Prince Carnival and Lady Lent. These schema formalised and monumentalised the material. The strategy of antithesis which invigorated his treatment of *kermis* is worked out on a more cosmic scale, and the spatial and temporal horizons are wider, covering the festive cycle from November to March. Instead of one festival, with contradictory attendant customs, the painting depicts many festivals, represented in a network of small scenes, as in the *Proverbs*. There is no country vista visible beyond the buildings. The traditional centres of village life — the church, the inn, the green — have urban equivalents, and urban polarity; the church and the inn face each other across the market square. This is a kind of ideal city.

The combination of older, formal visual models with the market setting allowed Bruegel scope for an extraordinarily rich array of significant counterpoints. One measure of the appeal of this painting for him is its role as a source for his later art; he reworked many of the motifs he devised here as separate later images. The subjects of Bruegel's two prints on festival plays, *The Dirty Bride* (fig. 73) and *The Masquerade of Orson and Valentine* (fig. 74), appear first in this painting. *Children's Games* (fig. 3) of the following year took up the motif of children playing with tops and rendered it more powerfully. Later in the 1560s, Bruegel gave the beggars and cripples their own paintings (*The Beggars* [or *The Cripples*], 1568, Louvre, Paris; *The Blind Leading the Blind*, 1568, Galleria Nazionale, Naples).

The *Battle Between Carnival and Lent* can be understood on many levels; through each path to an understanding of its subject has its pitfalls and dissatisfactions.[166] Like so many of Bruegel's works, the painting resists interpretation as a linear narrative. It is not a straightforward document of contemporary customs, any more than the *Proverbs* is a straight paremiology. If the picture is a contest, there is no winner.[167] The first key to its layers of meaning is its archaism. The feasts and customs depicted here were no longer celebrated in this way in the context of Antwerp in 1559. It is as important to understand what is being omitted as it is to investigate what is represented. Much becomes clearer when we consider the source materials fused in this design: the cyclical calendar and the allegorical battle.

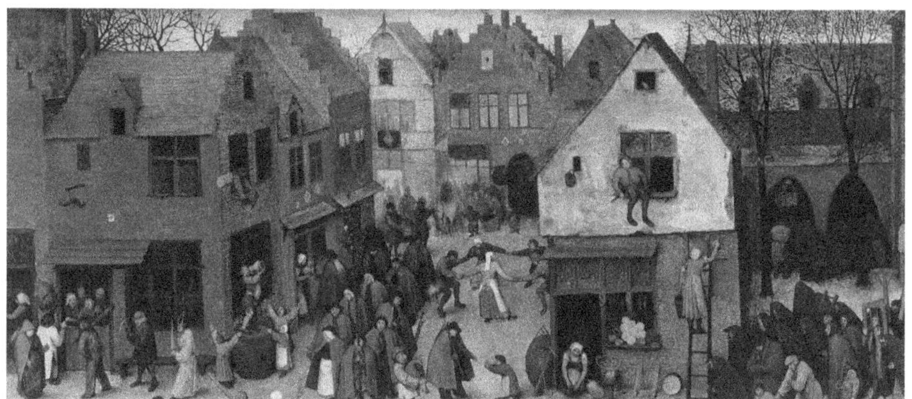

71 b Pieter Bruegel, Epiphany bonfire, Lepers' Procession, *Orson and Valentine*, detail, *Battle Between Carnival and Lent*

The oldest kind of pictorial calendar was the cycle of the Labours of the Months.[168] Familiar from carvings on cathedrals between Cambrai and Amiens, these Labours were initially conceived of in terms of the agricultural year. They show tasks typical to the season and the locale. Thirteenth-century manuscript illuminations show the fattening and the killing of pigs as the Labours of November and December.[169] Feasting appears only in winter, when work in the fields is over. Thus a single (male) month would be shown at a table with a goblet for January, or warming his feet at a fire for February.

Illuminated months flowered as a genre in the context of the Book of Hours. Following the innovations of the Limbourg brothers, the inhabitants of the months multiplied and their activities broadened. By the beginning of the sixteenth century, illuminators were including country

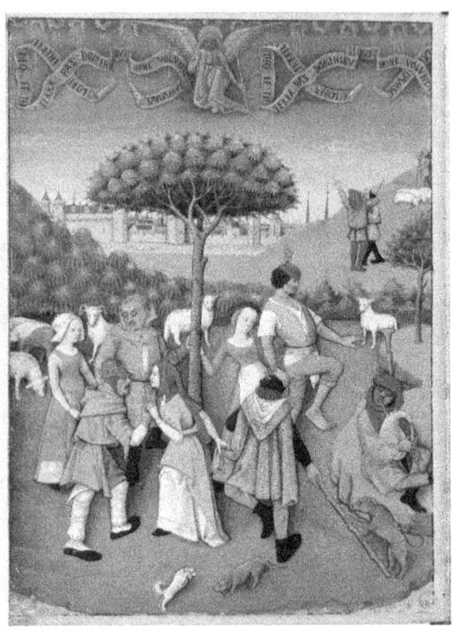

81 Anon, *peasants dancing a ronde*, in *Annonce aux bergers*, from the *Hours of Charles d'Angouleme*, Bibliothèque nationale, Paris, MS lat. 1173, fol. 20V

games and pastimes in the spring and summer months as well as in those of autumn and winter.[170] Peasant dances and crossbow practice were given their own pages in Books of Hours produced for Charles of Angouleme and Eleanor of Portugal.[171] Many of these books, produced in Ghent and Bruges early in the century, added small illustrations of children's games in the margins, around the larger illustrations of the months; these games too were organised seasonally. Characteristic of March and April, for example, were games with top and whip and parades with rattles.[172] In Charles' peasant *ronde*, the dancers' hats are decorated with holly leaves and berries, an authentic piece of folkloric observation (fig. 81). Specific pastimes were, of course, associated with specific times of year, though calendar classifications were by no means standardised at this date. The change from season to season naturally varied from region to region, and so did the representations of seasonal tasks across Europe. In the old Labours of the Months, the grape harvest appears in southern versions; lambing is sometimes placed in

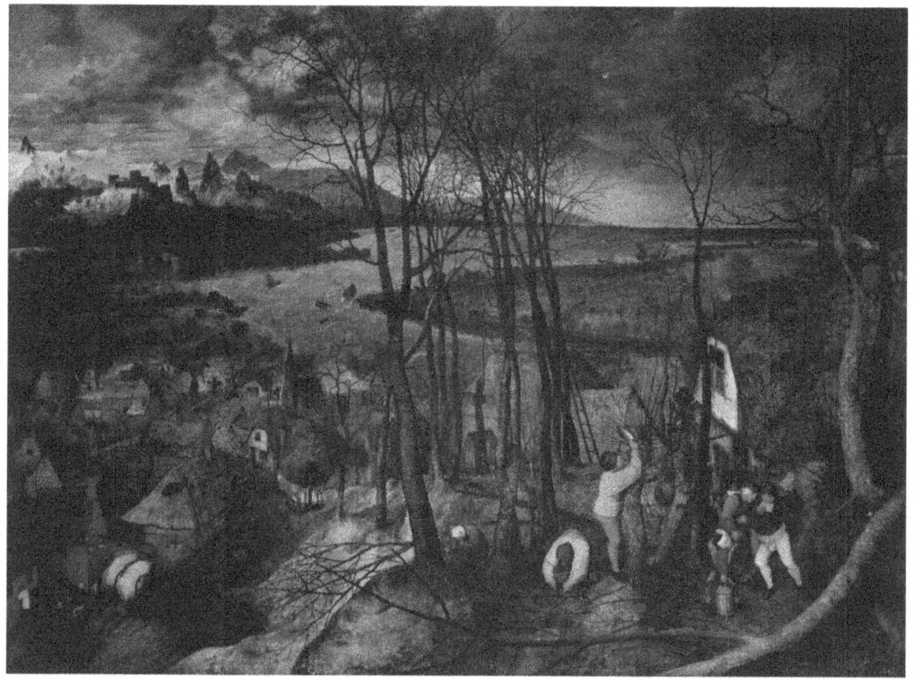

82 Pieter Bruegel, *The Dark Day*, 1565. Oil on panel, 118 x 163 cm. Kunsthistorisches Museum Wien oder KHM, Vienna. Inv GG 1837

March, sometimes in April or May. The date of the New Year changed from place to place; in Northern Europe it was often celebrated on the first of March, that is, at the beginning of Lent. Rural communities used local names for months and seasons; for example, December was known as *Wintermaand*, *Hoeremaand* and *Wijnmaand*.[173]

Broadening the idea of seasonal activities to include pastimes in itself tended to blur the old categories of the Labours. In Bruegel's *The Dark Day* (1565; fig. 82), the figures cutting and gathering branches are balanced by a family group; the man waves a waffle, the child wears a paper crown, part of a traditional game to celebrate the Feast of the Kings at Epiphany (fig. 82a).[174] Children wearing these crowns appear in the *Carnival and Lent* (at bottom left). The *Dark Day* belongs to Bruegel's beautiful series of the seasons; owned by the merchant-banker Nicholas Jongelinck in 1566. Five of this suite of paintings are extant. Work and play in *The Dark Day*, as they are in *The Harvesters* (Metropolitan Museum, New York) and *Hunters in the Snow* (Kunsthistorische Museum, Vienna). Though it is unclear how many paintings have been lost from the suite of months, it is more likely to have been one out of six than seven out of twelve. Each design therefore probably represents more than one calendar month.[175]

Bruegel made two other drawings for prints around this time, *Spring* (1565; fig. 83) and *Summer* (1568, fig. 84); these prints each carry under the image the names of three months. These also experiment with different balances of labour and leisure; the industrious garden of *Spring* has demarcated zones for gardening (March), sheep-shearing (April) and, in the background, May-games or *fêtes galantes*. *Summer* is altogether more rambunctious: out in the fields, order and disorder run into each other pictorially and in terms of subject. The great Michelangelesque young man in the foreground actually protrudes his foot and scythe out of the lower frame of the image, as he drinks deep from a round jug. This brilliant and unprecedented use of visual detail is also a pun; it refers to the expression *over de schreef gaan*, meaning *to cross permitted borders or go beyond all bounds*.[176] Evidently, Bruegel re-arranges and blurs boundaries in these experimental updates of the seasons, playing with the materials of the Labours of the Months.

Later in the century, this branching out from the original manuscript calendar imagery resulted in, on the one hand, new kinds of genre scenes such as Avercamp's winter views, and, in popular art, broadsheets such as *En Novembre c'est la Saison pour la Viande de Salaison*, which shows the progress of the pig from farm to sausage in twelve panels.[177] In the *Carnival and Lent*, as in the *Proverbs*, Bruegel was working with traditional subject matter at a key moment of transition. His own art undoubtedly had a hand in changing the way people thought about seasonal imagery, and its translation into new formats and genres.

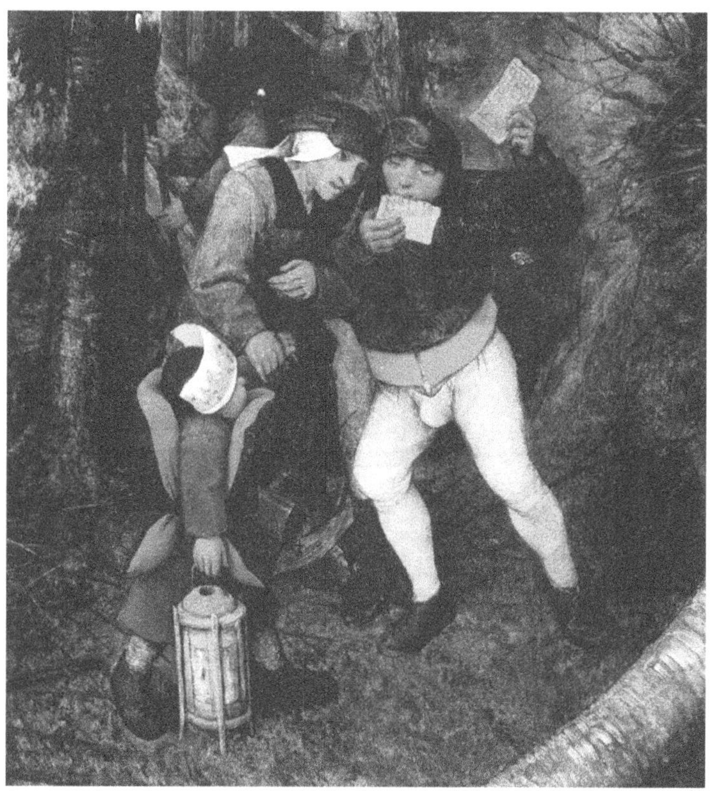

82a Pieter Bruegel, Shrovetide scene, detail, *The Dark Day*

With this background in mind, it is instructive to enter the world of the *Carnival and Lent* first through its depictions of labour. Among the many elements presented here, one important theme is that of work, particularly to do with food. Around the centre of the picture, behind the combatants and their trains, women prepare Lenten fish, men carry wine from the inn, and a woman makes waffles. These activities are of course seasonal tasks and festive preparations at the same time. The group of fishwives has a prominent position, right above the encounter between the two most fictional characters in the picture, the personifications of Lent and Carnival.

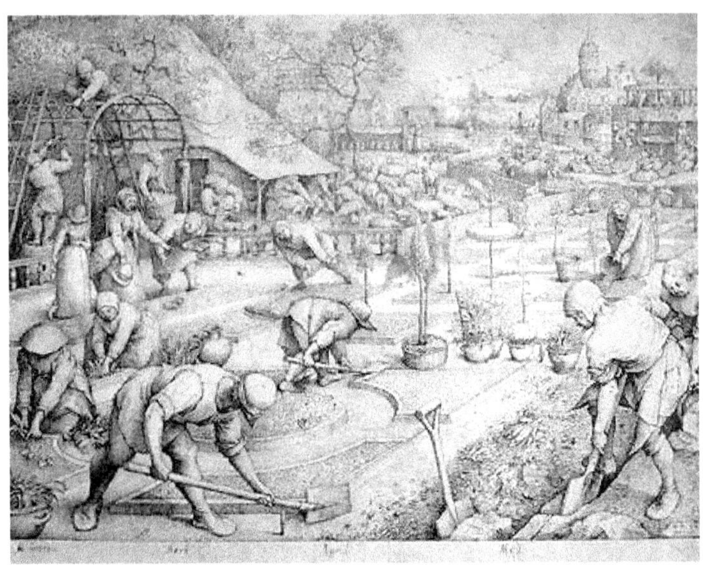

83 Pieter Bruegel, *Spring*, 1565. Pen and brown ink on paper, 22 x 29 cm. Graphische Sammlung Albertina, Vienna

Next to the women sorting fish, a girl draws water from the well, and pauses to divine from her reflection (a custom described, incidentally, in *Den Sack der Consten*). Like the fishwives, she is plainly dressed and a basket of vegetables at her feet shows that she has been to market. Next to the wine carriers, a little group in festival costume echoes the women's poses. Bruegel here blurs the line separating scenes of pastimes from seasonal work in contemporary Books of Hours. Work specific to feast-days includes the preparation of special foods, such as Shrovetide waffles or Lenten fish. These linked cameos subtly forestall the common accusation that feast days are wholly occasions of revelry and debauchery.

The picture represents a carefully tailored view of the mechanics of Carnival itself. The people who organised the street parades for festivals were craftsmen, working within the framework of guilds and confraternities. Prince Carnival himself is a butcher, wearing his pouch of

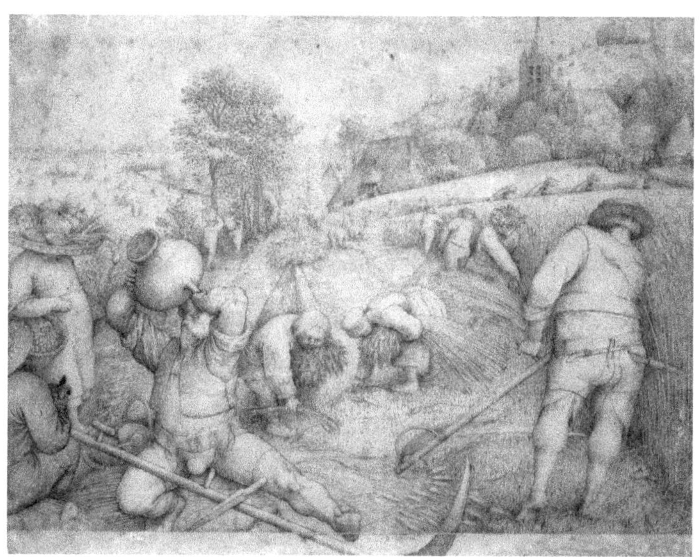

84 Pieter Bruegel, *Summer*, 1568. Pen on paper, 22 x28.6 cm. © Hamburger Kunsthalle. Inv. 21758. Photo: Elke Walford.

knives. It was, of course, the butchers who put the *carne* into Carnival: *the corporation of butchers... furnished the Carnival beef. At Nuremberg towards the middle of the 14th century, they were granted the privilege for organising the Carnival display for Lundi Gras.*[178] At Romans, the drapers traditionally organised the festivities (though their interest in meat took a rather different form as we will see in ch.5).

The craft of the craftsmen manufactured the masquerades, plays and farces of Carnival. This is the class to which Bruegel belonged. Yet none of the Carnival plays or masqueraders' costumes in this paintng reveal anything of the manufacturing skill which was the hallmark of festive productions of this time, nowhere more so than in the Antwerp *ommegangen*. The visual magnificence with which the cities celebrated seasonal feasts is excluded in favor of more archaic, home-made celebrations. The high viewpoint makes the city square into a stage: *Carnival may be seen as a huge play in which the main streets and squares become stages, the city becomes a theatre without walls and the inhabitants, the actors and spectators observing the scene from their balconies. In fact, there was no sharp distinction between actors and spectators.*[179] In the painting, people gaze at the various events from ground level windows, occasionally making contributions to the "actors." What interaction there is between the upper stories and the ground takes the form of two spouts of water: a man vomits from the *Blue Boat*; the "King" on a barrel is doused. Though formally visually linked, the groups otherwise do not attend to each other, and there is a good reason for this. Each group is living in a separate time of the year.[180]

Gaignebet was the first to realise that the picture is a kind of cyclic calendar, or seasonal clock, giving the ceremonies of the year from Christmas to Easter. A striking sign of this is the difference between the trees at the top left and right: from the bare branches of winter to the budding leaves of Easter. At the top of the painting is a Noël bonfire on a street-corner; below this, people celebrate Epiphany, the Feast of the Three Kings, when children wore crowns and adults played *Billets des Rois*,[181] below them, coming down the street, is an annual procession of lepers which took place on the second Monday of January (fig. 71b).[182] Candlemas was commemorated by the play of *Valentine and Ourson*, a performance of which is in progress at the first street corner on the left.[183] The catalogue can be followed down to the figure of Carnival and his train of masqueraders (fig. 71c).

Starting from Lent, the sequence of religious holidays between Lent and Easter moves backwards into the picture space, through the Church and out again, culminating at the house with the yellow upper story. The children behind Lent carry martelets, the rattle of which signifies the end of Lent. Their faces are marked with the cross for Ash Wednesday. Behind them the people coming out of the church carry branches, which in Flanders and France signify Palm Sunday. Gaignebet concluded:

The disposition of the series of ceremonies represented here is inspired

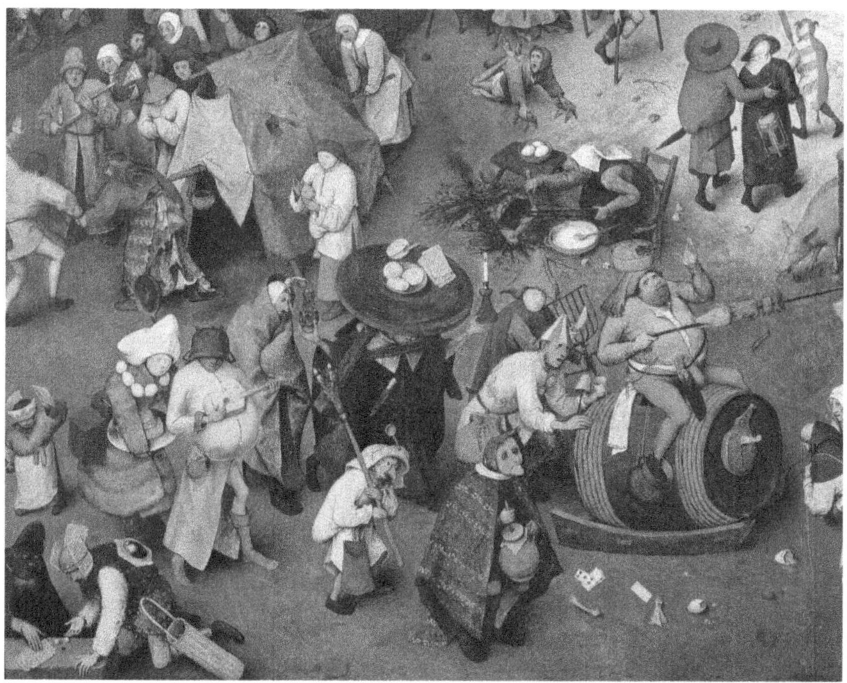

71c Pieter Bruegel, Prince Carnival and masqueraders, detail, *Battle Between Carnival and Lent*

by medieval circular calendars... The necessity of reconciling two contradictory medieval models, that of the... two antagonistic values of Carnival and Lent, and that of the cyclical passage, has obliged Bruegel to adapt the traditional iconography. In effect, the allegorical theme of the combat of Carnival and Lent brought together in space two personages who were in fact separated by the whole duration of Lent. The presence of the cross of ashes on the forehead of the old lady of Lent is symbolically justified. On the foreheads of the infants who chase her with the rattles of martelets on Samedi Saint, and participate in the Easter collection, the cross seeks in some sort to indicate the change. This sign brings together two burials, that of Carnival and that of Lent. One understands, moreover, why the succession of Carnival ceremonies appears with a clarity that could not be respected for those of Lent. Bruegel was forced, in order to conserve the struggle of Carnival and

> Lent, to oppose the unfolding of Carnivalesque time with a time of Lent, inverted to result in the Old Lady of Lent.[184]

The narrative implied by this language is slightly misleading. Rather than speak of Bruegel being forced or compelled by incompatibilities in his source materials to design the picture as it stands, it is more useful to think of Bruegel as compelling his sources — ethnographic observation and the ready-made formulae of allegorical discourse — thus opening the more interesting questions of how and why he did this. The motives for making new patterns come from the point of view of a particular historical reality. The "necessity" of revisiting old formulae is a core activity of art: to match inherited expressions and templates against the reality of present human experience, and make adjustments accordingly.

Gaignebet's explanation of detail and organisation in the painting, however, matches precisely what we see, and enables us to see more. Lenten time proceeds in and out of the church. While the mummers of Carnival solicit money at the left, churchgoers give alms to beggars at the right. The figure in Lenten costume between the merchants underlines both the fact that Lenten services were designed to reaffirm the normal social order after the upheaval of Carnival, and the obligation to charity which made that order more tolerable. Succouring the hungry was one of the Seven Acts of Mercy, related to the Catholic doctrine of Good Works, and practising the Seven Acts of Mercy, including the burial of the dead, was a declared *raison-d'être* of the civic and religious confraternities.

The woman washing windows, as the Lenten congregation streams out of the church, represents a return into profane time and profane tasks. At the other main entrance to the church, a person Gaignebet identifies as a confraternity member displays the relics of his brotherhood, to attract alms-givers.[185] The relics, like the displayed crucifix just inside the porch, are concrete examples of real sacred magic commanded by the Church — *supernatural power which could be dispensed to the faithful to help them in their daily problems* — as opposed to the illusory magic of Carnival.[186] Confraternities and the cult of relics were tightly bound together by Bruegel's day (see Chapter Five for further discussion).

In the original painting, this detail may have made more direct reference to the curative powers of relics, underlining the allusion to the orthodox transformative powers possessed by the Church. Figures later painted over in this part of the picture referred much more strongly to Lenten death or dearth, as opposed to Carnivalesque life or abundance. Next to this table, X-rays show that the artist placed two sick people under a coverlet, presumably to attract alms. An extremely thin person in a wagon once occupied the space just below the top-spinners. In the right corner, a corpse with a swollen stomach once lay under the pile of white linen, which still seems to bear the impression of his feet. These figures were erased from the original at some later date, after the picture had been copied several times by Pieter the Younger and his shop; they appear in these high quality facsimiles.[187] Their erasure diluted somewhat the strength of paired and balanced contradictions of sacred and profane.

It is clear, then, that Bruegel went to some pains in this design to create a balance between Carnival and Lent. Lenten time is shown as festive time; represented as structured in a parallel way. Lent is depicted as a popular festival, with customs, ritual and costume. Bruegel thus imposed the quality of Leach's pendulum swing on the whole cycle of religious observances and customs, from Lent to Easter. During festive time, people who were normally outcasts were (at least temporarily) reincorporated into the community. A notable instance of this is the lepers' procession at the back. A leper was pronounced legally dead and went through a mock burial ceremony. As a matter of course forced to shun contact with the living, once a year these mock-dead were allowed to walk formally into town, for reasons to do with the spirit of *communitas*.[188] This is the same myth of reconciliation at the heart of the story of Orson and Valentine, the popular play performed at Candlemas. Its climax is the return of Nameless, the wild man, into society, through the efforts of his brother, Love.[189]

The Battle

Turning from the traditions of representing seasonal time to the tradition of personified festivals in an allegorical combat, the other immediate parent of the *Carnival and Lent*. This convention was originally developed within the literary genre of the medieval dispute, employing formulas taken from epic poetry. Among the very earliest secular plays extant in Netherlandish drama is *Vanden Winter ende Vanden Somer*[190] from the fourteenth century. Allegorical disputes of this kind — between birds, towns, vices and virtues — were commonly used as vehicles to air a *thèse d'ordre sentimental, politique ou religieux*.[191]

Early literary Combats of Carnival and Lent seem to have been parodies of these more elevated forms of the dispute. Bruegel's parodic tournament ultimately descends from this comic branch of the tradition. Long descriptions of the cod-weaponry of the adversaries, their retainers, and successive phases of the combat, bulked large in this kind of text. Lent, for example, may deliver the mortal blow with a salmon.[192] Examples of the genre can be found in England, France, Germany and Italy from the thirteenth century on. Some took the form of mock-trials, others were parodies of chivalric combat. One version was staged at Tours in 1485.

Such literary treatments co-existed with oral traditions and folk performances, the details of which are harder to come by, though here the oral and literate evidently informed each other. At Norwich in 1443, John Gladman was prosecuted for taking part in a masque on *Fastengong Tuesday*. The New Year in Norwich was counted as beginning on March 1; so the forty days of Lent ended an extended festive period running from Christmas through Carnival. The defendants claimed that it was customary *in any city or borough through all this realm* to hold such parades at this time. The records of their trial give us a rare glimpse of folk masquerade. Gladman had played the role of *King of Christmas* on horseback. This King was followed by *Lenten... draped [with] herring skins and his horse with oyster shells*. They rode at the end of a parade of masquers, *each month, disguised after the season thereof... in token that all mirths should end with the twelve months of the year.* The rider playing Lent came last *in token that sadness and abstinence of mirth should follow and a holy time.*[193] It seems that the procession itself was the whole action, and the meaning resided in the formal shape and imagery. This parallels the focus on description in the older literary disputes.

By the turn of the century, like Elcke and Antigonus, the figuration had moved into the arena of public performance, which encouraged its development in more dramatic terms:

> Several separately developed elements of Carnival usage seem to have coalesced around 1500 to stimulate the idea of acting out the opposition between Carnival and Lent. The towns with their crowds demanded spectacle... Giving an overall sense to the occasion meant also sharpening the outcome. In the older literary versions of the combat the end of the battle was usually exile: whether Carnival or Lent won, the other was sure to return in such versions, as the seasons turned. But after 1490 texts appear in which Carnival dies or is killed.[194]

This more dramatic shape was further developed in literary sixteenth-century versions: *A poem called "The Expiration of Carnival," depicting the old fellow on his deathbed, was written in 1493 by a Milanese humanist. A "confession" of Carnival on the scaffold was published in 1516 at Bologna.*[195] In 1540, Jehan d'Abundance published his play on the combat, which ends with Carnival, defeated and about to die, making his farewells to his companions and pastimes.[196] Bruegel would have been aware of this repertoire and may well have witnessed some performance of this kind.

As a theme in painting, the most notable precedent is a treatment by Bosch, known through five copies of two main variants on the same composition.[197] These works are often cited in relation to Bruegel's *Carnival and Lent,*[198] and certain details, for instance the pig's head on a spit, may refer to this source. Otherwise, the Bosch copies present a completely different visual idea (fig. 85 a-b). The version represented in the Antwerp

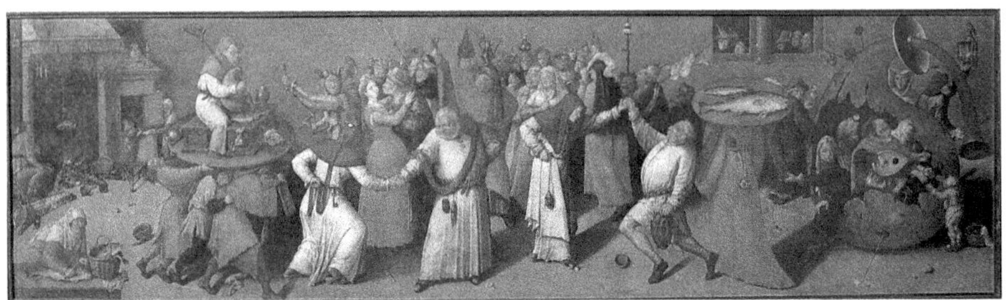

85a Follower of Hieronymus Bosch, Shrovetide and Lent, Museum Mayer van den Bergh. © IRPA-KIK, Brussels. Photo: Jean-Luc Elias (2004)

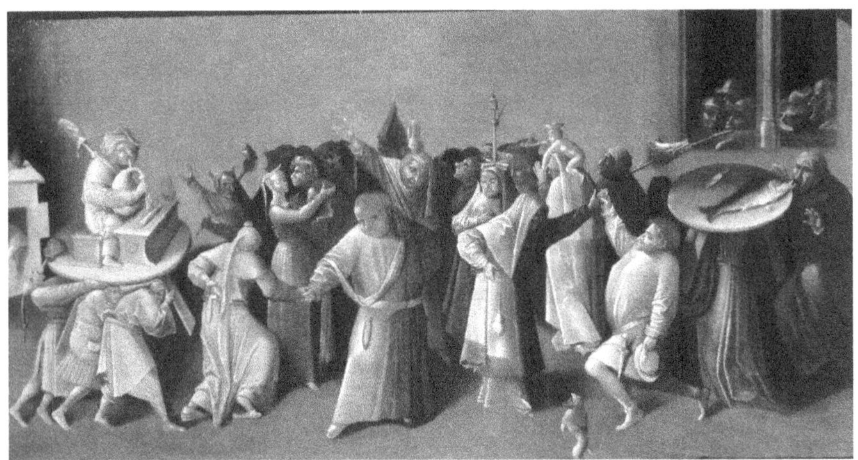

85b Follower of Hieronymus Bosch, *Shrovetide and Lent*, Southern Netherlands, 1555-1575. Oil on panel, 59.3 x 118.3 cm. Noordbrabants Museum, 's-Hertogenbosch. Photo: T. van der Vorst

and Amsterdam copies in particular reeks of degeneracy and folly. At right, a huge bulbous bagpipe, the bag of which is a broken eggshell, contains a grotesque merry company (fig. 85a). Lady Lent (if this indeed be she) is effectively effaced by the platter of fish on her head. The revellers resemble Bosch's hellbent carousers in works such as *The Haywain*. Some of the dancers wear monk's habits, recalling the festive clergy in Bosch's *Ship of Fools* (fig. 59). In the s'Hertogenbosch grisaille (fig. 85b), the two ends of the longer composition have been omitted and the central group only appears, markedly lessening the surreality of the scene. All variants include

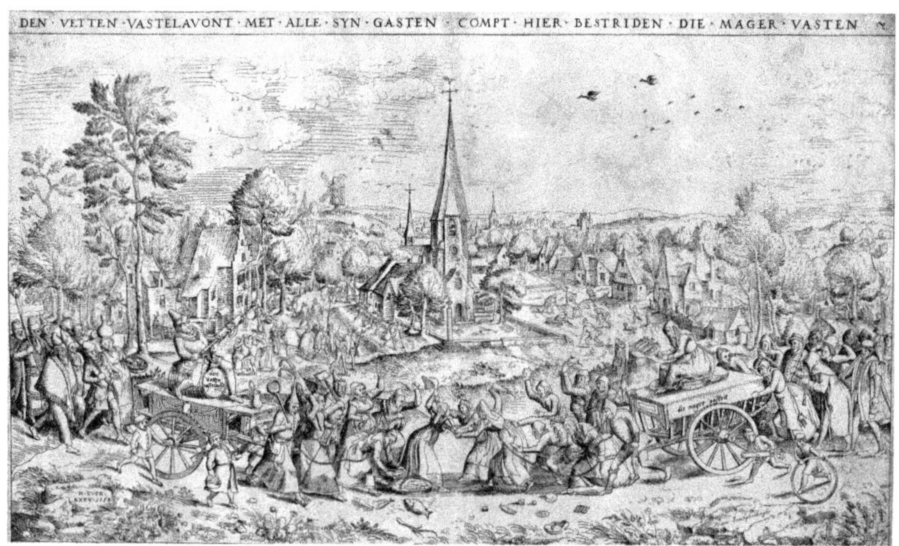

86 Frans Hogenberg, *The Fight Between Carnival and Lent*, 1558. Engraving, 32.7 x 51.8 cm. Bibliothèque Royale Belgique, Brussels S II 16150

a small duck-billed hybrid in the foreground. Attributes of Carnival and of Lent are not divided into separate halves of the design (so the bagpipe, for example, is beside Lent).[199]

In 1558 Hogenberg made a print on the subject (fig. 86).[200] Here, as in the *Proverbs* and *Cockaigne* designs, Hogenberg provided Bruegel with interesting ideas. His scene shows Carnival and Lent, fat and lean as they were usually shown, mounted high on carts, drawn by their followers. At the centre of the print, the two parades confront each other outside a town; the female followers fighting in a scene evocative of Griet's women and Battles for the Breeches. The print was published at the Four Winds the year before Bruegel's painting.

Strife between Carnival and Lent at this date could hardly escape alluding to strife between the daggers-drawn camps of the Reformation, as Stridbeck realised.[201] Protestants discarded and ridiculed the observance of Lent along with the other Catholic dogmas of Good Works. To Luther, almsgiving and fasting were of a piece with pilgrimages, indulgences, and the rest of the Catholic penitential structure, which guaranteed that designated Good Deeds on earth would be rewarded after death. Zwingli and his followers even ushered in the Swiss Reformation by ceremoniously eating sausages during Lent.

Hogenberg's idea of presenting the old combat or debate as an actual fight among rival followers was probably intended as a sarcastic comment on the virulence of current religious quarrels. This topical dimension of the subject is evident also in the painting at Boston, based on the central group from Bruegel's *Carnival and Lent* (Museum of Fine Arts, Boston).[202] In this later work, the two combatants are abstracted from their Bruegelian context as part of the cycle of feasts. The dispute takes place at closer quarters. Lady Lent is about to hit Carnival in the stomach with her paddle of fish. Bruegel kept his representations of carnivalesque mock clergy gentle and ambiguous; the Boston Lady Lent is garbed as a nun and mounted, like Carnival, on a barrel. Her skirt is hitched to show a bare leg, a rosary dangles from her waist. Instead of Bruegel's children and lay almsgivers, Lent's retainers include two figures in penitential hoods, such as those worn by flagellants. This is a considerably more biting representation than the even-handed oppositions of Hogenberg and Bruegel.

All three works make use of the structure familiar from the Battle of the Breeches tradition: Prince Carnival and Lady Lent's mock combat. The comic side of this is important. The advent of Lent had always been the occasion for rueful moans; even Catholics untainted by the new heresies hardly looked forward to its coming. Lent had its own rhetoric. A late comedy on this theme, Thomas Nashe's *Lenten Stuffe* (1599), parodies these woeful stories in a long discourse on the rise and fall of the Pope and the Herring. Carnival's calendar-fated demise occurs at the hands of the scrawny fishwife, Lent; recalling the inevitable victories of the dominant wife in *rederijker kluchtspelen*.[203]

The shape as well as the sex of the participants implied a deeper sort of conflict. A picture once in Vienna shows a fat man whose cheek is sucked

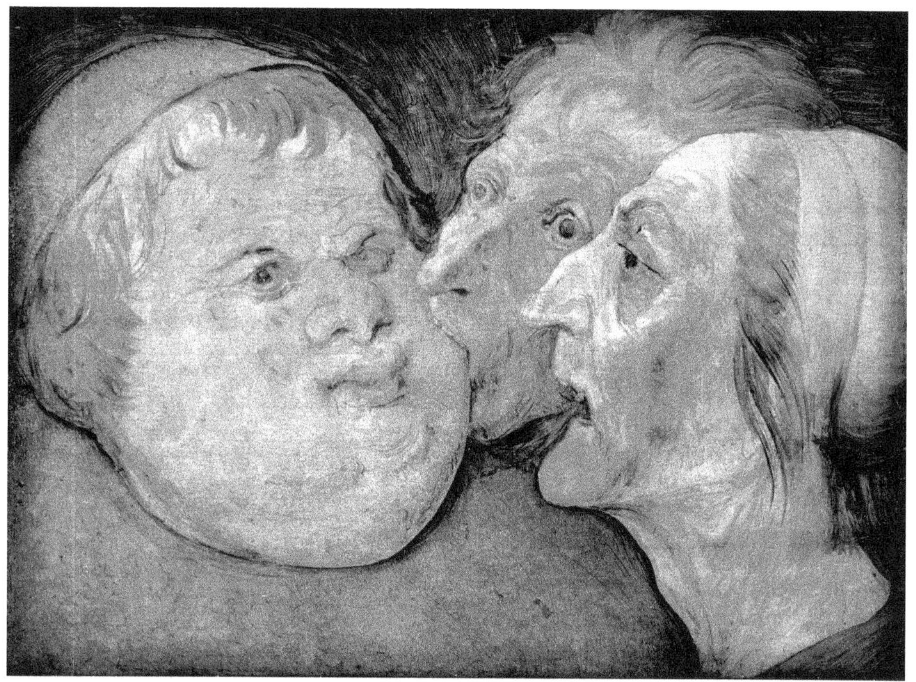

87 Circle of Pieter Bruegel, *Thin Couple Attacking Fat Man*, before 1569. Oil on panel. © Statens Museum for Kunst, Copenhagen. KMS 1639. Photo: SMK

on by a scrawny woman while behind a noseless younger man looks on. Behind them is a glimpse of a window and a picture on a wall. The scene is placed in a tondo on a larger rectangle. At the left side is a pie, a wine jug, and a piece of meat; to the right, leavened bread, mussel shells, etc. These still-life attributes led Glück to name the picture *Carnival and Lent*.[204]

The work seems to be a later sixteenth-century copy of a picture much closer to Bruegel's circle, the *Thin Couple Attacking a Fat Man* (fig. 87) in Copenhagen.[205] The fat man looks placid, as a wild-eyed thin man bites into his cheek, and the head of an equally scrawny woman fills the right-hand side. In the Copenhagen work, there is nothing to identify the protagonists as personifications of Carnival or Lent, and the attacking thin man is male, not female. These pictures express ideas related to those in *The*

Lean and the Fat Kitchens (figs. 66 a-b) with their blackly humorous treatment of famine and plenty.

The visual pairing of fat versus lean clearly had strong metaphorical resonance at mid-century. It was explored, for example, in John Lydgate's *The Fall of Princes* (London, 1554); an allegorical tale designed to illustrate that standard Renaissance trope, The Wheel of Fortune. In Lydgate's narrative, the only person immune to Fortune's caprices is Poverty:

> Once upon a time Fortune met Glad Poverty at a roadside and jeered and laughed at her. Poverty, a ragged, reckless woman, replied that she preferred to be poor and happy than wealthy and anxious. The dispute waxed bitter, and Poverty challenged Fortune to a wrestling match, the loser to obey the winner. In the bout, lean Poverty had the advantage over fat Fortune and overcame her.[206]

Illustrated books including this fable appeared in Bruges in 1474; further French editions in 1494 and 1527; two separate English versions in 1554. Despite the complexity and power of its reversal imagery, and the element of combat, the overall message is one of acceptance; the hierarchy is not challenged, and the poor are given the consolation of virtue. The real-life implications of the motif of the lean figure battling the fat are carefully controlled by its context.

Perhaps due to the rising intolerance of the fat, or wealthy, by the lean, or poor, this image came to appear too inflammatory. A seventeenth-century emblem-writer informs us, in order to explain an iconographic change he wishes to make, that *the ethnic tradition was to make Poverty not only ragged but pallid and angry*.[207] The visual idea of a confrontation between a hungry personification and a fat one, complete with the carnivalesque elements of reversal and social tension, was evidently underwritten in a myriad of different ways, apart from the tradition opposing Carnival and Lent.

These separate threads are united in Hogenberg's invention and in the strange paintings at Copenhagen and Boston. In the light of these choices, the scope of Bruegel's plan for his *Carnival and Lent* becomes apparent. Violence is intrinsic to the clashes of the Reformation, the *caesura* between feasting and fast days, and the cannibalistic encounters between lean and fat. But this aggression is entirely contained and softened in the 1559 painting. Where the artists responsible for the *Thin Couple* and the Boston *Combat* (perhaps the same person) could draw the bitterest implications from Bruegel's work, in Bruegel's original, the central "combat" between Carnival and Lent is integrated into the cycle of seasonal feasts. Carnival and Lent are not about to collide with each other. The Lenten cart pulled by the monk and the nun is about to pass between Prince Carnival and the viewer, while one of Carnival's sledge pullers holds up a flag as if to signify the end of the contest (fig. 71a).

Carnival and Lent as an image of the world

Bruegel to some extent countered the growing chorus of voices against Carnival among the Reforming groups by balancing the secular observations with the sacred ones. His Lenten cycle also has carnivalesque aspects. At the back of the picture (fig. 71b), the two kinds of festival merge into one: Noel, Epiphany; religious holidays celebrated with a traditional inextricable mix of secular and sacred customs. Beggars appear on both sides of the picture. Among the watchers as the Passover congregation files out of the church, a brightly dressed Fool holds a drumstick and a child carries deflated bagpipes. Even in the more clearly divided foreground scenes, then, the sacred and the secular are not kept rigidly apart but are deliberately "mixed." The fool in the Passover crowd has his opposite number in the mock clergyman in the Carnival play, the *Dirty Bride*.

Bruegel's choice of these details presents an implicit argument about the natural meaning and value of these customs by way of antithesis. The patterns of image and counter-image are strong also in the groupings around the well. These form a kind of inner circle, an overspill from the outer cycle of the calendar. Its pairs comment on each other. There is, for example, the productive and destructive use of pots: one woman stirs batter in a pot; across from her, adults break them in the course of a seasonal game. There is fire to cook the Carnival waffles and water used for divining.

Antithetical pairings radiate across the picture like the spokes of a wheel. Consider how the children's games are used to counterpoint adult games. The children playing with tops are placed next to the Church in the lee of the Lenten cycle. Opposite them, the action of children playing with dice is carnivalesque. They echo the adult dice players (whose stakes, innocuously, are waffles) at the bottom left-hand corner. The two groups of beggars bracket the women working with the fish. The wine carriers leaving the inn echo the wine carrier pulling Carnival's barrel; wine is an attribute of Carnival. The image of the two women with the fish cart, one holding it at the back, the other dragging it, echoes the action around Carnival's barrel. Work and play are again contrasted and pictorially linked. The living pig by the well is put in close relation to the whole pig's head on Carnival's stick. The opposition here involves a complex play on *raw* and *cooked*; the cooked pig's head is in itself being used as a prop, and the pig is not dead yet. But surely an excellent and humorous understanding of this part of Carnival — the slaughter of beasts, the preservation of meat, feasting and fast — lies behind this image.

Where these "spokes" meet, in the centre of the picture, a peasant couple are led by a Fool with a torch. This image has given commentators some difficulty. Because the lantern by the woman's side is dark, Stridbeck argued this must have a derogatory significance, since a lit lantern is a *common symbol* of reason and illumination. The dark lantern is balanced by the torch held by the Fool, and similarly therefore *a burning torch symbolised discord, disputes and destruction*.[208] Maybe so, but Bruegel, as we have seen, customarily adjusted allegorical meanings contextually. His command of emblematic puns and paradoxes demands caution in interpreting "common symbols" in his art.

Torches were customarily used for city processions and at festival time in the sixteenth century. They were also used symbolically in folk custom and ritual; and there were often torch processions on the first Sunday of Lent:[209]

> [torches] had their place in the Catholic pre-Lenten celebrations in the children's kingdom. Every year at Carnival time youngsters paraded with these torches, symbolically intended to kill rats... insect pests... and the field mice that harmed harvests... The ritual guaranteed a good harvest of apples and hemp for the next fall and eggs and chicks for Easter. It was a rite of purification and fertility... The shining... flame of the torches in the dark night before Mardi Gras dawned, naturally had its place in the scheme of Carnival.[210]

Torches, like bonfires, had a symbolic significance for rural festivals that naturally diminished in the towns; city governments in fifteenth century Burgundy could order householders to set torches above the doors along a processional route and this expressed no traditional views on their seasonal efficacy.[211] However, meaning is determined by the context here. Women carried torches in a heretical procession in Antwerp in 1526; the "symbolism" of this act seems to have been entirely modern.[212] Though a dark lantern may stand for ignorance, the Shrovetide child in *The Dark Day,* dressed in pillows and a Carnival crown, carries an unlit lantern (figure 71a); in this context, not a derogatory sign.

This enigmatic central group can best be considered as a collective identity: representing Everyman, like the figures in the *Netherlandish Proverbs*. Van Beselaere suggested the peasant couple stood for *de anonieme mensch,* the great mass of the people.[213] A miniature made after a festival held in Nuremberg in 1600 shows at the end of the procession a peasant and his wife, with a fool in motley behind them, aiming his club at the peasant.[214]

In Bruegel's two *kermis* designs, a fool with two children is placed in the centre foreground, like an emblem for the scenes behind.

The peasant was presented in a positive if somewhat ribald light, as an appropriate symbol for the community. At Antwerp in 1559, feasting peasants appeared on a sled as part of the parade to celebrate the Peace.[215] In 1565, peasants accompanied Fertility, the subject of an *ommegang* float.[216] On both occasions, the imagery correlates also with the spirit of incipient nationalism. The couple led by a fool in the *Carnival and Lent,* like peasants placed in *ommegangen,* may carry a message of this kind.

A puzzling detail in Bruegel's depiction of the couple is the hump on the man's back. Interpreting this as a sack hidden under his clothing, Stridbeck thought this detail could have been *inspired by one of the fables of Aesop, [in] which everybody carries two sacks. One of them hangs in front and contains the faults and crimes of others, while the other, which hangs on the back, contains one's own.*[217] Of course, there are problems with identifying the hump as a sack; but the visual idea of Aesop, the most famous hunchback of the day, is an illuminating suggestion. Aesop was a perennial favourite in oral and literate culture, enjoying another revival due to the predilection for printing *what everybody knows.* The *Wonderful and Joyous Life of Aesop* was reprinted with the original woodcuts at Antwerp in 1548. The frontispiece shows the hunchbacked author (fig. 88). Aesop's fables were part of commonplace wisdom in Bruegel's time. In view of the artist's liking for this kind of material, this Everyman and Wife, facing into the picture-space, away from the viewer, may be informed by this idea.

Whatever else it may mean, the placement of the peasant and his wife at the centre of an ideal city, at the hub of a cycle of feasts, is an archaism, and indeed the whole picture is a deliberate panorama of archaisms. Despite the city square setting, the painting depicts a strictly edited account of the seasonal year, describing festivals which scarcely existed any longer in Bruegel's Antwerp, while excluding all of the modern civic festivities which marked the city's year. The *Carnival and Lent* is in a sense, a memorial, tinged

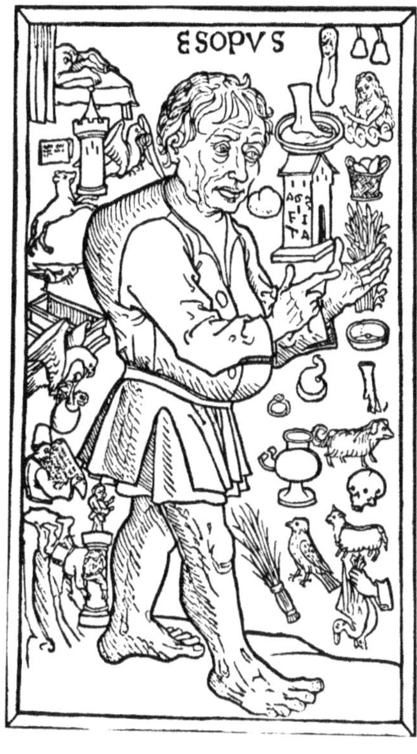

88 Anon, Aesop, title page, *Het Wonderlyck ende Genvelyck Leven van Esope*, publ Greg de Bonte (Antwerp, 1548)

with nostalgia, for an idealised Carnival whose days were over. The rambunctious chaos of the carnivalesque, so evident in the later psychological prints of James and Hermogenes, is here hardly characteristic of Carnival itself.

The painting in its structure harks back to the older tradition of the dispute, which was not initially an out-and-out combat. There was always a third party who arbitrated between the contestants.[218] If the peasant and his wife are arbitors, Bruegel has neatly twisted his materials by having them turn away from the contest. The idea of a farewell to Carnival thus runs through the whole picture, in its struture as much as in its imagery. The *Carnival and Lent* represents then a full circle; summing up the old parodic tradition of this Combat in a way that could only be done from the outside. As Gaignebet wrote:

> For it is not the triumph, but the farewell of Carnival which is represented in our tableau. The whole attitude of this personage, the gesture which he sketches with his left hand, his lifted eyes, mark this farewell. But to whom does he address this sign and this look? At the painter, and at ourselves.[219]

Carnival is in several ways past his day. Lent's vehicle is about to overtake that of Carnival, and come between Carnival and the viewer. Carnival's followers are orderly; the one scene of vomiting is quietly removed from the street. More people watch than participate. Beside the inn, a man is slumped, his head pillowed on his arms, in sleep or drunkenness, unaware of his proximity to the flames above him. The children's king stands drinking on a barrel, at the same time acclaimed by his "subjects" and doused with cold water. The douser makes plain his attitude to the celebrations. Apart from this intervention, Prince Carnival is the only other figure in the work who shows awareness of events going on outside of his own time.

The main formal idea for the *Carnival and Lent,* the circulation of the crowd in the town square, reworks the old folkloric year and its cycle of feasts. Bruegel's attempt in this painting to reconcile the popular and ecclesiastical festal calendars, at odds in real life,[220] reminds us also of the deeper philosophical dimensions, Neo-Platonic in origin, of his visual thought. Gaignebet cited Ortelius' contention that Bruegel *painted the things that could not be painted.*[221] Thomas offers this perception:

> In primitive societies the unfolding of the seasons and the life cycles of the inhabitants were sufficient to give man a sense of flux and decay but not of structural change. At a more advanced stage of historical development came the cyclical view of history, the view that change did occur, but that in the long run everything came back to where it started.

> This notion that history waxes and wanes like the moon, so influential in classical times, enjoyed a new vogue during the Renaissance.[222]

It is then perhaps the congruence between the "primitive" sense of time as cyclical, expressed in the popular calendar, and the Neo-Platonic idea that history itself was cyclical, that Bruegel sought to combine in his pictorial treatment of this subject. The *Carnival and Lent* is both comparative and conciliatory. This motive appears in the philosophy of the contemporary Neo-Platonists, eirenicists to a man and woman, then engaged in the considerably more arcane endeavour of producing a religious history, that would be both comparative and conciliatory:

> The most fundamental motive for using the *prisca theologia* was in order to have a past without breaks, a past that included and connected together the Christian and Jewish worlds, Greece and Rome, ancient Gaul and, for some, medieval France. In attempting this... with whatever mistakes in chronology and interpretation, they did also try to preserve the continuity of history, which... Christian revelation was always threatening to break. The consequences of this attempt were important in several ways... This wide unbroken view of history also entailed, and helped to support, religious liberalism... it remains true that most of the writers we have examined were more concerned with finding similarities than differences between various philosophies and religions.[223]

Since Bruegel chose to emphasise similarities rather than differences between the opposed observances of Carnival and Lent, the painting is thus evidence to support the view of Bruegel as an eirenicist. Beyond nostalgia, conscious archaism in this painting expresses the desire for a past without breaks, for continuity in the shape of an collective imaginary. The cycle of feasts is made to stand for an all-inclusive society held together and defined by its public festivals. This is a vision that could only be seen, as it were, from the outside, in retrospect. As in the case of the *Proverbs*, the appearence of this oral material in a fixed medium is a sign of its passing.

Notes to Chapter 4

[1] M. M. Bakhtin, *Rabelais and His World*, trans. Helene Iswolsky (Cambridge, 1968); still fundamental for early modern popular culture, though its application to Rabelais has been criticised, e.g., R. M. Berrong, *Rabelais and Bakhtin: Popular Culture in Gargantua and Pantagruel* (Lincoln, 1986).

[2] P. Burke, *Popular Culture in Early Modern Europe* (New York, 1978), 107f.

[3] See E. K. Chambers, *The Medieval Stage* (Oxford, 1903), I., ch. XIII and XIV, 274-335, on the history of this feast and its suppression.

[4] See, e.g., E. L. Eisenstein, "The Advent of Printing and the Protestant Revolt: A New Approach to the Disruption of Western Christendom," in R. M. Kingdon, ed., *Transition and Revolution: Problems and Issues of European Renaissance and Reformation History* (Minneapolis, 1974), 235-270.

[5] This is the burden of chapters 4 and 6 in R. W. Scribner, *For the Sake of Simple Folk: Popular Propaganda for the German Reformation* (Cambridge, 1981).

[6] In the essay on "The Symbolic Representation of Time," in E. Leach, *Rethinking Anthropology* (London, 1961); which follows from A. Van Gennep (1909), *The Rites of Passage*, trans. M. Vizedom and G. Caffee (Chicago, 1960), 114.

[7] E. R. Ladurie, *Carnival in Romans*, trans. M. Feeney (New York, 1979), 306-7.

[8] From the essay "Women on Top," in N. Z. Davis, *Society and Culture in Early Modern France* (Stanford, 1975), 153.

[9] cf. the related practice of *couvade*, where an expectant father, after or just before the birth, acts out many of the symptoms of pregnancy or takes to his bed after the delivery.

[10] See R. W. Scribner, "Reformation, Carnival and the World Turned Upside Down," *Social History* 3 (1978), 316; synthesising information from Van Gennep, ibid., and M. Gluckman, *Essays on the Ritual of Social Relations* (Manchester, 1962), 1-52.

[11] Davis, 153, summarising, *inter alia*, the arguments in the Introduction and ch. 3 of M. Gluckman (1962), and in ch. 4 of V. Turner, *The Forest of Symbols* (New York, 1967).

[12] V. Turner, "Comments and Conclusions," in B. Babcock, ed., *The Reversible World* (Ithaca, 1977), 280.

[13] Cf. E. Durkheim, *The Elementary Forms of the Religious Life*, trans. J. Swain (London, 1915), 347-9; analysed in terms of Carnival as reconciliatory, by M. D. Bristol, *Carnival and Theatre. Plebian Culture and the Structure of Authority in Renaissance England* (London, 1985), 30.

[14] M. Douglas, *Purity and Danger. An Analysis of the Concepts of Pollution and Taboo* (London, 1966), 88-93.

[15] See, e.g., R. Bernheimer, *Wild Men in the Middle Ages. A Study in Art, Sentiment and Demonology* (Cambridge, 1952), 3f.
[16] M. M. Bakhtin, *The Dialogic Imagination*, trans. M. Holquist and C. Emerson (Austin, 1981), 132; cf. Bristol, ibid., 24.
[17] Burke, 191-2. Probably this dispersal of the carnivalesque contributed to the "dilution" of the meaning of festival in comparison with "primitive" Carnival.
[18] Durkheim, loc. cit.
[19] Turner (1977), 284.
[20] Ibid., 287.
[21] Ibid., 282.
[22] Bakhtin (1968), 6f.
[23] Cf. e.g. Scribner (1978), 303-29.
[24] The best case for this is made by Davis, loc. cit.; arguing that "Women on Top" could foment actual revolt.
[25] The tale and its incarnation in folk drama is extensively dealt with in A. Dickson, *Valentine and Orson*, Early English Text Society, no. 204 (London, 1937).
[26] See discussion and references in E. P. Thompson, "Rough Music: Le Charivari anglais," *Annales: Economies, Societés, Civilisations* 27 (1972), 285-312.
[27] See documents and descriptions in S. Williams and J. Jacquot, "Ommegangs anversois du temps de Bruegel et de van Heemskert," *Les Fêtes de la Renaissance* II (Paris, 1957).
[28] On *Sotterie* in general, see Chambers, I, 380-3; and for the Netherlands specifically see the plays edited by A. H. Hoffmann von Fallersteben, *Altniederlandische Schaubuhne Abele Spelen ende Sottiernien* (Amsterdam, 1968), VI, many of which deal with the popular or folk themes of the domineering wife and the hen-pecked husband.
[29] See W. S. Gibson, "Artists and *Rederijkers* in the Age of Bruegel," *Art Bulletin* LXIII/3 (September, 1981), 426-46.
[30] On mock ceremonies, see Burke, 184; on mock abbeys and abbots, see "The Reasons of Misrule," in Davis, 97-123.
[31] Scribner (1981), 68.
[32] Scribner (1978), 306-7.
[33] Ibid., 308.
[34] See n. 26; also Davis, 298, n. 13; 300, n. 26; passim.
[35] Evidence for this view of the clergy is given in Kingdon's essay, "Was the Protestant Reformation a Revolution?" 53-104 in his collection cited in n. 4.
[36] Scribner (1978), 322, cf. 323, nn. 97-8; 324-9; also Bakhtin (1968), 9.
[37] Cf. e.g. ch. 2 of K. Thomas, *Religion and the Decline of Magic* (New York, 1971), and J. Delumeau, *Naissance et Affirmation de la Réforme* (Paris, 1965), 257-80.

[38] I draw this argument from the summary in S. Ozment, *The Age of Reform, 1250-1550* (New Haven, 1980), 330-2.
[39] Ibid., 331-2.
[40] H. P. Duerr, *Dreamtime: Concerning the Boundary between Wilderness and Civilization*, trans. F. Goodman (Oxford, 1985), 192-4.
[41] By the end of the sixteenth century, the Black Mass was firmly established in the minds of witchcraft inquisitors as a real practice; cf. discussion in J. Klaits, *Servants of Satan. The Age of the Witch Hunters* (Indiana, 1985), 52-53.
[42] Ibid., 53, for extracts from De Lancre's 200-page account of a carnivalesque sabbat. In 1609, De Lancre sent more than 80 women to the stake; his self-justificatory memoir of this exploit was published in 1612.
[43] See account in P. Minnaert, "A propos de Carnaval et Carême par Bruegel (Notes Folkloriques)," *Apollo: chronique des Beaux Arts* 23 (August-September 1943), 9.
[44] M. De Meyer, *De Volks- en Kinderprent in de Nederlanden, van de 15e tot de 20e eeuw* (Antwerp-Amsterdam, 1962), 573, reproduces a later *Dirty Bride* broadsheet illustrated with this sixteenth-century woodcut; but the woodcut itself is not truly "popular" since it seems to be copied from an etching by Daniel Hopfer, c. 1520, which shows the identical comic couple, this time labeled *Bolicana and Marcolfus*. Reproduced as fig. 59, 54 in E. Tietze-Conrat, *Dwarfs and Jesters In Art*, trans. E. Osburn (London, 1957).
[45] According to Minnaert, 9. Locher, the translator of Brant's *Ship of Fools*, also referred to Carnival costumes as aping the spirits of the dead; see translations in A. Pompen, *The English Versions of the Ship of Fools* (New York, 1967), 254.
[46] Scribner (1978), 323.
[47] Burke, 203.
[48] Quoted in Burke, 202; this metaphor was a persistent one. It appears again in a defense of Carnival by a Doctor of Auxerre who argued that since the clergy are *nothing but old wine-casks badly put together [they] would certainly burst if the wine of wisdom were allowed to boil by continued devotion to the Divine Service*, quoted in E. Welsford, *The Fool: His Social and Literary History* (New York,1935), 202.
[49] Scribner (1978), 72-3.
[50] Shakespeare, *Troilus and Cressida* (1601-2), I, iii, lines 109-10.
[51] See the chapter of that name in Burke, 107f.
[52] Ibid., 208.
[53] Ibid.
[54] Quoted ibid., 209.
[55] Scribner (1978), 265, n. 8.

[56] C. G. Stridbeck, "*Combat between Carnival and Lent* by Pieter Bruegel the Elder. An Allegorical Picture of the Sixteenth Century," *Journal of the Warburg and Courtauld Institutes* XIX (1956), 98.
[57] J. Huizinga, *The Waning of the Middle Ages. A Study of the Forms of Life, Thought, and Art in France and the Netherlands in the Fourteenth and Fifteenth Centuries*, trans. F. Hopman (Harmondsworth, 1972), 155; Jean-Chartier de Gerson, rector of the University of Pons, crusaded vehemently against the Feast of Fools.
[58] Ibid., 154.
[59] Ariès, 73.
[60] For a sample of the vast literature on masks and masking, see Scribner (1978), 311, nn. 31-3; Duerr, 232, n. 26; 278, n. 44.
[61] Duerr, 61, 268, n. 3.
[62] Scribner, ibid., 321, n. 84.
[63] R. Muchembled, *Popular Culture and Elite Culture in France 1400-1750*, trans. L. Cochrane (Baton Rouge-London, 1985), 165.
[64] Duerr, 233, n. 30.
[65] Ibid., 268, n. 4.
[66] Chambers, I, 401.
[67] Ibid., 401-2, n. 2, on relevant etymologies.
[68] Duerr, 232, n. 26; this is also the exact nomenclature used by Locher in his condemnation of Carnival fools (see n. 45 above).
[69] Ibid; for relationships between witches and masks, see K Meuli, "Maske un Maskereien," in E. Hoffmann-Krayer and H. Bächtold-Stäubli, eds., *Handwörterbuch des deutschen Aberglaubens*, V (Berlin, 1933), col. 1759.
[70] G. B. Spagnuoli (Mantuanus), *Fasti* (Strasbourg, 1518), Book 2; quoted in Burke, 190.
[71] Duerr, 236, n. 36.
[72] In the second edition of Locher's *Ship of Fools*, in Pompen, 254.
[73] J. Caro Baroja, ed., *Romances de ciego* (Taurus: Madrid, 1966), 84; Burke, 187.
[74] Burke, 187.
[75] Davis, 118; 307, n. 81.
[76] From a letter of 1604, in L. Vöet, *The Golden Compasses: A History and Evaluation of the Printing and Publishing Activities of the Officina Plantiniana at Antwerp* (Amsterdam, 1969), I, 18-19: *Plantin... towards nightfall... went out, accompanied by a lad to light his way... He had just left the street near the exchange where he lived, which led to the Meir Bridge, and had come to that familiar place where the crucifix now stands, when some drunken men in masks bore down upon him. They were looking for a zither player who had made fools of them... One of them immediately drew his dagger.*

[77] Muchembled, 161.
[78] Ibid., 160f.
[79] As Davis also notes, 107, 115, and passim; cf. Chambers, I, 403, n. 3.
[80] See Williams and Jacquot; also J. Wegg, *Antwerp, 1477-1559* (London, 1916), 84-5. The authorities also sponsored numerous parades to celebrate the Emperor's overseas battles. Since these were mainly victories in the way of religion, civic *ommegangen* had a particularly obvious political use here. They served to affirm loyalty and disarm the suspicions generated by the town's persistent reluctance to implement anti-heresy placards. Wegg, 85, 203, 211, 213, 266, 271.
[81] See A. van Gennep, *Le Folklore de la Flandre et du Hainaut Francais (Département du Nord)* (Paris, 1935), I, 156, on the first recorded dates of Giant processions in Belgian towns and regions.
[82] Wegg (1916), 50-1, on Kloppersdyke.
[83] See Gibson (1981), 432f., on *rederijker* floats for these events.
[84] The chief festival mainly because, it seems, of the clergy's involvement. A relic from the Holy Land was paraded. Wegg (1916), 85, mentions a Palm Procession, held on Palm Sunday, where, *a man representing Christ... sat on a wooden ass and was drawn to the Burg church. In 1487 it was ordered that none should take part in this but those who had been to the Holy Land.*
[85] The cathedral was dedicated to her and became a famous pilgrimage shrine from the 1470s on, complete with miracle-working statue. See Wegg (1916), 22, 224, 257, and discussion in Chapter Five.
[86] Muchembled draws on Guicciardini's descriptions of country *rederijkers*, 137.
[87] Gibson (1981), 433.
[88] Ibid, 440.
[89] See T. Weevers, *Poetry of the Netherlands in its European Context, 1170-1930* (London, 1960), 46-9; discussing *Elck* and the earliest secular plays.
[90] M. van Vaernewyck, quoted in S. L. Sumberg, *The Nuremberg Schembart Carnival* (New York, 1941), 136.
[91] Sumberg, loc. cit.
[92] On the *rederijkers* in general, see Hoffman von Fallersleben; on their serious topical dramas see Weevers, 102-7 and K. Moxey, *Aertsen, Beuckler and Secular Painting in the Reformation* (New York, 1977), 149-178; on their history in Antwerp, Wegg (1916), 64-5, 79-81, 127, 201-2, 214.
[93] Gibson (1981), 430; for more on the humanist poetry of the *rederijkers*, see Weevers, 67-87; S. Eringa, *La Renaissance et les Rhetoriqueurs Néerlandais* (Amsterdam, 1920), 25-50, 69-73.
[94] Gibson, ibid.; Moxey (1977), ibid.
[95] Van Gennep, I, 155, calls this *un caractère essential.*
[96] Bakhtin (1968), 6-10; 303-19.

[97] Michel de Montaigne, *Upon Some Verses of Virgil* (Essays, XV, 1575), in *Essays of Montaigne*, v. 8; trans. C. Cotton, rev. W. C. Hazlett (New York, 1910).
[98] Welsford, 200.
[99] Chambers, I, 294.
[100] Quoted in Muchembled, 127.
[101] Dates given in Muchembled, 140. See also n. 3 above.
[102] K. Moxey, "Pieter Bruegel and *The Feast of Fools*," *Art Bulletin* LXIV (4) (December, 1982), 642.
[103] All authorities are agreed on the young, unmarried and lowly status of the participants. See e.g., Moxey, *Feast of Fools*, 641; Welsford, 201; J. LeFebvre, *Les Fols et la Folie* (Paris, 1968), 171-212. Muchembled points to the fertility rite parallel, 140.
[104] See especially Davis, 97-109.
[105] Muchembled, 167.
[106] This is Muchembled's interpretation (pp. 168-9) of Davis' data (pp. 109-22), which I follow here.
[107] Muchembled, 167-8.
[108] Duerr, 236, n. 38.
[109] On the Blue Boat guilds see D. M. Enklaar, "De Blauuve Schvit," *Tijdschrift Voor Geschiedenis* XLVIII (1933); Minnaert, 9.
[110] Wegg (1916), 79.
[111] Ibid., 127-8. H. Pleij, "The Despisers of Rhetoric. Origins and Significance of Attacks on the Art of Rhetoric," in J. Koopmans et al, eds, *Rhetoric-Rhétoriqueurs-Rederijkers* (Amsterdam-Oxford, 1995), however, thinks the choice of this kind of name was an act of ironic self-defense responding to a tendency to mock the highly ornate language and style of the rhetoricians from the middle of the century on: "To eliminate that impression [of arrogance] some rederijkers adopted names... which humbly claim a great lack of knowledge: *The Uneducated* in Lier, *The Lightly Laden* in Ypres, *The Dull-witted* in Arnemuiden, *The Unesteemed* in Antwerp, *The Simple-Minded* in St. Niklaas, *Of Scant Wisdom* in Niewpoort... This insistence on one's own lack of education [is] a topos regularly found in prologues to medieval literary works... tak[ing] the form of competitive declarations of modesty and ineptitude" (168).
[112] Wegg (1916), 172, 213; cf. 271.
[113] Ibid., 82.
[114] Muchembled, 150.
[115] On Phillip's Joyous Entry, see Gibson (1981), 440; Wegg (1916), 261-5.
[116] Gibson, loc. cit.; the military guilds also had their fools, cf. Wegg (1916), 103-4; cf. E. H. van Heurck and G. J. Boekenoogen, *L'Imagerie Populaire des Pays-Bas Belgique-Hollande* (Paris, 1930), 12.

[117] Moxey, *Feast of Fools*, 642, and especially n. 20 discusses and reproduces a drawing (made after the event) of fools in motley at the Brussels *landjuweel*.
[118] Moxey, loc. cit.
[119] Ibid., 643.
[120] While Moxey (ibid., 644) does not find a common meaning in these, the information given in A. Dundes and C. A. Stibbe, "The Art of Mixing Metaphors. A Folkloristic Interpretation of the *Netherlandish Proverbs* by Pieter Bruegel the Elder," *Folklore Fellows Communications*, no. 230 (Helsinki), 1981, 16-17, referring to O. Fenichel, "The Long Nose," in *Collected Papers of Otto Fenichel* (New York, 1953), illuminates the connection.
[121] Dundes and Stibbe, 17.
[122] The carnivalesque aspect of this print is noted by Barnouw, who calls it a "make-believe kermis scene of Vanity Fair;" quoted in H. A. Klein, *Graphic Worlds of Pieter Bruegel the Elder* (New York, 1963), 263.
[123] On the print, its drawing and sources, see cat. 102-3 in N. Orenstein, ed., *Pieter Bruegel the Elder: Drawings and Prints*, Museum Boijmans Van Beuningen, Rotterdam; Metropolitan Museum of Art (New York, 2001), 232-4 .
[124] Moxey, *Feast of Fools*, 640.
[125] Wegg briefly mentions these gardens of the military guilds, 30, 44, 78, 103. It is not clear whether craft guilds or *rederijkerkammers* had their own gardens.
[126] On the *haagspel*, Edward van Even, *Het landjuweel van Antwerpen in 1561* (Leuven, 1861), 51; see M. D. Carroll, "Peasant Festivity and Political Identity in the Sixteenth Century," *Art History* 10 (September, 1987), 310, n. 70 and 311, n. 78.
[127] On shooting-guild members as festive actors, see T. Reintges, *Ursprung and Wesen der spatmittel alterlichen schutzengilden* (Bonn, 1963), 258-62.
[128] Welsford, 281.
[129] Ibid.
[130] Ben Jonson, *The Devil Is an Ass* (1616, published 1631), I, i, 81-5, 100-3.
[131] Guicciardini writing around 1560; Muchembled, 137.
[132] Ibid., 135.
[133] Carroll, as n. 123 above.
[134] Gibson (1981), 430.
[135] See account in Van Even.
[136] The Swiss forces, comprised of infantry and peasant archers, defeated Charles the Bold and his cavalry at Hericourt (November 1474), at Grandson (February 1476) and at Murton (June 1476). These victories culminated in their decisive battle at Nancy (January 1477), when Charles himself fell and the power of Burgundy was destroyed. In 1486, the German peasant leaders of the *Bundschuh* rebellion described their desire to be *at least as free as the Swiss, and, like the Hussites, to participate in the direction of religious affairs*; quoted in L. Rothkrug, "German Holiness

and Western Sanctity," *Historical Reflections* 15 (1) (1988), 182. On the Swiss in general and their archers see T. Brady, *Turning Swiss: Cities and Empire, 1450-1550* (Cambridge, 1985), 17-41. On the magical powers ascribed to archers, see Rothkrug, ibid, 183-4, n. 81, replying to R. Scribner's review in *European Studies Review* 13 (1983), 98.

[137] The nobility had for centuries complained that the crossbow was an "unfair' weapon. Cf. L. Rothkrug, "Holy Shrines, Religious Dissonance and Satan in the Origins of the German Reformation," *Historical Reflections* 14 (1987), 196-207.

[138] J. Sprenger and H. Kramer, *Malleus Maleficarum* (Speier, c. 1486), trans. M. Summers (London, 1971), 323-5; quoted in Rothkrug (1987), 197.

[139] Quoted in Chambers, I, 382.

[140] E.g. C. G. Stridbeck, *Bruegelstudien. Untersuchungen zu den ikonologischen Problemen bei Pieter Bruegel* (Stockholm, 1956), 162.

[141] Klein, 243.

[142] See L. P. V. Febvre (1946), *The Problem of Unbelief in the Sixteenth Century. The Religion of Rabelais*, trans. B. Gottlied (Cambridge, Mass., 1982), 393-5, on the rarity of clocks.

[143] Stridbeck, 164.

[144] This and following data are taken from Carroll, 229f.

[145] Quoted in Carroll, 299-300.

[146] Ibid., 298.

[147] Ibid., 295.

[148] See Burke, 184-5; Ladurie, 177; on St. George's Day customs in general see O. Reinsberg-Duringsfeld, *Traditions et Légendes de la Belgique* (Brussels, 1870), I, 262-7, and Reintges, 254-7.

[149] Wegg (1916), 50-1.

[150] Summarised in W. S. Gibson, *Pieter Bruegel the Elder: two studies*. Lawrence: Spencer Museum of Art, University of Kansas, 1991, 11-35

[151] Pieter van der Borcht *Peasant Kermis* (1559), Metropolitan Museum of Art, New York; on its text and imagery, A. Monballieu, "De *Kermis van Hoboken* bij P. Bruegel, J. Grimmer en G. Mostaert," *Jaerboek van het Koninklijk Museum voor Schone Kunsten Antwerpen* (1974), 146; Carroll, 301.

[152] Text and trans. from H. Miedema, "Realism and Comic Mode: The Peasant," *Simiolus* IX/4 (1977), 209.

[153] For an interpretation of these as denunciations of peasant leisure, see K. P. F. Moxey, "Sebald Beham's Church Anniversary Holidays: Festive Peasants as Instruments of Repressive Humour," in E. Uuman, ed., *Von der Macht der Bilder. Kunst der Reformationzeit* (Leipzig, 1983), 122f. and passim; the same arguement was presented in more detail in his later *Peasants, Warriors and Wives: Popular Imagery in the Reformation* (Chicago, 1989); on the other hand, Carroll, 301-2, relies on

variations in the captions, the evidence of proverbs advocating moderation over abstinence, and the peacefulness of the scene to make her case for the patriotic interpretation.

[154] Carroll's phrase, 299.

[155] Monballieu, 144.

[156] Muchembled, 133.

[157] A. Jans, "Enkele grepen uit de Kerkelijke wetgeving ten tijde vah pieter Bruegel," *Jaerboek van het koninklijk Museum voor Schone Kunsten Antwerpen* (1969), 105-11.

[158] J. O. Hand, catalogue entry, *The Age of Bruegel*, 100 (see n. 69 above).

[159] By Monballieu, 142-50.

[160] See A. Hamilton, *The Family of Love* (Cambridge, 1981), also H. de la Fontaine-Verwey, "Pieter Coecke van Aelst and the Publication of Serlio's book On Architecture," *Quaerendo* VI/2 (1976).

[161] This is the eirenicist position; also that of the *politique* party of Catherine de Medici in France. For eirenicism, see J. van Dorsten, *The Radical Arts* (London, 1973), ch. 2 and 3 on the *viri occulti et obscuri*; the general intellectual history on which these views were founded is given in W. J. Bouwsma, *Concordia Mundi: The Career and Thought of Guillaume Postel (1510-1581)* (Cambridge, 1957).

[162] Hamilton, 71. See also R. Boumans, "The Religious Views of Abraham Ortelius," *Journal of the Warburg and Courtauld Institutes* 17 (1954), 374-77.

[163] See J. Bossy, "Some Elementary Forms of Durkheim," *Past and Present*, XCV (1982), 3-18, and P. Biller, "Words and the Medieval Notion of *Religion*" *Journal of Ecclesiastical History* 36(3) (July 1985), 351-69.

[164] Scribner (1978), 69.

[165] Carroll, 301.

[166] Two main classic studies addressed the interpretative problems of this painting: C.G., Stridbeck, "*Combat between Carnival and Lent* by Pieter Bruegel the Elder. An Allegorical Picture of the Sixteenth Century," *Journal of the Warburg and Courtauld Institutes* XIX (1956), 96-109, who relates the work to the contemporary religious conflict and Coonhert's "middle way", and C. Gaignebet, "*Le combat de carnaval et de Carême* de P. Bruegel (1559), *Annales: Economies, sociétés, civilisations* 2 (March-April, 1972), 313-345. The following discussion draws on both of these, and from the older literature, on P. Minnaert, "A propos de Carnaval et Carême par Bruegel (notes folkloriques)", *Apollo: chronique des Beaux Arts* (Brussels) 23 (Aug-Sept 1943), 8-10, and G., Gluck, "Die Darstellungen des Karnevals und der Fasten von Bosch und Bruegel," *Gedenboek A. Vermeylen* (n. pl., 1932), 263-8.

[167] By Gaignebet's interpretation of the picture as a cycle, there can be no "winner" since one feast gives way to the next, and the cycle repeats.

[168] See, on this vast subject; J.C. Webster, *The Labors of the Months in Antique and Medieval Art to the end of the Twelfth Century* (Evanston-Chicago, 1938); mâle, 65-74; E. Panofsky, *Early Netherlandish Painting* (1953; New York, 1971), v. 2, 33-4, 373, n.1, 374, n. 10; J. Harthan, *The Book of Hours* (New York, 1977); for fine illustrations of sixteenth-century Books of Hours, see G. Bazin, *Le Livre des Saisons* (Geneva, 1948).

[169] E.g. Bibliotheque nationale, MS Lat. 1077 and 1394; cf. E. Mâle (1913), *The Gothic Image*, trans. D. Nussey (New York, 1958), 75, nn. 2-3.

[170] These developments have been studied by historians interested in the illustrations as documents of cultural activities; e.g. P. Aries, *Centuries of Childhood*, trans. R. Baldick (NewYork, 1962), 340-5; S. Hindman, "Pieter Bruegel's *Children's Games*, Folly, and Chance," *Art Bulletin*, LXIII (3) (September, 1981), 455-8, relates the tradition of calendar illustration to another *Theatrum Mundi* painting. On the development of adult seasonal pastimes in the sixteenth century in general see L. Sinanglou Marcus, *The Politics of Mirth* (Pittsburgh, 1980), chs. 1 and 2.

[171] *The Hours of Charles de Valois, Duc d'Angouleme*, Biblioteque Nationale, MS Lat. 1173, folio 20, V, For brief descriptions of this early sixteenth-century work see Aries, 340; Bazin, passim. The Breviary of Eleanor of Portugal is described and illustrated in J. Plummer, *Liturgical Manuscripts* (New York, 1964), 36, pl. 15.

[172] Hindman, 456-7, figs. 9-14a.

[173] *The Hours of Charles de Valois, Duc d'Angouleme*, Biblioteque Nationale, MS Lat. 1173, folio 20, V, For brief descriptions of this early sixteenth-century work see Aries, 340; Bazin, passim. The Breviary of Eleanor of Portugal is described and illustrated in J. Plummer, *Liturgical Manuscripts* (New York, 1964), 36, pl. 15.

[174] E. H. van Heurck and G. J. Boekenoogen, *L'Imagerie Populaire des Pays-bas Belgique-Hollande* (Paris 1930), 167, illustrate a printed cut-out crown from this period, to be worn by a child at Epiphany.

[175] For a summary of arguments about the identification of these pictures with specific months, see e.g. P. Bianconi, *The Complete Paintings of Bruegel* (New York, 1967), pp. 99-101. One issue is whether each painting represents one or two months, and hence how many from the putative whole series can be presumed missing. For the documents concerning Nicholas Jonghelinck, Marijnissen and Seidel, 58, n. 47.

[176] M. C. Plomp in N. M. Orenstein (2001), 243, n. 4.

[177] On this popular seventeenth-century broadsheet, Van Heurck and Boekenoog-en, 71f.

[178] Gaignebet, 336

[179] Burke, 182.

[180] Gaignebet, 324, credits this insight to G. Gluck (without precise references), quoting him as follows: *Les paysans ne se croient pas observés par le spectateur, et tout comme les bucherons de la tapisserie, vivent d'une vie bien a eux, sans relation aux exterieur.*

[181] A printed game involving many different characters, the rules for which have been lost, was apparently played at this time of year; possibly, it is this game, rather than a traditional custom, that is depicted at the back of the painting. Van Heurck and Boekenoogen, 116, reproduce two such *Billets de rois* broadsheets, 117, 129.
[182] Gaignebet, 343, illustrates a print from 1608 by C-J Visscher, in the Fondation Atlas van Stolk, Rotterdam; it shows a procession almost identical to the one in Bruegel's painting.
[183] For the history of this play, see introduction in Dickson (1937).
[184] Gaignebet, 327.
[185] Ibid., 337.
[186] K. Thomas, *Religion and the Decline of Magic* (New York, 1971), ch. 2: "The Magic of the Medieval Church," 32; cf. 25-50.
[187] Gaignebet, 337.
[188] J. Wegg (1916), *Antwerp, 1477-1559* (London, 1916), 145, mentions the legally dead status of the lepers at Antwerp; c.f. Gaignebet, 328, discusses customs surrounding lepers; S. Schama, *The Embarrassment of Riches* (New York, 1987), 579, mentions a similar procession for Amsterdam, on Printers' Monday, *in which particular dignitaries of the guild and of the leprozenhuis participated to emphasize this unbroken communitas.*
[189] Gaignebet, 329-31. Cf. R. Bernheimer's *Wild Men in the Middle Ages: A Study in Art, Sentiment, and Demonology* (Cambridge, Mass., 1952), 3, on the wild man as a median stage between human and beast: *The notion of the wild man must respond and be due to a persistent psychological urge. We may define this as the need to give external expression and symbolically valid form to the impulses of reckless physical self-assertion which are hidden in all of us but are normally kept under control.*
[190] For this play, see T. Weevers, *Poetry in the Netherlands in its European Context, 1170-1930* (London, 1960), 55; for similar forms, G. Lozinski, *La Bataille de Caresme et de Charnage*, critical edition with introduction (Paris, 1933), 85-90.
[191] Lozinski, 90.
[192] Ibid., 104. Lozinski lists versions from c. 1340 through to the seventeenth century.
[193] Documents in W. Hudson and J. Tingey, *Selected Records of the City of Norwich*, v. I (London, 1906), 345; quoted in Kinser, 50, who concludes: *There are some problems concerning the exact date on which this procession occurred and its political implications. It is probable that, notwithstanding the affirmation of the defendants... about the parade being customary on mardi gras, this parade in 1443 occurred in late January.*
[194] S. Kinser, *Rabelais's Carnival: Text, Context, Metatext.* (Berkeley, 1990), 54.
[195] Gaspare Visconti, *Il transito di Carnevale* in his *Rithmi* (Milan, 1493); the *Processo e confessione del Squaquarante Carneval* (1516), see P. Camporesi, *La maschera di Bertoldo* (Turin, 1976), 298-300; cited in Kinsey, 54.

[196] Jehan d'Abundance, *Le Testament de Carmentrant*, ed. J-C. Aubailly, *Deux jeux de Carnaval de la fin du moyen âge* (Paris, 1978), 71-87; published in his version at Lyons in 1540, on this and other sixteenth-century variations, Lozinski, 107f; on Italian carnival performances, ibid, 115-7.
[197] Of these, three are grisailles and two are in colour. They are illustrated in H. Swarzenski, "The Battle Between Carnival and Lent," *Bulletin of the Museum of Fine Arts* (Boston) XLIX (February, 1951), 2-11. Two of the grisailles are in private collections and have been little studied. One of the best known grisailles, formerly in the Lugano Collection is now at the Hague; our fig. 85b is in the Noordbrabants Museum, s'Hertogenbosch. Our fig. 85b is a coloured version in the Musee Mayer van den Bergh, Antwerp; for a useful note on the literature see J. De Coo's *Catalogus I* (Antwerp, 1966), 23-5; The other colour painting is in the Rijksmuseum, Amsterdam; this has the late inscription : *Dit is dans van Luther met syn none* ("this is the dance of Luther with his nun"). On both these last see G. Unverfehrt, *Hieronymous Bosch: die Rezeption seiner Kunst im fruhen Jahrhundert* (Berlin, 1980), cat. nos. 145, 146a, and 226; where they are classed as *Narrentanz.*
[198] E.g. by Stridbeck, 98-99, 105; Gluck, ibid.; De Coo, 24.
[199] The incoherence of this part of the design is atypical of Bosch, who marshaled his imagery in precise correspondences; it thus bears the hallmarks of one of the piecemeal compositions of Bosch's followers, as Unverfehrt thinks. Even if the bagpipe is an intrusion into the design after the style of Pieter Huys, its presence in a sixteenth-century copy of a *Carnival and Lent* suggests the association of metamorphic things with Carnival at this period.
[200] On this print and its relation to Bruegel's painting, Stridbeck, 105, W. S. Gibson, Bruegel (Oxford, 1977), 79, 81.
[201] This is the starting point for Stridbeck's analysis, which tries to derive Bruegel's religious views from the Painting's treatment of the subject.
[202] On the Boston work and other variants, see Swarzenski (1951), 2-11.
[203] Stridbeck, 101, 104-6, cites several *rederijker* plays that used images of Carnival and Lent to make points for or against the Reformed religion.
[204] Gluck, 267-8, is inclined to attribute the Vienna panel to Frans Francken. Unfortunately it has not been possible to obtain a photograph of this work.
[205] Ibid; Gluck compares the two panels and discusses their possible anteriority.
[206] Lydgate's lengthy text summarised by S. Chew, *The Pilgrimage of Life* (New Haven, 1962), 64. The original fable comes from a passage in Boccaccio's *De Casibus.*
[207] Martin Meyer, *Homo Microcosmus* (Frankfort, 1670); Chew, 65.
[208] Stridbeck, 108.
[209] R. Muchembled, *Popular Culture and Elite Culture in France 1400-1750,* trans. L. Cochrane (Baton Rouge-London, 1985), 57.

[210] E. Leroy Ladurie, *Carnival at Romans*, trans. M. Feeney (New York, 1979), 240.
[211] Ibid., 25.
[212] Wegg (1916), 163.
[213] Quoted in Stridbeck, 108.
[214] S. L. Sumberg, *The Nuremberg Schemart Carnival* (New York, 1941), 192.
[215] Carroll, 300.
[216] Ibid., 313, n. 96.
[217] Stridbeck, 108, n.5.
[218] Lozinski, 83-9.
[219] Gaignebet, 324.
[220] Marijnissen and Seidel, 58, n. 47:*The calendar in use... was the so-called Easter Calendar (Stylus Gallicanus), Camerancensis or Brabantiae) according to which the year began at Easter, on Good Friday or Saturday.*
[221] A. Ortelius, *Album Amicorum* (after 1550), MS Pembroke College, Cambridge, Gaignebet, 313; C. de Tolnay, *Pierre Bruegel l'Ancien* (Brussels, 1935), 61.
[222] Thomas, 428.
[223] D.P. Walker, "The *Prisca Theologia* in France," *Journal of the Warburg and Courtauld Institutes* XVII (1954), 258.

5 The Triumph of Death

> He dreamt that Death had appeared to him, as he is commonly painted and touched him with his dart.
>
> Samuel Coleridge, letter to Thomas Poole (1797)[1]

> Men shall speak with men who shall not hear them; their eyes shall be open and they shall not see; they will speak to them and there shall be no reply; they will ask pardon from one who has ears and does not hear; they will offer light to one who is blind, and to the deaf they will appeal with loud clamour.
>
> Leonardo, *Of the Worshipping of Pictures of Saints*[2]

> Men shall walk without moving, they shall speak with those who are absent, they shall hear those who do not speak.
>
> Leonardo, *Of Dreaming*[3]

Remedies Against Death

In his *Schilderboek*, Karl van Mander describes a work by Bruegel's *where all kinds of remedies are used against death*.[4] If this description fits any extant work by Bruegel, it must describe his extraordinary *Triumph of Death* (1566; fig. 89), which presents mankind warring with its dead over a barren, all-encompassing landscape. The picture tilts up at the back the better to present this panorama, in the manner of the *theatrum mundi*. The position of the tilt splits the picture into two horizontal sections, held together by antithetical patterns. The lower half is like a stage; in the upper half, ferocious dead armies swarm round careful topography and occupy strategic points in the highlands. Beyond them is the sea, no refuge for the living, and the sky, marked by the smoke of burning towns on the headland.

The theme is rare in Western art, and Bruegel's treatment of it is unique; he omits the presence of God and Judgement, which serve, in other Triumphs, to tie a classically-minded allegorical conceit into the Christian

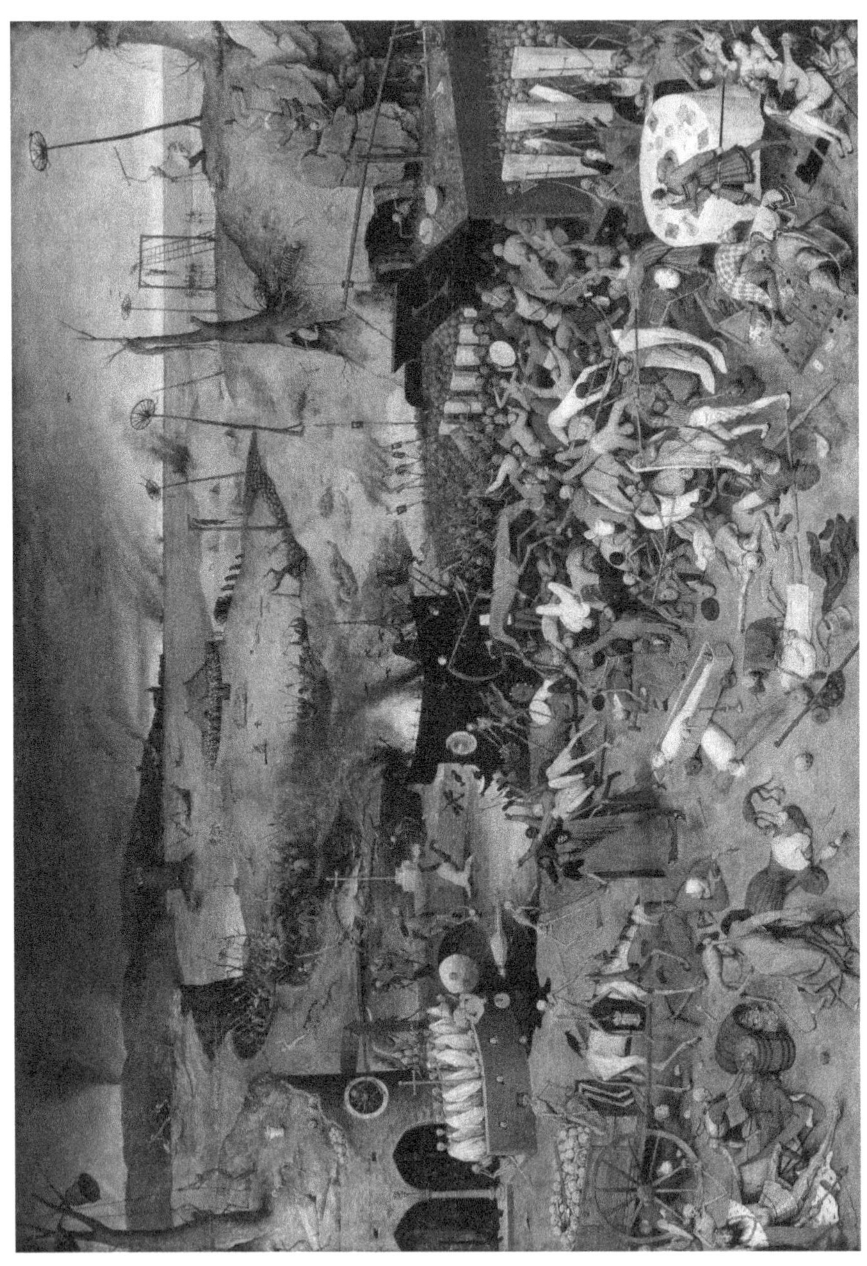

89 Pieter Bruegel, *The Triumph of Death*, c 1566. Oil on panel, 117 x 162 cm. © Museo Nacional del Prado, Madrid

cosmogony. Here I argue that Bruegel's great panel is a response to a revolution in the imaging of death, the shape and scope of which was the emotional core of the Reformation.

Any *Triumph of Death* is an image which grapples with the paradoxes that underlie all efforts to represent the hereafter in ritual and art. Van Mander's enigmatic comment about *remedies* takes us first into the lost mental world of sixteenth-century popular religion, where the supernatural was as real as the natural. Death, of course, had a natural and a supernatural aspect. *Remedies* imply mechanisms of alleviation: magical, physical, psychological. What is to be alleviated is not the condition of death itself, for this would be impossible; the dead themselves are (in the modern view) gone from the universe. The main target of this alleviation is rather the *relationship* between the dead and the living, which can indeed be figured in many different ways.

Bruegel depicted this relationship as violent and terrifying. To understand why, we must examine the impact of the Reformation on the ritual and representation of the dead. The painting takes up traditions for the figuration of death at a time of wholesale religious restructuring. Whatever the motives of leaders such as Luther, Erasmus and Calvin, whatever their concern with issues of priestly and bureaucratic corruption, one far-reaching result of their endeavours was to alter irrevocably the ancient representational structures surrounding death, starting with the cult of the saints and the ritual obligations woven around the idea of Purgatory. The Reformation changed the roles which the dead played in sixteenth-century life. What this means is that collective representations of the dead were altered or thrown into doubt, in the culturally constructed occult or unconscious dimension of death.

Representing the Dead

The continued existence of the dead did not arise as a question in the late Renaissance; if this was a "belief," it was a universal one. If, instead of thinking in terms of "beliefs," we ask, how were the living accustomed to interact with the dead, we move the discussion into the realm of representations — both aesthetic and religious — which lend themselves more readily to analysis. The living interact with the dead initially by representing them in particular ways. Most cultures distinguish, for example, between a *social soul* and a *wild spirit* of a dead person.[5] This was true of Bruegel's society, which articulated an idea of the Good Death, and of its opposite, as in the many versions of such late medieval tracts as the *Ars moriendi*. Folk culture, the oldest tier of thought about the place of the dead, maintained some forms of recognition of the wild, or anti-social dead; while an elaborate system administered by the church dealt with the social dead soul, ensuring its safe passage to the afterlife. In hindsight, these two forms of thought can be looked at as parts of one representational system, belonging to the culture as a whole, and characterised by an essentially magical use of imagery.

Let us consider first, then, a brief model of the ways in which people generally extract meaning from death. The dead exist on earth initially through two distinct kinds of representations: in memory, as a form of text; and as material remains, in the form of bones and their containers. All cultures, of course, are aware that these *are* representations, and not *the thing itself*, the dead spirit, which is accepted as being elsewhere. Though the spirit can sometimes be thought of as inhabiting its sign more or less fully — as is the case, for example, when the spirit of a saint is said to be present in its relics — this does not amount to a confusion between sign and signified.

The signs used for representing the departed person fall into two basic categories, corresponding to the classic structuralist axes of metaphor and metonomy.[6] Metaphorically, the dead can be remembered through abstract sign-systems, linguistic or visual. Metonymically, the material remains of the dead person are understood to represent the missing whole. These remains can in turn be read metaphorically, as referring to the living as well; since everyone knows that one day all of us will be representable in this way. Through ritual, the power of these basic sign-types can be harnessed, enhanced and administered. Ritual manipulates sign-systems to construct meaning from the absence of language at the centre of death: it works to *re-literate* this absence; to fill the void with signification. In this void, the missing spirit of the dead person is to be inscribed.

The simplest representations of the dead in a religious culture thus assert that absence is a sign of being. Other structures built on top of this assertion reiterate the idea with increasing degrees of elaboration: funerals, Last Rites, feast-days, institutions of remembrance, visions, ghost-stories. These are understood as signs of a continuing presence; evidence of a signified thing which exists elsewhere.

Early modern Europeans developed such patterns to a high level of detail. The clergy were the official custodians and administrators of complex, centuries-old representations constructed around the theory of the continuing presence of the dead. These institutions could generate, for example, the distinction between a saint and an ordinary dead soul. Their failures and successes in this area are important here. The foreground of Bruegel's *Triumph* shows some of the oldest complexes of this kind: a table set in a corner refers to the custom of the meal with the dead; (fig. 89c) the dead pilgrim in the centre, his hat covered with souvenirs from shrines, (fig. 89b) refers to the veneration of saints' relics.

All such practices were evidently linked still in Bruegel's day, but, after a half-century of Reformation, opinion was widely divided as to their virtue. Let us look in detail, then, at how these complexes were originally animated; how they grew out of the central metaphor of the continuing presence of the dead in Christian practice, and how the strength of this representation was first weakened, then fractured.

Purgatory and Charity

How then were the living accustomed to interact with the dead? These relationships in early modern Europe have very old roots in the history of the church and popular religion. The issue of the dead lay at the heart of Catholic doctrine, intertwined with the afterlife, the cult of the saints, pilgrimage and Purgatory. The Church taught that the living will be judged after death. Therefore every man and woman should act well, and, beyond this, everyone should go out of their way to act well; ideally, out of love of God, but at minimum, out of fear of punishment (the ultimate Bad Death of damnation). The Church systemised this precept in its doctrine of Good Works.

On the question of how one may act well towards the dead, the clergy had worked with inherited practices since the time of Constantine. Among pre-Christian customs, the idea of the *Totenmal* (meal with dead ancestors), persisted in several forms, and proved congruent with central Christian practices. Changes in the practice and meaning of *Totenmal* thus constitute an excellent barometer for the crisis to which Bruegel refers in his *Triumph*.

Long before the ratification of the mass in 1215 into a meal with and of the dead Christ, early Christians convened in cemeteries to celebrate the Eucharist on a martyr's tombstone, transformed for the moment into an altar. The sacred bodily remains, in these early communions, represented the presence of a spiritual ancestor, whose bones made the altar a sacred tool, and whose essential self, the soul, was with God. Later, the presence of relics became an essential foundation of Christian altars — so every altar was by definition a martyr's tomb.

Pope Gregory the Great famously advised his missionaries to build their churches on the pagan holy sites and graft the new religion as far as possible onto existing belief structures. Gregory hastened to send relics to England so that Augustine could convert pagan shrines into churches. The practice of "translation" — the movement of relics from one resting place to another — became a crucial strategy in the Christianisation of Europe. Peter Brown observed that,

> If the translation of relics had not gained a major place in Christian Piety, the spiritual landscape of [Christendom] might have been very different. It might have resembled that of the late Islamic world: the holy might have been permanently localised in a few privileged areas, such as the Holy Land, and in "cities of the saints" such as Rome. There might have been a Christian Mecca... but not the decisive spread of the cult of major saints, such as Peter and Paul, far beyond the ancient frontiers of the Roman world, as happened in Europe [in] the dark ages. Elsewhere, the holy might have been tied to the particularity of local graves that enjoyed little or no prestige outside their own region.[7]

By the time of William the Conqueror, these translations had become a means of magnifying the power and prestige of individual shrines; each time a saint was, as it were, re-interred, in a new custom-made resting place, the occasion was marked by a spate of miracles. In this way, the institution of relics enabled the spread of the cults of major saints across Europe, and became a mobile source of sacred capital. But the root of this was the early Christian custom of breaking bread with the dead martyr, who was in heaven. After the *Totenmal,* food would be given away to the poor, as remained customary at funerals down through the Middle Ages and into the early modern period.

During the conversion of Northern Europe to Christianity, the practice of sharing a meal with the blessed dead fused with the native Teutonic *Totenmal,* an annual feast to honour dead ancestors. Saints and ancestors became interwoven also in the early history of French funerary institutions, as Rothkrug explained,

> In earlier centuries aristocrats included holy persons in their family trees. Having entered into kinship with a saint, they sought burial near his tomb, which was usually included in a proprietary monastery that formed part of the noble's own dwellings. Ordinary pilgrims who visited the tomb were the saint's "children" and they were also buried in

> his cemetery. In the course of generations, the saint, the nobles and his "children" made up a dynasty thought to be located in the cemetery, just as St. Denis itself constituted France's *nécropole dynastique*. The pilgrimage site in the cemetery was [the most] holy place, even though the cemetery itself was sacred ground. Miracles came from the saint, not from the ground, and his wonders both sanctified the cemetery and glorified the valorous deeds ascribed to the nobility buried near him. So long as healing miracles glorified dynastic valour, nobility was perceived as multiple lineages largely legitimated by ancestral saints.[8]

Early in the Middle Ages, communities of monks ritually "kept alive" the dead by invocation and prayer for each name in continuous requiem masses. Special prayers were recited for the monastery's founder and for the souls of his ancestors. The practice of commemorative masses for the souls of the dead was further augmented by the aristocratic families who made the monastic system possible by endowments, ensuring that due attention would be paid to the welfare of their souls and to the dead souls of their line. From the twelfth century, groups of lay benefactors increasingly tried to associate themselves with monasteries, to derive advantage from the prayers of the monks. Ariès comments that,

> From the 13th and 14th centuries until the 18th, the authors of wills were obsessed by the fear that the clergy, church councils or recipients of their gifts would not carry out their obligations to the letter. Accordingly they posted publicly in church the terms of the contract, the gift that they had made, and a detailed list of the masses, services, and prayers that were due them.[9]

People had also begun to pay for masses in perpetuity. These endowments — *almost constant from the 12th to the 18th century* — represented a considerable amount of capital diverted away from economic activities, towards the salvation of souls and the perpetuation of the memory of the dead, as well as towards charitable and social work. A falling-off in endowments for memorial masses among Catholics dates from the later sixteenth century, and is, of course, a consequence of Reformation and Counter-Reformation.[10]

Another connected, though antagonistic, issue from this period should be noted here, as it emerged strengthened in Bruegel's time. In some regions, including the northern Netherlands, the cultural preference was to project reservoirs of sanctity into a living holy man, rather than a dead saint. While the first use of the word *martyr* referred to people literally martyred for Christ (i.e., the saints), after the conversion first of the Roman Empire, then of Europe, the meaning of the word was quickly enlarged to include people living in severe asceticism and self-abnegation (i.e., hermits, and, in theory, monks). The Church's claim to dominion over the powers of darkness was based largely on its command of the martyrs, particularly the dead ones. However, the idea of the holy man as a living ascetic, unsullied by worldly goods, persisted in lay circles, especially in the North.[11] As a representation, the idea of the living martyr indicates sources of sacred power, other than relics, beyond the control of the Church. This tradition contradicted the tenor of burgeoning payments for the care of the dead; and it was quick to resurface as an explicit alternative in Reformation plays and tracts. People still did not lose faith in the reality of the dead themselves; though in the long-term after 1700, faith in Hell was significantly eroded, and went into sharp decline after 1800.

These phenomena — relics, dead versus living martyrs, the financial care of the dead — were thus intimately linked long before Bruegel's lifetime. Binding them was a faith in the *efficacy* of these rituals and representations, as means of delivering power, aid and meaning between this world and the next. The issue that presented itself to the architects of the Reformation was *loss of faith in this efficacy*; disbelief in the power of the tools used to communicate with the afterlife. It is important to stress that everyone — Catholics and Radical Reformers alike, was in favour of reform in this area.

The first of these tools to be brought into question — by Luther, in 1517 — was the institution of indulgences — documents sold by the Church which reduced the amount of time a dead person would spend in Purgatory.

How did this come to be seen as invalid? The answer lies in complex interdependencies among relics, dead and living martyrs, and the financial care of the dead. These institutions and their rationales had become knotted together at every level of society, in *high* and *low* culture and in popular and official theory and practice. By the 1520s, they constituted a house of cards.

Meanwhile, in the urban society where Bruegel lived, the kernel of the *Totenmal* survived, mutated and evolved into other forms. After the fourteenth century, Western Europe witnessed a startling increase in the growth of religious confraternities:

> Beyond their special devotions to a particular saint or a special cult, these voluntary associations seemed to have functioned to a considerable extent as burial societies for their members. Virtually unknown in 1300 because of their communal and revolutionary overtones, these brotherhoods or *confratrias*, grew remarkably during the 15th century.[12]

The burial of the dead had been added to the biblical Six Works of Mercy in the twelfth century.[13] Subsequently, it became a central concern of lay charity and the particular responsibility of lay confraternities. The appearance of the Seventh Work of Mercy in iconography, *is contemporaneous with the confraternities; one finds it in the 14th century in Giotto's bas-reliefs in the Campanile in Florence. After the 15th century, its representation became commonplace. Of all the works of Mercy, the service for the dead became [a] main purpose of the confraternities.*[14]

These religious brotherhoods and the trade brotherhoods or guilds were strongly intertwined: *every functional association had a sort of religious counterpart, or double, that was a confraternity.*[15] Bruegel's Guild of St. Luke at Antwerp was no exception.[16] Wearing their confraternity hats, the guilds preserved some basic *Totenmal* practices. Seasonal feasts were held to honour the guild's deceased members, at which comprehensive lists of all members, dead and alive, were read aloud. Sebastian Frank, writing in

1534, deplored the custom, in the same terms as were used to rail against *kermissen*:

> There is much that could be told of the singular brotherhoods, saints, and altars of the craftsmen, how each craft has its own saint, brotherhood, and altar, good against any misfortune, or how, on their high days, they have a great banquet and celebrate the feast with much ceremony.[17]

Guild ordinances ensured that the dead were included in the roster of members at the annual or seasonal feast, that the dead were remembered in masses at the guild's own altar, and that members' funerals were well attended.[18]

This ideal of a close-knit community of deceased and living workers demonstrates how widely responsibilities to the dead had been spread by the beginning of the sixteenth century. Normal duties towards the dead for most people were explicated by the doctrine of Purgatory, belief in which had moved rapidly through the population from about 1350 onward.[19] Purgatory was represented as a place in the other world; a third possible destination, like Heaven and Hell, for the dead. It was in fact indistinguishable from Hell, except that it was possible to get out of it. This conception set in motion a decisive change in the Church's mechanisms for dealing with the dead; it meant a fundamental shift in the balance of power between the dead and the living.

Purgatory first of all imposed a new emphasis on the structures of communication between ourselves and the dead. The point of the cult of saints had been to obtain help from these powerful dead, Purgatory articulated the perception that it was now also necessary to send help from this world to those languishing in the afterlife. The Church taught that certain ones among the dead – martyrs – could intervene with God on behalf of the living. Saints had thus long been the only kind of dead people involved in Christian lay practice. Backed by the power of the martyrs, simultaneously present at the right hand of God, and in the bones or blood under the altar, the Church itself could intercede on behalf of its lay members whether they were alive or deceased. At the same time, the power of the saints was accessible to the layperson through the apparatus of pilgrimage and penance.

However, Purgatory quickly developed as a social institution in directions which were to change all this. At the time of the Avignon schism (1305-77,1378-1417), the papal court at Avignon obviously did not have access to the massed reserves of saints at Rome. It tried to assert its legitimacy in this respect by issuing indulgences: paper credit against time to be spent in Purgatory after death.[20] Indulgences were now given to people who made pilgrimages to shrines other than Rome, apparently as part of a program to undermine the importance of the rival papal court at the Vatican.

The invention of indulgences itself was in retrospect a crucial step in transferring intercessory power from the dead to the living. An indulgence could at first only be conferred upon a specific penitent who had performed a specific act of penitence such as a pilgrimage; in other words, they were non-transferrable. This meant that any individual could in theory accumulate on his or her own behalf an open-ended amount of remission for time in Purgatory. Also, there was no distinction of merit between the giving of alms to the poor, and payments to the Church for indulgences. The difference was that the Church had access to an infinite amount of "merit", and could accept any amount of "alms" in exchange.

The first papal bull to make indulgences generally available — by the Avignon Pope, Clement VI, in 1343 — likened its power in this respect to that of a treasury.[21] In 1476, Sixtus IV extended the scope of indulgences to make it possible for the living to buy other dead people out of Purgatory. There was a sliding scale of prices, depending on one's income. Indulgences thus became transferable. Sixtus used the same monetary metaphor — by now doctrine — in this Bull:

> It is our desire to use the Church's treasury of merit to assist those souls in Purgatory who would have gained this indulgence had they been alive. We therefore concede that parents, friends, or any others may secure the release of souls from the fires of Purgatory.[22]

The system of indulgences slowly shifted the onus for the fate of the dead onto the living, who could now intercede, and indeed felt deeply obliged to intercede, on behalf of their own dead. Leo X felt compelled to re-endorse the doctrine of Purgatory in 1513; Luther took his stand against indulgences four years later. Luther's indignant rejection of indulgences was, among other things, a rejection of the costs and responsibility transferable indulgences inflicted upon the living. The attack began as a criticism of these particular ritual practices, but was quickly thrust by internal logic on to the territory of a rejection of ritual *per se*.

For the reformers to reject Purgatory altogether was, however, from the Catholic point of view, a really heinous crime against the dead. The entire doctrine of penitence and good works — from the worth of the Seven Acts of Mercy to the value of pilgrimages — the whole idea, in short, that the right kind of human activity on earth could affect the fate of the dead, was put at stake in the attack on Purgatory. For these reasons, Catholic thinkers such as Sir Thomas More (1478-1535) ferociously fought to maintain its reality in the face of Protestant disbelief. In his *Supplication of Souls* (1529), More envisaged the dead piteously crying out for help from the living:

> If ye pity the blind, there is none so blind as we, which are here in the dark, saving for sights unpleasant, and loathsome, till some comfort come. If ye pity the lame, there is none so lame as we, that neither can creep one foot out of the fire, nor have one hand at liberty to defend our face from the flame. Finally, if ye pity any man in pain, never knew ye pain comparable to ours; whose fire as far passeth in heat all the fires that ever burned upon the earth, as the hottest of all those passeth a feigned fire, painted on a wall. If ever ye lay sick, and thought the night long and longed sore for day, while every hour seemed longer than five, bethink you then what a long night we silly souls endure, that lie sleepless, restless, burning and broiling in the dark fire, one long night

> of many days, of many weeks, and in sum of many years together... You have your physicians with you, that sometime cure and heal you; no physick will help our pain... Your keepers do you great ease and put you in great comfort; our keepers are such as God keep you from, cruel, damned sprites, odious, envious and hateful... despiteful tormentors, and their company more horrible and grievous to us than is the pain itself; and the intolerable torment that they do us, where with from top to toe they cease not continually to tear us.[23]

In Bruegel's, time the implications of the Reformers' claim that penitential practices were in fact invented rituals – without Biblical authority or supernatural weight — were discussed at all levels of society. The strength of concern is measured in the record number of public and secret meetings, and in the swelling ranks of radical cults such as the Anabaptists. The debate escalated in popular street demonstrations, frequently expressed in carnivalesque forms. The Reform-minded argued, first, that Purgatory itself had no proper biblical basis, second, that the abuses of these practices were in themselves sufficient reason for getting rid of them.

Charity and Limbo

This climate of debate, fanatical surety and uncertainty surrounded Bruegel's working life. Where then did Pieter Bruegel stand on these issues? Before his *Triumph of Death*, the artist made several works which involve these issues: *Caritas* (1559; fig. 90); *Christ's Descent into Limbo* (1561; fig. 91), and the *Death of the Virgin* (1564; fig. 92). None of these subjects are drawn from the Gospel proper. In the case of the latter two, Bruegel typically showed sympathy with and interest in the apocryphal tales taken for their own by the common people, such as the story of Mary's death. His design for the print of *Caritas* (1559, fig. 90), for example, in the *Virtues* series, represents all of the Seven Works of Mercy. The only elements of church symbolism in the picture are the pelican standing on Charity's head and the burning heart in her hand. The bird stands for Christ because the male pelican was supposed to feed his starving young with his heart's blood; he pecks at his breast to allow the blood to flow.

Instead of the three *putti* who are usually Charity's attributes, there are two, in contemporary dress, directing Lady Charity's attention to the scene of bread distribution at the left. One boy looks up at Charity and gestures with his open right hand towards a shockingly ravenous-looking group of people, lunging with open mouths at the proffered bread. The other child tugs at Charity's hand. This is all perfectly orthodox, but it is symptomatic of the times that none of the people represented as doing good in this picture are clergy. They are all typical Bruegelian laymen, in the archaic generalised costume favored by the artist.

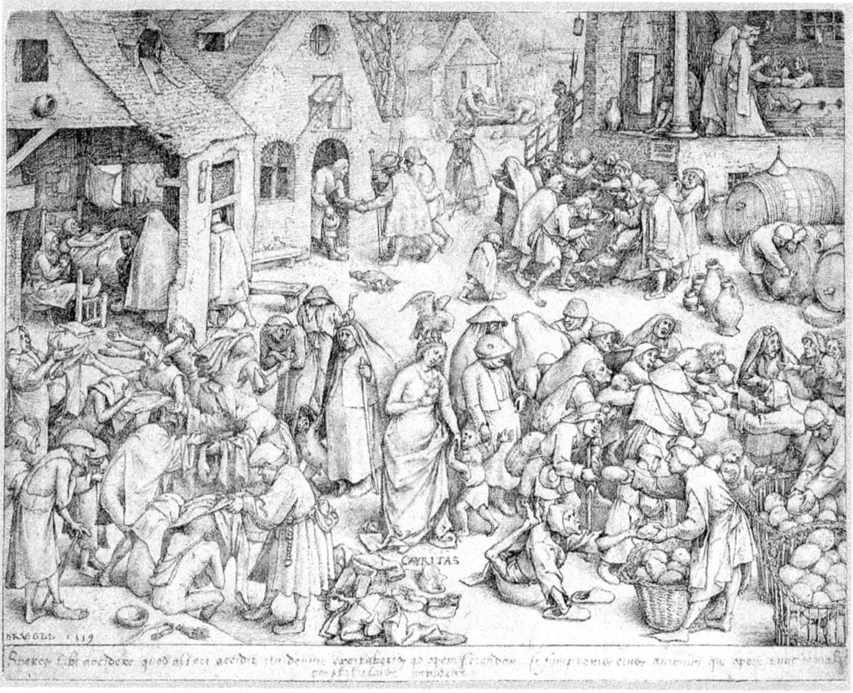

90 Pieter Bruegel, *Caritas*, 1559. Pen and brown ink on paper, 22.4 x 29.9 cm. Museum Boijmans van Beuningen, Rotterdam

This switch of focus on to the lay population, rather than the clergy, as agents of Good Works, can be found in other works by Antwerp masters. Discussing the relationship between Last Judgments and the Seven Works of Mercy, Harbison observed that,

> in the period after 1520, a pictorial relaxation of such doctrinal concepts as that of good works is often found. The Catholic Church did not by any means alter its teaching on this subject; but artists apparently felt the need to treat its portrayal more freely, to provide a more unified and simplified view of good Christians moving easily through the world performing various righteous Christian duties. In a painting like Bernhardt van Orley's large *Antwerp Triptych*, a sense of division and separation, of exacting doctrinal specification is lost. The painting was commissioned by the members of a charitable organization in Antwerp (*Les Aumoniers de la Chambre des Pauvres*), who are shown performing duties, which seem incidentally to correspond to the canonical seven works of mercy. Here, known contemporaries, not historical personages, exemplify model Christian behavior.[24]

By 1535, Good Works superseded indulgences quite literally in one instance from Antwerp:

> In old days a chest for money used to be placed beneath a cross in the naves of churches where pardons were sold. Now a picture was hung on the cross, instead of the chest beneath it, setting forth the Seven Works of Mercy, to show that these were the only pardons that brought souls to heaven.[25]

In *Caritas*, Bruegel carried this trend further than van Orley could in 1525. Two years after van Orley completed his Good Works picture, he was caught attending a secret religious (through not Protestant) service with friends and family, and narrowly escaped harsh punishment. Van Orley was interested, like many other Catholics of his time, in discussing Scripture and the religious issues of the day at private evangelical meetings with friends.

The Family of Love, whose members included Ortelius, Plantin, and possibly Bruegel, was a group of this kind. Their eirenicist attitudes were mentioned in the context of Carnival, as shedding some light on Bruegel's attitude to the mingling of sacred and profane. On matters of doctrine, the Family advocated complete liberty of conscience, while advising its members to stay within the framework of official orthodoxy of their region. For Ortelius and Plantin in the Netherlands, this meant staying within orthodox Catholicism, and indeed when Ortelius was investigated by a team of Spanish inquisitors in the 1570s, they could find no hard and fast evidence of his heterodoxy.[26]

Speaking of van Orley's trouble with the Inquisition, Harbison took the view that, *In such groups basic doctrine was not questioned as much as was its relevant application. Catholic orthodoxy was not rejected as long as its formalities and institutions could be both updated and purified.*[27] Such a path exemplifies the goals of the Family, and is precisely expressed in the nuances of the central group Bruegel's *Caritas*. This Lady Charity (with her Christ-pelican) herself embodies the Church's program of Good Works. Rather like a saint, she is a mediating source of divine love, to whom the children turn for help in the real world.

To the left of Bruegel's name in the lower right corner, there are a bowl and a belt. In the drawing (though not in the print), there is a third object, a bundle of twigs formed into a lash. The beggar's bowl stands for poverty, the belt for asceticism and self-deprivation, and the lash of twigs or branches for discipline, pain, suffering, etc.[28] These objects symbolise the orthodox apparatus of effective penitence, and so testify to Bruegel's adherence to Catholic doctrine at this time. The Latin caption of *Caritas* (again probably not written by Bruegel), reads: *Expect that what is befalling others will befall you. You will be aroused to render aid only if you make your own the feelings of the man who cries for help in the midst of adversity.* This careful wording — with its reformist tinge — could be read with approval in many different camps. It is equally illustrative of More's feelings about the dead, the principles of the Family of Love, and the tendency to make laymen the protagonists of Good Works. No group was unaffected by the "back-to-basics" change in the temperature of popular piety.

Two further works reveal something of Bruegel's own attitude to Purgatory and related issues. In the *Christ in Limbo*, from 1561 (fig. 91), Christ, surrounded by a protective bubble, descends into Hell after the Resurrection to liberate the holy men of the Old Testament. The text of this story comes from a composite apocryphal work, known as the *Gospel of Nicodemus*, or the *Acts of Pontius Pilate*. The source is worth remarking, given Calvin's well-publicised attacks on *Nicodemites*, by which he meant people secretly in sympathy with Reformation beliefs, who persisted in maintaining an outward profession of orthodoxy.[29] This describes the Family of Love quite well.

The *Christ in Limbo* should be seen in the context of contemporary arguments about the fate of the soul after death. In the wake of the Reformation, this naturally became the subject of much debate in the Netherlands and elsewhere. If the soul did not go to Purgatory, what happened to it? Spiritual "Libertines" such as Sebastian Brant argued that the soul must sleep peacefully until Judgement Day (psycho-pannychism), and that, in any case, the soul is the human rational spirit and therefore not to be held accountable after death for the sins of the flesh (antinomianism). Calvin and Luther had both attacked these ideas by the 1540s, while continuing to oppose Purgatory. Zupnick reasoned that,

> Bruegel's *Christ in Limbo* is [an] expression of his position in this controversy. In retaining the concept of punishment and imprisonment he rejects the libertine view completely and the Protestant views of Luther and Calvin to some extent. [The picture] seems to prove that in 1561 at least he accepted the idea of Purgatory, upon which the Catholics had built their superstructure of penitence, absolution, and indulgences.[30]

The caption given to this print is the last verse of *Psalms*, 24.7: *Lift up your heads, o ye gates, and be ye lift up ye everlasting doors, and the King of Glory shall come in*. The first two verses run as follows:

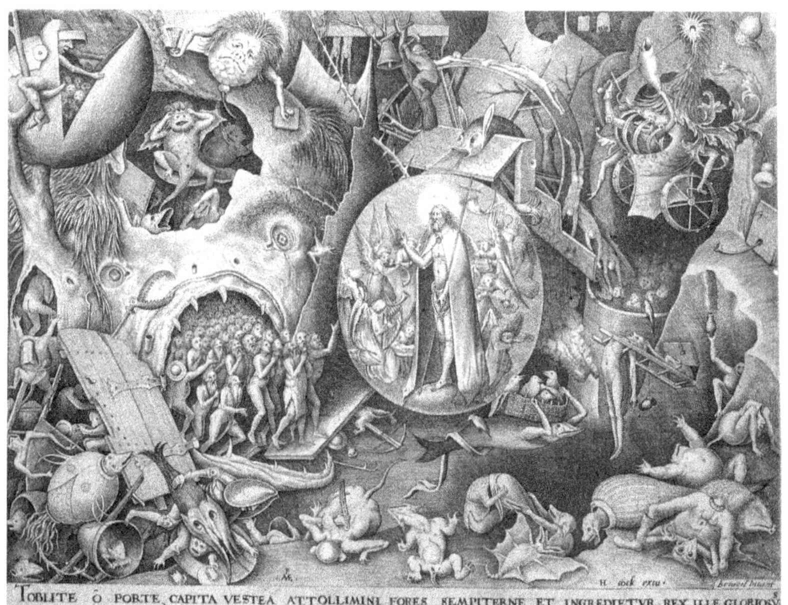

91 Pieter van der Heyden, after Pieter Bruegel, *Christ's Descent into Limbo*, 1561. Engraving, 23.2 x 29.1 cm. Bibliothèque Royale Belgique, Brussels. S 11 31214

> The earth is the Lord's, and the fullness thereof, the world and those who dwell therein. For He has founded it upon the seas and established it upon the rivers.
>
> Who shall ascend the hill of the Lord and who shall stand in His holy place? He who has clean hands and a pure heart, who does not lift up his soul to what is false...

He who does not lift up his soul to what is false resonates with the Familial call for freedom of conscience; it was also the cry used by the parish priests on Easter Sunday, the anniversary of the descent into Limbo. The priest would knock on all the doors that were closed as soon as the last stroke of midnight had struck and call out a folk variation of this text.[31]

If Bruegel "believed" in Purgatory – or at least accepted the philosophy of Good Works on which it was based – this may have been bound up with his sense of natural order, of interdependence among the natural, human and supernatural worlds, or with the Neo-Platonic idea of *homo chameleon*; that each human shapes the inner self by deeds. This general stance can be found in all his works.

On the other hand, this Limbo is comic-peculiar; its denizens do not terrify. The nightmarish elements suggest that Hell is here to be understood as a realm of the imagination. The metamorphic creatures in a row in the foreground are like early drafts for the flock of *Rebel Angels* (c. 1562; fig. 21), absorbed in their own change of state, or for the carnivalesque hybrids of the *Fall of Hermogenes*, intent on self-harm (1565; fig. 77). The Hell-mouth itself wears a doltish expression, like the one in *Dulle Griet* (c. 1562; fig. 35); it also sports what looks like a tonsure. Its head cracks open like an egg, to reveal a distraught Satan: an unimpressive figure, with noticeably perverse genitalia, clutching at his head. It is as if this were a bad dream Satan is having. The overall effect is theatrical and dissociated. Bruegel seems to have found it impossible to take the traditional iconography of Hell seriously. He saw Hell as an irrational space whose essence was the absence of reason. In the following year, he was to explore a different style of visual expression for this, in the background scenes of the *Dulle Griet*.

The Community of Believers

The third work that bears on Bruegel and Purgatory is his *Death of the Virgin* (fig. 92), a beautiful *grisaille* painting from around 1564, known also through the fine engraving by Philip Galle. This work is the only painting by Bruegel known to have belonged to Abraham Ortelius. It makes two

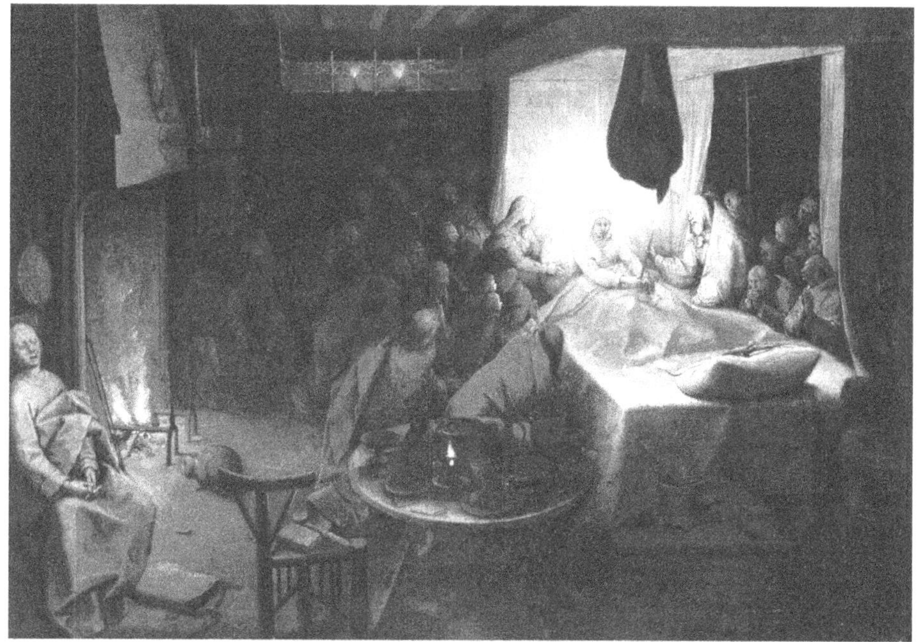

92 Pieter Bruegel, *Death of the Virgin*, c 1564. Oil on panel, 36 x 55 cm. ©NTPL/Angelo Hornak Upton House, The Bearsted Collection (The National Trust)

subtle and unusual references to the religious crisis. It raises the issue of what the community of believers is – and what its relationship to death should be. It also comments on the role of images in worship.

The first of these references is its depiction of the *sacra turba*, the holy crowd. Mary's mourners are specifically called a *sacra turba* in the Latin verses attached to the Galle engraving. Most of this inscription describes the emotions of the crowd, in a rhetorical address to the Virgin:

> And when you left the holy crowd whose support you had been, what sadness sprang up in you, how sad and also how joyful as they watched you going, was that pious group of yours and your son's. What pleased them more than for you to reign? What was so sad as to do without your face? This picture, painted by an artful hand, shows the happy bearing of sadness on the faces of the just.

In Bruegel's picture, the *sacra turba* number nearly forty people. They are of both sexes, of various ages, and there are two children present. Popular accounts of the Virgin's death give this account of their presence: *The people of Jerusalem streamed towards the scene of the miracle, and on touching the walls of the Virgin's house the sick recovered... A multitude of men and women assembled, crying out, Holy Virgin, that didst bear Christ our God, forget not the race of men.*[32] The presence of the crowd is rare in the iconographic tradition of the death of the Virgin. It becomes more explicable if the crowd is also identifiable as the *community of believers*. Urbach concluded that,

> in Bruegel's picture, most likely the *sacra turba* does not consist only of the Virgin's nearest relatives, but also [of] the flock of the believers coming to the dark room with the deathbed through the open door. Those coming in the hope of being healed might be among them. The depiction of the holy crowd in a time of religious dissension is certainly a veiled allusion to his [the artist's] inner belief... The community of believers was in the middle of the 16th century an important factor in the divided church.[33]

As an ideal, the community of the faithful was a key metaphor across the confessional board, warmly espoused by everyone from Luther and Calvin to Zwinglian communists and the Anabaptists.

What differentiated the Catholic concept of the community of believers from rivaling contemporary definitions was its traditional incorporation of the dead, wherein *communities perdured in time and their histories assumed transcendental meaning in the measure that each generation thought they helped somehow to carry out the purposes of their forebears.*[34]

In Protestant thought, while the community of believers included the dead, the living could not assist them. For Luther, the true church was an invisible assembly of the faithful of all times, present in spirit wherever and whenever communion was held, but immune to terrestrial interference: *It is meaningless to say we owe something to the dead or to assert that they can help us [for] the evening of history has arrived, and nothing remains but to preach the Gospel and look forward to the end.*[35] For Calvin equally, interaction with the dead went only one way, in as far as the dead had established the ethical norms which involuntarily shaped the behavior of living citizens. Thus the work of the dead lives on after them, assisting the living in a preordained corporate endeavour, which has its place in God's divine plan of history. The community is therefore for Calvin *the source and fountain of ethical concern.*[36] But it is famously central to his doctrine that nothing can be done in this life to affect a person's fate after death. Every soul is predestined by God.

This range of positions on the nature of the community of believers was philosophically founded on the utter rejection by Protestant theologians of the doctrine of free will. As such, it was abhorrent even to the most reform-oriented Catholics, Erasmus and his followers. The debate between Luther and Erasmus on free will reveals the philosophical and indeed the cosmological principles at stake in the argument. Luther took *Jeremiah* 18:6 for his text, where God likens his relationship with man to the potter's relationship with his clay: *As clay in the hand of the potter, so are you in my hand.*[37] As a metaphor, this text runs counter to the direction of similar Humanist analogies around 1500 for alternative models to Genesis.[38] Recall that Ficino, Pico and others had elevated the importance of the divine spark in humanity, over the clay out of which Adam was made. Erasmus' reply to Luther invoked both this Neo-Platonic emphasis that Man is created in God's image, and more orthodox concerns about Judgment and the afterlife:

> why does one so often hear of reward if there is no merit at all? How would disobedience of those following God's commandments be praised, and disobedience be damned? Why does Holy Scripture so frequently mention judgement if merit cannot be weighed at all... The life of us mortals abounds in many infirmities, imperfections, and vices. Whoever wishes to contemplate himself will easily lower his head. But we do not assume that even a justified man is capable of nothing but sin, especially because Christ speaks of rebirth, and Paul of a new creature. Why, you ask, is anything attributed to the freedom of the will then? It is in order... to prevent calumnies attributing cruelty and injustice to

> God; to prevent despair in us; to prevent a false sense of security; to stimulate our efforts... I answer [Luther], what's the good of the entire man, if God treats him like the potter his clay, or as he can deal with a pebble?[39]

Thus the relation between dead and living was argued by the professional theologians, though concerns besides the theological shaped the way in which the issue was framed. Both Erasmus and Calvin were interested in upholding the idea that historical practices have a point, whether these were to be defined as the ethical norms of a community or in terms of traditional Catholic exegesis. We can expect Bruegel to share the general Humanist desire that human history turn out to have significance. Thomas More's fierce defense of Purgatory was equally placed at the service of this principle.

In the *Death of the Virgin*, Bruegel thus again presented a Catholic meaning in Reformist dress. He showed the community of believers centred around the dying Virgin — a crucial figure in Heaven — yet with a cult distinguished quite clearly from those of the saints. Mary's cult grew enormously in size and importance in the fifteenth century; one or two aspects of its precepts are relevant here. Mary's bones are not on earth, since she was raised bodily into heaven; this Assumption became dogma in the 1490s. Thus she has no true relics — instead substitutes were used to sanctify her shrines — vials of her milk, items of clothing, and most especially, images. Her pictorial relationship with her son brings us to the second peculiar element in the *Death of the Virgin*:

> Though in iconographical tradition it is a *desideratum*, Jesus is not present at his mother's death in this strange composition by Bruegel. He is not present in person but in the shape of a *crucifix*. At the feet of Mary, this crucifix is laid on a pillow.[40]

Urbach explains:

> The dialogue between the Virgin and her son, who appears at the moment of her death, is an extremely dramatic point in literary tradition, and is usually referred to in painting. In Byzantine and West European iconographical traditions of the Dormition, Jesus always appears in his human shape, either on earth or in heaven, but never as a devotional object or as a sculpture (*imago*). [41]

This dying Mary fixes her eyes on a cross, an *imago,* at the foot of her bed; a symbolic representation of her son, rather than a mimetic vision of him. There is also a small statue, with a candle in front of it; fixed over the fire, the brightness of which balances the radiance round Mary's head. This points forward in time to cult of the saints.

Bruegel's reformist but not protestant position on the issue of images is most clearly indicated in this *Death of the Virgin.* The design refers to the power of images — in the medium — of course, of another image. This is strictly orthodox. At the same time the scene is naturalistic and restrained, in keeping with educated Reformist taste. The marvellous is kept to a minimum. The "miraculousness" of this image — its invitation for the viewer to suspend disbelief — is attached strongly to the power of Bruegel's illusionism. The choice of *grisaille* — traditionally a medium of representing figures inhabiting a separate plane of reality from the main scene — to imitate not statues but "real" people — underlines this further.

Images and Relics

The status of religious images was a flashpoint in the general crisis of death beliefs. The phenomenon of iconoclasm — violent attacks on images, starting in the 1520s, in Protestant and particularly Calvinist regions — directly expressed the collapse of confidence in ritual forms. Protestant iconoclasts attacked both religious images and relics. A wave of iconoclast destruction erupted in Antwerp in the *Wonderjaar* of 1566. The Reformers' iconoclasm was a symptom of the breakdown in effective ritual communication between the dead and the living. Images were attacked because they were intimately connected with the cult of relics, and therefore with the Protestant rejection of obligations to the dead in the persons of their most time-honoured representatives, the saints. The iconoclast "demystification" of relics thus corresponded to a shattering of the ties to the dead, which relics represented. When the relics of Geneva were dismantled in 1535, the arm of St. Antony was declared to be the penis of a stag, and the brain of St. Peter was described as a pumice stone.[42] Not only the power of the relics was denied but even their material origin as parts of dead humans.

The iconoclast attacks seem to have been an expression of the deep-rooted idea that there is a magical identity between an image and the thing it represents; that the metaphoric is actually really metonymic. The Church had gone to great pains for centuries to disabuse the common people of this conception, with little success, as Thomas showed for England and the Abbé Toussaert showed for Flanders.[43]

There is evidence to suggest that outbreaks of iconoclasm occurred only in regions which had experienced an upsurge in the magical powers of images shortly before the Reformation arrived locally. Netherlandish Catholic critics could not understand why the iconoclasts did away with images of Christ and the saints instead of *strange histories and pagan narratives*.[44] The answer is that the attacks were motivated in a complex way by anger and disillusionment at the *inefficacy* of the images, which had failed to provide an the other alternative auxiliary channel between the dead and the living.

Contemporary efforts to disentangle material and spiritual values in the case of images relied on the same underlying proposition: images of God are things we are liable to confuse with God himself. The Lutherans who compiled learned arguments to support reform in this area – Andreas

Karlstadt's *Von abtuhung der Bylder* (Wittenberg 1522) and Martin Bucer's *Das einigerlei Bild bei den Gotgläubigen* (Strasbourg 1530) – were forced to admit the power images exerted. Baxandall summarised the main points:

> The main topics are: evasion of the Second Commandment... is patently sophistical, and also ignores texts in the New Testament; St. Gregory's description of images as the illiterate's Bible is wrong because material images can show no more than the physical form; there is a lack of propriety in registering the godly in materials which, like wood, have such vulgar uses; yet if the material is precious, like gold, it diverts to itself the respect proper to the personage it is representing, [and] indeed we conflate the two; our lavish decoration and elaboration of images shows how much it is the images themselves we are honouring; *they encourage and are contaminated by the cult of saints and relics, which we are giving up...* the craftsmen who make them... are not competent to impart... knowledge of the divine... there is something quite comic and irrational, and indeed tasteless, about the spectacle of a human being abasing himself before a piece of wood and pigment; *the very fact that we are so powerfully attracted to them shows how dangerous they are.*[45] [Emphasis added.]

If images *can show no more than the physical form,* this means they cannot be animated by the presence of the saint. But if they cannot successfully represent the spiritual presence in a physical form, then why do they exert power over people? Exactly the same troubled points could be made using unschooled popular language. The following extract is from an anonymous pamphlet *Vanden Propheet Baruch,* written in the 1520s and reprinted in 1558. The view point is that of a townsman. His powerful visual metaphors show how these ideas could be expressed in vernacular thought:

> And is it not a great stupidity that someone says that the saints would be glad that people visit their images, which are wood and stone, or their bones, which are earth, because they died the death because they themselves did not want to do such things. They would also have preferred that we should permit ourselves to be burnt rather than allowing ourselves to be persuaded to visit their images and bones, *in*

what way could we help them by so doing? There is now an even greater idolatry committed than was ever the case with the idols of the Heathen, yes, much greater.... If they [the idols] are placed in houses, then their eyes become full of dust from the feet of those who come in, the papists lock them up so that they are not stolen, just as one does to someone whom the king is angry with, whom one places behind doors or *like a dead man that one buries*. They light their candles, lamps and lanterns, and many of these, which they [the idols] cannot see at all. They are like doorposts or bricks in a house. They say *the worms lick out their hearts* when they eat them up, together with their costumes and they feel nothing, their faces are black from the smoke, on their bodies and on their heads the night-owls fly.... And now that they are dead we visit them and decorate them with silver, gold and velvet and precious jewels, even though they do not need them. And the other poor living saints, who need them, are left naked and bare in hunger and thirst.[46]

The passages I have emphasised demonstrate a drastic logic that links the "deadness" of images and relics to disbelief in the ability of the dead to help the living, or vice versa. The author's complaint that the saints are not helped by visits to their images and bones reverses the causal relation previously held to exist; originally people visited saints' shrines to receive assistance from the sacred dead, not to proffer it.

The extraordinary poetic language strips away layers of penitential and aesthetic meaning. The essence of Renaissance illusionism, the basic challenge of rendering inert matter into a semblance of life, is here thrown aside as worse than useless as a ritual tool. A dead man — or the image of a dead man – for the two are the same — cannot and should not be treated as if it is alive. Only living holiness matters.

These sentiments appeared again and again in Netherlandish tracts and *rederijker* dramas around mid-century. The Council of Trent felt it necessary to begin its decree on images *with an assertion of the value of invoking the saints and venerating their relics; only then did it give the reasons for retaining images in churches and for honouring and worshipping them.*[47] The strength of popular belief in the magical identity of holy picture and holy person seems to have risen proportionally as the power of relics declined in specific geographical areas. The decline of relics was in turn directly linked to the crisis in beliefs about Purgatory.

One example will illustrate this point. Cardinal Albrecht of Brandenburg was the man behind the indulgence scheme that moved Luther onto the public scene. The Cardinal acquired a number of relics sufficient, according to his calculations, to procure 39,245,120 years of indulgence or remission of penance to be performed in Purgatory:

> Albrecht's belief that he possessed vast reserves of divine forgiveness made confession unnecessary and, at the same time, by converting the power of the relics into years of remission, the Cardinal radically diminished the religious efficacy of relics. For, as his own indulgence scheme illustrated, no one required relics to obtain indulgences.[48]

Albrecht was motivated to market indulgences in order to pay off his huge debt — *in excess of 26,000 ducats*[49] — to the Fuggers. Here, as elsewhere, we can see the Catholic penitential "Treasury" and early modern capitalism developing strikingly similar instabilities, in tandem, over the same time period. The structure of inflation in both is unmistakable. The cult of relics had been fatally linked to the inflation of pardons for Purgatory. In the places where such inflations took place, magical images were credited with the same kind of intercessory powers previously ascribed to relics. To understand these correlations, we need to think about how these images were being used, as the supernatural focus of pilgrimage shrines, immediately before the first waves of iconoclasm.

Discussing the various efforts made by Catholic reformers to get people to see the image as separate from the saint, Freedberg asked,

> Is it likely... that the countless men who went on pilgrimages to particular images, who sought aid from a favorite painting or sculpture, or who went to be healed by the miracle-working powers of a specific shrine made this kind of distinction? All the evidence suggests not. They expected such things not simply from St. Antony or the Virgin, but from specific physical embodiments of them, from a St. Antony in a

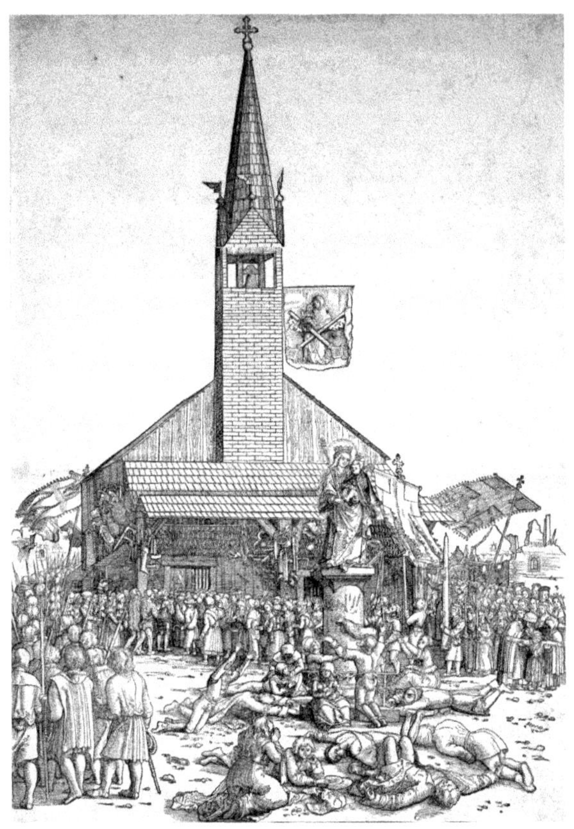

93 Michael Osendorfer, *Pilgrimages to the Church of the Schonen Maria*, 1521. Engraving. Kunstsammlung der Veste, Coburg / Germany

favoured chapel, from the Virgin at a renowned pilgrimage shrine.[50]

In the 1480s a statue of the Virgin at the Church of Our Lady in Antwerp began effecting *surprising miracles, and pilgrims flocked to her shrine.*[51] At Regensburg, a miracle-working image of the Madonna was installed in a shrine built in 1519 to commemorate the destruction of a synagogue. Over 200 miracles were recorded there in 1521.[52] An engraving by Michael Osendorfer shows the scene (fig. 93). According to an eyewitness report, pilgrims arriving in front of Mary's image,

> fell to the ground with terrifying shouts, sobbed, shook convulsively, and entered into frenzy when [as they believed] the Mother of God descended and, making herself visible, talked with them. During her conversation she showed them [visually] their fathers, mothers, brothers, and other souls being delivered from Purgatory.[53]

When Regensburg turned Protestant in 1542, the image of the Schoene Maria was shattered and her church was renamed. In these cases, magical images and subsequent bouts of iconoclasm were plainly connected with Purgatory.

Certain images thus became "windows into Purgatory" at the same time as the infinite power of relics was curtailed by converting them into set values in terms of indulgences. This represented a semiotic shift in the preferred media for accessing the spirit world, devaluing the metonymic (relics), and inflating the metaphoric (images). Miracle-working images became an advertisement for, or affirmation of, the efficacy of buying indulgences. This was a chancy policy, for it made the success of pilgrimage sites more reliant on mass hallucination. Come Luther's denunciation of the indulgence system, the escalated meaning of these images collapsed. Attacks by converts on images should thus be seen as motivated by anger and disillusionment at the "unmasking" of these images, which now appeared insufficiently miraculous. Since relics had themselves been deflated in favour of images, they too could be seen as equally valueless by the iconoclasts.

The sixteenth-century wave of miracle-working images can then be seen as one of the final unstable formats resorted to by popular piety, as the penitential machinery became caught in cycles of inflationary boom and collapse. Subsequent attacks upon these images manifest rage at the perceived *inefficacy* of material tools previously used to channel aid from the realm of the dead to that of the living.[54] For the Calvinists who organised teams of iconoclasts in Antwerp in 1566,[55] for the author of the *Vanden Propheet Baruch*, and indeed for everyone who had hearkened to Luther's message of *Solo Fides*, there were to be no more physical *remedies against*

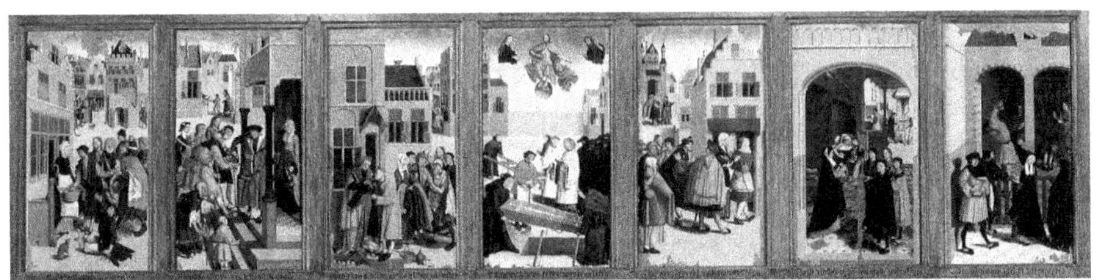

94 Master of Alkmaar, *Seven Works of Mercy*, polyptych, after restoration. Oil on panel, 101 x 54 cm. Rijksmuseum, Amsterdam. Sk-A-2815

death. At the Ghent Landjuweel of 1539, the set question for the main competition was, *What is the dying man's greatest support?* To this nearly all the participating chambers *gave a reformed answer stressing the importance of faith alone*; the answer given by the Violieren of St. Luke's was, *the resurrection of the flesh*.[56]

The iconoclasts' revolt started in the Southern Netherlands on August 10, 1566: *Within three weeks rioters had looted more than 400 churches, smashing statues, altarpieces, and stained glass windows, burning ritual objects, and desecrating graves*.[57] At Antwerp, about 200 people took part in a disciplined program of iconoclasm, out of a city of 100,000; most of the latter, including the city officials, were either apathetic or secretly in sympathy with the iconoclasts.[58] At the Antwerp cathedral: *The statues, images, pictures and ornaments, as they lay upon the ground, were broken with sledgehammers, hewn with axes, trampled, torn and beaten into shreds*.[59]

The targets of Netherlandish iconoclasm can be seen as even more specific than this, if one looks beyond the natural paranoia of literate commentators. An extraordinary instance of "directed" iconoclasm was connected to the disruption of funerary beliefs. This is the attack on a polyptych by the Master of Alkmaar, now in the Rijksmuseum (fig. 94a-b). The work's subject is the Seven Acts of Mercy.[60] It shows the charitable acts being carried out, as in Bruegel's *Caritas* and van Orley's triptych, by

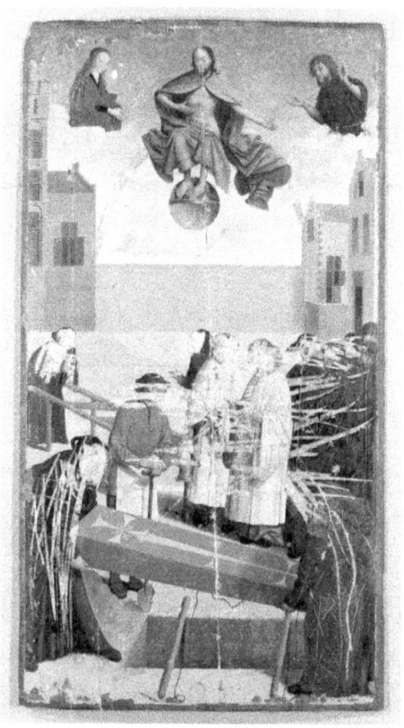
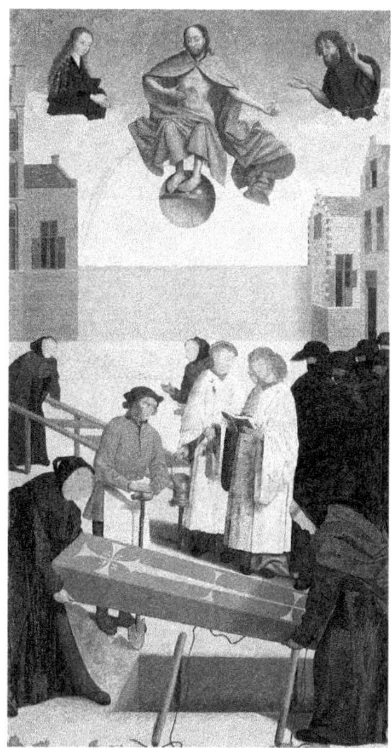

94a Master of Alkmaar, The Burial of the Dead, from *Seven Works of Mercy*, central panel, before restoration after iconoclast attack c. 1566

94b Master of Alkmaar, The Burial of the Dead, *Seven Works of Mercy*, after restoration

urban laymen. The restorer de Bruyn Kops described the purposeful manner of the savage slashes on the picture. The attacker(s) tried to erase the figure of Jesus, who hovers in the sky in the middle panel and presides over a confraternity burial. But the figures of the coffin-bearers in confraternity robes were slashed at as intensely, if not more so, as the figure of Jesus. Other burger figures had eyes and mouths attacked: *The intention clearly being to concentrate on the figures, faces, eyes, or even attributes of the persons performing the works of mercy.*[61] These attacked "attributes" were the distinctive robes of the confraternity members.

The role of the confraternities in the ever-escalating purgatorial crisis has already been touched on:

> [As] responsibility for spiritual care of the dead shifted gradually from the monastery to the private [sphere]... The Faithful enrolled their *own* dead into sodalities and confraternities that, by offering a maximum of penitential assistance, minimized the purgatorial ordeals... for each living and departed member. These lay penitential cooperatives — each usually a religious or cultic extension of a guild, the same people composing the two bodies — proliferated throughout the fourteenth and fifteenth centuries, vastly diversifying practices associated with penance... Furthermore, burgeoning brotherhoods promoted more and more access to indulgences, which, in turn, progressively desacralized relics and altered profoundly people's relations with their saints.[62]

And hence their relations to the dead. At the time of the iconoclasm at Antwerp Bruegel was living in Brussels, but still working intermittently for Cock's House of the Four Winds in Antwerp. His picture of *John the Baptist Preaching in the Wilderness* (fig. 95) chronicled the huge outdoor services, which characterised the summer before the iconoclasm; they were called *hage-preeken* (*hedge-* or *fence-preaching*), recalling the invisible zones implied in other *hag*-expressions.[63] The decision to clothe the Baptist's Sermon in the guise of a contemporary *hedge-preaching* drew attention to the Pauline common-ground of Erasmus, Luther and Calvin, and may even have gently rebuked the vicious actions of the Catholic authorities against contemporary advocates of adult baptism. The figures in the foreground wear costumes of many different nations; making another subtle eirenicist point for unity among Christians.

To view the *Triumph of Death* as a response to these turmoils — occurring either just before or just after the *Wonderjaar* of the iconoclasm — let us consider the evidence so far assembled about Bruegel's religious views, especially in the *Death of the Virgin*. In this small private painting for his friend Oretelius, a Reformist sympathiser, Bruegel used an iconographically unprecedented combination of motifs to treat the subject;

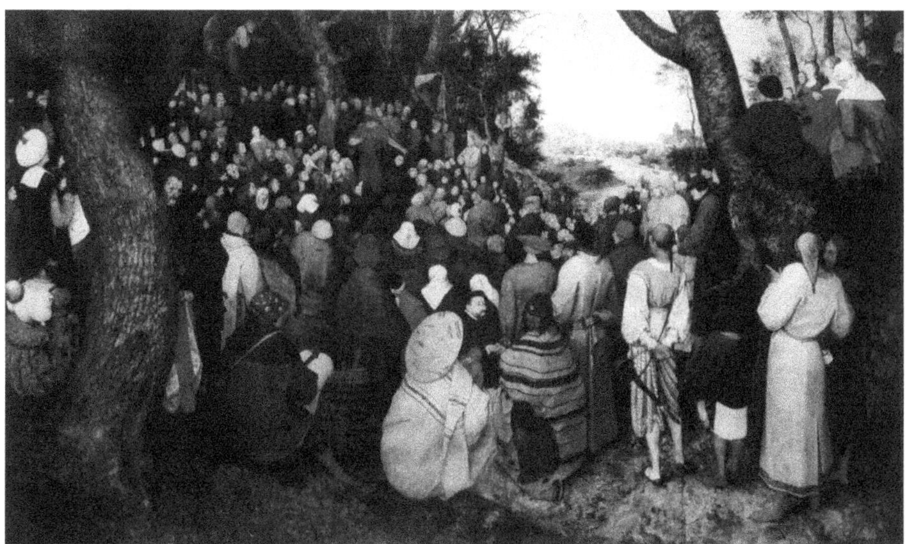

95 Pieter Bruegel, *The Sermon of St John the Baptist*, 1566, Oil on panel, 95 x 160.5 cm. Museum of Fine Arts, Budapest

making the *sacra turba* into an allegory for the community of believers. He abstracted the scene in *grisaille*, centring this "community" by light and composition on an *imago*, the cross at the feet of the illuminated Virgin. With deceptive simplicity, the *Death of the Virgin* achieved then a compromise between the call for a "purified" religion and the framework of orthodoxy. It seems that Bruegel, in line with Erasmian, (if not quite Familiast), rather than Reformed ideas about images, made an effort in this work to construct a religious picture of a type that would satisfy both sides.[64] Though formally Catholic, Bruegel's art on this issue remains best thought of, in Snow's phrase, as a *place from which to consider the paradoxes of his own time*.

Tolerance, however, as was clear by 1566, had increasingly little place in the mental world of the Reformation. In terms of the iconoclasm, Aertsen's reaction, as reported by van Mander, was probably typical:

> Pieter was often in an incensed state of mind, because the works which he had once hoped to leave to the world were destroyed in this tragic

way; and many times he had such bitter arguments with the enemies of art that he almost brought himself into danger.[65]

Bruegel's drawing for *Caritas* also suggests that at least before 1560, he publicly espoused the Doctrine of Good Works. Many Catholics had long found active practice of charity more satisfactory as a path to salvation than mercantile indulgence schemes, which were also technically "almsgiving." The replacement of money-chests with *Works of Mercy* pictures in the Antwerp churches demonstrates this shift. In terms of the *remedies against death* — pilgrimages, confraternity masses, indulgences — Good Works were apparently less subject to abuse than other parts of the penitential system. However, the relationship of Good Works to Purgatory certainly enshrined the idea that actions by the living influence events beyond the grave; on this point there could be no compromise.

The Unquiet Dead

The *Triumph of Death* seems to gather together the dark and frightening changes which made nonsense of the ideal of community between believers. In its scale and action the picture recalls the activities of the iconoclasts, *burning ritual objects and desecrating graves*. As we will see, it deals with the results of this collapse of confidence, both in *remedies against death* — ritual antidotes for purgatorial torments — and in the community between dead and living. Bruegel the fantasist discoverced the surreal potential of these narratives; Bruegel the ethnographer found his details in a panoply of folk-beliefs about death and the dead, sometimes at odds with orthodox thought, sometimes reinforcing it.

The mass protagonist in Bruegel's *Triumph* — the animated skeletal army — is a folk representation: it is technically an army of *revenants* (returning ghosts).[66] These are the wild dead, as opposed to the social souls. Their form is drawn from the sharp distinction made in traditional culture between one's own dead and the dead in general. While theologians tried to determine the fate of dead souls in debates about psycho-pannychism and antinomianism, most people had no doubt at all about the existence of *revenants* (returned ghosts) or the ability of the dead to protect or threaten the living.

Terrifying encounters with dead souls abound in folktale, clerical and popular anecdote from the twelfth century on, despite dogmatic denial that this was possible.[67] Whether seen as disembodied spirits or animated corpses, the "undead" were nocturnal, suggesting the intrusion of the world of dreams. They accost the living in their beds. William of Newburgh describes an ambulatory dead man, returned to terrorise his family in Buckingham in 1196:

> the corpse of [this] sinful man... crawls into bed with its widow, nearly crushing her with its weight, then attacks other family members when they try to intervene. Although the locals suggest to the bishop that the corpse must be disinterred and burnt to ashes, he convinces them that a letter of absolution for the man's sins, if laid in the tomb, will be just as effective — and it is.[68]

William adds tersely that *such things often happened in England*, and goes on to prove it by relating three more such cases.[69]

What was the situation then for the ghosts of those who did have "social souls," and who died the Good Death in the accredited manner? These too were more present on earth than orthodoxy would allow. In northern France and modern Belgium, All Saints' Day, the first of November, was equally All Souls' Day, *le jour de morts*, the time when villagers feasted and danced to honour the "age-group" of their dead:

> The group of the village dead was given the role of interceding for their heirs with the forces of death... Dead kin helped to purify and protect the village from the immense power of the numberless dead who peopled the supernatural world.[70]

In the thirteenth century, Rudolf von Schlettstadt related a tale about *the rector of the church of Basel, who reported that he saw the dead*. His account gives us an astonishing glimpse of what must have been a traditional folk dance with the age-set of the dead. It is notable that it starts with good dreams:

> He slept well and, after having had sweet dreams up until the hour of eleven, he awoke and got up to ease his bladder. Afterwards he returned to bed, with the window that looked out on to the cemetery still open... suddenly he saw many men in the cemetery, running to and fro with little torches and lamps, while others were performing a circle-dance and singing this song together in a deep voice:
>
> *wer ich da zw kurtzhaim / als ich bin zw langkhaim / so wolt ich vor meinem ende / gutz vil beywenden / und fur mich sendenn*
>
> [If I were still in the short home / As I am in the long home / Then I would, before my end / Turn towards many good things / And send them on my own behalf] [71]

Writing in Latin, Rudolf gave the words of the song in Middle High German and included its musical notation, strengthening the idea that here we have a genuine piece of ethnographic observation.

As in the case of Carnival, we can gauge how widespread and deeply rooted these customs were by clerical protests against them. Caciola summarises the tenor of these texts:

> As early as the eighth century, the *Indiculus superstitionum et paganiarum* headed its list of condemned practices with *sacrilege at the tombs of the dead*. In the ninth century, Hincmar of Reims discussed the traditional one-year anniversary rites for the dead, which included feasting and convivia in which the dead were represented among the living by masked revellers. In the early eleventh century, Burchard of Worms instructed confessors to enquire of their penitents, *Have you attended the vigils over the corpses of the dead, in which the bodies of Christians are guarded by a pagan ritual, and have you sung diabolical songs there and participated in dances*? Thomas of Cantimpre mentions identical practices in the thirteenth century, censuring the customary *games* played at vigils over the biers of the dead.[72]

It seems then that the age-set of dead kin had a protective local presence.[73] One's own dead could be relied upon. whereas the "numberless" dead were to be feared. Notwithstanding the official theological impossibility of such a return, the dead could be visualised in folk terms as a numberless army; the main visual idea of Bruegel's *Triumph*.

Family *revenants*, presumed to have a local attachment, also, of course had local residences in cemeteries and graves. This is where one went to meet ghosts. The idea of cemeteries as local hells, simultaneously homes of the dead on earth and portals to the spirit-world, was deeply implanted. The sagas viewed the tomb of the hero or bard as the natural place for an interview with its occupant; the shrines of the saints also successfully expressed this concept.

A rare view of a band of community ghosts in action comes from the period just prior to Luther's attack on indulgences. From the late fifteenth century on, the *Armenseelenkult* — the cult of the local dead — was an widespread aspect of Germanic folk religion, from Bavaria to the Baltic. German imagery illustrated tales told of the *Armenseelen — poor souls*, or *restless souls* in Purgatory. Two paintings, one from Kolberg (1492), one from the Marienkirche in Frankfurt an der Oder (1520; fig. 96), depicted similar stories of this kind. A knight has made a practice of saying prayers in a local cemetery for the souls lying there; he thus acts as their sponsor in Purgatory. When he is threatened by enemies, the dead jump out of their graves to defend him, each brandishing a tool appropriate to his walk of life; so the sailor has an oar; the tailor, scissors; the farmer a flail and so on.[74]

In folk terms, death was a social and existential metamorphosis. *Revenants* made up the train of *Den Verlooren Jagher*, the Wild Hunt or *carnival army*, anciently supposed to roam the countryside at Shrovetide.[75] Such ghosts had a bestial and demonic side to them, given visual shape, for example, by the antlered head of the leader of the *Verlooren Jagher*, Hearne

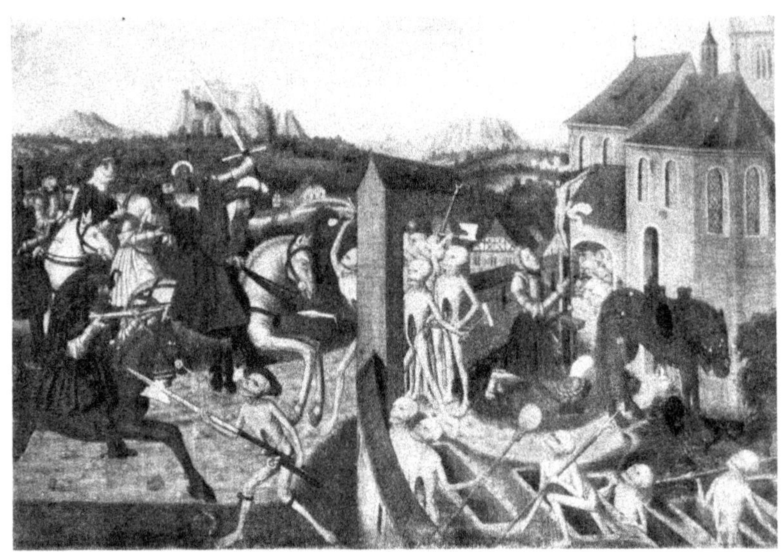

96 Anon, *Armenseelen attacking from a graveyard*, German, c 1520. Wall painting (destroyed), Marienkirche, Frankfort an de Oder. After Bucheit (1934), courtesy of Widener Library, Harvard College Library. 25212.164

the Hunter. Also part of Hearne's retinue were the ghosts of unbaptised children, never ritually received into the community, and so thought of as highly inimical to the living.

As an active belief system, this concept of the benevolent and malevolent dead was already archaic in late medieval Europe, lingering in rural communities, and more or less assiduously opposed by the Church. But it remained a powerful psychological metaphor. It may be that the concept of Purgatory took hold in the popular imagination because it was on one level a re-working of this ancient binary metaphor, with its directions of obligation and aid, a collective visual organisation of fear and desire.

In cultures which explicitly see the dead as an age-set — as in modern tribal societies — death is the last social rite of passage, following childhood, adolescence, adulthood and old age.[76] The corpse is transformed into a kindly ancestral spirit in a three-fold ritual. A full gamut of these three-stage funerals can be found in pre-Christian European burials. These steps were associated with the physical transformation of the body. In the first stage, immediately after death, the body itself is dangerously polluting for its nearest relatives. In the second stage, the family must either wait till the bones are clean of flesh, or expedite this cleansing. In the third and final stage, the bones were installed in an approved place, usually a family shrine or a communal ossuary.[77]

After Christianisation, the second cleansing stage was officially dropped; since the corrupted flesh now was to be resurrected at the end of time. The body was supposed to be buried straight away on consecrated ground, by way of a single-stage funeral. By the time the doctrine of Purgatory had been established, the welfare of the dead individual was in the hands of the mourning kin, rather than vice versa. However, the actual treatment of the body was shaped by less orthodox views. Division of the corpse, for example, remained a fashionable practice among the wealthy and the noble through the fifteenth century, despite papal bulls against it; more mundanely, the urban dead were exhumed anyway after a year and the clean bones laid to rest in charnel houses.[78]

Regional differences were important. In Northern Europe, *the corpse had to be protected and contained far more carefully [than in the South], since it was not believed to be fully dead, but potentially sensitive and active [it was] still continuous with the community it had left... until this "self" dissolved away into skeletal anonymity.*[79] The notion of a half-way house between life and death was expressed in medical theory and law. Alexander Neckham (1157-1217) asserted that three days before expiry, the pupils of a dying person would cease to reflect images, because, as everyone knew, the eyes died before the rest of the body.[80] The legal institution of *bier-right* meant the corpse had the right to confront its murderer, whom it might then identify by bleeding or gesturing.[81]

Folk custom treated the not-quite-dead as dangerous. In Flanders, one who dies open-mouthed is said to be calling another family member after him. According to a mid-nineteenth century writer, *until very recently it was the custom in some parts of France, Britain and Germany to open a window in any room where a corpse lay so that the soul might find its passage clear.*[82]

Popular attitudes toward the dead thus were multifaceted and ambivalent. At the very least, the ritual attention paid to family or village dead had in it some elements of propitiation and caution, if not outright fear. Such ideas were strongly intertwined with the view of the dead as alive in Purgatory. Down to the early twentieth century, Flemish folklore abounds with *revenant* kin, haunting descendants who fail to fulfil their last wishes or neglect to pay for enough masses for their souls. Unquiet spirits ranged from horrifying visitations by wandering corpses, like the tale told by William of Newburgh, to relatively mild ghosts making noises in a cupboard or cellar:

> *S'imaginait-on avoir revue une personne morte, ou entendue sa voix, ses plaintes, un bruit qu'elle faisait dans une armoire, dans la cave, au grenier... c'est qu'elle demandait une messe ou un pèlerinage; le prix de cette messe en argent ou en nature était remis au frère quêteur et porté par lui au monastère.*[83]

This was to become the standard structure of the ghost story in later periods. The needy or slighted family ghost, so central to purgatorial inflation, had begun to manifest the same kind of relationship towards the living as the malevolent "wild spirit."

Troublesome dead could be expelled from the locality by paying their ritual dues. On the other hand, we hear almost nothing of the troublesome dead before it became possible to pay these dues. Increasingly, the dead on earth were at best a nuisance, at worst a vengeful menace, and only in the case of the saints a source of local strength.

Ritual attention paid to family or local dead had been — among other things — a means of holding at bay the numberless dead, by keeping on the right side of the mediatory ghosts. In regions such as the Southern Netherlands and Northern France where the ties to the dead were institutionalised in church, confraternity and village practice, dire consequences might be expected to follow if these ritual safeguards between the two worlds were to be removed.

As it turned out, the dead were never "rejected" to this extent in these provinces. However, contemporary observers were alive to the possibility that they might be. The process of devaluing the mechanisms of penitence was tantamount to such a rejection in the eyes of counter-reformers such as More. The crisis in death-beliefs was felt as a cataclysm in popular culture. It crystallised a demonisation of the spirit-world, which had been gathering pace for a long time; with results visible also in newly negative visualisations of dreams, witches and the carnivalesque.

A Note on the *transi*

The strongest metaphor that folk culture contributed to the imagery of death was that of the *revenant*. In the *Armenseelen* scenes, as elsewhere in the visual arts, such dead, yet present, souls were represented as animated skeletal beings, like the personification of Death himself. They take the form of an animated *transi*; a figure in the first stage of decomposition, halfway between a skeleton and a corpse, but capable of movement. This was also the form used by Bruegel for the *Triumph*. Its meaning is complex and requires some disentangling.

First of all, there was a key difference between immobile and animated *transi*. These types were developed in different ways in the contexts of funerary art and popular culture. Both essentially addressed the issue of how the corrupting flesh itself may be construed as signifying the absent spirit. The immobile *transi* entered tomb sculpture in the late fourteenth century as a kind of rotting still-life.[84] Inscriptions on *transi* tombs exhorted the living to contemplate the transformation of great men into food for worms. Thus the *transi* of Pierre D'Ailly, Bishop of Cambrai (d. 1420), in the Notre Dame of that city, addressed the passerby:

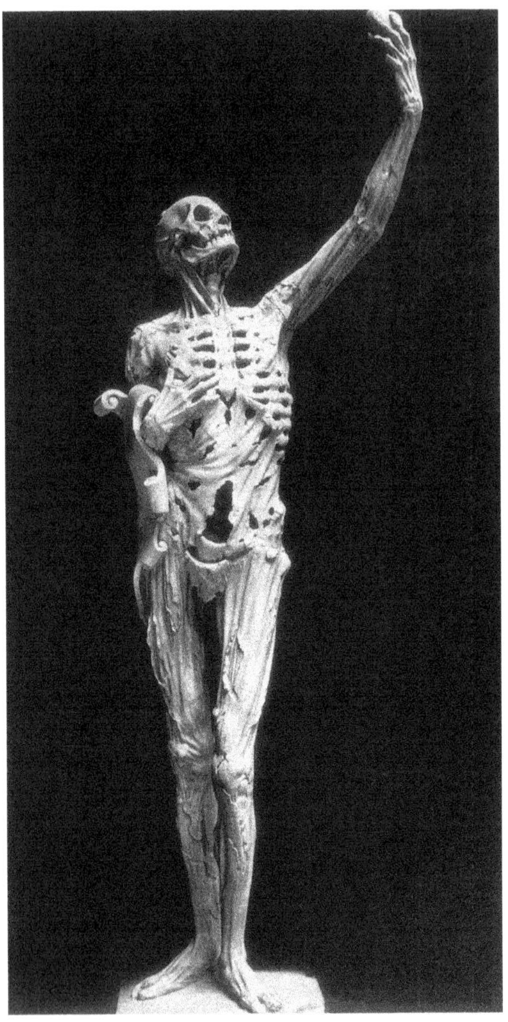

97 Ligier Richier, Tomb of René de Châlons, after 1544, Marble. St Étienne, Bar-le-Duc

The rotting body went beneath the rock / but the spirit of itself seeks the rock who is Christ / You, whoever are at hand, bring help by means of prayer... what wealth, what glory lasts? / Recently I possessed these things but now they are gone...[85]

The *transi* of Claude Bouton (d. 1556) in Notre Dame au Sablon, Brussels, reiterated the formula of lament for passing worldly glory, referred directly to himself in Purgatory, and asked the spectator to help with prayers.[86] Tomb *transi* sculpture represented the period of decay – the moment between the expiration of the soul and its skeletal endpoint – with an increasingly painful attention to detail which is itself worthy of remark. From the late fifteenth-century, German *transi* emphasise snake-like worms and other vermin feeding on the body; this macabre imagery can be found in other media all over the North.[87]

In the mid-sixteenth century, the Northern French sculptor Ligier Richier (c. 1500-67) made an astonishing *transi* (fig. 97), holding up a heart, for a monument, near the present Belgian border, containing the heart and entrails of René de Châlons, Prince of Orange (d. 1544); the rest of him was buried in the Grote Kerk at Breda. This "undead" figure brings a hallucinatory and even decorative intensity to the depiction of rags of flesh and skin. Though made for a supporter of Charles V, its sculptor adhered to the reformed religion; in 1560 his name appears on a petition appealing for freedom to practice the new faith; he fled religious persecution in Lorraine thereafter, ending his days in Calvinist Geneva.

The tomb *transi* thus found its apotheosis in sixteenth-century illusionism. Its artists were evidently professionally driven by the ferocious interest of their contemporaries in the significatory structures around death (which they naturally shared). They brought to their task the full battery of Renaissance mimesis, including the newly perfected arts of "virtual" space and landscape. But the salient implication of developing the *transi* in this way was indeed to focus attention on a frightening aspect of death, and thus to stress – almost to test to destruction – the most magical tenet of orthodox eschatology: the promise that the body would be renewed and reunited with its owner at the end of time.[88]

Death could be envisaged as a genuine metempsychosis too: metamorphosis into the new role of ancestor, if not rebirth in another body.

The early Fathers, faced with numerous pagan elaborations on this theme, had to make the stages of death conform to the unique Christian doctrine of the resurrection of the flesh. Thus, for instance, Ambrose, in an attack against Pythagorean reincarnation, tried to emphasise the special fate of the human corpse:

> those who say souls are immortal do not mollify me, since they allow me only partial redemption...What the state or activity of what we have in common with animals in our bodies is before the body exists is uncertain, and the truth cannot be gathered from contrary views...
>
> What is more excellent than to be convinced that the work of God does not perish and that those made after the likeness and image of God cannot be changed into the forms of beasts!... For how could man migrate, to whom all other living things are subject, if the better nature does not allow this? And if nature were to do so, grace would not.[89]

Ambrose argued that the dying human soul goes to an area where "natural" rules do not apply, before being reunited with the body on Judgement Day. This means death for humans is an exit from nature, by supernatural grace:

> For everyone ought to desire for himself above all else that "this corruptible body put on incorruption, and this mortal body put on immortality," so that we who now succumb to death through the frailty of the body, *being placed above nature*, may no longer have the possibility of fearing death.[90] [emphasis added]

Thomas Aquinas followed Ambrose and others in making a hard distinction between the rotting body and the body that would be resurrected.[91] This school of thought wanted to define the metamorphosis of death in absolutely non-material terms, by shifting it literally off the earth. This is one reason why most Renaissance artists avoided the *transi* completely in representations of the Resurrection of the Flesh. Luca Signorelli (c. 1445-1523), for example, designing Last Things for Orvieto Cathedral around 1500, depicted the resurrected dead as full skeletons and fully-fleshed bodies side-by-side, carefully avoiding any suggestion of a middle state. In his *Last Judgement* (fig. 100), Bruegel's resurrected arise out of the ground fully fleshed. As we have seen, these debates on the existential state of the dead body and its spirit were reignited by the Reformation.

Since the absent, waiting spirit had no external form, there would be inevitably some difficulty in conveying this visually. In the popular view, the visual appearance of the walking dead on earth was far more clearly articulated than that of souls in heaven. Actual skeletons of kin in pagan Europe (as elsewhere) worked as metonymic representations of ancestors, whose component parts had been correctly disposed of, and whose spirit had been successfully recuperated as a protective local ghost.[92] But the skeleton in Western art could not be made to represent a soul in heaven.

The image of the skeleton reasserts far too strongly that the thing it represents is down here, not up there. (This, of course, is how, metonymically, the relics of saints were supposed to operate; the saints maintained presence in both places). The funerary *transi* was a deconstructive solution to the impossible problem of showing the disembodied spirit. It was a kind of anti-portrait, where the skills of mimesis openly acknowledged that the absent soul cannot be represented directly. In the controlled context of a tomb, securely entrenched inside the church, and always flanked by other representations of the deceased (either in effigy or through memorial descriptions), the *transi* represented in the strongest terms the impossible and hence miraculous nature of the resurrection, by showing in gruesome detail what would have to be reversed for this to happen. It achieved its results through a curious metaphoric inversion, similar to the "dis-guising" at work in the rhetoric of the *Propheet Baruch*. At the same time, within the graphic energy of the image, the lively representation of decay started to work in unexpected ways as a stand-in for the vitality of the missing spirit; a substitute for the unrepresentable final state of the Christian soul.

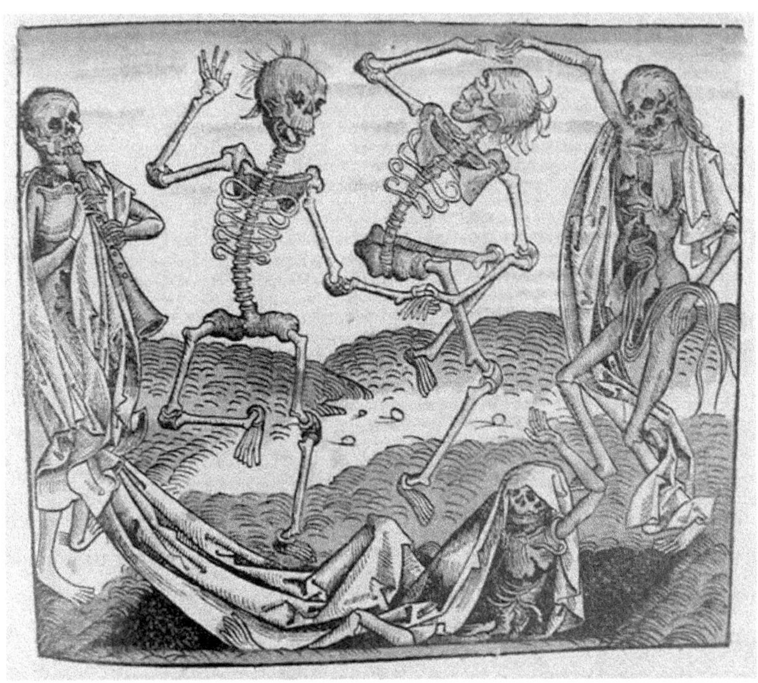

98 Michael Wohlgemut, *Dance of Death*, coloured woodcut from the *Nuremberg Chronicle*, f. CCLXIIIIv, by Hartmann Schedel,(1440-1514). University of Iowa Libraries, Iowa City, Iowa

The animated *transi* of popular art treated the image quite differently, significantly aided by the much more abstract medium of the wood-block printed image. Here, though the dead walk, their bodies are in a stable state, leathery and dry. They have been "wrongly" stabilised; their spirits are caught in flesh which cannot rot. The illusionistic *transi* of the tombs do not move to attack or defend the living: their "attack" on the viewer is aesthetic and psychological. The leathery folk *transi* on the other hand are much more active. Where the "movement" of rotting is shown, this is made on a par with the movement of the whole figure. So in the famous woodcut (fig 98) from the *Nuremberg Chronicle* (1493; with dozens of later editions), the capering figures represent a range of *transi*; the "wettest" one on the right has his entrails hanging out, the two in the middle are much closer to being true skeletons. These figures constitute in fact a serious piece of nonsense; a grotesque instance of the World-Upside-Down motif.

Why should the animated, active *transi* image come to signify particularly the wild, rather than the social, dead? The answer seems to be that the meaning of the folk *transi* was drawn from the first "lively" stage of death, trapped in its change of state. The skeleton, as metonym of the dead person, signified a departed spirit, its absent owner. The *transi* image is a monstrous hybrid, permanently *caught* in transit; like the wild spirit, it should not be here, but it is. A fascinating double-think is wrapped up in this image, stemming from the paradox inherent in the idea of the *revenant* itself. The French name provides a the key to this. The whole point of the *revenant* is that its spirit is supposed to have returned from somewhere, when in fact it has not gone anywhere, it has simply ceased to be. Materially, dead people do not leave this sphere nor do they exist in the abyss. As extinct entities, what is left of them is what is already here: bones, memories, images. They can therefore only be represented as present on earth through a representation which disguises this stark *remaining* as a *return*. To represent the *revenant* as a moving, thinking *transi* — animated bones thinly covered with "stopped" flesh — "re-wraps" the skeletal sign of absence as presence.[93] Its sign of inhabitation is its unnaturally arrested flesh. The animated *transi* signifies a *revenant* because it shows the genuinely present bones as inhabited by an impossibly present mind, presumed to have boomeranged back from beyond the grave. Bruegel's violent *transi* army belongs to this folk visualisation.

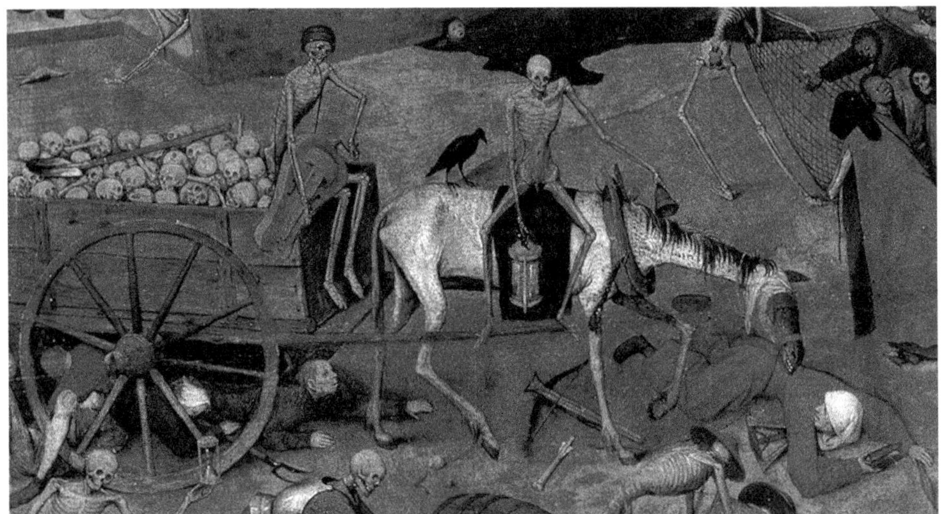

89a Pieter Bruegel, death's cart, detail, *The Triumph of Death*

Many currents run towards the theme of the Triumph of Death in popular artistic expression. From the wide range of models open to him, Bruegel selected a handful of the most striking and most archaic. Bruegel's later design for the print *The Triumph of Time* (fig. 99) showed that he was capable of handling a theme similar to a Triumph of Death in the language of classical allegory. Alternatively, he could have dealt with many of the same themes within the format of a *Last Judgment*, by reworking, perhaps, his 1558 print (fig. 100). Instead his main directions of visualisation were taken from popular models. Some details have sources in feast-day float designs, where topical and satirical subjects could be presented with some impunity. Others come from *memento mori* popular prints, such as woodcuts of the Dance of Death, constantly in print from about 1485 onwards. By the mid-sixteenth century, these "pictures of death" had been given a fine-art apotheosis in the famous series by Holbein the Younger (figs. 99a-b).

Bruegel drew on two traditions for his picture, one Italian and one Northern. The idea of Death mounted, trampling men, underfoot is Italian and derives from the *Apocalypse*.[94] Bruegel's Death Cart (fig. 89a) recalls the chariots central to many printed, painted and performed *Triumphs*, the idea for which ultimately derives from Petrarch. Pseudo-Petrarchan Triumphs were disseminated in the North through tapestry designs and engravings. They made their way into the public consciousness through the allegorical floats and processions of the *rederijkers*, in Antwerp and elsewhere in the Netherlands.

In 1561, when the *Violieren* presented a *Cycle of Human Vicissitudes*, this *ommgang* procession was really a series of seven allegorical Triumphs designed to show how each human condition causes the next. Thus the float showing the Triumph of Prosperity was followed by the Triumph of Pride, followed by Envy, then the Triumph of War, then Poverty, Humility, Peace, and finally Prosperity once more. Life was shown as a continuous cycle that ends only with the Last Judgment, which was the subject of the eighth and final float.

In 1563, Martin van Heemskerck made two drawings after floats from this procession: the *Triumph of Pride* and the *Triumph of Humility*; these were very similar in style to his designs on the evils of money (fig. 54). These floats often reworked ideas from contemporary art, as artists often designed and made the floats for the great processions. Bosch's *Haywagon*, for example, was turned into a float in 1563. The same Elck procession included one or two floats inspired by Bruegel engravings, specifically his print of the *Witch of Mallegem* from 1559 (fig. 40).[95]

Piero di Cosimo designed a notable procession on the theme of death for the Carnival of 1511 in Florence. Vasari's marvellous description of this event is worth quoting in full:

> The triumphal Car was covered with black cloth, and was of vast size, it had skeletons and white crosses painted upon its surface, and was drawn by buffaloes, all of which were totally black; within the Car

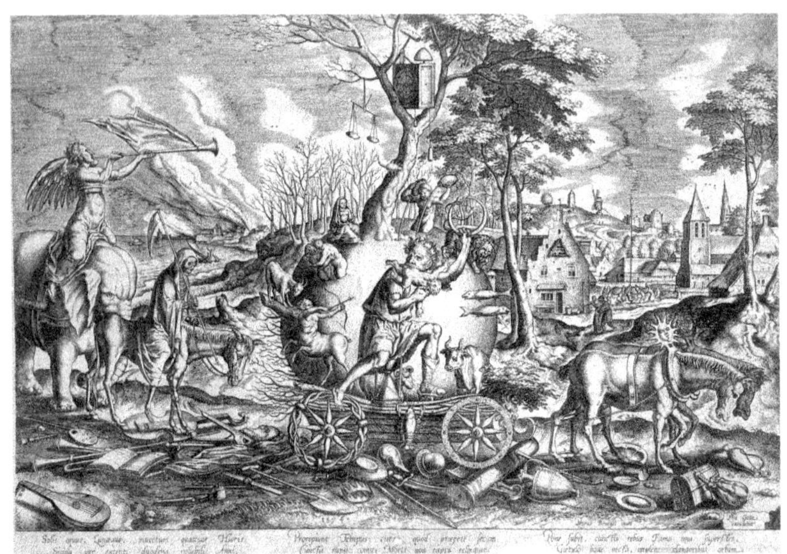

99 Philip Galle (?), after Pieter Bruegel, *The Triumph of Time*, published 1574. Engraving, Bibliothèque Royale Belgique, Brussels. S IV 2183

100 Pieter van der Heyden, after Pieter Bruegel, *The Last Judgement*, 1558. Engraving, 22.5 x 29.5 cm. Bibliothèque Royale Belgique, Brussels. S1 7609

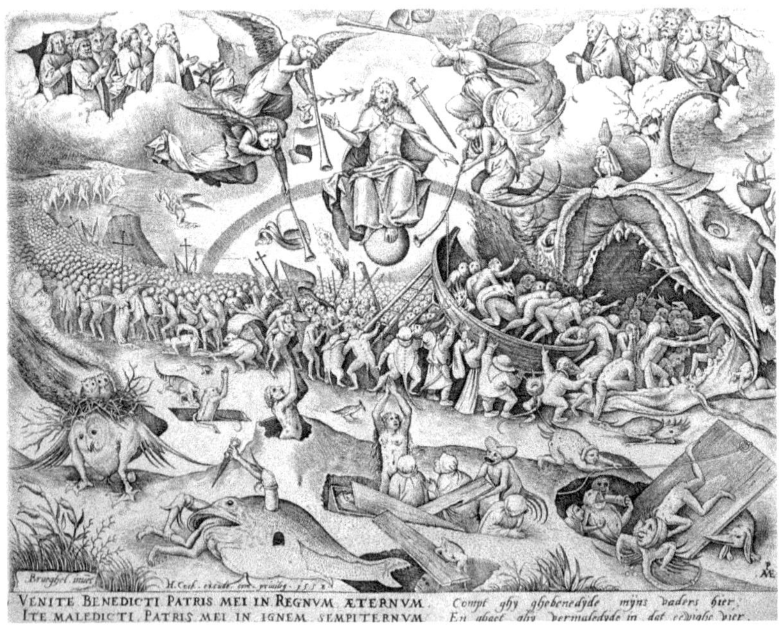

stood the colossal figure of Death, bearing the scythe in his hand, while around him were covered tombs, which opened at all the places where the procession halted... certain figures stole forth, clothed in black cloth, on these vestments the bones of a skeleton were depicted in white... which gleamed horribly forth on the black beneath. At a certain distance appeared figures bearing torches, and wearing masks, presenting the face of a death's head, both before and behind; these heads of death, as well as the skeleton neck beneath them, also exhibited to view, were not only painted with the utmost fidelity to nature, but had besides a frightful expression which was horrible to behold. At the sound of a wailing summons, sent forth with a hollow moan from trumpets of muffled yet inexorable tones, the figures of the dead raised themselves half out of their tombs, and seating their skeleton forms thereon, they sang the following words, now so much extolled and admired.

Before and after the Car rode a train of the dead on horses, carefully selected from the most wretched and meagre animals that could be found, the caparisons of these worn, half-dying creatures were black, covered with white crosses; each was conducted by four attendants, clothed in the vestments of the grave; these last... bearing black torches and a large black standard, covered with crosses, bones, and death's heads... each sang, with a trembling voice, and all in dismal unison, that psalm of David called the *Miserere*.

The novelty and the terrible character of this singular spectacle, filled the whole city, as I have before said, with a mingled sensation of terror and admiration, and although at the first sight it did not seem well calculated for a Carnival show, yet being new, and within the reach of every man's comprehension, it obtained the highest encomium... The old people who... witnessed [it] are never weary of extolling the extraordinary spectacle... I remember to have heard... that this invention was... believed at the time to... prefigure the return to Florence of the Medici family... [then] exiles, and so to speak *dead*, but dead that might be expected soon to arise again.[96]

This account, in all its lurid detail, appeared in Vasari's original 1550 edition of the *Lives of the Artists*, read and emulated in the Netherlands by the end of the decade. Vasari is explicit about the way that people looked for political overtones in this kind of material.

By 1580, the same imagery could be used to express explosive politico-religious tensions before the eyes of an alarmed burger population, in a tragic French carnival held that year. In the town of Romans, in the Rhône valley, craftsmen and laborers put up a show designed to touch the throbbing nerves of the community. Tax and class differentials had split the town when League craftsmen chose to dramatise these difficulties in metaphors drawn from the purgatorial crisis. Their carnival makes Bruegel's use of similar material look fairly restrained by comparision:

> From the beginning... the people's Carnival had focused on rituals celebrating death and calling for the burial or cannibalistic disposal of Evil, of the Old, the Corrupt, the Putrid.[97]

> The drapers were weaving a shroud for the Old World, a shroud they waved like an undertaker's pall. The[ir] pantomimes were pure folklore. But they rapidly turned political as they continued throughout the week... [There were] three primitive treatments — agrarian, martial, sacred — of the *initial* Carnival theme of death... *Warriors* (of the strictly Carnival variety) brandished swords during their dance, *peasants* beat flails and brandished threshing rakes... and the Confraternity of St. Blaise's, flaunted the pall. Crying *flesh of Christians, six deniers the pound*, the parading members of St. Blaise's fellowship... offered the crowd the flesh of corpses to eat. That was the fellowship's idea of black humor, since they were the ones in charge of burying the dead: eating the dead would therefore produce living flesh anew.[98]

A great difference in tone separates Piero's 1511 Triumph of Death and the 1580 Carnival of Death in Romans; from a pleasurable shudder, to a positive earthquake. The execution of Bruegel's painting falls midway between the two, but it is closer in time and spirit to that of Romans. Piero heralded the crisis; Bruegel envisaged its cosmic dimension; the drapers and ploughmen flaunted it in the faces of their alienated masters.

Key elements from the purgatorial crisis were present at Romans. The black side of the confraternities was well to the fore. That they should sell the meat of corpses — even in jest — represents not so much, as Ladurie suggested, *fantasies of cannibalism*,[99] but the old practice of *Totenmal*, twisted into a literal meaning: the feast with the dead as a feast on the dead. The radical wings of the Reformed party were convinced by this time that the confraternities subsisted on earnings from death. Like early insurance companies, their business was funerals, memorial masses and banquets and so forth. It was a short step to portray them as actually preying on the dead – *flesh of Christians, six deniers a pound* – an accusatory image already levelled against indulgence-mongers and the clergy in the Reformation war of prints (cf. figs. 37, 105, 106). The structure of the celebrations at Romans – with its agrarian, martial, and sacred treatments of death – illuminates much that is otherwise opaque about Bruegel's painting. It sharply restores a blasphemous tang of street carnival and its uncensored visual culture to the picture's subject.

The vocabulary of the Reformation coloured and shaped sixteenth-century carnivals of the dead. What of Bruegel's other principal inspiration, the *danse macabre* images? The rapid evolution of this genre from the fourteenth to the sixteenth century was manifestly linked to the looming problem of death, but its roots too went deeper than conscious sectarian differences.

The *Danse Macabre*

Like the feast-day death themes, the *pictures of death* (fig. 101 a-b)[100] by Hans Holbein the Younger (1497-1543) were first read as anti-clerical, and later, as the Reformation gathered pace, as anti-Catholic. In the sixteenth century, religious issues were, of course, political issues; however, this famous series, most often thought of as Protestant, contained no clear confessional bias. Holbein created his *pictures of death* in Basel (by 1526), they were printed at Lyons around 1540. Because they were prints, the meaning of Holbein's woodcuts could be turned around in a startlingly literal way. The blocks were first used by Catholic printers to produce the

1538 edition; they were then sold to a Protestant firm, who produced the 1542 and subsequent editions.[101] We can therefore compare side by side two endeavors, four years apart, to tie the woodcuts into the main confessional camps. Both sets of printers appended moralising verses under each print: redolent of Erasmian criticism in the Catholic edition, of Lutheran sympathy in the Protestant version. The pictures and the Bible quotations above them were not tampered with in any way. Holbein's images were clearly the main attraction for both editions.

Holbein took the familiar *personae* from the *danse macabre*, or Dance of Death, where a skeletal *transi* was depicted "dancing" in turn with typical members of classes and professions; Everyman wearing his social hat. Holbein separated these out into individual scenes with realistic backgrounds. This powerfully enhanced the drama of the theme, and also changed its narrative direction completely. The series is no longer a dance connecting the dead and the living. Each scene becomes a separate narrative, framing the confrontation between the individual and his or her death.

The imagery of the Dance of Death belonged at this point to a relatively young tradition, though it had evidently evolved from actual dances associated with All Saints' Day; recall the men with deep voices, singing in the churchyard, watched by the rector at the window. In the twelfth century, Gerald of Wales witnessed another such dance whose details uncannily prefigure the imagery and structure of the *danse macabre*:

> Here you may see men or girls, either in the church, in the cemetery, or in the circle-dance that winds through the cemetery with songs, suddenly fall to the ground. At first they are led into an ecstasy and are in a trance (*quietos*); then immediately, as if rapt into a frenzy, they leap up. Then they mime, with hands and feet, in front of everyone, whatever actions they are accustomed to engage in improperly on feast-days. You might see this one put his hand to the plough; another as if goading oxen. Each of them, as if to ease their work, emits trad-

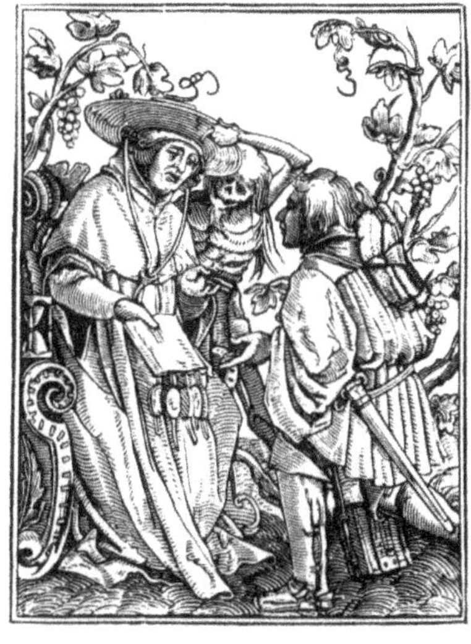

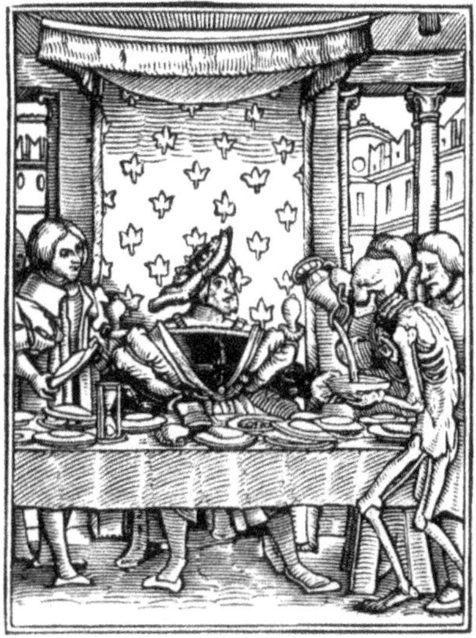

101a Hans Holbein the Younger, *The Cardinal*, from *The Dance of Death*, c. 1526. Cleveland Museum of Art. Inv 1922.149

101b Hans Holbein the Younger, *The King*, from *The Dance of Death*, c. 1526

itional cries in a barbarous tone. You might see this one imitate a cobbler, that one, a tanner; or a girl, as if she were carrying a distaff, now pulling out the thread at length with her hands and arms, and then, when it is out, winding it back on to the spindle. One, as she walks, seems to work fibre on the loom; another sits as if all is ready and tosses a shuttle from side to side, from hand to hand, and with flourishes and rhythm she seems to weave.[102]

These movements also recall the characterisation of the Armenseelen figures in the churchyard, each with tolls of histrade (fig. 96). By the early fourteenth century, *the danse macabre existed in the form of a morality play, to be publically performed with actors playing dead men in their winding-sheets and taking the hands of the living from all walks of life.*[103] By the early fifteenth century, it had become a theme in visual art. The first *Danse* that we know of was a mural painted at the cemetery of the Holy Innocents in Paris in 1424, where fifteen figures, paired with skeletons, were shown dancing.[104] Alternating clergy with lay characters, the *dramatis personae* included Pope and Emperor, lowly friar and infant:

> Irony and satire were traditional in the *danse macabre*. [its] anticlerical elements could be perceived by 15th century men as consistent with Catholicism [because] the satire... was predominantly social. The powerful and wealthy must also dance with that mocking, irreverent partner. The dead chide the living for their misdeeds... Criticism of the clergy is directed against failure to live up to the spiritual requirements of the office, and not against the office itself.[105]

The Parisian cemeteries were a public meeting place for "marginal" activities such as *peddling, chatting, soliciting and courting*, and it is plain from contemporary sources that these paintings were found *entertaining and even funny [by] their original audience*.[106] The reason for this lies in their complex folk-cultural roots. Caciola points out that, *the dance of the living with the dead, which to the monks was a symbol of the brevity of this life, may have been to others a celebration of the continuity of the living and the dead as one circular community*.[107]

Performed dances with the dead seem to have had a marked carnivalesque character; masks and singing are mentioned. Moved into an urban context, they represented an ultimate variation on the reversed world; the lowly got the same kind of vicarious pleasure as they did from World-Turned-Upside-Down prints, to see death turning the tables on the mighty.[108] These comic connotations are obvious in the *Nuremberg Chronicle* version, where the skeletal protagonists play musical instruments as well as dance (fig. 98), and in the much darker humour of Bruegel's *Triumph*.

Before Holbein, in the decades leading up to the Reformation, the *danse macabre* adorned the walls of convents and churches, usually with the bare minimum of scriptural references, often with none at all. When woodcut replicas of these paintings became available in the closing years of the fifteenth century, however, the same works appeared filled with radical potential:

> Having escaped the confines of the Church and the friar's spoken interpretation, the painted *danse macabre* could suggest ideas that lacked religious and even ethical content. The pictures *alone* have only one comment on death: it comes too high and low alike, and can come any time... Death need not be viewed as one of the crucial transitions of the Christian, but as the horrible physical end of life's sinful joys.[109]

The most potent anti-clerical aspect of Holbein's *pictures of death* was that they looked as if they cast doubt, not simply on the character of incumbents of clerical offices, but on the basic intercessory function of the priesthood itself. Death has no Last Rites in these pictures. When the images were framed separately, it was possible to read them as narratives with no references to God or the Church. In fact, Holbein was aware of the irreligious overtones, and designed introductory cuts showing the Creation, the Expulsion from Paradise, and a Last Judgement to end the set. Other artists around this time similarly felt it prudent to put the *Dance* in a Christian frame.[110]

These additions were not felt to have sufficiently neutralised the implications of the imagery to allow it to remain in print. Holbein's 1542 edition, essays and woodcuts together, was condemned by the Church and censured by the Faculty of Theology at Paris between 1544 and 1551. It also appears on a list from 1570 of books condemned in the Southern Netherlands; local authorities there had resisted the introduction of the Inquisition until after Bruegel's death (in 1569).[111]

As a point of comparison for Bruegel's *Triumph*, Holbein's imagery is important in several ways. The absence of God, at least in the individual scenes, is an obvious similarity. Holbein's key formal development was to set the action in realistic contemporary spaces: his frames are dense with landscape, streets, ships, and rooms. This was the path also taken by

Bruegel, master of the panoramic landscape. The realist treatment of space and *mise-en-scène* in the work of both artists adds greatly to the hallucinatory quality of their imagery. Finally, the history of how Holbein's series was framed, reframed, disseminated and suppressed, is evidence, among other things, of the malleable, polysemous quality of the imagery of death at this time. The wave of interest in *pictures of death* was not a simple matter of Protestants versus Catholics.

Holbein's series was much milder than some treatments. The *totentanz* painted by Niklaus Manuel (1484-1530) of Bern in the Dominikanerkloster was violent and political:

> In 1515, Manuel painted... a Dance of Death where Death stands on a platform holding a crossbow and a full quiver of arrows. The pope and the emperor stand among other figures beneath him as targets for his archery skill...[112]

Manuel was a politician, a playwright, and a Reformation activist, as well as a mystery-play. His popular dramas drew on mystery-play traditions and *Fastnachtsspiels*; he also employed the gruesome imagery of the *totenfressen*, Devourers of the Dead, used in Reformation prints (such as fig. 37), particularly in South Germany and Switzerland:

> In his plays of 1521 and 1523, the *devourers* of the dead come on stage one after the other in what for all the world appears as a Dance of Death transposed into theatrical guise for religious polemic... Sometimes in front of a corpse — the pope, a cardinal, a bishop, a priest, a monk, a nun, or other *devourer* recounts how he makes a sumptuous living from the dead... Funds given to relieve suffering in the next life enrich the *Totenfresser*.[113]

The metamorphosis of the *pictures of death*, from the gentle entertainment of the *danse macabre*, through the confessional passions projected into Holbein's realist scenes, to Bruegel's *Triumph*, was thus part of a wider metamorphosis in visual culture. From folk ritual dances, to *bose Fastnacht* in the streets of

Romans, the imagery of death darkened, becoming more grotesque and more surreal, in step with the general sea-change in carnival and the carnivalesque. This supports the picture of an escalating crisis, occurring at the grass-roots, as at Romans, among the masses of *common people, folk who have not much to lose*. Attacks made on the clergy in Antwerp in the days leading up to the iconoclastic riots demonstrate the strength of feeling behind the radical spirit now projected into *pictures of death*.

Danse Macabre and Carnival in the *Triumph of Death*

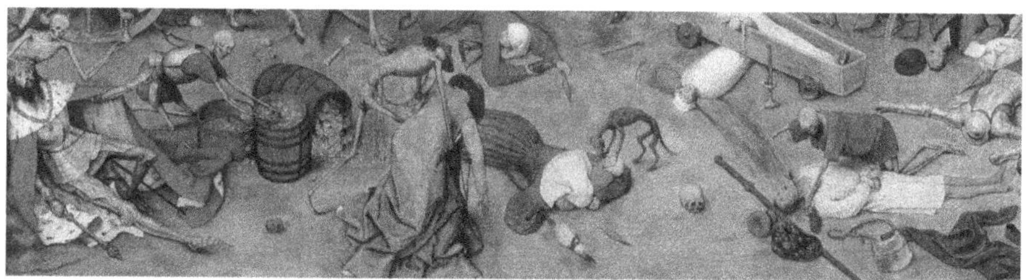

89b Pieter Bruegel, king, cardinal, pilgrim, detail, *The Triumph of Death*

Bruegel quoted motifs from the *Dance of Death* as a frieze in the foreground of his *Triumph of Death* (fig 89b); compare our two Holbeins (fig. 101a-b). From left to right across the painting, Death comes to a King, a Cardinal, a Mother, a Pilgrim, a Mercenary, a Fool, Lovers and a Maiden. Bruegel's cameos only include one clerical rank — the Cardinal. Tradition included equal numbers of clergy and laymen in the *danse macabre*; in later editions of Holbein the number of clergy increased.

From this tradition, Bruegel took the implicit violence of the confrontation between dead and living, the *transi* come to take the living body, minus any consolatory religious apparatus. The keys to the landscape are at the bottom of the picture, where a long strip of familiar characters from the *danse macabre* introduces the concerns of the picture with recognisable images. They form, as it were, the first parenthesis to the action.

Thus in the left corner, the king dies next to his gold. The gold stands in huge barrels, raided by a skeleton in full armour. A little to the right, a bending *transi* supports a slumped cardinal. As is traditional, the *transi* mimic the poses, costume and attitude of their victims: the one looking through the king's gold wears his armor, the one supporting the cardinal wears a cardinal's hat. On the far side of the painting, at bottom right, lovers playing music together are joined by a mandolin-playing *transi*. These figures — the king, the lovers, the maiden — all had separate popular models in the Northern *macabre* tradition.

The king evokes the motif of the *Three Living and the Three Dead Kings*, famous enough to be used as a street sign,[114] and given definitive visual shape around 1487 in a print by the Master of the House Book (fl. 1475-90). The original form here was a thirteenth-century poem centred around the dialogue between the living and the dead,[115] where the dead emerge to accost the kings out of the cemetery ground, as they do in the print. The subject was quite common in illuminations for the prayers for the dead, included in all Books of Hours.

The motifs of *Death and the Lovers*, and *Death and the Maiden*, were popular from early in the century. *Death and the Maiden* in particular branched out from the *danse macabre* to become its own genre in Northern art, with Lucas Cranach and Hans Beltung Grien among its most notable exponents. An early and extremely vicious sexual treatment of the motif comes in the middle of Nicolas Manual's monastic *Dance of Death*.[116] The theme was charged with a newfound eroticism, wherein death stood for desire itself, as much as for the end of it. Bruegel seems deliberately to quote types of lovers and maidens in the *Triumph* from more archaic *danse macabre* ensembles, so the viewer sees the painting as a whole as consciously referencing the familiar popular imagery of the *danse*.

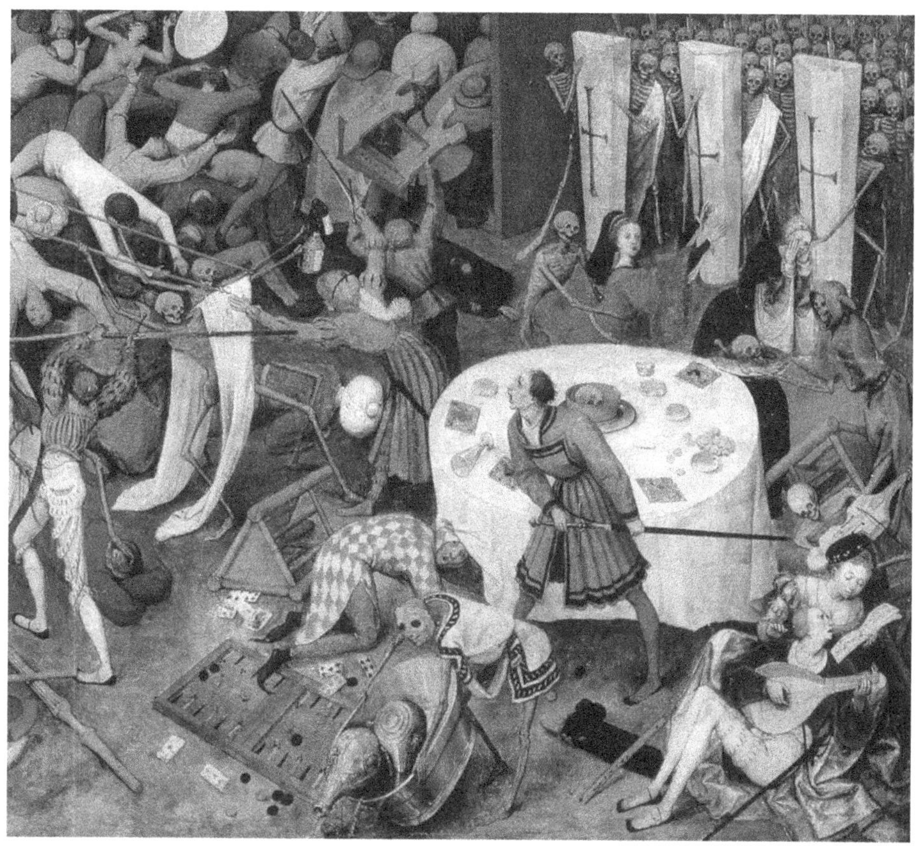

89c Pieter Bruegel, corner table, detail, *The Triumph of Death*

The lovers' corner is part of the larger table group, the second opening parenthesis of the painting (fig. 89c). Elements of *Totenmal* and carnival surround the table. Left of the lovers, a masked figure parodies, as if for carnival, *the entrance into fictive or sacred time*. This masquerading *transi* empties the festive flagons onto the ground. Behind him, a scared fool takes refuge under the table. His proximity to the playing cards makes him into an ironic version of the proverb, *Fools get the (best) cards*. This living fool is balanced by a *transi* fool on the opposite side of the table. He presents a well-dressed young woman with a skull and crossbones on a platter; recall the *totenfressen* imagery of Manuel's era, and the cry of the Romans Carnival *revenants* to come. This conventional imagery is used lightly and playfully; these corner-scenes of the painting announce themselves as quoted representations.

These actions swirl the viewer around the table. To the left, a young woman in court dress is boldly accosted by another *transi*. The white tablecloth frames the young nobleman drawing his sword. His head is encircled by the empty wineglass and pieces of bread, and by the skull in a bowl at the center of the table. This may be a visual pun alluding to the interesting phrase *croquer la tête du mort* (to munch on a dead man's head), which referred to the popularity of burial feasts in Flanders and Artois.[117] This last image turns the echo of *Totenmal* literally on its head; here is a literal feast of the dead, more restricted and restrained in Bruegel's vision than it was to be in the streets of Romans. The food is bones, not meat; it is an upside-down meal, rather than a blasphemous breach of taboo. But horror intrudes dynamically, from the top left, breaking into the circle round the table. Holding back the first onslaught of the dead, a group of German mercenaries are recognisable by their distinctive slashed clothing. Behind them on the ground lie overturned gaming boards; another swirl of scattered playing cards brings us back to the fool.

The king's greed, the lovers' lust, and the mercenaries' fashionable vanity may allude to the Seven Deadly Sins;[118] they are more likely to be allusions embedded in the *danse macabre* tradition itself, with its element of the dead chiding the living for their sins. Bruegel used the *danse macabre* figures in a theatrical way, as a curtain-opener; they work as a shorthand to show the action refers to the whole society of the living.

A different note altogether is struck at the centre of the picture, where, flanked by the foreground groups, a *transi* in a hair-shirt cuts the throat of a pilgrim (fig. 89b). One bony hand reaches for the purse. Next to the dying man's head is his hat, covered with souvenirs from the various pilgrimage sites he has visited;[119] a direct reference to contemporary penitential practices

This scene acts as an introduction to the central group. A female in a shroud, half under a coffin cart, is laid out on straw with a candle, as was the peasant custom.[120] This coffin is at the hub, visually and symbolically, of the drama, in the exact middle of the whole panorama, like the peasant couple at the centre of *Carnival and Lent*. The cart bears another shrouded corpse, a man, also on straw. A dead infant lies half in and half out of the coffin, its arms outstretched to the woman below. The coffin is wheeled, as in a contemporary funeral procession, by two *transi* wearing the penitential cowls and funerary robes of confraternity members (fig. 89d). To the right of this group is a third confraternity member. He wears the same robes but is alive and aghast, fallen under the foot of an especially elongated *transi*, which raise its arms to cut him down.

This sardonic central ensemble is crucial to the meaning of the painting as a whole. The pilgrim, the burial of the dead, the dead and living brethren; all are linked to the crisis of Purgatory. People enrolled their *own* dead in confraternities; hence the piteous dead family. The prime proponents (and profiteers) of the penitential economy were the Brotherhoods; recall the increasingly negative reactions to their purposes and function; the iconoclast attack on their robes; the scenes at Romans.

A slightly later Bruegel painting, known as *The Misanthrope* (1568; fig. 102), shows a similar theme. It depicts a confraternity member in funeral robes robbed by a symbol of the world. The caption — *Om dat de werelt is soe ongetru / Daer om gha ic in den ru* (*Because the world is so faithless, I wear mourning*) — seems to be a seventeenth-century addition;[121] however its author evidently recognised the significance of the costume. The World cuts the purse of one who ghoulishly accumulates money from the dead. In the

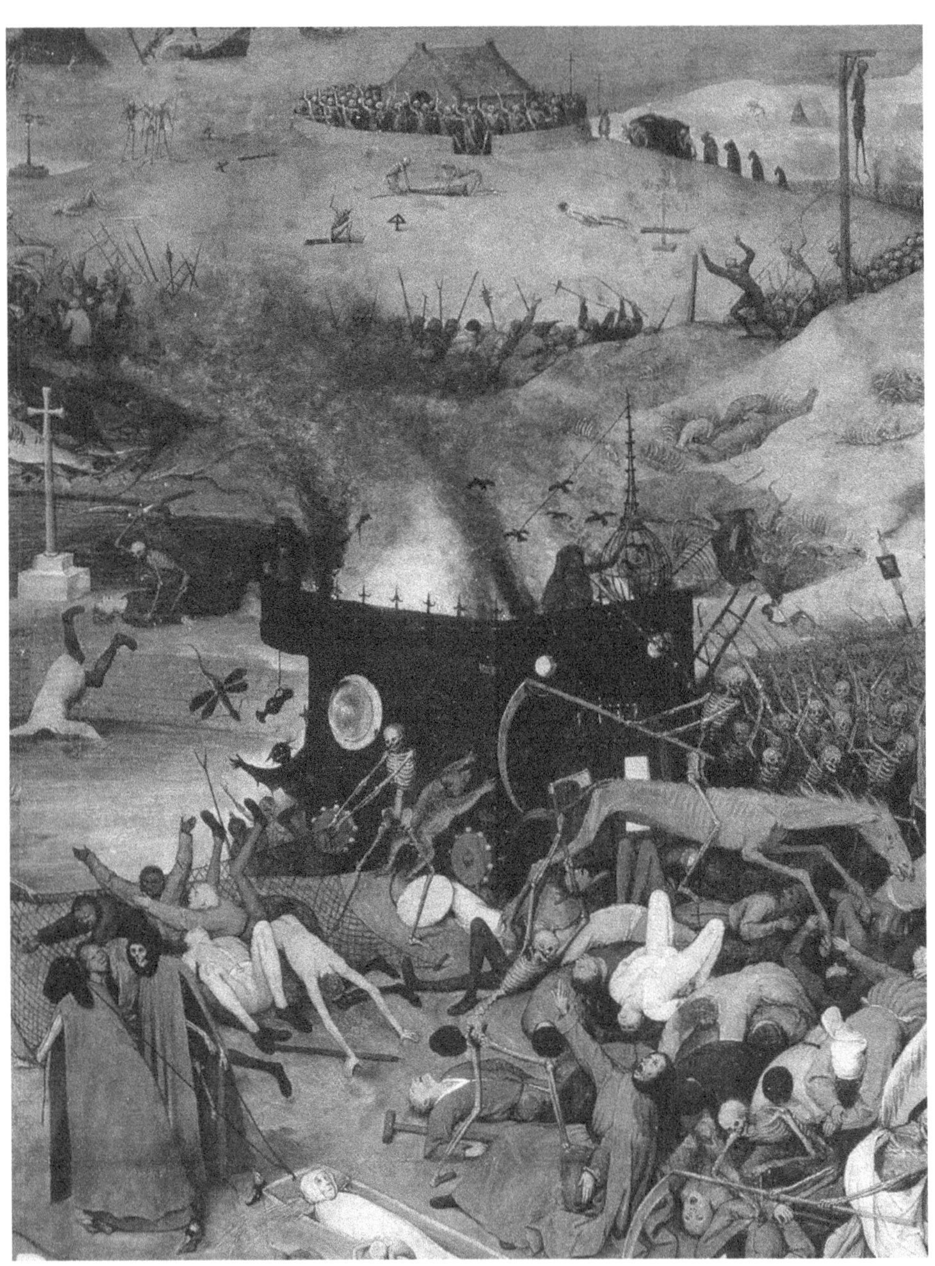

89d Pieter Bruegel, central section, *The Triumph of Death*

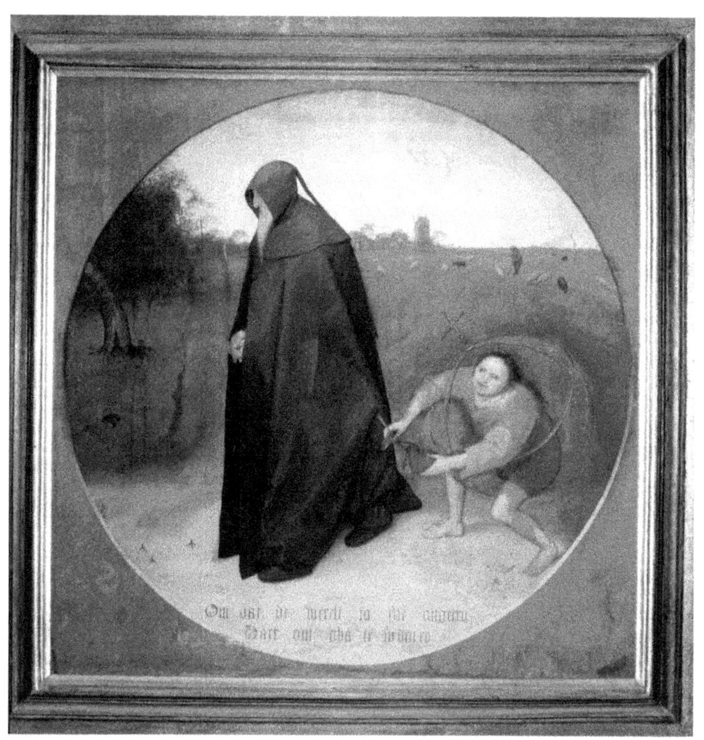

102 Pieter Bruegel, *The Misanthrope*, 1568. Oil on panel, 86 x 85 cm. Museo di Capodimonte, Naples. Photo © 2003. SCALA, Florence — courtesy of the Ministero Beni e Att. Culturali

background, a shepherd tends his flock by a windmill. The shepherd stands for Christ and the windmill for the Eucharist.[122] Both are presented as integrated parts of the world, fixtures in the landscape; in contrast to the miserable Brother, who, in addition to being robbed, also has tacks strewn in his path.

In Bruegel's *Triumph of Death*, the confraternity figures are at centre stage (fig. 89d, 89e). A net frames the cowled heads of the two skeletal Brethren. Two of the dead use it to catch the living (including two Africans). The image of the net is related pictorially to the doings of the Brothers; its edges parallel the edges of the coffin and of the pilgrim's staff; the group forms a balanced centre piece. The eye travels from the attack on

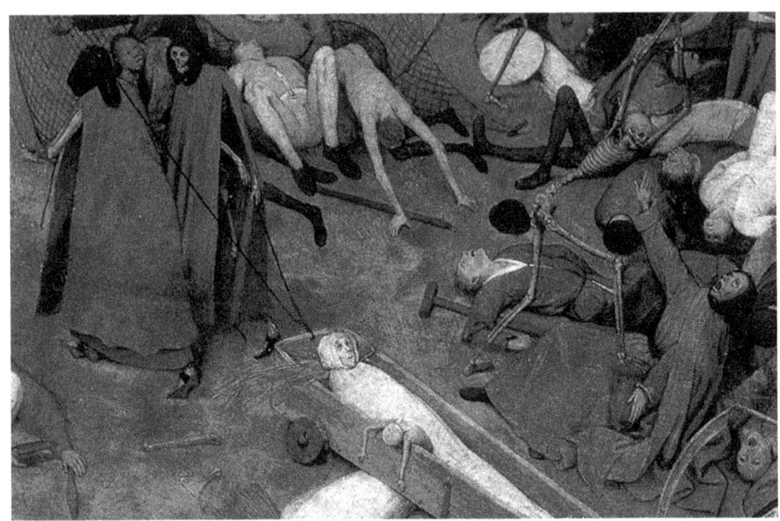

89e Pieter Bruegel, *transi* brethren and living brother, detail, *The Triumph of Death*

the pilgrim, to the geometrically arranged corpses, to the members of the brotherhood, to the net. The diagonal and narrative development of these figures points us into the picture.

To the left and right are two images of the Horsemen of Death. The left cart is a parody of a triumphal cart, filled with skulls and driven by a nag (fig. 89a). In keeping with the classical original, Bruegel has given the woman trampled by Death's nag the attributes of a classical Fate.[123] She holds distaff and shears, and is about to cut her thread. Right of the coffin's diagonal axis is a great wedge-like mass of the living. Nearest the viewer, the living are packed higgledy-piggeldy into an enormous pile, attacked here and there by individual *transi*. On the far side of this piled-up mass, an army of *transi* operates a military pincer maneuver, pushing the living into the mouth of an enormous coffin, which, big though it is, seems unable to hold them all. Made surreal through change of scale, this giant box dominates and organises this side of the painting. Between the confraternity mourners and the open lid of the box, an apocalyptic Horseman of Death rides directly over the piled-up bodies of the living (fig. 89d). For this figure,

Bruegel borrowed the Italian idea of Death the Rider, a *transi* armed with a scythe, as he can be seen at Palermo in the Galleria Nazionale.

The central coffin is drawn in one direction, diagonally into the painting. The two foreground horsemen move in the opposite direction. This structure is echoed further back in the picture, where a regiment of the mounted dead emerge from the lee of the cliff to the left and advances upon the living. At the top of the hill behind them, their movement is matched and opposed by a funeral procession, which moves up from the right, towards the top of the hill. This building — a church or charnel-house — is enclosed by a walled cemetery, packed with the ranks of the dead. This scene also recalls the *Armenseelen* in the churchyard (fig. 96); here the dead are waving at the viewer. Directly below this, at the foot of the hill, a crowd of living people holding crosses, hayforks, ladders, maces, are caught between the cavalry of the dead on their left and the infantry of the dead surging round the other side of the hill. These people are almost obscured by a cloud of infernal smoke, which rises from the fort, black and red in colour, at the centre of the picture. This whole background movement around the hill reflects and repeats the action of the foreground. Both involve funeral processions taking place in the midst of pincer attacks by the innumerable armies of the dead.

The hayforks and ladders bring to mind the Death Carnival in Romans, which had three thematic treatments of death: agrarian, martial, and sacred: *Flails, rakes, and brooms were also part of the traditional dances performed at the end of the wheat-growing cycle... The St. Blaise Carnival was a threshing rite... the death of the cereal cycle, a prelude to the rebirth that spring's sowing would represent.* The people danced *some carrying rakes, others brooms, yet others flails for threshing wheat... dressed in death shrouds... with others who cried that before three days were out the flesh of Christians would sell for six deniers the pound.*[124]

The movements of armies and funeral processions in Bruegel's *Triumph* correspond to martial and religious imagery. An agrarian theme is also alluded to. Carrying farm implements on high was a sign of revolt; *a few months before... an attorney turned protestor... had been arrested for having "carried the rake, exciting the people"* according to Catherine de Medici.[125] Hayforks, spears and ladders formed an otherwise inexplicable part of a carnival display at Nuremberg in 1539; the protest was aimed at the Lutheran Andreas Osiander, and the theme was *Hell.*[126]

The agrarian element in the Death Carnival justifies itself in two ways. The first is the traditional, eons-old parallel between death and agriculture. The second is the brandishing of agricultural tools, as a means of restoring the respect due to their wielders. Bruegel skillfully shaped such associations, feeding them into the total fabric of his picture. The reapers are caught in a reaping too big for them; a hayfork is caught in the net with its owner. These forms of protest are as little use against the dead as the swords of the *landsknechte*. The painting as a whole emphasises martial and religious aspects of death; the agrarian theme is no more than a grace-note there to deepen its harmony.

The Revenge of the Dead

The sheer scale on which the dead outnumber the living and the pointed references to penitential practices, express a world in the midst of the crisis of Purgatory. Other details support this interpretation. For example, everywhere the dead march under the sign of the cross. Crosses dot the landscape, but afford no protection to the living. On the bridge next to the fort, a man has his throat cut by a *transi* at the foot of a mounted cross (fig. 89f). This group is similar in effect to the murder of the pilgrim. Images are not a remedy against death.

On the hillside, with the packed cemetery at the top and the battle at the bottom, two more crosses each have a fresh corpse lying next to them. There is a close juxtaposition of two crosses at the summit of the hill. One is held by the living leader of the funeral procession. The other, slightly higher

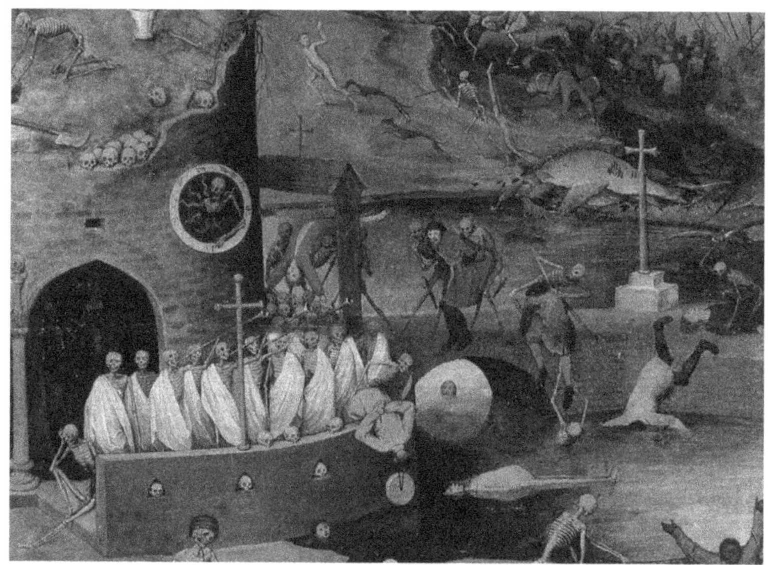

89f Pieter Bruegel, *transi* trumpeters and melancholic detail, *The Triumph of Death*

up, is held by one of the crowd of dead in the cemetery (waving in our direction). Whatever power the cross has is in the hands of the dead.

At the foot of the picture, above the music-playing lovers (fig. 89c), some of the dead assemble behind three huge coffins (marked with crosses). They occupy the position in Bruegel's pictures where the artist often places a liminal or mediating figure, who introduces the viewer to the action in the fashion of quattrocento painters; one instance is the quizzical notary guest at the *Wedding Dance* (Detroit Institute of Art). The shield-bearing *transi* in the front row have something of this quizzical characteristic. The two in the middle, dressed in winding sheets, peer interestedly out at the viewer. One stands with hand on hip. Others in the front row indicate the coffins, and particularly the crosses, with long bony fingers, again for the benefit of the viewer, whom the cross will not save from the coffin. These blackly funny details recall the spirit of Piero's Carnival.

Other pertinent features of the panorama refer to the punishment of criminals. In several prominent cameos, the dead execute the living as

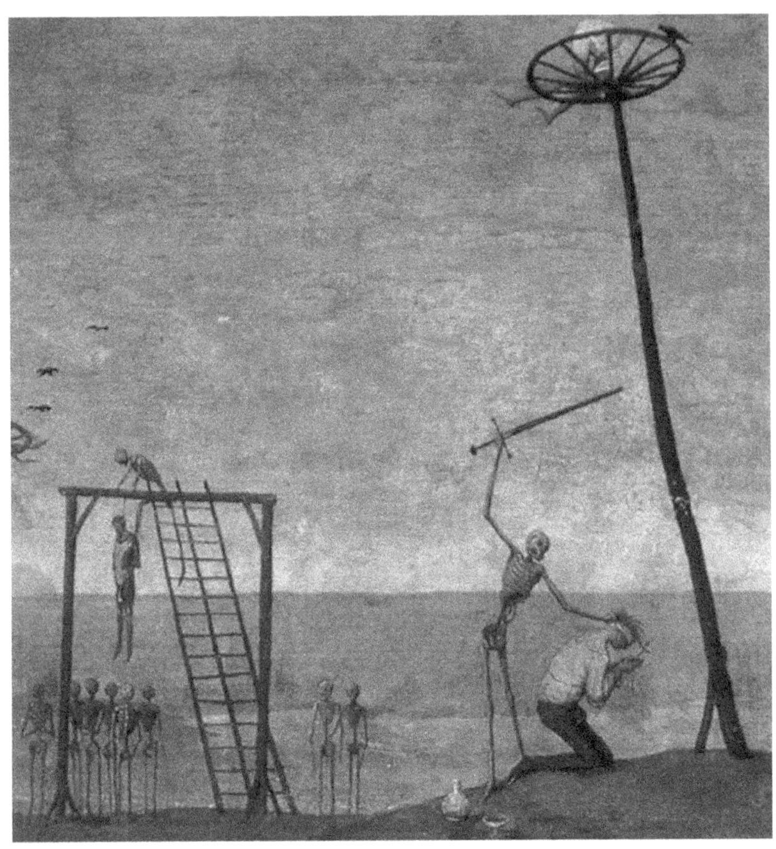

89g Pieter Bruegel, the dead executing the living, detail *The Triumph of Death*

though they were felons (fig. 89g). Above the cart of death, a group of dead, wearing their shrouds like togas, and therefore with an air of early Christian martyrs, stand behind a cross (fig. 89f). Some blow trumpets. They have a live prisoner, with bound hands and a millstone tied around his neck, about to be thrown into the water; a standard form of punishment for civil offenses. Left of this group sits an unrobed *transi* in the traditional position of melancholy, head in hand; a dreaming or melancholic figure, like the sleepers with hand to head (c.f., *The Peddler Pillaged by Apes*; fig. 31, or *Tondalus*, fig. 47).

Above and right of this figure, a *transi* bursts out of a clock face and indicates with his left hand the only legible number on the dial: the number one, placed where a six should be. The other markings imitate mystical signs. It was customary in parts of Flanders (as elsewhere) to stop the clock in a house when someone died there.[127] A giant clock with a human arm as its hand indicates that the eleventh hour has struck in *Desidia* (fig. 13); here, the living have been over-slothful in their responsibilities to the dead. The hour has struck for all the living, but the exact time at which this event is occurring remains deliberately unintelligible. The pleased-looking *transi* who flank the trumpeters at this execution are balanced by the skeletal melancholic, who turns his face away from the scene.

Most of the references to punishment are to be found in the top right-hand section of the painting. As in the *Griet*, the mood of the painting grows darker in the background scenes. These cameos are nightmarish for the same reasons as those in the *Griet*: they are *shorn of ethical and religious significance* (as Holbein's central images also were believed to be). Moving from right to left across the top, a *transi* dispatches with a sword a kneeling prisoner, underneath a torture wheel (fig. 89g). The prisoner is blindfolded, and clutches the small crucifix that was always given to condemned criminals. This little group is almost identical to one in Bruegel's *Justitia* print (1559, fig. 103). There too, we see in the distance the high torture wheels on which the broken and beaten bodies of criminals were displayed in the Netherlands: *the device was commonly employed north of the Alps... as a means of punishing lower-class criminals who had committed especially evil crimes.*[128] The print of *Justitia* focused on the misery of state punishment; it was evidently intended to have political and satirical resonance. In the *Triumph of Death*, the dead punish the living in the fashions appropriate for capital crimes.

To the left of the skeletal executioner with the sword, another group of *transi* hang a man on the gallows. Left of this, a long, unnaturally elongated corpse hangs from a tree. The bodies of executed criminals were

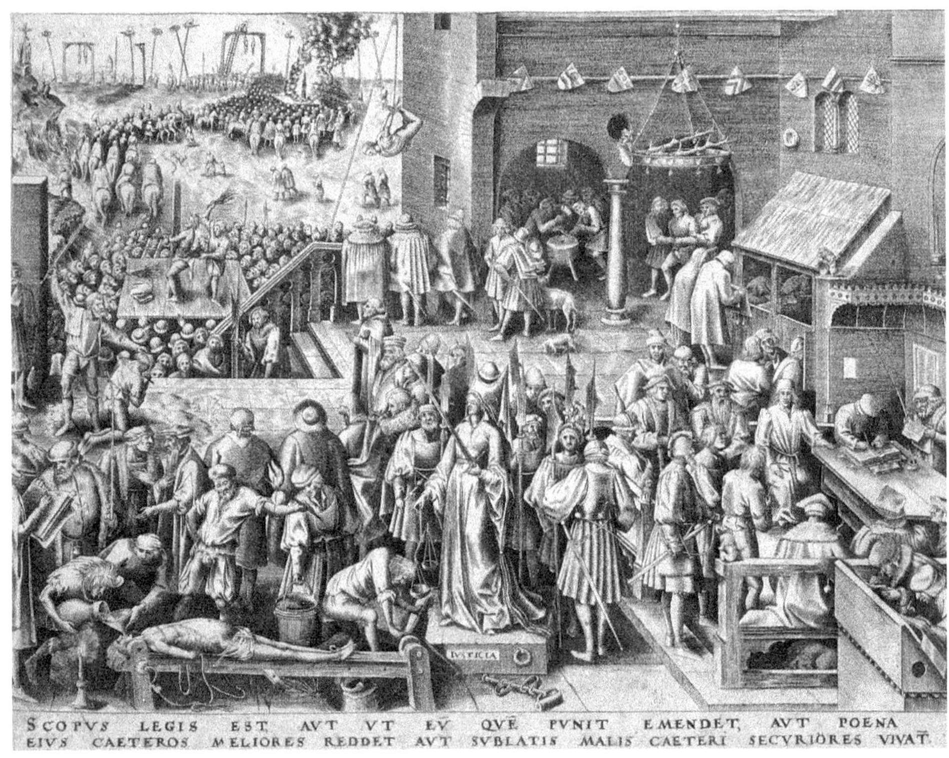

103 Philip Galle, after Pieter Bruegel, *Justitia*, 1559. Engraving, 23.3 x 28.7 cm. Bibliothèque Royale Belgique, Brussels. S II 135128

usually allowed to rot on the gallows; they were also sometimes placed in the tops of trees in cemeteries.[129] Moving again left, towards the hillside with the cemetery, a rotting corpse depends from a gallows, and two *transi* energetically cut down trees in the top left-hand corner. These vignettes may refer to the practice of putting the "wild" evil dead in trees.

On the hillside itself, there lie two unburied corpses outside of the cemetery walls. As Ariès explained, *Only social outcasts were left in the fields or, as the place was later called, the "dump"... Persons who had been excommunicated or prisoners who had been executed and not claimed by their families were left to rot unburied, with no more than a block of stone laid over them to preserve the appearance of the landscape.*[130] At the end of the fourteenth century, the poet Alain Chartier (c. 1392-1430) called the place where bodies of outcasts were thrown a *false atrium*, that is, a false cemetery: *It is a kind of false atrium / And there they throw the bodies of the damned / I saw more than four of them / blackened, rotting, left to lie / On the ground without a grave.*[131] Bruegel's skeletal figures on the hillside (and at the far right under the bell), disinterring coffins or pulling themselves out of the earth, evoke such beliefs concerning those who die the bad death, the death of criminals.

> Medieval man refused to give his enemy or the enemy of society the burial *ad sanctus*.... Sometimes... the dead were buried secretly, but the devils or angels did not always allow them to remain undisturbed in the placed they had usurped in the holy ground which they defiled with their presence. Either they dug them up by night and turned them out themselves, or else they caused unusual phenomena that alerted the clergy to the fraud. There exist forms that were used to petition the authorities for the right to exhume a corpse and eject it from a cemetery or church.[132]

Other details in Bruegel's panorama express the idea that the dead might be extracting their *just* revenge. Close by the demonic fort in the center of the picture, a bear springs after the wild figure of Death on horseback. The bear is traditionally the animal of *Ira*; one appears in the foreground of Bruegel's print of the subject (fig. 11). Bear-like creatures again appear in the print of *Justitia* (fig. 103); one sits with a shield above the table where the judge gives his verdict; another crouches in the foreground, carved or real, at the corner of the bench at the bottom right. These symbolic uses carry old connotations: *In archaic times a person who stood outside the law, the culture, was considered "dead" by ordinary people. In many instances the embodiment of these "dead" was the bear.*[133]

The wheeled fort itself (fig. 89d) resembles a form of *Hölle* (literally, a *Hell*), the German name given to all kinds of festival floats, whether or not their imagery expressed infernal themes. *Höllen* were commonly constructed as castles — for passion plays (as a prison for the damned) — and especially in pageant festivals. A *castle of hell* made for the Valenciennes Passion appears in a drawing from 1547.[134]

Like this one, *Höllen* might also be filled with fire. At the end of a mid-sixteenth-century parade at Nüremberg, participants, *laid siege to the Hölle with ladders, climbed up and set off the fireworks concealed in the pageant... the whole structure... was consumed in the flames.*[135] In 1548, a similar exploding float was among the pageants devised for Phillip's Joyous Entry into Antwerp.[136] Bruegel's hellish wheeled castle seems drawn from carnivalesque models of this kind.

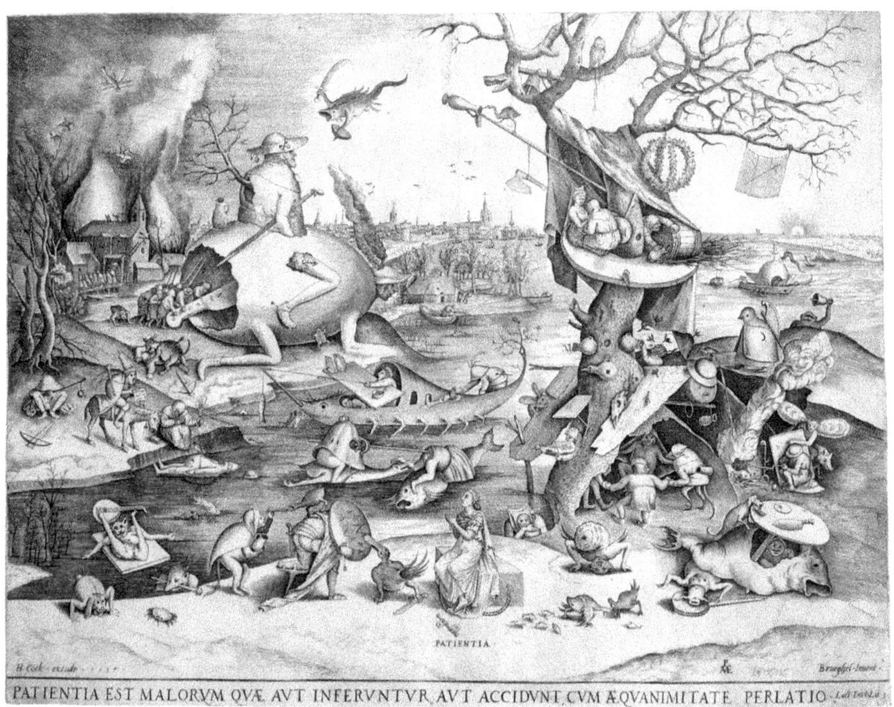

104 Pieter van der Heyden, after Pieter Bruegel, *Patientia*, 1557. Engraving, 34 x 44 cm. Bibliothèque Royale Belgique, Brussels. S 11 31216 plano

Prominent on one wall is a huge curved mirror — a *Vanitas* emblem (fig. 89d) — the only reference in the picture to the typical funerary caption or inscription, reminding the passer-by, *I was once as you are now*. The reflection this mirror would give, however, would be unrecognisably distorted. While its presence at a Triumph of Death requires no further explanation, its situation as part of the castle's decoration reflects the attribute-laden floats of the *rederijkers*; the globe in the cart of Father Time in the *Triumph of Time* (fig. 99) is similarly encircled with the symbols of the zodiac. In its train, half hidden at the rear, we see the silhouettes of figures who could be demonic spirits, or masked *transi* guisers; the painting leaves both options open. This wheeled-fort and its personnel are commensurate with the black carnival themes — the Carnival of Death, the Wild Hunt's *carnival army* — integrated into the painting.

Humanist Surrealism in *Patientia*

Some details are surreal in a quite different register; consider the huge grounded fish immediately below the cavalry of death. A closer look reveals several more shadowy fish behind it, apparently metamorphosing in the area where the infernal fumes from the fort envelope the victims of the cavalry attack. Beached or hybrid fish recur in Bruegel's art; apart from St Anthony's fish (fig. 32), and the *Big Fish Eat Little Fish* (fig. 36), the closest parallel here is the fish in Bruegel's print of *Patientia* (fig. 104).

Patientia, like *Justitia*, is, of course, one of the *Seven Virtues* (figs. 78, 90, 103, 104), the series designed (probably) in 1556, and published in 1557, to follow Bruegel's successful series of *Vices* (figs. 9-15).[137] As is often noted, most of the *Virtues* are in an entirely different allegorical style to that of the *Vices*. They are realistic where the *Vices* are surrealistic. The exception is *Patientia*; the style of which is far more like one of the *Vices* than the *Virtues*. Lady Patience kneels in a nightmarish landscape, extending out

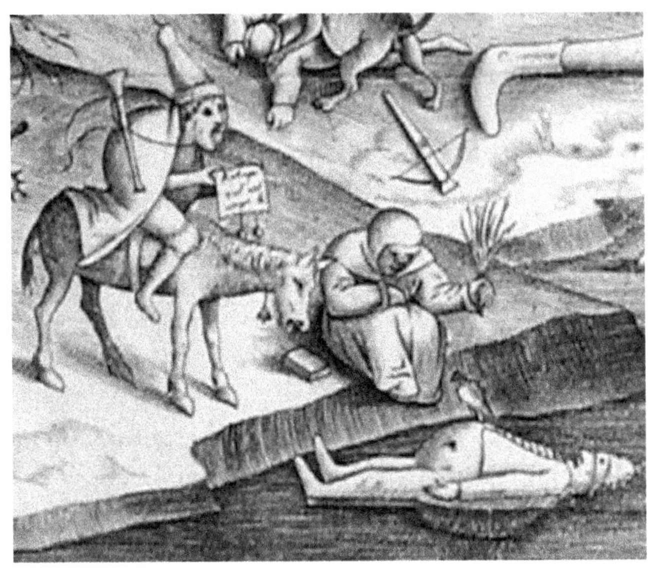

104a Pieter van der Heyden, after Pieter Bruegel, detail, *Patientia*.

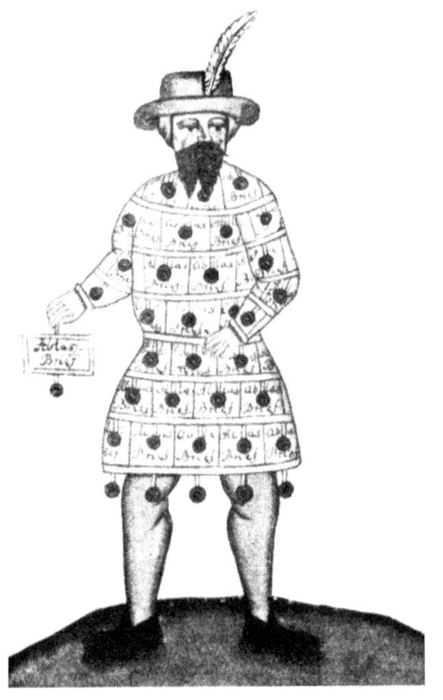

105 Anon, *Man in a Suit of Letters of Indulgence*, German, second half sixteenth century. Woodcut. Photo: after Jeannin (1957)

into the far distance (quite unlike the other *Virtues*). This is the world of Anthony's Temptation and Griet's deluded flight. Patience is represented as the only option in an insane world. As with the *Vices*, how exactly the world has gone mad is demonstrated explicitly by the nature of the bad dreams that surround her.

Apart from the *Triumph of Death*, this is the work where Bruegel most clearly criticised the politico-religious crisis, as opposed to finding positions from which to resolve it (as in the *Death of the Virgin* and *Caritas*). As Orenstein put it: *While there is debate about whether political content appears [elsewhere in Bruegel] there can be no doubt regarding its presence in Patientia. It seems clear from the clerical imagery and the large size of [this] print that Bruegel intended to make a statement of some sort about contemporary religious conflicts in the Netherlands.*[138]

Several of these political elements in *Patientia* prefigure motifs in the *Triumph of Death*; so the inter-play of imagery in the two works makes it possible, at least partially, to interpret each in the context of the other. Specific figures in *Patience* refer to the bankruptcy of penitential practices. A figure on horseback reads aloud from a document with seals attached. (fig. 104a). It is often identified as a papal bull; I think it is more like a letter of indulgence; we see such letters made into a coat here, for example, in a popular Protestant print (fig. 105). This rider seems to address his action to the drowned body floating in the water; similar to one in the *Triumph* (fig. 89f). The dead man is attended in the print by a monk who holds a switch of dry twigs over the body, in a parody of Last Rites.

The many-legged ship in the water (fig. 104b), resembles a striking image in an almost contemporary engraving, satirising the Ship of the Church (fig. 106) as a giant upside-down lizard. A smaller such boat glides on the water in the background of *Patientia*. Dominating the scene, a grotesque cardinal sits spliced into a giant egg-man, his characteristic hat on his head, a tree emerging from his hollow interior, and a papal bull omin-

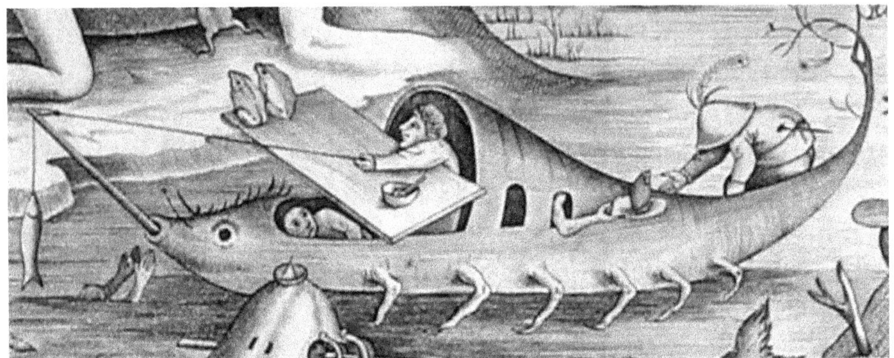

104b Pieter van der Heyden, after Pieter Bruegel, many-legged ship in water, detail, *Patientia*

106 Anon, *The Ship of the Papal Church*, German, second half sixteenth century. Printed pamphlet, 37.8 x 47.9 cm. © Staatliche Graphische Sammlung, Munich, Inv 209976 D

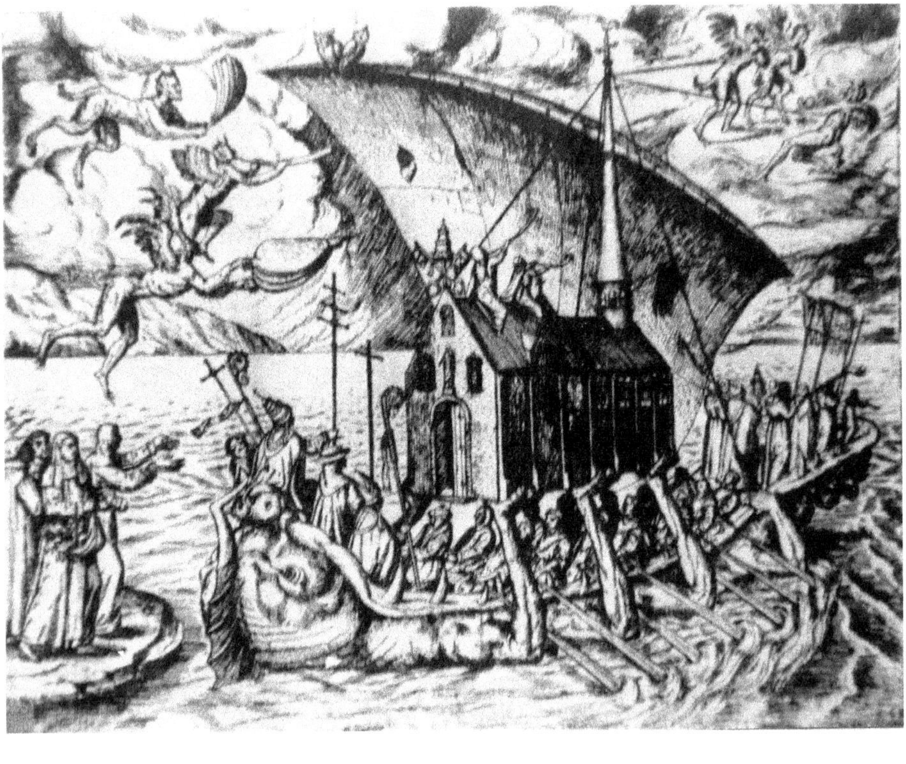

ously tucked into his waistband. A representation of Peter's keys decorates his hat; it indicates that this hollow and corrupt monster is a papal envoy. This detail was prudently omitted in the second impression.[139] In the background at the left, people stream out of a burning church; voting with their feet.

Despite all this, Bruegel's *Patientia* does not take a directly partisan stance. Concepts of Patience from all camps are merged. At least one of the metamorphs in the right-hand group can be interpreted as a stab at the divisive new creeds. This is the figure of the cloaked bird-head with the harp. Boon comments: *j'ai trouvé une explication dans une pièce des Rhétoricients, Van de Christe Kercke, il est dit d'un joueur de harpe qu'il trame une croyance étrange, une gecke devotie raemt.*[140] However this may be, the *evils that assail one* in *Patientia* include clear examples of the emptiness, or worse, perversion of the symbols and persons of the Church.

The cardinal is encased in his egg; the egg is also the body, on all fours, of a creature with the head of a peasant. Plumes of smoke rise from the peasant's hat, showing that his head is on fire. A group of people with a gargantuan knife and a ladder invade the inside of the egg man through the broken rear. The view this image presents of the relations between clergy and laymen is unusually explicit. Published at a time when Pope and Emperor were zealously prosecuting heretics in the Southern Netherlands,[141] this image must have been intended and read as referring to the current situation; it is much too specific to be taken as a general anti-clerical satire. The subject of Patience was taken up at this time by pro-Reformist Netherlandish artists, who gave the allegory a new "Neo-Stoical" iconography: *Patience with rock and chain.*[142] Bernard van Orley, Martin van Heemskerck and Joris Hoefnagel (whose riddling salute to Ortelius was touched on earlier), were among those whose creative use of Patience's attributes gave a contemporary spin to the old Virtue.[143]

Bruegel's design mobilises some of these ideas in the attributes of *Patientia* and in the Latin caption for the print: *Patience is the tranquil endurance of evils that assail you or happen to you.* from Book 5 of the *Institutiones*

Divinae of Lactantius. Lactantius was popular among Neo-Platonists as well as Protestants.[144] His characterisation of Patience as the *common virtue of most assistance to the just man who must live under the hegemony of the unjust*[145] had an unusually direct application to Antwerpers in 1556.

The figure of Patience herself is small and rather ineffectual. She looks up to heaven and holds a crucifix, like the condemned person in fig. 89g. Dragonflies and other infernal flying beasts occupy the right-hand corner of the print, similar to those to the left of the carnival fort in the *Triumph of Death*. A hollowed tree trunk behind her seems to be a gathering place for sinners, festooned with a horse's skull and various insects. A similar hollow tree rises prominently in the *Triumph*, above the giant coffin. A surreally elongated corpse hangs from its top, a naked man scrambles into its hollow, a javelin stuck in his back, animal bones and human skulls are scattered around it. This figure has been attacked from the rear, like certain figures in *Patientia*.

Monsters proliferating in the ocean and around the tree are familiar motifs used by Bruegel to convey the sense of the laws of nature and civilization gone hopelessly wrong. The outsize fish materialising out of the conjunction of smoke, earth, and death in Bruegel's *Triumph* symbolise the same kind of reversal of the laws of nature. When the dead rise to attack the living, the natural order is disrupted beyond repair. Bruegel's *Triumph* is his most apocalyptic and cosmological version of the World-Turned-Upside-Down.

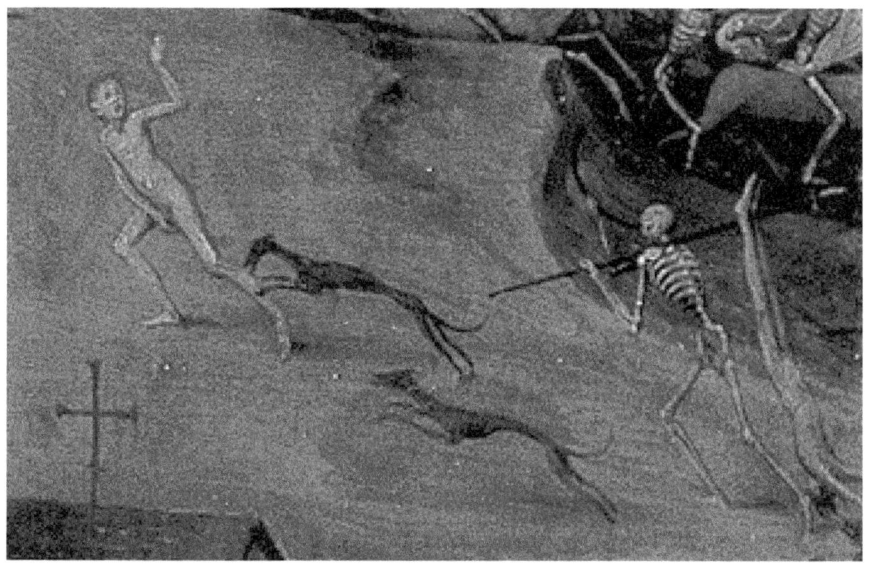

89h Pieter Bruegel, *transi* hunting a man, detail *The Triumph of Death*

Another key scene in the *Triumph*, to the left and above the fish shows a young naked man hunted by a fearsome *transi* with two hounds, hunting horn, and a pole on which to carry his human prey (fig. 89h). Such a scene inevitably evokes Acteon, the most famous person hunted by hounds, whose story is both a metamorphosis from human to stag and from hunter to victim.[146] In his Moralised Ovid, Pierre Bersuire associated the story of Acteon with Old Testament texts about vengeance: *Woe to you who spoil, will you not yourself also be spoiled?* (*Isaiah* 33:1), and *All who prey upon you, I will give for a prey* (*Jeremiah* 30:10).[147]

This is also a World Upside Down motif – the hunter hunted – with an independent tradition. It can be found in works by Cranach and George Pencz; a sixteenth-century mural in Vienna depicted the hunter

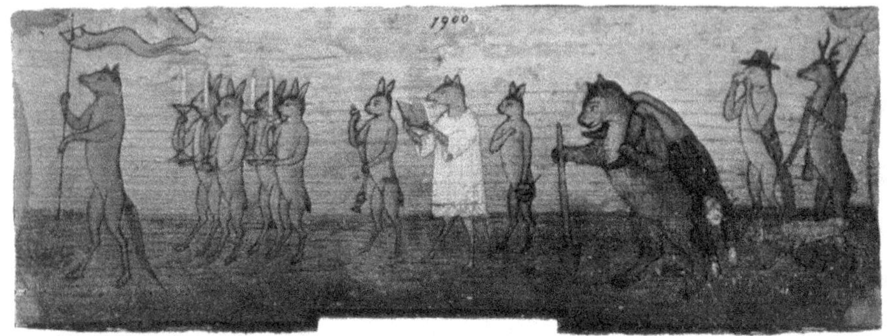

107 Anon, *Animals bring home the hunter* (World-Upside-Down motif), c. 1900. Paint on bark plaque. Photo: author

caught and subsequently eaten.[148] Another version of the theme was the *revenge of the animals*, often envisaged as a carnivalesque mock-funeral. A small piece of folk art from Eastern Europe shows the animals in a funeral procession: the bear carries the hunter over his back, rabbits hold candles and censer, the fox in a surplice reads the litany (fig. 107).[149] Many images of the three living and the three dead place the encounter in the context of the hunt – the version in the Flemish Grimani Breviary goes so far as to show the skeletal dead armed with javelins, pulling the living from their horses; this is close in context and conception to the action of the *Triumph*.[150]

All these were ready-made elements in the collective repertoire from which Bruegel drew the ingredients of his imagery. However, nowhere else in the imagery of death, as far as I am aware, is a naked man depicted, actually hunted by Death, as an animal would be hunted. Even Manuel, had his Death the Archer shoot at clothed figures, who were, of course, emblems of their class. In this small scene, naked as the distant crowds in the *Griet*, it is Man in Pico's sense – not just the collective Everyman of the *danse macabres*, defined by social roles and costume – who is treated as an animal by his own dead. Animal and human bones lie pointedly mingled,[151] all over the barren landscape of the *Triumph*, making the same point in a more Boschian shorthand. The bones add a Hamlet-like tone, and also make nonsense of the stress laid on Christian burial; human bones here are litter. Everyone is dying the bad death. Among the carcasses behind the fort, in a final irony, lie the oxen who pull Death's cart in earlier, merrier *Triumphs of Death,* by Piero and others.[152] What is left when the given Christian remedies against death fail is the fearsome anarchic dead of the popular imagination, the denizens of the Wild hunt, reducing humanity to the level of beasts, dust and bones.

Conclusion

By 1566, the *Wunderjaar* of the hedge-preachers and the iconcoclasts, Bruegel was living in Brussels, where he had moved in 1563. Sparked perhaps by the experience of watching aghast from afar the spectacular philistinism of the Antwerp iconoclasm, or by the opportunity of a conversation or commission, Bruegel made his *Triumph* a framework within which to present the broken relations of the quick and the dead as a cosmic apocalyptic drama. He set about this from his customary ethnographic point of view, marshalling the details of folk observance and belief with his usual attention to detail, deploying the *danse macabre* figures as a framing device, taking motifs from carnivalesque mock-ritual, and organising the whole in a gigantic panorama, developed from his earlier *theatro mundi* pictures. However, by giving this particular visual shape to these collective fears, Bruegel firmly situated them in the category of the imaginary. His *Triumph of Death* presents itself as an evil *dream* of the dead.

As a dissection of disrupted belief systems and inefficacious ritual, the action takes place in no identifiable eschatological place or time. There is no God, no Jesus, no Hell, no devils. This in itself creates an atmosphere of nightmare. The dead are shown acting as they might act if not constrained by Christian ritual and narrative. In the older tradition of the three living and the three dead, the dead come to warn the living; here the old identity this expresses between prophecy and history has been discarded.[153]

In the Holbein prints and in other dances of death, the skeletal *transi* was an abstraction — a personification of death himself. No one can *become* Death. In Bruegel's *Triumph*, due to their enormous numbers, the *transi* form becomes simply a mark of being dead. The *transi* figures are therefore newly fearsome, because, in zombie fashion, they kill in order to render the living the same as themselves. This concept of the dead does not occur in any Christian or millenarian framework or plan of history. Bruegel strongly endorsed human moral action elsewhere in his works in *Caritas*, in terms of Good Works, and in the *Rebel Angels* and the *Griet* in terms of Neo-Platonic psychology. No one who saw human nature in terms of *homo chameleon* would reject Erasmus's defence of the doctrine of free-will: *what is the good of the entire man, if God treats him like the potter his clay, or as he can deal with a pebble?* The stance of the *Triumph* is thus subjunctive: it envisages an alternative world, horrifying because it lacks this framework.

There are other dream elements in the painting. The classic Macrobian idea of the *phantasma* as *things out of all proportion* is evoked first by the mind-boggling scale of the dead armies, then by the giant coffin-like box, the focus of the action, into whose gaping black maw hordes of the living are swept by the dead (fig. 89d). Condensed into this image is, of course, a sublimated idea of the Hell-mouth, already seen by Bruegel as a pure sign, a theatrical prop, in his *Limbo* and *Griet*. The metamorphic fish and the man hunted by death also work as signs refined and abstracted from his earlier dream-scapes; following the progression from *St Anthony* (fig. 32), *Big Fish* (fig. 36), the *Vices* (figs. 9-15) and *Patientia* (fig. 104), through the *Griet* (fig. 35).

Around the centre of the painting, perspective collapses into chaos, as it does in the *Fall of the Magician* (fig. 77). Like these other, darker works of the mid-60s, the reversed world crossing over into nightmare is the visual focus here. The fiery wheeled fort — a mobile hell, part *ommgang* float, part old Carnival — produces metamorphoses around it in a different register from the rest of the imagery: giant insects fly round it; the fish appear emerging out of the ground in the wake of its smoke; it is manned and followed by figures as close to hybrid as any in the picture; yet still ambivalently legible as carnivalesque rather than demonic (fig. 89d). The glowing double portholes and door of this black box give it a face; this too is another kind of subliminal hell-mouth, a head inhabited by pure fire, accompanied by Ira's bear, manned by Griet's mannikens. The box-head is heading for the negative hole of the coffin-box, whose form and space it will fill.

The surreality of the *Triumph* emanates in part from these explicitly fantastical elements, and in part from the "lack" of divine apparatus, which above all announces the picture's status as fiction. A further powerful surreal dimension is inherent in its style and structure. The viewer is placed outside and above the world of the painting. Several kinds of distance and distancing techniques work to mediate the spectator's experience of the picture as visual pleasure. The first is the effect of Bruegel's spatialising philosophy, which offers a God-like command of the panorama. The second is the effect of his humour: enhancing the pleasure of detachment by carefully placed cameos, orchestrated like a string of emotional fire crackers, which evoke sharp little shocks of pleasurable horror, recognition and comedy.

At the same time, the painting shows a world crawling with the vengeful dead, treating the living as guilty of capital crimes. Its real subject is the collapse of the penitential system, which had also shattered ties to the dead at the level of folk religion. The purgatorial crisis, brewing for more than two hundred years, accelerated into violent moments of mass action. The first occurred in the time of Luther, when Bruegel was born; the second around and after 1560, in waves of religious persecutions and conversions, wars and revolts, when the artist was in his thirties. The third he did not live to see: the full-blown witch-hunt towards the close of the century, and the

Triumph of Lent in the next. This is the background out of which and against which we can understand the unprecedented aspects of Bruegel's *Triumph*.

The crises of Bruegel's culture were not, of course, restricted to the sphere of thanatological systems — the spread of capitalism as a system of (re-)structuring desire and its objects, the rise of gynophobia and misogyny, the repression and nocturnalisation of Carnival — these were inter-related yet distinct phenomena of the day. But the revolution in the institutions of death shook all these systems and discourses — indeed it continues to shake them. The reasons for this may by now be clearer.

The desire to get everybody out of Purgatory before the Last Judgement greatly inflated Catholic penitential mechanisms. In retrospect, the establishment of Purgatory was a watershed; the beginning of the end of Bruegel's *Triumph*. Since the existence of Purgatory was guaranteed and given social *gravitas* by the mechanisms which administered it, the more effort and attention were invested in these mechanisms, the more real Purgatory became; both in people's secret minds and in the social world. As we saw earlier, inflation in the system was assured by the fatal error of linking Purgatory to sources of sanctity derived from the dead themselves, and tying both to a monetary measure. The cult of saints turned around the cult of relics, and the Church's claim to ritual control of the spirit world depended on the support of the saints, who thus acted as a kind of "age-group of the dead" for the whole of Christendom.

It is thus important to note that the penitential crisis broke not on the position of death itself — everyone was clear there was an afterlife — but on the relation of the living to the dead. Starting with the saints, who were everybody's ancestors, obligations to and from the dead underwrote the whole of human relations and institutions: inheritance, kinship, peer associations, neighbourliness, law, legitimacy. The narrative usually drawn from this era is that the fragmentation of these systems enabled, and indeed necessitated, a new psychology privileging the private individual and so ushering in the Cartesian sense of the ego as a single-point consciousness.

What is clear is that the purgatorial crisis marks a shift in the balance between the collective and the individual self. As the fate of the individual became the new focus of cultural attention, the collective self faded in comparison. The emphasis laid by Luther, Calvin and others on *communitas* in itself suggests the problem; no one had felt the need to lay such stress the community of souls before it was broken. It was the personal self which was at stake in purgatory, no longer to be satisfied, like peasants dancing with their dead, by the movement from the *short home* to the *long home*.

Many of the phenomena we have encountered — from Holbein's splitting of the *danse macabre* into individual dramas, to the Family of Love's emphasis on freedom of conscience — spoke to the sudden collapse of collective notions of identity and the ascendancy, for better or worse, of isolated private consciousness.[154] By 1601, a year in which Bruegel would have been about 70, William Shakespeare wrote his most famous play, about a *revenant* and the psychological destruction it brings. *So have I heard and do in part believe it,* says Horatio, summing up the situation of the supernatural at the end of Bruegel's century (*Hamlet,* I.i.164). The fantastic nature of Bruegel's *Triumph,* for all its apparently archaic elements, is a measure of its modernity. Its only possible setting is in the arena of the imagination, which is where, in subsequent centuries, all subsequent encounters with the dead were to be located.

Notes to Chapter 5

[1] Referring to a dream of his father's, from an autobiographical *Letter to Thomas Poole*, 16th October 1797, last paragraph, in Earl Leslie Griggs, ed, *Collected Letters*, (London: Oxford Univ. Press, 1956-1971), v. 1, 355.
[2] Leonardo da Vinci, *Prophecies*, in *The Notebooks of Leonardo da Vinci*, ed. & trans. E. MacCurdy (1939; New York, 1955), 1106.
[3] Ibid.
[4] Karl van Mander, *Dutch and Flemish Painters*, trans. C. van de Wall (New York, 1936), 156.
[5] See introduction to M. Bloch and J. Parry, eds., *Death and the Regeneration of Life* (Cambridge, 1982), 15-18.
[6] The founding essay for this is Roman Jakobsen, *Two Aspects of Language and Two Types of Aphasic Disturbances, V. The Metaphoric and Metonymic Poles*, reprinted in K. Pomorska and S. Rudy, eds., *Language in Literature* The Jakobsen Trust, 1987.
[7] On Gregory the Great, see Bede (fl. c. 731), *Historia Ecclesiastica Anglorum*, trans. with intro. D. D. Knowles (London, 1975), I: XVIII; Brown, *The Cult of the Saints: Its Rise and Function in Latin Antiquity* (Chicago, 1981), 90.
[8] L. Rothkrug, "Religious Practices and Collective Perceptions: Hidden Homologies in the Renaissance and Reformation," *Historical Reflections/ Reflexions Historiques* 7 (1) (Spring, 1980), 3-61; cf. his further comments, considering the early history of French catholic death practices, in "German Holiness and Western Sanctity in medieval and Modern History," *Historical Reflections/ Reflexions Historiques* 15 (1) (Spring, 1988), 195.
[9] P. Ariès, *The Hour of Our Death*, trans. H. Weaver (New York, 1981), 181-3.
[10] Ibid., 182
[11] Ibid., on the institution of the *marterloyge*. Lay religiosity flourished in the Netherlands at an early date, for instance, the phenomenon of beguines and that of the Brethren of the Common Life. Cf. G. H. Williams, *The Radical Reformation* (London, 1962); E. W. McDonnell, *The Beguines and Beghards in Medieval Culture* (New Brunswick, 1954); L. K. Little, *Religious Poverty and the Profit Economy in Medieval Europe* (Ithaca, 1978), 113-45, esp. 128-34.
[12] W. Monter, *Ritual, Myth and Magic in Early Modern Europe* (Athens, OH.,1983), 13.
[13] C. Harbison, *The Last Judgement in Sixteenth Century Northern Europe* (New York, 1976), 107.
[14] Ariès, 185. I have changed *the* to *a* in the last sentence of this quotation.
[15] Ibid., 183; cf. the comments in two detailed local studies; M. Agulhon, *Penitents et Francs-Macons dans l'ancienne Provence* (Paris, 1967), 86f., and A. N. Galpern, *The Religions of the People in Sixteenth Century Champagne* (Cambridge, Mass., 1976), 157-60 and passim.

[16] J. Wegg, *Antwerp, 1477-1559* (London, 1916), 103. The altar of the Guild of St. Luke was in Great Church in Bruegel's time.
[17] Sebastian Franck, *Weltbuch* (Augsburg, 1534),134b; quoted in M. Baxandall, *The Limewood Sculptors of Renaissance Germany* (New Haven, 1980), 55.
[18] On St. Luke's funeral masses and burial regulations, see Wegg, (1916) 79-80; for comparison, see the instances given in A. Martindale, *The Rise of the Artist* (New York, 1972), 12f., and in E. Leroy Ladurie, *Carnival at Romans*, trans. M. Feeney (New York, 1980), 299.
[19] On Purgatory, see J. Le Goff, *The Birth of Purgatory*, trans. A. Goldhammer (Chicago, 1984), whose argument turns around the point that the appearance of the word *purgatorium* marks the beginning of its meaning as a definite place. This kind of interpretation is taken issue with in P. Biller's fascinating, and, to my mind, conclusive article, "Words and the Medieval Notion of *Religion*," *Journal of Ecclesiastical History* 36 (3) (July, 1985), 351-69; the lack of a special word is evidently more of a guide to the relatively unimportant status of Purgatory before the twelfth century than to its non-conception. Rothkrug (1980) starts from the opposite end of the scale by looking at rural shrines, pilgrimage and burial patterns to argue the importance of the shift in funerary beliefs in the two centuries before the Reformation (127-37).
[20] The previous mass use of indulgences had been as an inducement for the Crusades; see e.g. R. Seeberg, *Textbook of the History of Doctrines* (Grand Rapids, Michigan, 1964), 2:42-47; also T. N. Tentler, *Sin and Confession on the Eve of Reformation* (Princeton, 1977), 302-304, 328-30.
[21] Clement's bull is the first proclamation of the existence of the Church's *treasury of merit*; see discussion in S. Ozment, *The Age of Reform, 1250-1550* (New Haven, 1980); on the schism, 155-9; on the bulls of indulgence, 215-7, and biblio. The political motive of the Avignon papacy is I think a justifiable inference from available evidence. The church issued indulgences which pilgrims could earn by visiting specific shrines, and the schism in the church meant, among other things, rival claimants for the possession of its *treasury of merit*. On the extraordinary boom in inter-regional pilgrimage at this date, clearly linked to the relic-less growth of the cult of the Virgin and her shrines, see Rothkrug (1980), 15-36, with statistics on pre-Reformation shrines in his appendices; V. and E. Turner, *Image and Pilgrimage in Christian Culture: Anthropological Perspectives* (New York, 1978), 159ff.
[22] Cf. Ozment, 216.
[23] Thomas More, *Supplication of Souls*, in the 1557 ed. of his *English Works*; for background to this text, see e.g. A. G. Dickens, *The English Reformation* (New York, 1964), 5-6.
[24] Harbison, 110, summarises the evidence for Van Orley's religious beliefs.
[25] Letter from William Lok to Henry VIII, 20th July 1535, in Wegg, 191.

[26] See documents and discussion in R. Boumans, "The Religious Views of Abraham Ortelius," *Journal of the Warburg and Courtauld Institutes* 17 (1954), 374-77.
[27] Harbison, 111.
[28] H. A. Klein, *Graphic Worlds of Pieter Bruegel the Elder* (New York, 1963), 228.
[29] See L. Febvre (1942), *The Problem of Unbelief in the Sixteenth Century*, trans. B. Gottlieb (Cambridge, Mass., 1982), 126-127.
[30] I. Zupnick, "The Meaning of Bruegel's *Nobody* and *Everyman*," *Gazette des Beaux-Arts* LVII (May-June, 1966), 268.
[31] See documents in C. Gaignebet, "Le Combat de Carnaval et de Careme de P. Bruegel (1559)," *Annales: Societies, Economies, Civilisations* 2 (March-April, 1972), 318-320. In the context of the argument here, its use by Bruegel represents another piece of evidence for his traditional Christianity.
[32] Chapter 34 of the *Golden Legend*, augmented by another narrative ascribed to John the Evangelist. This and other texts are translated in M. R. James, *The Apocryphal New Testament* (London, 1924), 212ff; quoted in Z. Urbach, "Notes on Bruegel's Archaism. His Relation to Early Netherlandish Painting and Other Sources," *Acta Historiae Artium* (Academiae Scientiarum Hungaricae) XXIV (1978), 237-56.
[33] Urbach, 244-6.
[34] L. Rothkrug, *Holy Shrines, Religious Dissonance and Satan in the Origins of the German Reformation*, (1989), 25. My summary follows the argument presented in Rothkrug's book.
[35] In J. M. Headley, *Luther's View of Church History* (New Haven, 1963), 145; cf. M. Luther, "The Babylonian Captivity of the Church," (1520), trans. A. T. W. Steinhauser in *Three Treatises*, 167: *Hence it is a manifest and wicked error to offer or apply the mass... for the dead.*
[36] In K. McDonnell, *John Calvin: The Church and the Eucharist* (Princeton, 1967), 192. Cf. the passage from Calvin quoted in R. Wallace, *Calvin's Doctrine of the Christian Life* (Grand Rapids, 1959), 33, and in Rothkrug (1988), 205: *There is no limit to the extent to which sanctity may be diffused throughout all our works and concerns.*
[37] See E. F. Winter, ed. and trans., *Erasmus-Luther. Discourse on Free Will* (New York, 1961), 55, also S. Ozment, *The Age of Reform* (New Haven, 1980), 296.
[38] For Italian examples, see I. Lavin, "On the Sources and Meanings of the Renaissance Portrait Bust," *Art Quarterly* XXXIII (1970), 213-214.
[39] Erasmus, *De Libero arbitrio* (Basel, 1524), ed. cit. Winter, 81, 93.
[40] Urbach, 243.
[41] Ibid., 243-4.
[42] Monter, 25.
[43] K. Thomas, *Religion and the Decline of Magic* (New York, 1972); J. Toussaert, *Le sentiment religieux en Flandre a la fin du Moyen Age* (Paris, 1960).

[44] The poetess Anna Bijns and the theologian Martin Donk, in Freedberg, "The Hidden God: Image and Interdiction in the Netherlands in the Sixteenth Century," *Art History* 5 (June 1982), 135.
[45] M. Baxandall, *The Limewood Sculptors of Renaissance Germany* (New Haven, 1980), 70.
[46] S. Cramer and F. Piper, *Biblioteca Reformatoria Neerlandica* (The Hague, 1903-14), I, 261-71; trans. by K. Moxey, *Aertsen, Beuckelaer and Secular Painting in the Reformation* (New York-London, 1977), 145-6.
[47] Freedberg, (1982), 139.
[48] Rothkrug (1989), 86.
[49] Ozment, 251.
[50] Quoted in D. Freedberg, *Hidden God*, 139.
[51] Wegg, (1916), 22.
[52] Monter, 24-25.
[53] In Carl Theodor Gemeiner, *Die Regensbergische Chronik* (Regensberg, 1824), 4:393-94.
[54] Rothkrug, ibid., 59; 74-78; C. M. N. Eire, *Idolatry and the Reformation: A Study of the Protestant Attack on Catholic Worship in Germany, Switzerland, and France, 1500-1580*, Ph.D. diss., Yale University, 1979. Rothkrug considers iconoclasm to manifest itself among peoples who have weakened their links to their dead; Eire, on the other hand, correlates iconoclasm with the geographical distribution of the Great Peasant War.
[55] Antwerp iconoclasm is dealt with extensively in Moxey, 178-96; for selective bibliography is given in n. 3, 178-9.
[56] Moxey, (1977), 149-50; Wegg, (1916), 214; on the *landjuweel* of 1539 see L. M. van Dis, *Reformatorische Rederijkers-spelen* (Haarlem, 1937).
[57] Cf. R. Marijnissen and M. Seidel, *Bruegel* (New York, 1984), 19, n. 58-60; 59. In the course of his study *Iconoclasts and Their Motives* (Maarsen, 1985), 27, Freedberg observes that: *While there is plenty of evidence for the calculated orchestration of iconoclasm in the 16th century, we often find instances of what might loosely be termed primitive behavior... a delight in and a relishing of the sudden loosening of normal social and psychological restraints. Even though... iconoclasm is often planned, organised, and supervised, this loosening of... restraints is precisely what many of the commentators insist upon bringing to the fore... The evidence for the "abdication of self-control"... is abundant in the Southern Netherlands, but less so in the North."* This aspect of iconoclasm has been therefore well publicised; it is of interest here that the iconoclasts are said to behave *primitively*, as though released from "normal" social and psychological attitudes. The "norm" just prior to iconoclast outbreaks was, as we have seen, an inflated and gravely destabilised penitential system and, on the part of many people, a desire to make contact with miraculous images. Cf., ibid., 52, n. 93.

[58] It is clear that the Calvinists deliberately organised the outbreak. See P. M. Crew, *Calvinist Preaching and Iconoclasm in the Netherlands, 1544-1569* (Cambridge, 1978).
[59] J. J. Motley, *The Rise of the Dutch Republic* (London, 1904), vol. 1, 473-75; cf. the long unsympathetic account in J. Wegg, *The Decline of Antwerp under Philip of Spain* (London, 1924), ch. 2.
[60] The painting is briefly discussed in Harbison, 110, fig. 50, cat. 14.
[61] C. J. De Bruyn Kops, "*De Zeven Werken van Barmhartigheid* van de Meester van Alkmaar gerestaureerd," *Bulletin van Rijksmuseum* 23 (1975), part 4, 203-226, in Freedberg, *Iconoclasts*, 52, n. 97; cf. 29f; cf. figures 15-17.
[62] Rothkrug (1989), 58-9.
[63] We are told that people flocked to these services *by the thousands rather than the hundreds* and that these were chiefly *common people, folk who have not much to lose*. M. van Vaernewijk, in Marijnissen and Siedel, 27; the crowds frequently came armed — perhaps a sign of their readiness for action.
[64] Cf. E. Panofsky, "Erasmus and the Visual Arts," *Journal of the Warburg and Courtauld Institutes* XXXII (1969), 209-10; Erasmus and local writers like Anna Bijns, whose poetic diatribes against humanist nudes, etc., are well known, seem to have the most effect here since the Council of Trent's edicts were sternly resisted in the Netherlands (on the grounds not of aesthetics, but of local autonomy) until after Bruegel's death; cf. Moxey, 199-204, 215-228.
[65] Van Mander, 206.
[66] See Jean-Claude Schmitt, *Les revenants: les vivants et les morts dans la societé medievale* (Paris, 1994).
[67] The Church's explanation for the same phenomenon was that these were devils, not dead spirits. Cf e.g. Thomas of Cantimpre, *Bonum universale de apibus*, ii.57.8; first published as *Thomae Cantimpratani, S. Th. Doctoris, Ordinis S. Dominici, et Episcopi Suffraganei Cameracensis, Miraculorum, et exemplorum memorabilium sui temporis, libri duo* (Douai, 1597), 452; N. Caciola, "Wraiths, Revenants and Ritual in Medieval Culture," *Past and Present*, 152 (August, 1996): *The demonic-possession school of thought about revenants, as best represented by Thomas of Cantimpre and the hagiographer of Ida of Louvain, was distinctly a minority viewpoint*, 8.
[68] William of Newburgh, *Historia rerum Anglicarum*, v.22, in *Chronicles of the Reigns of Stephen, Henry II, and Richard I*, ed. Richard Howlett, 4 vols. (Rolls Series, London, 1884-9), 11, 475; in Caciola, nn. 56-7.
[69] Caciola, ibid.
[70] R. Muchembled, *Popular Culture and Elite Culture in France 1400-1750*, trans. L. Cochrane (Baton Rouge, 1985), 55; on All Souls Day, 54f; on the belief in a world peopled with dead souls (usually inimical), 62-5; on the "age group" conception of the dead, see N. Z. Davis, "Some Tasks and Themes in the Study of Popular

Religion," in C. Trinkaus and H. A. Oberman, ed., *The Pursuit of Holiness in Late Medieval and Renaissance Religion* (Leiden, 1974), 327-35.

[71] Rudolf von Schlettstadt, *Historiae memorabiles*, ch. 20, ed. Kleinschmidt, 72; in Caciola, 19, n. 128; she adds, *The verse is included in the text in Middle High German and is even set to musical notation. The use of a vernacular language in this context is a tantalizing clue to the story's oral foundation. Where did the Dominican collector of these tales hear the song in its original tongue and jot down the tune?... What is clear [is] that the verse derives from some local community where it was performed as a song of the dead. The references to the "short home" (kurtzhaim) and the "long home" (langkhaim) identify the singers with the dead, and also indicate how parallel the worlds of the living end the dead were thought to be: each has its proper realm or home, with distinct names and customs.*

[72] See documents in Caciola, nn. 130-33

[73] See e.g. Patrick J. Geary, *Living with the Dead in the Middle Ages* (Ithaca, 1994), 36.

[74] Briefly discussed in H. Buscheit, "Beitrage zum Armenseelenkultus," *Bayerischer Heimatschutz. Zeitschrift d. b. Landesvereins f. heimatschutz* 29 (1934), 70-1; figs. 43 and 44 respectively.

[75] H. P. Duerr, *Dreamtime: Concerning the Boundary between Wilderness and Civilisation*, trans. F. Gooodman (Oxford, 1985), 239-40, n. 45, quoting a seventeenth century German author on the antiquity of the wild hunt. See also C. Ginzburg, *The Night Battles* (Harmondsworth, 1985), 33-68, esp. 47-9; A. Van Gennep, *Le Folklore de la Flandre et du Hainaut Francais (Departement du Nord)*, (Paris, 1935), v. 2, 679-81.

[76] See Introduction, A. van Gennep (1909), *The Rites of Passage*, trans. M. Vizedom and G. Caffee (Chicago, 1960).

[77] Louis-Vincent Thomas, *Le cadavre: de la biologie à l'anthropologie*, Brussels: Complexe, 1980

[78] M. Camille, *Master of Death* (New Haven-London, 1996), 176. In part, this practice followed the lead of royalty who wanted their bodies to be dismembered so that the parts could be enshrined in a variety of religious foundations, like saints' relics. This in turn follows early medieval precedents; during the conversion of Europe, huge numbers of dead royals were conveniently discovered to be saints.

[79] See K. Park, "The Sensitive Corpse: Body and Self in Renaissance Medicine," *Fenway Court, 1990-91* (Boston, 1992), 77-87; and also her "The Life of the Corpse: Dissection and Division in Late Medieval Europe," *Journal of the History of Medicine and Allied Sciences* 50 (1995), 111-32. Cf. Camille, 171-2.

[80] Neckham, *De proprietibus rerum*

[81] H. Platelle, "La voix du sang: le cadavre qui saigne en présence de son meurtrier," in *La piété populaire au Moyen Âge, Actes du 99e congrès national des Sociétés Savantes*, Besançon, 1974; *Philologie et Histoire*, I (Paris 1977), 161-179.

[82] On the open-mouthed corpse, see Van Gennep, v. 1, 130-166; on the house-opening custom, see Edward Tylor (1871), *Religion in Primitive Culture* (New York, 1958), 36.
[83] Quoted in Van Gennep, v. 2, 676.
[84] That of the French doctor Guillaume de Harcigny is the earliest *transi* cited by K. Cohen, *Metamorphosis of a Death Symbol. The Transi Tomb in the Late Middle Ages and the Renaissance* (Berkeley, CA., 1973), 103, n. 20, figs. 1 and 2; her account of the origins of immobile *transi* on elite tombs, 12-47.
[85] Cohen, 14-15; the drawing of this tomb and its inscription are from Roger de la Gaignières' notebooks, ms 17025, f 34-35, Bib. nat., Paris.
[86] Ibid, 89-90; 90, n. 19.
[87] See eg. the transi tombs of Johannes Gemeiner (d. 1482), Sankt-Jakobs-Kirche, Straubing; Peter Niderwirt (d. 1522), Pfarrkirche, Eggenfelden, illustrated in Cohen.
[88] This is in the end Cohen's view — that the tomb *transi* was ultimately a symbol of life and resurrection. I agree that this is how it would have been viewed by the clergy and patrons. However, the sheer strength of interest in death and the fate of the dead suggests that the "over-development" of this part of the total compound sign of the tomb is itself a mark of purgatorial inflation and of thanatological crisis.
[89] St. Ambrose, *Funeral Orations*, "On his brother Satyrus: II," 128-33.
[90] St. Ambrose, 134-137. The quotation is a close paraphrase of a passage in Cicero's *De senectute* 23.85.
[91] On these debates see Walker Bynum, "Material Continuity, Personal Survival, and the Resurrection of the Body: A Scholastic Discussion in Its Medieval and Modern Contexts," in her *Fragmentation and Redemption: Essays on Gender and the Human Body in Medieval Religion* (Cambridge, Mass: Zone Books, 1991), 253-65.
[92] Bloch and Parry, 15-18.
[93] I take up this argument again in a study in preparation. The theory of occult representation as a kind of boomerang is derived from A. Gell,"Understanding the Occult," *Radical Philosophy*, Vol. 9 (Winter 1974), 17-26. The occult sign, Gell argued, operates by *disguising the invisible* (actually non-existent) workings of what are perceived to be aspects of literation hidden inside absence. Occult representation brings these *into the realm of the patent*.
[94] C. De Tolnay, *Pierre Bruegel l'Ancien* (Brussels, 1935), v. 1
[95] See W. S. Gibson, "Artists and *Rederijkers* in the Age of Bruegel," *Art Bulletin* LXIII (3) (September, 1981), 426-46, devoted to the subject, with particular reference to Bruegel; on the cycle, 433-437; on floats based on Bosch and Bruegel, 439.

[96] G. Vasari, *Lives of the Painters*, trans. Mrs. Jonathan Foster (London, 1898), v. 2, 417-8; cf. Gibson, *Bruegel* (London, 1977), 133, on the transmission of Vasari in the Netherlands.

[97] Le Roy Ladurie, 208.

[98] Ibid., 180.

[99] Ibid., 208, 390, n. 8.

[100] The pictures from the 1538 edition can be found at www.gutenberg.org /etext/21790

[101] N. Z. Davis, "Holbein's *Pictures of Death* and the Reformation at Lyons," *Studies in the Renaissance* 3 (1956): *within only a few years... these pictures were placed, and thought to fit with equal ease, in a framework of Catholic writings and interpretations and in one of Protestant writing and interpretation*, 97-130.

[102] Giraldus Cambrensis, *Itinerarium Kambriae*, ed. J. F. Dimock, *Giraldi Cambrensis Opera*, I. 2, (Rolls Series, London, 1868) 32-3; in Caciola, n.134.

[103] E. Male (1908), *Religious Art in France: the Late Middle Ages, a Study of Medieval Iconography and its Sources*, ed. H. Bober, trans. M. Mathews (Princeton, 1986), 329-30.

[104] For the vast literature on the *danse macabre*, James Clark, *The Dance of Death in the Middle Ages and in the Renaissance* (Glasgow, 1950), and two articles by J. H. M. Taylor, "Danse Macabré and Bande Dessinée: a Question of Reading," *Forum for Modern Language Studies*, XXV (1989), 356-69; and "Un miroir salutaire," in her edited vol., *Dies Illa: Death in the Middle Ages* (Liverpool, 1984), 29-43.

[105] Davis, 99.

[106] Camille, 159.

[107] Caciola, 23.

[108] See Jean Batany, "Un image en negatif du fonctionnalisme social: les danses macabre," in Taylor (1984), 15-28. Camille suggested the reason for their popularity had to do with a *traditional association between the body's liberated movement in dance and its degradation in death*, 159.

[109] Davis, 97-8.

[110] Ibid., 101; e.g., Manuel's painted *Dance of Death* at the Dominican monastery in Berne opens with the Fall, Moses Receiving the Commandments, and the Crucifixion.

[111] Ibid., 128.

[112] Rothkrug (1988), 202.

[113] Ibid, 204; these performances were titled, *Vom Papst und seiner Priesterschaft* (On the Pope and his Priests) and *Von Papsts und Christi Gegensatz* (On the Distinction between the Pope and Christ). On Manuel see C. Menz and H. Wagner, eds., *Niklaus Manuel Deutsch: Maler, Dichter, Staatsmann*, (Bern, 1979).

[114] Camille, 138.

[115] For the tradition of the *Three Living and the Three Dead*, its background, poems, etc., along with related *macabre* themes, see S. Chew, *The Pilgrimage of Life* (New Haven, 1962), ch. 8, 226-232. On the Master of the House Book 's print, see J. Filedt Kok, ed., *"Livelier than life:" The Master of the Amsterdam Cabinet or the Housebook Master* (Amsterdam, 1985) 152-6.

[116] Jean Wirth, *La Jeune Fille et la Mort. Recherche sur les themes macabres dans l'art germanique de la Renaissance* (Geneva, 1979); cf. Chew, 240f., 385, n. 14.

[117] Quoted in Muchembled, 133, n. 48; cf. Van Gennep, v. 1, 126f., who also gives the phrase *boire cervelle du mort*. Charles had attempted to place restrictions on funeral as well as marriage feasts from 1539 on, with as little success.

[118] Cf. P. Bianconi, *The Complete Paintings of Bruegel* (New York, 1967), 95.

[119] Pilgrimage badges could vary from a cheap printed *drapelet* to a copper medal; inexpensive lead figures could be pinned to hat or clothing; Muchembled, 102; E. H. van Heurck and G. J. Boekenoogen, *L'Imagerie Populaire des Pays-Bas Belgique-Hollande* (Paris, 1930), 9-14.

[120] Aries, 162; cf. Van Gennep, v. 1, 107-12, on crosses of straw and straw used to carpet the way to the graveyard.

[121] Marijnissen and Seidel, 50; the authors summarise views on the dating of the inscription and suggestions as to its "moralistic" meaning.

[122] See C. Rivals, "L'Image de moulin dans deux tableaux de Pieter Gruegel," *Image et Histoire: Actes du Colloques Paris-Censier* (May 1986), 128-36. Cf. R. W. Scribner, *For the Sake of Simple Folk: Popular Propaganda for the German Reformation* (Cambridge, 1981), who illustrates T. Stimmer's print *The Weird and Grotesque Mill*, Dahlem 1577, fig. 78, 107, a parody of this tradition.

[123] K. P. F. Moxey, "The Fates and Pieter Bruegel's *Triumph of Death*," *Oud-Holland* LXXXVII (1973), 49-51.

[124] Ladurie, 178-9.

[125] Ibid., 178.

[126] Scribner, 73-4, fig. 50.

[127] On *Desidia* and its proverbs, see A. Barnouw, *The Fantasy of Pieter Brueghel* (New York, 1947), 12; on clock-stopping, Van Gennep, v. 1, 105.

[128] S. Y. Edgerton, *Pictures and Punishment: Art and Criminal Prosecution in the Florentine Renaissance* (Ithaca, 1985), 135-6, n. 15.

[129] Aries, 44-5.

[130] Ibid., 42-3.

[131] Quoted in Aries, 43; 619, n. 38.

[132] Ibid., 45.

[133] Duerr, 61; 269, n. 5-10; cf. also the possible derivation of *berserker* from *bear-shirt*, ibid., 62.

[134] S. L. Sumberg, *The Nuremberg Schembart Carnival* (New York, 1941), on *most extensive use*, 143; on *Höllen* in general, 133-6; on the Valenciennes drawing (Bibliothèque National Fonds Francais MS 12536), 143, n. 67.
[135] Ibid., 139.
[136] Wegg, (1916), 165, on the exploding Eden scene.
[137] For both series, see cat. 42-54, 55, 64-77 in N. Orenstein, ed., *Pieter Bruegel the Elder: Drawings and Prints*, Museum Boijmans Van Beuningen, Rotterdam; Metropolitan Museum of Art (New York, 2001). Orenstein et. al group *Patientia* with the Vices, rather than the Virtues.
[138] Ibid, 162.
[139] K. G. Boon, "*Patientia* dans les gravures de la Reforme aux Pays-Bas," *Revue de l'Art* 56 (1982), 23, n. 105, notes a second state not listed by L. Lebeer, *Catalogue raisonné des estampes de Pierre Bruegel l'ancien*. Bibliothèque Royale Albert Ier, Brussels, 1969.
[140] The Inquisition was established by Imperial placard in 1550; at Antwerp, despite the city governors' reluctance to enforce the severest penalties, the numbers of executions for heresy rose steadily until by 1556 about two people were being publicly burnt every month. The chroniclers' accounts of these events are summarised in Wegg, (1916), 193-6, 205-7, 315-20
[141] Boon, 20, 24, n. 117; cf. J. Muller-Hofstede, "Zur Interpretation von Pieter Bruegels Landschaft. Aesthetischer Landschaftsbegriff und stoische Weltbetrachtung," in O. von Simson and M. Winner, ed., *Pieter Bruegel und seine Welt* (Berlin, 1979), 127-43, on the evidence for Ortelius's familiarity with Cicero and Seneca between 1550 and 1560.
[142] Boon, 7-18. Hoefnagel produced a manuscript of emblems on the theme of Patience while in exile in London in 1569; published and trans. by R. van Roosebroeck as, *Patientia, 24 politieke emblemata door Joris Hoefnagel* (Antwerp, 1935).
[143] Lactantius — like Origen — was among the pre-Augustine Fathers whose writings underwent revival in the sixteenth century. For Ficino, Pico, and later Neo-Platonists, Lactantius was a key verification source for the antiquity of the *prisca theologia* and a Christian apologist for Hermes Trismegistus; for radical reformers (e.g., Anabaptists), he was a representative of the purer religion of the early Church. See F. Yates, *Giordano Bruno and the Hermetic Tradition* (Chicago, 1964), 6-9, 14-16 and passim; H. Oliphaunt, *The Patristic Roots of Reformed Worship* (Zurich, 1975).
[144] J. Calvin, *Institutiones divinae* 4, 26, 27; 5, 22, 3; quoted in Boon, 20.
[145] Boon, 24, n. 115.
[146] Cf. Duerr, 63; 273, n. 24.
[147] W. D. Reynolds, *The "Ovidius Moralizatus" of Pierre Bersuire; An Introduction andTranslation*, Ph.D. diss., University of Illinois at Urbana-Champaign, 185.

Bersuire's commentary was written c. 1340-1342, published at Bruges in 1484, at Paris in 1493, and constantly reprinted in the sixteenth century.

[148] The Boon, 24, n. 115. The mural is in the Hasenhaus in Vienna; see fig.12 in ch. 16, "Caccia al Cacciatore," of G. Cocchiara's *Il mondo alla rovescia* (Turin, 1963).

[149] Ibid, 203-8; Cf. fig. 11.

[150] Lower marginal miniature under a death bed scene; the Grimani Breviary, Biblioteca Marciana, Venice, fol. 449v. Another Flemish illustration in the Book of Hours of Mary of Burgundy commemorates the manner of her death in a hunting accident in 1482 by showing her party themselves hunted by three skeletons; British Museum MS. Add. 35313, fol. 158v.; reproduced in T. S. R. Boase, *Death in the Middle Ages. Mortality, Judgement and Remembrance* (New York, 1972), 91, fig. 105. Cf. Chew, 230f.

[151] This detail occurs also in pictures of the *Three Living and Three Dead*, e.g., in the version by the Master of the House Book.

[152] See Chew, 232, on the oxen of Death. Oxen draw Death's cart in early fifteenth century Italian paintings (e.g. works by Matteo de Pasti in the Uffizi and by Lorenzo Costa at Bologna). Around 1460, Death appears mounted on a bullock as a new illustration for the prayers for the Dead in some Books of Hours. The source for the association of bulls and death is probably, as Chew suggests, *Isaiah* 34: 7. Cf. Comte de Laborde, *La Mort Chevauchant un Boeuf. Origine de cette illustration de l'Office des Morts dans certains Livres d'Heures de la fin du XVe siècle* (Paris, 1923).

[153] Chew, 232.

[154] I refer to a standard narrative of the evolution of individualism, usually presented as an active cultural achievement. For a nuanced version of this, see essays in R. Chartier ed. *A History of Private Life: III. Passions of the Renaissance* (Cambridge, Mass, 1989).

Questions and Conclusions

As a small child, I once watched one of these country fairs. I heard noise and lively shouting behind the garden fence. Looking through a crack... I saw campfires burning, with gypsies and other strange people clustered around them. The gypsies were gesticulating wildly, and everyone was loudly shouting at the same time... This scene created an impression of indescribable confusion, and I thought to myself that the goings-on in hell must be pretty much like this.

Memoir of the Wolf-man (1902)[1]

Dreams

Bruegel's artworks reveal much about how the discourses of Carnivals and dreams were inter-connected in his time, though his art is far from simply mirroring of the situation of the discourse. Both dreams and carnivals were complex networks of competing representations; when their non-cognitive aspects clashed in arenas of cognitive representation — in art, writing and law — the job of the cognitive representation was to resolve the discrepancy or make it disappear. Out of the decomposing matrix of the previous order, a new order was composed, or imposed.

This is clearly what was happening in the arenas of learned dream-theory and fine art. The proximate visual source on dream representation for Bruegel was the imagery of Bosch, which evoked the atmosphere of occult time and space principally by exploiting the possibilities of the hybrid or metamorphic body. Possibly the most startling aspects of this imagery from our point of view are its enormous popularity and instant mass recognisability as dream-like. Some of the reasons for this were discussed in Chapter One. Literally condensed in the hybrid body was a complex and weighty ancient and medieval tradition. Much more remains to be said about the ramifications of this tradition; here I have touched only on the most important areas of Renaissance thought through which such imagery was linked to dream fantasy: the changeable hybrid at the heart of the revival of Neo-Platonic and Hermetic thinking.

By the late fifteenth century, ruling philosophical habits of thought caused the *genus* of novel metamorphic imagery to be seen as expressing psychological concerns. For Italian and Northern Humanists, the hybrid was a "frozen" metamorphosis which could represent all kinds of things to do with the worlds inside the head and outside history, from the chameleon inner nature of man, to the otherworldly destinations of sleep. Possibly the most important and far-reaching legacy of the Neo-Platonists was to apply to their beloved hybrid imagery the exegetical tools devised to "reveal" Christian meanings "hidden" inside the enigmas of Ovidian metamorphosis. Hybrids were *infolded* visual riddles, never to be completely *unfolded*. This interpretative methodology of *unfolding* such an image resulted in infinitely expandable sequences of linked images. This goes some way to explaining one of the most striking features of the Boschian hybrid: its proliferation and "world-filling" qualities. It also forms an important chapter in the "pre-history" of the Freudian unconscious; these apparently endless chains of association inherent in the new imagery are structurally reminiscent both of Freud's central idea of the disparity in size and complexity between *dream-content* and *dream-thoughts*, and of Matte Blanco's effort to explain this relationship in his theory of the *unconscious as infinite sets*.[2] One area for further study here is the significance of this imagery in the decorative arts, where it underwent a rapid dissemination and development, between the sixteenth-and the later eighteenth-centuries, as grotesque decoration used to cover every imaginable surface.

Such then, was the state of the art on the causes and appearance of dreams at the start of Bruegel's century. The matrix of elite views on dreams may have been inconsistent and unsystematic, but it philosophically underwrote a few clear "stage-directions" which were of particular use and interest for artists. From Macrobius, best known and most copied of the

Neo-Platonic sources, came the descriptions of *kaleidoscopically changing things, distorted* and *out of all natural proportions in size*. These became the conventional markers for dream-representation in the modern era.

As conventions, they appear at the same time in folk accounts of dreams and in fine art, and this cannot be because the folk had read Macrobius (though we should not underestimate folk awareness of the literate canon), or because they had seen the art of Bosch (though eventually this visual culture entered peasant culture through the fantastical propaganda prints of the Reformation). Rather, they were alike because wider forces were at work, reshaping elite and folk representations at the same time. The reasons for this again demand further study.

One issue is the difficult question of "survivals" in folk culture. Macrobius, Pliny, Isidore of Seville et al. were, of course, themselves repositories of late ancient folklore, and it may make sense to see the profoundly conservative mechanisms of folk-culture as themselves primary sources for literate "discoveries" of magic, metamorphosis etc., over the long Middle Ages. However this may be, the Macrobian-Boschian key-notes of *kaleidoscopically changing things* and *things out of all proportion* certainly appear in the few sources of evidence we have for folk dream-discourse, as they do in tales and lore of the otherworld. Witch-trial transcripts and the *benandanti* testimonies, for example, refer to the motif of humans riding on animals that would normally be much too small to be used as steeds, such as hares or cats. Bosch also dealt with dream matter which was folkloric in the *benandanti* sense of the word, as in his wonderful *complicatio et explicatio* of the motif of the Fountain of Life, in the *Garden of Earthly Delights*. More study is needed on the whole subject of folk dreaming, its regional variation and evolution in this period.

Bruegel's use of the Boschian *language of bodies* amounted to a far greater engagement with the roots of this imagery than was the case, say, in Raimundi or Campagnola's emblematic quotations from Bosch. Closer in age to Shakespeare than to Bosch, Bruegel seems from the start to have been fascinated by the ways in which hybridity could be used to explore and dissect the social world. In the *Vices* series, Bruegel was already making connections between metamorphic dream imagery and the *found surrealism* of actual folk practices and folk motifs. It is Bruegel who shows us, albeit from the firm platform of literate Humanism, not so much how the folk dream, but the dream-like nature of folk-thought.

Carnivals

Carnivalesque imagery is collective folk fantasy from the culture theatre of festival practice and performance. The carnivalesque is a famous ancestor of surreal imagery. It becomes involved with dream imagery at a specific historical time, and its involvement is imbued with the politics of that situation. Carnival itself could plainly act as political institution, which is to say it could voice concerns, and deal with social conflict and resolution. Thus Carnival immediately became political in the cities of the first commercial revolution. The forms of old Carnival plays were transformed into theatre by guildsmen and *rederijkers*, themselves excluded from formal political participation, yet whose activities constituted the backbone of urban and provincial prosperity.

On a theoretical level, the political nature of Carnival has proved harder to pin down. Late medieval people defended it as a safety valve: the world was turned upside down to ensure that the world would turn the right way up again, with dissent vented, sated and silenced. Trade unionists in Brazil in the 1970s took the same view: Carnival turns the workers from their problems, diverting energies that might otherwise be directed to more lasting effect.[3] When early modern Carnival was used as a vehicle for popular protest — as, for example, in the case of Romans — it is difficult to estimate its success; the more political it got, the more likely it was to be crushed without mercy. In fact, it was the category of the carnivalesque, rather than Carnival itself, which emerged from the Reformation charged with several new kinds of political meaning.

The "transgressive" aspect of popular expression evidently could act as a set of brakes or limits on the build-up of power, by adjusting and reframing sense as nonsense. From the point of view of civic authority, carnivalesque nonsense — flying pigs, men wearing dresses, women dressed backwards, people banging frying pans or waving rattles, displaying vaginas, mooning, pissing, etc — punctures the illusion of rational activity, and so challenges the status quo and the plausibility of cause-and-effect based mentalities. On the eve of the French Revolution, masked revellers at the Paris Mardi Gras of 1789, for example, were called *chienlits* (shit-a-beds). Such resistance has inbuilt ambivalence; at any moment, there may be widely differing views as to what should be "resisted" and why. Thus, the carnivalesque became generally understood as a *style* of expressing cultural repression, used by the culturally repressed; a group which had expanded by the later modern era to include pretty much everyone.

At the end of the fifteenth century, Carnival itself was still a seasonal festival marking the end of festive winter, with feasting, masquerade, and symbolic contests, for instance, between Old Man Winter and Lady Summer or Spring. Even this was not as clear cut as it might appear. Recall the masquerade at Norwich, with King Christmas and the Lenten rider in a parade of the months, where the participants wound up in prison. Recall that Bruegel's *Carnival and Lent* itself is a kind of allegory, *not* a record of something Bruegel could have seen, since Carnival in the Netherlandish towns had been replaced by the City and Guilds with new kinds of processional celebrations. Bruegel has the personae of Carnival and Lent enact a nostalgic view of a whole repeating social world, but this was a world that was ending.

Against the separatist grain of most elite thinking at this time, it took all Bruegel's technical command of an ideal viewpoint to interweave Christian and profane activities in his painting, balancing rather than uniting the pub and the church in a dancing composition with intricate circles of revellers and worshippers. Like his kermis prints, this visualisation could be interpreted as radically nostalgic or progressively proto-nationalist. But the one clear point about these designs is the separation, through panoramic viewpoint and other compositional framing devices, of the spectator from the event. Excess of any kind, so central to the celebration of carnival, was unobtrusively edited out. At the same time, Bruegel gave this same excess free rein in his representations of madness, magic and chaos.

Bruegel's carnivalesque fantasy and his "ethnographic" works look completely different, but both are equally fictional. Chapter Four discussed the double structure of Carnival: its central "narratives" which the participants themselves point to as the *raison d'être* of the practice, and the exercise of license. In progressive interrogations of the *benandanti*, the accused rehearse over and over again the narrative which offered the "rationale" of their activities: that this was a seasonal struggle *against the witches* for the good of the harvest. But they also tell their inquisitors about swoops on local cellars and pissing in wine-casks, of "marriages" and revelry coming to and fro from their "battles" in the air.

License itself is a kind of anti-narrative. In any narrative account of Carnival, it can only be minimally represented (as something externally observed of others) or not represented at all. In Bruegel's surreal fantasy, license overwhelms narrative; "excess" is handled through potentially infinite chains of infolded and exfolded imagery, becoming the main visual point. This is true for the *Fall of the Magician*, the *Vices* and the *Griet*; also for works such as the *Battle of the Moneybanks and the Strongboxes*. The issue of revelry is where the real incommensurability between narrative and anti-narrative started to become visible. Bruegel's art goes far in the direction of moving the carnivalesque into a zone of dream-work-like excess, where it immediately begins to signify the overwhelming of sense, and so, by extrapolation, unconscious vice and nightmare.

Possibly because license was central to the participants' experience of

Carnival, concepts of license were the central focus for efforts to reform the festival. The aesthetic adoption by Bruegel and others of carnivalesque representation, and the cultural reformers' desire to control such representations, both reflect and express actual changes in the way Carnival and its representations were grounded in the real world. A modern attitude of surveillance and limited tolerance of carnivalesque enactment accelerated censorship of popular nonsense media around 1600. Religious turmoil gave city governments a pressing motive for the control and suppression of crowds. Fairs, theatres, outdoor preaching, Feasts of Fools and midsummer performances were banned or expelled from the city limits, in a Europe-wide effort, climaxing under the Puritan regimes of the seventeenth century.

The performative genres of nonsense were prime casualties of the cultural revolution instigated by the long Reformation, though, of course, much of this repertoire survived in print. The embedded folk image of Gargantua, for example, appears in French revolutionary prints, and in Honoré Daumier's lampoons of Louis-Phillipe as a pear. A new urban apparatus of prisons, asylums and work-houses, symbiotic with a "diagnostics" of criminology, psychiatry and utilitarianism, eradicated many of the private frames and public platforms from whence people had deployed the imagery and techniques of popular culture. This sustained effort at doing away with the "uncontrolled" was of course not wholly successful, yet it set in train a complex sequence of repercussions, instituting what Foucault called a *political technology of the body*, operating at *micro-physical* levels of power.[4] The internalised effects of the Triumph of Lent amounted to a demographic extension of aspects of self-regulation and *mentalité* which came to define civil elites.[5]

Nightmares

Why should all this go hand in hand with the transformation of the carnivalesque, not simply into the sphere of dreams, but into bad dreams? More research is needed fully to address this issue. However, three main cultural elements can be identified as shaping this transformation: melancholia, sexuality and the occult, definitions of which were themselves in flux during Briegel's lifetime.

Renaissance dream theory, mainly the domain of medicine and theology, changed as the imagination was revalued. This refocused attention on the causes of dreams, from the divine to the astrological, to the melancholic, and affected particularly the category of the *somnium naturale* – the only dream-type linked to the personal anxieties and desires of the dreamer. This was the category to which the nightmare belonged. When the personal dream took centre stage, its default form was the nightmare. The uncanny aspects of the *phantasma* became linked to the "disordered" visions of the melancholic, seen as creative by Ficino and other readers of Synesius, but as mad or disturbing by everyone else.

The second issue of sexuality is highly complex and again requires further study. A few starting points can be proposed here. The position of sexuality itself was changing. Recall that the "love philosophy" of the Neo-Platonists had gone some way to recuperating carnal love as a potential vehicle for sacred love. Shortly after, at the start of the sixteenth-century, Luther had done away with the celibacy requirement for priests, making it possible for the Protestant clergy to marry. Efforts were being made, then, in widely different quarters, to revalue sexuality, and to make it a subject for cultural debate. However, a millennium of Christian teaching on this subject was not to be overturned so easily. The whole bent of sixteenth-century official culture was patriarchal if not actively misogynist.

In psychoanalytic terms, sexuality is the central aspect of desire – the motive force of the unconscious mind – and the main way the Renaissance understood desire was as vice. When we sleep, *all our thoughts are nothing but texts to condemn us*, wrote Thomas Nashe, likening *the rest we take in our beds* to that of *the weerie traveller... in the coole soft grass in summer...*

thinking there to lye at ease... layeth his fainting head unawares on a loathsome nest of snakes. Bruegel's "Boschian" *Vice* designs illustrate this psychology, representing the "underbelly" of human desire as a mass of metamorphic hybrid personifications, witless and nonsensical.

Another perspective on desire is given by the case-history of women's carnivals, outlined in Chapter Two. While the repertoire of male carnivalesque fantasy expressed itself in terms of sports, fights, contests and flags, women's carnivals turned around midwifery, fertility, and household magic. The world-turned-upside-down was a crucial element in their ribaldry. As in Carnival generally, the core imagery of these festivals involved the portals of the body, especially the all-important extra oriface men lack. Women's carnivals seem to have been singled out early on for suppression by the (overwhelmingly masculine) forces of Lent. At the same time, visual representations demonstrate how rapidly and dramatically female carnivalesque motifs and practices were demonised over a very short period of time.

Part of the reason must be that the repression of women's carnivals itself created fear of women. Recall Cardan's terse comment in 1559, that women had been *forbidden by law* to behave in a *wild and senseless manner in public*, as they had done at *the old orgies* (i.e. women's carnivals). After this, they *gathered in secret*. When this also was forbidden, *they assembled only in thought.*[6] Once banned, the female carnivalesque — the world turned upside down by women — quickly came to be regarded as more dangerous, more transgressive, and also more senseless, than the male version. This was the beginning of the new male nightmare of the Sabbat, which retained many carnivalesque components.

It becomes clearer then why sixteenth-century society should come to think about bad dreams in terms of melancholia, witchcraft and gynophobia. Women held the role of the *Other*, the *not-man*, whose dominance in the home depended on psychological factors; will-power, one might say, rather than physical or legal power. Home was the arena where men might find themselves at the mercy of women, first in childhood, under the rule of the nursery, then in married life, in the kitchen and the bedroom.

By mid-century, older views about the instability of the female mind, and newer views of melancholia as the cause of "disordered" visions, shaped fears about the kinds of power women might wield under cover of the night. These fears were "really" negatively polarised desire. The desire of women became an object of fear; not simply fear of female sexual desire, though this was certainly an element, but fear of the consequences of driving female desire underground and out of sight. The more one group of humans oppresses another, the more that group comes to fear the people they have oppressed.

Bruegel made a quite extraordinary analysis of this shift in the form of his *Dulle Griet*. This picture uses women's carnival imagery to represent women's dreams in a complex and de-centred way. In the *Dulle Griet*, Bruegel played with — and to some extent deliberately made fun of — a tangle of shifting folk-ideas concerning the dreams of women, and male nightmares about these dreams. He realised this range of material had surreal potential; it could be treated in Boschian terms. He extrapolated from the folk imagery, subjecting its motifs to the operations of *explicatio* and *complicatio*. The central proverb of *tying a devil to a pillow* is thus perceived as a visual riddle, containing the idea of a occult victory during sleep. He set all this on the stage of a melancholic dream-scape. The female folk world was envisaged in terms of (male) nightmares, merging into castratory fantasy in the wings; evil desires projected as emanating from women.

Finally there is the issue of the occult. As discussed in Chapter Five, the Reformation marked a great rearrangement of the occult categories which had previously supported — among much else — the categories of dreams and nightmares. Once doubt was openly cast on the efficacy and authority of the rituals which provided access to the dead, a widespread destabilisation of the occult ensued. The Reformation itself can be seen in one sense as the primary cognitive response to a destabilisation of the occult which had been escalating for several centuries. Sixteenth-century Europeans did not lose their belief in spirits or the spirit-world; the problem was that they lost the cultural apparatus for controlling either. At the same time, cultural reformers in both camps recategorised as demonic everything occult that could not be brought within Christian rule. Recall Delumeau's statement, *After a millennium of assimilating animism came a total rejection of it, and the religion of a few was to be imposed on millions.*[7] In the Protestant regions, there were no longer any "good spirits," because ties to the saints had been cut, nor could the spirits of the dead be propitiated by prayer or ritual. At the same time previously positive or at least neutral aspects of the folk supernatural — belief in elves, kelpies, water-spirits etc — were now considered demonic. The result was a massive expansion of the negative supernatural sphere, and an expansion of the territory of bad dreams.[8]

This destabilisation connects the uncanny power of Bruegel's art with the shifting territory of the folkloric. Folkloric complexes redefined more or less exclusively in nocturnal terms were well on the way to being understood mainly as internal and psychological. The fact that the arena of Hermogenes and Griet is not day but night shapes the conceptualisation of their imagery.

Folk Culture and Surrealism

Bruegel's capacity to perceive folk culture as in some sense *surreal* brings us finally to the broader issues of representing folkloric beliefs in the second half of the sixteenth-century. At a general level, Bruegel's art worked to "fix" certain combinations of shapes from folkloric culture into forms which suited contemporary sensibilities. His works shows matters to do with dreams, carnival and witches; subjects caught in the act of decomposing and hardening into new shapes, under the pressure of literate scrutiny and religious reform. These shapes, up to that point, were not fixed in any single form. People expressed *variations* on sets of folk schema, moving the stress from one element to another. The significance of those aspects of peasant culture which most interested Bruegel was actually distorted by the very act of representing them – and so fixing them – shorn of their variability – in the discourse of fine art.

In semiotic and psychoanalytic terms, the sense of tantalising mystery in Bruegel's surreal imagery stems from condensations and displacements, made possible by the techniques of Renaissance illusionism. The novel images thus produced in fact constitute collisions between elements from recognisably distinct classificatory groups. Our minds seek a third term to mediate the impossibility. Failing to find this term, we assume that it is hidden. This generates an atmosphere of mystery and blocked, deflected desire, and the result is an experience of the occult or the uncanny. Bruegel's surrealism makes this psychoanalytic mechanism manifest. It renders its subject-matter as both comic and uncanny.

The gap between the "raw" folk materials and their deployment in this imagery contributes to this surreality in a subtle yet fundamental way. Separate sets of ideas from oral culture are forcibly brought together in the arena of two-dimensional illusionist art, in such a way as to bring out what seems to be their latent psychological meaning. This incommensurability of narrative context and aesthetic experience produces a pervading sense of absurdity – of having the "wrong" things put together – and a sense that there remains, somehow, "more to be said." This is the case as much in his apparently ethnographic works – such as the *Netherlandish Proverbs* or *Carnival and Lent* – as it is in the more clearly fantastical pictures such as in the *Dulle Griet*.

The poet Giorgos Seferis defined *style* as, *the difficulty which a person encounters in trying to express something*.[9] The success of Bruegel's art is essentially a success of its style: a series of solutions which wonderfully express the difficulties of expression inherent in the subjects of carnivals and dreams.

Notes to Questions and Conclusions

[1] From M. Gardiner, ed., *The Wolf-man and Sigmund Freud* (London, 1972; 1989), 5.
[2.] Ignacio Matte Blanco, *The Unconscious as Infinite Sets: an Essay in Bi-logic* (London, 1975).
[3] V. Turner, "*Carnaval* in Rio: Dionysian drama in an industrializing society," in his *The Anthropology of Performance* (New York: PAJ Publications), 124.
[4] M. Foucault, *Discipline and Punish: The Birth of the Prison*, trans. A. Sheridan (London, 1977), 26, 213-4; cf also "Prison talk: an interview with Michel Foucault," *Radical Philosophy* 16 (Spring, 1977), 10.
[5] See on this process, N. Elias, "The History of Manners" (1939), in his *The Civilising Process. Sociogenetic and Psychogenetic Investigations*, rev. ed., trans. Edmund Jephcott (1978); eds. E. Dunning et al. (Oxford, 1994).
[6] H. Cardan, *Offenbarung der Natur* (Basel, 1559), DCXLV; Duerr, 226, n. 6.
[7] I quoted this formulation in the Introduction; it is from Jean Delumeau's inaugural lecture at the Collège de France in 1975, in Monter, 90.
[8] For a definition of occult categories see A. Gell, "Understanding the Occult," *Radical Philosophy* 9 (Winter, 1974), 17-26. For an outline of an anthropological approach to occult Christian categories, see e.g., J. Le Goff, *The Medieval Imagination*, trans. A. Goldhammer (Chicago, 1988).
[9] Quoted in C. Stewart, *Demons and the Devil. Moral Imagination in Modern Greek Culture* (Princeton, NJ., 1991), 122.

Bibliography

Aarne, A. and Thompson, S., *The Types of the Folktale: A Classification and Bibliography*, 2nd rev. ed. Helsinki: Suomalainen Tiedeakatemia, 1961.

Ackermann, E. M., *"Das Schlaraffenland" in German Literature and Folksongs. Social Aspects of an Earthly Paradise, with an Inquiry into its History in European Literature*. PhD Diss., University of Chicago, 1944.

Adhémar, J., "French Caricatures of the Sixteenth Century," *Graphis*, 10 (54) (1954), 330-45.

Agnew, J-C., *Worlds Apart: The Market and the Theater in Anglo American Thought, 1550-1750*. Cambridge: Cambridge University Press, 1986.

Agulhon, Maurice, *Pénitents et Francs-Macons dans L'Ancienne Provence*. Paris: Fayard, 1968.

Aikema, Bernard, "Hieronymus Bosch and Italy?," in J. Koldeweij and B. Vermet with Barbera van Kooij, eds, *Hieronymus Bosch. New Insights into His Life and Work*. Ghent-Amsterdam: NAi Publishers/Ludion: 2001. 25-31.

Alpers, S., *The Art of Describing. Dutch Art in the Seventeenth Century*. Chicago: University of Chicago Press, 1983.

____, "Taking Pictures Seriously: A Reply to Hessel Miedema," *Simiolus* X (1978-9), 46-50.

Allan, M. J. B., *Marsiglio Ficino and the Phaedran Charioteer: introduction, texts, translations*. Berkeley: University of California Press, 1981.

Anglo, S., ed., *The Damned Art. Essays in the Literature of Witchcraft*. London-Henley-Boston: Routledge and Kegan Paul, 1977.

Antwerp's Golden Age. The Metropolis of the West in the 16th and 17th Centuries. Exhibition by the City of Antwerp and the Smithsonian Institution, 1973-5. Antwerp, 1973.

Ariès, P., *Centuries of Childhood*, trans. R. Bladick. New York: Vintage Books, 1962.

____, *The Hour of Our Death*, trans. H. Weaver. New York: Vintage Books, 1981.

Auduze, F., "Leroi-Gourhan, a philosopher of technique and evolution," *Journal of Archaeological Research* 10(4) (2002), 277-306.

Auerbach, E., *Mimesis. The Representation of Reality in Western Literature*, trans. W. R. Trask. Princeton: Princeton University Press, 1953.

Babcock, B., ed., *The Reversible World. Essays in Symbolic Inversion in Art and Society*. Ithaca: Cornell University Press, 1977.

Bakhtin, M. M., *Rabelais and His World*, trans. H. Iswolsky. Cambridge, Mass: M.I.T. Press, 1968.

____, *The Dialogic Imagination*, trans. M. Holquist and C. Emerson. Austin, TX: University of Texas Press, 1981.

Baldwin, T. W., *William Shakespeare's Small Latine and Lesse Greeke*. 2v. Urbana, IL: University of Illinois Press, 1944.

Ball, J. N., *Merchants and Merchandise. The Expansion of Trade in Europe, 1500-1623*. London: Croom Helm, 1977.

Baltrusaitis, J., *Le Moyen Age fantastique; antiquités et exotismes dans l'art gothique*. Paris: A. Colin, 1955.

Bamborough, J. B., *The Little World of Man*. London: Longmans, Green & Co., 1952.

Bangs, J. D., "Pieter Bruegel and History", *Art Bulletin*, LX (4), (1978), 704-5.

Barkan, L., *The Gods Made Flesh, Metamorphosis and the Pursuit of Paganism*. New Haven: Yale University Press, 1986.

Barnouw, A. J., *The Fantasy of Pieter Brueghel*. New York: Lear, 1947.

Baroja, Julio Caro, ed., *Romances de ciego*. Madrid: Taurus, 1966.

Bastelaer, R. van, and De Loo, G. H., *Pieter Bruegel l'Ancien, son oeuvre et son temps*. Brussels: G. van Oest & Cie, 1908.

Batany, Jean, "Un image en negatif du fonctionnalisme social: les danses macabre," in Jane H. M. Taylor, ed., *Dies illa: Death in the Middle Ages*. Liverpool: Francis Cairns Publications, 1984. 15-28.

Bax, D., *Hieronymous Bosch, His Picture Writing Deciphered*, trans. M. A. Bax-Botha. Rotterdam: A. A. Balkema, 1979.

Baxter, C., "Johann Weyer's *De Praestigiis Daemonum*: Unsystematic Psychopathology," in S. Anglo, ed., *The Damned Art*, 53-75.

Baxandall, M., *The Limewood Sculptors of Renaissance Germany*. New Haven: Yale University Press, 1980.

Bazin, G., *Le Livre des Saisons*. Geneva: Skira, 1948.

Benjamin, L., "Disguised Symbolism Exposed and the History of Early Netherlandish Painting." *Studies in Iconography*, 2 (1976), 11-24.

Bergman, M., *Hieronymus Bosch and Alchemy*, trans. D. Burton. Stockholm: Almquist & Wiksell International, 1979.

Bergmans, S., "Le Probleme de Jan van Hemessen, Monogrammiste de Brunswick," *Revue Belge d'Archeologie et de l'Histoire d'Art*, 24 (1955), 133-57.

Berlin, *Pieter Bruegel d. A. als. Zeichner: Herkunft und Nachfolge*. Staatliche Museen Preussischer Kulturbesitz, Kupferstichkabinett, 1975.

Bernheimer, R., *Wild Men in the Middle Ages. A Study in Art, Sentiment and Demonology*. Cambridge, Mass: Harvard University Press, 1952.

____, "Theatrum Mundi," *Art Bulletin* XXXVII (1956), 225-247.

Berrong, R. M., *Rabelais and Bakhtin: Popular Culture in Gargantua and Pantagruel*. Lincoln, NE.: University of Nebraska Press, c. 1986.

Bettelheim, B., *The Uses of Enchantment: The Meaning and Importance of Fairy Tales*. New York: Vintage Books, 1976.

Bialostocki, J., "Encompassing Themes and Archetypal Images," *Arte Lombarda* X (1965), 275-84.

Bianconi, P., *The Complete Paintings of Bruegel*, Intro. by R. Huges, notes and catalogue by P. Bianconi. New York: H. M. Abrams, 1970.

Biller, P., "Words and the Medieval Notion of 'Religion,'" *Journal of Ecclesiastical History* 36 (3) (July 1985), 351-69.

Bloch, M. and J. Parry, eds., *Death and the Regeneration of Life*. Cambridge: Cambridge University Press, 1982.

Boas, F., *The Religion of the Kwakiutl Indians*, vol 2. New York, 1930.

____, "Kwakiutl Culture as Reflected in Mythology," *Memoirs of the American Folklore Society* 28. New York, 1935.

Boas, G. (1930), *Essays on Primitivism and Related Ideas in the Middle Ages*. Baltimore: John Hopkins Press, 1948.

Boase, T. S. R., *Death in the Middle Ages. Mortality, Judgement and Remembrance*. London: Thames & Hudson, 1972.

Boétie, Etienne de la, *Le discours de la servitude volontaire*. ed. with an intro. by M. Abensour and M. Gauchet. Paris: Payot, 1976.

Boon, K. G., "Patientia dans les gravures de la Réforme aux Pays-Bays," *Revue de l'Art* 56 (1982), 7-25.

Bossy, J., "Some Elementary Forms of Durkheim," *Past and Present* XCV (1982), 3-18.

Boumans, R., "The Religious Views of Abraham Ortelius," *Journal of the Warburg and Courtauld Institutes* 17 (1954), 374-377.

Bouwsma, W. J., *Concordia Mundi: The Career and Thought of Guillaume Postel (1510-1581)*. Cambridge, Mass: Harvard University Press, 1957.

Bowers, Rick and Phayer, Thomas, "Thomas Phaer and the Boke of

Chyldren," *(1544) Medieval & Renaissance Texts & Studies*, v. 201 (March 1999).
Brady, T., *Turning Swiss: Cities and Empire, 1450-1550.* Cambridge: Cambridge University Press, 1985.
Briggs, K. M., *Pale Hecate's Team.* London: Routledge and Kegan Paul, 1962.
Brion, M., *Bosch.* Paris: Librairie Plon, 1938.
Bristol, M. D., *Carnival and Theatre. Plebian Culture and the Structure of Authority in Renaissance England.* New York: Methuen, 1985.
Brown, Peter, *The Cult of the Saints: Its Rise and Function in Latin Antiquity.* Chicago: University of Chicago Press, 1981.
Brussels. *Bruegel. Une dynastie de peintres.* Brussels: Palais des Beaux-Arts, 1980.
Bruyn, J., Letter, *Art Bulletin* LX(4) (December 1978), 741-2.
Bucheit, Hans, "Beitrage zum Armenseelenkultus," *Bayerischer Heimatschutz. Zeitschrift d. b. Landesvereins f. heimatschutz* 29 (1934).
Burke, Peter, *The Renaissance Sense of the Past.* London: Edward Arnold, 1969.
____, *Popular Culture in Early Modern Europe.* New York: New York University Press, 1978.
____, ed., *Economy and Society in Early Modern Europe. Essays from Annales.* London: Routledge & Kegan Paul, 1972
Bruyn Kops de, C.J., "De *Zeven Werken van Barmhartigheid,* van de Meester van Alkmaar gerestaureed," *Bulletin van Rijksmuseum* 23 (1975), part 4, 203-226.
Caciola, Nancy, "Wraiths, Revenants and Ritual in Medieval Culture," *Past and Present,* 152 (August, 1996), 3-45.
Cameron, A., *Daughters of Copper Woman.* Vancouver: Press Gang Publishers, 1981.
Camille, Michael, "Seeing and Reading: Some Visual Implications of Medieval Literacy and Illiteracy," *Art History* 9(1) (March, 1985), 26-49.
____, *Master of Death,* New Haven-London: Yale University Press, 1996.
Carroll, Margaret D., "Peasant Festivity and Political Identity in the Sixteenth Century," *Art History* 10(3) (September, 1987), 289-314.
Carvalho-Neto, P. de, *Folklore and Psychoanalysis.* Miami: University of Miami Press, 1972.
Cassirer, Ernst, Kristeller, P. O., Randall Jr., J. H., ed., *The Renaissance Philosophy of Man.* Chicago, 1948.
Céard, Jean, *La nature et les prodiges: l'insolite au 16e siècle, en France.* Geneva:

Droz, 1977.
Chambers, E. K., *The Medieval Stage,* 2v. Oxford: Oxford University Press, 1963 c. 1903.
Chartier, R., ed. *A History of Private Life: III. Passions of the Renaissance* Cambridge, Mass: Belknap Press of Harvard University Press, 1989.
Chew, Samuel, *The Pilgrimage of Life.* New Haven: Yale University Press, 1962.
Child, F. J. (1904), *English and Scottish Popular Ballads,* v. 5. New York, 1957.
Chrétien de Troyes, *Les Romans de Chrétien de Troyes*, ed. M. Roques, A. Micha, F. Lecoy. Paris: Champion, 1973.
Claire, Colin, *Christopher Plantin.* London: Cassell, 1960.
Clark, James, *The Dance of Death in the Middle Ages and in the Renaissance,* Glasgow: Jackson, Son & Company, 1950.
Cocchiara, Giuseppe, *Il mondo alla rovescia.* Turin: P. Boringhieri, 1963.
Cohen, Gustave (1926)., *Histoire de la mise en scène dans le théatre religieux francais du moyen age*, Paris: H. Champion, 1951.
Cohn, Norman, *The Pursuit of the Millenium*, rev. ed. New York: Oxford University Press, 1970.
Colie, R. L., *Paradoxia Epidemica: the Renaissance Tradition of Paradox.* Princeton: Princeton University Press, 1966.
Colonna, Francesco, *Hypnerotomachia Poliphili: The Strife of Love in a Dream* (1499), trans. and intro. J. Godwin. New York: Thames & Hudson, 1999.
Coo, J. de, "Forschungen zu Bruegels Dulle Griet," *Pantheon* XVIII (1960), 179-181, 232-36.
____, *Museum Mayer van den Bergh, Catalogus 1.* Antwerp: Museum Mayer van den Bergh, 1960.
Corwin, Nancy A., *The Fire Landscape: Its Sources and Its Development from Bosch through Jan Brueghel I, with Special Emphasis on the Mid-Sixteenth Century Bosch Revival*, Ph.D. diss., Univ. of Washington, 1976.
Coupe, W. A., *The German Illustrated Broadsheet in the Seventeenth Century.* Baden-Baden: Verlag Librairie Heitz, 1966-7.
Courcelle, Pierre, *Recherches sur les confessions de saint Augustin*. Paris: E. de Boccard, 1950.
Cox, P., "Origen and the Bestial Soul. A Poetics of Nature," *Vigilae Christianae* 36 (1982), 115-40.

Cramer, S. and Pijper, F., *Biblioteca Reformatoria Neerlandica,* 10v. The Hague: M. Nijhoff, 1903-14.
Crew, P. M., *Calvinist Preaching and Iconoclasm in the Netherlands, 1544-1569.* Cambridge: Cambridge University Press, 1973; 1978.
Curry, W. C., *Chaucer and the Medieval Sciences*, rev. ed. London: Allen & Unwin, 1960.
Curtius, E. R., *European Literature and the Latin Middle Ages.* trans. W. R. Trask (1953). Princeton, NJ: Princeton University Press, 1967.
Cuttler, C. D., *Northen Painting. From Pucelle to Bruegel.* New York: Holt, Reinhart & Winston, 1968.
Daly, M., *Gyn/Ecology. The Metaethics of Radical Feminism.* Boston: Beacon Press, 1978.
Darnall, J. and M. S. Weil, "Il *sacro bosco* di Bormarzo: Its Sixteenth-Century Literary and Antiquarian Context," *Journal of Garden History* 4 (1984), 1-94.
Davies, M., *National Gallery Catalogues. The Earlier Italian Schools*, 2nd ed. London: National Gallery, 1961.
Davies, M. G., *The Enforcement of English Apprenticeship: A Study in Applied Mercantilism, 1563-1642.* Cambridge, Mass: Harvard University Press, 1956.
Davis, N. Z., "Holbein's Pictures of Death and the Reformation at Lyons," *Studies in the Renaissance* 3 (1956), 97-130.
____, "Some Tasks and Themes in the Study of Popular Religion," in C. Trinkaus and H. A. Oberman, ed., *The Pursuit of Holiness in Late Medieval and Renaissance Religion.* Leiden: Brill, 1974. 327-335.
____, *Society and Culture in Early Modern France.* Stanford: Stanford University Press, 1975.
Deblaere, A., "Bruegel and the Religious Problems of his Time," *Apollo* CV (181) (March, 1977), 176-180.
Delevoy, R., *Bruegel.* Geneva: Skira, 1959.
Delumeau, J., *Catholicism between Luther and Voltaire.* London: Burns & Oates, 1977.
____, *Naissance et affirmation de la Réforme* (1965). Paris: Presses Universitaries de France, 1973.
Dentan, R. K., "Ethnographic Considerations of the Cross Cultural Study of Dreams," in J. Gackenbach, ed., *Sleep and Dreams. A Sourcebook.* New York: Garland, 1986. 317-358.

589

Desprez, F., *Les songes drolatiques de Pantagruel, où son contenues 120 figures de l'invention de Maitre Francois Rabelais; copiées en fac-simile par Jules Morel sur l'édition de 1565, pour la récréation des bons esprits, avec un texte explicatif et des notes par Le Grand Jacques (pseud)*. Paris, 1869.

Dickens, A. G., *The English Reformation.* London: B. T. Batsford, 1964.

Dis, L. M. van, *Reformatorische Rederijkers-spelen,* Haarlem, 1937.

Dickson, A., *Valentine and Orson*, Early English Text Society, no. 204. London, 1937.

Dixon, L., *Alchemical Imagery in Bosch's Garden of Delights Triptych.* Ann Arbor, MI: Garland, 1981.

Dobbs, B. J. T., *The Foundations of Newton's Alchemy: Or, the Hunting of the Greene Lyon.* Cambridge: Cambridge University Press, 1975.

Dorsten, Jan van, *The Radical Arts*. Oxford: University Press Leiden, 1970.

Douglas, M., *Purity and Danger. An Analysis of the Concepts of Pollution and Taboo* (1966). London: Ark Paperbacks, 1984.

Dreyer, P., "Bruegel's Alchimist von 1558; Versuch einer Deutung ad sensum mysticum," *Jahrbuch der Berliner Museeen* XIX (1977), 69-113.

Driesen, O., *Der Ursprung des Harlekin*. Berlin: A. Dunker, 1904.

Duerr, H. P., *Dreamtime: Concerning the Boundary Between Wilderness and Civilisation* (1978), trans. F. Goodman. Oxford: Basil Blackwell, 1985.

Dulaey, M., *Le Rêve dans la vie et la pensée de saint Augustin.* Paris: Etudes Augustiniennes, 1973.

Dundes, A., and Stibbe, C. A., "The Art of Mixing Metaphors. A Folkloristic Interpretation of the *Netherlandish Proverbs,* by Pieter Bruegel the Elder," *Folklore Fellows Communications,* No. 230. Helsinki: Suomalainen Tiedeakatemia, 1981.

____, *Life is Like a Chicken Coop Ladder. A Portrait of German Culture Through Folklore.* New York: Columbia University Press, 1984.

____, "The Psychoanalytic Study of Folklore," *Annals of Scholarship* 3(3), (1985), 1-42.

____, *Parsing Through Customs. Essays by a Freudian Folklorist.* Madison: University of Wisconsin Press, 1987.

Durkheim, E., *The Elementary Forms of the Religious Life,* trans. J. Swain. London, 1915.

Durling, R., "Deceit and Digestion in the Belly of Hell," in S. Greenblatt, ed., *Allegory and Representation.* Baltimore: John Hopkins University Press, 1981, 61-93.

Dvorak, M., *The History of Art as the History of Ideas, trans.* J. Hardy. London,

590

Boston: Routledge & Kegan Paul, 1984.
Edgerton, S. Y., *Pictures and Punishment. Art and Criminal Prosecution in the Florentine Renaissance.* Ithaca: Cornell University Press, 1985.
Eemans, M., *La Peinture Flamande de la Renaissance*. Brussels: Meddens, 1968.
Eire, Carlos M.N., *Idolatry and the Reformation: A study of the Protestant Attack on Catholic Worship in Germany, Switzerland, and France, 1500-1580,* PhD diss., Yale University, 1979.
Ehrenberg, R., *Capital and Finance in the age of the Renaissance.* London: J. Cape, 1928.
Eisenstein, E. L., "The Advent of Printing and the Protestant Revolt: A New Approach to the Disruption of Western Christendom," in R. M. Kingdon, ed., Transition and Revolution. *Problems and Issues of European Renaissance and Reformation History.* Minneapolis: Burgess, 1974. 235-270.
____, *The Printing Press as an Agent of Change,* 2v. Cambridge: Cambridge University Press, 1979.
Elias, Norbert, 'The History of Manners" (1939), in his *The Civilising Process. Sociogenetic and Psychogenetic Investigations,* rev. ed., trans Edmund Jephcott (1978); eds. E. Dunning, J. Goudblom, S Mennell. Oxford: Blackwell, 1994.
Enklaar, D. M., "De Blaue Schuit" *Tijdschrift Voor Geschiedenis* XLVIII (1933), 37-64, 145-61.
Eringa, S., *La Renaissance et les Rhétoriqueurs Néerlandais.* Amsterdam: Société Impimerie, 1920.
Evans, E. P., *The Criminal Prosecution and Capital Punishment of Animals.* London: W. Heinemann, 1906.
Even, E. van, *Het landjuweel van Antwerpen in 1561.* Leuven: Fonteyn, 1861.
Falkenburg, R. L. , *Joachim Patinir: Landscape as an Image of the Pilgrimage of Life,* trans. M. Hoyle. Amsterdam-Philadelphia: J. Benjamins Pub. Co., 1988.
____, "Pieter Aertsen, Rhyparographer," in J. Koopmans, et al, eds, *Rhetoric-Rhtoriqueurs-Rederijkers.* Amsterdam-Oxford: Royal Netherlands Academy of Arts and Sciences, 1995. 197-217.
Ferber, S., "Pieter Bruegel and the Duke of Alba," *Renaissance News* XIX (1966), 205-19.
Febvre, L. P. V., *The Problem of Unbelief in the Sixteenth Century. The Religion of Rabelais,* trans. by B. Gottlied. Cambridge, Mass: Harvard University Press, 1982.

591

Feinblatt, Ebria, *Prints and Drawings of Pieter Bruegel the Elder*. Exhibition, 22 March-7 May, 1961, Los Angeles County Museum.

Fenichel, O., "The Long Nose," in *Collected Papers of Otto Fenichel*, New York: W. W. Norton, 1953-54.

Ficino, Marsilio, *Marsilio Ficino: The Book of Life. A Translation by Charles Boer of Liber de Vita (or De Vita Triplici)*. Irving, TX.: Spring Shaftesbury, 1980.

Fierens, P., *Le Fantastique dans l'Art Flamand*. Brussels: Editions du Cercle d'art, 1947.

Filedt Kok, J. ed., *Livelier than Life: The Master of Amsterdam Cabinet or the Housebook Master*. Amsterdam: Rijksprentenkabinet/Rijksmuseum; Maarssey: Published in Association with Gary Schwartz, 1985.

Filipczak, Z. Z., *Picturing Art in Antwerp 1550-1700*. Princeton: Princeton University Press, 1987.

Fontaine-Verwey, H. de la, "Pieter Coecke van Aelst and the Publication of Serlio's Book on Architecture," *Quaerendo* 1-2 (1976), 166-194.

____, "The Family of Love," *Quaerendo* 6 (1976), 219-71.

Forbes, T. R., "Midwifery and Witchcraft," *Journal of the History of Medicine* (1962), 264-83.

____, ed., *The Midwife and the Witch*. New Haven: Yale University Press, 1966.

Foster, G. M., "Peasant Society and the Image of the Limited Good," *American Anthropologist* LXVII (1965), 307-8.

Foucault, Michel, *Discipline and Punish. The Birth of the Prison*, trans. A. Sheridan. New York: Vintage, 1977, 1979.

Fraenger, W., *Der Bauern-Bruegel und das deutsche Sprichwort*. Erlenbach-Zurich: E. Rentsch, 1923.

____, "Die Versuchungen des hl. Antonius von Hieronymus Bosch," *Archivio di Filosofia* 3 (1957), reprinted in *Hieronymous Bosch* (Dresden, 1975), 299-306.

Francastel, P., *La Figure et le lieu: l'ordre visuel du quattrocento*. Paris: Gallimard 1967.

Franck, J., "Geschichtes des Wortes 'Hexe,'" in Joseph Hansen, ed., *Quellen und Untersuchungen zur Geschichte des Hexenwahns und der Hexenverfolgung im Mittelalter*. Bonn: Giorgi, 1901.

Frank, R. H., "An Interpretation of *Land of Cockaigne* (1567) by Pieter Bruegel the Elder," *Sixteenth Century Journal* XXII (2) (1991), 299-329.

592

Frankfort, H., "The Archetype in Analytical Psychology and the History of Religion," *Journal of Warburg and Courtauld Institutes* XXI (July-December 1958), 166-78.
Freedberg, D., "The Hidden God: Image and Interdiction in the Netherlands in the Sixteenth Century," *Art History* 5 (June, 1982), 133-53.
____, *Iconoclasts and their Motives*. Maarsen: G. Schwartz, 1985.
French, P. J., *John Dee. The World of an Elizabethan Magus*. London: Routledge & K. Paul, 1972.
Freud, S., *On Dreams* (1901), trans J. Strachey. London: Hogarth Press, 1952.
____, *Wit and Its Relation to the Unconscious* (1905), trans. A.A. Brill. London: Keagan Paul, 1922.
____, *Character and Anal Erotism* (1908), trans. J. Strachey, in *Collected Papers* vol 2. New York: Basic Books, 1959. 45-50.
____, "The Occurrence in Dreams of Material from Fairy-tales" (1913), trans. J. Strachey *Collected Papers* IV. London: Hogarth, 1948. 236-43.
____, *Leonardo da Vinci. A Study in Psychosexuality* (1916) trans. A.A. Brill. New York: Random House, 1947.
____, *Interpretation of Dreams* (1900). The Standard Edition, ed. J. Strachey et al., vol 4. London: Hogarth Press, 1953.
Freud, S., and Oppenheim, D.E., *Dreams in Folklore,* trans. from the MS of 1911 by B.L. Pacella, New York: International Universities Press, 1958.
Friedlander, M.J., *Pieter Bruegel,* comments and notes by H. Panwels, trans. H. Norden. Leiden, 1976.
Fuller, T. *The Holy State, the Profane State*. London, 1662. London: W. Pickering, 1840.
Gackenbach, J., ed., *Sleep and Dreams. A Sourcebook*. New York: Garland, 1986 c. 1987.
Gaignebet, C., "*Le combat de carnaval et de Carême* de P. Bruegel (1559)," *Annales: Economies, sociétés, civilisations* 2 (March-April, 1972), 313-345.
Gandolfo, F., *Il 'dolce tempo'. Mistica, ermetismo e sogno nel cinquecento*. Rome: Bulzoni, 1978.
Geary, Patrick J., *Living with the Dead in the Middle Ages*, Ithaca: Cornell University Press, 1994.
Gell, Alfred, "Understanding the Occult," *Radical Philosophy,* Vol. 9 (Winter 1974), 17-26.

593

Gennep, A. van, *The Rites of Passage*, trans. M. Vizedom and G. Caffee. Chicago: University of Chicago Press, 1960.

____, *Le Folklore de la Flandre et du Hainaut Francais* (Departement du Nord), 2v. Paris: G. P. Maisoneuve, 1935-36.

Gersh, Stephen, *Middle Platonism and Neoplatonism: The Latin Tradition*, Publications in Medieval Studies, 23. University of Notre Dame Press: Notre Dame, IN, 1986.

Giametti, A. Bartlett, "Proteus Unbound: Some Versions of the Sea-God in the Renaissance," in P. Demetz, T. Greene, L. Nelson, Jr., ed., *The Disciplines of Criticism: Essays in Literary Theory, Interpretation and History*. New Haven: Yale University Press, 1968. 437-75.

Gibson, Walter S., *Hieronymous Bosch* (1972). Oxford: Oxford University Press, 1977.

____, "Hieronymus Bosch and the Mirror of Man. The authorship and iconography of the tabletop of the Seven Deadly Sins," *Oud Holland*, 87 (1973), 205-226.

____, *Bruegel*. New York: Thames and Hudson, 1977.

____, "Pieter Bruegel, *Dulle Griet*, and sexist politics in the sixteenth century," in *Pieter Bruegel und seine Welt*, ed. O. Von Simson and M. Winner. Berlin: Mann, 1979, 9-16.

____, "Some Flemish Popular Prints from Hieronymous Cock and His Contemporaries," *Art Bulletin* LX (1978), 673-81.

____, "Artists and *Rederijkers* in the Age of Bruegel," *Art Bulletin* LXIII/3 (September, 1981), 426-46.

____, *Mirror of the earth: the world landscape in sixteenth-century Flemish painting*. Princeton: Princeton University Press, 1989.

____, "Bosch's Dreams: A Response to the Art of Bosch in the Sixteenth Century," *Art Bulletin*, LXXIV (2) (June, 1992), 205-218.

____, *Pieter Bruegel the Elder: Two Studies*. Lawrence: Spencer Museum of Art, University of Kansas, 1991.

____, *Pieter Bruegel and the Art of Laughter*. Berkeley: University of California Press, 2006.

Ginzburg, C., *The Cheese and the Worms. The Cosmos of a Sixteenth-Century Miller* , trans. J. and A. Tedeschi. Baltimore: Johns Hopkins University Press, 1980.

____, *The Night Battles. Witchcraft and Agrarian Cults in the Sixteenth and Seventeenth Centuries* (1966), trans. J. and A. Tedeschi. Harmondsworth: Penguin, 1985

Gluck, G., "Die Darstellungen des Karnevals und der Fasten Von Bosch und Bruegel," *Gedenboek A. Vermeylen* (n.pl., 1932), 263-8.

Gluckman, M., *Essays on the Ritual of Social Relations*. Manchester: Manchester University Press, 1962.

Goff, J. Le, "Mentalities: a history of ambiguities," in J. Le Goff and P. Nora, ed., *Constructing the Past. Essays in Historical Methodology* Cambridge: Cambridge University Press, 1985. 166-80.

____, *La Civilisation de l'Occident Médiéval*. Paris: Arthaud, 1965.

____, *The Medieval Imagination*, trans. A. Goldhammer. Chicago: Chicago University Press, 1988.

Gordon, B., *Economic Analysis Before Adam Smith: Hesiod to Lessius*. London: Macmillan, 1975.

Goldman, I., *The Mouth of Heaven*. New York: Wiley, 1975.

Grant, H. F., "The World Upside-down," in R. O. Jones, ed., *Studies in Spanish Literature of the Golden Age Presented to Edward M. Wilson*. London: Tamesis, 1973. 103-135.

Grauls, J., *Volkstaal en Volksleven in het werk von Pieter Bruegel*. Antwerp-Amsterdam: Standaard-Boekandel, 1957.

Graus, F., "Social Utopias in the Middle Ages," *Past and Present* 38 (December, 1967), 3-19.

Graziani, R. "Pieter Bruegel's *Dulle Griet* and Dante", *Burlington Magazine* CXV, No. 841 (April, 1973), 209-219.

Greenblatt, S., "Murdering Peasants: Status, Genre and the Representation of Rebellion," *Representations* 1(1) (February, 1983), 1-29.

Grivot, D. and Zarnecki, G., *Gislebertus, Sculptor of Autun*. London: Trianon Press in Association with Collins, 1961.

Grossman, F., *Pieter Bruegel. The Paintings*. London, 1955.

____, "Bruegel, Pieter, the Elder," in *Encyclopedia of World Art*. New York: McGraw Hill, 1960, v. 2, col. 632-51.

Gudger, E. W., "Pliny's *Historia Naturalis*. The Most Popular Natural History Ever Published," *Isis* 6 (1924), 269-81.

Haavio, M., "The Upside-Down World," Essais Folkloriques, *Studia Fennica* 8 (1959), 207-221.

Hadzits, G. D., *Lucretius and his Influence*. New York: Coope Square Publishers, 1963.
Hajos, E., "The concept of an engravings collection in the year 1565: Quicchelberg, *Inscriptiones vel tituli theatri amplissimi*," *Art Bulletin* 40 (1958), 151-6.
Hamilton, A., *The Family of Love*. Cambridge: J. Clarke, 1981.
Harbison, C., *The Last Judgement in Sixteenth Century Northern Europe: A Study of the Relation Between Art and the Reformation*. New York-London: Garland Publ., 1976.
Harrebomée, P. J., *Spreekwoordenboek der Nederlandsche Taal*. Utrecht, 1858-70.
Harthan, John, *The Book of Hours*. New York: Crowell, 1977.
Hartlaub, G. F., "Giorgione im graphischen Nachbild," *Pantheon* XVIII (2) (1960), 76-85.
Haydn, H. C., *The Counter-Renaissance*. New York: Scribner, 1950.
Headley, J. M., *Luther's View of Church History*. New Haven: Yale University Press, 1963.
Heald, Suzette and Ariane Deluz, eds., *Anthropology and psychoanalysis: an encounter through culture*. London-New York: Routledge, 1994.
Helgerson, R., *The Elizabethan Prodigals*. Berkeley: University of California Press, 1977.
Heurck, E. H. van, and Boekenoogen, G. J., *L'Imagerie Populaire des Pays-Bays Belgique-Hollande*. Paris: Ducharte & Van Buggenhoudt, 1930.
Hindman, S., "Pieter Bruegel's *Children's Games*, Folly and Chance," *Art Bulletin* LXIII (3) (September, 1981), 447-75.
Hocke, G. R., *Labyrinthe de L'Art Fantastique. Le Manierisme dans l'Art European*, trans. C. Heim. Paris: Gonthier, 1967.
Hodgen, M., *Early Anthropology in the Sixteenth and Seventeenth Centuries*. Philadelphia: University of Pennsylvania Press, 1964.
Hoffman von Fallersleben, A. G., ed., *Altniederlandische Schaubuhne Abele Spelen ende Sottiernien* (*Horae Belgicae*, VI, Breslau, 1838), repr. Amsterdam, 1968.
Hofler, Otto., *Kultische Geheimbunde der Germanen*. Frankfurt-am-Main: Diesterweg, 1934.
Hsu, Francis L. K., ed., *Psychological anthropology; approaches to culture and personality*. Homewood, IL: Dorsey Press, 1961.

Huizinga, J., *The Waning of the Middle Ages. A Study of the Forms of Life, Thought, and Art in France and the Netherlands in the Fourteenth and Fifteenth Centuries* (1924), trans. F. Hopman from the Dutch editions (1919; 1921). Harmondsworth: Penguin, 1972.
Jacobowitz, E. S., and Stepanek, S. L., *The Prints of Lucas Van Leyden and His Contemporaries*, Exhibition catalogue, National Gallery, Washington, DC. Princeton: National Gallery of Art, 1983.
Jakobsen, Roman, *Two Aspects of Language and Two Types of Aphasic Disturbances, V. The Metaphoric and Metonymic Poles*, reprinted in K. Pomorska and S. Rudy, eds., *Language in Literature*, The Jakobsen Trust, Cambridge, Mass: Bellknap Press, 1987.
James, M. R., *The Apocryphal New Testament*. Oxford: Clarendon Press, 1924.
Jans, A., "Enkele grepen uit de Kerkelijke wetgeving ten tijde vah Pieter Bruegel," *Jaarboek van het koninklijk Museum voor Schone Kunsten Antwerpen:* Antwerp: Koninklijk Museum voor Schone Kunsten, 1969. 105-112.
Janson, H. W., *Apes and Ape Lore in the Middle Ages and the Renaissance*. London: Warburg Institute, University of London, 1952.
Jauss, H. R., "Form und Auffassung der Allegorie in der tradition der *Psychomachia*," in *Medium Aevum Vivum: Festschrift fur Walther Bulst*. Heidelberg: C. Winter, 1960. 179-206.
Jayne, S. R., "M. Ficino's Commentary on Plato's Symposium," *University of Missouri Studies* XIX, No. 1. 1944.
Jeannin, Pierre (a.k.a. Jean-Paul Clébert) *Les Marchands au XVIe siècle*. Paris: Edition du Seuil, 1957.
Jente, R., *Proverbia Communia*. Bloomington: Indiana University, 1947.
Jones, E., *Nightmare, Witches, and Devils*. New York: W.W. Norton and Company, 1931.
____, "Anal-Erotic Character Traits," in *Papers on Psychoanalysis* Boston: Beacon Press, 1961. 413-37.
Jung, C. G., *Collected Works*. v.12, 13. New York: Pantheon Books, 1953.
Katzenellenbogen, A., *Allegories of the Virtues and the Vices in Medieval Art*, trans. A. J. P. Crick. New York: W. W. Norton, 1964.
Kavaler, Ethan Matt, *Pieter Bruegel: parables of order and enterprise*. Cambridge: Cambridge University Press, 1999.
Kay, George, *The Penguin Book of Italian Verse*, introduced, edited, and translated by G. Kay. Harmondsworth: Penguin, 1965.

Kelly, H. A., *The Devil, Demonology and Witchcraft.* Garden City, N.Y., Doubleday, 1974.

Kennedy, J. G., and Langness, L. L., ed., *Ethos* (Journal of the Society for Psychological Anthropology) 9 (4) (Winter, 1981), with an introduction by the editors, 249-259.

Kingdon, R. M., ed., *Transition and Revolution. Problems and Issues of European Renaissance and Reformation History*. Minneapolis: Burgess Pub. Co., 1974.

Kinser, Samuel, *Rabelais's Carnival: Text, Context, Metatext*. Berkeley: University of California Press, 1990.

Kirschbaum, E., *Lexikon der Christlichen Ikonographie,* 8 vols. Freiburg: Herder, 1994.

Klaits, J., *Servants of Satan. The Age of the Witch Hunts*. Bloomington: Indiana University Press, 1985.

Klein, D. B., *The Unconscious: Invention or Discovery? A Historio-critical Inquiry*. Santa Monica: Goodyear Pub. Co., 1977.

Klein, H. Arthur, *Graphic Worlds of Pieter Bruegel the Elder*. New York: Dover Publications, 1963.

Klibansky, R., Panofsky, E., Saxl, F., *Saturn and Melancholy*. London: Nelson, 1964.

Koeman, C. *The History of Abraham Ortelis and his Theatrum Orbis Terrarum*. New York: American Elsevier Pub. Co., 1964.

Koldeweij, Jos, Paul Vandenbroeck and Bernard Vermet, *Hieronymus Bosch: The Complete Paintings and Drawings*. Ghent-Amsterdam: NAi Publishers/Ludion, 2001.

Koldeweij, Jos, and Bernard Vermet with Barbera van Kooij, eds, *Hieronymus Bosch. New Insights into His Life and Work*. Ghent-Amsterdam: NAi Publishers/Ludion, 2001.

Koopmans, Jelle, et al, eds, *Rhetoric-Rhétoriqueurs-Rederijkers*. Amsterdam: Royal Netherlands Academy of Arts and Sciences, 1995.

Kovel, Joel, *The Age of Desire*. New York: Random House, 1983.

Kris, E., *Psychoanalytic Explorations in Art*. New York: International Universities Press, 1952.

Kunzle, D., "Bruegel's Proverb Painting and the World Upside Down," *Art Bulletin* LIX (1977), 197-202.

____, "World Upside Down: The Iconography of a European Broadsheet Type" in B. Babcock, ed., *The Reversible World.* Ithaca: Cornell University Press, 1978, 39-94.

Laborde, Comte de, *La Mort Chevauchant un Boeuf. Origine de cette illustration de l'office des Morts dans certains Livres d'Heures de la fin du XVe siècle*. Paris: Francisque Lefrançois, 1923.
Ladurie, E. Le Roy, *Carnival in Romans*, trans. M. Feeney. New York: G. Brazillier, 1979.
Lavin, I., "On the Sources and Meaning of the Renaissance Portrait Bust," *Art Quarterly* XXXIII (1970), 207-226.
Leach, E. R. *Lévi-Strauss*. London: Fontana, 1970.
____, *Rethinking Anthropology*. London: University of London, Athlone Press, 1971.
Lebeer, L., "Le Pays de Cocagne (Het Luilekkerland)," in *Miscellanea Erwin Panofsky*. Brussels: Musées Royaux des Beaux-Arts, 1955. 199-214.
____, "De Blauwe Huyck," *Gentsche Bijdragen tot de kunstgeschiedenis* VI (1939-1940), 161-229.
____, *Catalogue raisonnée des estampes de Pierre Bruegel l'ancien*, Brussels: Bibliothèque Royale Albert, 1969.
LeFebvre, J., *Les fols et la folie*. Paris: Klincksieck, 1968.
Lehmann, P. *Die Parodie im Mittelalter*. Munich: Drei Masken Verlag, 1922.
Lenaghan, R. T., ed., *Caxton's Aesop*, with an intro. and notes. Cambridge, Mass: Harvard University Press, 1967.
Lenneberg, H. H., "Bosch's *Garden of Earthly Delights*, some musicological considerations and criticisms," *Gazette des Beaux-Arts* 103 (September, 1961), 135-144.
Lennep, J. van, *Art et Alchimie. Etude de l'iconographie Hérmetique et de ses influences*. Brussels: Editions Meddens, 1966.
Leonardo Da Vinci, *Prophecies*, in E. MacCurdy (1939), ed. and trans., *The Notebooks of Leonardo da Vinci*. New York: George Braziller, 1955.
Leroi-Gourhan, André, *Gesture and Speech* (1964), trans. A. Bostock Berger. Cambridge, Mass: MIT Press, 1993.
Lévi-Strauss, C., *The Savage Mind*. Chicago: University of Chicago Press, 1968.
Lichtman, R., *The Production of Desire*. New York: Free Press, 1982.
Lincoln, J. S., *The Dream in Primitive Cultures* London: Cresset Press, 1935.
Little, L. K., "Pride Goes Before Avarice: Social Change and the Vices in Latin Christendom," *The American Historical Review* 76 (February, 1971), 16-49.

____, *Religious Poverty and the Profit Economy in Medieval Europe*. Ithaca: Cornell University Press, 1978.

Lopez, R. S., *The Commercial Revolution of the Middle Ages, 950-1350*. Englewood Cliffs, NJ: Prentice Hall, 1971.

Lowry, M., *The World of Aldus Manutius*. Oxford: B. Blackwell, 1979.

Luther, Martin, "The Babylonian Captivity of the Church" (1520), trans. A. T. W. Steinhauser in *Three Treatises*, 2nd rev. ed. Philadelphia: Fortress Press, 1970.

McClellan, Catherine, "Wealth Woman and Frogs among the Tagish Indians," *Anthropos* 58 (1963), 121-8.

McDonnell, E. M., *The Beguines and Beghards in Medieval Culture*. New Brunswick, NJ: Rutgers University Press, 1954.

McDonnell, K., *John Calvin: The Church and the Eucharist*. Princeton: Princeton University Press, 1967.

MacLean, I., *The Renaissance Notion of Woman. A Study in the Fortunes of Scholasticism and Medical Science in European Intellectual Life*. Cambridge: Cambridge University Press, 1980.

McGowan, M. M., "Pierre de Lancre's *Tableau de l'Inconstance des Mauvais Anges et Demons*: The Sabbat Sensationalised," in S. Anglo, ed., *The Damned Art*, 182-201.

Macrobius, *Commentary on the Dream of Scipio*, trans. W. H. Stahl. New York: Columbia University Press, 1952.

Maeterlinck, L. "La genre satirique dans la peinture flamande," *Mémoires Couronnés et Autres Mémoires, L'Academie Royale des Sciences, des Lettres et des Beaux-Arts de Belgique* LXII(4) (March 1902-Jan. 1903). Gand: Librairie Néerlandaise, 1903.

____, "Nederlandsche Spreekworden," *Vlaamse Academie voor Taalen Letterkunde* 55 (1903), 109-29.

Mâle, Emile, *Religious Art in France: the Late Middle Ages, a Study of Medieval Iconography and its Sources* (1908), ed. Harry Bober ; trans. Marthiel Mathews. Princeton: Princeton University Press, 1986.

____, *The Gothic Image* (1913), trans. D. Nussey. New York, 1958.

Mander, Carel van, *The Lives of the Illustrious Netherlandish and German Painters, from the First Edition of the "Schilderboek" (1603–4)*, trans. & ed. Hessel Miedema. Doornspij: Davaco, 1994–99.

Mandiargues, A. P. de, *Die Monstren von Bomarzo*. Hamburg, 1969.

Marcus, L. Sinanoglou, *Childhood and Cultural Despair. A Theme and Variations in Seventeenth-Century Literature*. Pittsburgh: University of Pittsburgh Press, 1978.

____, *The Politics of Mirth*. Chicago: University of Chicago Press, 1986.

Margolin, J.C., & S. Matton, eds., *Alchimie et philosophie à la Renaissance. Actes du colloque international de Tours*, Paris: Vrin, 1993.

Marijnissen, R and M. Seidel, *Pieter Bruegel*. New York: Harrison House/Artabras, 1984.

Marlier, G., *Pierre Coeck d'Alost. La Renaissance Flamande*. Brussels: R. Finck, 1966.

Martin, G. and Cinotti, M., *The Complete Paintings of Bosch* (1966). New York: H. N. Abrams, 1971.

Martindale, A., *The Rise of the Artist In the Middle Ages and Early Renaissance*. New York: McGraw-Hill, 1972.

Martineau, Jane, ed., *Andrea Mantegna*, London-New York: Royal Academy of Arts - Metropolitan Museum of Art - Olivetti-Electa, 1992.

Marx, K., *Grundrisse: Foundations of the Critique of Political Economy*, trans. M. Nicolaus. New York: Vintage Books, 1973.

Matte Blanco, Ignacio, *The Unconscious as Infinite Sets: An Essay in Bi-logic*. London: Duckworth, 1975

Meijer, B. W., "From Leonardo to Bruegel: comic art in sixteenth-century Europe," *Word and Image* (Proceedings of the First International Conference on Word and Image) v.4, no. 1 (Jan-Mar. 1988), 405-41.

Meinel, C., ed., *Die Alchemie in der europäischen Kultur- und Wissenschaftsgesichte*, Wiesbaden: Harrassowitz, 1986.

Meiss, M., "Sleep in Venice. Ancient Myths and Renaissance Proclivities," *Proceedings of the American Philosophical Society* 110(5) (1966), 348-382.

Menz, Cäsar, and Wagner, Hugo. eds., *Niklaus Manuel Deutsch: Maler, Dichter, Staatsmann*, Bern: Kunstmuseum Bern, 1979.

Meyer, Maurits de, *De Volks- en Kinderprent in de Nederlanden, van de 15e tot de 20e eeuw*. Antwerp-Amsterdam: Standaard Wetenschappelijke Uitgeverij 1962.

____, "*De Blauwe Huyck*, La Cape Bleue de Jean van Doetinchem, datée 1577," *Proverbium* 16 (1971), 564-575.

Michel, E., *Bruegel*. Paris: Les Éditions G. Crès et Cie, 1931.

Miedema, H. "Realism and comic mode: the peasant," *Simiolus IX/4* (1977) 205-219.

Mielke, Hans, *Pieter Bruegel: die Zeichnungen*. Turnhout: Brepols, 1996.

Milne, L. S., *Dreams and Popular Beliefs in the Imagery of Pieter Bruegel the Elder*, PhD diss., Boston University, 1990.

Minnaert, Paul, "A propos de Carnaval et Carême par Bruegel (notes folkloriques)", *Apollo: chronique des Beaux Arts* (Brussels) 23 (Aug-Sept 1943), 8-10.

Monballieu, A., "De 'Kermis van Hoboken' bij P. Bruegel, J. Grimmer en G. Mostaert," *Jaerboek van het Koninklijk Museum voor Schone Kunsten* (1974), 139-169.

Montaigne, Michel de, (1580), *Essays of Montaigne*, 10v., trans. Charles Cotton (1685-6), rev. William Carew Hazlett. New York: Edwin C. Hill, 1910.

Monter, W., *Ritual, Myth and Magic in Early Modern Europe*. Athens, Ohio: Ohio University Press, 1983.

Moxey, Keith, "The Fates and Pieter Bruegel's *Triumph of Death*," *Oud-Holland* LXXVII (1973), 49-51.

____, *Aertsen, Beuckler and Secular Painting in the Reformation*. New York-London: Garland, 1977.

____, "Pieter Bruegel and *The Feast of Fools*," *Art Bulletin* LXIV (4) (December, 1982), 640-6.

____, "Sebald Beham's church anniversary holidays: festive peasants as instruments of repressive humor," in E. Uuman, ed., *Von der Macht der Bilder. Kunst der Reformationszeit*. Leipzig, 1983. 173-199.

____, *Peasants, Warriors and Wives: Popular Imagery in the Reformation*. Chicago: University of Chicago Press, 1989.

Muchembled, Robert, *Popular Culture and Elite Culture in France 1400--1750*, trans. L. Cochrane. Baton Rouge: Louisiana State University Press, 1985.

Muller-Hofstede, Justus, "Zur Interpretation von Pieter Bruegels Landschaft. Aesthetischer Landschaftsbergriff und stoische Weltbetrachtung," in O. von Simson and M. Winner, ed., *Pieter Bruegel und seine Welt*. Berlin, 1979. 127-143.

Nauert, C. G., *Agrippa and the Crisis of Renaissance Thought*. Urbana, IL: University of Illinois Press, 1965.

Noonan, J. T., Jr., *The Scholastic Analysis of Usury*. Cambridge, Mass: Harvard University Press, 1957.

Obrist, Barbara, "Visualization in Medieval Alchemy," *HYLE - International Journal for Philosophy of Chemistry*, 9 (2), (2003), 131-170.
____, *Les débuts de l'imagerie alchimique (XIV-Ve siècles)*, Paris: Le Sycamore, 1982.
Oliphaunt, H., *The Patristic Roots of Reformed Worship*. Zurich: Theologischer Verlag, 1975.
Ong, W. J., "Commonplace Rhapsody: Ravisius Textor, Zwinger and Shakespeare," in R. R. Bolgar, ed., *Classical Influences on European Culture A.D. 1500-1600*. Cambridge: Cambridge University Press, 1971. 91-126.
Orenstein, Nadine M., ed., *Pieter Bruegel the Elder: Drawings and Prints*, Museum Boijmans Van Beuningen, Rotterdam - Metropolitan Museum of Art, New York. New Haven: Yale University Press, 2001.
Owen, D. D. R., *The Evolution of the Grail Legend*. Edinburgh-London: Oliver & Boyd, 1968.
____, *The Vision of Hell*. Edinburgh: Scottish Academic Press LTD., 1970.
Ozment, S., *The Age of Reform, 1250-1550*. New Haven: Yale University Press, 1980.
Painter, G., Duncan, *The Hypnerotomachia Poliphili of 1499; an introduction on the dream, the dreamer, the artist, and the printer*. London: Eugrammia Press, 1963.
Park, K.,"The Life of the Corpse: Dissection and Division in Late Medieval Europe," Journal of the History of Medicine and Allied Sciences 50 (1995): 111-32.
____, "The Sensitive Corpse: Body and Self in Renaissance Medicine," Fenway Court, 1990-91, Boston: Isabella Stewart Gardner Museum, 1992, 77-87.
Panofsky, E., *Studies in Iconology. Humanistic Themes in the Art of the Renaissance* (1939). New York: Harper & Row, 1972.
____, *Early Netherlandish Painting* (1953), 2v., New York: Harper & Row, 1971.
Panse, F., and Schmidt, H. J., *Pieter Bruegels "Dulle Griet": Bildnis einer psychisch Kranken*. Berlin: Erhältich Durch Gebr. Mann, 1967.
Park, K., and Daston, L. J., "Unnatural Conceptions: The Study of Monsters in Sixteenth and Seventeenth Century France and England," *Past and Present* 92 (1981), 20-54.
Patch, H. R., *The Goddess Fortuna in Medieval Literature*. London: Cass, 1967.

____, *The Other World According to Descriptions in Medieval Literature*. Cambridge, Mass: Harvard University Press, 1950.

Pauw, de & de Veen, *Jérome Cock, Editeur d'estampes et graveur 1507?-1570*, Exhibition catalogue, Bibliothèque Royale Albert 1er, Brussels, 1970.

Peuckert, W. E., "Der Schoduvelstein," in W. Lang, ed., *Von fremden Volkern und Kulturen*. Dusseldorf: Droste, 1955.

Phillipps, M. M., *The 'Adages' of Erasmus. A Study with Translations*. Cambridge: Cambridge University Press, 1964.

Platelle, H., "La voix du sang: le cadavre qui saigne en présence de son meurtrier," in *La piété populaire au Moyen Âge, Actes du 99e congrès national des Sociétés Savantes*, Besançon, 1974; *Philologie et Histoire*, I (Paris 1977), 161-179.

Pleij, Herman, *Dreaming of Cockaigne: medieval fantasies of the perfect life*, trans. D. Webb. New York: Columbia University Press, 2001.

____, "*The Despisers of Rhetoric. Origins and Significance of Attacks on the Art of Rhetoric*," in J. Koopmans et al, eds, *Rhetoric-Rhétoriqueurs-Rederijkers*. Amsterdam: Royal Netherlands Academy of Arts and Sciences, 1995. 157-174.

Plummer, J., *Liturgical Manuscripts*. New York: 1964.

Pompen, A., *The English Versions of the Ship of Fools* (1925). New York: Octagon Books, 1967.

Popham, A. E., "Pieter Brueghel and Abraham Ortelius," *Burlington Magazine* LIX (1931), 184-8.

Propp, V., "Morphology of the Folktale" *International Journal of American Linguistics* 24 (1958), 1-135.

Quaife, G. R., *Wanton Wenches and Wayward Wives, Peasants and Illicit Sex in Early Seventeenth Century England*. London: Croom Helm, 1979.

Rank, O., *The Myth of the Birth of the Hero*. New York: Brunner, 1952.

Reintges, T., *Ursprung and Wesen der spatmittel alterlichen Schutzengilden* (Rheinisches Archiv, 58). Bonn: L. Röhrscheid, 1963.

Reinsberg-Duringsfeld, O., *Traditions et Légendes de la Belgique*, 2v. Brussels: F. Claassen, 1870.

Reynolds, W. D., *The "Ovidius Moralizatus" of Pierre Bersuire: An Introduction and Translation*. Ph.D. diss., University of Illinois at Urbana-Champaign, 1971.

Richter, Dieter, *Schlaraffenland. Geschichte einer populären Phantasie*. Cologne: Eugen Diederichs, 1984.

Riggs, T. A., *Hieronymous Cock (1510-1570): Printmaker and Publisher in Antwerp at the Sign of the Four Winds* (1971). New York: Garland, 1977.

____, "Bruegel and his Publisher," in O. von Simson and M. Winner, ed., *Pieter Bruegel und seine Welt* Berlin: Mann, 1979. 165-173.

Rivals, C., "L'Image de Moulon dans deux tableaux de Pieter Bruegel," *Image et Histoire: Actes du Colloque* Paris-Censier (May, 1986), 128-36.

Robertson, Clare, "Annibal Caro as Iconographer: Sources and Methods," *Journal of the Warburg and Courtauld Institutes* 45 (1982), 160-181.

Roheim, G., *The Gates of the Dream*. New York: International Universities Press, 1969.

Rooses, M., "Ortelius et Plantin," *Bulletin de la Société de Geographie d'Anvers* 5 (1880), 350-356.

Roosebroeck, R. van, *Patientia, 24 politieke emblemata door Joris Hoefnagel*. Antwerp, 1935.

Roscher, W. H., "Ephialtes: A pathological-mythological Treatise on the Nightmare in classical antiquity," trans. A.V. O'Brien, included in J. Hillman, *Pan and the Nightmare,* Irving, TX: Spring Publications, 1979. 1-58.

Rosoman, Leonard, *Leonard Rosoman, A.R.A., on Bruegel's Mad Meg*. London: Cassel, 1969.

Rothkrug, Lionel, "Popular religion and holy shrines," in J. Obelkevich, ed., *Religion and the People* Chapel Hill, NC: University of North Carolina Press, 1979. 20–86.

____, "Religious Practices and Collective Perceptions: Hidden Homologies in the Renaissance and Reformation," *Historical Reflections / Réflexions historiques* 7 (1980), 1-171.

____, "Peasant and Jew: Fears of Pollution and German Collective Perceptions," *Historical Reflections / Réflexions historiques* 10 (1983), 59-77.

____, "Holy Shrines, Religious Dissonance and Satan in the Origins of the German Reformation," *Historical Reflections / Réflexions historiques* 14 (1987), 143–286.

____, "German Holiness and Western Sanctity in Medieval and Modern History," *Historical Reflections / Réflexions historiques* 15 (1988), 161-249.

____, *Death, Trust, & Society: Mapping Religion & Culture*. Berkeley, CA: North Atlantic Books, 2006.

Rudwin, M. J., *The Origin of the German Carnival Comedy*. New York-Leipzig: G. E. Stecher & Co., 1920.

Ruvoldt, Maria, *The Italian Renaissance Imagery of Inspiration: Metaphors of Sex, Sleep, and Dream*. Cambridge: Cambridge University Press, 2004.
Sacks, O., *The Man Who Mistook his Wife for a Hat and Other Clinical Tales*. London: Duckworth, 1985.
Saunders, Richard, *The Astrological Judgement and Practice of Physic*. London, 1677.
Salet, F., *La Madelaine de Vézelay*. Melun: Librairie Argences, 1948.
Schama, S., *The Embarassment of Riches. An Interpretation of Dutch Culture in the Golden Age*. New York: Knopf, 1987.
Schapiro, M., "The Sculpture of Souillac," in W. R. W. Koehler, ed., *Medieval Studies in Memory of A. Kingsly Porter* Cambridge, Mass: Harvard University Press, 1939, v. 2, 359-87.
Scheicher, E., *Die Kunst- und Wunderkammern der Hapsburger*. Vienna: Molden, 1979.
Schlosser, Julius von, *Die kunst-und Wunderkammern der Spatrenaissance*. Leipzig: Klinkhardt & Biermann, 1908.
Schmidt, G. D., *The Iconography of the Mouth of Hell, Eighth-Century Britain to the Fifteenth Century*. Selinsgrove: Susquehanna University Press, 1995.
Jean-Claude Schmitt, *Les revenants: les vivants et les morts dans la societé medievale*. Paris: Gallimard, 1994.
Schneider, M., *Neurosis and Civilisation*. trans. M. Roloff. New York: Seabury Press, 1975.
Screech, M. A., "Commonplaces of Law, Proverbial Wisdom and Philosophy: their importance in Renaissance Scholarship (Rabelais, Joachim du Bellay, Montaigne)," in R. R. Bolgar, ed., *Classical Influences on European Culture A.D. 1500-1700.* Cambridge: Cambridge University Press, 1976. 127-134.
Scribner, R. W., "Reformation, Carnival and the World Turned Upside Down," *Social History* 3 (1978), 303-329.
____, *For the Sake of Simple Folk: Popular Propaganda for the German Reformation*. Cambridge, 1981.
Seeberg, R., *Textbook of the History of Doctrines.* Grand Rapids, Michigan: Baker Book House, 1964. 2:42-47.
Seipel, W., ed., *Pieter Bruegel d. im Kunsthistorisches Museum Wien*. Vienna: Kunsthistorisches Museum / Milan: Skira, 1998.
Serebrennikov, Nina, *Pieter Bruegel the Elder's series of "Virtues" and "Vices,"* PhD diss, University of North Carolina, Chapel Hill, 1986.

____, "'Dwelck den Mensche, aldermeest tot Consten verwect'. The Artist's Perspective," J. Koopmans, et al, eds, *Rhetoric-Rhétoriqueurs-Rederijkers* Amsterdam: Royal Netherlands Academy of Arts and Sciences, 1995. 219-246.

____, "Pieter Bruegel the Elder: The Draftsman Revealed," *Art Bulletin* (September, 2002), LXXXIV (3), 501-9.

Seznec, J., *The Survival of the Pagan Gods*, trans. B.F. Sessions. New York: Pantheon Books, 1953.

Shackle, G. L. S., *Epistemics and Economics: A Critique of Economic Doctrines*. Cambridge: Cambridge University Press, 1972.

Shulman, David, and Guy G. Stroumsa, eds., *Dream cultures: explorations in the comparative history of dreaming*. New York: Oxford University Press, 1999.

Silver, L., "The State of Research in Northern European Art of the Renaissance Era," *Art Bulletin* LXVIII (December, 1986), 518-35.

Simmel, G., *The Philosophy of Money*, trans. T. Bottomore and D. Frisby. London: Routledge & Kegan Paul, 1978.

Simson, O. von, and Winner, M., ed., *Pieter Bruegel und Seine Welt. Ein Colloquium Veranstaltel von Kunsthistorischen Institut der freien Universitat Berlin und dem Kupferstich Kabinett der Staatlichen Museen Stiftung Preussischer Kulterbesitz*, 13th and 14th November, 1975.

Siple, E. S., "A 'Flemish Proverb' Tapestry in Boston," *Burlington Magazine* 63 (1933), 29-35.

Sluys, F. and Cl., "Le Pays de Cocagne," *Problèmes-Revue de l'Association générale des étudiants en Médecine de Paris*, No. 77, 1961.

Snow, Edward, "'Meaning' in *Children's Games*: On the Limitations of the Iconographic Approach to Bruegel," *Representations* 2 (Spring, 1983), 27-60.

____, *Inside Bruegel: the Play of Images in Children's Games*. New York: North Point Press, 1997.

Snyder, J., ed., *Bosch in Perspective*. Englewood Cliffs, NJ.: Prentice Hall, 1973.

Spalding, K., *An Historical Dictionary of German Figurative Usage*. Oxford: Blackwell, 1952-81.

Sprenger, Jakob, and Kramer, Heinrich, *Malleus Maleficarum* (1486), trans. M. Summers (1928). London: Arrow Books, 1971.

States, B. O., *The Rhetoric of Dreams*. Ithaca: Cornell University Press, 1988.

Stobwer, A., ed., *Zur Geschichte des Volks-Aberglaubens in Anfange des XVI. Jahrhunderts. Aus der Emeis von Dr. Joh. Geiler von Kaiserberg.* 2nd ed. Basel 1985.

Strauss, Gerald, "A 16C Encyclopaedia: Sebastian Munster's Cosmography and its Editions," in *From the Renaissance to the Counter Reformation*, ed. C. H. Carter New York: Random House, 1965. 145-163.

____, *Manifestations of Discontent in Germany on the Eve of the Reformation.* Bloomington: Indiana University Press, 1971.

Stridbeck, C.G., "*Combat between Carnival and Lent* by Pieter Bruegel the Elder. An Allegorical Picture of the Sixteenth Century," *Journal of the Warburg and Courtauld Institutes* XIX (1956), 96-109.

____, *Bruegelstudien. Untersuchungen zu den ikonologischen Problemen bei Pieter Bruegel. d. Ä. sowie dessen Beiziehungen zum niederlandischen Romanismus.* Stockholm: Almquist & Wiksell, 1956.

Stuart, D. C., "The Stage Setting of Hell and the Iconography of the Middle Ages," *Romanic Review* IV (1913), 335-8.

Sullivan, M., "Madness and Folly: Pieter Bruegel the Elder's *Dulle Griet," Art Bulletin LIX (1) (1977), 55-66.*

Sumberg, S. L., *The Nuremberg Schembart Carnival.* New York: Columbia University Press, 1941.

Summers, D., *The Judgement of Sense. Renaissance Naturalism and the Rise of Aesthetics.* Cambridge: Cambridge University Press, 1987.

Sutton-Smith, B., "The Expressive Profile," in A. Paredes and R. Bauman, ed., *Towards New Perspectives in Folklore.* Austin: University of Texas Press, 1972.

Swarenski, H., "The Battle Between Carnival and Lent," *Bulletin of the Museum of Fine Arts Boston* XLIX (February, 1951), 2-11.

Sweerts, H., *De Tien Vermakelij-kheden des Houwelyks.* Amsterdam, 1684.

Synesius of Cyrene, *Essays and Hymns*, trans. w. intro and notes, A. Fitzgerald. Oxford: Oxford University Press, 1930.

Tannahill, R., *Flesh and Blood.* London: Hamilton, 1975.

Taylor, Archer, "The Shanghai Gesture," *Folklore Fellows Communications*, No. 166. Helsinki, 1956.

____, "Proverbial Phrases not Proverbs, in Breughel's Painting," *Proverbium* 3 (1965)

Taylor, F. Sherwood, *The Alchemists.* New York: H. Schuman, 1949.

Taylor, Jane H. M., ed., *Dies Illa: Death in the Middle Ages.* Liverpool: Francis Cairns Publications, 1984.

____, "Danse Macabré and Bande Dessinée: a Question of Reading," *Forum for Modern Language Studies*, 1989; XXV: 356 - 369.

Tedlock, Barbara, ed., *Dreaming: anthropological and psychological interpretations*. Cambridge: Cambridge University Press, 1987.

Tentler, T. N., *Sin and Confession on the Eve of Reformation*. Princeton: Princeton University Press, 1977.

Tervarent, Guy de, "Instances of Flemish Influence in Italian Art", *Burlington Magazine* 85 (1944), 290-4.

Theurillat, J., *Les mystères de Bomarzo et des jardins symboliques de la Renaissance*. Genève: Éditions les Trois Anneaux, 1973.

Thomas, K., *Religion and the Decline of Magic*. London: Weidenfield & Nicolson, 1971.

Thomas, Louis-Vincent, *Le cadavre: de la biologie à l'anthropologie*, Brussels: Complexe, 1980.

Thompson, E. P., "*Rough Music*: Le Charivari anglais," *Annales: Economies, Sociétés, Civilisations* 27 (1972), 285-312.

Thorndike, L., *A History of Magic and Experimental Science*, 6v. New York: Macmillan, 1923-1958.

Tietze-Conrat, E., *Dwarfs and Jesters in Art*, trans. E. Osburn. London: Phaidon Press, 1957.

Tolnay, C. de, *The Drawings of Pieter Bruegel the Elder*. London: A. Zwemmer, 1952.

____, *Pierre Bruegel l'Ancien*, 2v. Brussels: Nouvelle Sociéte Éditions, 1935.

Toussaert, J., *Le sentiment religieux en Flandre à la fin du Moyen Age*. Paris: Plon, 1963.

Trevor-Roper, H. R., *The European Witch Craze of the Sixteenth and Seventeenth Centuries and Other Essays*. Harmondsworth: Penguin, 1969.

Turner, V., *The Forest of Symbols*. Ithaca: Cornell University Press, 1967.

____, "Comments and Conclusions," in B. Babcock, ed., *The Reversible World* Ithaca: Cornell University Press, 1977. 276-96.

Unverfehrt, Gerd, *Hieronymus Bosch: die Rezeption seiner Kunst in frühen 16 Jahrhundert*. Berlin: Mann, 1980.

Urbach, Z., "Notes on Bruegel's Archaism. His relation to early Netherlandish painting and other sources," *Acta Historiae Artium* (Academiae Scientiarum Hungaricae) XXIV (1978), 237-56.

Vaernewijk, M. van, *Van die beroerlicke tijden in die Nederlanden en voornamelijk in Ghendt 1566-1568*, ed. F. Vanderhaeghen, 5v. Ghent, 1872-81.

Veldman, I. M., *Maerten van Heemskerck and Dutch Humanism in the Sixteenth Century*. Amsterdam: Mevlenhoff, 1977.
Verlinden, C., Craeybeckx, J. Scholliers, E., "Price and Wage Movements in Belgium in the Sixteenth Century," in P. Burke, ed., *Economy and Society in Early Modern Europe. Essays from "Annales"*. New York: Routledge, 1972. 55-84.
Vervoort, Renilde, "The Pestilent Toad. The Significance of the Toad in the Works of Bosch," in J. Koldeweij and B. Vermet, eds, *Hieronymus Bosch. New Insights into His Life and Work*. Rotterdam: Museum Boijmans Van Beuningen - Nai Publishers, 2001. 145-151.
Vetter, E. M., "Sant peters schifflin," *Kunst in Hessen und am Mittelrheing* (1969), 7-23.
Voet, L., *The Golden Compasses: A History and Evaluation of the Printing and Publishing Activities of the Officina Plantiniana at Antwerp*, 2v. Amsterdam: Van Gendt, 1969.
Walker Bynum, Caroline, *Fragmentation and Redemption: Essays on Gender and the Human Body in Medieval Religion.* New York: Zone Books, 1991.
Walker, D. P., "The Prisca Theologia in France," *Journal of the Warburg and Courtauld Institutes* XVII (1954), 204-259.
____, *Spiritual and Demonic Magic from Ficino to Campanella*. London: Warburg Institute, University of London, 1958.
____, *The Decline of Hell. Seventeenth Century Discussions of Eternal Torment*. London: Routledge & Kegan Paul, 1964.
Wallerstein, I., *The Modern World System: Capitalist Agriculture and the Origins of the European World Economy in the Sixteenth Century*. New York: Academic Press, 1974.
Warning, R., *Funktion und Struktur*. Munich: W. Fink, 1974.
Washington, D.C., National Gallery, *The Age of Bruegel: Netherlandish Drawings in the Sixteenth Century*. Cambridge, 1986.
Wauwermans, H. E., *Histoire de l'école cartographique Belge et Anversoise du XVIe siècle*. Brussels: Institut National de Géographie, 1895.
Weber, M., "Religious Rejections of the World and their Directions," in H. H. Gerth and C. W. Mills, ed. and trans., *From Max Weber: Essays in Sociology*. Oxford: Oxford University Press, 1958.
Webster, J. Carson, *The Labors of the Months in antique and medieval art.* Evanston, Ill.: Northwestern University, 1938.

Wee, H. van der, *The Growth of the Antwerp Market and the European Economy (fourteenth-sixteenth centuries)*, 3v. The Hague: Nishof, 1963.
____, "Anvers et les innovations de la technique financière aux XVIe et XVIIe siècles," *Annales: Economies, Sociétés, Civilisations* XXII (1967), 1067-89.
Weemans, Michel, "Herri met de Bles's sleeping peddler: an exegetical and anthropomorphic landscape," *Art Bulletin*, LXXXVIII (3), Sept, 2006, 459-482.
Weevers, T., *Poetry of the Netherlands in its European Context, 1170-1930*. London: Athlone Press, 1960.
Wegg, J., *Antwerp, 1477-1559*. London: Methuen, 1916.
____, *The Decline of Antwerp Under Philip of Spain*. London: Methuen, 1924.
Weigelt, H., *Sebastian Franck und die Lutherische Reformation*. Gutersloh: Gutersloher Verlaghaus G. Mohn, 1972.
Welsford, E., *The Fool: his Social and Literary History*. London: Faber & Faber, 1935.
Westerhoff, Jan C., "A World of Signs: Baroque Pansemioticism, the Polyhistor and the Early Modern Wunderkammer," *Journal of the History of Ideas* 62 (4) (October 2001), 633-650.
Williams, G. H., *The Radical Reformation*. Philadelphia: Westminister Press, 1972.
Williams, S. and Jacquot, J., "Ommegangs Anversois du temps de Bruegel et de van Heemskerk," *Les Fêtes de la Renaissance*. Paris: Centre National de la Recherche Scientifique, 1957, vol. 2. 359-388
Wilson, F. P., "The Proverbial Wisdom of Shakespeare," in W. Mieder and A. Dundes, eds., *The Wisdom of Many. Essays on the Proverb*. New York: Garland Publications, 1981. 174-189.
Wind, E., *Pagan Mysteries in the Renaissance*. London: Faber, 1968.
Winden, J. C. M. van, *Calcidius on Matter: His Doctrine and Sources. A Chapter in the History of Platonism*, trans. B. de Goede and S. J. P. van Dijk. Leiden: E. J. Brill, 1959.
Winter, E. F., ed. and trans., *Erasmus-Luther. Discourse on Free Will*. New York: Ungar, 1961.
Wirth, J., *La Jeune Fille et la Mort. Recherche sur les thèmes macabres dans l'art germanique de la Renaissance*. Geneva: Droz, 1979.

Wittkower, R. and M., *Born Under Saturn. The Character and Conduct of Artists: A Documented History from Antiquity to the French Revolution*. New York-London: W. W. Norton, 1963.

Wright, Sir Thomas, *A History of Caricature and Grotesque in Literature and Art* (1865), facs. ed. New York: Ungar, 1968.

Würtenberger, F., *Pieter Bruegel der Altere und die deutsche Kunst*. Wiesbaden, 1957.

Yates, F. A., *Giordano Bruno and the Hermetic Tradition*. Chicago: University of Chicago Press, 1964.

____, *The Art of Memory*. Chicago: University of Chicago Press, 1966.

____, *The Occult Philosophy in the Elizabethan Age*. London: Routledge & K. Paul, 1979.

Zagorin, Perez, "Looking for Pieter Bruegel," *Journal of the History of Ideas* 64,1 (2003), 73-96.

Zeydel, E. H., *"The Ship of Fools" by Sebastian Brant*(translated into rhyming couplets with introduction and commentary). New York: Columbia University Press, 1944.

Zehnpfennig, M., *Traum und Vision in Darstellungen des 16. und 17. Jahrhunderts*. Hanover: Tübingen, 1979.

Zupnick, I. L., "The Meaning of Bruegel's *Nobody* and *Everyman*," *Gazette des Beaux-Arts* LVII (May-June, 1966), 257-70.

____, "Bruegel and the Revolt of the Netherlands," *Art Journal* XXIII (4) (Summer, 1964), 283-9.

____, "Appearance and Reality in Bruegel's *Virtues*," *Actes du XXIIe Congrès International d'Histoire de l'Art* (Budapest, 1972), v. 1, 745-53.

____, "Bruegel's *Virtues* as the Epitome of Folly," in E. Castelli, ed., *L'Umanesimo e La Follia*. Rome, n. d.: Edizioni Abete, 1971. 89-106.

Index of authors, artists, and historical figures